INDEX TO FAIRY TALES, MYTHS AND LEGENDS:

SUPPLEMENT

INDEX TO
FAIRY TALES, MYTHS

AND

LEGENDS

SUPPLEMENT

BY

MARY HUSE EASTMAN
Wilmington (Del.) Institute Free Library

BOSTON
THE F. W. FAXON COMPANY
1937

PRINTED IN THE UNITED STATES OF AMERICA

You can pass muster in any drawing room and be ignorant of the date of Charlemagne's coronation, but if you don't know that the Sleeping Beauty was waked by a kiss, and if Cinderella's pumpkin-coach conveys no meaning to your mind, how can you pretend to be educated?

Josephine Daskam Bacon in "Open Market."

PREFACE

Not only have many volumes of folklore been issued since the 2d edition of the Index to Fairy Tales was published, but at that time there were many volumes which the compiler would have liked to include but which had to be omitted. Some of these were listed as time allowed in card index form for use in the Children's Department of the Wilmington Institute Free Library. It was suggested by Mr. Faxon that this might form the nucleus of a supplement which would include a fair representation of books published in the last ten years. A checking over of some of the recommended lists for children and storytellers, such as the Children's Catalog, the Guide to literature for character training, Bailey's Story-telling hour, and others, yielded a large list of books which appeared usable. Some of these were not immediately procurable, some on examination seemed not suitable for the index; but a fairly representative assortment of about five hundred books was finally assembled. Among these are books of a date early enough to have been indexed in the previous editions, which are included because they contain stories reprinted in recent collections, and knowledge of the original source has often proved useful.

The arrangement of the Supplement is practically the same as in the 2d edition. New features include a title list of the books indexed, a rather sketchy subject list, and several minor additions and changes which it is hoped will prove of value as time savers. For instance it was found that many titles which were in the 2d edition reappeared in the supplement. It would therefore be necessary to use both books to locate all available sources. To facilitate this the following note was added to such titles as could be verified: "For other entries, see 2d edition." Those which could not be verified were left unmarked. Also when it was found in checking entries that the story had appeared

in the 2d edition under two or more titles, a note was in-
serted to that effect. When a title referred to appears only
in the 2d edition, it has been so indicated by a special mark-
ing (#).

The cross references from one story to another have been
supplemented by the somewhat sketchy subject list already
referred to, of stories arranged under identifying "catch
words." This has so often aided the compiler in finding
a story to fit some special need that it has been added, in-
complete as it is, in the hope that it may be equally useful
to others. Also many subjects may be found by looking up
entries under the six words suggested by Kipling's verse:

"I keep six honest serving men (they taught me all I knew) ;
　Their names are What and Why and When and How and
　　Where and Who."

The list of books analyzed should be consulted to ascertain
what editions have been indexed. Different editions of an
author's works do not always contain the same stories, nor
are these stories always given the same titles. Variations
in titles and spelling have been taken care of as far as possible by cross references to the spelling or title used. To
distinguish editions the name of the editor, compilor, trans-
lator or publisher is used in parenthesis after the entry.

The asterisk (*) indicating versions for small children
has not been used since comparatively few graded readers
have been indexed in the supplement and in many cases the
book title indicates its field. The double asterisk (**) has
been used to indicate source material which might need
abridging or adapting before use.

Grateful acknowledgment is made to the friends who
aided in the compilation of the Supplement. Special thanks
are due the Greenwood Book Shop of Wilmington and the
Children's Department of the Philadelphia Free Library
for the loan of books for indexing, for helpful suggestions
and unflagging interest. Also, for years of friendly cooperation, I want to express sincere thanks to Arthur L.
Bailey, Librarian and the Board of Trustees of the Wilmington Institute Free Library. For help in editing and revis-
ing the manuscript I am deeply indebted to my brother

Charles whose collaboration has been invaluable. To his careful reading of the script, his logical criticism and wise suggestions, I owe more than I have words to express.

M. H. E.

Wilmington, Del.
    May 1937

CONTENTS

Index to Fairy Tales, Myths and Legends—Supplement

NOTE—# indicates: In 2d edition.

A

Abbott and the flea. Cooper. Argosy of fables.

Abdul Aziz and the pearl. Cooper. Argosy of fables.

Abel Stok's difficult task. Miller. My travelship: Holland. Olcott. Wonder stories from windmill land. (Jump, jump, jump the highest.)

Abelard and Heloise. Miller. My book of history. v. 3. (Quest for truth. *In* Ch. 11.)

Abijah's Fourth of July (poem). Bennett. Pigtail of Ah Lee Ben Loo.

Abner, the Jew, who had seen nothing. Hauff. Arabian days' entertainment.
See also Lost camel; Perplexity of Zadig.

Abou Hassan #.
See also Enchanted pomegranate branch and the beauty; Jester who fooled a king.

About an old man and an old woman, a cock and a hen, a fox and a wolf. Borski and Miller. Gypsy and the bear.

About ancestors. Canfield. Made-to-order stories. (Story about ancestors.)

About Jan the prince, Princess Wonderface, and the Flamebird. *See* Ivan and the gray wolf. II.

About Leviathan, king of the fish. **Gaster. Ma'aseh book. v. 2. (Man who obeyed his father's last will.)
For other entries, see 2d edition.

About Prince Surprise. *See* King Kajota.

About Smolinek. *See* Smolicheck.

About the hedgehog who became a prince. *See* Prince Hedgehog. II.

Abraham the carpenter. **Gaster. Ma'aseh book. v. 2.
See also Treasure of Hasan Taj.

Abram discovers God. *See* Star child. II.

Absent-minded saints. Guerber. Legends of Switzerland. (*In* Legends of Zurich.)

Absent-minded tailor. Shannon. California fairy tales.

Abu Taloot, Story of. Katibah. Other Arabian nights. (Story of Abu Taloot; or, When one's luck turns.)
See also Cogia Hassan Alhabbal.

I

Accidental candy. Denton. Homespun stories.
Accomplished and lucky tea kettle. Faulkner. Little
Peachling. (Wonderful tea-kettle—Bumbuku Chagama.)
Lee. Folk tales of all nations. (Miraculous tea-kettle.)
Mitford. Tales of old Japan.
Sugimoto. Picture tales from the Japanese. (Good-luck
teakettle.)
Whitehorn. Wonder tales of old Japan, (Wonderful tea-
kettle.)
For other entries, see 2d edition.
Achelous and Hercules. See Hercules and Deianeira.
Acheria, the fox. Carpenter. Tales of a Basque grand-
mother. (Asheria, the crafty red fox.)
Lee. Folk tales of all nations.
Achilles. Colum. Fountain of youth. (Story of Achilles.)
Rich. Read-aloud book. (Achilles and Hector.)
For other entries, see 2d edition.
Acid drops. Fyleman. Forty good-night tales. (Bag of
goodies, pt. 5.)
Acis and Galatea. Bryant. Children's book of celebrated
legends. (Triumph of Galatea.)
Bulfinch. Golden age. (In Ch. 26.)
For other entries, see 2d edition.
Acorn and the pumpkin. Bryce. Short stories for little
folks. (Man and the acorn.)
La Fontaine. Fables (Tilney).
See also Illuminating fig.
For other entries, see 2d edition.
Acqueduct of Caesarea. Vilnay. Legends of Palestine.
See also Palace of Pharaoh's daughter.
Act the truth. White. School management, p. 270.
Actæon. See Diana and Actæon.
Actor and the pig. Æsop. Fables (Jones. Clown and the
countryman.)
Æsop. Fables (Whitman ed. Buffoon and the countryman.)
Cooper. Argosy of fables. (Mountebank and the country-
man.)
Curry and Clippinger. Children's literature. (Mountebank
and the countryman.)
For other entries, see 2d edition.
Adalmina's pearls. Topelius. Canute Whistlewinks.
Adamant door. Beston. Starlight wonder book.
Adapa and the south wind. Miller. My book of history.
v. 1. (In Ch. 11.)
See also Wuchowson the wind-blower.
Admetus and Alcestis. Bulfinch. Golden age. (In Ch. 23.)
Curry and Clippinger. Children's literature. (Admetus
and the shepherd.)
Forbush. Myths and legends of Greece and Rome.
For other entries, see 2d edition.
Admetus and the shepherd. See Admetus and Alcestis.

Admiral of Babylon. Darton. Seven champions of Christendom.

Admiral's ghost (poem). Johnson and Scott. Anthology of children's literature.

Noyes. Poems.

Adonis. Bulfinch. Golden age. (Venus and Adonis. *In* Ch. 8.)

Forbush. Myths and legends of Greece and Rome. (Venus and Adonis.)

Lang. Book of myths. (Death of Adonis.)

Pyle. Tales from Greek mythology. (Aphrodite and Adonis.)

For other entries, see 2d edition.

Adopted child. Casserley. Michael of Ireland.

Adventure of a tiny little chicken who had not yet been born. *See* Why? why?

Adventure of my grandfather. *See* Bold dragoon.

Adventures of, etc. *See* the first important word of the title.

Adventurous cottontail. Bowman. Little brown bowl.

Adventurous cottontail and the princess. Bowman. Little brown bowl.

Adventurous Northmen. *See* Leif Ericson.

Adyevich. *See* Where love is, there God is also.

Æneas. Bulfinch. Golden age. (Adventures of Æneas. *In* Ch. 31.)

Farjeon. Mighty men from Achilles to Julius Caesar. (Burning of Troy.)

Rich. Read-aloud book. (Adventures of Æneas.)

See also Dido and Æneas.

For other entries, see 2d edition.

Æolus and the tower of the winds. *See* Ulysses and the bag of winds.

Æschylus and his destiny. La Fontaine. Fables (Tilney. *In* Horoscope.)

Æsop and the ass. Cooper. Argosy of fables.

Æsop and the impertinent fellow. Cooper. Argosy of fables.

For other entries, see 2d edition.

Æsop and the runaway slave. Cooper. Argosy of fables.

Æsop and the young rowdy. Cooper. Argosy of fables.

Æsop at play. Cooper. Argosy of fables.

For other entries, see 2d edition.

Afloat on a roof. Wiggin and Smith. Twilight stories.

Agamemnon. *See* Electra.

Age of the sorcerer. Carpenter. Tales of a Basque grandmother.

See also Rumpelstiltskin.

Aggo dah gauda. *See* King of the buffaloes.

Agib and the cheesecakes. *See* Noureddin Ali and his son.

Agnese and her fruit stand. Coe. Third book of stories.
Keyes. Five senses.

Ah Mee's invention. Chrisman. Shen of the sea.

Ah Tcha, the sleeper. Chrisman. Shen of the sea.
Harper. Ghosts and goblins.

"Aha!" said Pekka. *See* Pekka.

Aicha's stratagem. Chamoud. Picture tales from the
French. (Clever old woman of Carcassone.)
Coussens. Diamond story book.
See also Phantom banquet.
For other entries, see 2d edition.

Aileel and Ailinda. Beston. Starlight wonder book.

Ainsel. *See* My own self.

Aladdin; or, The Wonderful lamp. Arabian nights (Eliot).
Bruce. Treasury of tales for little folk.
Arthur Rackham fairy book.
Harper. Magic fairy tales.
Johnson and Scott. Anthology of children's literature.
Patten. Junior classics. v. 5.
Power. Blue caravan tales.
Quinn. Stokes' wonder book of fairy tales.
Wilson. Red magic.
See also How Cajusse was married; Magic lamp. II; Wish-
ing stone. III.
For other entries, see 2d edition.

Alaric. Niemeyer. Stories for the history hour.

Alber's pillar. Henderson and Calvert. Wonder tales of old
Tyrol.

Albolina. Wolff. Pale mountains.

Alcestis. *See* Admetus and Alcestis.

Alchemist. I. Farjeon. Tales from Chaucer. (Canon's
yeoman's tale.)
For other entries, see 2d edition.

Alcuin. Niemeyer. Stories for the history hour. (Charles
and Alcuin.)

Alenoushka and her brother. Ransome. Old Peter's Rus-
sian tales.
See also Brother and sister. I.
For other entries, see 2d edition.

Alexander Jones. Bryce. Folk lore from foreign lands.
For other entries, see 2d edition.

Alexander the Great. I. Farjeon. Mighty men from
Achilles to Julius Cæsar. (King of horses; Alexander the
king.)
Miller. My book of history. v. 2. (*In* Ch. 6.)
Power. Children's treasure chest. (Taming of Buceph-
alus.)
Terry. Tales from far and near. (Alexander the Great
and his horse.)
See also Gordian knot; Lesson in justice.
For other entries, see 2d edition.

Alexander the Great. II. Gaer. Magic flight. (Great legend: King Alexander's adventures.)
Landa. Aunt Naomi's Jewish fairy tales and legends. (King Alexander's adventures.)
See also Foolish Shah would fly; How Alexander the king got the water of life.

Alexander the Great. III. **Maspero. Popular stories of ancient Egypt. (Fragments . . . of the Romance of Alexander.)

Alexander the Great and the river Sambatyon. Gaer. Magic flight. (Great legend, pt. 2.)
Landa. Aunt Naomi's Jewish fairy tales and legends. (*In* King Alexander's adventures, pt. 3.)

Alexandria, Founding of. Lane. Tower legends. (Story told by the keeper of the Pharos.)
**Maspero. Popular stories of ancient Egypt. (*In* Fragment of a fantastic story.)

Alfie's Christmas boots. Campbell. Story of Christmas, p. 155.

Alfred the Great. *See* King Alfred.

Alhambra legend. Butterfield. Young people's story of architecture. (Red palace. *In* Ch. 22.)

Ali Baba and the forty thieves. Arabian nights (Eliot. Story of Ali Baba and the forty robbers.)
Arthur Rackham fairy book. (Ali Baba.)
Bruce. Treasury of tales for little folk.
Curry and Clippinger. Children's literature.
Patten. Junior classics. v. 5.
Quinn. Stokes' wonder book of fairy tales.
Rich. Read-aloud book. (History of Ali Baba and of the forty robbers.)
Wilson. Green magic.
See also How Jaffa was captured.
For other entries, see 2d edition.

Ali Cogia, a merchant of Bagdad. Arabian nights. Adventures of Haroun Er Raschid (Olcott).
See also Woman who hid her gold in a pot of honey.
For other entries, see 2d edition.

Alice and the mock turtle. Carroll. Alice's adventures in Wonderland. (Mock turtle's story. Ch. 9.)
(play). Knight. Dramatic reader. (Alice in Wonderland.)

Alice and the white knight. Carroll. Through the looking glass. ("It's my own invention." Ch. 8.)
For other entries, see 2d edition.

Alice in Wonderland. Large. Famous children of story-book land. (Abridged.)
See also Alice and the mock turtle; Alice and the white knight; Cheshire cat; Down the rabbit hole; Knave of hearts; Mad tea party; Tweedledum and Tweedledee.
For other entries, see 2d edition.

Aliquipiso. Partridge. Joyful Star.

All change #.
See also Merlicoquet; Travels of a fox.
All Fools' Day. *See* April Fools' Day.
All for the death of a flea. Katibah. Other Arabian nights.
  See also Spider and the flea.
All=powerful Khan. McNeer and Lederer. Tales from the
  crescent moon.
All Saints' Day. Manner. Silver treasury. (Judgement of
  Solomon.)
All too hard. Olcott. Wonder tales from China seas.
  See also Stone cutter.
All=wise Helen. Zeitlin. Skazki.
All women are alike #.
  See also Foxy gobé; Gullibles; Jack Hannaford; Visitor
  from hell; Visitor from paradise.
Allan=a=Dale's wedding (poem). Curry and Clippinger.
  Children's literature. (Allen-a-Dale.)
  See also Robin Hood.
  For other entries, see 2d edition.
Alligator and the jackal. *See* Little jackal and the alli-
  gator.
All's well that ends well. Lamb. Tales from Shakespeare.
Almansor, Story of. Hauff. Arabian days' entertainment.
Almond princess. Olcott. Wonder tales from goblin hills.
Almost=saved. I (poem). Coolidge. Poems.
  Independent (N. Y.). May 10, 1894, p. 1. (Legend of the
  almost-saved.)
  See also Brother of Christ #.
Almost=saved. II. Eells. Islands of magic. (Outside the
  door like the mother of St. Peter.)
  Carey. Flower legends. (Leek.)
Alnascher, Story of. *See* Barber's fifth brother.
Alone in the forest. Denton. Homespun stories.
Alphabet Park. Barrows and Cavanah. Favorite pages
  from Child Life.
Alphabet party. Fyleman. Forty good-morning tales.
  See also Mr. E. and the spelling man.
Alpheus. *See* Arethusa.
Alpine horn, Legend of. *See* How the Swiss came to use
  the Alpine horn.
Altchen and Berend=John. Miller. My travelship: Hol-
  land.
  Olcott. Wonder tales from windmill lands. (Willowman
  and Sunday's child.)
Always=late and Way=ahead. Cook. Red and gold stories.
Amadis of Gaul. Lanier. Book of giants. (Amadis among
  the giants.)
  For other entries, see 2d edition.
Amazon queen. I. Garnett. Ottoman wonder tales.
  See also Little Hyacinth's kiosk #.
Amazon queen. II. *See* Hippolyta.

Amazons. Eells. Magic tooth. (In the days of the Amazons.)

Amber, Origin of. *See* Phaeton.

Ambitious hunter and skilful fisher. Whitehorn. Wonder tales of old Japan. (Tamanoi; or, The jewel spring.)
For other entries, see 2d edition.

Ambitious old woman. Curtin. Fairy tales of Eastern Europe.
See also Fisherman and his wife.

America for Americans (play). Boeckel. Through the gateway.

Amerigo Vespucci. Colum. Voyagers. (Naming of the land.)

Amir and the Afghan. Atkins. Pot of gold.

Amleth. Adams. Swords of the vikings. (Amleth, Prince of Denmark.)
See also Hamlet.

Amys and Amylion. Darton. Wonder book of old romance.
For other entries, *see* 2d edition.

Ana Josepha. Shannon. Eyes for the dark.
See also Pan. II; Why the woodpecker's head is red. II.

Anansi and Nothing. Lee. Folk tales of all nations.

Anansi the spider-man, Stories of. *See* Conceited spider.

Anatomy of leadership. *See* Tail of the serpent. I.

Anchor house. Canfield. Made-to-order stories.

Ancient gods pursuing. Canton. Child's book of saints.

Ancient man, Story of the. Gate. Tales of the secret kingdom.

Ancient mariner (poem). Patten. Junior classics. v. 10. (Rime of the ancient mariner.)
Coleridge. Poems.

Ancient sparrow. Carey. Stories of the birds.

And if that isn't true . . . Williams-Ellis. Fairies and enchanters.

Ander's new cap. Piper. Folk tales children love. (Cap that mother made.)
Piper. Road in storyland. (Cap that mother made.)
For other entries, see 2d edition.

Androcles and the lion. Æsop. Fables (Jones. Slave and the lion.)
Curry and Clippinger. Children's literature. (Androcles; Androcles and the lion.)
Cooper. Argosy of fables. (Lion and the shepherd.)
Evans. Worth while stories.
Johnson and Scott. Anthology of children's literature.
For other entries, see 2d edition.

Androclus. *See* Androcles.

Andromeda. *See* Perseus.

Anemone. I. *See* Adonis #.

Anemone. II. Carey. Flower legends.
For other entries, see 2d edition.

Anemone. III. Patten. Junior classics. v. 8.

Anetka's carol. Kelly. Christmas nightingale.

Angel and the gargoyle. Brown. Under the rowan tree.

Angel from heaven. *See* Little Nell.

Angel gate. Guerber. Legends of Switzerland. (*In* Schaffhausen.)

Angel wife. Metzger. Tales told in Korea.

Angelus. Menefee. Child stories.

Angler and the little fish. *See* Fisher and the little fish.

Angry moon. Metzger. Tales told in Hawaii.

Angry polar bear. Canfield. Made-to-order stories.

Angus and the ducks. Flack. Angus and the ducks. Told under the blue umbrella.

Angus Og and Balor's son. Young. Celtic wonder tales. (Good action.)

Animal in the moon. La Fontaine. Fables (Tilney).

Animal party. Harriman. Stories for little children. Peck. Adventures of Mabel.

Animal races. De Huff. Taytay's memories. *See also* Deer and the rabbit; Fast runners; How deer won his antlers; How badger won a race.

Animals and birds play ball. *See* Birds' ball game.

Animals choose a king. *See* Dog and the kingship.

Animals' Christmas tree. I–II. *See* 2d edition.

Animals' Christmas tree. III. Bowman. Little brown bowl. (Christmas tree.) Harper. Merry Christmas to you. (Christmas tree.) For other entries, see 2d edition.

Animals, Fable of. *See* Animals get weapons.

Animals get weapons. Lee. Folk tales of all nations. (Fable of the animals.)

Animals in council. Eastman. Indian legends retold.

Animals' language. *See* Language of beasts.

Animals' New Year's eve. Bailey. Tell me another story. Lagerlöf. Further adventures of Nils. (*In* Ch. 10.)

Animals sick of the plague (poem). Cooper. Argosy of fables. (Animals sick with the plague.) La Fontaine. Fables (Tilney). For other entries, see 2d edition.

Animals take a bite. *See* Fox and his five hungry comrades.

Animals' winter quarters. Carrick. Animal picture tales from Russia. Carpenter. Tales of a Russian grandmother. (Winter's tale.) *See also* Rabbit and the other animals; Ram and the pig. For other entries, see 2d edition.

Anna's adventure. Fyleman. Forty good-night tales. (Twinkles, pt. 1.)

Anne of Brittany. Clément. Once in France. (That beloved Duchess Anne.)

Ant. Æsop. Fables (Jones).

Ant and a grasshopper. *See* Ant and the grasshopper.
Ant and the cricket. I (poem). Patten. Junior classics.
v. 10.
See also Ant and the grasshopper.
For other entries, see 2d edition.
Ant and the cricket. II. De Huff. Taytay's memories.
See also Ant and the grasshopper.
Ant and the cricket. III. Sheriff. Stories old and new.
(Cricket and the ant.)
Ant and the dove. Æsop. Fables (Artzybasheff. Dove and
the ant.)
Æsop. Fables (Whitman ed. Dove and the ant.)
Cooper. Argosy of fables.
Johnson and Scott. Anthology of children's literature.
(poem). Johnson and Scott. Anthology of children's litera-
ture. (Dove and the ant.)
For other entries, see 2d edition.
Ant and the flea (poem). Cooper. Argosy of fables.
Ant and the grasshopper. Æsop. Fables (Artzybasheff).
Æsop. Fables (Jones. Grasshopper and the ants.)
Æsop. Fables (Whitman ed.).
Æsop. Twenty four fables (L'Estrange. Ant and a grass-
hopper.)
Curry and Clippinger. Children's literature. (Grasshopper
and the ant.)
Johnson and Scott. Anthology of children's literature.
(Grasshopper and the ants.)
Rich. Read-aloud book.
See also Ant and the cricket. I–II; Grasshopper and the
bee; Thrifty squirrels.
For other entries, see 2d edition.
Ant and the pheasant. Lee. Folk tales of all nations.
Ant and the rat called "Jemez." De Huff. Taytay's mem-
ories.
See also Spider and the flea.
Antæus. *See* Hercules and his labors; Pygmies and the cranes.
Antelope and the jackal. Woodson. African myths.
Antigone. Bulfinch. Golden age. (*In* Ch. 23.)
Forbush. Myths and legends of Greece and Rome. (Anti-
gone, the faithful sister.)
Ants of Antic. Burnett. Children's book.
Antti and the wizard's prophecy. Bowman and Bianco.
Tales from a Finnish tupa.
See also Giant with the golden hair. I.
Anxious leaf. Curry and Clippinger. Children's literature.
For other entries, see 2d edition.
Ape. La Fontaine. Fables (Tilney).
See also Monkey who had seen the world.
Ape and the carpenter. *See* Carpenter and the ape.
In 2d edition there are entries under each title.

Ape and the dolphin. Æsop. Fables (Jones. Monkey and the dolphin.)
Æsop. Fables (Whitman ed. Monkey and the dolphin.)
Cooper. Argosy of fables. (Monkey and the dolphin.)
Price. Legends of the seven seas. (*In* Simo the dolphin.)
For other entries, see 2d edition.

Ape Sun Wu Kung #.
See also Arrogant ape and the sea dragon; Stone monkey.

Apelles. Richardson. Stories from old English poetry. (Campaspe and the painter.)
For other entries, see 2d edition.

Apes and the leopard (poem). Cooper. Argosy of fables.

Apes and the two travelers. Æsop. Fables (Jones).
Cooper. Argosy of fables.
For other entries, see 2d edition.

Ape's mango. Olcott. Wonder tales from pirate isles. (*In* String of pearls.)

Aphrodite. *See* Venus.

Aphrodite and Adonis. *See* Adonis.

Apollo and Daphne. *See* Daphne.

Apollo and Hyacinthus. *See* Hyacinthus.

Apollo and Pan. *See* Midas. II.

Apollo, Idas and Marpessa. *See* Idas and Marpessa.

Apollo's laurel. *See* Daphne.

Appeased wheelwright, Story of. **Arnold. Book of good counsels.

Apple-bump Ojii San. *See* Man with the wen.

Apple, Legend of. Newman. Fairy flowers.

Apple of contentment. Johnson and Scott. Anthology of children's literature.
Starbuck. Enchanted paths.
For other entries, see 2d edition.

Apple of discord. *See* Hercules and Minerva; Paris: Apple of discord.

Apple-seed John. *See* Johnny Appleseed.

Apple that talked. Bailey. Wonderful tree.

Apple tree May basket. Bailey. Wonderful tree.

Apple-tree witch. Noel. Magic bird of Chomo-lung-ma.

Apple tree's children. *See* How the apple blossom came back.

Apples of Venus. *See* Atalanta's race.

Apples of youth. I. *See* Iduna's apples.

Apples of youth. II. Curtin. Fairy tales of Eastern Europe.

April Fool blizzard. Bailey. Wonderful tree.

April Fool playhouse. Bailey. Wonderful tree.

April Fools' Day. *See* Actor and the pig; Bear says, North; Brahman and the goat; Brownie, Adventures of; Cock and the fox. V; Country fellow and the river; Devil's match; Emperor and the abbot #; Fool's story; Fox and the geese; French Puck; In the plate country; Jack the cunning thief; Knockmany, Legend of; Mare's nest; Oil merchant's

April Fools' Day—*continued.*
donkey; Pooka stories; Stupid wolf; Why cats always wash after eating; Wise fools of Gotham.
For other entries, see 2d edition.
April Fools' Day, Origin of. Evans. Worth while stories. (All fools' day.)
See also Jester who fooled a king.
Arab and his camel. I#.
See also Porcupine and the snakes; Puppies and their mother.
Arab and his camel. II. Æsop. Fables (Artzybasheff. Arab and the camel.)
Cooper. Argosy of fables. (Arab and the camel.)
Arab and the camel. *See* Arab and his camel. II.
Arabe duck. *See* Crane and the crab.
Arabian astrologer, Legend of. Irving. Tales from the Alhambra.
Arachne. Baldwin. Golden age. (Minerva. *In* Ch. 14.)
Evans. Worth while stories. (Legend of the spider web. Abridged.)
Forbush. Myths and legends of Greece and Rome. (Minerva and Arachne.)
Johnson and Scott. Anthology of children's literature.
Lang. Book of myths.
Power. How it happened. (How the spider was made.)
Pyle. Tales from Greek mythology.
Skinner. Child's book of country stories. (First spider.)
For other entries, see 2d edition.
Arbiter, the Hospitaller, and the hermit. La Fontaine. Fables (Tilney).
Arbor Day. *See* Crawfish and the great buzzard; Fairy in the oak; Gold in the orchard; Gourd and the pine; Happy clothes dryer; How K'tonton sent his tree a Shanah Tovah; How the elm tree grew; Johnny Appleseed; King who cut down the enchanted wood; Luck of the goldenrod; Oak planting festival; Old man and the three young men; Parable of the pomegranate; Pear tree and the wise man; Planting an orchard; Three apples. II and IV; Two apples on a tree.
See also in subject list: Tree legends; also names of trees.
For other entries, see 2d edition.
Arbor Day story. *See* Wonderful tree.
Arch of Stracena. Pogány. Hungarian fairy book.
Archer and his bow. *See* Bow.
Archer and the lion. Æsop. Fables (Jones).
Cooper. Argosy of fables. (Bowman and the lion.)
Archimedes. Lansing. Great moments in freedom. (Famous remark.)
Are you not satisfied? Coussens. Diamond story book. (Farmer and the noses.)
See also Stupid Tartaro.
For other entries, see 2d edition.

Arethusa. Bulfinch. Golden age. (*In* Proserpine. Ch. 6.)
Lang. Book of myths.
For other entries, see 2d edition.

Argonauts. Bulfinch. Golden age. (Golden fleece. *In* Ch. 17.)
Cady and Dewey. Picture stories from the great artists. (Golden fleece.)
Forbush. Myths and legends of Greece and Rome.
Kinney. Stars and their stories. (Ship Argo.)
Kinscella. Music appreciation readers. Book 5. (Golden fleece.)
Pyle. Tales from Greek mythology.
Rich. Read-aloud book.
For other entries, see 2d edition.

Ariadne. *See* Theseus.

Ariadne's crown. Bulfinch. Golden age. (Ariadne. *In* Ch. 21.)

Ariel. Burnett. Children's book. (Francese's fairy letter.)

Arion and the dolphin. Bulfinch. Golden age. (Arion. *In* Ch. 25.)
Forbush. Myths and legends of Greece and Rome. (Arion.)
Johnson and Scott. Anthology of children's literature.
Kinscella. Music appreciation readers. Book 5. (Lyre and the dolphin.)
Williamson. Stars through magic casements. (Dolphin who saved Arion.)
For other entries, see 2d edition.

Aristaeus and Proteus. *See* Bee-man of Arcadia.

Aristaeus, the bee-keeper. *See* Bee-man of Arcadia.

Aristotle and the Olympic victors. Cozad. Story talks.

Arlette, the tanner's daughter. Clément. Flowers of chivalry.

Armistice Day. *See* Boot is a league of nations; Ernest service; Family portrait; Frogs and the fighting bulls; Matter of arbitration; Price of victory; Soldier and his horse; There was a war; Two travelers and the oyster; Vintem.
See also in subject list: Peace; War.
For other entries, see 2d edition.

Armless, the fish-boy, Story of. Snell. Told beneath the northern lights.

Army of the sea king. Howes. Long bright land.

Army of two. Evans. Worth while stories.
Kinscella. Music appreciation readers. Book 3.
Patten. Junior classics. v. 7. (Rebecca the drummer.)
See also Castle Somlyo.

Arndt's night underground. Coe. Third book of stories.
See also John Dietrich. Adventures of #.
For other entries, see 2d edition.

Arrogant ape and the sea dragon. Price. Legends of the seven seas.
See also Ape Sun Wu Kung #; Stone monkey.

Arrow trail. Garett. Coyote stories.

Art of seeing. *See* Eyes and no eyes.
Artemis and Orion. *See* Orion.
Arthur and Sir Accalon. *See* Sir Accalon.
Arthur, King. *See* King Arthur.
Artist of Faloria. Wolff. Pale mountains.
Artist who forgot four colors. *See* How the artist forgot four colors.
Artistic pig. Shannon. California fairy tales.
Arum lily. Carey. Flower legends.
As Hai Low kept house. Chrisman. Shen of the sea.
  See also Epaminondas and his auntie; Prudent Hans.
As you like it. Lamb. Tales from Shakespeare.
  Patten. Junior classics. v. 5.
  Rich. Read-aloud book.
  Richardson. Stories from old English poetry. (Story of Rosalind; or, As you like it.)
Ascent of the Huebichenstein. Choate and Curtis. Little people of the hills.
Ash and the hazel. Darton. Wonder book of old romance.
Ash-maiden. *See* Cinderella.
Asheria. *See* Acheria the fox.
Ashiepattle and his goodly crew #.
  See also Flying ship; Hardy Hardback; How six men traveled through the wide world; Ship that sailed by land and sea.
Ashiepattle and the king's hares. Lee. Folk tales of all nations. (Osborn's pipe.)
  See also Eighteen rabbits; Jesper who herded the hares.
  For other entries, see 2d edition.
Ashiepattle who made the princess tell the truth at last #.
  See also Bet.
Ashik-Kerib. Chevalier. Noah's grandchildren. (Tale of Ashik-Kerib.)
Ashmedai and King Solomon. *See* King Solomon and the demon. I.
Aslaug and Ragner #. *See also* Ragnar Lodbrok.
Aspen tree. *See* Why the aspen leaves tremble.
Ass and his burdens. *See* Donkey and the salt.
Ass and his driver. Æsop. Fables (Jones).
  Cooper. Argosy of fables.
Ass and his master. I. *See* 2d edition.
Ass and his master. II. Æsop. Fables (Jones. Ass and his masters.)
  Cooper. Argosy of fables. (Ass and his masters.)
  See also Ass's wish; Discontented ass.
Ass and his purchaser. Æsop. Fables (Jones).
  Cooper. Argosy of fables.
  For other entries, see 2d edition.
Ass and his shadow. Æsop. Fables (Jones).
  Cooper. Argosy of fables. (Ass's shadow.)
Ass and the dog. I. *See* Ass, the dog, and the wolf.
Ass and the dog. II. Æsop. Fables (Jones).
Ass and the flute (poem). Cooper. Argosy of fables.

Ass and the frogs. Cooper. Argosy of fables.
For other entries, see 2d edition.
Ass and the grasshoppers. Cooper. Argosy of fables.
For other entries, see 2d edition.
Ass and the horse (poem). Cooper. Argosy of fables.
Ass and the lamb (poem). Cooper. Argosy of fables.
See also Envious wren.
Ass and the lap=dog. Æsop. Fables (Artzybasheff. Ass
and the little dog.)
Æsop. Fables (Jones).
Æsop. Fables (Whitman ed. Donkey and the lap-dog.)
Cooper. Argosy of fables.
For other entries, see 2d edition.
Ass and the lion hunting. *See* Lion and the ass hunting.
In 2d edition there are entries under each title.
Ass and the little dog. *See* Ass and the lap-dog.
Ass and the mule. *See* Horse and the loaded ass.
Ass and the nightingale. Cooper. Argosy of fables.
Ass and the old peasant. *See* Old man and his ass.
Ass and the old shepherd. *See* Old man and his ass.
Ass and the seal. Colum. King of Ireland's son. (*In* Fe-
delma.)
Ass and the wolf. Æsop. Fables (Jones).
Cooper. Argosy of fables.
Ass carrying an idol. Æsop. Fables (Jones. Ass carrying
the image.)
Æsop. Fables (Whitman ed.).
Cooper. Argosy of fables (Jackass in office.)
See also Ass carrying relics.
For other entries, see 2d edition.
Ass carrying salt. *See* Donkey and the salt.
Ass carrying the image. *See* Ass carrying an idol.
Ass eating thistles. Æsop. Fables (Artzybasheff).
For other entries, see 2d edition.
Ass in a tiger's skin. Cooper. Argosy of fables.
Ass in the lion's skin. Æsop. Fables (Artzybasheff).
Æsop. Fables (Jones).
Æsop. Fables (Whitman ed. Fox and the ass.)
Cooper. Argosy of fables.
Curry and Clippinger. Children's literature.
Rich. Read-aloud book.
For other entries, see 2d edition.
Ass laden with salt and with sponges. *See* Donkey and the
salt.
Ass pretending that he was ill. Cooper. Argosy of fables.
See also Ox who envied the pig.
Ass that lays money. *See* Table, the ass, and the stick. II.
Ass, the cock and the lion. Æsop. Fables (Artzybasheff).
Æsop. Fables (Jones).
Cooper. Argosy of fables.
See also Ass, the lion and the cock #.

Ass, the dog and the wolf. Æsop. Fables (Whitman ed.).
For other entries, see 2d edition.
Ass, the fox and the lion. *See* Lion, the fox and the ass. II.
Ass, the lion and the fox #.
See also Ass's brains #.
Ass, the ox and the labourer. Wheeler. Albanian wonder
tales. (Man who understood the speech of animals.)
Wilson. Green magic. (Man who understood animals' con-
versation.)
See also Language of beasts; Ohia and his sorrows.
For other entries, see 2d edition.
Assemoka, the sweet singer. Egan. New found tales.
Ass's brains #.
See also Ass, the lion and the fox; Lion, the fox and the stag.
Ass's mouth. Housman. Turn again tales.
Ass's wish. *See* Discontented ass. I.
In 2d edition there are entries under each title.
Astolpho, Adventures of. Echols. Knights of Charlemagne.
Astonishing story of the caliph's clock. *See* Caliph's clock.
Astronomer. Æsop. Fables (Jones).
Cooper. Argosy of fables.
At grandpa's farm. Harriman. Stories for little children.
At his post. Burnett. Children's book.
_ *See also* Knights of the silver shield.
At Marathon. *See* Darius and the Athenians.
At Mulberry farm. Cowles. Stories to tell.
At Pickle Palace. Cook. Red and gold stories.
At the back of the north wind. *See* Diamond and the north
wind.
At the behest of the pike. I. *See* 2d edition.
At the behest of the pike. II. Carpenter. Tales of a Rus-
sian grandmother. (By the pike's command.)
Gordon and Stockard. Gordon readers. 2d reader. (By
the pike's command.)
Ralston. Russian fairy tales. (Emilian the fool.)
See also Pike. I #.
At the door (poem). Wilson. Red magic.
Atagahi. James. Happy animals of Atagahi.
Atalanta's race. Bulfinch. Golden age. (Atalanta. *In* Ch.
18.)
Coussens. Diamond story book. (Apples of Venus.)
Johnson and Scott. Anthology of children's literature.
(Calydonian hunt and Atalanta's race.)
Forbush. Myths and legends of Greece and Rome. (Atal-
anta, the swiftest runner.)
Lang. Book of myths. (Atalanta.)
Pyle. Tales from Greek mythology.
Rich. Read-aloud book. (Atalanta.)
See also How the princess was beaten in a race #.
For other entries, see 2d edition.
Athena. *See* Minerva.

Athene and Ares in conflict. *See* Mars.

Athenian and the Theban. Æsop. Fables (Jones).

Athens. Bulfinch. Golden age. (*In* Minerva. Ch. 14.)
Curtis. Stories in trees. (Gift of the olive tree.)
For other entries, see 2d edition.

Atlantis, Story of. Colum. Voyagers. (Legend of Atlantis.)
For other entries, see 2d edition.

Atlantis, the lost land. Price. Legends of the seven seas.
See also Princess Bluegreen of the seven cities.

Atlas. Bulfinch. Golden age. (Perseus and Atlas. *In* Ch. 15.)
For other entries, see 2d edition.

Attila. Farjeon. Mighty men from Beowulf to William the Conqueror.
Lansing. Great moments in freedom. (*In* Venice, the first republic.)
Pogány. Hungarian fairy book. (Funeral of Attila.)
Seredy. Good master. (Skyway of warriors. *In* Ch. 7.)
For other entries, see 2d edition.

Atulagan. Phillips. Far peoples. (How a town was named.)

Aucassin and Nicolette. Coit. Kai Khosru.
(play). Coit. Kai Khosru.
For other entries, see 2d edition.

Augustus Caesar. Niemeyer. Stories for the history hour. (Augustus.)

Aunt Rhoda and the riddleman. Housman. Turn again tales.

Aunt Wind and Little Pomegranate. Olcott. Wonder tales from China seas.

Aunya's bargain. Young. Wonder smith and his son. (How the Gubbaun Saor welcomed home his daughter; How the Gubbaun quarreled with Aunya, and what came of it.)
See also Peasant's clever daughter; Queen's conquest.

Aurora and Tithonus. Bulfinch. Golden age. (*In* Ch. 26.)
For other entries, see 2d edition.

Avaricious woman, Story of. **Gaster. Ma'aseh book. v. 2.

Avenue of dreams. Marzials. Stories for the story hour.

Awakening of Ulster. Gregory. Cuchulain of Muirthemne.
Hull. Cuchulain. (Ulster, awake!)

Awful drunkard. Ralston. Russian fairy tales.

Awful fate of Mr. Wolf. Lee. Folk tales of all nations. (Awful fate of Brer Wolf.)
For other entries, see 2d edition.

Azazruk and the man-in-the-moon. *See* Man in the moon and the orphan boy.

Azores Islands, Origin of. Eells. Islands of magic. (Islands of flowers.)
See also Princess Bluegreen of the seven cities.

B

Baba Abdalla, Story of. Arabian nights. Adventures of Haroun Er Raschid (Olcott. Story told by the blind man, Baba Abdallah.)
For other entries, see 2d edition.

Baba Yaga. Ralston. Russian fairy tales.
Ransome. Old Peter's Russian tales.
See also Vasilisa, the beauty.
For other entries, see 2d edition.
　　In the second edition this story is also indexed under Witch. II.

Babes in the wood (poem). Curry and Clippinger. Children's literature.
Quinn. Stokes' wonder book of fairy tales.
Steel. English fairy tales.
For other entries, see 2d edition.

Babette. Crownfield. Feast of Noel.

Babiola. Aulnoy. Fairy tales (Planché. Babiole.)
Fairy garland (Dulac).
For other entries, see 2d edition.

Babiole. *See* Babiola.

Bablet. *See* Babiola.

Babouscka. Bailey. Stories children want. (Adapted.)
Smith and Hazeltine. Christmas in legend and story.
Walters. Book of Christmas stories.
For other entries, see 2d edition.

Baby bear story. Potter. Captain Sandman.

Baby bears' Christmas stocking. Walters. Book of Christmas stories.

Baby Gretel, Story of. Major. Merry Christmas stories.

Bacchus and the sailors. Bulfinch. Golden age. (*In* Bacchus. Ch. 21.)
For other entries, see 2d edition.

Bacchus and the vine. I. Shimer. Fairyland. (Miracle.)
See also First vineyard; Four qualities of drunkenness.

Bacchus and the vine. II. Teall. Batter and spoon fairies. (*In* Ch. 27.)

Bad Indian's ashes. Macmillan. Canadian wonder tales.
See also How mosquitoes came; Why mosquitoes bite people.

Bad little girl of Acoma. De Huff. Taytay's tales.

Bad little goblin's New Year. Skinner. Child's book of country stories.
Stewart. Tell me a story I never heard before.
For other entries, see 2d edition.

Bad little Indian boy. Hervey and Hix. Fanciful tales for children.

Bad poppy seeds. Carey. Flower legends. (Poppy.)
For other entries, see 2d edition.

Bad-tempered knife. Aspinwall. Can you believe me stories.

Bad-tempered squirrel. Evans. Worth while stories.

Bad wife. *See* Ghost of the spring and the shrew.

Badger and the bear. Sheriff. Stories old and new.
See also Kitpooseagunow the Avenger #.
For other entries, see 2d edition.

Badger's money. Mitford. Tales of old Japan.
For other entries,. see 2d edition.

Baedeker boy. Crew. Saturday's children.

Bag of dust. Bailey. Tell me another story. Bailey. Stories
children want.

Bag of gold. *See* Cobbler's song.

Bag of goodies. Fyleman. Forty good-night tales.

Bag of stories. Lee. Folk tales of all nations.
See also Jesper who herded the hares; King and the sage #.

Bags of the sun. Egan. New found tales.
See also Wise men of Merlingen.

Baile's strand, Story of. Gregory. Cuchulain of Muirthemne. (*In* Battle of Rosnaree.)

Baker boys and the bees. *See* Baker boys of Andernach.

Baker boys of Andernach. Evans. Worth while stories.
(Baker boys and the bees.)
For other entries, see 2d edition.

Baker's daughter. I. Williams-Ellis. Fairies and enchanters.
For other entries, see 2d edition.

Baker's daughter. II. Bianco. Street of little shops.

Baker's magic wand. Macmillan. Canadian wonder tales.
See also Go, I know not whither—fetch, I know not what.

Bala Lake. Henderson and Jones. Wonder tales of ancient
Wales. (Llyn Tegid.)
See also Syfaddon Lake.
For other entries, see 2d edition.

Balaton lake. Pogány. Hungarian fairy book. (Tale of the
Balaton.)

Balboa. Blaisdell. Log cabin days. (Balboa's reward.)
For other entries, see 2d edition.)

Bald huntsman. *See* Bald knight.

Bald knight. Æsop. Fables (Jones. Bald huntsman.)
Cooper. Argosy of fables.
For other entries, see 2d edition.

Bald man and the fly. Æsop. Fables (Jones).
Æsop. Fables (Whitman ed.)
For other entries, see 2d edition.

Balder. *See* Baldur.

Baldpate. Morris. Gypsy story teller.
Garnett. Ottoman wonder tales. (King's son and the der-
vish's daughter.)
Lee. Folk tales of all nations.
See also Faithful John.

Baldur and the mistletoe. Bulfinch. Golden age. (Death of
Baldur. *In* Ch. 40.)
Curry and Clippinger. Children's literature. (Death of
Balder.)
Johnson and Scott. Anthology of children's literature.

Baldur and the mistletoe—*continued.*
Lang. Book of myths. (Death of Baldur.)
Miller. My book of history. v. 3. (*In* Norse tales of creation and the gods. Ch. 7.)
Pyle. Tales from Norse mythology. (Death of Baldur.)
For other entries, see 2d edition.
Baleful cart. Clément. Once in France.
Ballad of Joseph and Damien (poem). Broomell. Children's story caravan.
Ballads and boots. *See* Minstrel and the cobbler.
Balloonist and the baron. Raspé. Children's Munchausen (Martin. *In* Ch. 7.)
Balor's defeat. Young. Celtic wonder tales. (Great battle.)
Bambi. Johnson and Scott. Anthology of children's literature. (How Bambi found the meadow.)
Bamboo=cutter and the moon=child. Nakazawa. Weaver of the frost. (Bamboo princess.)
Phillips. Far peoples. (Taketori-Hime.)
See also Bamboo maiden.
For other entries, see 2d edition.
Bamboo maiden. Metzger. Picture tales from the Chinese.
Bamboo princess. *See* Bamboo-cutter and the moon-child.
Banbury Cross. Hall. Godmother's stories.
Bandi Angel. Schwimmer. Tisza tales.
Bantagooma. Cooper. Tal. (*In* Ch. 15.)
Banyan deer. *See* Banyan deer king.
Banyan deer king. Johnson and Scott. Anthology of children's literature. (Banyan deer.)
Starbuck. Enchanted paths. (Banyan deer.)
For other entries, see 2d edition.
Bar Beach, Story about. Morley. I know a secret.
Bar of gold. Coussens. Diamond story book.
Starbuck. Far horizons.
For other entries, see 2d edition.
Baranga, the tree frog. Cendrars. Little black stories.
Barbarian against empire. *See* Hermann the Deliverer.
Barbarossa, Stories of. *See* Emperor's sleep; Pulling red hairs; Strange wedding gift; Sleeping king; Wonderful flower.
Barber. I. *See* 2d edition.
Barber. II. Capuana. Golden-feather.
Barber of Sari=Ann (poem). Bennett. Pigtail of Ah Lee Ben Loo.
Barber's clever wife. Williston. Hindu stories.
For other entries, see 2d edition.
Barber's fifth brother. Curry and Clippinger. Children's literature. (Story of Alnaschar.)
See also Brahman's dream; Brahman and the pans; Lazy Heinz; Milkmaid and her pail of milk; Poor man and the flask of oil.
For other entries, see 2d edition.

Bargain shop. Starbuck. Far horizons.

Barley sugar. Fyleman. Forty good-night tales. (Bag of goodies, pt. 6.)

Barmecide feast. Arthur Rackham fairy book. (Barmecide's feast.)

Evans. Worth while stories.

See also, Abi Fressah's feast #.

For other entries, see 2d edition.

Barnyard meeting. Skinner. Child's book of country stories.

Baron and the College of Physicians. Raspé. Children's Munchausen (Martin. *In* Ch. 14.)

Baron explores South Africa. Raspé. Children's Munchausen (Martin. *In* Ch. 24.)

Baron's amphibian chariot. Raspé. Children's Munchausen (Martin. *In* Ch. 22.)

Baron's steed. Raspé. Children's Munchausen (Martin. *In* Ch. 4.)

Raspé. Tales from the travels of Baron Munchausen.

See also White-horse-cut-in-two.

Barrel in the parlor. Williams-Ellis. Fairies and enchanters.

See also Ghost-laying stories.

Barrel-organ. Farjeon. Italian peepshow.

Barring of the door. I (poem). Johnson and Scott. Anthology of children's literature. (Get up and bar the door.)

For other entries, see 2d edition.

Barring of the door. II. Egan. New found tales. (Lawyer of Samarcand: Open door.)

Lee. Folk tales of all nations. (Farmer, his wife, and the open door.)

Barring of the door. I–II. *See also* Muffin man; Poffertjes pan.

Bart, Jean. Clément. Flowers of chivalry. (Let Jean Bart smoke.)

Bash-Chalek. *See* Steelpacha.

Bashichelik. *See* Steelpacha.

Basho, friend of moon and winds. Miller. My travelship: Japan.

This includes: Basho and the bees; Basho and the toad; Basho and the dragon-fly; Basho and the rustics; Basho's home at Yedo; Basho and the rich man.

Basil. *See* St. Basil.

Basilica of Julius. Butterfield. Young people's story of architecture. (*In* Churches of a new religion. Ch. 18.)

Basilisk. Bulfinch. Golden age. (Cockatrice; or, Basilisk. *In* Ch. 36.)

Basilisk of Utrecht. Miller. My travelship: Holland.

Basin of gold and the diamond lance. *See* Peronnik, Adventures of.

Basket (poem). Bennett. Pigtail of Ah Lee Ben Loo.

Basket of eggs. Lee. Folk tales of all nations.

Baskets of sunshine. Egan. New found tales.
Basque maiden and the king. Carpenter. Tales of a Basque grandmother.
See also Peasant's clever daughter.
Bass Rock, Story of. Lang. Red true story book. (How the Bass was held for King James.)
Bastuncedu dirigo. Hill and Maxwell. Napoleon's story book.
See also Table, the ass, and the stick.
Bat and the flying squirrel. *See* Birds' ball game.
Bat and the two weasels. Æsop. Fables (Jones. Bat and the weasels.)
Cooper. Argosy of fables. (Bat and the weasels.)
For other entries, see 2d edition.
Bat and the weasels. *See* Bat and the two weasels.
Bat, birds and beasts. I. Æsop. Fables (Artzybasheff. Birds, the beasts and the bat.)
Æsop. Fables (Jones. Birds, the beasts and the bat.)
Æsop. Twenty-four fables (L'Estrange).
Cooper. Argosy of fables. (Birds, the beasts and the bat.)
See also Crocodile's relatives.
For other entries, see 2d edition.
Bat, birds and beasts. II. Æsop. Fables (Whitman ed. Birds, the beasts and the bat.)
Bat, the bramble and the seagull. Æsop. Fables (Jones).
Bata, the Egyptian boy. Baikie. Wonder tales of the ancient world. (Tale of the two brothers.)
Lee. Folk tales of all nations. (Story of the two brothers.)
**Maspero. Popular stories of ancient Egypt. (Story of two brothers.)
See also Beaver medicine lodge; King finds a beautiful hair; Nothing child.
For other entries, see 2d edition.
Bath=boy's daughter. Garnett. Ottoman wonder tales. (Peris' god-daughter.)
For other entries, see 2d edition.
Batim, Story of. Morris. Gypsy story teller.
Battle between the fox and the wolf. *See* Reynard the fox.
Battle of Chevy Chase. *See* Chevy Chase.
Battle of fire and water. Metzger. Tales told in Hawaii.
Battle of Moytura. *See* Balor's defeat.
Battle of Rosnaree. *See* Baile's strand.
Battle of spirits. Howes. Long bright land.
Battle of the ape and the crab. *See* Crab and the monkey.
Battle of the birds. I. *See* 2d edition.
Battle of the birds. II. Howes. Long bright land.
See also Why the petrel lays its eggs on land.
Battle of the firefly and the apes #.
See also Cricket and the coyote.
Battle of the frogs and the mice. Forbush. Myths and legends of Greece and Rome.
For other entries, see 2d edition.

Battle of the owls. Metzger. Tales told in Hawaii.
Battle of the swans and peacocks. **Arnold. Book of good
counsels.
For other entries, see 2d edition.
Battle of the wizards. Olcott. Wonder tales from Baltic
wizards.
Battle that wasn't fought. *See* Sennacherib's defeat.
Baucis and Philemon. Bulfinch. Golden age. (*In* Ch. 6.)
Colum. Children who followed the piper. (Old couple's
house.)
Curry and Clippinger. Children's literature. (Miraculous
pitcher.)
Forbush. Myths and legends of Greece and Rome.
(play). Knight. Dramatic reader. (Miraculous pitcher.
Adapted.)
Pyle. Tales from Greek mythology. (Philemon and Bau-
cis.)
Starbuck. Familiar haunts. (Miraculous pitcher.)
See also Cedar tree of China; Stones in the kettle; Sunken
village.
For other entries, see 2d edition.
Bayard. I. Chandler. Magic pictures. (Bayard the brave.)
Clément. Flowers of chivalry. (Flowers of chivalry.)
Lang. Red true story book. (Monsieur de Bayard's duel.)
For other entries, see 2d edition.
Bayard. II. *See* Sons of Aymon.
Bayong of the lazy woman. Egan. New found tales.
Skipper. Jungle meeting-pool. (Lazy Tok. *In* Fifth meet-
ing.)
See also Wonderful pot.
Be=good fairy. Beard. Tucked-in tales.
Bean boy. Harper. More story-hour favorites.
Shannon. California fairy tales.
Bean Flower and Pea Blossom. Wilson. Red magic.
Bear and his mate. Cooper. Argosy of fables.
Bear and skrattel. Dasent. East of the sun and west of the
moon (Nielsen. Cat on the Dovrefell.)
Gordon and Stockard. Gordon readers. 2d reader. (Bruin
and the troll. Adapted.)
Rasmussen. East o' the sun and west o' the moon. (Cat on
the Dovrefell.)
For other entries, see 2d edition.
Bear and the beehives. Æsop. Fables (Artzybasheff).
See also Bees and the bears.
Bear and the bees. Bacon. Lion-hearted kitten.
Bear and the elephant. Cooper. Argosy of fables.
Bear and the fox. Æsop. Fables (Jones).
Cooper. Argosy of fables.
Bear and the fowls. Æsop. Fables (Whitman ed.).
For other entries, see 2d edition.
Bear and the hunter's stepson. Wilson. Red magic.

Bear and the leak. Sugimoto. Japanese holiday picture tales.
See also Valiant chattee-maker.

Bear and the little old woman #.
See also Bear's bad bargain; Signora Lupa and the fig tree.

Bear and the monkey. *See* Bear, the monkey, and the pig.

Bear and the old man's daughters. Carrick. More Russian picture tales.
See also Bluebeard.

Bear and the rabbit. Cooper. Argosy of fables.
See also Blue Jay, the imitator; Coyote imitates bear.

Bear and the tiger. Metzger. Tales told in Korea.

Bear and the travelers. *See* Travelers and the bear.

Bear goes fishing. *See* Why the bear has a stumpy tail.

Bear=man. Spence. Myths of the North American Indians. (*In* Ch. 6.)
See also Blackfoot and the bear; Boy who lived with grizzlies. II.

Bear says, North. Bowman and Bianco. Tales from a Finnish tupa. (Stupid bear.)
Harper. Fillmore folk tales.
Lee. Folk tales of all nations.
For other entries, see 2d edition.

Bear, the monkey, and the pig (poem). Cooper. Argosy of fables. (Bear and the monkey.)
For other entries, see 2d edition.

Bear, the wolf and the dog. Raspé. Children's Munchausen (Martin. *In* Ch. 19.)
Raspé. Tales from the travels of Baron Munchausen.

Bear woman. *See* Seven brothers.

Beard that grew and grew. Olcott. Wonder tales from windmill lands.

Bears and the bees. *See* Bees and the bears.

Bear's bad bargain. Faulkner. White elephant.
See also Bear and the little old woman # ; Signora Lupa and the fig tree.
For other entries, see 2d edition.

Bears make a visit. Shimer. Fairyland.
See also Three bears. I–II.

Bear's paw. Carrick. More Russian picture tales.

Bear's tail. *See* Why the bear has a stumpy tail.

Bearskin. I. Lee. Folk tales of all nations.
Williams. Tales from Ebony.
For other entries, see 2d edition.

Beatrice. Menefee. Child stories.

Beaumains. *See* Sir Gareth.

Beautiful hand. Evans. Worth while stories.

Beautiful mountain. Morris. Gypsy story teller.

Beautiful palace east of the sun and north of the earth. Coussens. Diamond story book.
For other entries, see 2d edition.

Beautiful star. *See* Child's dream of a star.

Beauty and the beast. Arthur Rackham fairy book.
Brock. Book of fairy tales.
Bruce. Treasury of tales for little folk.
Curry and Clippinger. Children's literature.
Evans. Worth while stories.
Faulkner. Road to enchantment.
Lee. Folk tales of all nations.
Mackenzie. Book of nursery tales.
Power. Blue caravan tales.
Quinn. Stokes' wonder book of fairy tales.
Starbuck. Familiar haunts.
See also Enchanted Tsarevich # ; Green serpent; Leaves that
hung but never grew; Speaking grapes, smiling apple and
tinkling apricot.
For other entries, see 2d edition.
Beauty and the horns. Harper. Fillmore folk tales.
For other entries, see 2d edition.
Beaver and porcupine. Spence. Myths of the North Amer-
ican Indians. (Beaver and the porcupine. *In* Ch. 7.)
Phillips. Indian tales for little folks. (Quarrel between
the beaver and the porcupine.)
For other entries, see 2d edition.
Beaver and the muskrat. Gearhart. Skalalatoot stories.
See also Beaver's tail.
Beaver and the porcupine. *See* Beaver and porcupine.
Beaver medicine legend. Spence. Myths of the North Amer-
ican Indians. (*In* Ch. 3.)
See also Bata, the Egyptian boy; Beaver stick #.
Beaver's tail. Pyrnelle. Diddie, Dumps and Tot. (*In* Ch.
16.)
See also Beaver and the muskrat; Klose-kom-bau, Story of.
Beaver's tree. Potter. Giant of Apple Pie Hill.
Becuma of the white skin. Stephens. Irish fairy tales.
Bed time. *See* Verotchka and the flowers.
Bedcats. Rounds. Ol' Paul.
Beder Basim, King of Persia, and the queen Johara the
jewel. *See* Gulnare of the sea.
Bedreddin Hassan. *See* Noureddin Ali and his son.
Bee and a housefly. Phillips. Far peoples. (Story of a bee
and a housefly.)
Bee and Jupiter. *See* Jupiter and a bee.
Bee and the fox. De Huff. Taytay's tales.
Bee and the goats. *See* Goats in the turnip field.
Bee and the orange tree. Aulnoy. Fairy tales (Planché).
For other entries, see 2d edition.
Bee-keeper. Æsop. Fables (Jones).
Bee-man of Arcadia. Bulfinch. Golden age. (Aristaeus,
the bee-keeper. *In* Ch. 24.)
Forbush. Myths and legends of Greece and Rome. (Aris-
taeus and Proteus.)
Lang. Book of myths. (Aristaeus, the bee keeper.)
For other entries, see 2d edition.

Bee-man of Orn. Stockton. Reformed pirate.
For other entries, see 2d edition.

Bee queen and the ant king. Noel. Magic bird of Chomo-
lung-ma.

Bee, the harp, the mouse, and the bum-clock. Hutchinson.
Chimney corner fairy tales.
Johnson and Scott. Anthology of children's literature.
See also Princess who would not smile # ; Three cows. III.
For other entries, see 2d edition.

Bee, the mouse, the muskrat, and the boy. Tappan. Little
lady in green.
See also Golden lantern, the golden goat and the golden cloak ;
Old man's son.

Beech and the oak. Patten. Junior classics. v. 8.

Beech tree. I. Baumbach. Tales from the Swiss alps.

Beech tree. II. Tuttle. Frightened tree and other stories.
(Queen tree.)

Beer and bread. Carpenter. Tales of a Russian grandmother.
(Wonderful beer of poor Petrusha.)
Ralston. Russian fairy tales. (*In* Legends about saints.
Ch. 6.)
For other entries, see 2d edition.

Bees and the bears (poem). Cooper. Argosy of fables.
(Bears and the bees.)

Bees and the katydids. Meeker. Folk tales from the Far
East.

Bees and the sugar. I. *See* 2d edition.

Bees and the sugar. II. Blaisdell. Rhyme and story second
reader. (What became of the sugar.)

Bees, the drones and the wasp. Cooper. Argosy of fables.
For other entries, see 2d edition.

Beeves and the butchers. *See* Oxen and the butchers.

Beggar. Otero. Old Spain in our Southwest.

Beggar and the king. Bowman. Little brown bowl.

Beggar woman's twins. *See* Beggar's curse. II.

Beggar's Christmas feast. Starbuck. Far horizons.
For other entries, see 2d edition.

Beggar's curse. I. Olcott. Wonder tales from windmill
lands. (Three hundred and sixty-five children.)
For other entries, see 2d edition.

Beggar's curse. II. Guerber. Legends of Switzerland.
(*In* Legends of Zurich.)
Henderson and Calvert. Wonder tales of old Tyrol. (Elder
tree.)
Schwimmer. Tisza tales. (Beggar woman's twins.)

Beggar's curse. III. Lee. Folk tales of all nations.

Beggar's gold. Atkins. Pot of gold.
See also Poor man and the rich man # ; Rich brother and
poor brother #.

Beginning of all life. *See* Creation of the world (Eskimo).

Beginning of death. *See* Death.

Bel and the dragon. Wilson. Red magic.

Believing husbands #.
See also Mad man, the dead man and the devil; Silly men and cunning wives.
Bell of Atri. ' Evans.   Worth while stories.
Patten.   Junior classics.   v. 8.   (Horse that aroused the town.)
See also Bell of justice; Dome of the chain.
For other entries, see 2d edition.
Bell of justice.   I.   Guerber.   Legends of Switzerland.   (*In* Legends of Zurich.)
For other entries, see 2d edition.
Bell of Müdera.   *See* Benkei and the bell.
Bell of Munot.   Guerber.   Legends of Switzerland.   (*In* Schaffhausen.)
Bell of the earth and the bell of the sea.   Beston.   Starlight wonder book.
Bell that would go home.   *See* Benkei and the bell.
Belle=Belle; or, The Chevalier Fortuné.   Aulnoy.   Fairy tales (Planché).
For other entries, see 2d edition.
Bellerophon.   *See* Pegasus.
Belling the cat.   Æsop.   Fables (Jones. Mice in council.)
Æsop.   Fables (Whitman ed.   Mice in council.)
Cooper.   Argosy of fables.   (Mice in council.)
(poem).   Cooper.   Argosy of fables.   (Council held by the rats.)
Curry and Clippinger.   Children's literature.   (Mice in council.)
Johnson and Scott.   Anthology of children's literature.
Rich.   Read-aloud book.   (Mice in council.)
For other entries, see 2d edition.
Bellini and the Sultan of Turkey.   Steedman.   Knights of art.   (Bellini.)
Bells of China.   *See* Wind bells.
Bells of Christmas.   Blondell.   Keepsakes.
Egan.   New found tales.
See also Three bells; Three silver bells # ; Why the chimes rang.
Bells of Malket.   Brown.   Under the rowan tree.
Bells of Santa Cruz.   Otero.   Old Spain in our Southwest.
Bells that ring=a=ting=a=ling.   Olcott.   Wonder tales from windmill lands.
Belly and the members.   Æsop.   Fables (Artzybasheff).
Esop.   Fables (Jones).
Cooper.   Argosy of fables.
Evans.   Worth while stories.   (Discontented members.)
For other entries, see 2d edition.
Beloved warrior.   Brown.   Curious book of birds.   (Good hunter.)
See also Unseen friends.
For other entries, see 2d edition.

Belshazzer and the strange cat. Cowles. Stories to tell.

Ben Ali the Egyptian (poem). Bennett. Pigtail of Ah Lee Ben Loo.

Bendigeid Bran. *See* Bran the blessed.

Benead and the moor elves (play). Going. Folklore and fairy plays.
See also Kippie-kappie; Knockgrafton, Legend of; You must not work on Sunday #.

Benefactors. Cooper. Argosy of fables.

Beneficent frog. *See* Benevolent frog.

Benevolent frog. Aulnoy. Fairy tales (Planché. Beneficent frog.)
For other entries, see 2d edition.

Benjy in Beastland. Evans. Worth while stories. (Benny in Beastland.)
Ewing. Lob Lie-by-the-fire.
See also Gerald's dream; Johnny's rabbit; Little boy pie; Robin's eggs.
For other entries, see 2d edition.

Benkei and the bell. Henderson and Calvert. Wonder tales of old Japan. (Benkei and the bell of Müdera.)
Kinscella. Music appreciation readers. Book 6. (Bell that would go home.)
Whitehorn. Wonder tales of old Japan. (Wonderful bell.)
For other entries, see 2d edition.

Benny in Beastland. *See* Benjy in Beastland.

Beowulf. Bailey. Stories of great adventures.
Barbour. Old English tales retold.
Cruse. Young folk's book of epic heroes.
Evans. Worth while stories.
Farjeon. Mighty men from Beowulf to William the Conqueror. (Grendel the monster.)
Johnson and Scott. Anthology of children's literature. (Beowulf's fight with Grendel.)
Lang. Book of myths.
Lang. Red book of animal stories.
Miller. My book of history. v. 3. (*In* Ch. 13.)
Power. Bag o' tales. (How Beowulf came to Daneland.)
Tappan. Old world hero stories.
For other entries, see 2d edition.

Ber Rabbit and Ber Wolf. *See* Brother Rabbit and Brother Wolf.

Berries, Origin of. *See* First strawberries.

Bertha. *See* Queen Bertha.

Bertha and the black boar. *See* Leaves that hung but never grew.

Bertha Goldfoot. Farjeon. Old nurse's stocking basket.

Best wish. I. *See* 2d edition.

Best wish. II. Harper. Fillmore folk tales.
For other entries, see 2d edition.

Bet. Schwimmer. Tisza tales.
See also Ashiepattle who made the princess tell the truth at last # ; Jack and the king who was a gentleman # ; Shepherd who won the king's daughter by a single word #.
Beth Gellert. Cady and Dewey. Picture stories from the great artists.
See also Brahman and the mongoose ; Faithful Bruno ; Kindness misunderstood ; Knight and the greyhound.
For other entries, see 2d edition.
Betrothal gifts #.
See also Frog princess.
Betsey's mistake. Burnett. Children's book.
Better of it. Olcott. Wonder tales from pirate isles.
Better than that. Coussens. Diamond story book.
See also King and the miller of Mansfield.
For other entries, see 2d edition.
Betty's ride. Curry and Clippinger. Children's literature.
Beuno. *See* St. Beuno.
Bevis of Hampton. *See* Sir Bevis.
Beware of bad company. I. *See* 2d edition.
Beware of bad company. II. **Arnold. Book of good counsels. (Heron and the crow.)
Beware of bad company. III. Woodson. African myths.
Beware of the chest. Clément. Once in France.
See also Bluebeard ; Forbidden room.
Bewitched violin. Lee. Folk tales of all nations.
See also Jew among the thorns.
Bharata's quest. *See* Slippers of the king.
Biburg See. Henderson and Calvert. Wonder tales of old Tyrol.
See also Sunken city in Zug lake.
Bidabe and his witch bride. Carpenter. Tales of a Basque grandmother.
Biddy O'Bride. Housman. Turn again tales.
Big boaster and little boaster. Metzger. Picture tales from the Chinese.
Big Booboo and the little Booboo. Harriman. Stories for little children.
Big brother's valentine. Bailey and Lewis. For the children's hour (1920 ed.).
See also Elaine's valentines.
For other entries, see 2d edition.
Big Claus and Little Claus. *See* Little Claus and Big Claus.
Big dog Rover and Woody Woodchuck. La Rue. Under the story tree.
Big fish and the frogs. Cooper. Argosy of fables.
See also Frog and the snake #.
Big hippo who was too noisy and clumsy. Lobagola. Folk tales of a savage.
Big horn mountain sheep and coyote. Hogner. Navajo winter nights.
Big long man and mountain lion. Hogner. Navajo winter nights.

Big long man and the giant. Hogner. Navajo winter nights.
See also Giant and the boy.
Big long man goes hunting. Hogner. Navajo winter nights.
Big long man's corn patch. Hogner. Navajo winter nights.
See also Tar baby stories; Rabbit and tar wolf; Master Rabbit again encounters the pine-gum baby.
Big music. Field. American folk and fairy tales.
Big-nosed bogey. Henderson and Jones. Wonder tales of ancient Wales. (Bwca'r Trwyn; or, The big-nosed bogey.)
See also Boggart # ; Brownie and the thievish maids #.
Big snake of Pecos. James. Tewa firelight tales.
Big tree. Told under the blue umbrella.
Big, white woolly lamb. Shannon. California fairy tales.
Big worm. Fuller. Book of dragons.
Bigger, Adventures of. See Outlandish adventures of Bigger.
Bilinck and the three waves. Carpenter. Tales of a Basque grandmother.
Billy Beg and the bull. Adams and Atchinson. Book of giant stories.
Hutchinson. Chimney corner fairy tales. (Billy Beg and his bull.)
Johnson and Scott. Anthology of children's literature.
See also Wonderful horns.
For other entries, see 2d edition.
Billy Boy and his friends. See Bremen town musicians.
Billygoat's barnyard. Skinner. Happy tales.
Billy's garden. Elson and Runkel. Child-library readers. Book 2.
Bimini and the fountain of youth #.
See also Ponce de Leon and the fountain of youth.
Binding of Fenris. See Binding of the Fenris wolf.
Binding of the Fenris wolf. Curry and Clippinger. Children's literature. (How the Fenris wolf was chained.)
Evans. Worth while stories. (Binding of Fenrir.)
Pyle. Tales from Norse mythology.
For other entries, see 2d edition.
Birch and the star. Thorne-Thomsen. Birch and the star, and other stories.
Topelius. Canute Whistlewinks.
Bird. I. See 2d edition.
Bird. II. Bailey. Tell me another story.
Bird and the monkeys. See Birds and the monkeys. II.
Bird bride. Partridge. Joyful Star.
Bird-cage maker. Faulkner. Road to enchantment.
For other entries, see 2d edition.
Bird-call (poem). Cooper. Argosy of fables.
Bird-catcher, the partridge, and the cock. See Fowler, the partridge, and the cock.
Bird Day. See Ben Flicker's mistake # ; Bobby Bluebird's adventures #. Cuckoo comes to Ireland ; Eider duck ; Fairy lamps ; Fairy wren ; Feeding of the emigrants ; Gun for

Bird Day—*continued.*

sale; How K'tonton saved the birds on Shabbath Shirah; How the birds came; How the little bird reached home; Killing the birds; Little boy pie; Moon bird; New neighbors; R. D. P. society; Robin's eggs; Scarecrow; Why the birds sing different songs.

See also in subject list: Bird legends; also names of birds.

For other entries, see 2d edition.

Bird Feng, Story of. Dulac. Edmund Dulac's fairy book.

Bird=found. *See* Fundevogel.

Bird from the waterfall. Cendrars. Little black stories.

See also Man with the bag; Monkey's bargains # ; Travels of a fox.

Bird=man and the singing girl. Kennedy. Red man's wonder book.

Bird monsters. *See* How the birds came. II.

Bird=of=gold, Story of. Colum. Boy apprenticed to an enchanter.

Bird of love. Purnell and Weatherwax. Talking bird.

Bird of Saint Martin. Cooper. Argosy of fables.

Bird of sorrow #.

See also Catherine and her destiny; Trouble when one's young.

Bird songs #.

See also Why the birds sing different songs.

Bird that sings. Topelius. Canute Whistlewinks.

Bird with two beaks. Cooper. Argosy of fables.

See also Rival roosters.

Birdcatcher and the lark. *See* Fowler and the lark.

Birdhouse of Lincoln logs. Morley. I know a secret.

Birds and the monkeys. I. **Arnold. Book of good counsels. (Weaver birds and the monkeys.)

Cooper. Argosy of fables. (Weaver birds and the monkeys.)

For other entries, see 2d edition.

In 2d edition this story is also indexed under the title "Monkey and the crows."

Birds and the monkeys. II. Mackenzie. Jackal in Persia. (Bird and the monkeys.)

See also Ape, the glow-worm and the popinjay # ; Monkeys, the firefly and the bird; Monkeys' house.

Birds and their nests. I. *See* 2d edition.

Birds and their nests. II. Hervey and Hix. Fanciful tales for children. (Why the cuckoo has no nest.)

Birds' ball game. Bailey. Stories from an Indian cave. (How the squirrel won the ball game.)

Gearhart. Skalalatoot stories. (Bat and the flying squirrel.)

James. Happy animals of Atagahi. (Tournament day.)

Rich. Why-so stories. (Animals and birds play ball.)

For other entries, see 2d edition.

Birds go to war. I. *See* 2d edition.

Birds go to war. II. De Huff. Taytay's tales. (*In* War between the birds and the animals.)
See also Battle of the birds. II; Why the petrel lay its eggs on land.

Birds go to war. III. Sexton. Gray wolf stories. (Swallows war against the snakes.)

Birds of passage (poem). Cooper. Argosy of fables.

Birds on Midsummer Day. Graham. Happy holidays.

Birds, the beasts and the bat. *See* Bat, birds and beasts.

Birth of Athene. *See* Minerva.

Birth of Bran. *See* Finn MacCool.

Birth of Sin. *See* Fine-weather woman.

Birthday candles (poem). Potter. Giant of Apple Pie Hill

Birthday of the Infanta. Bailey. Tell me another story. (Adapted.)
For other entries, see 2d edition.

Birthday party. Casserley. Michael of Ireland.

Birthday pie. Potter. Giant of Apple Pie Hill.

Birthday present. Bailey. Tell me another story.
For other entries, see 2d edition.

Bishop Hatto and the rats. *See* Mouse tower.

Bishop's chairs. Broomell. Children's story caravan.

Biter bit. I. *See* 2d edition.

Biter bit. II. Lanier. Book of giants.

Bitter waters. Chrisman. Wind that wouldn't blow.

Bittern and the mussel. *See* Oyster and the heron.

Bizhan and Manizha. Coit. Ivory throne of Persia.

Biwag. *See* Toribio.

Black Agnace of Dunbar. Coe. Third book of stories. (How Black Agnes kept her castle.)
For other entries, see 2d edition.

Black beetle that didn't wish to work. Lobagola. Folk tales of a savage.

Black bull of Norroway. Rhys. English fairy book.
Steel. English fairy tales.
For other entries, see 2d edition.

Black bull of the Castle of Blood. Williams-Ellis. Fairies and enchanters. (Secret room.)
For other entries, see 2d edition.

Black cat. I. *See* 2d edition.

Black cat. II. Harriman. Stories for little children. (Tale of a black cat.)
For other entries, see 2d edition.

Black cat and the pumpkin. *See* Hallowe'en story.

Black cat of the witch=dance=place. Harper. Ghosts and goblins.

Black charger. Gunterman. Castles in Spain.

Black doll. Rhys. English fairy book.

Black Douglas. Terry. Tales from far and near. (How a strong castle was taken.)
For other entries, see 2d edition.

Black dragon of the Sea of Dunting. *See* Dragon princess.

Black dwarf. Friedlander. Jewish fairy tales (Dutton).

Black egg. Capuana. Italian fairy tales.

Black-headed crow and a little yellow canary, Story of. Mamin. Verotchka's tales.

Black-headed one. Martin. Fatma was a goose.

Black horse. Price. Legends of the seven seas. (Prince Underwave and the earth king's son. Adapted.)

Black leopard who lost the man in the tree. Lobagola. Folk tales of a savage.

Black magic. *See* Master and his pupil.

Black Prince. Patten. Junior Classics. v. 7. (Boy heroes of Crecy and Poitiers.)

Tappan. Old world hero stories. (Edward, the Black Prince.)

For other entries, see 2d edition.

Black rider. *See* Hunted hare.

Black rooster and the red rooster. *See* Rival roosters.

Black sheep. Macmanus. Donegal wonder book.

See also Cinderella.

Black snake and the golden chain. *See* Crow and the snake. II.

Black Thief and Knight of the Glen. Colum. Big tree of Bunlahy. (Story that shattered King Cormac's cup and the story that put it together again.)

Macmanus. Donegal wonder book. (Steed o' Bells.)

For other entries, see 2d edition.

Black-toothed prince. Cook. To-day's stories of yesterday.

Black tulip. Miller. My travelship: Holland.

Blackamoor. Æsop. Fables (Jones).

Cooper. Argosy of fables.

For other entries, see 2d edition.

Blackbird and the fox. Brown. Curious book of birds.

See also Clever woodpecker.

Blackfoot and the bear. Macmillan. Canadian wonder tales.

See also Bear-man.

Blacksmith. Henderson and Calvert. Wonder tales of old Tyrol.

See also Smith and the devil.

Blacksmith and his dog. Æsop. Fables (Jones).

Æsop. Twenty-four fables (L'Estrange. Smith and his dog.)

Cooper. Argosy of fables. (Brazier and his dog.)

Blacksmith of the gods. *See* Vulcan.

Blacksmith's sons #.

See also Little Princess Sunshine; Peter and the birch tree dryad.

Blacksmith's wife of Yarrowfoot. Harper. Ghosts and goblins. (Witch's shoes.)

Olcott. Wonder tales from fairy isles. (Witch's shoes.)

For other entries, see 2d edition.

Blackthorn. I. *See* St. Patrick's thorn.

Blackthorn. II. *See* Wicked tree.

Bladder=Campion. *See* Boy who caught flies.

Blessed bread and cheese. Guerber. Legends of Switzerland., (*In* Fribourg.)

Blessed gift of joy is bestowed upon man. Rasmussen. Eagle's gift.

Blind boy who killed a bear. Snell. Told beneath the northern lights.

Blind hen. Cooper. Argosy of fables.

Blind man and the cripple. Ralston. Russian fairy tales.

Blind man and the cub. Æsop. Fables (Jones).

Blind man and the elephant. *See* Blind men and the elephant.

Blind man and the snake. Cooper. Argosy of fables.
For other entries, see 2d edition.

Blind man and the whelp. Cooper. Argosy of fables.
For other entries, see 2d edition.

Blind man, Story of. *See* Baba Abdallah, Story of.

Blind man, the deaf man, and the donkey. Lee. Folk tales of all nations.
Pyle. Fairy tales from India.
For other entries, see 2d edition.

Blind men and the elephant (poem). Broomell. Children's story caravan.
(poem). Cooper. Argosy of fables. (Six men of Indostan.)
Evans. Worth while stories. (Blind man and the elephant.)
(poem). Johnson and Scott. Anthology of children's literature.
(poem). Power. Children's treasure chest. (Six men of Indostan.)
(poem). Saxe, J. G. Poems.
See also Chameleon; Red-bud tree.
For other entries, see 2d edition.

Blixie Bimber, Story of. Sandburg. Rootabaga stories.
Sandburg. Rootabaga country.

Blockhead Hans. *See* Hans Clodhopper.

Blooming fruiting winter. Olcott. Wonder tales from windmill lands.

Blooming of the white thorn. *See* Thorn of Glastonbury.

Blossom makers. Nakazawa. Weaver of the frost.

Blotter, the pen and the ink. Cozad. Story talks.

Blue and green eggs. Elson and Runkel. Child-library readers: Book 2.

Blue Beard. *See* Bluebeard.

Blue belt. Dasent. East of the sun and west of the moon (Nielsen).
Sheriff. Stories old and new.
For other entries, see 2d edition.

Blue bird. I. Aulnoy. Fairy tales (Planché).
Dulac. Edmund Dulac's fairy book.
Fairy garland (Dulac).
For other entries, see 2d edition.

Blue bird. II. Skinner. Merry tales.
See also Land where people never die.
For other entries, see 2d edition.
Blue bird. III. *See* 2d edition.
Blue bird. IV. Gordon and Stockard. Gordon readers. 2d
reader.
Blue bonnets. I. Blondell. Keepsakes.
Egan. New found tales.
Blue bonnets. II. American Home magazine. July, 1936,
p. 24. (*In* Beautiful legends of Texas' wild flowers.)
Blue flower. I–II. *See* 2d edition.
Blue flower. III. Van Dyke. Blue flower.
Blue flower. IV. *See* Land of the blue flower.
Blue hill. Bacon. Mercy and the mouse.
Blue jackal. **Arnold. Book of good counsels. (Dyed
jackal.)
Cooper. Argosy of fables. (Dyed jackal.)
For other entries, see 2d edition.
Blue Jay the imitator. Spence. Myths of the North Ameri-
can Indians. (Blue Jay and Ioi go visiting. *In* Ch. 7.)
See also Iktomi goes visiting; Coyote and porcupine; Coyote
imitates bear; Coyote's adventures; Bear and the rabbit.
For other entries, see 2d edition.
Blue Jay visits the ghosts. Spence. Myths of the North
American Indians. (Blue Jay and Ioi: marriage of Ioi.
In Ch. 7.)
For other entries, see 2d edition.
Blue Jay's wife. *See* Ghost wife. V; Ghost land. III.
Blue light. Curry and Clippinger. Children's literature.
Grimm. Fairy tales (Olcott).
For other entries, see 2d edition.
Blue lotus. Farjeon. Old nurse's stocking basket.
Blue moon. Housman. Doorway in fairyland.
Blue mountains. Coussens. Diamond story book.
For other entries, see 2d edition.
Blue ribbon. Evans. Worth while stories.
Blue robin. Broomell. Children's story caravan.
For other entries, see 2d edition.
Blue rowan tree. Olcott. Wonder tales from fairy isles.
Blue silver. Sandburg. Rootabaga pigeons.
Blue wings, Story of. Skinner. Child's book of country sto-
ries.
Bluebeard. Arthur Rackham fairy book.
De La Mare. Told again.
Quinn. Stokes' wonder book of fairy tales.
Rich. Read-aloud book.
Wilson. Red magic.
See also Bear and the old man's daughters; Castle of Com-
orre; Cliff dweller and the corn maiden # ; Forbidden room.
I–II; Indian Bluebeard; Prophecy of the djinn; St. Try-
phene; Three chests.
For other entries, see 2d edition.

Bluebell. I. *See* 2d edition.

Bluebell. II. *See* Hyacinthus.

Bluebells. Marzials. Stories for the story hour.

Bluebird and coyote. Parker. Skunny Wundy and other Indian tales. (How the bluebird gained the color of the sky and the gray wolf gained and lost it.)

Phillips. Indian tales for little folks. (Why the bluebird is blue and the coyote is gray.)

For other entries, see 2d edition.

Bluebird and the crow. De Huff. Taytay's memories.

Boadicea. Farjeon. Mighty men from Beowulf to William the Conqueror. (Little island, pt. 3.)

Boar, Tale of the. Darton. Wonder book of old romance.

Boar and the chameleon. Cooper. Argosy of fables.

See also How the ox and the crab ran a race.

Boar who was a man. Davis. Truce of the wolf.

Boaster and the baby. *See* Manabozho and his toe.

Boastful bamboo tree. Faulkner. Little Peachling.

Boastful frogs. Sheriff. Stories old and new.

Boastful geese. *See* Geese whose ancestors saved Rome.

Boastful menehune. Metzger. Tales told in Hawaii.

See also Me-ne-hu-ne #.

Boastful pigeon. Carey. Stories of the birds.

See also Butterfly that stamped.

Boastful stranger. Metzger. Tales told in Hawaii.

See also How Maui won a place for himself in the house.

Boasting elephant and the fighting hooked lizards. Lobagola. Folk tales of a savage.

Boasting traveler. Æsop. Fables (Jones).

Cooper. Argosy of fables.

For other entries, see 2d edition.

Bob=cat. Brown. Under the rowan tree.

Bob Cratchit's Christmas dinner. *See* Cratchit's Christmas dinner.

Bobbie, the powder boy. Evans. Worth while stories.

Bobby Squirrel plays a joke. Skinner. Happy tales.

Bobby's fairy shoes. *See* Timothy's shoes.

Bobby's mud=pie man. Harriman. Stories for little children.

Bodach and the boy. MacManus. Lo, and behold ye!

See also Jack and his master ; Keep cool #.

Boettger, Johann. *See* Powdered wig.

Bog of Ecsed. Pogány. Hungarian fairy book. (Bog of Ecsed and the will-o'-the-wisp.)

Bogdynek. Byrde. Polish fairy book.

Bogey beast. Steel. English fairy tales.

Boiled owl. Housman. Turn again tales.

Bold blackbird. *See* Valiant blackbird.

Bold dragoon. Irving. Bold dragoon, and other ghostly tales.

Sechrist. Little book of Hallowe'en. (Adventure of my grandfather. Adapted.)

Bold giant. Fyleman. Forty good-night tales.

Bold rabbit with cock eyes and a short tail. Mamin. Verotchka's tales.

Bones of Djuling. Martens. Wonder tales from far away. (Youngest of seven sisters and the Djulungdjulung fish. *In* Two Cinderella stories.)
See also Cinderella.

Boniface. *See* St. Boniface.

Boniface and Keep=it=all. Perkins and Danielson. Mayflower program book.
Stocking. Golden goblet.
See also Closed hand; Tommy's Christmas stocking; Troll's Christmas.

Bontche Schweig. *See* Bontsie Silent.

Bontsie Silent. Manner. Silver treasury.
Schwarz. Jewish caravan. (Bontche Schweig.)

Booby. Faulkner. Road to enchantment.
Lee. Folk tales of all nations.
For other entries, see 2d edition.

Boodle and the bottles. Fyleman. Forty good-night tales. (Mrs. Moodle, pt. 2.)

Boodle's adventure. Fyleman. Forty good-morning tales. (Mrs. Moodle. II.)

Book for Jerry. Van Buren and Bemis. Christmas in storyland.

Booker Washington's examination. McVenn. Good manners and good conduct. (Booker T. Washington arrives at Hampton.)

Boone, Daniel. Bailey. Stories children want. (Road that went out West.)

Boot is a league of nations. Broomell. Children's story caravan.

Boots and his brothers. Adams and Atchinson. There were giants. (Poucinet.)
Curry and Clippinger. Children's literature.
Faulkner. Road to enchantment. (Peter, Paul, and Espen.)
Hutchinson. Chimney corner fairy tales.
Johnson and Scott. Anthology of children's literature.
Piper. Road in storyland.
Rasmussen. East o' the sun and west o' the moon. (Three brothers.)
Told under the green umbrella.
Whiteman. Playmates in print.
See also Fool and the prince; Hans Clodhopper; Princess whom nobody could silence.
For other entries, see 2d edition.

Boots and the troll. Kinscella. Music appreciation readers. Book 4. (Boy who fooled the troll.)
Rasmussen. East o' the sun and west o' the moon. (Lad who fooled the troll and won the princess.)
For other entries, see 2d edition.

Bo=peep (poem). Skinner. Merry tales. (How the sheep found Bo-peep.)

Borah of Byamee, the Wirreenun. Wells. How the present came from the past. Book 1, pt. 2.

Boris takes a walk. Mitchell. Here and now story book.

Boro Budur temple. Olcott. Wonder tales from pirate isles. (Legend of the Boro-Budur.)

Borrowed plumage. Wiggin and Smith. Twilight stories.

Borrowed wings. Metzger. Tales told in Hawaii.

Boton and the emperor of the Greeks. Pogány. Hungarian fairy book.

Botticelli, Alessandro. Steedman. Knights of art.

Böttger, Johann. *See* Powdered wig.

Bottle=hill, Legend of. Lee. Folk tales of all nations.
For other entries, see 2d edition.

Bound princess. Housman. Doorway in fairyland.
This includes: Fire eaters; Galloping plough; Thirsty well; Princess Melilot; Burning rose; Camphor worm.

Bow. Cooper. Argosy of fables. (Archer and his bow.)
For other entries, see 2d edition.

Bow of Ulysses. *See* Ulysses' return.

Bower in the woods. Burnett. Children's book.

Bowl of mist. Marzials. Stories for the story hour.

Bowman and the lion. *See* Archer and the lion.

Box tortoise's shell. Parker. Skunny Wundy and other Indian tales.

Box with something pretty in it. Bryce. Folk tales from foreign lands. (What was in the box.)
For other entries, see 2d edition.

Boy and his coat. Cady and Dewey. Picture stories from the great artists.

Boy and his dream. Buckingham. Elephant's friend.

Boy and his sister. *See* Sun a prisoner. I.

Boy and his three helpers. Macmillan. Canadian wonder tales.
See also Beautiful bride. II # ; Great Heart and the three tests #.

Boy and his wife. Linderman. Kootenai why stories.

Boy and the dancing fairy. *See* Magical dancing doll.

Boy and the deer. Fleming. Round the world in folk tales.

Boy and the elf. Lagerlöf. Wonderful adventures of Nils. (*In* Ch. 4.)

Boy and the fairies. Silvester and Peter. Happy hour stories.

Boy and the filberts. Æsop. Fables (Jones).
Cooper. Argosy of fables.
Johnson and Scott. Anthology of children's literature.
See also Monkey and the peas; Owl and the two rabbits.
For other entries, see 2d edition.

Boy and the moonlight. Miller. My travelship: Japan.

Boy and the near-boy. Wiggin and Smith. Twilight stories.

Boy and the nettle. Æsop. Fables (Jones. Boy and the nettles.)
Cooper. Argosy of fables.
Rich. Read-aloud book.
For other entries, see 2d edition.
Boy and nightingale. *See* Nightingale and the pearl.
Boy and the Nis. Choate and Curtis. Little people of the hills.
Boy and the pig. De Huff. Taytay's tales.
Boy and the rainbow (poem). Cooper. Argosy of fables.
Boy and the robber's magical booty. Macmillan. Canadian wonder tales.
Boy and the scorpion. Cooper. Argosy of fables.
Boy and the snails. Æsop. Fables (Jones).
Boy and the thief. *See* Thief and the boy.
Boy bathing. Æsop. Fables (Jones).
Cooper. Argosy of fables.
For other entries, see 2d edition.
Boy=catcher. James. Tewa firelight tales.
Boy drummers in Holland. *See* Drummers' day.
Boy heroes of Crecy and Poitiers. *See* Black Prince.
Boy in the jug. Sheriff. Stories old and new.
For other entries, see 2d edition.
Boy in the moon. I–II. *See* 2d edition.
Boy in the moon. III. Spence. Myths of the North American Indians. (*In* Ch. 7.)
Boy in the moon. IV. Bailey. Stories from an Indian cave. (Boy who went to the sky.)
Boy magician. Lee. Folk tales of all nations.
Spence. Myths of the North American Indians. (*In* Ch. 4.)
Boy martyr. Farjeon. Tales from Chaucer. (Prioress's tale.)
For other entries, see 2d edition.
Boy of Cadore. Miller. My Bookhouse. v. 4.
Boy of great strength and the giants. Macmillan. Canadian wonder tales.
See also Morning star. I.
Boy of Italy who could tame all animals. *See* St. Francis of Assisi ; Wolf of Gubbio.
Boy Pu=nia and the king of the sharks. Colum. Fountain of youth.
For other entries, see 2d edition.
Boy, the coyote, and the magic rock. De Huff. Taytay's tales.
Boy who became a robin. *See* How the robin came.
Boy who became a walrus. Snell. Told beneath the northern lights.
Boy who became emperor. Lee. Folk tales of all nations.
For other entries, see 2d edition.
Boy who brought the light. Snell. Told beneath the northern lights.

Boy who caught flies. Carey. Flower legends. (Bladder-Campion.)
For other entries, see 2d edition.

Boy who conquered himself. Forbes. Good citizenship. (*In* Ch. 8.)

Boy who cried for the moon. Metzger. Tales told in Hawaii.
See also Child that cried for the moon.

Boy who cried "Wolf." Æsop. Fables (Artzybasheff. Shepherd boy and the wolf.)
Æsop. Fables (Jones. Shepherd's boy and the wolf.)
Æsop. Fables (Whitman ed. Shepherd boy and the wolf.)
Cooper. Argosy of fables. (Shepherd-boy and the wolf.)
Curry and Clippinger. Children's literature. (Shepherd's boy.)
Evans. Worth while stories.
Johnson and Scott. Anthology of children's literature. (Shepherd's boy and the wolf.)
Rich. Read-aloud book. (Shepherd boy and the wolf.)
White. School management, p. 246. (Wolf.)
For other entries, see 2d edition.

Boy who fooled the troll. *See* Boots and the troll.

Boy who forgot. *See* Rhœcus.

Boy who had morning star for playmate. Sexton. Gray wolf stories.

Boy who heard the silent speak. Topelius. Canute Whistlewinks.

Boy who invented sails. Metzger. Tales told in Hawaii.

Boy who kept his promise. Tappan. Prince from nowhere.

Boy who killed the dif. Wheeler. Albanian wonder tales.

Boy who learned the language of the beasts. *See* Three languages.

Boy who lived with grizzlies. I. Sexton. Gray wolf stories.

Boy who lived with grizzlies. II. Spence. Myths of the North American Indians. Ch. 3. (Sacred bear spear.)
See also Mooin the bear's child # ; Bear man.

Boy who played the bousouka. Wheeler. Albanian wonder tales.

Boy who recommended himself. White. School management, p. 242.

Boy who sang with the birds. *See* Walter von der Vogelweide.

Boy who set a snare for the sun. *See* Sun a prisoner. I.

Boy who stole the nightingale that was called Gizari. Wheeler. Albanian wonder tales.

Boy who talked with the birds. Carpenter. Tales of a Basque grandmother.

Boy who took the letter to the world where the dead live. Wheeler. Albanian wonder tales.

Boy who wanted to play always. Evans. Worth while stories.
  See also Quentin and the clock.
Boy who was brother to the Drague. Wheeler. Albanian wonder tales.
  See also Two brothers. IV.
Boy who was easily pleased. Tappan. Prince from nowhere.
Boy who was fated to be a king. Wheeler. Albanian wonder tales.
  See also False prince and the true # ; Golden armlet.
Boy who was initiated into buffalo herd. Sexton. Gray wolf stories.
Boy who was reared by buffaloes. Sexton. Gray wolf stories.
Boy who went to the sky. *See* Boy in the moon. III.
Boy who would a robber be. Dane. Once there was and was not.
Boy who wouldn't wash his face. Potter. Giant of Apple Pie Hill.
Boy whom his parents, the king, and the giant conspired to kill. Ryder. Twenty-two goblins.
Boy without a name. *See* First Christmas present. III.
Boys and the frogs. Æsop. Fables (Jones).
  Cooper. Argosy of fables.
  Johnson and Scott. Anthology of children's literature.
  For other entries, see 2d edition.
Boys and the giant. Macmillan. Canadian wonder tales.
Boy's visit to Santa Claus. Skinner. Christmas stories.
  Walters. Book of Christmas stories.
  For other entries, see 2d edition.
Boys who did not get a magic cow. Olcott. Wonder tales from Baltic wizards. (*In* What happened to some Lapp children.)
Boys who went to the sun. James. Tewa firelight tales.
  See also Sun children kill the great monsters.
Bradamante, Adventures of. Echols. Knights of Charlemagne. (Many enchantments; Roger and Bradamante.)
Brahman and the goat, Story of. **Arnold. Book of good counsels.
  Cooper. Argosy of fables. (Brahman and the three goats.)
  See also Farmer, the sheep and the robbers # ; Foolish Brahmin # ; King's curing; Magic cap.
  For other entries, see 2d edition.
Brahman and the mongoose. Cooper. Argosy of fables.
  See also Beth Gellert #.
Brahman and the pans, Story of. **Arnold. Book of good counsels.
  Cooper. Argosy of fables.
  See also Barber's fifth brother ; Broken pot #.
Brahman and the three goats. *See* Brahman and the goat.

Brahman and the tiger. *See* Brahman, the tiger, and the jackal.

Brahman saved by a crab. Cooper. Argosy of fables.

Brahman, the thief, and the ghost. *See* Hermit, the thief, and the demon.

Brahman, the tiger, and the jackal. Bruce. Treasury of tales for little folk. (Brahman, the tiger and the six judges.)

Curry and Clippinger. Children's literature. (Tiger, the Brahman, and the jackal.)

Faulkner. White elephant. (Brahmin and the tiger.)

Johnson and Scott. Anthology of children's literature. (Tiger, the Brahman, and the jackal.)

Pyle. Fairy tales from India. (Brahmin, the tiger, and the seven judges.)

See also How the fox used his wits.

For other entries, see 2d edition.

Brahman, the tiger, and the seven judges. *See* Brahman, the tiger, and the jackal.

Brahman, the tiger and the six judges. *See* Brahman, the tiger and the jackal.

Brahman who died because of poison. Ryder. Twenty-two goblins.

Brahman's dream. Lee. Folk tales of all nations.

See also Barber's fifth brother; Brahman and the pans; Broken pot #; Milkmaid and her pail.

Brahman's star. Lane. Tower legends.

Brahmin. *See* Brahman.

Owing to the variation in spelling of this title in different books, it has been decided to enter them all as "Brahman."

Bramble. Cooper. Argosy of fables.

Bramble=bush king. Chidley. Fifty-two story talks.

Curry and Clippinger. Children's literature. (Bramble is made king.)

Gaer. Burning bush. (*In* Bramble that would be king.)

See also Trees choosing a king.

Bramble is made king. *See* Bramble-bush king.

Bramble that would be king. *See* Bramble-bush king.

Bran. I. *See* Finn MacCool.

Bran. II. *See* Bran the blessed; Branwen, the daughter of Llyr.

Bran the blessed. Lanier. Knightly legends of Wales. (*In* Branwen, the daughter of Llyr.)

Morris. Book of the three dragons. (Wonderful head.)

Branch of almond blossom. Gunterman. Castles in Spain.

See also Alhambra legend.

Brandan. *See* St. Brandan.

Branwen, the daughter of Llyr. Farjeon. Mighty men from Beowulf to William the Conquerer. (Quarrelsome brother.)

For other entries, see 2d edition.

Brave boy. Lee. Folk tales of all nations.
  See also Brave little tailor; Brave against his will #; Gipsy
    and the dragon. II.
Brave drummer boy of France. Kinscella. Music apprecia-
    tion readers. Book 3.
Brave grenadier. Beston. Starlight wonder book.
Brave little bowman. Aspinwall. Jataka tales. (Valiant
    dwarf.)
  Freeman. Child-story readers. 3d reader.
  For other entries, see 2d edition.
Brave little Glory. Olcott. Wonder tales from China seas.
Brave little Kombe. Martens. Wonder tales from far away.
Brave little tailor. Adams and Atchinson. Book of giant
    stories. (Gallant tailor.)
  Harper. Magic fairy tales.
  Power. Bag o' tales.
  Quinn. Stokes' wonder book of fairy tales. (Valiant little
    tailor.)
  Williams. Tales from Ebony. (Valiant little tailor.)
  See also Brave boy; Devil and the tailor; Gypsy and the
    dragon. II; Johnny Gloke; Thomas Berennikov; Stan
    Bolovan.
  For other entries, see 2d edition.
Brave man, the wise man, and the clever man. Ryder.
    Twenty-two goblins.
  See also Four clever brothers.
Brave mountaineer. *See* Tell, William.
Brave mouse. Gordon and Stockard. Gordon readers. 2d
    reader.
Brave prince. Pogány. Hungarian fairy book.
Brave queen of Hungary. Patten. Junior classics. v. 7.
Brave Seventee Bai. Pyle. Fairy tales from India.
  For other entries, see 2d edition.
Brave tailor. *See* Gipsy and the dragon. II.
Brave three hundred. Curry and Clippinger. Children's lit-
    erature. (Pass of Thermopylae.)
  Farjeon. Mighty men from Achilles to Julius Caesar. (Se-
    cret path.)
  Miller. My book of history. v. 2. (Leonidas at Thermopy-
    lae. *In* Ch. 4.)
  Patten. Junior classics. v. 7. (Fight at the pass of Ther-
    mopylae.)
  See also Kenewa, the bravest of the Penacooks; Sachem of the
    white plume.
  For other entries, see 2d edition.
Brave tin soldier. Andersen. Fairy tales (Siewers tr.
    Steadfast tin soldier.)
  Andersen. Fairy tales (Stickney. v. 1. Steadfast tin sol-
    dier.)
  Bruce. Treasury of tales for little folk. (Valiant tin sol-
    dier.)

Brave tin soldier—*continued.*
Curry and Clippinger. Children's literature. (Hardy tin soldier.)
Johnson and Scott. Anthology of children's literature. (Steadfast tin soldier.)
Rich. Read-aloud book. (Hardy tin soldier.)
Starbuck. Familiar haunts. (Steadfast tin soldier.)
Through story-land with the children.
For other entries, see 2d edition.

Brave young warrior who was a dearly loved son. *See* Cygnus.

Brav-o-lona, Story of. Browne. Indian nights.

Brazen Hold; or, Seven stages. Coit. Ivory throne of Persia.

Brazier and his dog. *See* Blacksmith and his dog.

Bread-and-butter sandwich. Potter. Giant of Apple Pie Hill.

Bread-and-butter town. Potter. Giant of Apple Pie Hill.

Bread of gold. *See* Sovereign of the mineral kingdom.

Bread stone, Legend of the. Schwimmer. Tisza tales.

Breda. Miller. My travelship: Holland. (Capture of Breda.)

Bremen town musicians. Bruce. Treasury of tales for little folk. (Travelling musicians.)
Curry and Clippinger. Children's literature. (Traveling musicians.)
De La Mare. Told again. (Musicians.)
Evans. Worth while stories. (Traveling musicians. Abridged.)
Grimm. Fairy tales (Olcott).
Grimm. Tales from Grimm (Wanda Gag. Musicians of Bremen.)
Harriman. Stories for little children. (Billy Boy and his friends. Adapted.)
Hutchinson. Chimney corner stories.
Johnson and Scott. Anthology of children's literature. (Travelling musicians.)
Kinscella. Music appreciation readers. Book 3. (Town musicians.)
Quinn. Stokes' wonder book of fairy tales. (Traveling musicians.)
Starbuck. Familiar haunts. (Traveling musicians.)
Told under the green umbrella. (Street musicians.)
Whiteman. Playmates in print.
Wilson. Green magic. (Musicians of Bremen.)
See also Krencipal and Krencipalka ; Three companions. II ; Traveling cat.
For other entries, see 2d edition.

Brer. *See* Brother.
Owing to the inconsistent use of the terms "Brer" and "Brother" in the same books, and because the same stories

Brer—*continued.*
> appear in various books under different titles, it has been decided to enter them all under "Brother."
> *See also* entries under "Mister."

Briar rose. *See* Sleeping beauty. I.

Bricriu's feast. Gregory. Cuchulain of Muirthemne.

Bridal gift. Hart. Picture tales from Holland.

Bridal march. Wilson. Green magic.

Bride, St. *See* St. Bridget.

Bride and her Christmas dream. *See* St. Bride.

Bride of broken waters. Browne. Indian nights.

Bride of the southland. *See* How the seasons came to be. IV.

Bridegroom of O Chu San. *See* Rats and their son-in-law.

Bridge builder. Fleming. Round the world in folk tales.

Bridge of Avignon. Kinscella. Music appreciation readers. Book 3. (Shepherd boy who built a bridge.)

Bridge of meetings. Vilnay. Legends of Palestine.

Bridge of the kist. *See* Pedlar of Swaffham.

Bridget. *See* St. Bridget.

Bright=cloud woman. *See* Raven gets fish for his people.

Bright=Hawk's feather. Carpenter. Tales of a Russian grandmother. (Little feather of the splendid falcon.)
> Lee. Folk tales of all nations. (Little feather of Fenist the bright falcon.)
> For other entries, see 2d edition.

Bright May morning. Marzials. Stories for the story hour.

Bright moon=cakes and the money tree. *See* Chinese emperor's visit to the moon.

Bright sun brings it to light #.
> *See also* Meinrad's watchers; Singing bone.

Brigid. *See* St. Bridget.

Brisingamen, Story of. *See* Freyja.

Bristlepate and the sad princess. Meeker. Folk tales from the Far East.
> *See also* Golden goose. I; Hans who made the princess laugh.

Britomart. Richardson. Stories from old English poetry. (Adventures of fair Florimel.)

Broad man, the tall man, and the man with eyes of flame. Bruce. Treasury of tales for little folk. (Long, Broad, and Quick-eye.)
> Curtin. Fairy tales of Eastern Europe. (Long, Broad, and Swift Glance.)
> Johnson and Scott. Anthology of children's literature. (Long, Broad, and Sharpsight.)
> Lee. Folk tales of all nations. (Long, Broad, and Sharpsight.)
> Power. Bag o'tales.
> For other entries, see 2d edition.

Broken engagement. *See* Sir One Long Body and Madame Thousand Feet.

Broken wing. I. See 2d edition.
Broken wing. II. *See* Wuchowson the windblower.
Bronze boar. Andersen. Fairy tales (Siewers tr. Bronze pig.)
Andersen. Fairy tales (Stickney). v. 2. (Metal pig.)
See also Chop Chin and the golden dragon # ; Man who did not believe in fairies; White elephant. V.
For other entries, see 2d edition.
    In 2d edition this story is also indexed under the title "Metal pig."
Bronze Buddha and the whale. *See* Idol and the whale.
Bronze-heart. Newman. Fairy flowers.
Bronze horse. Capuana. Italian fairy tales.
Bronze pig. *See* Bronze boar.
Bronze ring. Coussens. Diamond story book.
For other entries, see 2d edition.
Brook and the fountain (poem). Cooper. Argosy of fables.
Brook Chorny. Carpenter. Tales of a Russian grandmother. (Rivers that talked.)
Ralston. Russian fairy tales. (*In* Ch. 3.)
Broom. Fyleman. Tea time tales.
Broom and the juniper. Carey. Flower legends.
Broomstick and Snowflake. Falkberget. Broomstick and Snowflake.
Broomstick and the East Mountain giant. Falkberget. Broomstick and Snowflake.
Broomstick and the giant maiden. Falkberget. Broomstick and Snowflake.
Brother and sister. I. Grimm. Fairy tales (Olcott. Little brother and little sister.)
Lang. Old friends among the fairies.
Quinn. Stokes' wonder book of fairy tales. (Enchanted stag.)
See also Alenoushka and her brother.
For other entries, see 2d edition.
Brother and sister. II. Æsop. Fables (Jones).
Æsop. Fables (Whitman ed.).
For other entries, see 2d edition.
Brother Bernard. *See* Monk and the bird's song.
Brother Mole. Sale. Tree named John. (Brer Mole swaps his eyes for Brer Frawg's tail.)
Brother of Christ #.
See also Almost saved. I.
Brother Rabbit and Brother Bear. Lee. Folk tales of all nations. (Brer Rabbit and Brer Bear.)
Brother Rabbit and Brother Wolf. Lee. Folk tales of all nations. (Ber Rabbit and Ber Wolf.)
See also Cat and the mouse in partnership; Wolf's butter.
Brother Rabbit and the mosquitoes. Field. American folk and fairy tales.
For other entries, see 2d edition.

Brother Rabbit conquers Brother Lion. Sale. Tree named John. (*In* Gittin' well.)
See also Lion and the hare. I.
For other entries, see 2d edition.
Brother Rabbit's cool air swing. Babbitt. Animals' own story book. (Mr. Rabbit's cool-air swing.)
For other entries, see 2d edition.
Brother Rabbit's cradle. Patten. Junior classics. v. 9.
For other entries, see 2d edition.
Brother Rabbit's laughing place. Babbitt. Animals' own story book. (Mr. Rabbit's laughing place.)
For other entries, see 2d edition.
Brother Rabbit's riding-horse #.
See also Master Rabbit has a ride # ; Wolf as bridegroom #.
Brother Square-toes. Kipling. Rewards and fairies.
Brother Wolf makes a mistake. Lee. Folk tales of all nations. (Brer Wolf makes a mistake.)
Brotherhood of long ago. Coe. Third book of stories.
Brotherless girl. Wilson. Green magic.
Brothers who went out into the world. Tappan. Little lady in green.
Brown bear of the Green Glen. Morris. Gypsy story teller
Brown bull of Cooley. *See* Cattle raid of Cooley.
Brown cow. Casserly. Whins on Knockattan.
Brownie and the children. Hall. Godmother's stories.
Brownie and the farmer. Bryce. Folk lore from foreign lands.
Brownie and the thievish maids. Olcott. Wonder tales from fairy isles. (Here's a piece that wad please a brownie— the dairymaid's tale.)
For other entries, see 2d edition.
Brownie in the house. Starbuck. Enchanted paths.
For other entries, see 2d edition.
Brownie of Blednock. Johnson and Scott. Anthology of children's literature.
Starbuck. Familiar haunts.
For other entries, see 2d edition.
Brownie turns cook. *See* Over the cat to the kitchen.
Brownie's mother. Potter. Giant of Apple Pie Hill.
Brown's little Brownie. Beard. Tucked-in tales.
See also Owl's answer to Tommy #.
Bruce, Robert. Cruse. Young folk's book of epic heroes. (King Robert the Bruce.)
Gordon and Stockard. Gordon readers. 2d reader. (Miller and the king.)
Hodgkins. Atlantic treasury of childhood stories. (Story of an outlaw king.)
See also Heart of the Bruce.
For other entries, see 2d edition.

Bruce and the spider. Evans. Worth while stories.
Lansing. Great moments in freedom. (*In* Robert the Bruce.)
For other entries, see 2d edition.
Bruin and Reynard partners. I. *See* 2d edition.
Bruin and Reynard partners. II. Bowman and Bianco.
Tales from a Finnish tupa. (Farmers three.)
Lee. Folk tales of all nations. (Partners; Harvest.)
For other entries, see 2d edition.
Bruin and Reynard partners. I–II. *See also* Hare, hippopotamus and elephant; Laborer and his master; Outwitting the bogie; Peasant and the bear.
Bruin and the troll. *See* Bear and skrattel.
Brunelleschi's crucifix. Untermeyer. Donkey of God. (*In* Florence.)
Brunhilda. Bulfinch. Golden age. (Brunhild. *In* Ch. 40.)
For other entries, see 2d edition.
Brutus, king of Britain. *See* Gogmagog.
Bubble, the shoe, and the straw. Kovalsky and Putnam.
Long-legs, Big-mouth, Burning-eyes.
See also Straw, the coal and the bean.
Bucca and the Cornish maid. Price. Legends of the seven seas.
See also Flying Dutchman.
Buccoleon. *See* Dragon of Ghent; Turk, turban, tulip and dragon #.
Bucephalus. *See* Alexander the Great. I.
Buchettino. Lee. Folk tales of all nations.
For other entries, see 2d edition.
Buckwheat. Andersen. Fairy tales (Stickney). v. 2.
See also Proud foxglove.
For other entries, see 2d edition.
Buddha and Kujira. *See* Idol and the whale.
Budulinek. Harper. More story-hour favorites.
See also Cat, the cock and the fox. II; Wolf and the seven little kids.
For other entries, see 2d edition.
Buffalo and the cow. *See* Water-buffalo and the cow.
Buffalo and the mean old bear. Parker. Skunny Wundy and other Indian tales.
Buffalo cave. Sexton. Gray wolf stories. (Adventures in buffalo cave.)
Buffaloes and the herons. Meeker. Folk tales from the Far East.
Buffaloes who held a feast. Lobagola. Folk tales of a savage.
Buffalo's hump and the brown birds. Parker. Skunny Wundy and other Indian tales.
Buffoon and the countryman. *See* Actor and the pig.
Builder of ability and the builder of haste #.
See also Mud people.

Building of Balor's dune. Young. Wonder Smith and his son.

Building the Rockies. Rounds. Ol' Paul.

Bulb=show. Skinner. Child's book of country stories.

Bull and a ram. Æsop. Twenty-four fables (L'Estrange).

Bull and the calf. Æsop. Fables (Jones).
Cooper. Argosy of fables.
See also Ox and the calf.
For other entries, see 2d edition.

Bull and the goat. Cooper. Argosy of fables.
For other entries, see 2d edition.

Bull of Earlstoun. *See* Gordon of Earlstoun.

Bull of Siva. Lee. Folk tales of all nations.

Bull Shan, the two jackals, Damnah and Lilah, and the lion. *See* Lion and the bull. II.

Bull that demanded fair treatment. Cabot. Course in citizenship. (Ox who won the forfeit.)
Harriman. Stories for little children. (Ox who won the forfeit.)
For other entries, see 2d edition.

Bullfinch who was once a wicked grocer. Carey. Stories of the birds.

Bumble bees and clover. *See* Honied clover.

Bumble bees, tumble weeds and eagles. Allen. Whispering wind. (Spider woman.)

Bumbuku=Chagama. *See* Accomplished and lucky tea kettle.

Bun. Hutchinson. Candlelight stories.
For other entries, see 2d edition.

Bundle of sticks. Æsop. Fables (Artzybasheff. Old man and his sons.)
Æsop. Fables (Jones. Father and sons.)
Boeckel. Through the gateway.
Cabot. Course in citizenship. (Old man and his sons.)
Curry and Clippinger. Children's literature. (Old man and his sons.)
Power. Children's treasure chest.
See also Judas tree. II; Seven sons of Sandy Saunderson.
For other entries, see 2d edition.

Bundle of straw. Kinscella. Music appreciation readers. Book 6.

Bunny Cottontail and the crane. De Huff. Taytay's tales.

Bunny in the moon. *See* Hare in the moon. II.

Bunny Rabbit and the King of Beasts. De Huff. Taytay's tales.

Bunny Rabbit and turtle. *See* Hare and the tortoise.

Bunny Rabbit's journey. Skinner. Happy tales.
See also Easter rabbit.

Bunny the brave. Mackenzie. Jackal in Persia. (Tiger and the hare.)
Mukerji. Hindu fables.
See also Lion and the hare; Tiger and the shadow.

Bunny the brave saves Brahmin the priest. *See* Tiger gets his deserts. II.

Bunnyfluffkins. Quinn. Stories for the six-year-old. (Abridged.)

Bunyan, Paul. Field. American folk and fairy tales. (Winter of the blue snow ; Old home camp.)

Rounds. Ol' Paul. (Ol' Paul and his camp.)

Wadsworth. Paul Bunyan. (Hero of the woods.)

See also Winter of the blue snow ; Little blue ox.

Burial of poor Cock Robin. *See* Cock Robin.

Buried moon. Coussens. Diamond story book.

Dulac. Edmund Dulac's fairy book.

Through story-land with the children.

For other entries, see 2d edition.

Buried treasure. I. *See* Gold in the orchard.

Burning of Abbot Spiridion. Canton. Child's book of saints.

Burning of the books. Miller. My book of history. v. 4. (*In* Growth of China. Ch. 5.)

Burning of the rice fields. McVenn. Good manners and right conduct. Book 2.

For other entries, see 2d edition.

Burning of Troy. *See* Æneas ; Trojan war.

Burning rose. Housman. Doorway in fairyland. (Bound princess, pt. 5.)

Bush cow and the elephant. Lee. Folk tales of all nations.

Busybody land. Housman. Turn again tales.

Butcher and his customers. Æsop. Fables (Jones).

Buttercups. Marzials. Stories for the story hour.

Butterfly. I. Andersen. Fairy tales (Stickney). v. 2.

For other entries, see 2d edition.

Butterfly and the bee. I (poem). Cooper. Argosy of fables.

Butterfly and the bee. II. Cooper. Argosy of fables.

Butterfly and the kite. Kinscella. Music appreciation readers. Book 2.

Butterfly and the maidens. Egan. New found tales.

Butterfly blossom. Stewart. Tell me a story I never heard before.

Butterfly boy. Buckingham. Elephant's friend.

Butterfly that stamped #.

See also Boastful pigeon.

Butterfly's ball (poem). Johnson and Scott. Anthology of children's literature.

See also Down in the meadow.

Butterfly's children. *See* Lesson of faith.

Buttons and rings and various things. *See* Secret of success.

Buz and Hum. Skinner. Child's book of country stories.

For other entries, see 2d edition.

Buy a father. Chrisman. Shen of the sea.

Bwca'r Trwyn. *See* Big-nosed bogey.

By the pike's command. I. Byrde. Polish fairy book. (Lie-a-stove.)
For other entries, see 2d edition.
By the pike's command. II. *See* At the behest of the pike. II.
By the weeping waters. Cross. Music stories.
By yarrow and rue. *See* Voyage of the red cap.

C

Cabbages, Origin of. Teall. Batter and spoon fairies. (*In* Ch. 27.)
Cabbage patch. Bancroft. Goblins of Haubeck.
Cabrakan. *See* Killing of Cabrakan.
Cactus, Legend of. Martinez Del Rio. Sun, the moon and a rabbit. (Eagle and the snake.)
Miller. My book of history. v. 4. (*In* Aztec conquerors. Ch. 11.)
Purnell and Weatherwax. Talking bird. (Eagle and the snake.)
Cadmus and the dragon's teeth. Bulfinch. Golden age. (Cadmus. *In* Ch. 12.)
Forbush. Myths and legends of Greece and Rome.
Pyle. Tales from Greek mythology. (Story of Cadmus.)
See also Europa.
For other entries, see 2d edition.
Caedmon, the herdsman poet. Smith and Hazeltine. Christmas in legend and story. (Christmas song of Caedmon.)
See also Robber who became a poet.
For other entries, see 2d edition.
Caesar and Cleopatra. Miller. My book of history. v. 2. (*In* Ch. 10.)
Caesar, Julius. Cooke. Stories of Rome.
Farjeon. Mighty men from Achilles to Julius Caesar. (Roads of Rome.)
Patten. Junior classics. v. 7. (Julius Caesar crossing the Rubicon.)
See also Augustus Caesar.
For other entries, see 2d edition.
Caesar Rodney's ride. Blaisdell. Log cabin days.
Cage=bird and the bat. Æsop. Fables (Jones).
Cain's ducklings. Mackaye. Tall tales of the Kentucky mountains.
Calabash of winds. Metzger. Tales told in Hawaii.
See also Ulysses and the bag of winds.
Calandrino and the pig. Davis. Truce of the wolf.
Caligula, Emperor of Rome. Farjeon. Mighty men from Beowulf to William the Conqueror. (Little island, pt. 1.)
Caliph Haroun=al=Raschid, Adventures of. Arabian nights. Adventures of Haroun Er Raschid (Olcott).
For other entries, see 2d edition.

Caliph Stork. Hauff. Arabian days' entertainment.
McNeer and Lederer. Tales from the crescent moon. (Stork kalif. Adapted.)
For other entries, see 2d edition.
Calipha the camel child. Martin. Fatma was a goose.
Caliph's clock. Bennett. Pigtail of Ah Lee Ben Loo. (Astonishing story of the caliph's clock.)
See also First clock.
Call of the cuckoo. Stewart. Tell me a story I never heard before.
Callisto and Arcis. Bulfinch. Golden age. (Callisto. *In* Ch. 4.)
Kinney. Stars and their stories. (Great bear and the little bear.)
Williamson. Stars through magic casements. (Callisto and Arcas.)
For other entries, see 2d edition.
Cally Coo-coo o' the woods. MacManus. Donegal wonder book.
For other entries, see 2d edition.
Calydonian hunt. Bulfinch. Golden age. (Meleager and Atalanta. *In* Ch. 18.)
Johnson and Scott. Anthology of children's literature. (Calydonian hunt and Atalanta's race.)
Lang. Book of myths.
For other entries, see 2d edition.
Calypso. Bulfinch. Golden age. (*In* Ch. 29.)
Forbush. Myths and legends of Greece and Rome. (*In* Ulysses.)
Cam, Tam, and the genie. Olcott. Wonder tales from China seas.
See also Cinderella.
Camaralzaman and Badoura, Princess of China #.
See also Noureddin Ali and his son.
Cambuscan bold, Story of. Farjeon. Tales from Chaucer. (Squire's tale.)
Kinscella. Music appreciation readers. Book 5. (King and the brazen horse.)
See also Candace, Story of; Enchanted horse.
For other entries, see 2d edition.
Camel. Cooper. Argosy of fables.
(poem). Johnson and Scott. Anthology of children's literature. (Camel and the floating sticks.)
See also Fox and the lion.
For other entries, see 2d edition.
Camel and the ass. Cooper. Argosy of fables.
Camel, and the floating sticks. *See* Camel; What was it?
Camel and the pig. Bailey. Tell me another story.
Bryce. Short stories for little folks.
Curry and Clippinger. Children's literature.
For other entries, see 2d edition.

Camel and the ram. Carrick. Still more Russian picture tales.

Camel and the rat. Johnson and Scott. Anthology of children's literature.
Cooper. Argosy of fables.
Skinner. Happy tales.

Camel and the shrub. Cooper. Argosy of fables.

Camel driver and the adder. Cooper. Argosy of fables. (Camel driver and the snake.)
See also Foolish fish; Man and the snake; Snake's thanks; Way of the world. I.
For other entries, see 2d edition.

Camel driver and the snake. *See* Camel driver and the adder.

Camel of Bethlehem. Walters. Book of Christmas stories.

Camel, the lion and his court. *See* Crow, the jackal, the wolf and the camel.

Camel's complaint (poem). Harper and Hamilton. Winding roads. (Plaint of the camel.)

Camel's load. *See* Old Hump.

Camilla. Bulfinch. Golden age. (*In* Ch. 33.)

Campanula. *See* Venus's looking glass.

Campaspe and the painter. Richardson. Stories from old English poetry.

Campbells are coming. Kinscella. Music appreciation readers. Book 5. (Marching music.)

Camphor princess. Olcott. Wonder tales from pirate isles.

Camphor-worm. Housman. Doorway in fairyland. (Bound princess, pt. 6.)

Can and Could. Hartshorne. Training in worship. (*In* Faith in oneself. Adapted.)
For other entries, see 2d edition.

Can men be such fools as all that? Farjeon. Old nurse's stocking basket.

Canary=dog. Aspinwall. Can you believe me stories.
See also Cat that barked; Kitten that forgot how to mew.

Candace, Story of. Richardson. Stories from old English poetry.
See also Cambuscan bold; Enchanted horse.

Candle fly. Egan. New found tales.

Candle of Etienne Leblanc. Crownfield. Feast of Noel.

Candlemas Day. Graham. Happy holidays.

Candlemas eve. Stewart. Tell me a story I never heard before.

Candles. I. Johnson and Scott. Anthology of children's literature.
For other entries, see 2d edition.

Candy box. La Rue. Under the story tree.

Canek the Chieftain. Miller. My book of history. v. 4. (*In* Ch. 10.)

Canon's yeoman's tale. *See* Alchemist. I.

Canova, Antonio. Evans. Worth while stories.
For other entries, see 2d edition.
Canterbury bell. *See* Venus's looking glass.
Canute Whistlewinks. *See* Knut Spelevink.
Cap. Fyleman. Tea time tales.
Cap o' rushes. Lee. Folk tales of all nations.
Starbuck. Far horizons.
Steel. English fairy tales.
Williams-Ellis. Fairies and enchanters.
For other entries, see 2d edition.
Cap that mother made. *See* Ander's new cap.
Capella; or, Wonderful goat. Kinney. Stars and their
stories.
Capful of moonshine. Housman. Moonshine and clover.
Capons fat and lean. Æsop. Fables (Artzybasheff).
Capture of Breda. *See* Breda.
Caradoc and the Emperor of Rome. Farjeon. Mighty men
from Beowulf to William the Conqueror. (Little island,
pt. 2.)
Caramel. Fyleman. Forty good-night tales. (Bag of good-
ies, pt. 2.)
Caravan. Hauff. Arabian days' entertainment.
Caraway brodchen. Olcott. Wonder tales from goblin hills.
Cardinal and his courier. Untermeyer. Donkey of God.
(*In* Orvieto-Perugia-Assisi.)
Caribou and moose. Macmillan. Canadian wonder tales.
(Strange tale of caribou and moose.)
Caribs, Origin of. *See* Korobona, the strong of heart.
Carl and Carlo. Baldwin. Pedlar's pack.
Carl Krinken: his Christmas stocking. *See* Christmas
stocking; Stocking's story.
Carl of the drab coat. Stephens. Irish fairy tales.
Carlanco. Sawyer. Picture tales from Spain. (Terrible
Carlanco.)
For other entries, see 2d edition.
Carlo Magno and the giant. Gunterman. Castles in Spain.
Carlos and the magic horse. Shimer. Fairyland.
Carnation. Carey. Flower legends.
Carob tree, Legend of. Vilnay. Legends of Palestine. (*In*
Throne of Solomon.
See also King Solomon and the demon. II.
Carolers. Proudfoot. Child's Christ tales.
Carp rider. Nakazawa. Weaver of the frost.
See also Coming of the paper carp.
Carpenter and the ape. **Arnold. Book of good counsels.
(Monkey and the wedge.)
Cooper. Argosy of fables. (Monkey and the wedge.)
Mackenzie. Jackal in Persia. (Inquisitive monkey.)
For other entries, see 2d edition.
Carrie=Barry=Annie. Fyleman. Tea time tales.
Carthage. *See* Delenda est Carthago.

Cask (poem). Cooper. Argosy of fables.
Cassabianca (poem). Patten. Junior classics. v. 10.
   (poem). Hemans. Poems.
   (poem). Power. Children's treasure chest.
   For other entries, see 2d edition.
Cassim. Shimer. Fairyland. (How Cassim became king.)
Cassiopeia. Bulfinch. Golden age. (Perseus and Andro-
   meda. *In* Ch. 15.)
   Kinney. Stars and their stories. (Tale of a vain queen.)
   See also Perseus.
Castle Bousin. Nemcova. Disobedient kids.
Castle of Bim. Stockton. Reformed pirate.
   For other entries, see 2d edition.
Castle of Blanderon. *See* St. Anthony of Italy.
Castle of Comorre. Masson. Folk tales of Brittany.
   See also Bluebeard.
Castle of echoes. Cook. Red and gold stories.
Castle of fairies. Pogány. Hungarian fairy book.
Castle of frowns. Cook. To-day's stories of yesterday.
Castle of the hawk. Guerber. Legends of Switzerland. (*In*
   Aargau.)
   For other entries, see 2d edition.
Castle of Thou shalt go and not return. Dane. Once there
   was and was not.
   See also Master-maid. I.
Castle of Zeta. Pogány. Hungarian fairy book.
Castle Somlyo. Schwimmer. Tisza tales.
   See also Army of two.
Castle that came out of an egg (Castello dell' Ovo). Un-
   termeyer. Donkey of God.
Castle-treasure. Olcott. Wonder tales from Baltic wizards.
Castor and Pollux. Bulfinch. Golden age. (*In* Ch. 20.)
   Forbush. Myths and legends of Greece and Rome.
   Williamson. Stars through magic casements. (Twin broth-
   ers.)
   For other entries, see 2d edition.
Cat and mouse. *See* Cat and the mouse. I.
Cat and mouse keep house. *See* Cat and the mouse in part-
   nership.
Cat and the birds. Æsop. Fables (Jones).
   See also Hen and the cat. II.
   For other entries, see 2d edition.
Cat and the captain. Wiggin and Smith. Twilight stories.
Cat and the cock. Æsop. Fables (Jones).
   See also Wolf and the lamb. I.
   For other entries, see 2d edition.
Cat and the dog. *See* Why the dog and cat are enemies. VI.
Cat and the fox. I. *See* Fox and the cat. I.
Cat and the fox. II. *See* Fox and the cat. IV.
Cat and the hen #.
   In 2d edition this story is also indexed under the title
   "Hen and the cat."

Cat and the looking glass. Cooper. Argosy of fables.
Cat and the mice. I. Æsop. Fables (Artzybasheff).
Æsop. Fables (Jones).
Cooper. Argosy of fables.
For other entries, see 2d edition.
Cat and the mice. II. Lee. Folk tales of all nations.
Metzger. Picture tales from the Chinese.
Cat and the mouse. I. Curry and Clippinger. Children's
literature.
Hutchinson. Fireside stories. (Cat and mouse.)
Lee. Folk tales of all nations.
Power. Bag o' tales.
See also Tail of Katoos; Why the monkey still has a tail.
For other entries, see 2d edition.
Cat and the mouse. II. *See* 2d edition.
Cat and the mouse. III. *See* Cat and the mouse in partner-
ship.
Cat and the mouse in partnership. De La Mare and Quayle.
Readings. (Pot of fat.)
Grimm. Tales from Grimm (Wanda Gag. Cat and mouse
keep house.)
Williams. Tales from Ebony. (Cat and the mouse.)
See also Compair Lapin and Compair L'Ours; Fox and the
mole; Fox as partner. I #; Jan and Jantje; Mr. Rabbit
nibbles up the butter; Telltale grease; Three sons and
the chest; Winter.
For other entries, see 2d edition.
Cat and the rat. Cooper. Argosy of fables.
Lee. Folk tales of all nations.
Cat and the sparrows. I (poem). Cooper. Argosy of
fables. (Cat and the two sparrows.)
See also Why cats always wash after eating.
For other entries, see 2d edition.
Cat and the stork. Cooper. Argosy of fables.
Cat and the two sparrows. *See* Cat and the sparrows. I.
Cat learns to dance. Cowles. Stories to tell.
See also Cat-cat and Mouse-mouse #.
Cat of Rat-a-rat Town. Retner. That's that.
Cat on the Dovrefell. *See* Bear and skrattel.
Cat that barked. Potter. Giant of Apple Pie Hill.
See also Canary-dog; Kitten that forgot how to mew.
Cat that came to Mabel's house. Potter. Captain Sandman.
Cat that could not be killed. De La Mare and Quayle. Read-
ings.
For other entries, see 2d edition.
Cat that walked by himself #.
See also First friend.
Cat, the cock, and the fox. I. Lee. Folk tales of all na-
tions.
For other entries, see 2d edition.

Cat, the cock, and the fox. II. Faulkner. Road to enchantment.
For other entries, see 2d edition.

Cat, the cow, the dog, and the dairymaid (poem). Bennett. Pigtail of Ah Lee Ben Loo.

Cat, the monkey and the chestnuts (poem). Cooper. Argosy of fables. (Monkey and the cat.)
La Fontaine. Fables (Tilney. Monkey and the cat.)
For other entries, see 2d edition.

Cat, the rat, the cheese, and the fox. Babbitt. Animals' own story book.
See also Matter of arbitration.

Cat who became head-forester. *See* Fox and the cat. IV.

Cat who served the lion. *See* Lion, the mouse, and the cat.

Caterpillar and the butterfly (poem). Cooper. Argosy of fables.

Caterpillar and the lark. *See* Lesson of faith.

Caterpillar and the wild animals. Lee. Folk tales of all nations.
See also Rabbit and the other animals.

Catfish and the moose. I. Cooper. Argosy of fables.

Catfish and the moose. II. Phillips. Indian tales for little folks. (Why the catfish has a flat head.)

Cathedral bell and the hermitage bell (poem). Cooper. Argosy of fables.

Cathedral under the sea. Gibson. Golden bird.
See also Ys, Story of.

Catherine and her destiny (poem). St. Nicholas. June, 1888, p. 572. (Caterina and her destiny.)
See also Bird of sorrow; Trouble when one's young.
For other entries, see 2d edition.

Cato the censor. *See* Delenda est Cartago.

Cat's beautiful wife. Cooper. Argosy of fables.

Cats and fowls. Woodson. African myths.

Cats and mice. Cowles. Stories to tell.

Cat's cup of Vlaardingen. Miller. My travelship: Holland.

Cat's tail, Story of. Lee. Folk tales of all nations.
See also How the rabbit lost his tail; Monkey's bargains; Travels of a fox.

Cats that clawed to heaven. Mackaye. Tall tales of the Kentucky mountains.

Cat's trousers. Fyleman. Forty good-night tales.

Catskin. I. Coussens. Diamond story book.
Rhys. English fairy book.
Steel. English fairy tales.
See also Cinderella.
For other entries, see 2d edition.

Catspaw. Housman. What-o'clock tales.

Cattle of Mohos. Pogány. Hungarian fairy book.

Cattle raid of Cooley. Gregory. Cuchulain of Muirthemne. (War for the bull of Cuailgne; Two bulls.)

Cattle raid of Cooley—*continued.*
Hull.   Cuchulain.   (Meave demands the brown bull of Cooley.)
For other entries, see 2d edition.
Cattle that came. Starbuck. Far horizons.
For other entries, see 2d edition.
Cause of tides. I–II. *See* 2d edition.
Cause of tides. III. Metzger. Tales told in Hawaii. (Why we have tides.)
See also Old woman and the tides.
Cave of Rakim. Vilnay. Legends of Palestine.
Cave of the little people. Kennedy. Red man's wonder book
Cavern of Steenfoll. Hauff. Arabian days' entertainment.
For other entries, see 2d edition.
Cecilie. *See* St. Cecilie.
Cedar tree of China. Curtis. Stories in trees.
See also Baucis and Philemon.
Ceiling-people, Story of the. Aspinwall. Can you believe me stories.
Cenerentola. Faulkner. Road to enchantment. (Cenorientola.)
Martens. Wonder tales from far away. (Two Cinderella stories.)
See also Cinderella.
Cenorientola. *See* Cenerentola.
Centaurs. Bulfinch. Golden age. (*In* Ch. 16.)
Cephalus and Procris. Bulfinch. Golden age. (*In* Ch. 3.)
For other entries, see 2d edition.
Ceres and her daughter. *See* Proserpina.
Ceres and Proserpine. *See* Proserpina.
Ceyx and Halcyone. *See* Halcyon birds.
Chain of anger. Egan. New found tales.
See also Who killed the otter's babies?
Chameleon (poem). Cooper. Argosy of fables.
See also Blind men and the elephant; Red-bud tree.
For other entries, see 2d edition.
Championship of Ulster. Adams and Atchinson. Book of enchantment.
Gregory.   Cuchulain of Muirthemne.
See also Carving of MacDatho's boar #.
Change about. *See* Man who was going to mind the house.
Changeling. I. *See* 2d edition.
Changeling. II. Masson. Folk tales of Brittany.
Changeling. III. Price. Legends of the seven seas.
Changeling stories. *See* Spriggan's child; Ulda's old mother; Child and the fiddle.
Chapel of Karcsa. Pogány. Hungarian fairy book.
Charcoal burner and the fuller. Æsop. Fables (Jones).
Cooper.   Argosy of fables. (Collier and the fuller.)
For other entries, see 2d edition.
Charger and the ass. *See* Horse and the ass. I.
Charger and the miller. *See* War-horse and the miller.

Charity. Schwarz. Jewish caravan.

Charlemagne. Lansing. Great moments in freedom. (Charlemagne at school.)
> Miller. My travelship: Holland. (Charlemagne legend of Sittard.)
> Niemeyer. Stories for the history hour. (Charles and Alcuin.)
> For other entries, see 2d edition.

Charlemagne and the bridge of moonbeams (poem). Olcott. Wonder tales from goblin hills.

Charlemagne and the magic ring. Guerber. Legends of Switzerland. (*In* Legends of Zurich.)
> Olcott. Wonder tales from goblin hills. (Enchanted ring of Fastrada.)
> For other entries, see 2d edition.

Charles and Alcuin. *See* Charlemagne.

Charmed ring. *See* Wonderful ring.

Charon. Harshaw. Council of the gods. (Hermes goes to Pluto's kingdom.)

Chase of the Gilla Dacar. Young. Tangle-coated horse and other tales. (Tangle-coated horse.)
> *See also* Finn MacCool.
> For other entries, see 2d edition.

Chasing the rainbow. Schwimmer. Tisza tales.

Chat about the clock. Fun folk and fairy tales.

Chattering aspen. *See* Why the aspen leaves tremble. III.

Chaucer, Geoffrey. Miller. My book of history. v. 3. (*In* Ch. 13.)

Cheese floor. Guerber. Legends of Switzerland. (*In* Glarus and Grisons.)
> *See also* Girl who trod on the loaf.

Cheeses that ran away. Hutchinson. Candlelight stories. (Wise man of Gotham.)
> Lee. Folk tales of all nations. (Of sending cheeses. *In* Wise men of Gotham.)
> *See also* Wise men of Gotham.
> For other entries, see 2d edition.

Chekilli the Creek boy, Adventures of (play). Lamkin and Jagendorf. Around America with the Indians.
> In some editions, not indexed here, this story has the title "Only son Rabbit."

Cheops and his pyramid. Butterfield. Young people's story of architecture. (*In* Ch. 2.)

Cherry blossom, Legend of the. Newman. Fairy flowers.

Cherry of Zennor. Rhys. English fairy book.
> *See also* Sick fairy.
> For other entries, see 2d edition.

Cherry tree. Burnett. Children's book.

Cherry tree adventure. Bailey. Wonderful tree.

Cheshire=cat. Carroll. Alice's adventures in Wonderland. (*In* Pig and Pepper. Ch. 6.)

Chess game of a monkey and a queen. Rowe. Moon's birthday.

Chestnut kettle. Spence. Myths of the North American Indians. (Wonderful kettle. *In* Ch. 4.)

Lee. Folk tales of all nations. (Wonderful kettle.)

For other entries, see 2d edition.

Chestnut man. Fyleman. Tea time tales.

Chests of dust. Egan. New found tales.

See also Mother Holle.

Chevalier Fortuné. *See* Belle-Belle.

Chevy Chase. Bailey. Stories of great adventures. (Battle of Chevy Chase.)

Greenwood. Stories from famous ballads.

For other entries, see 2d edition.

Chi-wee and the rabbit. Harper and Hamilton. Winding roads.

Moon. Chi-wee.

Chib, Adventures of. *See* Three strong men.

Chick, D. D. Harper. Merry Christmas to you.

Chick, chick, halfchick. *See* Little half-cock.

Chickadee makes a shoomesh bow. Garett. Coyote stories.

Chicken-Licken. *See* Chicken-Little.

Chicken-Little. Arthur Rackham fairy book. (Henny-Penny.)

Bruce. Treasury of tales for little folk. (Henny-Penny.)

Curry and Clippinger. Children's literature. (Henny-Penny.)

Hutchinson. Chimney corner stories. (Henny Penny.)

Johnson and Scott. Anthology of children's literature. (Henny-Penny.)

Lee. Folk tales of all nations. (Henny-Penny.)

Piper. Gateway to storyland.

Power. Bag o' tales. (Story of Chicken-Licken.)

Steel. English fairy tales. (Henny-Penny.)

(play). Wheelock. Kindergarten children's hour. v. 2. (Folk lore tale of Henny-Penny. *In* Ch. 14.)

See also Fatma was a goose; Fowls on pilgrimage; Hungry fox # ; Snapper brothers; Timid hare.

For other entries, see 2d edition.

Chicken Little and Duckie Dee. Blaisdell. Rhyme and story second reader.

Chicken Little's umbrella. Blaisdell. Rhyme and story second reader.

Chickens in the field. Morley. I know a secret.

Chicken's mistake (poem). Cooper. Argosy of fables.

(poem). Carey. Poems.

Chickpeatina. Capuana. Italian fairy tales.

Child and the burro. Otero. Old Spain in our Southwest. (*In* Early schooling in New Mexico.)

Child and the fiddle. Lee. Folk tales of all nations.

Child from the sea. Rasmussen. Eagle's gift.

Child husband. Metzger. Tales told in Korea.

Child=Improver. Aspinwall. Can you believe me stories.
Child of long ago. Harper and Hamilton. Winding roads.
Child of the thunder. Blondell. Keepsakes. (Good thunder.)
For other entries, see 2d edition.
Child that cried for the moon. De La Mare and Quayle. Readings.
See also Boy who cried for the moon.
Child that dropped from the clouds. Baldwin. Pedlar's pack.
Child who saw Santa Claus. Bailey. Stories children want.
Bailey. Tell me another story.
Childe Charity, Story of. Johnson and Scott. Anthology of children's literature.
For other entries, see 2d edition.
Childe Rowland. Coe. Third book of stories.
Johnson and Scott. Anthology of children's literature.
Steel. English fairy tales.
For other entries, see 2d edition.
Children in the moon. I–II. *See* 2d edition.
Children in the moon. III. Gordon and Stockard. Gordon readers. 2d reader. (In moon land.)
For other entries, see 2d edition.
Children of Eric the Red. *See* Gudrid the Fair ; Leif Ericson.
Children of Lir. *See* Fate of the children of Lir.
Children of Mt. Carmel. *See* Wisdom of the men of Jerusalem.
Children of Spinalunga. Canton. Child's book of saints.
Children of the House of Dawn. Eells. Magic tooth.
Children of the sun. Wolff. Pale mountains.
Children of the wolf. *See* Romulus and Remus.
Children of wind and the clan of peace. Smith and Hazeltine. Christmas in legend and story.
For other entries, see 2d edition.
Children who were changed into swallows. *See* Swallows, Origin of. I.
Children's crusade. Cather. Pan and his pipes. (Stephen, the child crusader.)
Kinscella. Music appreciation readers. Book 3. (Stephen, boy crusader.)
Miller. My book of history. v. 3. (*In* Ch. 10.)
Tappan. Old world hero stories.
Terry. Tales from far and near. (Little soldiers of the cross.)
Children's league of nations. Broomell. (Children's story caravan.
Children's new dresses. *See* New dresses.
Child's dream of a star. Coussens. Diamond story book.
Kaphan. Tell us a Dickens story. (Beautiful star. Adapted.)
Wilson. Red magic.
For other entries, see 2d edition.

Child's wish. Cowles. Stories to tell.
Skinner. Happy tales.
See also Mischievous Knix #.
Chimæra. *See* Pegasus.
Chimalma, the sorceress. Martinez Del Rio. Sun, the moon and a rabbit.
Chimmapanzy and Pollymalloy. Farjeon. Old sailor's yarn box.
Chimney imps. Harper. More story-hour favorites.
Chimneys of Kampen. King. Golden cat head.
Chin-chin Kobakama. Faulkner. Little Peachling.
For other entries, see 2d edition.
Chinese artist. Davis. Baker's dozen. (Chinese fairy tale.)
Housman. Moonshine and clover. (Chinese fairy tale.)
Chinese boy's garden. Kinscella. Music appreciation readers. Book 2.
Chinese emperor's visit to the moon. Olcott. Wonder tales from China seas. (Bright moon-cakes and the money tree.)
Lane. Tower legends. (Moon that shone on the Porcelain Pagoda.)
Chinese fairy tale. *See* Chinese artist.
Chinese nightingale. *See* Nightingale. I.
Chinese princess and her silk dress. *See* Silkworm. I.
Chinese Red Riding Hood. *See* Tiger aunt.
Chinese student who got in the cellar. Canfield. Made-to-order stories. (Very last story of all.)
Chinese tale. Fyleman. Tea time tales.
Chinny. Aspinwall. Can you believe me stories.
Chinooks visit the supernaturals. *See* Ghost land. III.
Chip and Munkey. Burnett. Children's book.
Chipmunk and Owl-woman. Garett. Coyote days.
Linderman. Kootenai why stories. (Co-pee.)
Partridge. Joyful Star. (Ogress and mother.)
See also Chipmunk's stripes. V.
Chipmunk's stripes. I. Cowles. Stories to tell. (Faithful chipmunk.)
For other entries, see 2d edition.
Chipmunk's stripes. II. See 2d edition.
Chipmunk's stripes. III. Parker. Skunny Wundy and other Indian tales. (How Rock-dweller, the chipmunk, gained his stripes.)
For other entries, see 2d edition.
Chipmunk's stripes. IV. See 2d edition.
Chipmunk's stripes. V. Field. American folk and fairy tales. (Why the chipmunk's back is striped.)
See also Chipmunk and Owl-woman.
For other entries, see 2d edition.
Chipmunk's stripes. VI. Hogner. Navajo winter nights. (Teel-get, the monster.)
Chip's Thanksgiving. Bailey. Tell me another story.
Choice of Midas. *See* Midas. II.

Choo Chin and the dragon #.
See also Gods know; White elephant. V.

Chop sticks. Chrisman. Shen of the sea.

Chorny Ruchei. See Brook Chorny.

Christ-child. I. Harper. Merry Christmas to you. (Legend of the Christ-child.)
Harrison. Christmas tide. (Legend of the Christ-child.)
Van Buren and Bemis. Christmas in storyland.
Walters. Book of Christmas stories. (Legend of the Christ-child.)
For other entries, see 2d edition.

Christ-child. II. See 2d edition.

Christ-child. III. Smith˙and Hazeltine. Christmas in legend and story. (Christmas legend.)
See also Christmas tree. I ; Little friend ; Stranger child. I.
For other entries, see 2d edition.

Christ-child. IV. Bowman. Little brown bowl. (Tale of the Christ-child.)

Christ-child and the clay birds. Untermeyer. Donkey of God. (In Donkey of God.)
(poem). Smith and Hazeltine. Christmas in legend and story. (Little mud sparrows.)
For other entries, see 2d edition.

Christ-child and the palm tree. See Flight into Egypt. I.

Christ of the Andes. Boeckel. Through the gateway, p. 23.

Christening of Maui. Metzger. Tales told in Hawaii.

Christian and Hopeful in Doubting Castle. Power. Bag o' tales.

Christmas. See Baby Gretel ; Boniface and Keep-it-all ; Boy's visit to Santa Claus ; Camel of Bethlehem ; Child who saw Santa Claus ; Closed hand ; Cosette's Christmas eve ; Dame Quimp's quest ; Eager heart ; Earl Sigurd's Christmas eve ; Ebenezer Scrooge's Christmas ; Fairies of the kitchen ; Family portrait ; Felix the wise man ; Fir tree that found something to do ; First Christmas presents ; Flight into Egypt ; Four-footed Santa Claus ; Gift of love ; Gift of the magi ; Gift that grew ; Gissing and the telephone ; Gretchen, Story of ; Hilarion ; His Christmas turkey ; Holly, Legend of ; Holly-tree elf ; How Johnny Cricket saw Santa Claus ; How old Mr. Long-tail became a Santa Claus ; How the animals kept Christmas ; How the Christmas pudding came ; Jimmy Scarecrow's Christmas ; Jolly good boots ; Kitten that wanted to be a Christmas present ; Kitten's Christmas wish ; Letter to Santa Claus ; Little Roman Shepherd ; Magic curtain ; Man in the Christmas moon ; Marble boy ; Miss Merry Christmas ; Mr. Bear ; Mr. Fox's Christmas dinner ; Margil vine ; Mother Christmas ; Mother Popple's Christmas pudding ; Night with Santa Claus ; Nutcracker and Mouseking ; Other wise man ; Perez the mouse. I ; Perfect ring ; Pine tree's dress of gold ; Royal engine ; Star # ; Star bearer ; Star of Bethlehem ; Stars and the child ; Strange story of Mr. Dog and Mr. Bear ; St. Bridget ; St. Boniface ;

Christmas—*continued.*

St. Zita; Spirit of Christmas; Stocking's story; Surprise Christmas tree; Talkative Christmas tree; Three bells; Three purses; Tim Puss's Christmas; Tomorrow is Christmas; Tree that trimmed itself; Troll's Christmas; Two little stockings; Two little wooden shoes; Walking doll; When Toinette sang; Why Father Christmas got married; Why the top sings; Youngest thief.

See also titles beginning: Christmas; Santa Claus.

For other entries, see 2d edition.

Christmas angel. I. *See* 2d edition.

Christmas angel. II. Coe. Third book of stories.

See also Ebenezer Scrooge's Christmas.

Christmas apple of Hermann the clockmaker. Harper. Merry Christmas to you. (Christmas apple.)

Harper. More story-hour favorites. (Christmas apple.)

For other entries, see 2d edition.

Christmas at the Hollow Tree Inn. Skinner. Christmas stories.

Walters. Book of Christmas stories.

Christmas before last. Stockton. Reformed pirate.

For other entries, see 2d edition.

Christmas bells. *See* Why the chimes rang.

Christmas cake. I. Walters. Book of Christmas stories.

For other entries, see 2d edition.

Christmas cake. II. Potter. Giant of Apple Pie Hill.

Christmas candle. I. See 2d edition.

Christmas candle. II. Bailey. Wonderful tree.

Major. Merry Christmas stories.

Christmas carol (Dickens). *See* Cratchit's Christmas dinner; Ebenezer Scrooge's Christmas; Spirit of Christmas.

Christmas chimes. Cozad. Story talks.

Christmas cuckoo. Harper. Merry Christmas to you.

Harper. More story-hour favorites.

Starbuck. Enchanted paths.

Walters. Book of Christmas stories.

For other entries, see 2d edition.

Christmas garden. Bailey. Stories children want.

Bailey. Tell me another story.

See also Christmas rose, Legend of. I.

Christmas hold-up. Burnett. Children's book.

Christmas in many lands (play). Skinner. Christmas stories.

Christmas in the mouse-hole. Wiggin and Smith. Twilight stories.

Christmas in the movies. Wiggin and Smith. Twilight stories.

Christmas in the playroom. Walker. Sandman's Christmas stories.

Christmas in the woods. Harper. Merry Christmas to you.

Potter. Fairy caravan. (*In* Demarara sugar. Ch. 14.)

Christmas joke. Bailey. Wonderful tree.
Major. Merry Christmas stories.
Christmas kings. *See* Christmas promise of the three kings.
Christmas land. Skinner. Christmas stories. (Christmas-land.)
Christmas lanterns. Kinscella. Music appreciation readers. Book 6.
Christmas legend. I. *See* Hilarion.
Christmas legend. II. *See* Christ-child. III.
Christmas night. *See* Shepherd's gift.
Christmas nightingale. Kelly. Christmas nightingale.
Christmas party. Major. Merry Christmas stories.
See also Stocking's story.
Christmas promise of the three kings. Skinner. Christmas stories. (Christmas kings.)
Walters. Book of Christmas stories. (Three kings. Abridged.)
For other entries, see 2d edition.
Christmas pudding. I. Buckingham. Elephant's friend. (How the Christmas pudding came.)
Christmas pudding. II. Child life. Dec. 1925. (Mother Popple's Christmas pudding.)
Christmas rose, Legend of. I. Good Housekeeping. Dec. 1907, p. 605.
Harper. Merry Christmas to you.
Smith and Hazeltine. Christmas in legend and story.
See also Christmas garden.
For other entries, see 2d edition.
Christmas rose, Legend of. II. Carey. Flower legends. (Christmas rose.)
Smith and Hazeltine. Christmas in legend and story. (First Christmas roses.)
See also Christ child. III; Chrysanthemum; Field of angels.
For other entries, see 2d edition.
In 2d edition this story is also indexed under the title "Shepherd maiden's gift."
Christmas rose, Legend of. III. Baumbach. Tales from the Swiss alps.
Graham. Welcome Christmas.
For other entries, see 2d edition.
Christmas rose, Legend of. IV. *See* 2d edition.
Christmas rose, Legend of. V. Bailey. Stories children want.
Walters. Book of Christmas stories.
Christmas song of Caedmon. *See* Caedmon, the herdsman poet.
Christmas spruce tree. *See* Fir tree. III.
Christmas stocking. I. *See* 2d edition.
Christmas stocking. II. Graham. Welcome Christmas.
Warner. Carl Krinken.
Christmas town. I. *See* 2d edition.
Christmas town. II (poem). Skinner. Happy tales.

Christmas tree.   I.   Cabot.   Course in citizenship.   (Legend of the Christmas tree.)
Campbell.   Story of Christmas, p. 131.
Harriman.   Stories for little children.   (Stranger child.)
Wheelock.   Kindergarten children's hour.   v. 2.   (Origin of the Christmas tree.   *In* Ch. 12.)
See also Christ-child.   III.
For other entries, see 2d edition.
Christmas tree.   II.   *See* 2d edition.
Christmas tree.   III.   Van Buren and Bemis.   Christmas in storyland.
For other entries, see 2d edition.
Christmas tree.   IV, V, VI.   *See* 2d edition.
Christmas tree.   VII.   *See* Animals' Christmas tree.
Christmas tree.   VIII.   *See* Thorn of Glastonbury.
Christmas tree.   IX.   Potter.   Giant of Apple Pie Hill.
Christmas tree.   X.   Kinscella.   Music appreciation readers. Book 1.
Christmas tree for cats.   Bailey.   Stories children want.
For other entries, see 2d edition.
Christmas tree for Santa Claus.   Faulkner.   Story lady's Christmas stories.
Christmas tree in the barn.   Bailey.   Tell me another story.
Christmas tree of the animals.   *See* Animals' Christmas tree ; Christmas at the Hollow Tree Inn ; Christmas tree in the barn.
Christmas tree that went walking.   Bailey.   Wonderful tree.
Major.   Merry Christmas stories.
Christmas witch.   Lindsay.   Choosing book.
Christmas wreath.   Bailey.   Wonderful tree.
Major.   Merry Christmas stories.
Christmasland.   *See* Christmas land.
Christopher, Saint.   *See* St. Christopher.
Christ's brother.   Ralston.   Russian fairy tales.   (*In* Legends about saints.   Ch. 6.)
Chrysanthemum.   Carey.   Flower legends.
See also Christ child.   III ; Christmas rose.   II ; Field of angels.
Chudo Yudo with twelve heads.   *See* Ivan Buikovich.
Chundun Rajah.   Pyle.   Fairy tales from India.
For other entries, see 2d edition.
Church and the crown.   *See* William the Conqueror.
Churl of the Town of Mischance.   Colum.   King of Ireland's son.   (*In* Gilly of the goatskin.)
See also Keep cool # ; Son of strength.
Cid, The.   Cruse.   Young folk's book of epic heroes.
Johnson and Scott.   Anthology of children's literature. (Knighting of Rodrigo.)
Miller.   My book of history.   v. 3.   (*In* Ch. 12.)
Tappan.   Old world hero stories.
For other entries, see 2d edition.

Cincinnatus. Cooke. Stories of Rome.
> Lansing. Great moments in freedom. (*In* Driving the Kings out of Rome.)
> For other entries, see 2d edition.

Cinder-lad and his six brothers. Shimer. Fairyland.

Cinderella; or, The little glass slipper. Arthur Rackham fairy book.
> Bruce. Treasury of tales for little folk.
> Curry and Clippinger. Children's literature.
> De La Mare. Told again.
> Evans. Worth while stories.
> Grimm. Fairy tales (Olcott. Ash-maiden.)
> Grimm. Tales from Grimm (Wanda Gag).
> Harper. Magic fairy tales.
> Hutchinson. Chimney corner stories.
> Johnson and Scott. Anthology of children's literature.
> Lang. Old friends among the fairies.
> Lee. Folk tales of all nations.
> Mackenzie. Book of nursery tales.
> Power. Bag o' tales.
> Power. Blue caravan tales.
> Quinn. Stokes' wonder book of fairy tales.
> Rich. Read-aloud book.
> Starbuck. Familiar haunts.
> Rhys. English fairy book.
> Told under the green umbrella.
> *See also* Black sheep; Bones of Djulung; Cam, Tam, and the genie; Catskin; Cenerentola; Despised maiden; Different Cinderella; Ditu Migniulu; Fairy flowers; Kongi and Potgi; Liisa and the prince; Little Cinderella; Little Scar Face; Princess Hotaru; Sheepskin coat; Tewa Cinderella; Tomato peeler; Turkey maiden.
> For other entries, see 2d edition.

Cinderella's sisters. Baker. Tell them again tales.

Circe's palace. *See* Ulysses.

City garage. Emerson. Merry-go-round of modern tales.

City mouse and the garden mouse. *See* Country mouse and the town mouse.

City of the seven hills. *See* Titus, Emperor of Rome.

City of the winter sleep. Beston. Starlight wonder book.

City of wise men. Egan. New found tales.

City's Christmas tree. *See* Fir Tree. IV.

Claelia, the hostage. Cooke. Stories of Rome. (*In* Heroes of early Rome.)

Clare, St. *See* St. Clare.

Clarke Colvill. Williams-Ellis. Fairies and enchanters.

Clean hands. White. School management, p. 270.

Clear round gift. *See* Mirror of Matsuyama.

Clematis. Carey. Flower legends.

Clerk of Oxford's tale. *See* Patient Griselda.

Clever Alice. Grimm. Tales from Grimm (Wanda Gag. Clever Elsie).
Grimm. Fairy tales (Olcott. Clever Elsie.)
For other entries, see 2d edition.
Clever ape and the foolish wolf. Cooper. Argosy of fables.
Clever Chang. Shimer. Fairyland.
Clever, clever, clever. *See* Fox, the bear and the poor farmer.
Clever daughter. *See* Maiden who was wiser than an emperor.
Clever dog. Carrick. Tales of wise and foolish animals.
Clever Elsie. *See* Clever Alice.
Clever girl and the king. Schwimmer. Tisza tales.
See also Clever prince # ; Sage damsel.
Clever Grethel. De La Mare. Told again.
For other entries, see 2d edition.
Clever Hans. *See* Prudent Hans.
Clever judge. Schwarz. Jewish caravan.
Clever little fisherman. Fleming. Round the world in folk tales.
See also Fairy nets; Laka and the menehunes.
Clever little hermit crab. Meeker. Folk tales from the Far East.
Clever little rabbit. Lebermann. New German fairy tales.
Clever old woman of Carcassonne. *See* Aicha's stratagem.
Clever peasant. Lee. Folk tales of all nations.
See also What the four were for.
Clever prince #.
See also Clever girl and the king.
Clever Semiletka. Carpenter. Tales of a Russian grandmother.
See also Peasant's clever daughter; Sage damsel.
Clever tailor. I. *See* 2d edition.
Clever tailor. II. Kinscella. Music appreciation readers Book 3. (Of a tailor and a bear.)
Clever Tom and the Leprechaun. *See* Field of Boliauns.
Clever Tom and the little people. Choate and Curtis. Little people of the hills.
See also Curmudgeon's skin.
Clever woodpecker. Kovalsky and Putnam. Long-legs, Bigmouth, Burning-eyes.
See also Blackbird and the fox; Jackal and the partridge #.
Cliff-dweller and the corn maiden #.
See also Bluebeard; Pueblo Bluebeard.
Clipped penny. Capuana. Italian fairy tales.
See also Wonderful pot.
Clock. I. *See* 2d edition.
Clock. II. *See* Chat about the clock.
Clock and the sun-dial (poem). Johnson and Scott. Anthology of children's literature.
(poem). Cooper. Argosy of fables.

Clock in the kitchen. Kinscella. Music appreciation readers. Book 2.
See also Matter of habit; Three sillies.
Clocks of Rondaine. Stockton. Reformed pirate.
For other entries, see 2d edition.
Clock-tick who ran away. Aspinwall. Can you believe me stories.
Closed hand. Walker. Sandman's Christmas stories.
See also Boniface and Keep-it-all.
Cloth of endless length. Sugimoto. Picture tales from the Japanese.
See also Two wishes that came true; How the good gifts were used by two.
Clothes make the man. Keller. Fat of the cat.
Cloud-carrier and the star-folk. Spence. Myths of the North American Indians. (*In* Ch. 3.)
Cloud climbers. Cook. Red and gold stories.
Cloud trip. Cooper. Tal. (*In* Ch. 5.)
Cloud-woman (poem). Colum. King of Ireland's son. (*In* Fedelma.)
Clouds, Origin of. Metzger. Tales told in Hawaii.
See also Earth and the sky.
Clover field. Potter. Captain Sandman.
Clover's story. *See* Great Uncle Nathaniel's teeth.
Clovis. Niemeyer. Stories for the history hour.
Clown and the countryman. *See* Actor and the pig.
Clown of God. Gibson. Golden bird.
Clown of San Cristobal. Otero. Old Spain in our Southwest.
See also King John and the Abbot of Canterbury.
Clumsy hippo and the happen-to-be-clumsy gazelle. Lobagola. Folk tales of a savage.
Clurican. *See* Jumping fire; Little shoe; Seeing's believing.
Clytie. Bulfinch. Golden age. (*In* Ch. 13.)
Carey. Flower legends. (Heliotrope.)
Johnson and Scott. Anthology of children's literature. (Clytie, the heliotrope.)
Lang. Book of myths.
Power. Bag o' tales.
Whiteman. Playmates in print.
For other entries, see 2d edition.
Coal-scuttle. Canfield. Made-to-order stories.
Coat of arms of Putsk. Borski and Miller. Gypsy and the bear.
Cobbler. I. See 2d edition.
Cobbler. II. Cooper. Tal. (*In* Ch. 12.)
Cobbler. III. Marzials. Stories for the story hour.
Cobbler and the financier. *See* Cobbler's song.
Cobbler and the king. Power. Children's treasure chest. (Merry tale of the king and the cobbler.)
See also Gudeman of Ballengeich.
For other entries, see 2d edition.
Cobbler dog. *See* Dog as cobbler.

Cobbler turned doctor. Æsop. Fables (Jones).
Æsop. Fables (Whitman ed.).
Cooper. Argosy of fables.
For other entries, see 2d edition.
Cobbler's lad. Lee. Folk tales of all nations.
See also Giant who had no heart.
For other entries, see 2d edition.
Cobbler's song. LaFontaine. Fables (Tilney. Cobbler and
the financier.)
(poem). Cooper. Argosy of fables. (Cobbler and the finan-
cier.)
Egan. New found tales. (Contented poor man.)
Kinscella. Music appreciation readers. Book 5. (Hundred
crowns for a song.)
Retner. That's that. (Bag of gold. Adapted.)
For other entries, see 2d edition.
Cobwebs. Rhys. English fairy book.
Cock-a-doodle-do. Carpenter. Tales of a Basque grand-
mother. (*In* Manesh and Mayi at home.)
For other entries, see 2d edition.
Cock and a diamond. *See* Cock and the jewel.
Cock and the bean. Carrick. More Russian picture tales.
(poem). Quinn. Stories for the six-year-old.
See also Cock and the hen in the nut wood.
Cock and the cats who bore his litter. Cooper. Argosy of
fables.
Cock and the fox. I. *See* 2d edition.
Cock and the fox. II. Æsop. Fables (Whitman ed.).
Piper. Folk tales children love. (Rooster and the fox.)
Piper. Road in storyland. (Rooster and the fox.)
See also Fox and the woodcock.
For other entries, see 2d edition.
Cock and the fox. III. Carrick. Animal picture tales from
Russia. (Fox and the cock.)
For other entries, see 2d edition.
Cock and the fox. IV (poem). Curry and Clippinger. Chil-
dren's literature.
Farjeon. Tales from Chaucer. (Nun's priest's tale.)
Kinscella. Music appreciation readers. Book 1.
For other entries, see 2d edition.
Cock and the fox. V. Babbitt. Animals' own story book.
(Rooster and the fox.)
See also Partridge and the fox.
For other entries, see 2d edition.
Cock and the fox. VI. Æsop. Fables (Jones. Dog, the cock
and the fox.)
Carrick. More Russian picture tales. (Dog and the cock.)
Cooper. Argosy of fables. (Dog, the cock and the fox.)
For other entries, see 2d edition.
Cock and the fox. VII. Æsop. Fables (Whitman ed. Fox
and the cock.)

Cock and the fox. VIII. Kinscella. Music appreciation
readers. Book 1. (An old fable of the cock.)
Cock and the hen. I–II. *See* 2d edition.
Cock and the hen. III. Elson and Runkel. Child-library
readers. Book 2.
See also Little cock and little hen.
Cock and the hen in the nut wood #.
See also Cock and the bean ; Pedelesta and Mustaccio ; Rooster
and the hen.
Cock and the jewel. Æsop. Fables (Artzybasheff).
Æsop. Fables (Jones).
Æsop. Twenty four fables (L' Estrange. Cock and a dia-
mond.)
(poem). Cooper. Argosy of fables. (Cock and the pearl.)
Power. Children's treasure chest. (Cock and the jewel.)
For other entries, see 2d edition.
Cock and the mouse. Cowles. Stories to tell.
Cock and the pearl. *See* Cock and the jewel.
Cock and the raven (poem). Cooper. Argosy of fables.
Cock Robin. Curry and Clippinger. Children's literature.
(Courtship, marriage and dinner of Cock Robin and Jenny
Wren ; Burial of poor Cock Robin.)
(poem). Johson and Scott. Anthology of children's litera-
ture. (Who killed Cock Robin?)
(poem). Power. Bag o' tales.
For other entries, see 2d edition.
Cock, the cat, and the young mouse. *See* Mouse, the cat and
the cock.
Cock, the mouse and the little red hen.
Hutchinson. Chimney corner stories.
Lefevre. Cock, the mouse and the little red hen.
Piper. Gateway to storyland.
For other entries, see 2d edition.
Cockatrice. *See* Basilisk.
Cocks and a partridge. *See* Partridge and the cocks.
Cock's stone. *See* Stone in the cock's head.
In 2d edition there are entries under each title.
Cocoanut monkey (poem). Olcott. Wonder tales from pirate
isles.
Coconut tree. I. Metzger. Tales told in Hawaii. (Origin
of the coconut tree.)
Coconut tree. II. Lee. Folk tales of all nations. (Where
the coconut came from.)
Coffin-lid. Ralston. Russian fairy tales.
Coggelty-Curry. Mason. Wee men of Ballywooden.
Cogia Hassan Alhabbal, History of. Arabian nights. Ad-
ventures of Haroun Er Raschid (Olcott. Story told by
Cogia Hassan Alhabbal).
See also Abu Taloot ; Luck and blessing ; One cannot help an
unlucky man ; Three gifts. III #.
For other entries, see 2d edition.

Colbert, Jean Baptiste. Chambers' miscellany. v. 5. (Story of Colbert.)

Cold heart. *See* Stone-cold heart.

Cold iron. Kipling. Rewards and fairies.
See also Huon of Bordeaux.

Collier and the fuller. *See* Charcoal burner and the fuller.

Colt. Cooper. Argosy of fables.

Colum. *See* St. Columba.

Columba. *See* St. Columba.

Columbine, Origin of. Stewart. Tell me a story I never heard before. (Cry of the eagle.)

Columbus, Christopher. Colum. Voyagers. (Great admiral; Naming of the land.)
Cozad. Story talks. (Who discovered America.)
Curry and Clippinger. Children's literature. (How Columbus got his ships.)
See also Little brother of long ago; Persian Columbus.
For other entries, see 2d edition.

Columbus in the new world. Blaisdell. Log cabin days.

Columns with a maiden's beauty. *See* Ionians build to Diana.

Comb. Cooper. Argosy of fables.

Comedy of errors. Lamb. Tales from Shakespeare.

Coming of Angus and Bride. Olcott. Wonder tales from fairy isles. (Snowdrops of Bride.)
For other entries, see 2d edition.

Coming of Arthur. *See* King Arthur's coming.

Coming of Finn. Young. Tangle-coated horse. (Lordship of the Fianna.)
See also Finn MacCool.

Coming of horses to Navajo land. Hogner. Navajo winter nights.

Coming of Lugh. *See* Lugh, the long-handed.

Coming of Merlin. *See* Merlin the enchanter; Why the red dragon is the emblem of Wales.

Coming of the corn. *See* First corn. I.

Coming of the Norsemen. *See* Leif Ericson.

Coming of the old-world fairies. Kennedy. Red man's wonder book.
See also Fairies' passage.

Coming of the paper carp. Nakazawa. Weaver of the frost.

Coming of the prince. Harper. Merry Christmas to you.
For other entries, see 2d edition.

Coming of the water-lily. *See* Star maiden. I.

Compair Bouki and the monkeys. Lee. Folk tales of all nations.

Compair Bouki, Compair Lapin, and the birds' eggs. Lee. Folk tales of all nations.

Compair Lapin and Compair L'Ours. Lee. Folk tales of all nations.
See also Cat and the mouse in partnership.

Compair Lapin and Madam Carencro. Field. American folk and fairy tales.
See also Why the turkey buzzard is bald-headed. I.
Compair Lapin and the earthworm. Lee. Folk tales of all nations.
Compair Tareau and Jean Malin. *See* Jean Malin and the bull-man.
Companion-in-suffering-in-the-glade. Colum. Bright islands.
Companions of Ulysses. La Fontaine. Fables (Tilney).
Company in the parlor. Potter. Giant of Apple Pie Hill.
Conary Mor. *See* Destruction of Da Derga's hostel.
Conceited ant. De Huff. Taytay's tales.
Conceited apple branch. Andersen. Fairy tales (Stickney). v. 2.
For other entries, see 2d edition.
Conceited elephant and the very lively mosquito. Lobagola. Folk tales of a savage.
Conceited mouse. Harriman. Stories for little children.
Conceited partridge. Carey. Stories of the birds.
Conceited spider. Lee. Folk tales of all nations.
See also Anansi the spider-man #.
Conchubar. *See* Conor MacNessa.
Confident parrot (poem). Cooper. Argosy of fables.
See also Parrot. II #.
Confucius. Metzger. Picture tales from the Chinese. (Wise man and the boy.)
Conjure wives. Harper. Ghosts and goblins.
For other entries, see 2d edition.
Conn-Eda, Story of. I. *See* 2d edition.
Conn-Eda, Story of. II. *See* Black Thief and Knight of the Glen.
Conn the boaster. Dunbar. Sons o' Cormac.
Conn the hundred-fighter. Young. Tangle-coated horse. (*In* Lordship of the Fianna.)
Connla and the fairy maiden. Curry and Clippinger. Children's literature.
For other entries, see 2d edition.
Connor cows. Egan. New found tales.
Conor MacNessa, King of Ulster. *See* Fergus MacRogh and the kingship of Ulster; Vengeance of Mesgedra.
Conrad of the Red Town. Baldwin. Pedlar's pack.
Constans, the emperor. Gibson. Golden bird. (Tale of King Coustans, the emperor.)
For other entries, see 2d edition.
Constant green jerkin. Dunbar. Sons o' Cormac.
See also How Cormac lost his kingdom.
Constantes and the Dhrako. Garnett. Ottoman wonder tales. (How Hasanek outwitted the dev.)
Lee. Folk tales of all nations. (Constantes and the dragon.)
See also Esben and the witch.
For other entries, see 2d edition.

Constantes and the dragon. *See* Constantes and the Dhrako.
Constantine the Great. Bryant. Children's book of celebrated legends. (St. Helena and the cross.)
Contented poor man. *See* Cobbler's song.
Contest. I. *See* Hare and the pig.
Contest. II. *See* Magic singing.
Contest for a tiger tooth. Phillips. Far peoples.
Contests. Eells. Magic tooth.
Contests of Manawyddan against the Thief of the Sea. Morris. Book of the three dragons.
Contrary Chueh Chun. Chrisman. Shen of the sea.
Conversion of St. Wilfrid. Kipling. Rewards and fairies.
Converted miser. *See* Miser converted.
Coocooburrah bird and the dawn. *See* How the sun was made.
Cook's tale. *See* Sir Gamelyn.
Copee. *See* Chipmunk and Owl-woman.
Copernicus and his book. Lansing. Great moments in freedom. (Old man's dream.)
Copetuengh. *See* Magic awl.
Coppelia, the mysterious doll. Kinscella. Music appreciation readers. Book 5.
Copper kettle fairy. Potter. Captain Sandman.
Coquerico. *See* Half-Chick.
Corals and pearls. Katibah. Other Arabian nights.
Corentin. *See* St. Corentin.
Coriolanus. Cooke. Stories of Rome.
   Farjeon. Mighty men from Achilles to Julius Caesar. (Man with the name of a city.)
   For other entries, see 2d edition.
Cormac's disappearance. *See* How Cormac MacArt went to faery.
Cormac's judgement. Egan. New found tales. (Judgement of Cormac MacArt.)
   Rolleston. High deeds of Finn. (Judgement of Cormac.)
Cormorants of Udröst. Wilson. Green magic. (Ut-Röst cormorants.)
   See also Belinck and the three waves.
   For other entries, see 2d edition.
Corn chooses a mate #.
   See also Fair earth.
Corn for Italy. Botsford. Picture tales from the Italian.
Corn, Origin of. *See* Chekilli, the Creek boy; First corn; Seven corn maidens # ; Spirit of the corn # ; Turkey-given corn.
Cornelius. Niemeyer. Stories for the history hour.
Corner in babies. Burnett. Children's book.
Cornflower. *See* Cornflower youth.
Cornflower youth. Carey. Flower legends. (Cornflower.)
   For other entries, see 2d edition.
Coronation of Inez de Castro (poem). Hemans. Poems.
   Lang. Red true story book.

Corsa, Story of. Hill and Maxwell. Napoleon's story book. (*In* Why the fairies went to Corsica.)

Cortez. Martinez Del Rio. Sun, the moon and a rabbit. (Fair gods; Fleet on fire.)

Cosette's Christmas eve. Skinner. Christmas stories.

Cottager and his cat #.
See also Fortune-seekers. I ; Master Mustapha of the whiskers.

Cotton-tail and the turtle. De Huff. Taytay's memories.

Cotton-Woolleena. Housman. Turn again tales.

Coucy, Regnault de. Cather. Pan and his pipes. (When knighthood was in flower.)

Council held by the rats. *See* Belling the cat.

Councilor and the orphan. Noel. Magic bird of Chomo-lung-ma.
See also Language of birds. I.

Count Angewiller and the fairy. Henderson. Wonder tales of Alsace-Lorraine.

Count Eberstein's cook. Henderson. Wonder tales of Alsace-Lorraine.

Count La Cerda's treasure. Otero. Old Spain in our Southwest.

Counted as men. Egan. New found tales.

Countess Bertha's honey-feast. Spurr. Dumas fairy tale book.

Countess Itha. Canton. Child's book of saints.
For other entries, see 2d edition.

Countess Wilhelmine's long walk. Guerber. Legends of Switzerland. (*In* Legends of Neuchatel.)
See also Tichborne dole.

Country bumpkin and the hobgoblin. Masson. Folk tales of Brittany.

Country cat. Bailey. Tell me another story.
For other entries, see 2d edition.

Country maid and her milk can. *See* Milkmaid and her pail of milk.

Country mouse and the city mouse. *See* Country mouse and the town mouse.

Country mouse and the town mouse. I. Æsop. Fables (Artzybasheff. Country mouse and the city mouse.)
Æsop. Fables (Jones. Town mouse and the country mouse.)
Æsop. Fables (Whitman ed. Town mouse and country mouse.)
Cooper. Argosy of fables.
(poem). Curry and Clippinger. Children's literature.
Curry and Clippinger. Children's literature. (Field mouse and the town mouse.)
Evans. Worth while stories. (Country mouse and the city mouse.)
Johnson and Scott. Anthology of children's literature. (Town mouse and the country mouse.)

Country mouse and the town mouse—*continued.*
Piper. Folk tales children love. (Country mouse and the city mouse.)
Piper. Road in storyland. (Country mouse and the city mouse.)
Power. Children's treasure chest. (Country mouse and town mouse.)
Rich. Read-aloud book.
Starbuck. Familiar haunts. (Town mouse and the country mouse.)
Told under the green umbrella. (Town mouse and the country mouse.)
Wilson. Red magic.
For other entries, see 2d edition.
Country mouse and the town mouse. II (poem). Curry and Clippinger. Children's literature. (City mouse and the garden mouse.)
Country of arched entrances. *See* First arch.
Country of gentlemen. Lee. Folk tales of all nations.
Olcott. Wonder tales from China seas.
Country of the stupid folk. *See* Fortune seekers. I.
Country where the mice eat iron. Aspinwall. Jataka tales. (Stolen ploughshares.)
Cooper. Argosy of fables. (Merchant's son and the iron scales.)
Lee. Folk tales of all nations. (Mice that ate an iron balance.)
Mackenzie. Jackal in Persia. (Story of the trusty friend.)
Phillips. Far peoples. (Merchant and his friend.)
See also Mouse-deer and King Solomon.
For other entries, see 2d edition.
   In 2d edition this story is also indexed under the titles "Merchant and his iron," and "Stolen plow."
Countryman and the snake. I. Cooper. Argosy of fables.
Æsop. Fables (Whitman ed.).
See also Camel driver and the snake.
For other entries, see 2d edition.
Countryman and the snake. II. Æsop (Jones. Farmer and the viper.)
Courage in danger. White. School management, p. 277.
Court cards, Story of the. Fyleman. Tea time tales.
Courtship, marriage, and dinner of Cock Robin and Jenny Wren. *See* Cock Robin.
Courtship of Emer. Gregory. Cuchulain of Muirthemne. (Courting of Emer.)
Hull. Cuchulain. (How Cuchulain wooed his wife.)
Courtship of Hilbert and Japiky. Miller. My travelship: Holland.
Courtship of Mr. Stork and Miss Heron. Brown. Curious book of birds.
Covetous man. *See* Miser. I.

Cow Golden Horn. Mukerji. Hindu fables.

Cow, his capital. *See* Cow that went to college.

Cow of plenty. Young. Celtic wonder tales.
See also Wonderful cow #.

Cow that went to college. McVenn. Good manners and right conduct. (Cow, his capital.)

Cow, the goat, the sheep, and the lion. *See* Lion's share. III.

Cowboy and his fairy. *See* Herdboy and the weaving princess.

Cowslip. I. *See* 2d edition.

Cowslip. II. Carey. Flower legends.
For other entries, see 2d edition.

Coyote and buffalo bull. Linderman. Kootenai why stories.

Coyote and chickadee. Garett. Coyote stories.

Coyote and deer. Hogner. Navajo winter nights.

Coyote and evening star. James. Tewa firelight tales.

Coyote and grizzly. I. *See* 2d edition.

Coyote and grizzly. II. Linderman. Kootenai why stories. (Coyote and grizzly bear.)

Coyote and horned toad. Hogner. Navajo winter nights.

Coyote and lynx cat. Hogner. Navajo winter nights.

Coyote and Old=Man's eyes. *See* Old-Man's eyes.

Coyote and porcupine. Hogner. Navajo winter nights.
See also Blue Jay the imitator ; Coyote imitates bear ; Iktomi goes visiting.

Coyote and red fox. De Huff. Taytay's memories.

Coyote and rolling rock. Sexton. Gray wolf stories.
For other entries, see 2d edition.

Coyote and the badger. Hogner. Navajo winter nights.

Coyote and the blackbirds. De Huff. Taytay's tales.
For other entries, see 2d edition.

Coyote and the buffalo. Garett. Coyote days.

Coyote and the donkey. De Huff. Taytay's memories.

Coyote and the fox. De Huff. Taytay's tales.
Lee. Folk tales of all nations.

Coyote and the rock lizards. Hogner. Navajo winter nights.

Coyote and the turtle. De Huff. Taytay's tales.
Lee. Folk tales of all nations.
See also Why turtles stay near the water.

Coyote and wood=tick. Garett. Coyote stories.

Coyote fights some monsters. Garett. Coyote stories.

Coyote imitates bear and kingfisher. Garett. Coyote stories.
See also Blue Jay the imitator.

Coyote juggles his eyes. *See* Coyote's eyes.

Coyote laughs. Hogner. Navajo winter nights.

Coyote lives with ten grizzlies. Sexton. Gray wolf stories.

Coyote marries. Sexton. Gray wolf stories. (Coyote marries the daughter of Thunder.)

Coyote meets wind and some others. Garett. Coyote stories.

Coyote pushes in Mountain Lion's face #.
See also How wild cat lost his nose and tail.

Coyote quarrels with mole. Garett. Coyote stories.

Coyote steals a blanket #.
See also Rolling stone.

Coyote, the grey giant and the beautiful maiden. Hogner. Navajo winter nights.
See also Three tests.

Coyote, the hungry. I. *See* 2d edition.

Coyote, the hungry. II. Rich. Why-so stories. (Why coyotes are hungry.

Coyote transforms a monster. Sexton. Gray wolf stories.
See also Devouring hill.

Coyote's adventures. Linderman. Kootenai why stories.
See also Blue Jay the imitator; Coyote imitates Bear; How Master Rabbit went fishing; I know what I have learned.

Coyote's eyes. I. Morris. Stories from mythology: North American. (*In* Ch. 12.)
Garett. Coyote stories. (Coyote juggles his eyes.)

Coyote's eyes. II. Hogner. Navajo winter nights. (How coyote got yellow eyes.)

Coyote's eyes. I–II. *See also* Crab and the jaguar; Fox's eyes; Old-Man's eyes #; Wonderful bird #.

Crab. *See* Doctor Know-all.

Crab and his mother. Æsop. Fables (Artzybasheff. An old crab and a young one.)
Æsop. Fables (Jones).
Cooper. Argosy of fables. (Crab and her mother.)
For other entries, see 2d edition.

Crab and the elephant. Aspinwall. Jataka tales.

Crab and the fox. I. *See* 2d edition.

Crab and the fox. II. Æsop. Fables (Jones).
Cooper. Argosy of fables.
See also Fox and the crabs #.

Crab and the jaguar. Carrick. Picture folk tales.
See also Coyote's eyes; Wonderful bird.

Crab and the monkey. I. Mitford. Tales of old Japan. (Battle of the ape and the crab.)
Whitehorn. Wonder tales of old Japan. (Story of monkey and crab.)
See also Dreadful boar; Ito and his friends.
For other entries, see 2d edition.

Crab and the monkey. II. De Leeuw. Java jungle tales.

Crackling mountain. *See* Farmer and the badger.

Crafty fox and industrious goose. Lee. Folk tales of all nations. (Fox and the goose.)
For other entries, see 2d edition.

Crafty servant. Chamoud. Picture tales from the French.
See also My own self.

Crane and the crab. **Arnold. Book of good counsels.
Cooper. Argosy of fables.
Mackenzie. Jackal in Persia. (Crane, the crab and the fish.)
Phillips. Far peoples. (Heron and the crab.)
Sawyer. Picture tales from Spain.
Shimer. Fairyland. (Crane, the fish, and the lobster.)
See also Pelican's punishment; Undan the pelican.
For other entries, see 2d edition.
Crane and the crow. *See* Why the crow is black. III.
Crane and the heron. Ransome. Old Peter's Russian tales.
(*In* Christening in the village.)
For other entries, see 2d edition.
Crane in the wheat fields. Starbuck. Familiar haunts. (*In* Wise men of Gotham.)
For other entries, see 2d edition.
Crane, the crab and the fish. *See* Crane and the crab.
Crane, the fish and the lobster. *See* Crane and the crab.
Crane who quarrelled with his mate. Cooper. Argosy of fables.
Cranes of Ibycus. Bulfinch. Golden age. (Ibycus. *In* Ch. 25.)
Forbush. Myths and legends of Greece and Rome.
Lang. Book of myths.
See also Meinrad's watchers; Will on the wind.
Cratchit's Christmas dinner. Dickens. Christmas carol.
Evans. Worth while stories. (Tiny Tim.)
Kinscella. Music appreciation readers. Book 2. (Tiny Tim. Adapted.)
Kaphan. Tell us a Dickens story. (Tiny Tim. Adapted.)
Large. Famous children of storybook land. (Tiny Tim.)
Manner. Silver treasury. (Bob Cratchit's Christmas dinner.)
Walters. Book of Christmas stories.
See also Ebenezer Scrooge's Christmas.
For other entries, see 2d edition.
Crawfish and grizzly bear. Garett. Coyote stories.
Crawfish and the great buzzard. James. Happy animals of Atagahi.
Crazy Jim and the pixies. Hall. Godmother's stories.
Crazy priestess and her crazy daughters. *See* Three sillies. II.
Creaking wheels. *See* Oxen and the axle trees.
Cream tarts. Arabian nights. Adventures of Haroun Er Raschid (Olcott. Famous history of the cream tarts.)
See also Noureddin Ali and his son.
Creation, Legend of. Untermeyer. Donkey of God. (*In* Donkey of God.)
Creation of giants and trolls. Smith. Made in Sweden.
(*In* Fabrics of Scania.)
See also Giants and fairies. II; Titans #.

Creation of Ireland. Young. Celtic wonder tales. (Earth-shapers.)

Young. Tangle-coated horse. (*In* Night of the nights.)

Creation of man (Greek). Pyle. Tales from Greek mythology.

For other entries, see 2d edition.

Creation of man (Indian). Browne. Indian nights. (Story of Klose-kom-bau.)

Lee. Folk tales of all nations. (Creation of man.)

Leland. Algonquin legends. (How Glooskap made the elves and fairies and then man.)

Macmillan. Canadian wonder tales. (Glooskap's country.)

Phillips. Indian tales for little folks. (*In* How Napi made the animals.)

Whitman. Navaho tales. (Five worlds.)

For other entries, see 2d edition.

Creation of man (Mexican). Miller. My book of history. v. 4. (Story of creation. *In* Ch. 10.)

Martinez Del Rio. Sun, the moon, and a rabbit. (Gods seek company.)

Creation of man (Norse). Pyle. Tales from Norse mythology. (*In* Sun, moon and stars and day and night.)

See also Creation of the world (Norse).

Creation of man (Polynesian). Howes. Long bright land. (Man and woman.)

See also How the monkey was made.

Creation of man.
For other versions, *see* How the races obtained their colors; Why the negro is black.

Creation of the world (African). Woodson. African myths. (Creation.)

Creation of the world (Babylonian). Miller. My book of history. v. 1. (How Marduk created the world. *In* Ch. 11.)

Creation of the world (Chinese). Applegarth. Missionary stories for little folks. 1st series. (Dragon that swallows the sun.)

Creation of the world (Eskimo). Rasmussen. Eagle's gift. (Story about the beginning of all life.)

For other entries, see 2d edition.

Creation of the world (Greek). Pyle. Tales from Greek mythology.

For other entries, see 2d edition.

Creation of the world (Indian). Hogner. Navajo winter nights. (Navajo land.)

James. Happy animals of Atagahi. (Crawfish and the great buzzard.)

Morris. Stories from mythology: North American.

Rich. Why-so stories. (How a bird made the world.)

Rich. Why-so stories. (Navaho story of the swallow.)

Spence. Myths of the North American Indians. (Creation myths. *In* Ch. 2.)

Creation of the world (Indian)—*continued.*
Whitman. Navaho tales. (Five worlds.)
For other entries, see 2d edition.
Creation of the world (Japanese). Miller. My book of history. v. 4. (*In* Japan and the Japanese. Ch. 5.)
Teall. Batter and spoon fairies. (*In* Ch. 26.)
Creation of the world (Mexican). Miller. My book of history. v. 4. (*In* Story of creation. Ch. 10.)
Creation of the world (Norse). Miller. My book of history. v. 3. (Norse tales of creation and the gods. *In* Ch. 7.)
Pyle. Tales from Norse mythology. (How the world was made.)
For other entries, see 2d edition.
Creation of the world (Polynesian). Howes. Long bright land. (In the beginning.)
See also Earth and the sky.
Creation of the world (South American). Eells. Magic tooth. (Karu and Rairu.)
Creation of woman. Metzger. Tales told in Hawaii.
See also First woman #.
Creigfryn's bargain. *See* Curse of Pantannas.
Cricket and the ant. *See* Ant and the cricket.
Cricket and the coyote. Bailey. Story-telling hour.
See also Battle of the firefly and the apes #.
Crime and punishment. * * Gaster. Ma'aseh book. v. 1.
See also Meinrad's watchers; Will on the wind.
Crimson slippers. McNeer and Lederer. Tales from the crescent moon.
Cripple and the bully. Cooper. Argosy of fables.
Crispin. *See* St. Crispin.
Critical parrot (poem). Cooper. Argosy of fables.
Crocodile pagoda. Burnett. Children's book.
Crocodile tale and a monkey tail. *See* Monkey and the crocodile.
Crocodile's ingratitude. De Leeuw. Java jungle tales.
Olcott. Wonder tales from pirate isles. (Friend Mouse-deer.)
See also Foolish fish; Tiger gets his deserts; Way of the world. I.
Crocodile's relatives. Woodson. African myths.
See also Bat, birds and beasts.
Crocus. Carey. Flower legends.
See also Why crocus holds up his golden cup.
Crœsus and Solon. Curry and Clippinger. Children's literature.
Crœsus' dream. Farjeon. Tales from Chaucer. (Crœsus. *In* Monk's tale.)
Crœsus, the gold=lover. *See* Virgilius the sorcerer.
Crom Duv, the giant. Colum. King of Ireland's son. (House of Crom Duv.)
Crooked mouse. Blaisdell. Rhyme and story second reader.
Cross grandmother rabbit. Potter. Giant of Apple Pie Hill.

Cross of the dumb (poem). Smith and Hazeltine. Christmas in legend and story.
(poem). Macleod. Poems.
Cross=patch. Baker. Tell them again tales.
Cross=surety. Ralston. Russian fairy tales.
See also Joseph the Sabbath lover.
Crow. I. Byrde. Polish fairy book. (About the black crow.) •
For other entries, see 2d edition.
Crow. II. *See* Fox and the crow. I.
Crow and Mercury. Æsop. Fables (Whitman ed.).
Cooper. Argosy of fables.
For other entries, see 2d edition.
Crow and the cheese. *See* Fox and the crow. I.
Crow and the daylight. Lee. Folk tales of all nations.
For other entries, see 2d edition.
Crow and the partridge. Blaisdell. Rhyme and story second reader. (Crow and the pigeon.)
Carey. Stories of the birds. (Raven who tried to walk like the dove.)
Johnson and Scott. Anthology of children's literature.
Rich. Why-so stories. (Crow and the pigeon. *In* Tales of the crow.)
See also Kites and the swans.
For other entries, see 2d edition.
In 2d edition this story is also indexed under the title "Partridge and the crow."
Crow and the peacock. *See* Why the crow is black. IV.
Crow and the pigeon. *See* Crow and the partridge.
Crow and the pitcher. Æsop. Fables (Artzybasheff).
Æsop. Fables (Jones).
Æsop. Fables (Whitman ed.).
Cooper. Argosy of fables. (Crow and the water jar.)
Curry and Clippinger. Children's literature.
Johnson and Scott. Anthology of children's literature.
For other entries, see 2d edition.
Crow and the raven. Æsop. Fables (Jones).
Cooper. Argosy of fables.
Crow and the serpent. *See* Crow and the snake. I.
Crow and the sheep. Æsop. Twenty-four fables (L'Estrange. Sheep and a crow.)
Cooper. Argosy of fables.
Crow and the snake. I. Æsop. Fables (Jones).
Cooper. Argosy of fables. (Crow and the serpent.)
Crow and the snake. II. **Arnold. Book of good counsels. (Black snake and the golden chain.)
Cooper. Argosy of fables. (Black snake and the golden chain.)
Mackenzie. Jackal in Persia.
Phillips. Far peoples. (Snake and the crow.)
Sawyer. Picture tales from Spain. (Crow's nest.)
See also Hen and the snake ; Sparrows and the falcon.

Crow and the swan. Æsop. Fables (Jones).
See also Why ravens croak.
Crow and the water jar. *See* Crow and the pitcher.
Crow children. Rich. Why-so stories. (*In* Tales of the crow.)
For other entries, see 2d edition.
Crow, Tales of the. Rich. Why-so stories.
Crow, the jackal, the wolf, and the camel. * * Arnold. Book of good counsels. (Camel, the lion, and his court.)
Cooper. Argosy of fables. (Camel, the lion and his court.)
Mackenzie. Jackal in Persia. (Crow, the wolf, the jackal and the tiger.)
For other entries, see 2d edition.
Crow, the wolf, the jackal and the tiger. *See* Crow, the jackal, the wolf and the camel.
Crown. Blondell. Keepsakes.
Crown of gold. Atkins. Pot of gold.
Crown of St. Stephen. Patten. Junior Classics. v. 7. (Brave Queen of Hungary.)
Crowning of Ines de Castro. *See* Coronation of Inez de Castro.
Crown's warranty. Housman. Moonshine and clover.
Crows and the owls. Cooper. Argosy of fables.
Crow's children. I (poem). Cary. Poems.
(poem). Cooper. Argosy of fables.
For other entries, see 2d edition.
Crow's children. II. Rich. Why-so stories. (Why the crow hates the hawk.)
See also Frog's beautiful son; Jupiter and the monkey; One's own children are always the prettiest.
Crow's children. III. Carey. Stories of the birds. (Ugly little crows.)
Crow's nest. *See* Crow and the snake. II.
Cruachan. *See* Queen Maeve of Connaght.
Cruche, Legend of. Carpenter. Tales of a Basque grandmother.
See also Midas. I.
Cruise of the Long Serpent. Dunlap. Stories of the Vikings.
Crumb in the beard. Coussens. Diamond story book.
See also King Thrushbeard.
Cry fairy. Bailey. Tell me another story.
Cry of the eagle. Stewart. Tell me a story I never heard before.
Crystal egg (poem). Colum. King of Ireland's son. (Sending of the crystal egg. *In* Fedelma.)
Cu-beag of the Willow-wood. MacManus. Donegal wonder book.
Cub and the crocodile. Bacon. Lion-hearted kitten.
Cuchulain. *See* Cuhulain.
Cuchulain's adventures in shadow-land. See Scathach, woman warrior.

Cuckoo (poem). Cooper. Argosy of fables.
For other entries, see 2d edition.
Cuckoo and the eagle. Cooper. Argosy of fables.
For other entries, see 2d edition.
Cuckoo and the hoopoe. Lee. Folk tales of all nations.
See also Fisherman and his wife.
Cuckoo comes to Ireland. Stein. When fairies were friendly.
(*In* How Nial won the beautiful princess.)
Cuckoo, the carved door and the white knights. Wiggin and Smith. Twilight stories.
Cuckoo whose nest was made for her. Housman. Turn again tales.
Cuhulain. Cruse. Young folk's book of epic heroes. (Cuchulain.)
Gregory. Cuchulain of Muirthemne. (Boy deeds of Cuchulain.)
Hull. Cuchulain. (Boy-corps of King Conor.)
Johnson and Scott. Anthology of children's literature. (How Cuchulain got his name.)
Miller. My book of history. v. 3. (*In* Ch. 13.)
Power. Bag o' tales. (Cuchulain's wedding.)
For other entries, see 2d edition.
Cuhulain's son. *See* Death of Conla, son of Aiffe.
Cunning monkey and the boar. *See* Sagacious monkey and the boar.
Cunning partner. *See* Rogue and the simpleton.
Cupid and folly (poem). Cooper. Argosy of fables.
Cupid and Psyche. Bulfinch. Golden age. (*In* Ch. 11.)
Forbush. Myths and legends of Greece and Rome.
Johnson and Scott. Anthology of children's literature.
Lang. Book of myths. (Psyche.)
Lee. Folk tales of all nations. (Psyche.)
Pyle. Tales from Greek mythology. (Eros and Psyche.)
For other entries, see 2d edition.
Curious birthday. Untermeyer. Last pirate.
Curlew and the saint. *See* St. Beuno and the curlew.
Curly-locks. Hall. Godmother's stories.
See also Twelve huntsmen; White steed Bufanin.
Curse of Pantannas. Choate and Curtis. Little people of the hills. (Creigfryn's bargain.)
See also Syfaddon lake.
For other entries, see 2d edition.
Curse on Dasaratha. Mukerji. Rama.
Cursed Alp. Guerber. Legends of Switzerland. (*In* Glarus and Grisons.)
Cusi-Coyllur. *See* Love of Joyful Star.
Cuthbert. *See* St. Cuthbert.
Cyclops. *See* Ulysses and Polyphemus.
Cygnus. Kinney. Stars and their stories. (Brave young warrior who was a dearly loved son.)
Cymbeline. Lamb. Tales from Shakespeare.

Cynical hoopoe. Carey. Stories of the birds.
See also King Solomon and the hoopoe.

D

Dædalus and Icarus. Barry and Hanna. Wonder flights of long ago.
Bryant. Children's book of celebrated legends.
Bulfinch. Golden age. (Dædalus. *In* Ch. 20.)
Curry and Clippinger. Children's literature. (Icarus and Dædalus.)
Evans. Worth while stories. (Wax wings.)
Forbush. Myths and legends of Greece and Rome.
Johnson and Scott. Anthology of children's literature. (Icarus and Dædalus.)
Lang. Book of myths. (Icarus.)
Miller. My book of history. v. 2. (*In* Ch. 1.)
Pyle. Tales from Greek mythology.
Rich. Read-aloud book. (Dædalus.)
See also Winged hero.
For other entries, see 2d edition.
Daffy-down-dilly. Marzials. Stories for the story hour.
Dafydd Meurig of Betws Bledrws. Henderson and Jones. Wonder tales of ancient Wales.
See also David and the silver bell.
Dagda's harp. I. Kinscella. Music appreciation readers. Book 2. (Magic harp of Dagda.)
For other entries, see 2d edition.
Dagda's harp. II. Young. Celtic wonder tales. (Good action.)
Dahlia. Newman. Fairy flowers. (Monsieur Rosette.)
Dahut. *See* Ys, Story of.
Dairy-woman and the pail of milk. *See* Milkmaid and her pail of milk.
Dairymaid's tale. *See* Brownie and the thievish maids.
Dairywoman and the pot of milk. *See* Milkmaid and her pail of milk.
Daisy. I. Andersen. Fairy tales (Stickney). v. 2.
For other entries, see 2d edition.
Daisy. II. *See* Little white daisy.
Daisy and Double and the wolf. Potter. Fairy caravan. (*In* Ch. 9.)
Dame Gudbrand. Johnson and Scott. Anthology of children's literature. (Gudbrand on the hillside.)
Lee. Folk tales of all nations. (Gudbrand on the hillside.)
Rasmussen. East o' the sun and west o' the moon. (Gudbrand-on-the-hillside.)
For other entries, see 2d edition.
Dame Nancy and her fairy child. Choate and Curtis. Little people of the hills.

Dame Quimp's quest. Van Buren and Bemis. Christmas in storyland.

Dame Wiggins of Lee and her seven wonderful cats (poem). Curry and Clippinger. Children's literature. (poem). Hutchinson. Candlelight stories.
For other entries, see 2d edition.

Damien, Father. Broomell. Children's story caravan. (Ballad of Joseph and Damien.)

Damnah is taken into the service of the lion. Mackenzie. Jackal in Persia.

Damnah the jackal. Mackenzie. Jackal in Persia. (Treacherous conduct of the jackal Damnah to the bull Shan.)
See also Reynard the fox.

Damon and Pythias. Evans. Worth while stories.
McVenn. Good manners and right conduct. Book 2.
See also Five races of men.
For other entries, see 2d edition.

Dance of death. I. Cross. Music stories. (Danse macabre.)
Kinscella. Music appreciation readers. Book 5. (Ghost story told in music.)

Dance of death. II. Leland. Algonquin legends. (Dance of old age. *In* Weewillmickq. II.)
Macmillan. Canadian wonder tales.
Partridge. Joyful Star. (Maiden with the beautiful face and the evil heart.)

Dance of old age. *See* Dance of death. II.

Dance of the nymphs. Olcott. Wonder tales from windmill lands.

Dance of the shoes. Potter. Fairy caravan. (*In* Ch. 17.)

Dance of the Tylwythe Teg. *See* Rhys and Llywelyn.

Dancer in the sky. Kinscella. Music appreciation readers. Book 6.
See also Paup-Puk-Keewis.

Dancing. Metzger. Tales told in Hawaii. (Origin of dancing.)

Dancing blanket. *See* Raven's dancing blanket.

Dancing gypsy. Carpenter. Tales of a Basque grandmother.

Dancing kitten. Fyleman. Forty good-night tales.

Dancing monkeys. Cooper. Argosy of fables.
See also Venus and the cat.

Dancing pike. Bernhard. Master wizard.

Dancing princesses. *See* Twelve dancing princesses.

Dancing shoes. I. *See* Twelve dancing princesses.

Dandaka the monk. Lee. Folk tales of all nations.

Dandelion. I. Bailey. Stories children want. (Legend of the dandelion.)
For other entries, see 2d edition.

Dandelion. II. *See* Prairie dandelion.

Danger of traveling in the dark. * * Gaster. Ma'aseh book. v. 2.

Daniel Meek. Fyleman. Forty good-morning tales.

Daniel O'Rourke. Olcott. Wonder tales from fairy isles. (Up to the moon.)
See also Far adventures of Billy Burns; Trip to the moon.
For other entries, see 2d edition.
Danse Macabre. See Dance of death. I.
Dante. See Beatrice.
Daphne. Bailey. Tell me another story. (Story of the laurel.)
Bryant. Children's book of celebrated legends. (Apollo and Daphne.)
Bulfinch. Golden age. (Apollo and Daphne. In Ch. 3.)
Curtis. Stories in trees. (Apollo's laurel.)
Forbush. Myths and legends of Greece and Rome. (Apollo and Daphne.)
Johnson and Scott. Anthology of children's literature.
Lang. Book of myths. (Apollo and Daphne.)
Pyle. Tales from Greek mythology. (Phœbus and Daphne.)
See also When Cavillaca ran away.
For other entries, see 2d edition.
Darab. Coit. Ivory throne of Persia.
Darius and the Athenians. Lansing. Great moments in freedom. (At Marathon.)
Darius Green and his flying machine (poem). Johnson and Scott. Anthology of children's literature.
Dark Patrick's blood=horse. MacManus. Lo, and behold ye!
Dark place. Spaulding and Bryce. Aldine readers. Book 2. rev. ed.
Dark pony. Burnett. Children's book.
Darning=needle. Andersen. Fairy tales (Stickney). v. 1.
De La Mare and Quayle. Readings.
For other entries, see 2d edition.
Darrah, Lydia. Blaisdell. Log cabin days. (Lydia Darrah outwits the British.)
Date=stone of forgetfulness. Olcott. Wonder tales from China seas.
See also Dreamer the giant; Paksuni and the chess game; Rip Van Winkle; Vision of Tsunu.
Daughter of the dragon king. Olcott. Wonder tales from China seas.
Daughter of the King of Naples. Eells. Islands of magic.
Daughter of the lion. Untermeyer. Donkey of God.
Daughter of the Prince of Bakhtan and the possessing spirit. See Journey of Khensu to Bekhten.
David. See St. David.
David and the good health elves. Andress. Journey to Health-land.
David and the silver bell. Kinscella. Music appreciation readers. Book 5.
See also Dafydd Meurig.
David Cameron's fairy godmother. St. Nicholas. Dec. 1891, p. 130.

David's valentines. Bailey. Wonderful tree.
Davis, Sam. Evans. Worth while stories.
Dawn, twilight and midnight. Curtin. Fairy tales of eastern Europe.
Day and night. I. *See* 2d edition.
Day and night. II. Johnson and Scott. Anthology of children's literature. (Determination of night and day.)
For other entries. see 2d edition.
Day and night. III. Pyle. Tales from Norse mythology. (Sun, moon and stars and day and night.)
Day and night.
For other versions, *See* Dragon that swallows the sun every day; Flying head. II; How night came; Rescue of rabbit.
Day-dreaming. *See* Brahman and the pans; Brahman's dream; Broken pot; Lazy Heinz; Lean Liesl and Lanky Lenz; Milkmaid and her pail of milk; Poor man and the flask of oil; Three sillies.
Day of misfortunes. Johnson and Scott. Anthology of children's literature.
Day of the scholars. MacManus. Lo, and behold ye!
See also Miller at the professor's examination; Wise weaver.
Daylight, Origin of. I–IV. *See* 2d edition.
Daylight, Origin of. V #.
See also Lady in the sun.
Daylight saving. Broomell. Children's story caravan.
Days of chivalry. *See* King Arthur.
Dead game and the jackal. *See* Greedy jackal.
Dead mother. Ralston. Russian fairy tales.
For other entries. see 2d edition.
Dead, Tales of. Ralston. Russian fairy tales. (*In* Ch. 5.)
This includes: Coffin-lid; Ride on the gravestones; Soldier and the vampire; Two friends.
For other entries, see 2d edition.
Dead witch. Ralston. Russian fairy tales.
Deadly moss. Metzger. Tales told in Hawaii.
Deadly tree. Egan. New found tales. (Lawyer of Samarcand: Deadly tree.)
Dearest wish of your heart. *See* Washington does not go to sea.
Death. I. Lee. Folk tales of all nations. (Beginning of death.)
Death. II. Woodson. African myths. (Beginning of death.)
Death and an old man. *See* Death and the woodman.
Death and the woodman. Æsop. Fables (Artzybasheff. Old man and death.)
Æsop. Fables (Jones). Old man and death).
Æsop. Twenty-four fables (L'Estrange. Death and an old man.)
(poem). Cooper. Argosy of fables.
For other entries, see 2d edition.

Death of Abu Nowas and his wife #.
See also Jester who fooled a king.
Death of Adonis. *See* Adonis.
Death of Balder. *See* Baldur and the mistletoe.
Death of Baldur. I. *See* Baldur and the mistletoe.
Death of Baldur. II. Adams. Swords of the Vikings.
 (Death of Balder the Beautiful.)
Death of Conla, son of Aiffe. Gregory. Cuchulain of Muir-
 themne. (Only son of Aoife.)
 Hull. Cuchulain. (Fight of Cuchulain with his son Conla.)
Death of Earl Haakon. Dunlap. Stories of the Vikings.
 (Olaf returns to his own.)
Death of King Haakon the good. Dunlap. Stories of the
 Vikings. (On the wings of an arrow.)
Death of little Yei-T'so. Hogner. Navajo winter nights.
Death of the greedy jackal. *See* Greedy jackal.
Debtor and his sow. Æsop. Fables (Jones).
Deceitful maidens. Metzger. Tales told in Hawaii.
December weds May. *See* Merchant's tale.
Decision of Paris. *See* Paris: Apple of discord.
Decius Mus. *See* How Decius Mus saved Rome #.
Dedi the wizard, and the Sun-god's babies. Baikie. Won-
 der tales of the ancient world.
Deeds of Nanaboojoo. *See* Manabozho.
Deep waters. Housman. What-o'clock tales.
Deer and the coyote. De Huff. Taytay's tales.
Deer and the rabbit. Babbit. Animals' own story book.
 (How the deer won his horns.)
 Bailey. Stories from an Indian cave. (How the deer won
 his antlers.)
 Cooper. Argosy of fables. (How the deer got his horns.)
 Gearhart. Skalalatoot stories. (How the deer got his ant-
 lers.)
 Rich. Why-so stories. (How the deer got his horns.)
 See also Animal races; Fast runners #.
 For other entries, see 2d edition.
Deer and the snail. Phillips. Far peoples. (Race between
 the deer and the snail.)
 Woodson. African myths.
 See also Hare and the hedgehog.
Deer and the what-fruit tree. Babbitt. Animals' own story
 book.
Deer's child. Nusbaum. Seven cities of Cibola.
 Nusbaum. Zuni Indian tales.
Deer's sandals. Purnell. Merry frogs.
Deer's teeth. Linderman. Kootenai why stories. (Deer-
 persons.)
 See also Why the deer's teeth are blunt.
Deha. *See* Flood (Indian).
Deianeira. *See* Hercules and Deianeira.
Deirdre. Gregory. Cuchulain of Muirthemne. (Fate of the
 children of Usnach.)

Deirdre—*continued.*
Hull. Cuchulain. (Deirdre of contentions; Sorrowful death of Usna's sons.)
Lang. Book of myths.
For other entries, see 2d edition.
      In 2d edition this story is also indexed under the title "Fate of the sons of Usna."
Delenda est Carthago. Cooke. Stories of Rome. (Fate of Carthage.)
Miller. My book of history. v. 2. (Cato the censor. *In* Ch. 10.)
For other entries, see 2d edition.
Deluded dragon. *See* Gipsy and the dragon. II.
Demades and his fable. *See* Power of fables.
Demerara sugar. *See* Christmas in the woods.
Demeter. *See* Proserpina.
Democritus and the people of Abdera. La Fontaine. Fables (Tilney).
Demon of Adachi plain. *See* Goblin of Adachigahara.
Demon servant of Erloch Castle. Guerber. Legends of Switzerland. (*In* Bern.)
Demon's marriage. * * Gaster. Ma'aseh book. v. 2. (Proud prince who unwittingly gave his daughter in marriage to a demon.)
For other entries, see 2d edition.
Demon's mother-in-law. Boggs and Davis. Three golden oranges. (Don Demonio's mother-in-law.)
For other entries, see 2d edition.
Denis. *See* St. Denis.
Departure. Grahame. Dream book.
Grahame. Kenneth Grahame book.
Derido; or, The giant's quilt. Adams and Atchinson. There were giants.
For other entries, see 2d edition.
Derrick's downfall. Emerson. Merry-go-round of modern tales.
Deserted woman and her daughter. Morris. Stories from mythology: North American. (*In* Ch. 3.)
Despised maiden. Egan. New found tales.
See also Cinderella.
Destruction of Da Derga's hostel. Gregory. Cuchulain of Muirthemne. (High king of Ireland.)
Young. Celtic wonder tales. (Conary Mor.)
See also Sons of Doel Dermat.
For other entries, see 2d edition.
Destruction of Roll. Guerber. Legends of Switzerland. (*In* Bern.)
Destruction of Sennacherib. *See* Sennacherib's defeat.
Destruction of Treasure Valley. *See* King of the Golden River.
Determination of night and day. *See* Day and night.
Determination of the seasons. *See* Seasons.

Deucalion and Pyrrha. Bulfinch. Golden age. (*In* Ch. 2.)
Miller. My book of history. v. 1. (*In* Ch. 3.)
Pyle. Tales from Greek mythology.
See also Sura's seeds.
For other entries, see 2d edition.
Devapala. Williston. Hindu stories.
Devil and the gipsy. *See* Gipsy and the dragon. III.
Devil and the tailor. Williams-Ellis. Fairies and enchant-
ers.
Devil and Tom Walker. Irving. Bold dragoon.
Devil-fish's daughter. Spence. Myths of the North American
Indians. (*In* Ch. 7.)
Devil's bridge. I–II. *See* 2d edition.
Devil's bridge. III. Guerber. Legends of Switzerland. (*In*
Forest cantons.)
See also Fairy bridge of Licq; Why goats have short tails.
Devil's hide. Lee. Folk tales of all nations.
See also Keep cool #.
For other entries, see 2d edition.
Devil's mother=in=law. Lee. Folk tales of all nations.
Devoted daughter. Partridge. Joyful Star.
Devouring hill. Spence. Myths of the North American In-
dians. (How the rabbit slew the devouring hill. *In* Sioux
myths.)
Diamond and the north wind (play). Knight. Dramatic
reader.
Macdonald. At the back of the north wind. (*In* Ch. 1, 5,
8.)
Diamonds and toads. Arthur Rackham fairy book. (Toads
and diamonds.)
Chidley. Fifty-two story talks. (Tale about words.)
Curry and Clippinger. Children's literature. (Toads and
diamonds.)
Harper. Magic fairy tales. (Toads and diamonds.)
Hutchinson. Candlelight stories. (Toads and diamonds.)
Johnson and Scott. Anthology of children's literature.
(Toads and diamonds.)
Lang. Old friends among the fairies. (Toads and dia-
monds.)
Quinn. Stokes' wonder book of fairy tales.
See also Rose queen; Three heads of the well.
For other entries, see 2d edition.
Diana and Actæon. Bulfinch. Golden age. (*In* Ch. 4.)
For other entries, see 2d edition.
Diana and Endymion. *See* Endymion.
Diary of a lonely rooster. Wiggin and Smith. Twilight
stories.
Dick Whittington and his cat. Arthur Rackham fairy book.
(Dick Whittington.)
Curry and Clippinger. Children's literature. (Whittington
and his cat.)
De La Mare. Told again. (Dick Whittington.)

Dick Whittington and his cat—*continued.*
Evans. Worth while stories.
Harper. Magic fairy tales. (History of Whittington.)
Lang. Old friends among the fairies. (History of Whittington.)
Mackenzie. Book of nursery tales.
(poem). Noyes. Tales of the Mermaid tavern. (Flos Mercatorum.)
Power. Children's treasure chest. (History of Dick Whittington and his cat.)
Quinn. Stokes' wonder book of fairy tales. (Dick Whittington.)
Rhys. English fairy book. (Dick Whittington.)
Steel. English fairy tales.
Terry. Tales from far and near. (Dick Whittington.)
See also Honest penny ; Miller's boy and his cat ; Three copecks.
For other entries, see 2d edition.
Dickens, Charles. Buckingham. Elephant's friend. (Boy and his dream.)
Dicky Dick's master. Rhys. English fairy book.
Dicky the brave. Brown. Under the rowan tree.
See also Lexy and the dogs on his street.
Dido and Æneas. Bulfinch. Golden age. (*In* Adventures of Æneas. Ch. 31.)
Miller. My book of history. v. 2. (Founding of Rome. *In* Ch. 8.)
See also Æneas.
Dietrich of Berne, and Laurin the dwarf king. Henderson and Calvert. Wonder tales of old Tyrol. (*In* King Lareyn's garden.)
Different Cinderella. Cook. To-day's stories of yesterday.
See also Cinderella.
Different family. Cozad. Story talks. (Eye-traps.)
Dinabuc. *See* Giant of St. Michael's Mount.
Dinah, the dinosaur. Burnett. Children's book. (Dinah.)
Dinewan the emu. *See* Emu and the crows.
Dinner bell. Told under the blue umbrella.
Dinner bells. Potter. Giant of Apple Pie Hill.
Dinner horses. Mitchell. Here and now story book.
Diogenes the wise man. Bryant. Children's book of celebrated legends. (Diogenes in the market place.)
For other entries, see 2d edition.
Diomed's man=eating mares. Bryant. Children's book of celebrated legends. (Mares of Diomed.)
For other entries, see 2d edition.
Dionysius and Jupiter's cloak. Cozad. Story talks. (*In* Up-side-down world.)
Dipper. Piper. Folk tales children love. (Star dipper.)
Piper. Road in storyland. (Star dipper.)
Wheelock. Kindergarten children's hour. v. 3. (Legend of the great dipper. *In* Ch. 49.)

Dipper—*continued.*
See also Great bear.
For other entries, see 2d edition.
Dirty Tom. Evans. Worth while stories.
Disappearance of Cormac. *See* How Cormac MacArt went to faery.
Disappointed peacock. Purnell. Merry frogs.
Discomfiture of Cabrakan. *See* Killing of Cabrakan.
Discontented ass. I. Æsop. Fables (Whitman ed.).
Æsop. Twenty-four fables (L'Estrange. Ass's wish.)
See also Ass and his master. II ; Jupiter and the ass.
For other entries, see 2d edition.
Discontented ass. II. Baker. Tell them again tales. (Discontented donkey.)
Discontented donkey. *See* Discontented ass. II.
Discontented fir tree. *See* Little pine tree who wished for new leaves.
Discontented grass plant. I. *See* 2d edition.
Discontented grass plant. II #.
See also Keang-Njamo.
Discontented members. *See* Belly and the members.
Discontented mill window. Broomell. Children's story caravan.
For other entries, see 2d edition.
Discontented ox. *See* Ox who envied the pig.
Discontented pendulum. Curry and Clippinger. Children's literature.
Johnson and Scott. Anthology of children's literature.
Power. Children's treasure chest.
For other entries, see 2d edition.
Discontented rooster. Lebermann. New German fairy tales.
Discontented squirrel. Cabot. Course in citizenship.
Perkins and Danielson. Second year Mayflower program book.
Discontented tailor. Evans. Worth while stories.
See also Man with the wen.
Disease, Origin of. Bailey. Stories from an Indian cave. (When the plants were kind.)
For other entries, see 2d edition.
Dish of lentils. Schwimmer. Tisza tales.
See also King and the miller of Mansfield.
Dish land. Fun folk and fairy tales.
Dishonest trucker. King. Golden cat head.
Disobedient daughter's marriage. Woodson. African myths.
Disobedient dicky bird. Evans. Worth while stories.
For other entries, see 2d edition.
Disobedient kids. Nemcova. Disobedient kids.
See also Wolf and the seven little kids.
Disobedient woodpeckers. Brown. Curious book of birds.
See also Thirsty heron.
Ditch of Csorsz. Pogány. Hungarian fairy book.

Ditu Migniulu. Hill and Maxwell. Napoleon's story book.
See also Cinderella ; Thumbelina.
Dividing the cheese. *See* Matter of arbitration.
Divine musician. *See* Orpheus and Eurydice.
Dnieper and Sozh. Ralston. Russian fairy tales. (Sozh and Dnieper.)
Dnieper, the Volga, and the Dvina. Carpenter. Tales of a Russian grandmother. (Rivers that talked.)
Ralston. Russian fairy tales. (Metamorphosis of the Dnieper, the Volga, and the Dvina.)
Do and did. Retner. That's that.
Dobbin, Story of. Told under the blue umbrella.
Doctor and his patient. Cooper. Argosy of fables.
Doctor Dolittle, Story of. Harper and Hamilton. Winding roads.
Dr. Johnson and his father. Chidley. Fifty-two story talks. (Repentance of Samuel Johnson.)
For other entries, see 2d edition.
Doctor Know-all. Grimm. Fairy tales (Olcott).
Grimm. Tales from Grimm (Wanda Gag. Doctor Know-it-all.)
Lee. Folk tales of all nations. (Crab.)
Williams. Tales from Ebony.
For other entries, see 2d edition.
Doctor of medicine. Kipling. Rewards and fairies.
Doctor of physic's tale. *See* Virginia.
Dog, a donkey, a cat, and a cock. Borski and Miller. Gypsy and the bear.
Dog and a shadow. *See* Dog and his shadow.
Dog and his master. *See* Traveler and his dog.
Dog and his shadow. Æsop. Fables (Artzybasheff. Dog and the shadow.)
Æsop. Fables (Jones. Dog and the shadow.)
Æsop. Fables (Whitman ed. Dog and the shadow.)
Æsop. Twenty-four fables (L'Estrange. Dog and a shadow.)
Cooper. Argosy of fables. (Dog and the shadow.)
Curry and Clippinger. Children's literature. (Dog and the shadow.)
Johnson and Scott. Anthology of children's literature.
Piper. Road in storyland.
Rich. Read-aloud book. (Dog and the shadow.)
See also Fox and the piece of meat ; Wolf and the fox. II.
For other entries, see 2d edition.
Dog and the cock. *See* Cock and the fox. VI.
Dog and the cook. *See* Dog invited to supper.
Dog and the corpse. Ralston. Russian fairy tales.
Dog and the crocodile. Æsop. Fables (Whitman ed.).
Cooper. Argosy of fables.
For other entries, see 2d edition.
Dog and the horse. *See* Perplexity of Zadig.
Dog and the jester. Bowman. Little brown bowl.

Dog and the kingship. Babbitt. Animals' own story book (Animals choose a king.)
For other entries, see 2d edition.

Dog and the leopard. I. *See* 2d edition.

Dog and the leopard. II. Woodson. African myths.

Dog and the loaf of bread. Cooper. Argosy of fables.

Dog and the oyster. Cooper. Argosy of fables.
For other entries, see 2d edition.

Dog and the shadow. *See* Dog and his shadow.

Dog and the sow. Æsop. Fables (Jones).

Dog and the sparrow. De La Mare, and Quayle. Readings.
See also Spider's visit; What the fox did to the wolf.
For other entries, see 2d edition.

Dog and the wolf. I. Æsop. Fables (Artzybasheff).
Æsop. Fables (Jones).
Æsop. Fables (Whitman ed. Wolf and the mastiff.)
Cooper. Argosy of fables. (House-dog and the wolf.)
For other entries, see 2d edition.

Dog as cobbler. Borski and Miller. Gipsy and the bear. (Cobbler dog.)
Carrick. Tales of wise and foolish animals.
See also Sidi Lion's shoemaker.

Dog chasing a wolf. Æsop. Fables (Jones).

Dog dance. I. Spence. Myths of the North American Indians. (Young dog-dance. *In* Ch. 3.)

Dog dance. II. Sexton. Gray wolf stories. (Shaggy dog dance. *In* Boy who was reared by buffaloes.)

Dog in the manger. Æsop. Fables (Artzybasheff).
Æsop. Fables (Jones).
Æsop. Fables (Whitman ed.).
Cooper. Argosy of fables.
Johnson and Scott. Anthology of children's literature.
For other entries, see 2d edition.

Dog invited to supper. Æsop. Fables (Artzybasheff).
Æsop. Fables (Jones. Dog and the cook).
Æsop. Fables (Whitman ed.).
For other entries, see 2d edition.

Dog market in Buda. Schwimmer. Tisza tales.

Dog of Helvellyn. Cabot. Course in citizenship.

Dog of Pompeii. Untermeyer. Donkey of God.

Dog rose. Carey. Flower legends.

Dog Sultan. *See* Old Sultan.

Dog that stole a ride. Buckingham. Elephant's friend.

Dog, the cock and the fox. *See* Cock and the fox. VI.

Dog, the snake and the cure of headache. Lee. Folk tales of all nations.

Dog Tray. White. School management. p. 251.

Dog who carried his master's dinner. La Fontaine. Fables (Tilney).

Dog with his ears cropped. La Fontaine. Fables (Tilney).

Dogs and the fox. Æsop. Fables (Jones).
 Cooper. Argosy of fables.
Dogs and the hides. Æsop. Fables (Jones).
 Cooper. Argosy of fables.
 Kinscella. Music appreciation readers. Book 2. (Foolish little dogs.)
 For other entries, see 2d edition.
Dog's clock. Botsford. Picture tales from the Italian.
 See also Old Mother Hubbard.
Dog's diploma. *See* Why the dog and cat are enemies. III.
Dog's house. Cooper. Argosy of fables.
Dogs on his street. *See* Lexy and the dogs on his street.
Doing an angel's work. White. School management, p. 271.
Doll house. Broomell. Children's story caravan.
Doll in the grass. Bailey. Tell me another story.
 Hutchinson. Candlelight stories.
 Johnson and Scott. Anthology of children's literature.
 For other entries, see 2d edition.
Doll merchant's visit. Cook. Red and gold stories.
Doll under the briar rosebush. Told under the blue umbrella. (Doll under the rosebush.)
 For other entries, see 2d edition.
Dollar watch and the five jack=rabbits. Sandburg. Rootabaga stories.
Dolls' house. Fyleman. Forty good-night tales.
Dolls, Origin of. I. Snell. Told beneath the northern lights. (First doll.)
 For other entries, see 2d edition.
Dolls, Origin of. II. *See* Toymaker. I.
Doll's wish. Skinner. Christmas stories.
Dollykin. Capuana. Golden-feather.
Dolph Heyliger. Irving. Bold dragoon.
Dolphin who saved Arion. *See* Arion and the dolphin.
Dolphins and the sprat. *See* Dolphins, the whales, and the sprat.
Dolphins, the whales, and the sprat. Æsop. Fables (Jones).
 Cooper. Argosy of fables. (Dolphins and the sprat.)
Dome of the chain. Vilnay. Legends of Palestine.
 See also Bell of Atri.
Dominick's magic shoes. Perkins and Danielson. Mayflower program book.
 See also. Duty shoes.
Dominick=Tekun. Carpenter. Tales of a Basque grandmother.
Don Calico Corn. Shannon. California fairy tales.
Don Demonio's mother=in=law. *See* Demon's mother-in-law.
Don Fernan and the orange princess. Gunterman. Castles in Spain.
 See also Three orange peris # ; Three oranges.
Don Joean and the old witch. Olcott. Wonder tales from pirate isles.

Don Quixote. Curry and Clippinger. Children's literature. (Stories from Don Quixote.)

Rich. Read-aloud book. (Don Quixote and the adventures of the windmills.)

For other entries, see 2d edition.

Donal O'Donnell's standing army. MacManus. Lo, and behold ye!

See also Table, the ass and the stick.

Donald and his neighbors. *See* Hudden and Dudden and Donald O'Neary.

Donkey and the lap-dog. *See Ass* and the lap-dog.

Donkey and the rock. Egan. New found tales.

Donkey and the salt. Æsop. Fables (Jones. Ass and his burdens.)

Æsop. Fables (Whitman ed. Ass laden with salt and with sponges.)

Cooper. Argosy of fables. (Ass carrying salt.)

For other entries, see 2d edition.

Donkey boy. Rowe. Moon's birthday.

Donkey cabbage. Grimm. Fairy tales (Olcott. Donkey cabbages.)

See also Princess of Tiflis.

For other entries, see 2d edition.

Donkey of God. Untermeyer. Donkey of God.

Donkey=skin. Bruce. Treasury of tales for little folk.

For other entries, see 2d edition.

Donkeys. Cooper. Argosy of fables.

Donkeys! dogs! cats! rats! Botsford. Picture tales from the Italian.

See also Why the dog and cat are enemies. III.

Donkey's eggs. Chamoud. Picture tales from the French.

See also Mare's nest.

Donkey's story. Piper. Folk tales children love.

Piper. Road in storyland.

Segur. Memoirs of a donkey. (*In* Ch. 1.)

Don't mention it. Shannon. Eyes for the dark.

Doomed prince. *See* Prince and the three fates.

Door of opportunity. *See* Opportunity.

Dora Miller's wonder ball. *See* Wonder balls. II.

Dorani. Barry and Hanna. Wonder flights of long ago. (Flying stool.)

For other entries, see 2d edition.

Dorchester giant (poem). Adams and Atchinson. Book of giant stories.

Dorji and Tipsi. Noel. Magic bird of Chomo-lung-ma.

See also Prince Vivien and Princess Placida.

Dorothea. *See* St. Dorothea.

Dorothy's dream. Evans. Worth while stories. (Dorothy's dream of happiness.)

Dou, Gerard. Miller. My travelship: Holland. (Gerard Dou, the little master.)

Doubleturk. Olcott. Wonder tales from goblin hills.
See also Rumpelstiltskin.
Douglas, James. *See* Heart of the Bruce.
Dove and the ant. *See* Ant and the dove.
Dove and the heron. *See* Jackal and the heron.
Dove who spoke truth. Brown. Curious book of birds.
For other entries, see 2d edition.
Dover straits, Origin of. Wilson. Green magic. ("Merry
Dun of Dover.")
Doves of Alix. Crownfield. Feast of Noel.
Down-cellar onion. Potter. Captain Sandman.
Down in the meadow. Quinn. Stories for the six-year-old.
Down the rabbit hole. Carroll. Alice's adventures in Won-
derland. (*In* Ch. 1.)
Johnson and Scott. Anthology of children's literature.
Drachenfels, Legend of. *See* Siegfried with the horny skin.
Dragon. Fyleman. Forty good-night tales.
See also Reluctant dragon.
Dragon and his grandmother. Grimm. Tales from Grimm
(Wanda Gag).
For other entries, see 2d edition.
Dragon and the prince. Harper. Fillmore. Folk tales.
(Dragon's strength.)
For other entries, see 2d edition.
Dragon at hide-and-seek. No. 2 Joy Street.
Dragon fly. I. Hartshorne. Training in worship. (Two
worlds. Adapted.)
For other entries, see 2d edition.
Dragon fly. II. *See* Dragon fly of Zuni.
Dragon fly and the water-lily. Patten. Junior classics.
v. 8.
Dragon fly of Zuni. Nusbaum. Seven cities of Cibola.
(Dragon fly.)
Nusbaum. Zuni Indian tales. (Dragon fly.)
Dragon Fragrance ink. Olcott. Wonder tales from China
seas.
Dragon land. Metzger. Tales told in Korea.
Dragon of Dunsmore Heath. Darton. Seven champions of
Christendom.
Dragon of Ghent. Lane. Tower legends.
See also Golden dragon of the Boringue # ; Turk, turban,
tulip and dragon #.
Dragon of the north. Fuller. Book of dragons.
For other entries, see 2d edition.
**Dragon of the seven conflicts, and the glory of Gwron Brif-
fardd Prydain.** Morris. Book of the three dragons.
Dragon of Wantley. Wilson. Red magic.
For other entries, *see* 2d edition.
Dragon prince. Barry and Hanna. Wonder flights of long
ago.
Byrde. Polish fairy book.
See also East o' the sun and west o' the moon.

Dragon princess. Fuller. Book of dragons.
   Price. Legends of the seven seas. (Black dragon of the Sea
      of Dunting. Adapted.)
   For other entries, see 2d edition.
Dragon Sin. Carey. Flower legends.
   Fuller. Book of dragons.
   For other entries, see 2d edition.
Dragon slayer. Evans. Worth while stories.
Dragon that swallows the sun every day. Applegarth. Mis-
   sionary stories for little folk. 1st series.
   See also Creation of the world (Chinese).
Dragon with seven heads. I. Carpenter. Tales of a Basque
   grandmother. (Dragon with the seven heads.)
Dragon with seven heads. II. Phillips. Far peoples.
   See also Four clever brothers; Prince Ahmed and the fairy
      Perie Banou; Brave man, the wise man, and the clever
      man.
Dragons of Lucerne. *See* Good-natured dragons.
Dragon's story. St. Nicholas. Sept. 1889, p. 816.
Dragon's strength. *See* Dragon and the prince.
Drake, Francis (poem). Johnson and Scott. Anthology of
   children's literature. (Admiral's ghost.)
   Kipling. Rewards and fairies. (Simple Simon.)
   For other entries, see 2d edition.
Drakesbill and his friends. Bruce. Treasury of tales for
   little folk. (Drakestail goes to see the king.)
   Coussens. Diamond story book. (Drakestail.)
   Curry and Clippinger. Children's literature. (Drakestail.)
   Hutchinson. Fireside stories. (Drakestail.)
   Johnson and Scott. Anthology of children's literature.
      (Drakestail.)
   Lang. Old friends among the fairies. (Drakestail.)
   Shimer. Fairyland.
   See also How the speckled hen got her speckles; Little rooster
      and the Turkish sultan; Poor woman's rooster; Valiant
      blackbird; Why? Why?
   For other entries, see 2d edition.
Drakestail. *See* Drakesbill and his friends.
Drakestail goes to see the king. *See* Drakesbill and his
   friends.
Drawing of the sword. *See* King Arthur's coming.
Dreadful boar. Metzger. Picture tales from the Chinese.
   (Grandmother and the boar.)
   See also Crab and the monkey; Ito and his friends; Masha
      and her friends.
   For other entries, see 2d edition.
Dream about King Arthur. *See* Dream of Rhonabwy.
Dream of a great prophet. Gaer. Burning bush.
Dream of Angus Og. *See* Fairy swan song.
Dream of Owen O'Mulready. Lee. Folk tales of all nations.
   For other entries, see 2d edition.

Dream of Paradise. Friedlander. Jewish fairy tales (Dutton).
**Gaster. Ma'aseh book. (Wife of R. Hanina and the
miracles that occurred to her.)
See also Third leg.
Dream of Rhonabwy. Colum. Fountain of youth. (Dream
about King Arthur.)
For other entries, see 2d edition.
Dream of the white lark. Canton. Child's book of saints.
See also Little cup of tears # ; Miller's daughter. I.
Dreamer. Lee. Folk tales of all nations.
Dreamer=the=giant. Sharman. Bamboo.
See also Date-stone of forgetfulness; Vision of Tsunu.
Dreams of gold. Stewart. Tell me a story I never heard before.
Drimin the cow, Adventure of. Casserley. Michael of Ireland.
Dripping. *See* Valiant Chattee-maker.
Driving out of the Red=and=whites. Kennedy. Red man's
wonder book.
Drop of rain. Cooper. Argosy of fables. (Rain drop.)
For other entries, see 2d edition.
Drop of the water of light. See Water of light #.
Drop of water. Andersen. Fairy tales (Stickney). v. 2.
For other entries, see 2d edition.
Drouth witches. James. Tewa firelight tales.
Drowned child. Spence. Myths of the North American Indians. (*In* Ch. 5.)
Drum and the lily. Kinscella. Music appreciation readers.
Book 1.
Drum that saved lambkin. *See* Lambikin.
Drum that talked. Kinscella. Music appreciation readers.
Book 3.
Drummers' Day. Kinscella. Music appreciation readers.
Book 2. (Boy drummers in Holland.)
Drums of the storm. Egan. New found tales.
Dry land mermaid, Adventures of. Potter. Giant of Apple
Pie Hill.
Dryope. Bulfinch. Golden age. (*In* Ch. 8.)
For other entries, see 2d edition.
Duck and the serpent. Cooper. Argosy of fables.
Johnson and Scott. Anthology of children's literature.
For other entries, see 2d edition.
Duck with red feet. Leland. Algonquin legends. (How one
of the partridge's wives became a Sheldrake duck.)
Macmillan. Canadian wonder tales.
Duckie Dee paints the aster. Blaisdell. Rhyme and story
second reader.
Duckling with golden feathers. Olcott. Wonder tales from
Baltic wizards.
See also Princess Rosette. I.

Ducky Widdle-waddle, and Fishy Flip-flop. Harriman. Stories for little children.

Duel of the giants. **Arnold. Book of good counsels.

Dugong, dugong, where from? Olcott. Wonder tales from pirate isles.

Duke Vortigern. Farjeon. Mighty men from Beowulf to William the Conqueror.

Duke William's treasure. Johnson and Scott. Anthology of children's literature.
   See also Treasure in the chest.

Dulce domum. Grahame. Kenneth Grahame book.

Dulcetta. Garnett. Ottoman wonder tales. (Stolen prince.)
   For other entries, see 2d edition.

Dumb princess. Adams and Atchinson. Book of princess stories.
   For other entries, see 2d edition.

Dummling's goose. *See* Golden goose. I.

Dummling's request. Evans. Worth while stories.
   See also Good bargain; Sir Cleges.

Dun horse. Cowles. Stories to tell.

Dust-raising adventures of the carpet-sweeper and the broom. Emerson. Merry-go-round of modern tales.

Dust under the rug. Cabot. Course in citizenship.
   Through story-land with the children.
   For other entries, see 2d edition.

Dutch Boor and his horse. Coe. Third book of stories.

Dutch cheese. De La Mare. Dutch cheese.

Dutiful daughter. Metzger. Tales told in Korea. (Sim Chung, the filial daughter.)
   Phillips. Far peoples. (Sim Chung.)
   For other entries, see 2d edition.

Dutton, Joseph. Broomell. Children's story caravan. (Ballad of Joseph and Damien.)

Duty shoes. Bowman. Little brown bowl.
   See also Dominick's magic shoes; New shoes; Timothy's shoes.

Duty that was not paid. Cather. Educating by story-telling.

Dwarf and the cobbler's sons. Harper. Merry Christmas to you.
   Harper. More story-hour favorites.

Dwarf king. Gordon and Stockard. Gordon readers. 2d reader.

Dwarf people #.
   See also Pygmies. II.

Dwarfs and the fairies. Evans. Worth while stories. (Odin and the dwarfs. Abridged.)
   See also Giants and fairies. II.
   For other entries, see 2d edition.

Dwarfs' banquet. Choate and Curtis. Little people of the hills.
   For other entries, see 2d edition.

Dwarf's gifts. Pyle. Tales from Norse mythology. (Sif's golden hair.)

Dwarf's new cheese. Guerber. Legends of Switzerland. (*In* Forest cantons.)

Dwarfs of Red Smoke Hill. Kennedy. Red man's wonder book.

Dwarfs' tailor. Martens. Wonder tales from far away. (Tailor of the dwarfs.)
For other entries, see 2d edition.

Dyed jackal. *See* Blue jackal.

Dymchurch flit. *See* Fairies' passage. II #.

Dy=yoh=wi and his eagle. De Huff. Taytay's tales.

E

Eabani. *See* Gilgamesh.

Eager Heart, Story of. Wheelock. Kindergarten children's hour. v. 3. (*In* Ch. 49.)
(play). Campbell. Story of Christmas, p. 209.

Eagle. I. *See* 2d edition.

Eagle. II. Lee. Folk tales of all nations.

Eagle and his captor. Æsop. Fables (Jones).

Eagle and the arrow. Æsop. Fables (Jones).
Æsop. Fables (Whitman ed.).
Cooper. Argosy of fables.
See also Oak and the woodcutter.
For other entries, see 2d edition.

Eagle and the beetle. Æsop. Fables (Jones).
Æsop. Fables (Whitman ed.).
Cooper. Argosy of fables.
For other entries, see 2d edition.

Eagle and the cocks. Æsop. Fables (Jones).

Eagle and the crow. Æsop. Fables (Jones. Eagle, the jackdaw and the shepherd.)
Æsop. Fables (Whitman ed.).
Cooper. Argosy of fables. (Eagle and the jackdaw.)
For other entries, see 2d edition.

Eagle and the fox. Æsop. Fables (Jones).

Eagle and the jackdaw. *See* Eagle and the crow.

Eagle and the kite. Cooper. Argosy of fables.

Eagle and the owl. Botsford. Picture tales from the Italian.
See also One's own children are always the prettiest.
For other entries, see 2d edition.

Eagle and the serpent. *See* Eagle and the worm.

Eagle and the snake. *See* Cactus, Legend of.

Eagle and the spider. Cooper. Argosy of fables.

Eagle and the worm (poem). Cooper. Argosy of fables.
Cooper. Argosy of fables. (Eagle and the serpent.)
(poem). Johnson and Scott. Anthology of children's literature.

Eagle and the wren. Chamoud. Picture tales from the French.
For other entries, see 2d edition.

Eagle myth about flying swallows and a wolf dance. Rasmussen. Eagle's gift.

Eagle, the cat and the sow. Æsop. Fables (Jones. Eagle, the cat and the wild sow.)
Cooper. Argosy of fables. (Eagle, the cat and the wild sow.)
See also Jackal and the cat.
For other entries, see 2d edition.

Eagle, the cat, and the wild sow. *See* Eagle, the cat, and the sow.

Eagle, the jackdaw and the shepherd. *See* Eagle and the crow.

Eagle warrior. Purnell and Weatherwax. Talking bird.

Eagles of opportunity. Egan. New found tales.
See also Great shell of Broad House.

Ear of wheat. Carey. Stories of the birds.
Rich. Why-so stories. (Why Europe loves the robin.)
See also St. Leonor.

Earl Gerald. Colum. Big tree of Bunlahy. (Wizard Earl.)
For other entries, see 2d edition.

Earl Mar's daughter. Bailey. Stories of great adventures.
For other entries, see 2d edition.

Earl-of-eating. Cook. To-day's stories of yesterday.

Earl of idleness. Cook. Red and gold stories.

Earl Sigurd's Christmas eve (poem). Smith and Hazeltine. Christmas in legend and story.

Early girl. Brown. Curious book of birds.

Earth and the sky. Lee. Folk tales of all nations. (Rangi and Papatua; or, The heavens and the earth.)
Metzger. Tales told in Hawaii. (How heaven and earth were kicked apart.)
See also How Ma-ui lifted up the sky; Sun of water.
For other entries, see 2d edition.

Earth giants. *See* Zipacna.

Earth shapers. *See* Creation of Ireland.

Earthen pot and the pot of brass. Æsop. Fables (Jones. Two pots.)
Æsop. Fables (Whitman ed. Two pots.).
Cooper. Argosy of fables. (Two pots.)
For other entries, see 2d edition.

Earthquakes. Wells. How the present came from the past. Book 1, pt. 2.

East o' the sun and west o' the moon. Dasent. East of the sun and west of the moon (Nielsen).
Hutchinson. Chimney corner fairy tales.
Johnson and Scott. Anthology of children's literature.
Power. Bag o' tales.
Rasmussen. East o' the sun and west o' the moon, and other tales.

East o' the sun and west o' the moon—*continued.*
See also Dragon prince ; Parrot of Limo Verde.
For other entries, see 2d edition.

East wind and north wind. Partridge. Joyful Star. (Triumph of the East wind's daughter.)
For other entries, see 2d edition.

Easter. *See* Blue and green eggs ; Boy who discovered the
spring ♯ ; Bunny Rabbit's journey ; Flax ; Forgotten bell ;
Golden willow ; Little Gretchen's lily ♯ ; Mrs. Topknot's
Easter surprise ; Molly's Easter hen ; Snowdrop. I ♯ ;
Springtime. II ♯ ; Why the robin has a red breast. V ;
Wonder egg ♯.
See also Titles commencing with the word "Easter."
For other entries, see 2d edition.

Easter bunnies and the lily. Bowman. Little brown bowl.

Easter lily. Newman. Fairy flowers. (Princess Lily.)

Easter rabbit. I. Arnold. Folk tales retold.
For other entries, see 2d edition.

Easter rabbit. II. *See* 2d edition.

Easter rabbit. III. Piper. Folk tales children love.
Piper. Road in storyland.
For other entries, see 2d edition.

Easter rabbit. IV–VI. *See* 2d edition.

Easter rabbit. VII. Skinner. Happy tales. (Bunny rabbit's journey.)

Easter story. Bailey. Tell me another story.
See also Lesson of faith.

Eastern garden. *See* Nightingale and the pearl.

Ebenezer Scrooge's Christmas. Dickens. Christmas carol.
(play). Knight. Dramatic reader.
Large. Famous children of storybook land. (Tiny Tim.)
Walters. Book of Christmas stories. (Scrooge's Christmas.
Adapted.)
See also Christmas angel. II ; Cratchit's Christmas dinner ;
Spirit of Christmas.

Ebenezer Teaser. Beard. Tucked-in tales.

Eben's cows. Mitchell. Here and now story book.

Echo. I. White. School management, p. 264.
See also Unhappy echo.

Echo. II. Metzger. Tales told in Hawaii. (Saucy fairy.)

Echo and Narcissus. Bulfinch. Golden age. (*In* Ch. 13.)
Carey. Flower legends. (Narcissus.)
Curry and Clippinger. Children's literature. (Narcissus.)
Cross. Music stories. (Narcissus.)
Johnson and Scott. Anthology of children's literature.
Lang. Book of myths.
Power. How it happened. (How the echo and the narcissus
were made.)
Pyle. Tales from Greek mythology.
For other entries, see 2d edition.

Echo and the owl. Cooper. Argosy of fables.

Echo chief of the invisibles. Hillyer. Box of daylight. (Town of the air.)

Echo well, Tale of. Miller. My travelship: Holland.

Edam cheese. Hart. Picture tales from Holland.
See also Moon in the mill-pond.

Edelweiss. Carey. Flower legends.

Edric the Wild. *See* Wild Edric.

Education. La Fontaine. Fables (Tilney).

Education of dear Jim. Richards. More five minute stories.

Education of the delightful boy. Richards. More five minute stories.

Education of the lion. Cooper. Argosy of fables. (Education of the young lion.)
For other entries, see 2d edition.

Edward, the Black Prince. *See* Black Prince.

Eean the fisherman's son, Story of. Colum. Boy apprenticed to an enchanter.

Eel and the snake. Cooper. Argosy of fables.

Eggs or beans. Lee. Folk tales of all nations.
See also Maid with her basket of eggs.

Egori the brave and the gipsy. Ralston. Russian fairy tales. (*In* Legends about saints. Ch. 6.)
For other entries, see 2d edition.

Eider duck. White. School management, p. 255.

Eighteen rabbits. Morris. Gypsy story teller.
See also Jesper who herded the hares; Ashiepattle and the king's hares #.

Eighty-one brothers. Faulkner. Little Peachling. (Prince of the reed plains.)
Sugimoto. Japanese holiday picture tales. (Rabbit and the god of happiness.)
Whitehorn. Wonder tales of old Japan. (White rabbit and the crocodiles.)
See also Mouse-deer, the crocodile and the tiger.
For other entries, see 2d edition.

Ei-niin-mita. *See* Go, I know not whither—fetch, I know not what. II.

Einon and Olwen. Henderson and Jones. Wonder tales of ancient Wales.

Eiveen Cold-heart. Dunbar. Sons o' Cormac.

Ekorn the squirrel. Johnson and Scott. Anthology of children's literature. (Ekorn; Nest.)

Elaine's valentines. Harriman. Stories for little children.
See also Big brother's valentine.
For other entries, see 2d edition.

Elba. Wolff. Pale mountains. (Children of the sun, pt. 1.)

Elder tree. *See* Beggar's curse.

Elder-tree mother. I. Andersen. Fairy tales (Stickney). v. 1.
Bailey. Tell me another story. (Adapted.)
For other entries, see 2d edition.

Electra. Bulfinch. Golden age. (Agamemnon, Orestes, and Electra. *In* Ch. 28.)

Electric light and the candle. Emerson. Merry-go-round of modern tales.

Eleio the fleet. Metzger. Tales told in Hawaii.

Elena the fair. *See* Princess to be kissed at a charge.

Elephant and Jupiter's ape (poem). Cooper. Argosy of fables. (Elephant and the ape of Jupiter.)
  La Fontaine. Fables (Tilney).

Elephant and the ape of Jupiter. *See* Elephant and Jupiter's ape.

Elephant and the dog. I. *See* Elephant who was lonely #.

Elephant and the dog. II. Buckingham. Elephant's friend.

Elephant and the frog. Babbitt. Animals' own story book. (Mr. Elephant and Mr. Frog.)
  Cooper. Argosy of fables. (Frog's saddle horse.)
  For other entries, see 2d edition.

Elephant and the jackal. **Arnold. Book of good counsels. (Old jackal and the elephant.)
  Cooper. Argosy of fables. (Old jackal and the elephant.)
  See also Lion and the bull. II.
  For other entries, see 2d edition.

Elephant and the monkey. Piper. Folk tales children love.
  Piper. Road in storyland.
  For other entries, see 2d edition.

Elephant and the pug dog. Cooper. Argosy of fables.

Elephant and the rats. Babbitt. Animals' own story book.
  See also Lion and the mouse.
  For other entries, see 2d edition.

Elephant and the whale. *See* How the elephant and the whale were tricked. I.

Elephant has a bet with the tiger. De Leeuw. Java jungle tales. (Elephant makes a wager with the tiger.)
  Lee. Folk tales of all nations.
  Skeat. Tiger's mistake.
  For other entries, see 2d edition.

Elephant in favor. Cooper. Argosy of fables.
  For other entries, see 2d edition.

Elephant makes a wager with the tiger. *See* Elephant has a bet with the tiger.

Elephant princess and the prince. Skeat. Tiger's mistake.

Elephants and their masters (poem). Cooper. Argosy of fables.

Elephant's child. Evans. Worth while stories. (Elephant's trunk. Abridged and adapted.)
  For other entries, see 2d edition.

Elephant's friend. *See* Elephant and the dog. II.

Elephant's trunk. *See* Elephant's child.

Elephant-trainer's luck. Aspinwall. Jataka tales.

Elf and the cow. Fyleman. Forty good-morning tales.

Elf and the dormouse. Evans. Worth while stories. (How we came to have umbrellas.)

Elf and the dormouse—*continued.*
  (poem). Harriman. Stories for little children.
  (poem). Hervey and Hix. Fanciful tales for children.
  For other entries, see 2d edition.
Elf gifts. Olcott. Wonder tales from fairy isles.
Elfin cricketer. Rhys. English fairy book.
Elfin pup. Field. Eliza and the elves.
Elfod the priest. Henderson and Jones. Wonder tales of
  ancient Wales.
Elf's umbrella. *See* Elf and the dormouse.
Elijah and the poor hasid. **Gaster. Ma'aseh book. v. 2.
Elijah and the three sons who watched in the garden.
  **Gaster. Ma'aseh book. v. 1.
Elijah the prophet and St. Nicholas. Carpenter. Tales of
  a Russian grandmother. (Peasant, the saint, and the
  prophet.)
  Ralston. Russian fairy tales. (Elijah the prophet and
    Nicholas.)
  For other entries, see 2d edition.
Elizabeth of Hungary. *See* St. Elizabeth of Hungary.
Elizabeth of Stein, Romance of. Guerber. Legends of
  Switzerland. (*In* Legends of Vaud and Valais.)
Elk. Sexton. Gray wolf stories. (How the strange young
  man rid the country of great elk.)
  See also Youth and Fire-boy and the giant elk.
Elschen. Olcott. Wonder tales from goblin hills.
Elves and the cobbler. *See* Elves and the shoemaker.
Elves and the envious neighbour. *See* Man with the wen.
Elves and the shoemaker. Arnold. Folk tales retold.
  (Shoemaker and the elves.)
  Curry and Clippinger. Children's literature.
  Egan. New found tales. (Happy elves. Adapted.)
  Evans. Worth while stories. (Shoemaker and the elves.)
  Grimm. Fairy tales (Olcott).
  Harriman. Stories for little children. (Old Jan the cob-
    bler.)
  Hutchinson. Chimney corner stories.
  Johnson and Scott. Anthology of children's literature.
    (Elves and the cobbler.)
  Kinscella. Music appreciation readers. Book 2. (Elves
    and shoemaker.)
  Piper. Road in storyland.
  Piper. Folk tales children love. (Shoemaker and the elves.)
  Power. Bag o' tales.
  Quinn. Stokes' wonder book of fairy tales.
  Starbuck. Familiar haunts.
  Told under the green umbrella.
  Whiteman. Playmates in print.
  See also Llew.
  For other entries, see 2d edition.
Emarie. Barbour. English tales retold.
Emilian the fool. *See* At the behest of the pike. II.

Emma of Haarlem. King. Golden cat head.
See also Wives of Weinberg.
Emperor and the bird's nest. Cowles. Stories to tell. (Emperor's bird's nest.)
For other entries, see 2d edition.
Emperor and the goose boy. Evans. Worth while stories. (Goose boy and the king.)
For other entries, see 2d edition.
Emperor's bird's nest. *See* Emperor and the bird's nest.
Emperor's garden. Krohn and Johnson. Scales of the silver fish.
Emperor's invisible robe. *See* Emperor's new clothes.
Emperor's new clothes. Andersen. Fairy tales (Siewers. Emperor's new suit.)
Arthur Rackham fairy book.
Bailey. Tell me another story. (Adapted.)
Bruce. Treasury of tales for little folk.
Curry and Clippinger. Children's literature.
Johnson and Scott. Anthology of children's literature.
Power. Children's treasure chest.
Rich. Read-aloud book.
Shimer. Fairyland. (Emperor's invisible robe.)
Starbuck. Familiar haunts.
For other entries, see 2d edition.
Emperor's sleep. Olcott. Wonder tales from goblin hills. (Barbarossa.)
(poem). Olcott. Wonder tales from goblin hills. (Barbarossa.)
See also Fairy horse dealer.
For other entries, see 2d edition.
Empty birdhouse. Potter. Giant of Apple Pie Hill.
Empty drum. Williams. Tales from Ebony.
For other entries, see 2d edition
Emu and the crows. Lee. Folk tales of all nations. (Dinewan the emu and Wahn the crows.)
Enamtues, the wishing stone. Garett. Coyote stories.
Enchanted baby. Beston. Starlight wonder book.
Enchanted bed. Darton. Seven champions of Christendom.
Enchanted castle. I. Cook. Red and gold stories.
Enchanted castle. II. Olcott. Wonder tales from goblin hills.
Enchanted cat. Olcott. Wonder tales from fairy isles.
Enchanted cave of Cesh Corran. Stephens. Irish fairy tales.
Enchanted cow. Davis. Truce of the wolf.
Harper. Ghosts and goblins.
Enchanted doughnuts. Byrde. Polish fairy book.
Enchanted feather. Tappan. Little lady in green.
Enchanted fish of Polaman. Olcott. Wonder tales from pirate isles.
Enchanted forest. Wahlenberg. Old Swedish fairy tales.

Enchanted garden. I. Stewart. Tell me a story I never heard before.

Enchanted garden. II. *See* St. David of Wales.

Enchanted grouse. Bowman and Bianco. Tales from a Finnish tupa. (Kalle and the wood grouse.)
Harper. Fillmore folk tales.
See also Magic egg.
For other entries, see 2d edition.

Enchanted gypsy. Shannon. California fairy tales.

Enchanted hare. *See.* Witch hare.

Enchanted hind. *See* Hind in the forest.

Enchanted horse. Adams and Atchinson. Book of enchantment. (Story of enchanted horses.)
Barry and Hanna. Wonder flights of long ago. (Flying horse of Firouz Schah.)
See also Cambuscan bold.
For other entries, see 2d edition.

Enchanted isles of the genii. Olcott. Wonder tales from China seas.

Enchanted knight. *See* Ogier the Dane.

Enchanted lake. I. *See* 2d edition.

Enchanted lake. II. Kinscella. Music appreciation readers. Book 6.
See also Magic well.

Enchanted lime tree. Carpenter. Tales of a Russian grandmother.
See also Fisherman and his wife.

Enchanted man. Morris. Gypsy story teller.

Enchanted mesa. Allen. Story-teller's house.

Enchanted palace. Eells. Islands of magic.

Enchanted peafowl. *See* Nine peahens and the golden apple

Enchanted pig. Adams and Atchinson. Book of enchantment.
For other entries, see 2d edition.

Enchanted pillow. Lee. Folk tales of all nations.

Enchanted pomegranate branch and the beauty #.
See also Abou Hassan; Golden armlet; Quest of world's desire.

Enchanted princess. I–III. *See* 2d edition.

Enchanted princess. IV (poem). Adams and Atchinson. Book of princess stories.

Enchanted princess. V. Denton. Homespun stories.

Enchanted ring of Fastrada. *See* Charlemagne and the magic ring.

Enchanted snake. Lee. Folk tales of all nations. (Snake who became the king's son-in-law.)
See also Snake #.
For other entries, see 2d edition.

Enchanted soldier, Legend of. Adams and Atchinson. Book of enchantment.
Irving. Alhambra.

Enchanted stag. I. *See* Brother and sister. I.

Enchanted stag. II. *See* St. Denis.

Enchanted tapestry. Cooper. Tal. (*In* Ch. 3.)
See also Tapestry prince.

Enchanted whistle #.
See also Jesper who herded the hares; One hundred hares.

Enchanter's wife. Gate. Tales from the secret kingdom.

Enchantments of Ewinwen, daughter of the sea-wave.
Morris. Book of the three dragons.

End of the Round Table. *See* King Arthur's death.

End of the world. I. *See* 2d edition.

End of the world. II. Bowman and Bianco. Tales from a
Finnish tupa.
See also Chicken-Little.

Endless tale. I. Skinner. Happy tales. (Treasure.)
For other entries, see 2d edition.

Endless tale. II–III. *See* 2d edition.

Endless tale. IV. Hart. Picture tales from Holland. (Tale
without end.)
Nemcova. Disobedient kids. (Tale without end.)
For other entries, see 2d edition.

Endymion. Bulfinch. Golden age. (*In* Ch. 26.)
Forbush. Myths and legends of Greece and Rome. (Diana
and Endymion.)
Lang. Book of myths.
For other entries, see 2d edition.

Enemy of Rome. *See* Hannibal.

Envious coyote. De Huff. Taytay's tales.

Envious wren (poem). Cooper. Argosy of fables.
See also Ass and the lamb.

Eochy. *See* Etain and Midir; Deirdre.

Epaminondas and his auntie. Hutchinson. Chimney corner
stories.
Manner. Silver treasury. (Story of Epaminondas and his
auntie.)
See also As Hai Low kept house; George Washington Jackson.
For other entries, see 2d edition.

Eperjes, Legend of. Schwimmer. Tisza tales.

Ephemera. Curry and Clippinger. Children's literature.

Epimetheus. *See* Prometheus.

Eric=fine of Lugh. *See* Fate of the children of Turenn.

Eric Shrewdspoken. Adams. Swords of the Vikings. (Quick
wit of Erik.)

Eric the Red, Saga of. Colum. Voyagers. (Children of
Eric the Red.)

Erik Bold-ax and Haakon the Good. Dunlap. Stories of
the Vikings.

Erisichthon. *See* King and the oak.

Erl-king. Cross. Music stories.
(poem). Olcott. Wonder tales from goblin hills.

Ermine is carried off by the young eagle. Rasmussen.
Eagle's gift. (Blessed gift of joy is bestowed upon man.)

Ernest service. McVenn. Good manners and right conduct. Book 2.

Eros and Psyche. *See* Cupid and Psyche.

Erratic clock. Cozad. Story talks.

Errua the madman. Lee. Folk tales of all nations.
See also Devil's hide; Fanch Scournac; Jack and his master · Keep cool #.

Esben and the witch #.
See also Bee, the mouse, the muskrat, and the boy; Constantes and the Dhrako; Golden lantern, the golden goat and the golden cloak; Thirteenth son; Tartaro and Petit Perroquet.

Escape of Hugo de Groot. *See* Grotius, Hugo.

Escape of the mouse #.
See also Three subtle crafts of Manawyddan.

Escape of the penguins. Morley. I know a secret.

Escape of the Stag Barasingh. Mukerji. Hindu fables.

Escaped jackdaw. Æsop. Fables (Jones).

Escaped mermaid. Rhys. English fairy book.
See also Mermaid of Edam.

Eskimo girl who fled to the Indians. Morris. Stories from mythology: North American. (*In* Ch. 3.)

Eskimo twins. Harriman. Stories for little children.
Perkins. Eskimo twins. (*In* Ch. 1–2.)

Est! est! est! Untermeyer. Donkey of God. (Cardinal and his courier. *In* Orvieto-Perugia-Assisi.)

Esther. *See* Queen Esther.

Estinne, André. *See* Brave drummer boy of France.

Eta maiden and the Hatamoto. Mitford. Tales of old Japan.

Etain and Midir. Lee. Folk tales of all nations. (Etain.)
Young. Celtic wonder tales. (Golden fly.)
For other entries, see 2d edition.

Etana and his flight to heaven, Story of. Miller. My book of history. v. 1. (*In* Ch. 11.)
See also Sun conqueror, Sanpati.

Etheldrinda's fairy. Housman. Turn again tales.

Ethlenn o' the mist. Dunbar. Sons o' Cormac.

Eudes. Niemeyer. Stories for the history hour.
See also St. Genevieve.

Eumaeus. Bulfinch. Golden age. (Telemachus. *In* Ch. 30.)
Power. Bag o' tales. (How the swineherd welcomed Odysseus.)
See also Ulysses' return.
For other entries, see 2d edition.

Eumenes. *See* King Eumenes.

Euphemia. *See* Princess of the lost island.

Eureka! Lansing. Great moments in freedom. (*In* A famous remark.)
See also Archimedes.
For other entries, see 2d edition.

Euripides. White. School management, p. 267. (An oath.)

Europa. Forbush. Myths and legends of Greece and Rome. (Cadmus.)
  Kinney. Stars and their stories. (Europa's strange voyage.)
  Pyle. Tales from Greek mythology.
  For other entries, see 2d edition.
Eurydice. *See* Orpheus and Eurydice.
Evander. Bulfinch. Golden age. (*In* Ch. 33.)
Evangeline. Patten. Junior Classics. v. 7. (Evangeline of Acadia.)
  For other entries, see 2d edition.
Everyday (play). Skinner. Christmas stories.
Everything in its right place. Andersen. Fairy tales (Stickney). v. 2.
  For other entries, see 2d edition.
Evil of haste. Katibah. Other Arabian nights.
Executioner of Titipu. *See* Mikado.
Extravagant mouse, Story of. Mackenzie. Jackal in Persia.
Eye=traps. Cozad. Story talks.
Eyes and no eyes. Curry and Clippinger. Children's literature. (Eyes and no eyes; or, The art of seeing.)
Eyes for the dark. Shannon. Eyes for the dark.

F

Fable of, etc. *See* the first important word of the title.
Faery and the kettle. Lee. Folk tales of all nations.
  See also Fairy borrowing #; Hillman and the housewife.
Faint heart failed. Broomell. Children's story caravan.
Fair Ailinn. Dunbar. Sons o' Cormac.
Fair earth. Stewart. Tell me a story I never heard before.
  See also Corn chooses a mate; First corn.
Fair exchange. *See* Giotto.
Fair Florimel. *See* Florimel.
Fair gods. Martinez Del Rio. Sun, the moon and a rabbit.
Fair=haired magician. Kennedy. Red man's wonder book.
Fair Jehane. Gibson. Golden bird.
Fair one with golden locks. Aulnoy. Fairy tales (Planché. Fair with golden hair.
  Harper. Magic fairy tales. (Story of pretty Goldilocks.)
  Quinn. Stokes' wonder book of fairy tales.
  For other entries, see 2d edition.
Fair princess of Behkten. *See* Journey of Khensu to Behkten.
Fair Snow=White. *See* Snow-White and the seven dwarfs.
Fair unknown. Barbour. English tales retold. (Strange quest.)
  Darton. Wonder book of old romance.
  For other entries, see 2d edition.
Fairies. I–III. *See* 2d edition.
Fairies. IV. Olcott. Wonder tales from fairy isles. (The fairies! The fairies!)

Fairies. V (poem). Harper and Hamilton. Winding roads.

Fairies' concert. Kinscella. Music appreciation readers. Book 2.

Fairies' kittens. *See* Pussy willows, Origin of. IV.

Fairies of the Caldon Low (poem). Howitt. Poems. (poem). Johnson and Scott. Anthology of children's literature.
For other entries, see 2d edition.

Fairies, Origin of. *See* Dwarfs and the fairies; Giants and the fairies; How Glooskap made the elves and fairies.

Fairies' passage. I–II. *See* 2d edition.

Fairies' passage. III. Olcott. Wonder tales from fairy isles. (Much noise, no fairies.)
See also Coming of the old world fairies.

Fairy and the electric tram. Fyleman. Forty good-morning tales.

Fairy and the spinning woman. Carpenter. Tales of a Basque grandmother.
See also My own self.

Fairy bakeshop. Buckingham. Elephants friend. (I've come for Poly.)

Fairy bridge of Licq. Carpenter. Tales of a Basque grandmother.

Fairy bridegroom. Untermeyer. Last pirate.

Fairy caught. I. Rhys. English fairy book. (Skillywidden.)
For other entries, see 2d edition.

Fairy caught. II. Olcott. Wonder tales from fairy isles. (My Shilo.)

Fairy cobbler. Fyleman. Tea time tales.

Fairy cow. I. *See* 2d edition.

Fairy cow. II. *See* Stray cow.

Fairy eye-glasses. Burnett. Children's book.

Fairy Fancy. Stewart. Tell me a story I never heard before.

Fairy farmers. Rhys. English fairy book.

Fairy fish queen. Evans. Worth while stories.

Fairy flowers. Capuana. Golden-feather.
See also Cinderella.

Fairy folk (poem). Patten. Junior classics. v. 10.
For other entries, see 2d edition.

Fairy forest. Howes. Long bright land.

Fairy frog. **Gaster. Ma'aseh book. v. 1. (R. Hanina and the frog.)
For other entries, see 2d edition.

Fairy funeral. Rhys. English fairy book.
For other entries, see 2d edition.

Fairy gentleman and his dumpling wife. Field. Eliza and the elves.

Fairy gifts. Coussens. Diamond story book.
For other entries, see 2d edition.

Fairy girl's tune. Casserley. Whins on Knockattan.

Fairy gold. Lee. Folk tales of all nations.
See also Furze blossom gold.
Fairy harp. Kinscella. Music appreciation readers. Book 5.
(Golden harp.)
For other entries, see 2d edition.
Fairy horn. Rhys. English fairy book.
For other entries see 2d edition.
Fairy horse dealer. Rhys. English fairy book.
See also Emperor's sleep ; King Arthur's cave.
Fairy hunt. Rhys. English fairy book.
Fairy huntsman. Shimer. Fairyland.
See also Rip Van Winkle.
For other entries, see 2d edition.
Fairy in the oak. Bailey. Story-telling hour.
Potter. Fairy caravan. (*In* Ch. 23.)
See also Happy clothes-dryer.
Fairy lamps. Skinner. Child's book of country stories.
For other entries, see 2d edition.
Fairy mirror. *See* Mirror of Matsuyama.
Fairy nets. Colum. Bright islands. (*In* Little people of Ao-
tea-roa.)
Howes. Long bright land.
See also Clever little fisherman ; How Kahukura learned to
make nets ; Laka and the menehunes.
Fairy nurse #.
See also Sick fairy.
Fairy nursling. *See* "Fary" nursling.
Fairy ointment. Rhys. English fairy book. ("Fary" oint-
ment.)
For other entries, see 2d edition.
Fairy opera. *See* Hansel and Grethel. II.
Fairy philtre. Rhys. English fairy book.
Fairy prince, cloud-chariot and the serpent Shell-crest.
Ryder. Twenty-two goblins.
Fairy revolt. Brown. Under the rowan tree.
Fairy riddle. Cook. To-day's stories of yesterday.
Fairy rose. Newman. Fairy flowers.
Fairy rowan tree. *See* Fairy tree of Dooros. II.
Fairy shoemaker. I. *See* 2d edition.
Fairy shoemaker. II. Starbuck. Enchanted paths.
For other entries, see 2d edition.
Fairy stories. *See* Story-telling time.
Fairy swan-maidens. Gregory. Cuchulain of Muirthemne.
(Only jealousy of Emer.)
Hull. Cuchulain.
Fairy swan song. Gregory. Cuchulain of Muirthemne.
(Dream of Angus Og.)
For other entries, see 2d edition.
Fairy tail. Beard. Tucked-in tales.
Fairy tools. Rhys. English fairy book.
Fairy treasure. Rhys. English fairy book.
Fairy tree of Dooros. I. *See* 2d edition.

Fairy tree of Dooros. II. Colum. King of Ireland's son. (Story of the fairy rowan tree.)
See also Mountain ash, Legend of. II.

Fairy went a=marketing (poem). Harper and Hamilton. Winding roads.

Fairy whistle. Gordon and Stockard. Gordon readers. 2d reader.
See also Enchanted whistle #.

Fairy who grew up. Hartshorne. Training in worship.

Fairy who fell into a letter=box. Fyleman. Forty good-night tales.

Fairy who lived in a dairy. Fyleman. Tea time tales.

Fairy wife. I. *See* 2d edition.

Fairy wife. II. Woodson. African myths.

Fairy wife. III. Metzger. Tales told in Hawaii.

Fairy wives. *See* Star wives.

Fairy wren. Gordon and Stockard. Gordon readers. 2d reader.

Fairyfoot. Curry and Clippinger. Children's literature. (Story of Fairyfoot.)
For other entries, see 2d edition.

Fairy's gift. Eells. Brazilian fairy book.

Faith in oneself. *See* Can and Could.

Faithful Augustus. White. School management, p. 247.

Faithful Bruno. Evans. Worth while stories.
See also Beth Gellert.

Faithful cat. Mitford. Tales of old Japan. (Story of the faithful cat.)

Faithful chipmunk. *See* Chipmunk's stripes. I.

Faithful Constance. Farjeon. Tales from Chaucer. (Man of law's tale.)
Richardson. Stories from old English poetry. (Pious Constance.)
For other entries, see 2d edition.

Faithful dancing=girl wife. I. Metzger. Tales told in Korea. (Spring fragrance.)
For other entries, see 2d edition.

Faithful dancing=girl wife. II. Metzger. Tales told in Korea. (Faithful dancing girl.)

Faithful dog. *See* Thief and the dog.

Faithful John. Quinn. Stokes' wonder book of fairy tales.
See also Baldpate; Leppa Polkky and the blue cross; Old soldier; Princess Red-white-and-black # ; Witch's curse. II.
For other entries, see 2d edition.

Faithful little Hollander. *See* Leak in the dike.

Faithful little squire. Clément. Once in France.

Faithful maiden. Adams. Swords of the Vikings.

Faithful minstrel. *See* Richard Coeur de Leon.

Faithful Rajpoot, Story of. * * Arnold. Book of good counsels.
Ryder. Twenty-two goblins. (King Shudraka and Hero's family.)

Faithful Rajpoot, Story of—*continued.*
For other entries, see 2d edition.

Faithful Svend #.
See also Laugh with them who laugh.

Falconer and the partridge. *See* Partridge and the fowler.

Fall of the golden man. *See* King Harold of England.

Falling Eagle. Martinez Del Rio. Sun, the moon and a rabbit.

Falling leaves. Marzials. Stories for the story hour.

Falling star. *See* Star boy. II.

False=alarm clock. Emerson. Merry-go-round of modern tales.

False oath. Egan. New found tales.

False prince. *See* Sham prince.

False prince and the true #.
See also Golden armlet.

False woman who became a night owl. Rasmussen. Eagle's gift.

Family portrait, Story of a. Hartshorne. Training in worship.

Family reunion. Eells. Brazilian fairy book.

Family too large for the pie. Fun folk and fairy tales.

Famished bear. Cooper. Argosy of fables.

Famous remark. *See* Archimedes; Eureka.

Fanch Scouarnec #.
See also Errua, the madman; Stupid Tartaro.

Far adventures of Billy Burns. MacManus. Lo, and behold ye!
See also Daniel O'Rourke.

Far to voyage. Chrisman. Wind that wouldn't blow.

Faridun. Coit. Ivory throne of Persia. (Faridun, Story of; or, Last days of Zahhak.)

Farm at the end=of=the=water. *See* Turkey-given corn.

Farm house. Bailey. Tell me another story.

Farm yard cock and the weather cock. Andersen. Fairy tales (Stickney). v. 2.
For other entries, see 2d edition.

Farmer and fortune. Æsop. Fables (Jones).
See also Traveler and Fortune.

Farmer and his dogs. Æsop. Fables (Jones).
Cooper. Argosy of fables. (Farmer and the dogs.)

Farmer and his sons. I. *See* Gold in the orchard.

Farmer and his two daughters. *See* Father and his daughters.

Farmer and the badger. Henderson and Calvert. Wonder tales from old Japan. (Hare and the badger.)
Lee. Folk tales of all nations. (Crackling mountain.)
Mitford. Tales of old Japan. (Crackling mountain.)
Whitehorn. Wonder tales of old Japan. (Kachi-kachi yama; or, Crackling mountain.)
For other entries, see 2d edition.

Farmer and the crane. Cooper. Argosy of fables.
See also Farmer, his boy and the rooks.
Farmer and the dogs. *See* Farmer and his dogs.
Farmer and the fox. Æsop. Fables (Jones).
For other entries, see 2d edition.
Farmer and the hill-man. Bailey. Tell me another story.
(Farmer and the troll.)
For other entries, see 2d edition.
Farmer and the hoe. Metzger. Picture tales from the Chinese.
Farmer and the humming bird. *See* Father "Lime-Stick" and the flower pecker.
In 2d edition there are entries under each title.
Farmer and the lion. Cooper. Argosy of fables.
Farmer and the money lender. Power. Bag o' tales.
For other entries, see 2d edition.
Farmer and the noses. *See* Are you not satisfied?
Farmer and the stork. Æsop. Fables (Artzybasheff. Husbandman and the stork.)
Æsop. Fables (Jones).
Cooper. Argosy of fables. (Husbandman and the stork.)
For other entries, see 2d edition.
Farmer and the troll. *See* Farmer and the hill-man.
Farmer and the viper. *See* Countryman and the snake. II.
Farmer boys. La Rue. Under the story tree.
Farmer Brown's gray pony. Kinscella. Music appreciation readers. Book 2.
See also Little gray pony.
Farmer, his boy and the rooks. Æsop. Fables (Jones).
See also Farmer and the crane.
Farmer, his wife, and the open door. *See* Barring of the door. II.
Farmer of Liddesdale. Lee. Folk tales of all nations.
For other entries, see 2d edition.
Farmer saint. Sugimoto. Picture tales from the Japanese.
Farmer tries to sleep. Mitchell. Here and now story book.
See also Little rooster.
Farmer Weatherbeard. Lee. Folk tales of all nations.
(Farmer Weathersky.)
See also Mistress of magic; Oh.
For other entries, see 2d edition.
Farmer Weathersky. *See* Farmer Weatherbeard.
Farmer's ass #.
See also Silly weaver girl.
Farmer's horse and his dog. Cooper. Argosy of fables.
Farmers three. *See* Bruin and Reynard partners. II; Fox as partner. III.
Farmer's wife and the raven (poem). Cooper. Argosy of fables.
For other entries, see 2d edition.
Farthing rushlight. *See* Lamp and the sun.

"Fary" nursling. Rhys. English fairy book. (Fairy nursling.)
For other entries, see 2d edition.

"Fary" ointment. *See* Fairy ointment.

Fast runners #.
See also Animal races ; Deer and the rabbit.

Fat gnome and the Rag=bag Boy. Shannon. California fairy tales.

Fat of the cat. Keller. Fat of the cat, and other stories.

Fat old elephant and the cross old rhinoceros. Lobagola. Folk tales of a savage.

Fatal imitation. Lee. Folk tales of all nations.

Fatal marriage. Æsop. Fables (Artzybasheff).

Fatal pride of Vukub. *See* Hero twins. I.

Fate. I. *See* 2d edition.

Fate. II #.
See also We cannot escape our fate ; Fore-ordained match ; Prince and the foundling.

Fate. III. Curtin. Fairy tales of Eastern Europe.
See also Man who went to find his angel.

Fate and the three fishes. *See* Three fish. I.

Fate of Carthage. *See* Delenda est Carthago.

Fate of little Jack Sparrow. *See* Fate of Mr. Jack Sparrow.

Fate of Mr. Jack Sparrow. Lee. Folk tales of all nations. (Fate of little Jack Sparrow.)
For other entries, see 2d edition.

Fate of the boy witch. De Huff. Taytay's tales.

Fate of the children of Lir. Adams and Atchinson. Book of enchantment. (Children of Lir.)
Lang. Book of myths. (Children of Lir.)
Young. Celtic wonder tales. (Children of Lir.)
For other entries, see 2d edition.

Fate of the children of Turenn. Young. Celtic wonder tales. (Eric-fine of Lugh.)
For other entries, see 2d edition.

Fate of the children of Usnach. *See* Deirdre.

Fate of the Silver Prince. Skeat. Tiger's mistake. (Fate of the Silver Prince and Princess Lemon-grass.)

Fate of the sons of Usna. *See* Deirdre.
In 2d edition there are entries under each title.

Fate of the witch wife. De Huff. Taytay's tales.
See also First rattlesnake #.

Father and his daughters. Æsop. Fables (Jones).
Cooper. Argosy of fables. (Farmer and his two daughters.)
See also Wise priest.

Father and son who married daughter and mother. Ryder. Twenty-two goblins.

Father and sons. *See* Bundle of sticks.

Father Bruin in the corner. Rasmussen. East o' the sun and west o' the moon. (Father Bruin.)
For other entries, see 2d edition.

Father "Follow=my=nose." Skeat. Tiger's mistake. (Father "Follow-my-nose" and the four priests.)

Father "Lime=Stick" and the flower=pecker. Skeat. Tiger's mistake.

In 2d edition this story is also listed under the title, "Farmer and the humming bird."

Father of the gods. Martinez Del Rio. Sun, the moon and a rabbit.

Father's advice. Noel. Magic bird of Chomo-lung-ma.

Father's story. *See* Happy-go-lucky Henery.

Fatima's rescue. Hauff. Arabian days' entertainment.

Fatma was a goose. Martin. Fatma was a goose.
See also Chicken-Little.

Fatty. Olcott. Wonder tales from pirate isles.

Fault finders. Egan. New found tales.

Faust. Menefee. Child stories. (How Margaret led Faust through the perfect world.)
For other entries, see 2d edition.

Fawn and his mother. Æsop. Fables (Artzybasheff. Fawn and her mother.)
Æsop. Fables (Jones).
Cooper. Argosy of fables.
For other entries, see 2d edition.

Feast. Bowman and Bianco. Tales from a Finnish tupa.
See also Fox and the cat. V.

Feast day. Lee. Folk tales of all nations.

Feast of magic peaches. Olcott. Wonder tales from China seas.
See also Stone monkey.

Feast of St. Nicholas. I. Chandler. Magic pictures.

Feast of St. Nicholas. II. Dodge. Hans Brinker. (*In* Ch. 9.)
Graham. Welcome Christmas.
See also St. Nicholas.

Feast of the durians. Skipper. Jungle meeting-pool. (*In* Fifth meeting.)

Feast of the new fire. Martinez Del Rio. Sun, the moon and a rabbit.

Feather woman. *See* Maid who married the morning star; Scar Face. III.

Feathered serpent. I. Purnell and Weatherwax.• Talking bird.

Feathered serpent. II. Martinez Del Rio. Sun, the moon and a rabbit. (Feathered snake.)

February, the month of no horns. *See* How deer won his antlers. II.

Fedelma, the enchanter's daughter. Colum. King of Ireland's son.
See also Mastermaid; Morraha.

Feeding of the emigrants. Housman. Moonshine and clover.

Felicia, and the pot of pinks. *See* Fortunée.

Felix. Smith and Hazeltine. Christmas in legend and story.
See also Gift of love.

Felix, the wise man. Stocking. Golden goblet.

Fenetta, the water nymph. Guerber. Legends of Switzerland. (*In* legends of Vaud and Valais.)

Fenette the Alpine shepherdess. *See* How the Swiss came to use the Alpine horn.

Ferdinand and the taste for cheese. Morley. I know a secret.

Fergus MacRogh and the Kingship of Ulster. Gregory. Cuchulain of Muirthemne. (*In* Birth of Cuchulain.)

Hull. Cuchulain. (How Conor became King of Ulster.)

Ferragus, who owned the brazen head. Lanier. Book of giants.

See also Roland. II.

Ferro and Forte. *See* Giants of the clock.

Festival of the weaver and the herdsman. *See* Sky bridge of birds.

Fiddle=diddle=dee. Harriman. Stories for little children.

For other entries, see 2d edition.

Fiddlebow of the nixie. Baumbach. Tales from the Swiss alps.

See also Little Fred and his fiddle #.

Fiddler in hell. Ralston. Russian fairy tales.

Fiddler in the fairy ring. Coussens. Diamond story book.

See also Rhys and Llywelyn.

For other entries, see 2d edition.

Fidelity in duty. White. School management, p. 278.

Field. Bailey. Tell me another story.

Field crosses of the farmers. Otero. Old Spain in our Southwest.

Field mouse and the town mouse. *See* Country mouse and the town mouse.

Field of angels, Story of. Van Buren and Bemis. Christmas in storyland.

See also Christmas rose, Legend of. II.

Field of Boliauns. Faulkner. Road to enchantment. (Clever Tom and the Leprechaun.)

For other entries, see 2d edition.

Field of the cloth of gold. Chandler. Magic pictures.

For other entries, see 2d edition.

Field of the pious. White. School management, p. 245. (Filial love.)

Fiend. Ralston. Russian fairy tales.

Fifine and the white mare. Carpenter. Tales of a Basque grandmother.

Fig=tree and his branches. Cooper. Argosy of fables.

Fight at Svoldar Island. *See* King Olaf.

Fight at the pass of Thermopylae. *See* Brave three hundred.

Fight of Cuchulain with his son Conla. *See* Death of Conla, son of Aiffe.

Fight with dragons. Burnett. Children's book.

Fighting witch tree. Tuttle. Frightened tree and other stories.

Filial love. *See* Field of the pious.

Filial son and daughter. Metzger. Tales told in Korea.

Filmy White. Baumbach. Tales from the Swiss alps.

Finding dreams in the land of sleep. Harriman. Stories for little children.

For other entries, see 2d edition.

Finding of the new world. *See* Columbus, Christopher.

Finding of the treasure. Skinner. Christmas stories.

Fine, fine. Cendrars. Little black stories.

Fine weather woman. Spence. Myths of the North American Indians. (Birth of Sin. *In* Ch. 7.)

Finette Cendron. Aulnoy. Fairy tales (Planché).

For other entries, see 2d edition.

Finland's greatest fisherman. *See* Fox and the peasant.

Finn and the Great Bear. Williamson. Stars through magic casements.

Finn MacCool. De La Mare and Quayle. Readings. (Running; jumping; swimming.)

Gregory. Cuchulain of Murthemne.

Hull. Cuchulain, the hound of Ulster.

Stephens. Irish fairy tales. (Boyhood of Fionn; Birth of Bran.)

Young. Tangle-coated horse.

For other entries, see 2d edition.

Finn MacCool and the seven brothers. Lanier. Book of giants. (Giant hand.)

Dulac. Edmund Dulac's fairy book. (Queen of the many-colored bedchambers.)

Finnochio of St. Francis. Untermeyer. Donkey of God. (*In* Gubbio-San Gimignano-Siena.)

Finny and Funny. Potter. Captain Sandman.

Fionn. *See* Finn MacCool.

Fir-tree. I. Andersen. Fairy tales (Siewers tr.).

Andersen. Fairy tales (Stickney). v. 1.

Curry and Clippinger. Children's literature.

Graham. Welcome Christmas.

Harper. Merry Christmas to you.

Johnson and Scott. Anthology of children's literature.

Starbuck. Familiar haunts.

Walters. Book of Christmas stories.

For other entries, see 2d edition.

Fir tree. II. Van Buren and Bemis. Christmas in storyland. (Little fir tree.)

For other entries, see 2d edition.

Fir tree. III. Skinner. Christmas stories. (Christmas spruce tree.)

Walker. Sandman's Christmas stories. (Little fir tree.)

Fir tree. IV. Buckingham. Elephant's friend. (City's Christmas tree.)

Fir tree and the bramble. Æsop. Fables (Jones).

Cooper. Argosy of fables.

For other entries, see 2d edition.

Fir=tree and the palm (poem). Cooper. Argosy of fables. Heine. Poems.

Fir=tree that found something to do. Hartshorne. Training in worship.

Firdausi. Coit. Ivory throne of Persia.

Fire and beauty, Legend of. Olcott. Wonder tales from pirate isles.

Fire=ball dwarf tree. Tuttle. Frightened tree and other stories.

Fire=bird. I. See 2d edition.

Fire=bird. II. Barry and Hanna. Wonder flights of long ago.
Dulac. Edmund Dulac's fairy book.

Fire=bird, the horse of power, and the Princess Vasilissa. Ransome. Old Peter's Russian tales.
For other entries, see 2d edition.

Fire boys. James. Tewa firelight tales.

Fire=eaters. Housman. Doorway in fairyland. (Bound princess, pt. 1.)

Fire fairy. Fyleman. Forty good-morning tales.

Fire! fire! fire! Olcott. Wonder tales from fairy isles.
See also Horned women.

Fire=ghost of Neuchatel. Guerber. Legends of Switzerland. (*In* Legends of Neuchatel.)

Fire=jewel and the Midnight Axe. Martens. Wonder tales from far away.

Fire=makers. Lee. Folk tales of all nations.
Wells. How the present came from the past. Book 1, pt. 2.
See also Wonderful lizard; Secret of fire.

Fire neglected burns the house. Tolstoi. Twenty-three tales.

Fire, Origin of. I. See 2d edition.

Fire, Origin of. II. Lansing. Great moments in freedom. (Fire stories.)
For other versions, *see* How fire was brought to the Indians. I; Secret of fire; Wonderful lizard.

Fire that would not burn. Bailey. Tell me another story.

Firecracker that went off. Bailey. Wonderful tree.

Fireflies, Origin of. I. See 2d edition.

Fireflies, Origin of. II. Mitchell. Gray moon tales. (Mammy and the fireflies.)

Firefly. Cooper. Argosy of fables.

Fireless island. Howes. Long bright land.

First arch. Butterfield. Young people's story of architecture. (*In* Country of arched entrances. Ch. 12.)

First aviator of the Pacific. Metzger. Tales told in Hawaii.

First battle. I. *See* 2d edition.

First battle. II. Partridge. Joyful Star. (How the first battle came to be fought.)

First burro. Shannon. Eyes for the dark. (Outlandish adventures of Bigger.)

First buttercups. Kinscella. Music appreciation readers. Book 3.
>*See also* How buttercups came #.
>For other entries, see 2d edition.

First butterflies. I. Johnson and Scott. Anthology of children's literature. (Story of the first butterflies.)
>For other entries, see 2d edition.

First butterflies. II. Metzger. Picture tales from the Chinese.

First butterflies. III. Mitchell. Gray moon tales. (Mammy and the butterflies.)

First camel. Æsop. Fables (Artzybasheff. Jupiter and the horse.)
>Cooper. Argosy of fables. (Jupiter and the horse.)
>For other entries, see 2d edition.

First Christmas. Major. Merry Christmas stories. (Star angel.)

First Christmas gift. *See* First Christmas present. III.

First Christmas present. I. Walters. Book of Christmas stories. (First Christmas presents.)
>For other entries, see 2d edition.

First Christmas present. II. *See* 2d edition.

First Christmas present. III. Cozad. Story talks. (First Christmas gift.)
>Campbell. Story of Christmas, p. 36. (Boy without a name.)

First Christmas roses. *See* Christmas rose. II.

First Christmas tree. I. *See* 2d edition.

First Christmas tree. II. *See* Thorn of Glastonbury.

First clock. Lansing. Man's long climb. (Man who was always in a hurry.)
>Lansing. Great moments in science. (Water thief.)
>*See also* Caliph's clock.

First coquette. Metzger. Tales told in Hawaii.

First corn. I. Macmillan. Canadian wonder tales. (Coming of the corn.)
>For other entries, see 2d edition.

First corn. II. Spence. Myths of the North American Indians. (Maize spirit. *In* Ch. 3.)
>Power. Children's treasure chest. (Mondawmin, friend of all mankind.)
>For other entries, see 2d edition.

First corn. III. Johnson and Scott. Anthology of children's literature. (How Indian corn came into the world.)
>Power. How it happened. (How maize was given to the Red Indians.)
>Spence. Myths of the North American Indians. (Maize spirit. *In* Ch. 3.)
>For other entries, see 2d edition.

First corn. IV–V. *See* 2d edition.

First corn. VI. Skinner. Child's book of country stories. (Origin of Indian corn.)
>For other entries, see 2d edition.

First corn. VII–IX. *See* 2d edition.
First corn. X. Bailey. Stories from an Indian cave. (*In* Three sisters.)
Stewart. Tell me a story I never heard before. (Fair earth.)
First corn. XI. Browne. Indian nights. (Origin of corn.)
See also First corn. VI.
First corn.
For other versions, *see* Chekilli the Creek boy; How corn and beans came to be.
First doll. Snell. Told beneath the northern lights.
See also Toymaker. I.
First fire. I–II. *See* 2d edition.
First fire. III. *See* How fire was brought to the Indians. VI.
"First friend." Through story-land with the children. (Story of Lup.)
See also Cat that walked by himself.
First gang. Through story-land with the children.
First good cry. Snell. Told beneath the northern lights.
First great adventure in thinking. Miller. My book of history. v. 1. (*In* Ch. 9.)
First great woman of history. Miller. My book of history. v. 1. (*In* Ch. 9.)
First harp. Blondell. Keepsakes.
Colum. Big tree of Bunlahy.
First hat. Shannon. California fairy tales.
See also Queen's hat.
First kantele. *See* How the harp came to Finland.
First little boy. Krohn and Johnson. Scales of the silver fish.
First man and first woman. Whitman. Navaho tales. (*In* Five worlds.)
First Marathon race. Lansing. Great moments in freedom. (*In* At Marathon.)
See also Swiss Marathon.
First moles. *See* Moles, Origin of.
First mosquitoes. I. *See* 2d edition.
First mosquitoes. II. *See* Pitcher, the witch and the black cats.
First moss rose. *See* Moss rose, Legend of.
First moving pictures. Metzger. Tales told in Hawaii.
First Noel (play). Skinner. Christmas stories.
First pig and porcupine. Leland. Algonquin legends. (Young man who was saved by a rabbit and a fox.)
Macmillan. Canadian wonder tales.
First plumbers. Krohn and Johnson. Scales of the silver fish. (It was lucky Noah invited the elephants.)
First snowdrops. I. *See* 2d edition.
First snowdrops. II. Carey. Flower legends. (Snowdrop.)
For other entries, see 2d edition.
First spider. *See* Arachne.

First strawberries. Bailey. Stories from an Indian cave. (How strawberries came to the earth. Adapted.)
Browne. Indian nights. (Origin of berries.)
Gearhart. Skalalatoot stories. (Where strawberries came from.)
For other entries, see 2d edition.
First Thanksgiving. Bailey. Tell me another story.
Cabot. Course in citizenship.
See also Thanksgiving.
First thimble. Chamoud. Picture tales from the French.
See also Lady Yolanda's thimble.
First vinyard. I. Friedlander. Jewish fairy tales. (Dutton. *In* Giant Og.)
See also Giant of the flood; Bacchus and the vine.
For other entries, see 2d edition.
First vinyard. II. *See* Grapes. Origin of.
First water lily. *See* Star maiden.
First wings. *See* Wings. II.
First woman #.
See also Creation of woman.
First woodpecker. *See* Why the woodpecker's head is red. I.
Fish and a butterfly. Menefee. Child stories.
Fish and the ring. Steel. English fairy tales.
For other entries, see 2d edition.
Fish-boy. Shannon. Eyes for the dark.
Fish in the forest. *See* How a fish swam in the air and a hare in the water.
Fish that leaped from the frying pan. Cooper. Argosy of fables.
Fish that took the biggest bite. Krohn and Johnson. Scales of the silver fish.
Fisher and the little fish. Æsop. Fables (Jones. Fisherman and the sprat.)
Æsop. Fables (Whitman ed. Angler and the little fish.)
Cooper. Argosy of fables. (Angler and the little fish.)
For other entries, see 2d edition.
Fisher Joe. Lee. Folk tales of all nations.
Fisher-boy Urashima. *See* Uraschimataro and the turtle.
Fisherman. I–IV. *See* 2d edition.
Fisherman. V. *See* Fisherman and troubled water.
Fisherman and his wife. Curry and Clippinger. Children's literature.
Grimm. Fairy tales (Olcott).
Grimm. Tales from Grimm (Wanda Gag).
Hutchinson. Chimney corner fairy tales.
Johnson and Scott. Anthology of children's literature.
Power. Blue caravan tales.
Starbuck. Familiar haunts.
Told under the green umbrella.
Williams. Tales from Ebony.
See also Ambitious old woman; Cuckoo and the hoopoe; En-

Fisherman and his wife—*continued.*
chanted lime tree; Girl who wanted everything; Keang-Njamo; Ludwig and Marleen; Magic tree; Restless cuckoos; Woman who had what she wanted.
For other entries, see 2d edition.

Fisherman and the genie. Arabian nights (Eliot. Story of the fisherman.)
Evans. Worth while stories. (Adapted.)
Lee. Folk tales of all nations. (Story of the fisherman and the genie; More about the fisherman and the genie.)
Price. Legends of the seven seas. (Adapted.)
For other entries, see 2d edition.

Fisherman and the goldfish. Schwimmer. Tisza tales.

Fisherman and the monkey. Eells. Brazilian fairy book.
See also Puss in boots.

Fisherman and the nymphs. Phillips. Far peoples.

Fisherman and the sprat. *See* Fisher and the little fish.

Fisherman and troubled water. Æsop. Fables (Whitman ed.).
Cooper. Argosy of fables. (Fisherman.)
For other entries, see 2d edition.

Fisherman piping. Æsop. Fables (Jones).
Cooper. Argosy of fables.

Fishermen. Cooper. Argosy of fables.
See also Helmsman and the sailors.

Fishing net, Tale of. *See* How Kahukura learned to make nets.

Five Chinese boys. *See* Five queer brothers.

Five Heads. Lee. Folk tales of all nations. (Story of Five Heads.)

Five little babies. Mitchell. Here and now story book.

Five little red caps. Arnold. Folk tales retold.

Five mice in the cupboard. Potter. Giant of Apple Pie Hill.

Five peas in a pod. *See* Pea blossom.

Five pennies. Arnold. Folk tales retold.
See also Mouse merchant; Only a penny #. One straw.

Five queer brothers. Arnold. Folk tales retold. (Five Chinese boys.)
For other entries, see 2d edition.

Five races of men. Egan. New found tales.
See also Damon and Pythias.

Five servants. Grimm. Tales from Grimm (Wanda Gag. Six servants.)
Morris. Gypsy story teller. (Frosty.)
See also Hans and the four giants.
For other entries, see 2d edition.

Five wise words of the Guru. Egan. New found tales. (Wise words of the Guru.)

Five wonderful eggs. Shimer. Fairyland.

Five worlds. Hogner. Navajo winter nights. (Navajo land.)
Whitman. Navaho tales.

Five worlds—*continued*.
See also Creation of the world (Indian).
Flag that waved in the north. Forbes. Good citizenship.
(*In* Ch. 9.)
Flanagan pig and his piece of gold. Casserley. Michael of
Ireland. (Piece of gold.)
Flanagan pig's soup. Casserley. Michael of Ireland.
Flax. Andersen. Fairy tales (Stickney). v. 2.
Johnson and Scott. Anthology of children's literature.
Wheelock. Kindergarten children's hour. v. 3. (*In* Ch.
36.)
For other entries, see 2d edition.
Flea. *See* King's flea. II.
Flea and the camel. Cooper. Argosy of fables.
See also Gnat and the bull; Waggoner and the butterfly.
Flea and the man. I. Æsop. Fables (Jones).
Cooper. Argosy of fables.
Cooper. Argosy of fables. (Prince and the flea.)
Flea and the man. II (poem). Cooper. Argosy of fables.
(Man and the flea.)
Flea and the ox. Æsop. Fables (Jones).
Cooper. Argosy of fables.
Flea and the wrestler. Cooper. Argosy of fables.
Flea=huntin'dest night. Mackaye. Tall tales of the Ken-
tucky mountains.
Fleamie and the hornets. Nakazawa. Weaver of the frost.
(Sting me!)
Fleamie the tree=frog. Nakazawa. Weaver of the frost.
Fleet on fire. *See* Cortez.
Flies and the honey=pot. Æsop. Fables (Whitman ed.).
Cooper. Argosy of fables.
Johnson and Scott. Anthology of children's literature.
(Flies and the pot of honey.)
For other entries, see 2d edition.
Flies and the pot of honey. *See* Flies and the honey-pot.
Flies of Mendiondo. Carpenter. Tales of a Basque grand-
mother.
Flight. Byrde. Polish fairy book.
Flight into Egypt. I. Smith and Hazeltine. Christmas in
legend and story.
For other entries, see 2d edition.
Flight into Egypt. II. Eells. Islands of magic. (Why the
Alveloa bird received a blessing.)
Flight into Egypt. III. Campbell. Story of Christmas,
p. 47.
Flight of Astrid. Dunlap. Stories of the Vikings.
Flight of the beasts. *See* Timid hare.
Flight of the golden bird. Martin. Fatma was a goose.
Flight of the stone canoe. *See* In the land of souls.
Flight of Tiri. Eells. Magic tooth.
See also Hansel and Grethel. I.
Flip the penguin. Farjeon. Old sailor's yarn box.

Floating island. *See* How the races obtained their colors (Indian).

Floating prince. Stockton. Reformed pirate.

Floating sticks. *See* What was it?

Flood (Babylonian). Miller. My book of history. v. 1. (*In* Story of the strong man, Gilgamesh. Ch. 11.)

Flood (Greek). *See* Deucalion and Pyrrha.

Flood (Indian). Curtis. Stories in trees. (Tall pine tree.) De Huff. Taytay's tales. (Deha.)

Hogner. Navajo winter nights. (Great flood.)

Sexton. Gray wolf stories. (Thunder sends the great flood upon the earth.)

Whitman. Navaho tales. (*In* Five worlds.)

Flood (Latin American). Eells. Magic tooth. (How the great flood began.)

Martinez Del Rio. Sun, the moon and a rabbit. (*In* Sun of water.)

Purnell. Merry frogs. (Three birds and a little black dog.)

Flood.
For other versions *see.* in 2d edition: Deluge; Flood; Great flood; Indians' flood; Manabozho and the lake magicians; Olelbis; Wisakaha slays the cloud manitous.

Flora doll, Story of. Buckingham. Elephant's friend.

Florimel. Richardson. Stories from old English poetry. (Adventures of Fair Florimel.)

Floris and Blanchefleur. Darton. Wonder book of old romance.

Flos mercatorum. *See* Dick Whittington and his cat.

Flower-blooming old man. *See* Old man who made withered trees to bloom.

Flower drink. McNeer and Lederer. Tales from the crescent moon.

Flower o' content. Burnett. Children's book.

Flower of Lanai. Metzger. Tales told in Hawaii.

Flower of life. Dane. Once there was and was not.
See also Singing bone.

Flower=towers. *See* Iris. IV.

Flower without a name. Farjeon. Italian peepshow.

Flowering stick. Buckingham. Elephant's friend. (*In* Butterfly boy.)

Flowers, Legend of. Egan. New found tales. (Passing of the flowers.)

Fleming. Round the world in folk tales.

Power. How it happened. (How the flowers and the bees returned to the earth.)

Wells. How the present came from the past. Book 1, pt. 2.

Flowers of chivalry. *See* Bayard. I.

Flowers' party. Silvester and Peter. Happy hour stories.

Flute contest of the musical foxes. Hogner. Navajo winter nights.

Flute music. Olcott. Wonder tales from goblin hills.
See also Song of the spring.

Flute player. Marzials. Stories for the story hour.
Flute, Story of. I. Eells. Magic tooth.
Flute, Story of. II. *See* Pan. I.
Flute that blew from fairyland. Fun folk and fairy tales.
 Stewart. Tell me a story I never heard before. (Flute
 which blew from fairyland.)
Fly and the chariot. *See* Fly upon a wheel.
Fly and the draught mule. Æsop. Fables (Jones).
 Æsop. Fables (Whitman ed.).
 Cooper. Argosy of fables.
 For other entries, see 2d edition.
Fly in Saint Paul's cupola. Cooper. Argosy of fables.
 For other entries, see 2d edition.
Fly of Kolumbatsh. *See* Knight and the dragon.
Fly upon a wheel. Æsop. Fables (Artzybasheff).
 Cooper. Argosy of fables. (Fly and the chariot.)
Flying Dutchman #.
 See also Bucca and the Cornish maid.
Flying=fish. Cooper. Argosy of fables.
Flying head. I. Morris. Stories from mythology: North
 American. (Great Head. *In* Ch. 4.)
 For other entries, see 2d edition.
Flying head. II. Spence. Myths of the North American In-
 dians. (Blackfoot day-and-night myth. *In* Ch. 3.)
Flying horse of Firouz Schah. *See* Enchanted horse.
Flying kitten. Bacon. Mercy and the mouse.
Flying ship. Bruce. Treasury of tales for little folk.
 Faulkner. Road to enchantment.
 Lee. Folk tales of all nations.
 Ransome. Old Peter's Russian tales. (Fool of the world
 and the flying ship.)
 Told under the green umbrella.
 See also Ashiepattle and his goodly crew # ; Ship that sailed
 by land and sea.
 For other entries, see 2d edition.
Flying stool. *See* Dorani.
Flying taro. Metzger. Tales told in Hawaii.
Flying trunk. Andersen. Fairy tales (Siewers tr.).
 Andersen. Fairy tales. (Stickney). v. 2.
 Barry and Hanna. Wonder flights of long ago.
 Shimer. Fairyland.
 See also Winged hero.
 For other entries, see 2d edition.
Fog boat story. Mitchell. Here and now story book.
Fog princess. Gates. Tales from the secret kingdom.
Folly of avarice. Cooper. Argosy of fables.
 See also Miser. I.
Fool and the birch=tree. Ralston. Russian fairy tales.
Fool and the prince. Kovalsky and Putnam. Long-legs;
 Big-mouth ; Burning-eyes.
 See also Boots and his brothers ; Hans Clodhopper.
Fool family. Metzger. Tales told in Hawaii.

Fool in the moon. Gaer. Magic flight.

Fool of the world and the flying ship. *See* Flying ship.

Fool remains a fool. Gaer. Magic flight.

Fool who was willing, Story of. Bennett. Pigtail of Ah Lee Ben Loo.

Fool who went to school. Eells. Brazilian fairy book.

Foolhardy jackal. *See* Foolhardy wolf.

Foolhardy wolf. Aspinwall. Jataka tales. (Foolhardy jackal.)

See also Fox who served a lion.

For other entries, see 2d edition.

Fooling the cat. Freeman. Child-story readers. 3d reader.

Foolish brother and the wonderful bush. Morris. Gypsy story teller.

See also Princess on the glass hill.

Foolish coyote. Purnell. Merry frogs.

Foolish fish. I. Cendrars. Little black stories. (Why no one ever carries the alligator down to the water.)

Cooper. Argosy of fables. (Man and the crocodile.)

See also Camel driver and the snake; Crocodile's ingratitude; Little Jackal and the alligator; Way of the world. I.

For other entries, see 2d edition.

Foolish fishermen. Botsford. Picture tales from the Italian.

See also Wise men of Gotham.

Foolish Fred. Evans. Worth while stories.

See also Lazy Jack; Prudent Hans; Silly Matt.

Foolish John. Wilson. Green magic.

Foolish little dogs. *See* Dogs and the hides.

Foolish Mabel. Fyleman. Forty good-night stories.

Foolish mother goat. Noel. Magic bird of Chomo-lung-ma.

Foolish Shah, Kai Kaus. Coit. Ivory throne of Persia. (Foolish Shah.)

Foolish Shah would fly. Coit. Ivory throne of Persia. (Foolish Shah again.)

See also Alexander the Great. II.

Foolish teacher. Lee. Folk tales of all nations. (Foolish teacher, the foolish pupils, and the cat.)

Foolish timid rabbit. *See* Timid hare.

Foolish tortoise. I. Æsop. Fables (Jones. Tortoise and the eagle.)

Cooper. Argosy of fables. (Tortoise and the eagle.)

Power. Children's treasure chest. (Tortoise and the eagle.)

For other entries, see 2d edition.

Foolish young emperor. Starbuck. Far horizons.

Armfield. Tales from Timbuktu.

Fool's story. Marzials. Stories for the story hour.

Forbidden fountain. Olcott. Wonder tales from fairy isles. (Tylwith Teg.)

For other entries, see 2d edition.

Forbidden room #.

See also Three chests.

Forest and the woodcutter. *See* Woodman and the trees.
Forest bride. Bowman and Bianco. Tales from a Finnish
tupa. (Mouse bride.)
Harper. Fillmore folk tales.
See also Three feathers.
For other entries, see 2d edition.
Forest maiden. Partridge. Joyful star.
Forest mother. Lindsay. Choosing book.
Forester Etin. Power. Bag o' tales.
For other entries, see 2d edition.
Forest's foster daughter. Wahlenberg. Old Swedish fairy
tales.
Forge of Vulcan. *See* Vulcan.
Forget=me=not. I. *See* 2d edition.
Forget=me=not. II. Carey. Flower legends.
For other entries, see 2d edition.
Forget=me=not. III–V. *See* 2d edition.
Forget=me=not. VI. Buckingham. Elephant's friend. (For-
get-me-nots.)
Forget not the best. *See* Wonderful flower. I.
Forgetful carpenter (poem). Wheelock. Kindergarten chil-
dren's hour. v. 2. (*In* Ch. 17.)
Forgetful duck. Bowman. Little brown bowl.
Forgetful kingfisher. Brown. Curious book of birds.
Carey. Stories of the birds. (Kingfisher.)
Rich. Why-so stories. (How the kingfisher got its color.)
Forging of the magic sampo. *See* Ilmarinen the smith;
Sampo.
Forgiving Indian. Cabot. Course in citizenship.
White. School management, p. 261.
Forgotten bell. Baumbach. Tales from the Swiss alps.
Fortunata. Fairy garland (Dulac).
Fortunate shoemaker. *See* Pedlar of Swaffham.
Fortunatus. Rhys. English fairy book. (Old Fortune.)
Wilson. Green magic. (Fortunatus and the wishing cap.)
For other entries, see 2d edition.
Fortune and the beggar #.
See also Pail of gold; Stone lion. I.
Fortune=seekers. I. Chamoud. Picture tales from the
French.
Grimm. Fairy tales (Olcott. Three luck-children.)
Evans. Worth while stories. (Three lucky sons.)
Tappan. Little lady in green. (Country of the stupid folk.)
See also Cottager and his cat #; Master Mustapha of the
whiskers.
For other entries, see 2d edition.
Fortune=tellers. La Fontaine. Fables (Tilney).
Fortunée. Aulnoy. Fairy tales (Planché).
Aulnoy. White cat. (Pot of carnations.)
Harper. Magic fairy tales. (Felicia and the pot of pinks.)
Quiller-Couch. Twelve dancing princesses. (Felicia; or,
The pot of pinks.)

Fortunée—*continued.*
For other entries, see 2d edition.
Fortunes of Said. *See* Said, Adventures of.
Forty=first brother. Lee. Folk tales of all nations. (Story of the forty-first brother.)
For other entries, see 2d edition.
Forty=seven Ronins. Mitford. Tales of Old Japan.
Forty=nine dragons. Fuller. Book of dragons. (Two brothers and the forty-nine dragons.)
For other entries, see 2d edition.
Foster brother. Masson. Folk tales of Brittany.
Founding of Rome. *See* Romulus and Remus.
Fountain of beauty. Capuana. Italian fairy tales.
See also Green serpent. I.
For other entries, see 2d edition.
Fountain of Giant Land. Adams and Atchinson. There were giants.
For other entries, see 2d edition.
Fountain of youth. *See* Ponce de Leon and the fountain of youth.
Four brothers. I–II. *See* 2d edition.
Four brothers. III. *See* Four clever brothers.
Four brothers who brought a dead lion to life. Ryder. Twenty-two goblins.
See also Rash magician ; Lion makers.
Four chiefs of the four winds. *See* War of the winds.
Four clever brothers. De La Mare. Told again. (Four brothers.)
See also Brave man, the wise man, and the clever man ; Dragon with seven heads. II ; Four scientific suitors ; Hush-a-bye baby ; Prince Ahmed and the fairy Perie Banou ; Three brothers. I ; Three gifts. V ; Three lovers who brought the dead girl to life.
For other entries, see 2d edition.
Four comrades who wanted to travel round the world. Rasmussen. Eagle's gift.
See also Rip Van Winkle.
Four=footed Santa Claus. Burnett. Children's book.
Four friends. I. *See* 2d edition.
Four friends. II. *See* True friendship. II.
Four friends. III. Sugimoto. Picture tales from the Japanese. (Japanese big four.)
Four generals. Chrisman. Shen of the sea.
Four gifts. Masson. Folk tales of Brittany.
For other entries, see 2d edition.
Four grizzly bears capture the camp. Sexton. Gray wolf stories.
Four hunters. Morris. Gypsy story teller.
See also Longstaff, Pinepuller and Rockheaver.
Four=leaf clover. Evans. Worth while stories.
For other entries, see 2d edition.
Four leaved clover. I–II. *See* 2d edition.

Four leaved clover. III. Curry and Clippinger. Children's literature.

Four peas. Fyleman. Forty good-morning tales.

Four qualities of drunkenness. Independent (N. Y.). May 31, 1894, p. 708.
See also Bacchus and the vine ; First vinyard ; Grapes, Origin of.

Four scientific suitors. Ryder. Twenty-two goblins.
See also Four clever brothers.

Four seasons. *See* Twelve months. I.

Four underground kingdoms. Carpenter. Tales of a Russian grandmother.

Four weavers. Lee. Folk tales of all nations.

Four winds. I. *See* 2d edition.

Four winds. II. Cooper. Tal. (*In* Ch. 18.)

Fourchette and the kittens. Morley. I know a secret.

Fourth of July. *See* Firecracker that went off ; Stars and the sky rocket ; Stolen Fourth ; That lazy Ah Fun ; Yankee balloon.

Fourth of July tent. Bailey. Wonderful tree.

Fourth of July story. Faulkner. Story lady's book.

Fowler and the birds. Æsop. Fables (Whitman ed.).
For other entries, see 2d edition.

Fowler and the lark. Æsop. Fables (Jones).
Cooper. Argosy of fables. (Birdcatcher and the lark.)
For other entries, see 2d edition.

Fowler and the pigeons. *See* Pigeon-king and Mouse-king.

Fowler and the quails. *See* Quails.

Fowler and the viper. Cooper. Argosy of fables.

Fowler, the partridge and the cock. Æsop. Fables (Jones).
Cooper. Argosy of fables. (Bird-catcher, the partridge and the cock.)

Fowls on pilgrimage. Brown. Curious book of birds.
See also Chicken-Little.

Fox. *See* Miraculous fox.

Fox and a goat. *See* Fox and the goat. I.

Fox and a raven. *See* Fox and the crow.

Fox and coyote and whale. Garett. Coyote stories.

Fox and grapes. *See* Fox and the grapes.

Fox and his five hungry comrades. Lee. Folk tales of all nations. (Animals take a bite.)
For other entries, see 2d edition.

Fox and his flute. Kinscella. Music appreciation readers. Book 3.
See also Indian boy and his flute.

Fox and the ape. *See* Fox, the monkey, and the animals.

Fox and the ass. *See* Ass in the lion's skin.

Fox and the blackbird. Carrick. More Russian picture tales.
See also Fox and the dove #.

Fox and the bramble. Æsop. Fables (Jones).
Cooper. Argosy of fables.
See also Serpent and the file.
For other entries, see 2d edition.

Fox and the cat. I. Æsop. Fables (Artzybasheff. Cat and the fox.)
Æsop. Fables (Whitman ed. Cat and the fox.)
La Fontaine. Fables (Tilney. Cat and the fox.)
See also Hundred-wit, Thousand-wit and Single-wit.
For other entries, see 2d edition.

Fox and the cat. II. *See* 2d edition.

Fox and the cat. III. Lee. Folk tales of all nations.
For other entries, see 2d edition.

Fox and the cat. IV. Curtin. Fairy tales of Eastern Europe. (Cat and the fox.)
Ransome. Old Peter's Russian tales. (Cat who became head-forester.)
For other entries, see 2d edition.

Fox and the cat. V #.
See also Feast.

Fox and the clay pot. Quinn. Stories for the six-year-old.

Fox and the cock. I–II. *See* 2d edition.

Fox and the cock. III. *See* Cock and the fox. III.

Fox and the cock. IV. *See* Cock and the fox. VII.

Fox and the countryman. Æsop. Fables (Artzybasheff. Fox and the woodman.)
Æsop. Fables (Whitman ed.).
Cooper. Argosy of fables. (Fox and the woodman.)
For other entries, see 2d edition.

Fox and the crab. *See* How the fox and the crab ran a race.

Fox and the crabs #.
See also Crab and the fox. II.

Fox and the crane. Carrick. Still more Russian picture tales.
See also Fox and the stork ; Merry little fox.
For other entries, see 2d edition.

Fox and the crow. I. Æsop. Fables (Artzybasheff).
Æsop. Fables (Jones).
Æsop. Fables (Whitman ed.).
Æsop. Twenty-four fables (L'Estrange. Fox and a raven.)
(poem). Cooper. Argosy of fables. (Fox and the raven.)
Harriman. Stories for little children. (Crow and the cheese.)
Johnson and Scott. Anthology of children's literature.
Rich. Read-aloud book.
Rich. Why-so stories. (*In* Tales of the crow.)
For other entries, see 2d edition.

Fox and the crow. II. Bowman and Bianco. Tales from a Finnish tupa. (Wily fox.)
See also Jackal and the heron ; Owl, the fox and the crow.
For other entries, see 2d edition.

Fox and the crows. De Huff. Taytay's tales.

Fox and the dove #.
See also Fox and the blackbirds.

Fox and the drum, Story of. Mackenzie. Jackal in Persia.
See also Fox and the piece of meat ; Jackal and the drum.
In 2d edition this story is also indexed under the title
"Fox, the hen, and the drum."

Fox and the fireflies. Morris. Stories from mythology:
North American. (*In* Ch. 12.)

Fox and the foolish blue jay. Babbitt. Animals' own story
book.
See also Fox and the wolf. V ; Rival roosters.

Fox and the fowls. *See* Fox and the piece of meat.

Fox and the geese. Kinscella. Music appreciation readers.
Book 3. (How sly fox lost his dinner.)
See also Stupid wolf ; Why cats always wash after eating.
For other entries, see 2d edition.

Fox and the goat. I. Æsop. Fables (Artzybasheff).
Æsop. Fables (Jones).
Æsop. Fables (Whitman ed.).
Æsop. Twenty-four fables (L'Estrange. Fox and a goat.)
Cooper. Argosy of fables.
See also Fox in the well. II #.
For other entries, see 2d edition.

Fox and the goat. II. Woodson. African myths.

Fox and the goose. *See* Crafty fox and industrious goose.

Fox and the grapes. Æsop. Fables (Artzybasheff).
Æsop. Fables (Jones).
Æsop. Fables (Whitman ed.).
Æsop. Twenty-four fables (L'Estrange. Fox and grapes.)
Cooper. Argosy of fables.
Curry and Clippinger. Children's literature.
Johnson and Scott. Anthology of children's literature.
Rich. Read-aloud book.
For other entries, see 2d edition.

Fox and the grasshopper. Æsop. Fables (Jones).

Fox and the hare. Carrick. Still more Russian picture tales.
See also Little white rabbit. II.

Fox and the hedgehog. I. See 2d edition.

Fox and the hedgehog. II. *See* Fox and the mosquitoes.

Fox and the icicle. Cooper. Argosy of fables.

Fox and the Indians. De Huff. Taytay's tales.

Fox and the leopard. Æsop. Fables (Jones).
For other entries, see 2d edition.

Fox and the lion. Æsop. Fables (Artzybasheff).
Æsop. Fables (Jones).
Æsop. Fables (Whitman ed.)
Cooper. Argosy of fables.
See also Camel.
For other entries, see 2d edition.

Fox and the lizard. De Huff. Taytay's tales.
Lee. Folk tales of all nations.

Fox and the lobster. Carrick. Still more Russian picture tales.
See also How the fox and the crab ran a race.
Fox and the mask. Æsop. Fables (Whitman ed.).
Cooper. Argosy of fables.
For other entries, see 2d edition.
Fox and the mice. De Huff. Taytay's tales.
Lee. Folk tales of all nations.
See also Fox that lost his tail.
For other entries, see 2d edition.
Fox and the mole. Babbitt. Animals' own story book.
See also Cat and the mouse in partnership.
Fox and the monkey. Æsop. Fables (Jones).
Cooper. Argosy of fables.
Fox and the mosquitoes. Æsop. Fables (Jones. Fox and the hedgehog.)
Cooper. Argosy of fables. (Fox and the hedgehog.)
For other entries, see 2d edition.
Fox and the peasant. Carrick. Still more Russian picture tales.
Bowman and Bianco. Tales from a Finnish tupa. (Finland's greatest fisherman.)
See also Hungry fox and his breakfast.
Fox and the piece of meat. Mackenzie. Jackal in Persia. (Story of the fox and the fowls.)
See also Dog and his shadow; Lion and the hare. III; Owl and the two rabbits; Wolf and the fox. II.
For other entries, see 2d edition.
Fox and the prairie dogs. De Huff. Taytay's memories.
See also Fox and the skunk; Scheme of skunk and coyote.
Fox and the quails. De Huff. Taytay's memories.
Fox and the rabbit. I. *See* 2d edition.
Fox and the rabbit. II. Bowman and Bianco. Tales from a Finnish tupa.
See also Hares and the frogs.
Fox and the raven. *See* Fox and the crow. I.
Fox and the sheep. I. *See* 2d edition.
Fox and the sheep. II. De Huff. Taytay's tales.
Fox and the sick lion. *See* Lion, the fox and the beasts.
Fox and the skunk. De Huff. Taytay's memories.
De Huff. Taytay's tales.
See also Raccoon and the three roasting geese; Scheme of skunk and coyote.
Fox and the snake. Æsop. Fables (Jones).
Fo and the snowbirds. De Huff. Taytay's memories.
Fox and the stork. Æsop. Fables (Artzybasheff).
Æsop. Fables (Jones).
Æsop. Fables (Whitman ed.).
Cooper. Argosy of fables.
(poem). Cooper. Argosy of fables.
See also Fox and the crane; Fox and the toucan; Merry little fox.

Fox and the stork—*continued.*
For other entries, see 2d edition.
Fox and the tiger. I. *See* 2d edition.
Fox and the tiger. II. Cooper. Argosy of fables.
For other entries, see 2d edition.
Fox and the toucan. Eells. Brazilian fairy book.
See also Fox and the stork.
Fox and the turkey. De Huff. Taytay's tales.
Lee. Folk tales of all nations.
Fox and the turtledoves. De Huff. Taytay's memories.
Fox and the wolf. I–IV. *See* 2d edition.
Fox and the wolf. V. Æsop. Fables (Whitman ed.).
See also Fox and the foolish blue jay.
Fox and the wolf. VI. De Huff. Taytay's memories.
Fox and the woodcock. Carrick. Still more Russian picture
tales.
See also Cock and the fox. II.
Fox and the woodman. *See* Fox and the countryman.
Fox and the woodpecker. De Huff. Taytay's memories.
Fox and the young turkeys. La Fontaine. Fables (Tilney).
Fox as a shepherd. *See* Fox as herdsboy.
Fox as herdsboy. Carrick. Tales of wise and foolish animals.
(Fox as a shepherd.)
Harriman. Stories for little children. (Why the tail of a
fox has a white tip.)
Johnson and Scott. Anthology of children's literature.
(Why the tail of the fox has a white tip.)
Power. How it happened. (Why the fox has a white tip
to his tail.)
See also Rabbit's tail. I; Why the fox has a dark tail.
For other entries, see 2d edition.
Fox as judge. *See* Reward of kindness.
Fox as partner. I–II. *See* 2d edition.
Fox as partner. III. Bowman and Bianco. Tales from a
Finnish tupa. (*In* Farmers three.)
For other entries, see 2d edition.
Fox in the well. I. Æsop. Fables (Artzybasheff).
Æsop. Fables (Whitman ed.).
See also Merry little fox.
For other entries, see 2d edition.
Fox in the well. II #.
See also Fox and the goat. I.
Fox in the well. III. Dorey. Three and the moon. (How
Master Renard enticed Ysegrim to eat the moon and how
he was judged by the court of the lion.)
Fox-physician. Ralston. Russian fairy tales.
Fox sings. I. James. Tewa firelight tales.
Fox sings. II. Bowman and Bianco. Tales from a Finnish
tupa. (Song of the fox.)
Fox that flew. De Huff. Taytay's tales.

Fox that lost his tail. Æsop. Fables (Artzybasheff. Fox without a tail.)
Æsop. Fables (Jones. Fox without a tail.)
Æsop. Fables (Whitman ed. Fox without a tail.)
Cooper. Argosy of fables. (Fox without a tail.)
See also Fox and the mice.
For other entries, see 2d edition.
Fox that traveled. *See* Travels of a fox.
Fox, the bear and the poor farmer. Sawyer. Picture tales from Spain. (Clever, clever, clever.)
See also Well done, ill paid # ; More with mind than with force.
For other entries, see 2d edition.
Fox, the cock and the crane. Carrick. Still more Russian picture tales.
Fox, the hen, and the drum. *See* Fox and the drum.
In 2d edition there are entries under each title.
Fox, the monkey, and the animals. Æsop. Fables (Jones. Monkey as king.)
Æsop. Fables (Whitman ed. Fox and the ape.)
Cooper. Argosy of fables. (Monkey who would be king.)
For other entries, see 2d edition.
Fox who asked for a night's lodging. *See* Travels of a fox. II.
Fox who served a lion. Æsop. Fables (Jones).
Cooper. Argosy of fables. (Lion and the fox.)
See also Foolhardy wolf.
Fox who was the cause of his own death, Story of. Mackenzie. Jackal in Persia.
See also Frogs and the fighting bulls.
Fox wife. Metzger. Picture tales from the Chinese.
Fox without a tail. *See* Fox that lost his tail.
Fox woman. Metzger. Tales told in Korea.
Foxes and the river. Æsop. Fables (Jones).
Foxes' gratitude. *See* Grateful foxes.
Foxes' wedding. Mitford. Tales of old Japan.
Fox's eyes. De Huff. Taytay's memories.
See also Coyote's eyes.
Fox's trick. Eells. Brazilian fairy book.
Foxy gobé. McNeer and Lederer. Tales from the crescent moon.
See also All women are alike #.
Fra Angelico's vision. Untermeyer. Donkey of God. (*In* Florence.)
Francese's fairy letter. Burnett. Children's book.
See also Prospero and Miranda.
Francis of Assisi. *See* St. Francis of Assisi.
Franconia Notch, Story of. *See* Old man of the mountain ; Pipe of peace.
Franklin, Benjamin. Blaisdell. Log cabin days. (Honest Ben.)

Franklin, Benjamin—*continued.*
  Cozad. Story talks. (Benjamin Franklin and the speckled axe.)
Franklin's tale. *See* Rocks removed.
French drummer boy. Chidley. Fifty-two, story talks.
Fresh figs. Eells. Islands of magic.
Fretful porcupine. *See* How the shad came #.
Frey. *See* Wooing of Gerd.
Freyja. Lang. Book of myths. (Freya, queen of the Northern gods.)
  Evans. Worth while stories. (Freyja's necklace. Adapted.)
  Pyle. Tales from Norse mythology. (Story of Brisingamen.)
  See also How Loki stole a necklace.
Friar and the boy. Dulac. Edmund Dulac's fairy book.
  See also Jew among the thorns ; Silver flute.
Friar Bacon and the brazen head. Richardson. Stories from old English poetry. (Friar Bacon's brass head.)
  Williams-Ellis. Fairies and enchanters. (Head of brass.)
  For other entries, see 2d edition.
Friar Bacon's brass head. *See* Friar Bacon and the brazen head.
Friar's tale. *See* Summoner and the fiend.
Friday. Ralston. Russian fairy tales.
Friedrich and his child garden. Menefee. Child stories.
Friend mouse=deer. *See* Crocodile's ingratitude.
Friend of Achilles. *See* Patroclus.
Friend of the devil. Eells. Islands of magic.
Friendly robin. Fyleman. Forty good-night tales.
Friendly skeleton. *See* Island of skeletons.
Friends that quarreled. *See* Why the dog and cat are enemies. IV.
Friendship. Curry and Clippinger. Children's literature.
Friendship of the squirrel and the creeping fish. Lee. Folk tales of all nations.
  Skeat. Tiger's mistake. (Friendship of Tupar the squirrel and Ruan the creeping fish.)
  See also Monkey and the crocodile.
Frigg's gift. *See* How flax was given to men.
Frightened tree. *See* Why the aspen leaves tremble. V.
Frithiof. Bailey. Stories of great adventures. (Frithjof, the Viking.)
  Power. Bag o' tales. (Frithiof's journey to the Orkneys.)
  For other entries, see 2d edition.
Fritz=and=Franz. Brown. Under the rowan tree.
Fritz the master=fiddler. Bennett. Pigtail of Ah Lee Ben Loo.
Froebel, Friedrich. Menefee. Child stories. (Friedrich and his child garden.)
Frog. *See* If heaven will it. II.
Frog and an oxe. *See* Frog and the ox.
Frog and Belinka. Nemcova. Disobedient kids.

Frog and the antelope. Harper. More story-hour favorites.
Linderman. Kootenai why stories.
See also Hare and the hedgehog; How a turtle outwitted a
wolf.
Frog and the crab. Cooper. Argosy of fables.
Frog and the crow. Lee. Folk tales of all nations.
Skinner. Happy tales.
See also Fox and the geese; Why cats always wash after
eating.
Frog and the frogling (poem). Cooper. Argosy of fables.
Frog and the hen. Cooper. Argosy of fables.
For other entries, see 2d edition.
Frog and the leopard #.
See also Race between a reindeer and a tom-cod.
Frog and the ox. Æsop. Fables (Artzybasheff).
Æsop. Fables (Jones. Ox and the frog.)
Æsop. Fables (Whitman ed. Frog who wished to be as big
as an ox.)
Æsop. Twenty-four fables (L'Estrange. Frog and an oxe.)
Cooper. Argosy of fables.
Curry and Clippinger. Children's literature.
See also Kenewai and the water buffalo; Wren.   I.
For other entries, see 2d edition.
Frog and the serpent. Cooper. Argosy of fables.
See also Sagacious snake.
Frog and the wild hog. Coussens. Diamond story book.
Frog bride. *See* Frog queen.
Frog king. *See* Frog prince.
Frog prince. Grimm. Fairy tales (Olcott. Frog king; or,
Iron Henry.)
Grimm. Tales from Grimm (Wanda Gag).
Hutchinson. Fireside stories.   (Adapted.)
Johnson and Scott. Anthology of children's literature.
Quinn. Stokes' wonder book of fairy tales.
White. School management, p. 279.   (Abridged.)
Williams. Tales from Ebony.
See also Little white dog; Plain gold ring.
For other entries, see 2d edition.
Frog princess. I–II. *See* 2d edition.
Frog princess. III. *See* Frog queen.
Frog princess. IV. Tappan. Little lady in green.
See also Betrothal gifts # ; Three feathers.
Frog queen. Byrde. Polish fairy book. (Frog princess.)
Carpenter. Tales of a Russian grandmother.   (Frog bride.)
Phillips. Far peoples. (Princess frog.)
For other entries, see 2d edition.
Frog, the crab and the serpent. Mackenzie. Jackal in
Persia. (Story of the frog, the weasel, and the snake.)
See also Herons and the mongoose.
For other entries, see 2d edition.
Frog, the weasel and the snake. *See* Frog, the crab and the
serpent.

Frog travellers. Faulkner. Little Peachling. (Two frogs.)
Henderson and Calvert. Wonder tales of old Japan. (Two
frogs.)
Through story-land with the children. (Two frogs.)
Whitehorn. Wonder tales of old Japan. (Travels of two
frogs.)
See also Journey of the Breton fishermen; Peasant's journey.
For other entries, see 2d edition.

Frog who wished to be as big as an ox. *See* Frog and the ox.

Frog wife. Bryce. Folk lore from foreign lands. (Frog
wife.)

Frog=witch. Eells. Magic tooth.

Froglet. Capuana. Italian fairy tales.

Frogs and the fighting bulls. Cooper. Argosy of fables.
See also Fox who was the cause of his own death.
For other entries, see 2d edition.

Frogs and the old serpent. *See* Sagacious snake.

Frogs and the well. *See* Two frogs and the well.

Frogs asking for a king. *See* Frogs who asked for a king.

Frog's beautiful son. Cooper. Argosy of fables.
See also Crow's children.

Frog's complaint against the sun. Æsop. Fables (Jones).

Frogs desired a king. *See* Frogs who asked for a king.

Frog's saddle horse. *See* Elephant and the frog.

Frogs who asked for a king. Æsop. Fables (Artzybasheff.
Frogs desired a king.)
Æsop. Fables (Jones. Frogs asking for a king.)
Æsop. Fables (Whitman ed. Frogs desiring a king.)
Cooper. Argosy of fables. (Frogs asking for a king.)
Curry and Clippinger. Children's literature. (Frogs desir-
ing a king.)
For other entries, see 2d edition.

Frohburg castle. Guerber. Legends of Switzerland. (*In*
Legends of Soleure.)

From the land of the sky=blue water. Cross. Music stories.

Frost. *See* King Frost. I.

Frost king's bride. *See* King Frost.

Frosty. *See* Five servants.

Frozen music. Raspé. Children's Munchausen (Martin. *In*
Ch. 5.)
Raspé. Tales from the travels of Baron Munchausen.

Fulfilled. Told under the green umbrella.
For other entries, see 2d edition.

Funakoshi Jiuyémon. Mitford. Tales of old Japan. (Wonderful adventures of Funakoshi Jiuyémon.)

Fundevogel. Grimm. Fairy tales (Olcott. Bird-found.)
For other entries, see 2d edition.

Funeral march of a marionette. Cross. Music stories.

Funnel makers. Meeker. Folk tales from the Far East.

Funny story. Pyle. Fairy tales from India.
For other entries, see 2d edition.

Furnace who made a mistake. Aspinwall. (Can you believe me stories.)
Furrows of Satan. Pogány. Hungarian fairy book.
Furze blossom gold. Olcott. Wonder tales from fairy isles.
See also Fairy gold; Pedlar of Swaffham.

G

Gabottu and the bears. Botsford. Picture tales from the Italian.
Ga=do=waas and his star=belt. Williamson. Stars through magic casements.
Gai Gai, the snake warrior. Olcott. Wonder tales from pirate isles.
Gagliuso. Faulkner. Road to enchantment. (Good cat.)
For other entries, see 2d edition.
Galahad. *See* Sir Galahad.
Galatea. I. *See* Acis and Galatea.
Galatea. II. *See* Pygmalion and Galatea.
Galileo. Lansing. Great moments in science. (Galileo and the pendulum.)
For other entries, see 2d edition.
Gallant captains. Martinez Del Rio. Sun, the moon and a rabbit.
Gallant tailor. *See* Brave little tailor.
Galleeny's, Story of the. Housman. Turn again tales.
Gallimaufry. *See* Many-furred creature.
Galloping plough. Housman. Doorway in fairyland. (Bound princess, pt. 2.)
Gambler's loss. Allen. Whispering wind. (Loss of a great gambler.)
Game=cocks and the partridge. *See* Partridge and the cocks.
Gamelyn. I. *See* Sir Gamelyn.
Gamelyn. II. Housman. What-o'clock tales.
Gamelyn the dressmaker. Housman. Moonshine and clover.
Gander and his geese. Housman. Turn again tales.
Ganymede. Bulfinch. Golden age. (Hebe and Ganymede. *In* Ch. 19.)
For other entries, see 2d edition.
Garden and the dragon. *See* Hercules and his labors.
Garden down in Kiang Sing. Chrisman. Wind that wouldn't blow.
Garden farm. Richards. More five minute stories.
Garden of bluebells. Wheelock. Kindergarten children's hour. v. 4. (*In* Ch. 14.)
Garden of paradise. I. *See* 2d edition.
Garden of paradise. II. Martens. Wonder tales from far away.
Garden of twilight. Blondell. Keepsakes.
Gardener and his dog. Æsop. Fables (Jones).
For other entries, see 2d edition.

Gardener and his landlord. La Fontaine. Fables (Tilney).
Gardener and the bear. Mackenzie. Jackal in Persia.
For other entries, see 2d edition.
Gardener and the nightingale. See Rustic and the nightingale.
Gardener to the king. Smith. Made in France. (*In* Ch. 8.)
Gareth and Lynette. See Sir Gareth.
Gargantua. Guerber. Legends of Switzerland. (*In* Legends of Vaud and Valais.)
For other entries, see 2d edition.
Garofano. Botsford. Picture tales from the Italian.
Gaston, Comte de Foix. Lang. Red true story book. (Story of Orthon ; Piteous death of Gaston.)
Gasworks. Fyleman. Forty good-morning tales.
Gate of honor. Wahlenberg. Old Swedish fairy tales.
Gate that would not open. Perkins and Danielson. Second year May-flower program book.
Gateway to fairyland. Bowman. Little brown bowl.
Gatterang. Phillips. Far peoples. (How two towns were named.)
Gautama. See Lover of men #.
Gay godmother. Bowman. Little brown bowl.
Gay little king. Skinner. Child's book of country stories.
Stewart. Tell me a story I never heard before.
For other entries, see 2d edition.
Gazelle. Lang. Old friends among the fairies. (Story of a gazelle.)
See also Prince Csihan ; Puss in boots.
For other entries, see 2d edition.
Gazelle who took care of lion cubs. Lobagola. Folk tales of a savage.
Geese and the cranes. Cooper. Argosy of fables.
For other entries, see 2d edition.
Geese and the tortoise. See Talkative tortoise.
Geese save Rome. Cooke. Stories of Rome. (*In* Coming of the Gauls.)
See also Geese whose ancestors saved Rome.
For other entries, see 2d edition.
Geese=swans. Cowles. Stories to tell.
Geese whose ancestors saved Rome. Cooper. Argosy of fables. (Boastful geese.)
Johnson and Scott. Anthology of children's literature.
White. School management, p. 274. (Russian fable.)
See also Geese save Rome.
Gefion's plow. Dunlap. Stories of the Vikings. (*In* Wonder prince from Aasgaard.)
Geirrod and Thor. Pyle. Tales from Norse mythology. (Thor and Geirrod.)
See also Thorkill.
For other entries, see 2d edition.
Gellert, Story of. See Beth Gellert.
Genevieve. See St. Genevieve.

Genie Plum tree and Genie Pomegranate. Olcott. Wonder stories from China seas.

Gentle cockatrice. Housman. Moonshine and clover.

Gentle maiden. *See* Wakontas and the two maidens.

Gentle Olga and spiteful Vera. *See* King Frost. II.

Gentle sunshine. *See* Twelve months.

Geoffrey, knight of the Round Table. *See* Sir Geoffrey.

George, Saint. *See* St. George.

George Washington Jackson. Silvester and Peter. Happy hour stories.

See also Epaminondas and his auntie.

Geraint and Enid. *See* Sir Geraint.

Gerald's dream. Bowman. Little brown bowl.

See also Benjy in beastland.

Geranium. *See* Red geranium.

German legend. *See* Stranger child.

Gertrude and the cake. *See* Why the woodpecker's head is red. I.

Get up and bar the door. *See* Barring of the door.

Getting even. Broomell. Children's story caravan.

Geynleyn. *See* Fair unknown.

Gheczy castle. Schwimmer. Tisza tales.

Ghiberti's doors. Butterfield. Young people's story of architecture. (In Great artists and architects. Ch. 45.)

Ghirlandaio. Steedman. Knights of art. (Domenico Ghirlandaio.)

Ghos'es. *See* Ghost story. II.

Ghost and the shadow. Baker. Pedlar's wares.

Ghost land. I–II. *See* 2d edition.

Ghost land. III. Spence. Myths of the North American Indians. (Heaven sought bride; Chinooks visit the Supernaturals. *In* Ch. 7.)

Ghost land.
For other versions, *see* How a man found his wife in the land of the dead; In the land of souls; Land of the Hereafter #; Sayadio in spirit land; Talking birds; Tooboo the short.

Ghost=laying stories. Henderson. Folk lore of the Northern counties. (*In* Ch. 10.)

See also Barrel in the parlor; Ghost of Sakura; Peter's Ghost.

For other entries, see 2d edition.

Ghost of muskrat village. Harper. More story-hour favorites.

Ghost of Sakura. Mitford. Tales of old Japan.

Ghost of the great white stag. Harper. Ghosts and goblins. Parker. Skunny Wundy and other Indian tales.

Ghost of the spring and the shrew. Carpenter. Tales of a Russian grandmother. (Bad wife.)

Ralston. Russian fairy tales. (Bad wife.)

For other entries, see 2d edition.

Ghost of the spring and the shrew—*continued.*
In 2d edition this story is also indexed under the title "Quarrelsome wife."

Ghost of Watz Mountain. Henderson and Calvert. Wonder tales of old Tyrol.

Ghost story. I. *See* 2d edition.

Ghost story. II. **Sale. Tree named John. (Ghos'es.)

Ghost story of Egypt. Maspero. Popular stories of ancient Egypt. (Fragment of a ghost story).

Ghost tree. *See* White birch. II.

Ghost wife. I. Harper. Ghosts and goblins.
For other entries, see 2d edition.

Ghost wife. II–III. *See* 2d edition.

Ghost wife. IV. Egan. New found tales. (Shadow land.)
For other entries, see 2d edition.

Ghost wife. V. Spence. Myths of the North American Indians. (Blue Jay and Ioi. *In* Ch. 7.)

Ghosts of Forefathers' Hill. Harper. Ghosts and goblins.
For other entries, see 2d edition.

Ghosts of Kahlberg. Harper. Ghosts and goblins.
Henderson. Wonder tales of Alsace-Lorraine.

Giacco and his bean. Botsford. Picture tales from the Italian.
See also Travels of a fox.

Giacomo Robusti. *See* Tintoretto.

Giant. I. *See* 2d edition.

Giant. II (poem). Adams and Atchinson. Book of giant stories.

Giant and the boy. De Huff. Taytay's memories.
See also Big long man and the giant.

Giant and the fairy. Fyleman. Tea time tales.

Giant and the herdboy. Starbuck. Far horizons.
For other entries, see 2d edition.

Giant and the small boy. De Huff. Taytay's memories.

Giant and the mite. Farjeon. Italian peepshow.

Giant and the twins. De Huff. Taytay's memories.

Giant behind the waterfall. *See* Grettir the Strong.

Giant builder. Bulfinch. Golden age. (How Thor paid the mountain giant his wages. *In* Ch. 38.)
Pyle. Tales from Norse mythology. (How a wall was built around Asgard.)
For other entries, see 2d edition.

Giant Crump and Lady moon #.
See also Owl and the moon.

Giant Einheer. Guerber. Legends of Switzerland. (*In* Thurgau.)

Giant Energy and Fairy Skill. Bailey. Tell me another story.
For other entries, see 2d edition.

Giant Flint. James. Happy animals of Atagahi.

Giant ghost. Sechrist. Little book of Hallowe'en.

Giant hand. *See* Finn MacCool and the seven brothers.

Giant=hunters. Kennedy. Red man's wonder book.

Giant King of Limburg. Olcott. Wonder tales from windmill lands. (Ratteretalleratteratattertatatattertela.)

Giant Lampong. Meeker. Folk tales from the Far East.

Giant lizard. De Huff. Taytay's memories.

Giant loses his wife. Rhys. English fairy book.

Giant of Apple Pie Hill. Potter. Giant of Apple Pie Hill and
other stories.

Giant of Band=Beggars' Hall. Adams and Atchinson. Book
of giant stories. (Giant of Bang Beggars' Hall.)
For other entries, see 2d edition.

Giant of St. Michael's Mount. Lanier. Book of giants.
See also King Ryence's challenge; King Arthur.

Giant of the black mountains. Adams and Atchinson. There
were giants.
For other entries, see 2d edition.

Giant of the flood. Friedlander. Jewish fairy tales. (Dut-
ton. Giant Og.)
See also First vinyard.
For other entries, see 2d edition.

Giant of the sea. Snell. Told beneath the northern lights.

Giant Og. *See* Giant of the flood.

Giant Pot=ear. Adams and Atchinson. There were giants.
Mukerji. Rama. (*In* Death of Kumbhakarna.)

Giant pyramid builder. Lanier. Book of giants.

Giant that was caught. Olcott. Wonder tales from fairy
isles.

Giant twins. Byrde. Polish fairy book.
See also Longstaff, Pinepuller, and Rockheaver.

Giant who did not like bones. Olcott. Wonder tales from
Baltic wizards.

Giant who had no heart. Adams and Atchinson. Book of
giant stories. (Giant who had no heart in his body.)
Dasent. East of the sun and west of the moon (Nielsen.
Giant who had no heart in his body.)
Lanier. Book of giants. (Giant who had no heart in his
body.)
Lee. Folk tales of all nations. (Giant who had no heart
in his body.)
Rasmussen. East o' the sun and west o' the moon. (Giant
who had no heart in his body.)
Through story-land with the children.
See also Cobbler's lad.
For other entries, see 2d edition.

Giant who had no heart in his body. *See* Giant who had no
heart.

Giant who kicks people down cliffs. Hogner. Navajo winter nights.

Giant who married a mortal princess. Marzials. Stories
for the story hour.

Giant who rode on the ark. Adams and Atchinson. There
were giants.
For other entries, see 2d edition.
Giant who shines in the sky. *See* Orion.
Giant with the golden hair. I. Adams and Atchinson.
Book of giant stories. (Giant with three golden hairs.)
Williams. Tales from Ebony. (Three golden hairs.)
See also Antti and the wizard's prophecy; Seven doves #;
Wanderer who had forgotten who he was.
For other entries, see 2d edition.
Giant with the golden hair. II. Power. Stories to shorten
the road. (Three golden hairs of the old man Vsevede.)
Lee. Folk tales of all nations. (Three golden hairs of
Grandfather Allknow.)
Morris. Gypsy story teller. (Three golden hairs of the Sun
King.)
Curtin. Fairy tales of Eastern Europe. (Three golden
hairs of Grandfather Know All.)
For other entries, see 2d edition.
Giant with three golden hairs. *See* Giant with the golden
hair. I.
Giants and fairies. I. *See* 2d edition.
Giants and fairies. II. Pyle. Tales from Norse mythology.
(*In* How the world was made.)
See also Dwarfs and the fairies.
Giants and the dwarfs. Miller. My travelship: Holland.
Giant's baby. I. Baldwin. Pedlar's pack.
Giant's baby. II. Potter. Captain Sandman.
Giant's bird. Potter. Giant of Apple Pie Hill.
Giant's boot. *See* Wind's tale of the giant's boot.
Giants' cave. Lanier. Book of giants. (*In* Introduction.)
Giant's duck. Potter. Giant of Apple Pie Hill.
Giants of the clock. Untermeyer. Donkey of God. (*In*
Venice.)
Giants of the Sill valley. Henderson and Calvert. Wonder
tales of old Tyrol.
Giants of Towedneck. Williams-Ellis. Fairies and enchant-
ers.
See also Tom Hickathrift.
Giant's plaything. *See* Toy of the giant child.
Giants' pot. Starbuck. Enchanted paths.
For other entries, see 2d edition.
Giant's quilt. *See* Derido.
Giant's stairs. Adams and Atchinson. There were giants.
For other entries, see 2d edition.
Giant's wig. Marzials. Stories for the story hour.
Gift of fishes. Gunterman. Castles in Spain.
Gift of love. Faulkner. Story lady's Christmas stories.
See also Felix.
Gift of swiftness. Cendrars. Little black stories.
See also Hare afraid of his ears. II.

Gift of the flutes. Nusbaum. Seven cities of Cibola.
Nusbaum. Zuni Indian tales.
Gift of the gnomes. *See* How the Swiss came to use the Alpine horn.
Gift of the olive tree. *See* Athens.
Gift of the sea king. *See* Sea king's gift.
Gift of the shining stranger. Perkins and Danielson. Second year Mayflower program book.
Gift that grew. Bailey. Wonderful tree.
Gifts of the north wind. *See* Lad who went to the north wind.
Gifts the trees gave #.
See also Luck of the goldenrod; Palm tree; Plucky prince #;
Why the laurel makes wreaths.
Gigi and the magic ring. Tappan. Prince from nowhere.
(Wishing ring.)
See also Grateful beasts. II #; Magic ring. I.
For other entries, see 2d edition.
Gil Dong. *See* Hong Kil Tong.
Gila monster's tobacco ranch. *See* How chipmunk got small
feet.
Gilgamesh. Miller. My book of history. v. 1. (Story of the strong man, Gilgamesh. *In* Ch. 11.)
Wells. How the present came from the past. Book 2, pt. 2.
(Izdubar or Gilgamesh, Story of. Abridged.)
Gilly of the goatskin. Colum. King of Ireland's son. (*In* Sword of light.)
Ginger and Sandy. Baker. Tell them again tales.
Gingerbread boy. I. Bailey. Story-telling hour.
(poem). Bruce. Treasury of tales for little folk. (Gingerbread man.)
Evans. Worth while stories. (Gingerbread man.)
Harriman. Stories for little children.
See also Irrepressible pie.
For other entries, see 2d edition.
Gingerbread boy. II. Piper. Gateway to storyland.
Gingerbread man. I. *See* Gingerbread boy. I.
Gingerbread man. II (poem). Skinner. Happy tales.
For other entries, see 2d edition.
Gingerbread man. III. *See* 2d edition.
Gingerbread man. IV. *See* Timothy Brown.
Giorgione. Steedman. Knights of art.
Giotto. Chambers' miscellany. v. 9. (Cimabue and Giotto.
In Anecdotes of the early painters.)
Cozad. Story talks. (Fair exchange.)
Miller. My book of history. v. 3. (*In* Ch. 16.)
Steedman. Knights of art.
For other entries, see 2d edition.
Giotto's O. Steedman. Knights of art. (*In* Giotto.)
Giotto's tower. Lane. Tower legends. (Goblin of Giotto's
tower.)
Gipsy and the bear. *See* Gipsy and the dragon. III.

Gipsy and the dragon. I. *See* Stan Bolovan.
Gipsy and the dragon. II. Schwimmer. Tisza tales. (Brave tailor.)
   Morris. Gypsy story teller. (Deluded dragon.)
   See also Brave boy; Stan Bolovan.
Gipsy and the dragon. III. Borski and Miller. Gipsy and the bear. (Gipsy and the bear.)
   Lee. Folk tales of all nations. (Devil and the gipsy.)
   See also Giant and the tailor; Johnny Gloke; Stan Bolovan.
Gipsy winds up in a belfry. Shannon. Eyes for the dark.
Giraffe and the palms. Silvester and Peter. Happy hour stories.
Giraffe who thought that she had a good heart. Lobagola. Folk tales of a savage.
Girl Alarana and her brother who were eaten by wolves and became caribou. Rasmussen. Eagle's gift.
Girl and the frog. Carrick. Animal picture tales from Russia.
Girl who adored jewels. *See* Tarpeia.
Girl who could spin gold from clay and long straw. Bruce. Treasury of tales for little folk. (Titelli-Ture.)
   See also Rumpelstiltskin.
   For other entries, see 2d edition.
Girl who did not do as she was told. Sheriff. Stories old and new.
   See also Lassie and her godmother.
Girl who had to be carried. Olcott. Wonder tales from pirate isles.
Girl who knew more than the emperor. *See* Maiden who was wiser than an emperor.
Girl who rejected her cousin #.
   See also Scar Face II; Snow-man husband.
Girl who ruled over all. *See* Young head of the family.
Girl who showed great devotion to a thief. Ryder. Twenty-two goblins.
Girl who sought her nine brothers. *See* Little sister.
Girl who took a snake for husband. Wheeler. Albanian wonder tales.
   See also Snake prince.
Girl who transposed the heads of husband and brother. Ryder. Twenty-two goblins.
   See also Silent princess #.
Girl who trod on the loaf. Wheelock. Kindergarten children's hour. v. 3. (Adapted. *In* Ch. 14.)
   See also Cheese floor.
   For other entries, see 2d edition.
Girl who wanted everything. Evans. Worth while stories.
   See also Fisherman and his wife.
Girl with the goat's face. *See* Goat-faced girl.
Girl's affection which first killed a man and afterwards brought him back to life. Rasmussen. Eagle's gift.
Gissing and the telephone. Morley. I know a secret.

Gissing Pond. Morley. I know a secret.
Giufa and the morning-singer. Lee. Folk tales of all na-
  tions.
Giving game. Mitchell. Gray moon tales. (Mammy and
  the wicked elves.)
Glass ball. Casserley. Whins on Knockattan.
Glass mountain. Byrde. Polish fairy book.
  For other entries, see 2d edition.
    In 2d edition this story is also indexed under the title
  "Princess on the glass mountain."
Glaucus. Bulfinch. Golden age. (Glaucus and Scylla. *In*
  Ch. 7.)
  For other entries, see 2d edition.
Glimminge castle. Freeman. Child-story readers. 3d
  reader.
  Lagerlöf. Wonderful adventures of Nils. (*In* Ch. 4.)
Glob and Alger. Coussens. Diamond story book.
  For other entries, see 2d edition.
Gloomy hippopotamus. Bacon. Lion-hearted kitten.
Glooskap. Macmillan. Canadian wonder tales. (Glooskap's
  country.)
Glooskap and Malsum, the wolf. Leland. Algonquin leg-
  ends. (Of Glooskap's birth and of his brother Malsum, the
  wolf.)
  Macmillan. Canadian wonder tales. (*In* Glooskap's coun-
  try.)
  Spence. Myths of the North American Indians. (Glooskap
  and Malsum. *In* Ch. 3.)
  For other entries, see 2d edition.
Glooskap and the baby. *See* Why the baby says "Goo."
Glooskap and the bullfrog. Macmillan. Canadian wonder
  tales. (*In* Glooskap's country.)
  For other entries, see 2d edition.
Glooskap and the fairy. Macmillan. Canadian wonder tales.
Glooskap and the magic gifts. I. *See* 2d edition.
Glooskap and the magic gifts. II. Leland. Algonquin leg-
  ends. (How Glooskap made a magician of a young man.)
  Macmillan. Canadian wonder tales. (*In* Passing of Gloos-
  kap.)
  For other entries, see 2d edition.
Glooskap and the magic gifts. III. Leland. Algonquin
  legends. (How Glooskap, leaving the world, . . . gave
  gifts to men.)
  Macmillan. Canadian wonder tales. (*In* Passing of Gloos-
  kap.)
  For other entries, see 2d edition.
Glooskap and the magic gifts. IV. Leland. Algonquin
  legends. (Of other men who went to Glooskap for gifts.)
  Macmillan. Canadian wonder tales. (*In* Passing of Gloos-
  kap.)
  For other entries, see 2d edition.
Glooskap and the magic gifts. V–VI. *See* 2d edition.

Glooskap and the magic gifts. VII. Leland. Algonquin legends. (Of Glooskap and the three other seekers.)
Spence. Myths of the North American Indians. (Glooskap's gifts. *In* Ch. 3.)

Glooskap and the turtle #.
See also How turtle came.

Glooskap's country. *See* Glooskap.

Glooskap's departure. Macmillan. Canadian wonder tales. (Passing of Glooskap.)

Glooskap's gifts. *See* Glooskap and the magic gifts.

Gloria victis. Clément. Flowers of chivalry.

Gloriana. Kipling. Rewards and fairies.

Gloves of Gwron Gawr. Morris. Book of the three dragons.

Glowworm and the jackdaw #.
See also Monkeys, the firefly and the bird.

Gnat and the bull. Æsop. Fables (Artzybasheff).
Æsop. Fables (Jones).
Cooper. Argosy of fables.
See also Flea and the camel; Waggoner and the butterfly.
For other entries, see 2d edition.

Gnat and the lion. *See* Lion and the gnat. I.

Gnome king. Denton. Homespun stories.

Gnome who became a little boy. Fyleman. Forty goodnight tales.

Gnome's revenge. Guerber. Legends of Switzerland. (*In* Forest cantons).

Gnomes who tried to stop Thanksgiving. Deihl. Holiday-time stories.

Go, I know not whither—fetch, I know not what. I. Zeitlin. Skazki. (Whither no one knows.)
See also Baker's magic wand; Boy who took the letter to the world where the dead live; Castle of Thou shalt go and not return; Town of nothing.
For other entries, see 2d edition.

Go, I know not whither—fetch, I know not what. II. Bowman and Bianco. Tales from a Finnish tupa. (Ei-Niin-Mita; or, No-So-What.)
See also Pali's luck; Schmat-Razum #.

Go-to-sleep story. Harriman. Stories for little children. (Go-sleep story.)
For other entries, see 2d edition.

Goat. *See* Wolf, the she-goat and the kid.

Goat and the goatherd. *See* Goatherd and the goat. I.

Goat and the horse (poem). Cooper. Argosy of fables.

Goat and the hyena. Berry. Black folk tales.
See also Goat and the ram.

Goat and the lion. *See* Wolf and the goat.

Goat and monkey. De Leeuw. Java jungle tales.

Goat and the ram. Carrick. More Russian picture tales.
Quinn. Stories for the six-year-old.
See also Goat and the hyena.

Goat and the vine. Æsop. Fables (Jones).
  Cooper. Argosy of fables. (Vine and the goat.)
Goat=faced·girl. Tappan. Prince from nowhere. (Girl with
  the goat's face.)
  For other entries, see 2d edition.
Goatherd and the goat. I. Æsop. Fables (Jones).
  Cooper. Argosy of fables. (Goat and the goatherd.)
Goatherd and the goat. II. *See* Goatherd and the wild
  goats.
Goatherd and the wild goats. Æsop. Fables (Jones).
  Cooper. Argosy of fables. (Goatherd and the goats.)
Goatherd who won a princess. Boggs and Davis. Three
  golden oranges.
  See also Lying for a wager.
Goats in the turnip field. Kinscella. Music appreciation
  readers. Book 1. (Bee and the goats.)
  Piper. Folk tales children love. (Olaf and the three goats.)
  Piper. Road in storyland. (Olaf and the three goats.)
  Told under the green umbrella. (Three goats.)
  See also Important gnat; Little white rabbit, II; Table, the
  ass, and the stick.
  For other entries, see 2d edition.
Gobborn seer. Young. Wonder smith and his son.
  For other entries, see 2d edition.
Goblin and the braces. Fyleman. Forty good-morning tales.
Goblin and the rose. Davis. Truce of the wolf.
Goblin house. Howes. Long bright land.
Goblin in the cellar. Baumbach. Tales from the Swiss alps.
Goblin of Adachigahara. Sugimoto. Picture tales from Jap-
  anese. (Demon of Adachi plain.)
  For other entries, see 2d edition.
Goblin of Giotto's tower. Lane. Tower legends.
Goblin of the mountains. Howes. Long bright land.
Goblin of the pitcher. Harper. Ghosts and goblins.
Goblin who was turned into a door knocker. Fyleman.
  Tea time tales.
Goblins of Haubeck. Bancroft. Goblins of Haubeck.
God knows how to punish man. Lee. Folk tales of all na-
  tions.
God sees the truth, but waits. Tolstoy. Ivan the fool.
God with a bad memory. Shannon. Eyes for the dark.
Goddess of Fuji=San. Henderson and Calvert. Wonder tales
  of old Japan.
Godfather Death. *See* Strange godfather.
Godfrey de Bouillon. Schwarz. Jewish caravan. (Rashi
  and the Duke of Lorraine.)
  See also King for three days.
  For other entries, see 2d edition.
Godiva. Graham. Happy holidays. (Lady Godiva's Day.)
  For other entries, see 2d edition.

Gods know. Bruce. Treasury of tales for little folk.
See also Chop Chin and the dragon # ; White elephant. V.
For other entries, see 2d edition.

Gods of the sun and the moon. Garett. Coyote stories.

Gods seek company. Martinez Del Rio. Sun, the moon and a rabbit.

Gods wishing to instruct a son of Jupiter. La Fontaine. Fables (Tilney).

Gog and Magog. *See* Gogmagog.

Goggle-eyes. Morris. Gypsy story teller.

Gogmagog. Lanier. Book of giants.
Olcott. Wonder tales from fairy isles. (Legend of Gogmagog.)

Going to meet Christmas. Skinner. Christmas stories.

Gold and lead. Cooper. Argosy of fables.

Gold and silver clubs. Metzger. Tales told in Korea.

Gold axe. *See* Golden hatchet.

Gold-bearded man. Pogány. Magyar fairy tales. (Golden bearded man.)
For other entries, see 2d edition.

Gold bell. Casserley. Whins on Knockattan.

Gold bread. *See* Golden loaf.

Gold Buckskin Whincher. *See* Blixie Bimber, Story of.

Gold-children. *See* Golden lads.

Gold ducat. Wahlenberg. Old Swedish fairy tales.

Gold girl and the tar girl. *See* Mother Holle.

Gold in the orchard. Æsop. Fables (Jones. Farmer and his sons.)
Bailey. Tell me another story. (Ploughman and his sons.)
Cooper. Argosy of fables. (Farmer and his sons.)
(poem). Johnson and Scott. Anthology of children's literature. (Plowman and his sons.)
Power. Children's treasure chest. (Farmer and his sons.)
See also Wink, the lazy bird and the red fox.
For other entries, see 2d edition.

Gold Maria and Pitch Maria. Williams-Ellis. Fairies and enchanters. (Lazy Maria.)
See also Mother Holle.
For other entries, see 2d edition.

Gold-spinners #.
See also Petru.

Gold tree. Baumbach. Tales from the Swiss alps.

Gold-tree and Silver-tree. Adams and Atchinson. Book of princess stories.
For other entries, see 2d edition.

Golden age of the Alps. Guerber. Legends of Switzerland. (*In* Legends of Vaud and Valais.)

Golden apple with the silver seeds. Atkins. Pot of gold.

Golden apple-tree and nine peahens. *See* Nine peahens and the golden apples.

Golden apples of Lough Erne. *See* Conn-Eda, Story of.

Golden armlet. Martens. Wonder tales from far away.
See also Boy who was fated to be a king; Enchanted pomegranate branch and the beauty; False prince and the true #.

Golden ball. Lee. Folk tales of all nations.
Steel. English fairy tales.
For other entries, see 2d edition.

Golden-bearded man. *See* Gold-bearded man.

Golden bird. I. *See* 2d edition.

Golden bird. II. Bruce. Treasury of tales for little folk.
Grimm. Fairy tales (Olcott).
Hutchinson. Chimney corner fairy tales.
Power. Blue caravan tales.
See also Firebird, the horse of power and Princess Vasilissa; Golden bird and the good hare; Ivan and the grey wolf; Miraculous fox; Red heron.
For other entries, see 2d edition.

Golden bird. III. *See* White-headed Zal.

Golden bird. IV. Cook. Red and gold stories.

Golden bird and the good hare. Cowles. Stories to tell. (Adapted.)
Morris. Gypsy story teller.
See also Golden blackbird #.

Golden boat. Metzger. Picture tales from the Chinese.

Golden boy. Newman. Fairy flowers.

Golden branch. Aulnoy. Fairy tales (Planché).
For other entries, see 2d edition.

Golden Butterfly. I. Cook. To-day's stories of yesterday.

Golden Butterfly. II. Olcott. Wonder tales from pirate isles.

Golden cat head. King. Golden cat head and other tales.

Golden chick and the magic frying pan. Chardon. Golden chick and the magic frying pan.

Golden cock. I. *See* 2d edition.

Golden cock. II. Zeitlin. Skazki.

Golden cow-bell. Guerber. Legends of Switzerland. (*In* Glarus and Grisons.)

Golden door that spoke. Cooper. Tal. (*In* Ch. 2.)

Golden dreams. *See* Wolfert Webber.

Golden eagle. Farjeon. Old nurse's stocking tales.

Golden eggs. I. *See* 2d edition.

Golden eggs. II. Olcott. Wonder tales from pirate isles.

Golden-feather. Capuana. Golden-feather.

Golden fir-cones. Hart. Picture tales from Holland.
See also Silver cones #.

Golden fish. I. Carrick. Picture folk tales.
Faulkner. Road to enchantment.
Phillips. Far peoples. (Goldfish.)
Ransome. Old Peter's Russian tales.
See also Fisherman and his wife.
For other entries, see 2d edition.

Golden-fish, the wonder-working tree, and the golden bird. Curtin. Fairy tales of Eastern Europe.
See also Three sisters. I.

Golden fleece. I. *See* Argonauts.

Golden fleeced lamb. Schwimmer. Tisza tales.
See also Golden goose. I.

Golden fly. *See* Etain and Midir.

Golden fountain. Darton. Seven champions of Christendom.

Golden gift of the genii of the padi-field. Olcott. Wonder tales from pirate isles.

Golden goblet. Perkins and Danielson. Second year Mayflower program book.
For other entries, see 2d edition.

Golden goblets of gladness. Newman. Fairy flowers.

Golden goose. I. Evans. Worth while stories. (Dummling's goose.)
Grimm. Fairy tales (Olcott).
Johnson and Scott. Anthology of children's literature.
Williams. Tales from Ebony.
See also Bristlepate and the sad princess ; Little lady in green ; Wonderful lamb.
For other entries, see 2d edition.

Golden Hair and the three bears. *See* Three bears. I.

Golden harp. *See* Fairy harp.

Golden hatchet. Martens. Wonder tales from far away.
Olcott. Wonder tales from Baltic wizards. (Gold axe.)

Golden helmet, Legend of. Olcott. Wonder tales from windmill lands. (Legend of the golden helmet.)
For other entries, see 2d edition.

Golden Hood. I. *See* Little Goldenhood.

Golden Hood. II. Colum. Children who followed the piper. (Golden Hood ; Valentine ; Nest of eagles ; Sleeping maiden.)
Colum. Fountain of youth.

Golden lads. Grimm. Fairy tales (Olcott. Gold-children.)
For other entries, see 2d edition.

Golden lantern, the golden goat, and the golden cloak. Williams. Jolly old whistle. (Pinkel and the fur coat.)
See also Bee, the mouse, the muskrat and the boy ; Esben and the witch ; Old man's son ; Tartaro and Petit Perroquet.
For other entries, see 2d edition.

Golden loaf. Faulkner. Road to enchantment. (Gold bread.)
For other entries, see 2d edition.

Golden locks. Denton. Homespun stories.

Golden lynx. Byrde. Polish fairy book.

Golden Mead, Legend of. Olcott. Wonder tales from goblin hills.

Golden melon. *See* Two melons.

Golden mouse. *See* Mouse merchant.

Golden oranges. Capuana. Italian fairy tales.

Golden parrot. Boggs and Davis. Three golden oranges.

Golden pitcher. Gunterman. Castles in Spain.
Williams. Jolly old whistle.
Golden=rod and Star=blue grass. Newman. Fairy flowers.
Golden roses and apples red. Canton. Child's book of
saints.
Golden ship. Bowman and Bianco. Tales from a Finnish
tupa. (Hidden Laiva ; or The golden ship.)
Golden=skin the mouse. *See* Mouse-king's story.
Golden skittle. Choate and Curtis. Little people of the hills.
Golden snuff box. *See* Jack and his golden snuff box.
Golden spear. *See* Lost spear.
Golden strawberries. Olcott. Wonder tales from goblin
hills. (Moss wifie.)
Golden thread. Pogány. Hungarian fairy book.
Golden touch. *See* Midas. I.
Golden twins. Wilson. Green magic.
Golden willow. Cozad. Story talks.
Golden wonder. Crew. Saturday's children.
Golden wood. Chardon. Golden chick.
Goldenhair and Goldenhand. *See* Prince with the golden
hand.
Goldfish. *See* Golden fish. I.
Goldfish bowl. I. Forbes. Good citizenship. (*In* Ch. 7.)
Goldfish bowl. II. Metzger. Picture tales from the Chinese.
Goldheart and Promise. Pogány. Magyar fairy tales.
See also Master-maid. I ; Yvon and Finette.
Goldsmith's niece and the fisherman's faithful son. Mar-
tens. Wonder tales from far away.
Goliath. Lanier. Book of giants. (Son of Anak.)
Golovikka. Ralston. Russian fairy tales.
Gondoliers. *See* Stolen prince. II.
Gonzaga, Frederigo. *See* Little Frederigo Gonzaga.
Good action. Young. Celtic wonder tales.
Good and bad weather. Harper and Hamilton. Winding
roads.
For other entries, see 2d edition.
Good bargain #.
See also Dummling's request.
Good cat. *See* Gagliuso.
Good for evil. White. School management, p. 273.
Good=for=nothing. I. *See* 2d edition.
Good=for=nothing. II. Lee. Folk tales of all nations.
Good for nothing Ganiche. Carpenter. Tales of a Basque
grandmother.
Good, good smell. Potter. Captain Sandman.
Good hunter. *See* Beloved warrior.
Good joke. Bryce. Folk lore from foreign lands.
Good Little Corn and bad Big Corn. Martinez Del Rio.
Sun, the moon and a rabbit.
Good little mouse. Aulnoy. Fairy tales (Planché).
Aulnoy. White cat.
For other entries, see 2d edition.

Good-luck tea kettle. *See* Accomplished and lucky tea kettle.

Goodman is always right. *See* What the goodman does is sure to be right.

Good-natured dragons. Fuller. Book of dragons. (Dragons of Lucerne.)
Guerber. Legends of Switzerland. (*In* Forest cantons.)
See also Shepherd and the dragon.
For other entries, see 2d edition.

Good-natured hyena and the little lion children. Lobagola. Folk tales of a savage.

Good natured little boy. Curry and Clippinger. Children's literature.

Good natured raven. *See* How fire was brought to the Indians. II.

Good neighbors. Hall. Godmother's stories.

Good night, my brave Michael. Lee. Folk tales of all nations.

Good Orphan Sunblossom. Bernhard. Master wizard. (Good Orphan Sunblossom and the enchanted treasure.)

Good Samaritan. Curry and Clippinger. Children's literature.

Good Thanksgiving (poem). Harriman. Stories for little children.
(poem). McVenn. Good manners and right conduct. Book 2. (Good time.)
Spaulding and Bryce. Aldine readers, Book 2.
For other entries, see 2d edition.

Good thunder. *See* Child of the thunder.

Good time. *See* Good Thanksgiving.

Good and the ills. Æsop. Fables (Jones).

Goodwife of Kittlerumpit. Choate and Curtis. Little people of the hills.

Goody 'Gainst-the-stream. Lee. Folk tales of all nations.
Power. Stories to shorten the road.
See also Mary, Mary, so contrary.
For other entries, see 2d edition.

Goody Two-Shoes. Curry and Clippinger. Children's literature. (Renowned history of Little Goody Two-Shoes.)
Johnson and Scott. Anthology of children's literature. (Renowned history of Little Goody Two-Shoes.)
Quinn. Stokes' wonder book of fairy tales.
For other entries, see 2d edition.

Goolahwilleel. *See* Top-knot, pigeons.

Goose. I. *See* 2d edition.

Goose. II. Kovalsky and Putnam. Long-legs, Big-mouth, Burning eyes.
See also How the mayor carved the goose.

Goose. III. *See* Goose and the swans. II.

Goose and the golden eggs. *See* Goose that laid golden eggs.

Goose and the goldfinch (poem). Cooper. Argosy of fables.

Goose and the swans. I. *See* 2d edition.

Goose and the swans. II. Cooper. Argosy of fables. (Goose.)

Goose boy and the king. *See* Emperor and the goose boy.

Goose girl. I. Grimm. Fairy tales (Olcott).
Lang. Old friends among the fairies.
Quinn. Stokes' wonder book of fairy tales.
See also Three feathers. II.
For other entries, see 2d edition.

Goose girl. II. *See* Goose girl at the well.

Goose girl at the well. Evans. Worth while stories. (Goose girl.)
Grimm. Fairy tales (Olcott).
For other entries, see 2d edition.

Goose that laid golden eggs. Æsop. Fables (Artzybasheff. Goose and the golden eggs.)
Æsop. Fables (Jones).
Æsop. Fables (Whitman ed. Goose with the golden eggs.)
Cooper. Argosy of fables. (Goose with the golden eggs.)
Curry and Clippinger. Children's literature. (Goose with the golden eggs.)
Johnson and Scott. Anthology of children's literature. (Goose with the golden eggs.)
See also Hen that laid golden eggs; Woman and the fat hen.
For other entries, see 2d edition.

Goose who tried to keep the summer. Bailey. Tell me another story.

Goose with the golden eggs. *See* Goose that laid golden eggs.

Gooseherd's reward. Henderson and Calvert. Wonder tales of old Tyrol.

Gootom and the tree fairy. Meeker. Folk tales from the Far East.
See also Table, the ass and the stick.

Gordian knot. Bulfinch. Golden age. (Midas. *In* Ch. 6.)
See also Alexander the Great.

Gordon of Earlstoun. Lang. Red true story book. (Adventures of the Bull of Earlstoun.)

Gore-Gorinskoe. Martens. Wonder tales from far away. (Rich brother and poor brother.)
Ralston. Russian fairy tales. (Woe.)
Ransome. Old Peter's Russian tales. (Little Master Misery.)
See also Luck, luck in the red coat; Sorrow.
For other entries, see 2d edition.

Gorgeous goldfinch. *See* How the finch got her colors.

Gorgon's head. *See* Perseus.

Gorsedd of the gods. Morris. Book of the three dragons.

Gotham men and the cuckoo. Starbuck. Familiar haunts. (*In* Wise men of Gotham.)
For other entries, see 2d edition.

Gracieuse and Percinet. *See* Graciosa and Percinet.

Graciosa and Percinet. Aulnoy. Fairy tales (Planché. Gracieuse and Percinet.)

Aulnoy. White cat.

For other entries, see 2d edition.

Gradual fairy. Broomell. Children's story caravan.

For other entries, see 2d edition.

Graelent of Brittany (play). Going. Folklore and fairy plays.

Grain of corn. Faulkner. White elephant.

For other entries, see 2d edition.

Grain that was like an egg. Egan. New found tales. (Old man and the grain of wheat.)

Ralston. Russian fairy tales. (*In* Legends about saints. Ch. 6.)

For other entries, see 2d edition.

Grainne the haughty. Dunbar. Sons o' Cormac.

Grand Sagamore who wandered afar. Parker. Skunny Wundy and other Indian tales.

Grandfather Pig's spectacles. Harriman. Stories for little children.

Grandfather's eyes. Lee. Folk tales of all nations. (Jezinkas.)

For other entries, see 2d edition.

Grandfather's penny. Bailey. Stories children want.

Grandfather's willow whistle. Skinner. Child's book of country stories.

Grandma's spoon story. Burnett. Children's book.

Grandmother and the boar. *See* Dreadful boar.

Grandmother Spider's transformation. De Huff. Taytay's memories.

Grandmother's golden dish. Broomell. Children's story caravan. (Merchants and the golden bowl.)

Grandmother's spectacles. Perkins and Danielson. Second year Mayflower program book.

For other entries, see 2d edition.

Granny's Blackie. Cabot. Course in citizenship.

For other entries, see 2d edition.

Granny's garden. *See* Tulip bed. III.

Grape arbor tea room. Morley. I know a secret.

Grapes, Origin of. Gaer. Burning bush. (*In* Tower that wasn't completed.)

See also Four qualities of drunkenness.

For other entries, see 2d edition.

Grass fairy. Gordon and Stockard. Gordon readers. 2d reader.

Grasshopper. James. Tewa firelight tales.

Grasshopper and the ants. *See* Ant and the grasshopper.

Grasshopper and the bee. White. School management, p. 253.

See also Ant and the grasshopper.

Grasshopper and the dove. Spaulding and Bryce. Aldine
  readers. Book 2, rev. ed.
  See also Nightingale and the glow-worm.
Grasshopper and the owl. *See* Owl and the grasshopper.
Grasshopper and the snail. Blaisdell. Rhyme and story sec-
  ond reader.
  See also Hare and the tortoise.
Grateful animals. *See* Prince Wicked and the grateful ani-
  mals.
Grateful animals and ungrateful man. I. *See* Prince
  Wicked and the grateful animals.
Grateful animals and ungrateful man. II. Bryce. Folk
  lore from foreign lands. (Gratitude.)
  Cowles. Stories to tell. (Grateful animals and the ungrate-
  ful man.)
  Phillips. Far peoples.
  Woodson. African myths. (Ingrate.)
  See also Fortunes of Shikrantha #; Grateful beasts. II;
  Prince Wicked and the grateful animals.
Grateful elephant. Cabot. Course in citizenship. (King's
  white elephant.)
  Faulkner. White elephant and other tales. (White ele-
  phant.)
  For other entries, see 2d edition.
Grateful foxes. Henderson and Calvert. Wonder tales of old
  Japan. (Foxes' gratitude.)
  Mitford. Tales of old Japan.
  For other entries, see 2d edition.
Grateful Indian. Evans. Worth while stories.
  Harper and Hamilton. Winding roads.
Grateful mouse. Aspinwall. Jataka tales.
Grateful sparrows. I. *See* 2d edition.
Grateful sparrows. II. *See* Swallow King's rewards.
Grateful squirrels. Metzger. Tales told in Korea.
Gratitude. *See* Grateful animals and ungrateful man.
Gray. *See also* Grey.
Gray hare. Bailey. Tell me another story.
Gray manikin. Olcott. Wonder tales from goblin hills.
Gray mare is the best. *See* Money makes the mare to go.
Great admiral. *See* Columbus, Christopher.
Great and the little fishes. Cooper. Argosy of fables.
Great artist. Eckford. Wonder windows.
Great battle. *See* Balor's defeat.
Great bear. I–III. *See* 2d edition.
Great bear. IV. *See* King Arthur's dream; Round Table,
  Founding of. II.
Great bear and the little bear. I. *See* Callisto and Arcis.
Great bear and the little bear. II. Eckford. Wonder win-
  dows. (Little bear and the big bear.)
  See also Great bear. III #.
Great bear in the sky. I–II. *See* 2d edition.

Great bear in the sky. III. Spence. Myths of the North American Indians. (Seven brothers. *In* Ch. 3.)
For other entries, see 2d edition.
Great bell. Allen. Story-teller's house. (Soul of the great bell.)
Gibson. Golden bird. (Story of the great bell of Pekin.)
See also Voice of the bell.
For other entries, see 2d edition.
Great-big=man. Newman. Fairy flowers.
Great chief of the animals. Lee. Folk tales of all nations.
See also Greedy cat.
Great Claus and Little Claus. *See* Little Claus and Big Claus.
Great dipper, Legend of. *See* Dipper.
Great dream. Kinscella. Music appreciation readers. Book 2.
Great festival. Martinez Del Rio. Sun, the moon and a rabbit.
Great flapjack griddle. Wadsworth. Paul Bunyan. (Paul's great flapjack griddle.)
Great flood. *See* Flood (Indian).
Great giant Bungah. Cooper, Tal. (*In* Ch. 19.)
Great god Wah=Nee=Chee's nonsense pot. Shannon. California fairy tales.
Great gray touring car. Emerson. Merry-go-round of modern tales.
Great head. I. Spence. Myths of the North American Indians. (Great head and the ten brothers. *In* Ch. 4.)
See also Widow and her seven sons.
For other entries, see 2d edition.
Great head. II. *See* Flying head.
Great head and the ten brothers. *See* Great head. I.
Great healing. *See* Orion.
Great King Eagle. Through story-land with the children.
Great hero Pulowech. *See* Pulowech and the sea maiden.
Great queen. *See* Tide jewels.
Great sea=serpent. Farjeon. Old sailor's yarn box.
Great shell of Broad House. Allen. Whispering wind.
Whitman. Navaho tales.
See also Eagles of opportunity.
Great stone face. Bailey. Stories children want.
Elson and Keck. Junior high school literature.
Field. American folk and fairy tales.
Hartshorne. Training in worship.
See also Old man of the mountain; Pipe of peace.
For other entries, see 2d edition.
Great stone fire eater. Lee. Folk tales of all nations.
For other entries, see 2d edition.
Great uncle Nathaniel's teeth. Canfield. Made-to-order stories. (Clover's story.)
Great walled country. *See* In the great walled country.

Great white bear. Harper. Ghosts and goblins.
Harriman. Stories for little children.
For other entries, see 2d edition.
Greatest=egg=beater=of=them=all. Emerson. Merry-go-round
of modern tales.
Greatest race that ever was. Skipper. Jungle meeting-pool.
(*In* Second meeting.)
Greatest thing in the world. Skipper. Jungle meeting-pool.
(*In* Third meeting.)
See also Rats and their son-in-law.
Grecian king and the physician Douban. Lee. Folk tales
of all nations. (Story of the Grecian king and the sage
Douban.)
For other entries, see 2d edition.
Grecian music contest. *See* Narcissus; Orpheus. II.
Greedy antelope. Broomell. Children's story caravan.
Greedy blackbird. *See* When the blackbird was white.
Greedy cat. I. Bailey. Stories children want.
Lee. Folk tales of all nations.
See also Great chief of the animals; Possible-impossible.
For other entries, see 2d edition.
Greedy cat. II. *See* Old woman's cat.
Greedy daughter. Lee. Folk tales of all nations.
Greedy jackal. ** Arnold. Book of good counsels. (Dead
game and the jackal.)
Cooper. Argosy of fables. (Death of the greedy jackal.)
For other entries, see 2d edition.
Greedy lad. Eells. Brazilian fairy book.
Greedy merchant. Katibah. Other Arabian nights.
Greedy priest. *See* Priest with the envious eyes. II.
Greedy raven. Carey. Stories of the birds.
Greedy shepherd. Bailey. Stories children wan   (Adapted.)
Starbuck. Enchanted paths.
For other entries, see 2d edition.
Greedy spider and the magpies. Berry. Black folk tales.
(Magpies and greedy spider.)
See also Spider and the crows #.
Greek minstrel's tale of the Trojan war. *See* Trojan war.
Greek princess and the young gardener. Adams and Atch-
inson. Book of princess stories.
For other entries, see 2d edition.
Green bird. I. *See* 2d edition.
Green bird. II. Housman. Moonshine and clover.
Housman. What-o'clock tales.
Green bird. III. Martens. Wonder tales from far away.
Green coat. Wahlenberg. Old Swedish fairy tales.
Green Corn, Yellow Corn, and the dancing fox. De Huff.
Taytay's tales.
Green Corn, Yellow Corn, and the two deer. De Huff.
Taytay's memories.
Green donkey. Cooper. Argosy of fables.

Green dragon. *See* Green serpent.
Green-feather, Adventures of. Kennedy. Red man's wonder book.
Green grass on the wall. Olcott. Wonder tales from windmill lands.
Green horse. Cooper. Tal. (*In* Ch. 6.)
Green kitten. Farjeon. Old sailor's yarn box.
Green lizard. Harriman. Stories for little children.
Green man of No Man's Land. Morris. Gypsy story teller.
See also Battle of the birds; Morraha.
Green page. Fyleman. Forty good-night stories.
Green parrot. De Huff. Taytay's memories.
Green sergeant. Eells. Brazilian fairy book.
Green serpent. I. Aulnoy. Fairy tales (Planché).
Dulac. Edmund Dulac's fairy book.
Fairy garland. (Dulac. Green dragon.)
Fuller. Book of dragons. (Green dragon.)
See also Beauty and the beast; Fountain of beauty.
For other entries, see 2d edition.
Green serpent. II. Purnell and Weatherwax. Talking bird. (Green serpents.)
Green shoes (poem). Field. Eliza and the elves.
Green shoes with buckles. Casserley. Michael of Ireland.
Green willow #.
See also Willow tree ghosts.
Greenies. Andersen. Fairy tales (Stickney). v. 1.
For other entries, see 2d edition.
Grendel the monster. *See* Beowulf.
Gretchen, Story of. Perkins and Danielson. Second year Mayflower program book.
Gretta's Christmas. Graham. Welcome Christmas.
Gretta's riches. Cook. To-day's stories of yesterday.
Grettir the Strong. Lanier. Book of giants. (Giant behind the waterfall.)
For other entries, see 2d edition.
Grey. *See also* Gray.
Grey hare. Casserley. Michael of Ireland.
Grey owl's feather. Casserley. Michael of Ireland.
Grey rabbit plays a trick. Hogner. Navajo winter nights.
Grief and his due. Æsop. Fables (Jones).
Griffin. Bulfinch. Golden age. (*In* Ch. 16.)
Griffin and the minor canon. Starbuck. Far horizons.
For other entries, see 2d edition.
Griffin, William (poem). Broomell. Children's story caravan. (True ballad of the extraordinary fortitude of William Griffin.)
Grim Griffin (poem). Adams and Atchinson. There were giants.
Grimpy Grumps. *See* Castle of frowns.
Grindelwald oath. Guerber. Legends of Switzerland. (*In* Bern.)

Grisell Baillie's sheep's head. Lang. Red true story book.
Grizel Cochrane. Chambers' miscellany. v. 5. (*In* Scottish traditionary stories.)
  Patten. Junior Classics. v. 7. (Adventure of Grizel Cochrane.)
Groac'h of the Isle of Loc. Harper. Ghosts and goblins. (Witch of Lok Island.)
  Masson. Folk tales of Brittany. (Witch of Lok Island.)
  For other entries, see 2d edition.
Grocery man. Mitchell. Here and now story book.
Grombuskin (poem). Buckingham. Elephant's friend.
Grotius, Hugo. Miller. My travelship: Holland. (Escape of Hugo de Groot.)
Groundhog's story. Buckingham. Great idea.
  See also Candlemas.
Ground pigeon. Brown. Curious book of birds.
Grumble corner. *See* Mr. Horner of Grumble corner.
Grumbler. Egan. New found tales. (Sowittan, the grumbler.)
Gryphon. *See* Griffin.
Guardians of the door. Canton. Child's book of saints.
Gubbaun Saor. *See* Gobborn seer.
Gubbaun Saor's secret. Young. Wonder smith and his son. (How the Gubbaun Saor went into the country of the ever young.)
Gudbrand of the dales. Lang. Red true story book.
Gudbrand on the hillside. *See* Dame Gudbrand.
Gudeman of Ballengeich. Fun folk and fairy tales.
  See also Cobbler and the king.
  For other entries, see 2d edition.
Gudrid the fair. Colum. Voyagers. (Children of Eric the Red.)
Guelphs, Origin of. *See* Beggar's curse.
Guests from Gibbet Island. Irving. Bold dragoon.
Guido and his pupil. Wheelock. Kindergarten children's hour. v. 4. (*In* Ch. 11.)
Guillaume's flute. Crownfield. Feast of Noel.
Guilty dogs. Broomell. Children's story caravan.
Guinea pig's tail. Baker. Tell them again tales.
Guinea-fowl and the hen. Cooper. Argosy of fables.
Guinea-hen and the crocodile. Cooper. Argosy of fables.
  See also Jackal and the crocodile.
Gull and the kite. Cooper. Argosy of fables.
Gullibles. Egan. New found tales.
  See also All women are alike.
Guilliver's travels. De La Mare and Quayle. Readings. (Abridged.)
  For other entries, see 2d edition.
Gulliver's travels: Brobdingnag. Patten. Junior classics. v. 5. (Gulliver in the land of the giants.)
  For other entries, see 2d edition.

Gulliver's travels: Lilliput land. Johnson and Scott. Anthology of children's literature. (Gulliver is taken captive.)
Patten. Junior classics. v. 5. (Gulliver is shipwrecked.)
Rich. Read-aloud book. (Voyage to Lilliput.)
For other entries, see 2d edition.
Gulnare of the sea, Story of. Arabian nights. Adventures of Haroun Er Raschid. (Olcott. Story of Gulnare of the Sea ; Story of Beder Basim, King of Persia.)
See also Queen Lab and the magic cakes.
For other entries, see 2d edition.
Gun for sale. Buckingham. Great idea.
Gunawolf. Fun folk and fairy tales. (Gunnewolf.)
For other entries, see 2d edition.
Gushtasp, Adventures of. Coit. Ivory throne of Persia.
Gustavus I of Sweden. *See* How Gustavus Vasa won his kingdom.
Guy Mannering. Patten. Junior classics. v. 5. (Abridged.)
Guy of Godolphin goes hunting. Lindsay. Choosing book.
Guy of Warwick. Barbour. English tales retold.
Darton. Wonder book of romance.
For other entries, see 2d edition.
Gwalana, the happy river. Egan. New found tales.
Gypsy. *See* Gipsy.
Gypsy and the dragon. *See* Stan Bolovan.

H

Ha! Ha! the kabouter mannikins. *See* Kabouter mannikins.
Haarlem. Olcott. Wonder tales from windmill lands. (Name of the City of Flowers.)
Habbitrot. *See* Habetrot and Scantlie Mab.
Habetrot and Scantlie Mab. Coussens. Diamond story book.
Choate and Curtis. Little people of the hills. (Habetrot with a distaff.)
Potter. Fairy caravan. (Habbitrot. *In*. Ch. 11.)
For other entries, see 2d edition.
Habetrot with a distaff. *See* Habetrot and Scantlie Mab.
Hacon. *See* King Hakon.
Hading, Adventures of. Adams. Swords of the Vikings. (Five adventures of Hading.)
This includes: Enemy forgiven ; Golden ring ; Hading dies for a friend ; Treacherous daughter ; Weariness of peace.
Hadrian and the aged planter. Schwarz. Jewish caravan.
Haensel and Grethel. *See* Hansel and Grethel.
Hafiz the stonecutter. *See* Stone cutter.
Hagoromo. *See* Robe of feathers.
Hags of the long tooth. De La Mare and Quayle. Readings.
Haida demi-gods. Spence. Myths of the North American Indians. (*In* Ch. 7.)
Hairy boggart. *See* Outwitting the bogie.

Hal o' the draft. Kipling. Rewards and fairies. (Wrong thing.)
Halcyon birds. Brown. Curious book of birds. (Halcyone.)
Bulfinch. Golden age. (Ceyx and Halcyone. *In* Ch. 9.)
Forbush. Myths and legends of Greece and Rome. (Ceyx and Halcyone.)
Lang. Books of myths. (Ceyx and Halcyone.)
Pyle. Tales from Greek mythology. (Ceyx and Halcyone.)
Rich. Why-so stories. (How the kingfisher came to be.)
For other entries, see 2d edition.
Halcyone. *See* Halcyon birds.
Half boys. Egan. New found tales.
Half=chick. Bailey. Stories children want. (Little Half Chick.)
Bruce. Treasury of tales for little folk.
Johnson and Scott. Anthology of children's literature.
Lee. Folk tales of all nations.
Martens. Wonder tales from far away. (Coquerico.)
Piper. Folk tales children love. (Little Half-chick.)
Piper. Road in storyland. (Little Half Chick.)
Starbuck. Familiar haunts. (Story of Coquerico.)
Tappan. Prince from nowhere. (Sad story of Halfcock.)
For other entries, see 2d edition.
Halibut's story. Gaer. Burning bush. (Miracle that happened to a fish.)
Hallowe'en. *See* Andrew Coffey #; *Broom; *Chestnut #; Cold lady #; Far Darrig in Donegal #; Jack-o'-lantern and the Indians #; *Jenny Pumpkin and the black witch; *Laughing Jack-o'-lantern; Man who did not believe in fairies; Mr. Bad 'Simmon Tree #; Peony lantern #; Simon and the black-gum tree #; Teig O'Kane and the corpse #; *Three pumpkins; Tomson's Hallowe'en; *Twilight fairy; *Twinkling Feet's Hallowe'en; Voyage of the red cap; Witch of Windy Hill.
For other entries, see 2d edition.
Hallowe'en adventure. Bailey. Wonderful tree.
Hallowe'en steeplechase. Teall. Batter and spoon fairies. (*In* Ch. 30.)
Hallowe'en story. I. Harriman. Stories for little children
For other entries, see 2d edition.
Haman. *See* Queen Esther.
Hamlet, prince of Denmark. Lamb. Tales from Shakespeare.
See also Amleth.
Hammer and saw and plane. Mitchell. Here and now story book.
Han and Kewan. Housman. What-o'clock tales.
Han Hsin. *See* High as Han Hsin; How little Han Hsin made princes laugh.

* Suitable for small children.

Handel, George Frederick. Kinscella. Music appreciation
readers. Book 2. (Handel and the spinet.)
Kinscella. Music appreciation readers. Book 3. (Famous
water music.)
Handful of clay. Blondell. Keepsakes.
See also Its mission.
For other entries, see 2d edition.
Hannibal, hero of Carthage. Baldwin. Thirty more fa-
mous stories.
Cooke. Stories of Rome.
Farjeon. Mighty men from Achilles to Julius Caesar. (Han-
nibal with the one eye.)
Miller. My book of history. v. 2. (Enemy of Rome. *In*
Ch. 9.)
Hanno. *See* Voyage of Hanno.
Hans. *See* Hans the shepherd boy. II.
Hans and his dog. Elson and Runkel. Child-library read-
ers. Book 2. (Prince, the faithful dog. Adapted.)
For other entries, see 2d edition.
Hans and the four giants. Arnold. Folk tales retold.
See also Five servants.
Hans and the north wind. *See* Lad who went to the north
wind.
Hans Brinker. Large. Famous children of storybook land.
(Abridged.)
See also Feast of St. Nicholas. II.
Hans Clodhopper. Coussens. Diamond story book. (Block-
head Hans.)
Johnson and Scott. Anthology of children's literature.
See also Boots and his brothers; Fool and the prince.
For other entries, see 2d edition.
Hans Hannekemaier. King. Golden cat head, and other
tales. (Golden cat head.)
Hans Hannekemaier in Hindeloopen. Miller. My travel-
ship: Holland.
Olcott. Wonder tales from windmill lands. (Three meals
shorten the day.)
Hans Hannekemaier in Middleburg. Miller. My travel-
ship: Holland.
Hans Hecklemann's luck. Starbuck. Far horizons.
For other entries, see 2d edition.
Hans in luck. Evans. Worth while stories.
Faulkner. Road to enchantment.
Hutchinson. Fireside stories. (Adapted.)
Lee. Folk tales of all nations.
For other entries, see 2d edition.
Hans my hedgehog. Grimm. Fairy tales (Paull).
Lang. Green fairy book. (Jack the hedgehog.)
Hans the hunter. Shimer. Fairyland. (Sister without a
name.)
For other entries, see 2d edition.

Hans the otherwise. Bennett. Pigtail of Ah Lee Ben Loo.
For other entries, see 2d edition.
Hans the shepherd boy. I. *See* 2d edition.
Hans the shepherd boy. II. Baker. Tell them again tales.
(Hans.)
Hans, who made the princess laugh. Power. Stories to
shorten the road.
See also Bristlepate and the sad princess.
For other entries, see 2d edition.
Hansel and Grethel. I. Arthur Rackham fairy book.
Bruce. Treasury of tales for little folk. (Hansel and
Gretel.)
Grimm. Fairy tales (Olcott. Haensel and Grethel.)
Grimm. Tales from Grimm (Wanda Gag, Hansel and
Gretel.)
Harper. Magic fairy tales. (Hansel and Grettel.)
Johnson and Scott. Anthology of children's literature.
Kinscella. Music appreciation readers. Book 4. (Hansel
and Gretel.)
Lang. Old friends among the fairies. (Hansel and Grettel.)
Lee. Folk tales of all nations.
Power. Blue caravan tales.
Quinn. Stokes' wonder book of fairy tales. (Hansel and
Gretel.)
Quinn. Stories for the six-year-old. (Hansel and Gretel.)
Rich. Read-aloud book. (Hansel and Gretel.)
See also Flight of Tiri.
For other entries, see 2d edition.
Hansel and Grethel. II. Cross. Music stories. (Hansel
and Gretel.)
Kinscella. Music appreciation readers. Book 4. (Fairy
opera.)
For other entries, see 2d edition.
Hansel and Grettel. *See* Hansel and Grethel.
Hanuman, the baboon god. Mukerji. Rama.
Happiest doll. Bowman. Little brown bowl.
Happy=boy. De Huff. Taytay's memories.
Happy Boz'll. Williams-Ellis. Fairies and enchanters.
Happy Brown Lady. Bowman. Little brown bowl.
Happy clothes=dryer #.
See also Fairy in the oak.
Happy elves. *See* Elves and the shoemaker.
Happy family. Andersen. Fairy tales (Stickney). v. 1.
Bailey. Tell me another story. (Adapted.)
For other entries, see 2d edition.
Happy forest. Housman. What-o'clock tales.
Happy=go=lucky Henery. Canfield. Made-to-order stories.
(Father's story.)
Happy little hobgoblin. Potter. Captain Sandman.
Happy little song. Blaisdell. Rhyme and story second
reader.

Happy man. Chidley. Fifty-two story talks.
Happy prince. Curry and Clippinger. Children's literature.
Harper. Merry Christmas to you.
Harper. Selfish giant.
Perkins and Danielson. Second year Mayflower program book.
Starbuck. Far horizons.
For other entries, see 2d edition.
Happy returns. Housman. Moonshine and clover.
Happy squirrel. Bryce. Short stories for little folks.
Hapsburgs, Origin of. *See* Castle of the hawk.
Harald. *See* Harold.
Harbour buoy's story. Marzials. Stories for the story hour. (Harbour buoy.)
Hardy Hardback. Williams-Ellis. Fairies and enchanters.
See also Ashiepattle and his goodly crew #.
Hardy tin soldier. *See* Brave tin soldier.
Hare afraid of his ears. I. Æsop. Fables (Whitman ed.).
Hare afraid of his ears. II. Carrick. Tales of wise and foolish animals. (Hare and his shadow.)
(poem). Cooper. Argosy of fables. (Hare's ears.)
See also Gift of swiftness.
Hare and his shadow. *See* Hare afraid of his ears. II.
Hare and many friends. *See* Hare with many friends.
Hare and the baboons. Worthington. Little wise one.
Hare and the badger. *See* Farmer and the badger.
Hare and the buffalo. Worthington. Little wise one.
Hare and the dog. Carrick. Animal picture tales from Russia.
Hare and the elephant. I. *See* Timid hare.
Hare and the elephant. II. Lee. Folk tales of all nations. (Hare and the elephants.)
Hare and the frog. *See* Hares and the frogs.
Hare and the frog, their mother-in-law and her daughter. Worthington. Little wise one.
Hare and the hedgehog. De La Mare. Told again.
Hutchinson. Fireside stories.
Piper. Road in storyland.
Told under the green umbrella. (Race between hare and hedgehog.)
Whiteman. Playmates in print. (Hedgehog and the hare.)
See also Deer and the snail; Frog and the antelope; How a turtle outwitted a wolf; How the gopher raced.
For other entries, see 2d edition.
Hare and the hound. Æsop. Fables (Jones).
Cooper. Argosy of fables.
For other entries, see 2d edition.
Hare and the lion. *See* Lion and the hare.
Hare and the partridge. La Fontaine. Fables (Tilney).
For other entries, see 2d edition.
Hare and the pig. Power. Bag o' tales. (Contest.)
For other entries, see 2d edition.

Hare and the python. Worthington. Little wise one.
Hare and the sparrow. Cooper. Argosy of fables.
Hare and the tortoise. I. Æsop. Fables (Artzybasheff).
Æsop. Fables (Jones).
Æsop. Fables (Whitman ed.).
Cooper. Argosy of fables.
(poem). Cooper. Argosy of fables.
Curry and Clippinger. Children's literature.
Johnson and Scott. Anthology of children's literature.
Kinscella. Music appreciation readers. Book 2. (Bunny
    Rabbit and turtle.)
Power. Bag o' tales.
See also Grasshopper and the snail; How turtle got his tail;
    Turtle and the fowl; Wolf and the hare.
For other entries, see 2d edition.
Hare and the tortoise. II. Worthington. Little wise one.
Hare and the wart-hog. Worthington. Little wise one.
Hare at the water hole. Worthington. Little wise one.
See also Lion and the hare; Tiger and the shadow.
Hare, hippopotamus and elephant. Carrick. Tales of wise
    and foolish animals.
See also Bruin and Reynard partners.
Hare, his father-in-law, and the tortoise. Worthington.
    Little wise one.
See also Mr. Rabbit nibbles up the butter.
Hare, his mother, and his master. Worthington. Little wise
    one.
Hare in the moon. I. Johnson and Scott. Anthology of chil-
    dren's literature. (Why there is a hare in the moon.)
For other entries, see 2d edition.
Hare in the moon. II. Aspinwall. Jataka tales. (Hare's
    self-sacrifice.)
Mukerji. Hindu fables. (Bunny in the moon.)
See also Old man of Teutli.
For other entries, see 2d edition.
Hare in the moon. III. *See* Moon's message #.
Hare in the moon. IV. Martinez Del Rio. Sun, the moon,
    and a rabbit. (Sun, the moon and a rabbit.)
Hare that ran away. *See* Timid hare.
Hare that was sent to York. Lee. Folk tales of all nations.
    (Of sending rent. *In* Wise men of Gotham.)
See also Wise men of Gotham.
For other entries, see 2d edition.
Hare, the buffalo, the lion, and the bees. Worthington. Lit-
    tle wise one.
Hare, the chickens, the dog, and the snake. Worthington.
    Little wise one.
Hare, the chickens, the goats, and the rats. Worthington.
    Little wise one.
Hare, the fox, and the wolf. Mackenzie. Jackal in Persia.
    (Story of the wolf, the hare and the fox.)
For other entries, see 2d edition.

Hare, the honey-bird, and the elephant. Worthington. Little wise one.

Hare, the lion, and the fleas. Worthington. Little wise one.

Hare, the lion, the antelopes, and the old woman. Worthington. Little wise one.

Hare, the lion, the hyena and the tortoïse. Worthington. Little wise one.

Hare, the lion, the man, and his dogs. Worthington. Little wise one.

Hare, the old man, the bull frog, the otter, the crocodile, and the hippopotamus. Worthington. Little wise one.

Hare, the otter, the old man and his daughter. Worthington. Little wise one.

Hare, the secretary bird, the owl, the hyena and the crocodile. Worthington. Little wise one.

See also Brother Rabbit and Mr. Wildcat.

Hare with many friends (poem). Cooper. Argosy of fables. (Hare and many friends.)

(poem). Curry and Clippinger. Children's literature.

Johnson and Scott. Anthology of children's literature.

For other entries, see 2d edition.

Hares and the foxes. Cooper. Argosy of fables.

For other entries, see 2d edition.

Hares and the frogs. Æsop. Fables (Artzybasheff).

Æsop. Fables (Jones).

Æsop. Fables (Whitman ed.).

Æsop. Twenty-four fables (L'Estrange).

Carrick. Still more Russian picture tales. (Hare and the frog.)

Cooper. Argosy of fables.

See also Fox and the rabbit; Hare's lip. I; Rabbit's self respect.

For other entries, see 2d edition.

Hares and the lions. Cooper. Argosy of fables.

Hare's ears. *See* Hare afraid of his ears. II.

Hare's lip. I. Hart. Picture tales from Holland.

See also Hares and the frogs; Rabbit's self respect.

Hare's lip. II. Lee. Folk tales of all nations. (How the hare got his split lip.)

Power. How it happened. (Why the hare has a split lip.)

Hare's lip. III. Parker. Skunny Wundy. (How the rabbit's lip was split.)

See also Moon's message #.

Hare's self sacrifice. *See* Hare in the moon. II.

Harkhuf, the explorer. Miller. My book of history. v. 1. (*In* Ch. 7.)

Harold Fair Hair. Dunla'p. Stories of the Vikings. (Why Harald would not cut his hair.)

Harold, King of England. *See* King Harold of England.

Haroun-Er-Raschid and the beautiful Zutulbe. *See* Robber Caliph.

Harp King Alfred played. *See* King Alfred.

Harp, Origin of. Colum. Big tree of Bunlahy. (First harp.)
Harp that saved England. *See* King Alfred.
Harper's promise. *See* Promise. II.
Harpies. Bulfinch. Golden age. (*In* Ch. 31.)
For other entries, see 2d edition.
Harping of Alawn Alawon. Morris. Book of the three dragons.
Hart and the vine. *See* Stag and the vine.
Harvest. *See* Bruin and Reynard partners. II.
Harvestin' o' Dermond. Dunbar. Sons o' Cormac.
Hary Janos. Schwimmer. Tisza tales.
Hasty word. Ralston. Russian fairy tales.
Hats for horses. Bianco. Street of little shops.
Haughty aspen (poem). Smith and Hazeltine. Christmas in legend and story.
Haughty butter=dealer. Lebermann. New German fairy tales.
Haughty slave. Aspinwall. Jataka tales.
Havelok the Dane. Barbour. English tales retold.
Darton. Wonder book of old romance.
For other entries, see 2d edition.
Hawk and mole. Wilson. Red magic.
Hawk and the fowl. *See* Hen and the falcon.
Hawk and the kite, Story of. Mackenzie. Jackal in Persia.
Hawk and the nightingale. Æsop. Fables (Jones. Nightingale and the hawk.)
Æsop. Fables (Whitman ed.).
(poem). Cooper. Argosy of fables. (Kite and the nightingale.)
For other entries, see 2d edition.
Hawk, the kite and the pigeons. Æsop. Fables (Jones).
See also Kite and the pigeons.
Hawks and their friends. Aspinwall. Jataka tales.
For other entries, see 2d edition.
Haydn, Joseph. Kinscella. Music appreciation readers. Book 2. (Little Joseph and the parade.)
Haystack cricket. · Sandburg. Rootabaga country.
Sandburg. Rootabaga pigeons.
Haze of Indian summer. *See* Indian summer.
Hazel nut. Marzials. Stories for the story hour.
Hazel scepter. Masson. Folk tales of Brittany.
Hazelnuts of long nourishment. Morris. Book of the three dragons.
He aimed high and hit the mark. McVenn. Good manners and right conduct. Book 2.
He of the little shell. *See* Morning star. I.
He who asks little receives much. Lee. Folk tales of all nations.
For other entries, see 2d edition.
He who picked up sticks. *See* Man in the moon. II.
Head and tail of the snake. *See* Tail of the serpent. I.
Head of brass. *See* Friar Bacon and the brazen head.

Head or tail. *See* Tail of the serpent. I.
Headdress of stars. Bailey. Stories from an Indian cave.
Headless princess. *See* Princess in the chest.
Heads of gold. *See* Prairie dandelion.
Healing waters. *See* Hidden waters.
Heart of the Bruce (poem). Patten. Junior classics. v. 10.
Heart's ease, Legend of. Carey. Flower legends. (*In* Pansy.)
    For other entries, see 2d edition.
Heathen who honored his father. **Gaster. Ma'aseh book. v. 1.
Heather blossoms. *See* How the blossoms came to the heather.
Heavens and the earth. *See* Earth and the sky.
Heaven-sought bride. *See* Ghost land. III.
Hebe and Ganymede. *See* Ganymede.
Hector. Bulfinch. Golden age. (*In* Ch. 27.)
    Farjeon. Mighty men from Achilles to Julius Caesar. (Death of Hector.)
    Forbush. Myths and legends of Greece and Rome. (*In* Trojan war : Hector and Achilles.)
    Power. Bag o' tales. (Slaying of Hector.)
    Rich. Read-aloud book. (Achilles and Hector.)
    For other entries, see 2d edition.
Hedge-king. *See* King Wren.
Hedgehog and the dog. Cooper. Argosy of fables.
Hedgehog and the hare. *See* Hare and the hedgehog.
Hedgehog who became a prince. *See* Prince Hedgehog.
Heidelberg adventure. Crew. Saturday's children. (Adventure in Heidelberg.)
Heidi. Large. Famous children of storybook land. (Abridged.)
Heifer and the ox. Æsop. Fables (Jones).
    Cooper. Argosy of fables.
Helena, St. *See* St. Helena.
Heliotrope. *See* Clytie.
Helmsman and the sailors. Cooper. Argosy of fables.
    See also Fishermen.
Helping hands. Housman. What-o'clock tales.
Hen, a heron and a deer. Martinez Del Rio. Sun, the moon and a rabbit.
Hen and the cat. I#. *See* Cat and the hen. I#.
    In 2d edition there are entries under each title.
Hen and the cat. II. Æsop. Fables (Artzybasheff).
    Cooper. Argosy of fables.
    See also Cat and the birds ; Hen and the fox.
Hen and the Chinese mountain turtle. Applegarth. Missionary stories for little folks. 1st series. (Turtle-tales and chicken tails.)
    For other entries, see 2d edition.
Hen and the falcon. Mackenzie. Jackal in Persia. (Hawk and the fowl.)
    For other entries, see 2d edition.

Hen and the fox. Æsop. Fables (Whitman ed.).
See also Hen and the cat. II.
For other entries, see 2d edition.
Hen and the snake. De Leeuw. Java jungle tales.
See also Crow and the snake. II.
Hen and the swallow. Cooper. Argosy of fables.
For other entries, see 2d edition.
Hen that laid golden eggs. Curry and Clippinger. Children's literature. (Hen with the golden eggs.)
See also Goose that laid golden eggs.
Hen that laid diamonds. Cowles. Stories to tell.
Hen with the golden eggs. *See* Hen that laid golden eggs.
Hengist and Horsa, Adventures of. Farjeon. Men of might from Beowulf to William the Conqueror. (Kings of Kent.)
Olcott. Wonder tales from windmill lands.
Henny Penny. *See* Chicken Little.
Hens' Christmas picnic. Potter. Fairy caravan. (*In* Ch. 14.)
Hephaestus. *See* Vulcan.
Her blanket. I. Cross. Music stories.
Her blanket. II. Eckford. Wonder windows. (Navajo blanket.)
Her blanket. I–II. *See also* Indian's blanket; Rugmakers.
Her father's daughter. *See* Maid of Zaragoza.
Her friend and her flag. *See* Joan of Arc's banner.
Her roadway. Eggleston. Stories for special days in the church school.
See also Road of the loving heart.
Herb of fear. Farjeon. Italian peepshow.
Herbert Jones, P. C. and the fairy. Fyleman. Forty goodnight tales.
Hercules and Deianeira. Bailey. Tell me another story. (Horn of plenty.)
Bulfinch. Golden age. (*In* Hercules. Ch. 19.)
Bulfinch. Golden age. (Achelous and Hercules. *In* Ch. 23.)
For other entries, see 2d edition.
Hercules and his labors. Adams and Atchinson. Book of giant stories. (Pygmies.)
Adams and Atchinson. There were giants. (Three golden apples.)
Bryant. Children's book of celebrated legends. (Mares of Diomed.)
Bryant. Children's book of celebrated legends. (Hercules killing Nessus.)
Bulfinch. Golden age. (Hercules. *In* Ch. 19.)
Curtis. Stories in trees. (Tree with strange apples.)
Forbush. Myths and legends of Greece and Rome. (Hercules the strongest man.)
Forbush. Myths and legends of Greece and Rome. (Pygmies and the cranes.)
Johnson and Scott. Anthology of children's literature. (Three golden apples.)

Hercules and his labors—*continued.*
Kinney. Stars and their stories. (Strongest man in the world; Garden and the dragon.)
Pyle. Tales from Greek mythology. (Labors of Hercules.)
Rich. Read-aloud book. (Story of the twelve labors of Hercules.)
Williamson. Stars through magic casements. (Twelve labors of Hercules.)
See also Spinning-wheel of Omphale.
For other entries, see 2d edition.

Hercules and Minerva. *See* Hercules and Pallas.

Hercules and Pallas. Æsop. Fables (Jones. Hercules and Minerva.)
Æsop. Fables (Whitman ed.).
For other entries, see 2d edition.

Hercules and Plutus. Æsop. Fables (Jones).
For other entries, see 2d edition.

Hercules and the carter. *See* Hercules and the wagoner.

Hercules and the wagoner. Æsop. Fables (Artzybasheff).
Æsop. Fables (Jones).
Cooper. Argosy of fables.
Johnson and Scott. Anthology of children's literature. (Hercules and the carter.)
Power. Bag o' tales. (Put your shoulder to the wheel.)
For other entries, see 2d edition.

Hercules' choice. Bulfinch. Golden age. (*In* Hercules. Ch. 19.)

Herd boy and the weaving maiden. Phillips. Far peoples. (Cowboy and his fairy.)
For other entries, see 2d edition.

Herdboy and the weaver. *See* Sky bridge of birds.

Herdsman and the lost bull. Æsop. Fables (Jones).

Here's a piece that wad please a brownie. *See* Brownie and the thievish maids.

Hereward. Cruse. Young folk's book of epic heroes.

Hermann the Deliverer. Lansing. Great moments in freedom. (Barbarian against empire.)

Hermes and Apollo. Cather. Pan and his pipes. (Tortoise that gave the world music.)
Forbush. Myths and legends of Greece and Rome. (Mercury the mischievous.)
For other entries, see 2d edition.

Hermes goes to Pluto's kingdom. *See* Charon.

Hermes Trismegistus. Colum. Boy apprenticed to an enchanter. (*In* Story of Bird-of-gold.)

Hermit. **Voltaire. Zadig. (*In* Ch. 17.)
For other entries, see 2d edition.

Hermit and the mouse. *See* Mouse king's story; Mouse who became a tiger; So born, so die.

Hermit of the pillar. Canton. Child's book of saints.

Hermit, the thief, and the demon. Lee. Folk tales of all nations. (Brahman, the thief, and the ghost.)
For other entries, see 2d edition.
Hermod and Hadvor. Coussens. Diamond story book.
For other entries, see 2d edition.
Hero and Leander. Bulfinch. Golden age. (*In* Ch. 13.)
Pyle. Tales from Greek mythology.
See also Orrelana, Story of.
For other entries, see 2d edition.
Hero of the woods. *See* Bunyan, Paul.
Hero twins. I. Adams and Atchinson. There were giants.
Lanier. Book of giants. (Fatal pride of Vukub.)
Lee. Folk tales of all nations. (Vukub-Cakix, the great macaw.)
Miller. My book of history. v. 4. (*In* Story of creation. Ch. 10.)
For other entries, see 2d edition.
Herod and the bubbles. Darton. Wonder book of old romance.
Heroine of France. *See* Joan of Arc.
Heroine of Monmouth. *See* Molly Pitcher.
Heron and the crab. *See* Crane and the crab.
Heron and the crow. *See* Beware of bad company. II.
Herons and the mongoose, Story of. **Arnold. Book of good counsels.
Cooper. Argosy of fables.
See also Frog, the crab and the serpent.
Herons, Story of. Housman. Moonshine and clover.
Hero's tasks. Aspinwall. Jataka tales.
Herr Korbes #.
See also Krencipal and Krencipalka.
Hester's Easter offering. Evans. Worth while stories.
Hestia. *See* Vesta.
"Heyo, house" #.
See also Lion and the jackal.
Hiawatha. Cather. Pan and his pipes. (Songs of Hiawatha.)
Morris. Stories from mythology: North American. Ch. 6.
Spence. Myths of the North American Indians. (*In* Ch. 4.)
For other entries, see 2d edition.
Hickamore and Hackamore. Marzials. Stories for the story hour. (Sunbeams.)
Hick'ry pick=tooth. Field. American folk and fairy tales.
Mackaye. Tall tales of the Kentucky mountains.
Hidden Laiva. *See* Golden ship.
Hidden maiden. Olcott. Wonder tales from Baltic wizards.
Hidden treasure. I. See 2d edition.
Hidden treasure. II. Gaer. Magic flight.
Hidden waters. Lee. Folk tales of all nations. (Healing waters.)
Spence. Myths of the North American Indians. (Healing waters. *In* Ch. 4.)
For other entries, see 2d edition.

Hidesato of the rice bale. *See* Lord Bag of Rice.
Hiding of the church bell. Starbuck. Familiar haunts. (*In* Wise men of Gotham.)
For other entries, see 2d edition.
High as Han Hsin. Chrisman. Shen of the sea.
See also How little Han Hsin made princes laugh.
High emprise for the cuirass. Maspero. Popular stories of ancient Egypt.
High emprise for the throne of Amon. Maspero. Popular stories of ancient Egypt.
High Hop Low Lee. Burnett. Children's book.
High king of Ireland. *See* Destruction of Da Derga's hostel.
High tea. Broomell. Children's story caravan.
Highwayman and the priest. Cooper. Argosy of fables.
Hilarion. Skinner. Christmas stories. (Christmas legend.)
Hilary. *See* St. Hilary.
Hildebrand. Untermeyer. Donkey of God. (*In* Ravello, Salerno, Paestum.)
Hill. Cowles. Stories to tell.
Richards. Golden windows.
Hill of the fairy calf. Choate and Curtis. Little people of the hills.
For other entries, see 2d edition.
Hillman and the housewife. Bailey. Tell me another story. (Magic saucepan. Adapted.)
Harriman. Stories for little children. (Adapted.)
Hutchinson. Candlelight stories.
Johnson and Scott. Anthology of children's literature.
For other entries, see 2d edition.
Hina, the woman in the moon. Howes. Long bright land. (Marama and Ina.)
Metzger. Tales told in Hawaii. (Woman in the moon.)
For other entries, see 2d edition.
Hina's voyage. Colum. Bright islands. (How Hina voyaged to the island of the king of the fishes.)
Price. Legends of the seven seas. (Ina, the fairy voyager.)
Hind in the forest. Aulnoy. Fairy tales. (Planché. Hind in the wood.)
Dulac. Edmund Dulac's fairy book. (Hind of the wood.)
Wilson. Red magic. (Enchanted hind.)
For other entries, see 2d edition.
Hind in the wood. *See* Hind in the forest.
Hind of the golden apple. Lee. Folk tales of all nations.
Hind of the wood. *See* Hind in the forest.
Hinemoa. Howes. Long bright land.
Hi'nun. Spence. Myths of the North American Indians. (*In* Ch. 4.)
Hinzelmann. Bancroft. Goblins of Haubeck.
See also Slapdash and slambang.
For other entries, see 2d edition.
Hippocras. Darton. Wonder book of old romance. (Physician and his cousin.)

Hippogriff. Echols. Knights of Charlemagne. (Winged horse; Orc and the Hippogriff.)

Hippolyta, Queen of the Amazons. Bulfinch. Age of fable. (*In* Hercules. Ch. 19.)

Hiram, King of Tyre. Gaer. Burning bush. (*In* Man who thought he was a god.)
For other entries, see 2d edition.

His Christmas turkey. Walters. Book of Christmas stories.

History of, etc. *See* the first important word of the title.

Hobby of Hugh Midity. Shannon. California fairy tales.

Hobyahs. Bailey. Stories children want.
Through story-land with the children.
For other entries, see 2d edition.

Hodgepodge hold=fast. Olcott. Wonder tales from windmill lands.
See also Golden goose; Monkey's bargains #; Rat's wedding; Travels of a fox.

Hofus the stone=cutter. *See* Stone-cutter.

Hog inn=and=out ag'in! Mackaye. Tall tales of the Kentucky mountains.

Hok Lee and the dwarfs. Coussens. Diamond story book.
Freeman. Child-story readers. 3d reader.
For other entries, see 2d edition.

Hokusai. Eckford. Wonder windows. (Great artist.)

Holbein. Chambers' miscellany. v. 9. (Hans Holbein. *In* Anecdotes of the early painters.)

Hole among the rocks. Casserley. Whins on Knockattan.

Hole and three. Buckingham. Great idea.

Holidays are busy days. Bailey. Tell me another story. (Holiday.)

Hollow tree store. De La Mare and Quayle. Readings.

Holly. I. Marzials. Stories for the story hour.
Skinner. Child's book of country stories.
For other entries, see 2d edition.

Holly. II. Newman. Fairy flowers.

Holly=tree elf. Elson and Runkel. Child-library readers. Book 2.

Holy bird. *See* Nightingale. IV.

Holy Child of Chimayo. Otero. Old Spain in our Southwest.

Holy Cross. Untermeyer. Donkey of God.

Holy Grail. Allen. Tales from Shakespeare.
Cather. Pan and his pipes.
See also King Arthur; Lohengrin; Sir Galahad; Sir Percival.
For other entries, see 2d edition.

Holy man and the Darwesh. Mackenzie. Jackal in Persia.

Holy night. I. *See* Shepherd's gift.

Holy night. II. *See* 2d edition.

Holy night. III. Menefee. Child stories.

Holy Sunday. *See* Why the swallow lives in warm climates.

Home=bred boy. Lee. Folk tales of all nations. (Story of the home-bred boy.)

Home is home. Blaisdell. Rhyme and story second reader.

Homeless spirit. Metzger. Tales told in Hawaii.
Homes a=fire. Olcott. Wonder tales from windmill lands.
Honest ass. **Gaster. Ma'aseh book. v. 1. (Honest ass of R. Jose.)
Honest Ben. Blaisdell. Log cabin days.
Honest bootblack. White. School management, p. 252.
Honest coin. Bowman. Little brown bowl.
Honest penny. Rasmussen. East o' the sun and west o' the moon. (Righteous penny.)
See also Dick Whittington and his cat.
For other entries, see 2d edition.
Honest woodman. Æsop. Fables (Jones. Mercury and the woodman.)
Cooper. Argosy of fables. (Mercury and the woodman.)
Curry and Clippinger. Children's literature. (Mercury and the woodman.)
Olcott. Wonder tales from Baltic wizards. (Poor man and Never-enough.)
For other entries, see 2d edition.
Honesty and dishonesty. See Rogue and the simpleton.
Honesty the best policy. White. School management, p. 276.
For other entries, see 2d edition.
Hong Kil Tong. Metzger. Tales told in Korea.
This includes: Gil Dong, the boy; Gil Dong, the outlaws, and the monks; Gil Dong and the king; Gil Dong and the captive maid.
For other entries, see 2d edition.
Honi the circle maker. See Praying for rain. I.
Honi=ha=Me'aggel. See Praying for rain. I; Sleep of one hundred years.
Honied clover. Johnson and Scott. Anthology of children's literature.
Honour, fire and water. Cooper. Argosy of fables.
Hoodie=crow. Lee. Folk tales of all nations. (Tale of the hoodie.)
For other entries, see 2d edition.
Hop=o'=my=Thumb. I. Arthur Rackham fairy book.
Brock. Book of fairy tales.
Lang. Old friends among the fairies. (Little Thumb.)
Mackenzie. Book of nursery tales.
Quinn. Stokes' wonder book of fairy tales.
For other entries, see 2d edition.
Hope. See Pandora.
Hoppaway. Fyleman. Forty good-morning tales.
Hoppie's famous kick. Nakazawa. Weaver of the frost.
Horatius at the bridge. Cooke. Stories of Rome. (Heroes of early Rome.)
Lansing. Great moments in freedom. (In Driving the kings out of Rome.)
(poem). Patten. Junior classics. v. 10.
(poem). Power. Children's treasure chest.

Horatius at the bridge—*continued.*
Terry. Tales from far and near. (Keeping of the bridge.)
For other entries, see 2d edition.
Horn, Adventures of. Barbour. English tales retold.
Horn of plenty. *See* Hercules and Deianeira.
Horned animals give a party. Babbitt. Animals' own story
book.
See also Why the dog and cat are enemies.
Horned viper that spoke to the hooked lizard. Lobagola.
Folk tales of a savage.
Horned women. Curry and Clippinger. Children's litera-
ture.
Lee. Folk tales of all nations.
See also Fire! fire! fire!
For other entries, see 2d edition.
Horns of the black goat. Casserley. Whins on Knockattan.
Horoscope. La Fontaine. Fables (Tilney).
See also Æschylus and his destiny; King's son and the painted
lion.
Horse. *See* Mazeppa.
Horse and a hog. *See* Horse and the hog.
Horse and an ass. *See* Horse and the ass. I.
Horse and his rider. I. Æsop. Fables (Jones).
For other entries, see 2d edition.
Horse and his rider. II. *See* Soldier and his horse.
Horse and the ass. I. Æsop. Fables (Artzybasheff).
Æsop. Fables (Jones).
Æsop. Twenty-four fables. (L'Estrange. Horse and an
ass.)
Æsop. Fables (Whitman ed.).
Cooper. Argosy of fables. (Charger and the ass; Horse and
the ass.)
For other entries, see 2d edition.
Horse and the ass. II. Cooper. Argosy of fables.
Horse and the groom. Æsop. Fables (Artzybasheff).
Æsop. Fables (Jones).
Cooper. Argosy of fables.
For other entries, see 2d edition.
Horse and the hog. Æsop. Twenty-four fables. (L'Estrange.
Horse and a hog.)
For other entries, see 2d edition.
Horse and the lion. Æsop. Fables (Artzybasheff).
For other entries, see 2d edition.
Horse and the loaded ass. Æsop. Fables (Jones. Ass and
the mule.)
Æsop. Twenty-four fables (L'Estrange. Laden ass and a
horse.)
Cooper. Argosy of fables.
For other entries, see 2d edition.
Horse and the stag. Æsop. Fables (Jones).
Æsop. Fables (Whitman ed.).
Cooper. Argosy of fables.

Horse and the stag—*continued.*
For other entries, see 2d edition.
Horse and the wild boar. Æsop. Fables (Artzybasheff).
Horse Gullfaxi and the sword Gunnfoder. Lang. Old friends among the fairies.
For other entries, see 2d edition.
Horse=headed monster. Pogány. Hungarian fairy book.
Horse of Siena. Untermeyer. Donkey of God.
Horse that aroused the town. *See* Bell of Atri.
Horse that b'leeved he'd get there. Broomell. Children's story caravan.
See also Little engine that could.
For other entries, see 2d edition.
Horse with the hump. Housman. What-o'clock tales.
Horses of King Manus. Colum. Boy apprenticed to an enchanter.
Horses with wings. *See* Pelops.
Horseshoe of Luck. Lawrence. Magic of the horseshoe, p. 107. (Abridged.)
For other entries, see 2d edition.
Horus the Hawk. *See* Isis and Osiris.
Hound and the fox. Æsop. Fables (Jones).
Hound and the hare. Æsop. Fables (Jones).
Cooper. Argosy of fables.
Hound of the Hill of Spears. MacManus. Donegal wonder book.
House built of beautiful men and women. Metzger. Tales told in Hawaii.
House=dog and the wolf. *See* Dog and the wolf.
House in the forest. Wolff. Pale mountains.
House in the storm. Casserley. Whins on Knockattan.
House in the valley of the yew tree. Young. Tangle-coated horse.
House in the wood. Grimm. Fairy tales (Olcott. Little house in the wood.)
Johnson and Scott. Anthology of children's literature. (Hut in the forest.)
Ransome. Old Peter's Russian tales. (Hut in the forest.)
Williams. Tales from Ebony.
For other entries, see 2d edition.
In 2d edition this story is also indexed under the title "Hut in the forest."
House lady. Housman. Turn again tales.
House of beautiful days. Elson and Runkel. Child-library readers. Book 2. (Magic ladder. Adapted.)
For other entries, see 2d edition.
House of cards. Nemcova. Disobedient kids.
House of Crom Duv. *See* Crom Duv. the giant.
House that burned down. Miller. My travelship: Japan.
House that grew up. Fyleman. Tea time tales.

House that Jack built. Curry and Clippinger. Children's literature. (This is the house that Jack built.)
(poem). Johnson and Scott. Anthology of children's literature.
For other entries, see 2d edition.
House that would not stay still. Emerson. Merry-go-round of modern tales.
How a bird made the world. See Creation of the world (Indian).
How a clever cottager outwitted seven thieves. See Magic cap.
How a cloister came to Utrecht. Olcott. Wonder stories from windmill lands. (Blooming fruiting winter.)
How a fairy breeze helped. Cook. To-day's stories of yesterday.
How a fish swam in the air and a hare in the water. Harper. Fillmore folk tales. (Susan Walker, what a talker.)
Lee. Folk tales of all nations. (Fish in the forest.)
For other entries, see 2d edition.
How a fishbone and a princess started Michael on a career. Dorey. Three and the moon.
How a flute saved Wee Lamb. See Wolf and the kid. II.
How a girl saved a fort. See Zane, Betty.
How a man found his wife in the land of the dead. Lee. Folk tales of all nations.
See also Ghost land.
How a man was bewitched. Mitford. Tales of old Japan. (How a man was bewitched and had his head shaved by the foxes.)
How a plowman won a battle. Kinscella. Music appreciation readers. Book 6.
How a sensible peasant cured his wife's curiosity. See Language of beasts.
How a single bunny overcame a herd of elephants. See Rabbits and the elephants.
How a skyscraper and a railroad train got picked up. Sandburg. Rootabaga pigeons.
How a strong castle was taken. See Black Douglas.
How a town was named. Phillips. Far peoples.
How a turtle fooled a little boy. Babbitt. Animals' own story book.
Lee. Folk tales of all nations. (Tortoise.)
See also How the monkeys escaped being eaten.
How a wall was built around Asgard. See Giant builder.
How Alexander the king got the water of life #.
See also Alexander the Great. II.
How Alfred made the peace. See King Alfred; King Alfred and Guthrum #.
How animals came into the world. Woodson. African myths.
See also Borah of Byami.

How an old man lost his wen. *See* Man with the wen.

How Ariadne helped Theseus. *See* Theseus.

How arrow heads came. Bailey. Stories from an Indian cave.
See also Rabbit scatters Flint to the winds; Why the flint rock cannot fight back.

How Arthur became king. *See* King Arthur's coming.

How Arthur proved his kingship. *See* King Arthur's coming.

How Aunya tricked Balor's messenger. Young. Wonder smith and his son. (How the djinn . . . brought a message.)
See also Gobborn seer #.

How badger won a race. Hogner. Navajo winter nights.
See also Animal races.

How Bambi found the meadow. *See* Bambi.

How Beowulf came to Daneland. *See* Beowulf.

How Bimbo the Snip's thumb stuck to his nose. Sandburg. Rootabaga stories.

How Black Agnes kept her castle. *See* Black Agnace of Dunbar.

How black became white. Eells. Fairy tales from Brazil.

How Blanca the haughty became gentle. Gunterman. Castles in Spain.
See also King Thrushbeard.

How Bozo the Button Buster busted all his buttons. Sandburg. Rootabaga pigeons.
Sandburg. Rootabaga country.

How Brother Rabbit fooled the whale and the elephant. *See* How the elephant and the whale were tricked. I.

How Bruin the bear sped with Reynard the fox. *See* How Bruin tried to bring Reynard to court.

How Bruin tried to bring Reynard to court. Curry and Clippinger. Children's literature. (How Bruin the bear sped with Reynard the fox.)
Miller. My book of history. v. 3. (Reynard and Bruin. *In* Ch. 11.)

How bunny was named. Whiteman. Playmates in print.

How buttercups came #.
See also First buttercups.

How butterflies came. I. *See* 2d edition.

How butterflies came. II. Hogner. Navajo winter nights. (White butterfly boy and rain boy.)

How Cajusse was married. Lee. Folk tales of all nations.
See also Aladdin.

How Cassim became king. *See* Cassim.

How Catherine Douglas tried to save King James of Scotland.
Patten. Junior classics. v. 7.

How cats came to purr. Bennett. Pigtail of Ah Lee Ben Loo. For other entries, see 2d edition.

How Chief Bear lost his tail. *See* Why the bear has a stumpy tail.

How Ching and Anam and Menes counted. Smith. Number stories of long ago.

How chipmunk got small feet. Hogner. Navajo winter nights. (Gila monster's tobacco ranch ; or, How chipmunk got small feet.)

How color came to the redbird. Bailey. Stories from an Indian cave.

See also How the birds got their colors.

How Columbus got his ships. *See* Columbus, Christopher.

How Conor became King of Ulster. *See* Fergus MacRogh and the kingship of Ulster.

How Cormac lost his kingdom. Dunbar. Sons o' Cormac.

See also Constant green jerkin.

How Cormac MacArt went to faery. Colum. Big tree of Bunlahy. (King Cormac's cup.)

Rolleston. High deeds of Finn. (Disappearance of Cormac.)

For other entries, see 2d edition.

How corn and beans came to be. I. *See* 2d edition.

How corn and beans came to be. II. Bailey. Stories from an Indian cave. (Three sisters.)

See also First corn. X.

How coyote got yellow eyes. *See* Coyote's eyes. II.

How coyote got white spots on his nose. Hogner. Navajo winter nights.

How coyote happened to make the black moss food. Garett. Coyote stories.

How coyote's fur grew rough. Hogner. Navajo winter nights.

How Cuchulain got his name. *See* Cuhulain.

How Cuchulain went to fairyland. *See* Fairy swan-maidens.

How Cuchulain wooed his wife. *See* Courtship of Emer.

How curiosity killed the cat. Shannon. Eyes for the dark. (Hugh Midity tells a story.)

How daisy chains came. Cook. To-day's stories of yesterday.

For other entries, see 2d edition.

How dandelions were made. Power. How it happened.

How Deep Red Roses goes back and forth. Sandburg. Rootabaga pigeons.

How deer won his antlers. I. *See* Deer and the rabbit.

How deer won his antlers. II. Hogner. Navajo winter nights. (February, the month of no horns ; or, How deer won his antlers.)

De Huff. Taytay's memories. (Animal races.)

How Dippy the Wisp and Slip Me Liz came in the moonshine. Sandburg. Rootabaga pigeons.

How emeralds came. Phillips. Far peoples.

How Esther became queen. *See* Queen Esther.

How Finn obtained the tooth of knowledge. Young.
Tangle-coated horse. (Silver pool.)
See also Finn MacCool.

How fire came to the cave people. *See* How fire was brought
to the Indians. VI.

How fire came to the earth. I–II. *See* 2d edition.

How fire came to the earth. III. *See* Wren who brought
fire.

How fire came to the earth. IV. Phillips. Indian tales for
little folks. (How the fire got into the rocks and trees.)
See also Daylight, Origin of. IV.

How fire was brought to the Indians. I. Cowles. Stories
to tell.
Lee. Folk tales of all nations. (Origin of fire.)
For other entries, see 2d edition.

How fire was brought to the Indians. II. Carey. Stories
of the birds. (Good-natured raven.)
For other entries, see 2d edition.

How fire was brought to the Indians. III. Morris. Stories
from mythology: North American. (Theft of fire. *In*
Ch. 7.)
For other entries, see 2d edition.

How fire was brought to the Indians. IV–V. *See*
2d edition.

How fire was brought to the Indians. VI. Bailey. Stories
from an Indian cave. (How fire came to the cave people.)
James. Happy animals of Atagahi. (First fire.)
Rich. Why-so stories. (How the water spider brought the
fire.)

How fire was brought to the Indians. VII. Hervey and
Hix. Fanciful tales for children. (Fire bird.)

How fire was brought to the Indians. I–VII.
For other versions, *see* Fire, Origin of; Mis' Swallow;
Wren who brought fire.

How five little angels lost their wings. Stewart. Tell me
a story I never heard before.

How flax was given to men. Power. How it happened.
(How flax was given to the world.)
Pyle. Tales from Norse mythology. (Frigg's gift.)
For other entries, see 2d edition.

How Fox and Raccoon tricked one another. Parker.
Skunny Wundy and other Indian tales.

How Frey won a bride and lost a sword. *See* Wooing of
Gerd.

How Genetaska deserted her trust. Partridge. Joyful Star.
Spence. Myths of the North American Indians. (Peace
queen. *In* Ch. 4.)
See also White goddess.

How George the tadpole lost his tail. Freeman. Child-story
readers. 3d reader.

How Jack went to seek his fortune. Hutchinson. Candle-light stories.
  Steel. English fairy tales. (How Jack went out to seek his fortune.)
  For other entries, see 2d edition.
How Jaffa was captured. Baikie. Wonder tales of the ancient world. (How Tahuti took the town of Joppa.)
  **Maspero. Popular stories of ancient Egypt. (How Thutiyi took the city of Joppa.)
  Vilnay. Legends of Palestine.
  See also Ali Baba and the forty thieves.
How Joeagah, the raccoon, ate the crabs. Parker. Skunny Wundy and other Indian tales.
How Johnny the Wham sleeps . . . and Joe the Wimp shines. Sandburg. Rootabaga pigeons.
How Kahukura learned to make nets. Lee. Folk tales of all nations. (Huia; or, The tale of the fishing net.)
  See also Fairy nets; Laka and the menehunes.
  For other entries, see 2d edition.
How Kana brought back the sun, moon and stars. Colum. Bright islands.
  See also Little Bear #.
How Kitty used her umbrella. Burnett. Children's book.
How K'tonton drove Satan out of the shofar. Weilerstein. Adventures of K'tonton.
How K'tonton entertained holy guests in his succah. Weilerstein. Adventures of K'tonton.
How K'tonton masqueraded on Purim. Weilerstein. Adventures of K'tonton.
How K'tonton prayed for rain. *See* Praying for rain. II.
How K'tonton rejoiced and was merry on Simhath Torah. Weilerstein. Adventures of K'tonton.
How K'tonton saved the birds on Shabbath Shirah. Weilerstein. Adventures of K'tonton.
How K'tonton sent his tree a Shanah Tovah. Weilerstein. Adventures of K'tonton.
How K'tonton took a ride on a chopping knife and wished he hadn't. Weilerstein. Adventures of K'tonton.
  See also Tom Thumb; Thumbling.
How K'tonton was forgiven on Yom Kippur. Weilerstein. Adventures of K'tonton.
How K'tonton went to synagogue and swung on a lulav. Weilerstein. Adventures of K'tonton.
How K'tonton wished a wish on Shevouth night. Weilerstein. Adventures of K'tonton.
How Lawiswis was rescued by the white roses. *See* Why roses have thorns. II.
How Leif the Lucky found Vineland the Good. *See* Leif Ericson.
How little bunny rabbit caught the sun. *See* Sun a prisoner. II.

How little Duke Jarl saved the castle. Housman. Moonshine and clover.

How little Hans Hsin made princes laugh. Fun folk and fairy tales.
See also High as Hans Hsin.
For other entries, see 2d edition.

How little Peter saved the life of Peter the Great. Burnett. Children's book.

How little prairie dog was made. Hogner. Navajo winter nights.

How Livia won the brooch. Patten. Junior classics. v. 7.

How Loki saved a peasant's son. *See* Skrymsli.

How Loki stole a necklace. Pyle. Tales from Norse mythology.
See also Freyja ; Heimdall and Loki.

How maize was given to the Red Indians. *See* First corn. III.

How maple sugar came. I. *See* 2d edition.

How maple sugar came. II. Bailey. Stories children want.
For other entries, see 2d edition.

How Marduk created the world. Miller. My book of history. v. 1. (*In* Ch. 11.)

How Margaret led Faust through the perfect world. Menefee. Child stories.

How Master Rabbit gave himself airs. *See* How rabbit lost his tail. II.

How Master Rabbit went fishing. Leland. Algonquin legends. (Amazing adventures of Master Rabbit.)
For other entries, see 2d edition.

How Master Rabbit went to a wedding. *See* How rabbit lost his tail. II.

How Master Renard enticed Ysegrim to eat the moon. *See* Fox in the well.

How Master Renard persuaded Master Ysegrim to enter Holy Orders. Dorey. Three and the moon.
See also Why the bear has a stumpy tail.

How Master Renard tricked three fishermen. *See* Hungry fox and his breakfast.

How Maui fished up the great island. Howes. Long bright land. (Maui and the fish.)
Metzger. Tales told in Hawaii. (Why the Hawaiian islands are in a row.)
For other entries, see 2d edition.

How Maui lifted up the sky #.
See also Earth and sky.

How Maui snared the sun. *See* Sun a prisoner. V.

How Maui strove to win immortality for men. Howes. Long bright land. (Maui and death.)
Metzger. Tales told in Hawaii. (Laugh of the swamp-rail.)
See also Why we do not live forever on this earth.
For other entries, see 2d edition.

How Maui won a place for himself in the house. Howes.
Long bright land. (Maui's boyhood.)
Metzger. Tales told in Hawaii. (Maui the baby.)
For other entries, see 2d edition.
How men rebelled against the Sun=god. Baikie. Wonder
tales of the ancient world.
How Michael fought Gunhild, the Dane. Dorey. Three and
the moon.
How Miska got married. Pogány. Magyar fairy tales.
How Mr. Rabbit lost his fine bushy tail. James. Happy
animals of Atagahi. (Rabbit and possum lose their tails.)
For other entries, see 2d edition.
How moose and turkey scalped the giants. Parker. Skunny
Wundy and other Indian tales.
How mosquitoes came. I–V. *See* 2d edition.
How mosquitoes came. VI. Lee. Folk tales of all nations.
(How the mosquitoes came to Oneata.)
See also Bad Indian's ashes.
How much land does a man need. Broomell. Children's
story caravan.
How music won two wives. James. Tewa firelight tales.
How Napi made the animals. Phillips. Indian tales for
little folks.
How night came. Eells. Fairy tales from Brazil.
Harper and Hamilton. Winding roads.
See also Day and night ; Why the owl rules the night.
For other entries, see 2d edition.
How Nonu was saved. Metzger. Tales told in Hawaii.
How Odin became the wisest of the wise. *See* Odin's search
for wisdom.
How Odysseus returned to his own land. *See* Ulysses' re-
turn.
How Old Man Rabbit helped Father Coon. Buckingham.
Elephant's friend.
How old Mr. Long=Tail became a Santa Claus. Harper.
Merry Christmas to you.
Harper. More story-hour favorites.
Van Buren and Bemis. Christmas in storyland.
How one of partridge's wives became a Sheldrake duck.
See Duck with red feet.
How pansies came colored. Carey. Flower legends. (*In*
Pansy.)
For other entries, see 2d edition.
How partridge built the birds' canoes. Leland. Algonquin
legends. (How the partridge built good canoes for all the
birds.)
Macmillan. Canadian wonder tales. (*In* Partridge and his
drum.)
For other entries, see 2d edition.
How Perseus slew the Gorgon. *See* Perseus.
How Phidias helped the image=maker. Patten. Junior
classics. v. 7.

How Pink Peony sent Spuds, the ballplayer, up to pick four moons. Sandburg. Rootabaga country.
Sandburg. Rootabaga pigeons.

How Primrose went to the party. Bailey. Stories children want.
Bailey. Tell me another story.

How Rabbi Akiba became rich. **Gaster. Ma'aseh book. v. 1.

How Rabbit lost his tail. I. Eells. Fairy tales from Brazil. (How the rabbit lost his tail.)
See also Cat's tail; Monkey's bargains.

How Rabbit lost his tail. II. Leland. Algonquin legends. (How Master Rabbit went to a wedding; How Master Rabbit gave himself airs.)
Macmillan. Canadian wonder tales.
Rich. Why-so stories.

How Rabbit lost his tail. III. Bailey. Stories from an Indian cave. (Why the rabbit has a short tail.)
See also Rabbit and otter #.

How Rabbit lost his tail. IV. Mitchell. Gray moon tales. (Mammy and the rabbit.)

How Rabbit lost his tail. V. Sale. Tree named John. (When Brer Rabbit thundered.)
See also Why the bear has a stumpy tail.

How Rabbit lost his tail. I–V.
For other versions, *see* How Mr. Rabbit lost his fine bushy tail.

How Rag Bag Mammy kept her secret. Sandburg. Rootabaga country.
Sandburg. Rootabaga pigeons.

How Robin Hood won the golden arrow. Bailey. Stories of great adventures.

How robin's breast became red. *See* Why the robin's breast is red. V.

How Robin's kite learned to fly. Bailey. Stories children want.

How Rock=dweller, the chipmunk, gained his stripes. *See* Chipmunk's stripes. III.

How Ryochi found his mother. Sugimoto. Japanese holiday picture tales.

How St. George fought the dragon. *See* St. George and the dragon.

How Satni=Khamois triumphed over the Assyrians. *See* Sennacherib's defeat.

How sense was distributed. Bryce. Folk lore from foreign lands. (How the animals got sense.)
For other entries, see 2d edition.

How Sigurd won the hand of Brynhild. *See* Sigurd the Volsung.

How six men traveled through the wide world. Evans. Worth while stories. (Mighty men. Adapted.)

How six men traveled through the wide world—*continued.*
Grimm. Fairy tales (Olcott. How six men got on in the world.)
See also Ashiepattle and his goodly crew # ; Five companions; Long-legs, Big-mouth, and Burning-eyes; Longstaff, Pinepuller and Rockheaver.
For other entries, see 2d edition.

How six pigeons came back to Hatrack the horse. Sandburg. Rootabaga country.
Sandburg. Rootabaga pigeons.

How six umbrellas took off their straw hats. Sandburg. Rootabaga country.
Sandburg. Rootabaga pigeons.

How Skadi chose her husband. Miller. My book of history. v. 3. (*In* Norse tales of creation and the gods. Ch. 7.)
Pyle. Tales from Norse mythology. (Skadi chooses a husband for herself.)
For other entries, see 2d edition.

How sleep came. Eells. Magic tooth.

How sly fox lost his dinner. *See* Fox and the geese.

How Spot found a home. Mitchell. Here and now story book.

How stars and fireflies were made. Power. How it happened.
See also How we got our first daisies.

How strawberries came to the earth. *See* First strawberries.

How strife came to the world. Eells. Magic tooth.

How summer came to Canada. *See* How summer came to the earth. II.

How summer came to the earth. I. *See* 2d edition.

How summer came to the earth. II. Johnson and Scott. Anthology of children's literature. (How Glooskap found the summer.)
Macmillan. Canadian wonder tales. (How summer came to Canada.)
Spence. Myths of the North American Indians. (How Glooskap caught the summer. *In* Ch. 3.)
For other entries, see 2d edition.

How summer came to the earth. III. Rich. Why-so stories. (Why the birds go south in winter.)
See also South wind, Tale of; Stealing the springtime.
For other entries, see 2d edition.

How Supersmart ate the elephant. Lee. Folk tales of all nations.

How Tahuti took the town of Joppa. *See* How Jaffa was captured.

How Tajima Shumé was tormented by a devil of his own creation. Mitford. Tales of old Japan.

How the alligator got his scales. Eells. Magic tooth.

How the Alpine horn came to the herdsman. *See* How the Swiss came to use the Alpine horn.

How the animals got sense. *See* How sense was distributed.

How the animals kept Christmas. Walker. Sandman's Christmas stories.

How the animals lost their freedom. I. Borski and Miller. Gypsy and the bear.
See also Why the dog and cat are enemies. III.

How the animals lost their freedom. II. Katibah. Other Arabian nights. (Fable of the men and the beasts.)

How the animals lost their tails and got them back. Sandburg. Rootabaga country.
Sandburg. Rootabaga stories.
Through story-land with the children. (How the animals lost their tails.)

How the Apaches escaped from their underworld. Sexton. Gray wolf stories.

How the apple blossoms came back. Evans. Worth while stories. (Apple tree's children. Adapted.)
For other entries, see 2d edition.

How the aristocrats sailed away. Stockton. Reformed pirate.
For other entries, see 2d edition.

How the artist forgot four colors. Applegarth. Missionary stories for little folks. 1st series.
Perkins and Danielson. Second year Mayflower program book. (*In* Colors.)

How the baboons got their tails. Wells. How the present came from the past. Book 1, pt. 2.

How the baby named herself. Burnett. Children's book.

How the baron rescued the prisoners. Raspé. Tales from the travels of Baron Munchausen.
Raspé. Children's Munchausen (Martin. *In* Ch. 17.)

How the Bass was held for King James. Lang. Red true story book.

How the bat saved the world. Purnell. Merry frogs.

How the birds and the flowers were given their colors. Power. (How it happened.)
See also How the birds got their colors. I; How the finch got her colors.

How the birds came. I. Skinner. Child's book of country stories.
For other entries, see 2d edition.

How the birds came. II. Hogner. Navajo winter nights. (Bird monsters.)
Whitman. Navaho tales. (Quest of the war gods: Tsenahale the winged.)

How the birds chose a king. De Leeuw. Java jungle tales.
See also King Wren.

How the blackbird spoiled his coat. *See* When the blackbird was white.

How the blossoms came to the heather. Bryce. Folk lore
from foreign lands. (Heather blossoms.)
For other entries, see 2d edition.

How the bluebird came by its color. *See* How the bluebird got its color.

How the bluebird crossed. Brown. Curious book of birds.

How the bluebird gained the color of the sky. *See* Bluebird and Coyote.

How the bluebird got its color. Babbitt. Animals' own
story book. (How the bluebird came by its color.)
For other entries, see 2d edition.

How the bluebird was chosen herald. Skinner. Child's
book of country stories.
For other entries, see 2d edition.

How the bogatirs were destroyed in Holy Russia. Zeitlin.
Skazki.

How the Brazilian beetles got their gorgeous coats. Eells.
Fairy tales from Brazil.

How the bread came to the children. Bowman. Little
brown bowl.
Harriman. Stories for little children. (Hungry-boy.)

How the buffalo and the grizzly bear went to war. Phillips. Indian tales for little folks.

How the buzzard got his black coat. *See* Why the turkey-
buzzard is bald-headed.

How the camel got his hump. Werner's recitations.
No. 51.
See also Old Hump.
For other entries, see 2d edition.

How the camel got his proud look. Metzger. Picture tales
from the Chinese.

How the cat and the mouse became enemies. *See* Who is
guilty?

How the chase began. Bailey. Stories from an Indian cave.

How the Christmas pudding came. Buckingham. Elephant's friend.

How the conifers flaunt the promise of spring. *See* Why
the evergreen trees keep their leaves in winter. III.

How the coyote danced with the blackbirds. Johnson and
Scott. Anthology of children's literature.

How the crow came to be black. *See* Why the crow is
black. III.

How the deer got his horns. *See* Deer and the rabbit.

How the deer won his antlers. *See* Deer and the rabbit.

How the dog became the friend of man. Woodson. African myths.
See also Dog and the leopard. I #.

How the ducks got their fine feathers. Applegarth. Missionary stories for little folks. 1st series.
For other entries, see 2d edition.

How the echo and the narcissus were made. *See* Echo
and Narcissus.

How the elephant and the whale were tricked. I. Babbitt. Animals' own story book. (Tug of war between a whale and an elephant.)
Carrick. Picture folk tales. (Elephant and the whale.)
Lee. Folk tales of all nations. (Tug of war.)
Piper. Road in story land. (How Brother Rabbit fooled the whale and the elephant.)
See also Spider, the hippopotamus, and the elephant; Tale from Timbuktu.
For other entries, see 2d edition.

How the elephant and the whale were tricked. II. Lee. Folk tales of all nations. (How the tortoise overcame the elephant and the hippopotamus.)
Martens. Wonder tales from far away. (Land turtle and the hippopotamus.)
For other entries, see 2d edition.

How the elm tree grew (play). Bailey. Story-telling hour.

How the emu lost his wings. Rich. Why-so stories.

How the engine learned the knowing song. Mitchell. Here and now story book.

How the evergreens came. *See* Why the evergreen trees keep their leaves in winter. II.

How the Fenris wolf was chained. *See* Binding of the Fenris wolf.

How the finch got her colors. Brown. Curious book of birds. (Gorgeous goldfinch.)
Rich. Why-so stories. (Why the finch's feathers are ruffled.)
See also Gorgeous goldfinch.
For other entries, see 2d edition.

How the fire got into the rocks and trees. *See* Daylight, Origin of; How fire came to the earth. IV.

How the first battle came to be fought. *See* First battle. II.

How the five rusty rats helped a new village. Sandburg. Rootabaga stories.

How the flowers and the bees returned to the earth. *See* Flowers, Legend of.

How the flowers came. Bailey. Tell me another story.
For other entries, see 2d edition.
    In 2d edition this story is also indexed under the title "Query Queer and the flowers."

How the flying squirrel got his wings. Johnson and Scott. Anthology of children's literature. (Nuts of Jonisgyout.)
Rich. Why-so stories.
For other entries, see 2d edition.

How the fox and the crab ran a race. Babbitt. Animals' own story book. (Fox and the crab.)
Shimer. Fairyland. (Fox and the crab.)
See also Fox and the lobster.
For other entries, see 2d edition.

How the fox used his wits. Eells. Magic tooth.
See also Brahman, the tiger, and the jackal.
How the ghost monkey and the ape tried to fool each other. De Leeuw. Java jungle tales.
How the gobbler got his warwhoop. *See* Why the turkey gobbles. II.
How the gods made war and peace with one another. Pyle. Tales from Norse mythology.
How the good gifts were used by two. Walters. Book of Christmas stories.
See also Cloth of endless length; Two wishes that came true; Two pine cones.
For other entries, see 2d edition.
How the gopher raced. Nusbaum. Seven cities of Cibola.
Nusbaum. Zuni Indian tales.
See also Hare and the hedgehog.
How the great flood began. *See* Flood (Latin American).
How the griffin taught school. McVenn. Good manners and right conduct. Book 2.
See also Griffin and the minor canon.
How the Gubbaun Saor got his trade and proved himself. Young. Wonder smith and his son.
How the Gubbaun tried his hand at matchmaking. *See* How the son of the Gobhaun Saor sold the sheepskin.
How the Gubbaun Saor welcomed home his daughter. *See* Aunya's bargain.
How the hare got his split lip. Lee. Folk tales of all nations.
See also Moon's message #; Rabbit and the moon #.
How the harp came to Finland. Fillmore. Wizard of the North. (First kantele. *In* Ch. 24.)
Kinscella. Music appreciation readers. Book 2.
How the hat ashes shovel helped Snoo Foo. Boeckel. Through the gateway.
Sandburg. Rootabaga stories.
How the home was built. Lindsay. Mother stories.
Perkins and Danielson. Mayflower program book.
For other entries, see 2d edition.
How the hunter became a partridge #. *See* Magic wigwam.
In 2d edition there are entries under each title.
How the hyacinth was made. *See* Hyacinthus.
How the Indian pipe came. Newman. Fairy flowers. (Indian pipe.)
For other entries, see 2d edition.
How the Indians got tobacco. I #.
See also Fair earth.
How the Indians got tobacco. II. Power. How it happened. (How tobacco was given to the world.)
How the Indians obtained fish. *See* Raven gets fish for his people.

How the jellyfish lost his bones. *See* Monkey and the jelly-fish.

How the Kapys saved their castle. Schwimmer. Tisza tales.

How the kingfisher came to be. *See* Halcyon birds.

How the kingfisher got his bill. Rich. Why-so stories.

How the kingfisher got its color. *See* Forgetful kingfisher.

How the lake was made. Howes. Long bright land.

How the little bird reached home. Evans. Worth while stories.

How the little demon earned his stolen crust of bread. Broomell. Children's story caravan. (Imp and the crust. Adapted.)

For other entries, see 2d edition.

How the long-eared owl came by his name. *See* Owl's tufted cap.

How the magic mead was brought to Asgard. *See* Odin and the mead.

How the Mayor carved the goose. Harper and Hamilton. Winding roads.

Retner. That's that.

See also Goose. II.

How the monkey and the goat earned their reputations. Eells. Fairy tales from Brazil.

See also Spider's visit.

How the monkey became a trickster. Eells. Fairy tales from Brazil.

How the monkey got a drink when he was thirsty. Eells. Fairy tales from Brazil.

How the monkey got food when he was hungry. Eells. Fairy tales from Brazil.

How the monkey saved his troop. Aspinwall. Jataka tales. (Monkey's heroic self-sacrifice.)

For other entries, see 2d edition.

How the monkey was made. Power. How it happened.

How the monkeys escaped being eaten. Eells. Fairy tales from Brazil.

See also How a turtle fooled a little boy.

How the moon was kind to her mother. *See* Why all men love the moon.

How the mosquitoes came to Oneata. *See* How mosquitoes came. VI.

How the mouse got into his hole. Lee. Folk tales of all nations.

For other entries, see 2d edition.

How the nightingale got his beautiful voice. Blondell. Keepsakes. (Why everyone loves the nightingale.)

Carey. Stories of the birds.

Kinscella. Music appreciation readers. Book 2. (How the nightingale got its voice of gold.)

Purnell and Weatherwax. Why the bee is busy. (Why everyone loves the nightingale.)

How the nightingale got his beautiful voice—*continued.*
See also Why the nightingale sings better than the dove.
How the old lady lost her pain. Retner. That's that.
How the partridge built good canoes for all the birds.
See How partridge built the birds' canoes.
How the partridge got his whistle. *See* How the terrapin lost his whistle.
How the path grew. Brown. Under the rowan tree.
How the peacock got its beautiful tail. *See* Io.
How the peacock was given coloured feathers. Power. How it happened.
See also Why the peacock's tail is spotted.
How the pied piper came. *See* Pied piper of Hamelin.
How the pigeon became a tame bird. Eells. Fairy tales from Brazil.
See also Three lemons; Three oranges.
How the Potato Face Blind Man enjoyed himself. Sandburg. Rootabaga stories.
How the princess' pride was broken. Adams and Atchinson. Book of princess stories.
For other entries, see 2d edition.
How the princess was beaten in a race. Evans. Worth while stories. (Princess loses the foot race.)
See also Atalanta's race.
For other entries, see 2d edition.
How the pussies came on the willows. Bowman. Little brown bowl.
How the rabbit caught the sun. *See* Sun a prisoner. II.
How the rabbit escaped from the wolves. Cooper. Argosy of fables.
How the rabbit fooled the elephant. *See* Rabbits and the elephants.
How the rabbit fooled the lion. Babbitt. Animals' own story book.
How the rabbit got its cotton tail. *See* Rabbit's tail. II.
How the rabbit lost his tail. *See* How rabbit lost his tail. I.
How the rabbit slew the devouring hill. Spence. Myths of the North American Indians. (*In* Sioux myths.)
See also Coyote transforms a monster.
How the rabbit's lip was split. *See* Hare's lip. III.
How the races obtained their colors (African). Phillips. Far peoples. (Where the white man came from.)
See also Why the negro is black.
How the races obtained their colors (Chinese). Phillips. Far peoples. (*In* Ch. 1.)
How the races obtained their colors (East Indian). Phillips. Far peoples. (*In* Ch. 1.)
How the races obtained their colors (Indian). Kennedy. Red man's wonder book. (Floating island.)

How the races obtained their colors (Latin American). Eells. Magic tooth.
See also Why the negro is black.
How the red bird came to be red. Babbitt. Animals' own story book.
How the red bird got his color. Cooper. Argosy of fables. Rich. Why-so stories.
How the red squirrel got his white eyelids. Gearhart. Skalalatoot stories.   .
How the robin came. Carey. Stories of the birds. (Boy who became a robin.)
 Johnson and Scott. Anthology of children's literature. (Boy who became a robin.)
 Rich. Why-so stories. (Why the robin brings the spring.)
 Shimer. Fairyland. (Origin of the robin.)
 For other entries, see 2d edition.
How the robin got his red breast. *See* Why the robin has a red breast. I.
How the rosemary was given its sweet scent and its flow=ers. Power. How it happened.
How the Sarts tribe learned to sing. White. Made in Russia. (*In* Ch. 7.)
See also Why the birds sing different songs.
How the seasons came to be. I–II. *See* 2d edition.
How the seasons came to be. III. Bailey. Stories from an Indian cave. (How the seasons came to earth.)
See also Little ice man #.
How the seasons came to be. IV. Browne. Indian nights. (Bride of the southland.)
 Hillyer. Box of daylight. (Tchamsen regulates the seasons.)
How the seasons came to be. I–IV.
 For other versions, *see* Day and night.
How the selfish Goannas lost their wives. Lee. Folk tales of all nations.
See also Punishment of the stingy.
How the sheep found Bo=peep. *See* Bo-peep.
How the singing water got to the tub. Mitchell. Here and now story book.
How the sly fox caught the jaguar. Babbitt. Animals' own story book.
How the snail gained his wonderful eyes. Parker. Skunny Wundy and other Indian tales.
How the son of the Gobhaun Saor shortened the road. *See* Shortening of the road.
How the son of the Gobhaun Saor sold the sheepskin. Power. Stories to shorten the road.
 Young. Celtic wonder tales.
 Young. Wonder smith and his son. (How the Gubbaun tried his hand at matchmaking; How the son of the Gubbaun met with good luck.)
See also Sage damsel.

How the sparrow hawk won freedom. Purnell and Weatherwax. Why the bee is busy.

How the speckled hen got her speckles. Eells. Fairy tales from Brazil.

Power. How it happened.

See also Drakesbill and his friends.

How the spider ate the hyena cubs' food. Lee. Folk tales of all nations.

How the spider was made. *See* Arachne.

How the squirrel won the ball game. *See* Birds' ball game.

How the strange young man rid the country of the great elk. *See* Elk.

How the sun was made. Power. How it happened.

Wells. How the present came from the past. Book 1, pt. 2.

See also Why the cock crows at dawn.

How the swallow came to be. *See* Procne and Philomela; Swallows, Origin of.

How the swineherd welcomed Ulysses. *See* Eumaeus.

How the Swiss came to use the Alpine horn. Fun folk and fairy tales. (Gift of the gnomes.)

Kinscella. Music appreciation readers. Book 4. (Legend of the Alpine horn.)

Lee. Folk tales of all nations. (Fenette the Alpine shepherdess.)

Lee. Folk tales of all nations. (How the Alpine horn came to the herdsman.)

For other entries, see 2d edition.

How the terrapin escaped from the wolves. Cooper. Argosy of fables.

How the terrapin lost his whistle. Bailey. Stories from an Indian cave.

Rich. Why-so stories. (How the partridge got his whistle.)

How the Tewa tribe divided. James. Tewa firelight tales.

How the three wild Babylonian baboons went away. Sandburg. Rootabaga country.

Sandburg. Rootabaga pigeons.

How the Thunder-bird scared the turtle. *See* Turtle and Thunder-bird.

How the tiger got his stripes. Eells. Fairy tales from Brazil.

How the toad got his bruises. Eells. Fairy tales from Brazil.

How the Tongans came to Fiji. Lee. Folk tales of all nations.

How the tortoise conquered his enemies. Eells. Magic tooth.

How the tortoise overcame the elephant and the hippopotamus. *See* How the elephant and the whale were tricked. II.

How the treaty of peace was made. Partridge. Joyful Star.

How the tulips came to have bright colors. *See* Tulip bed. II.

How the turkey got his beard. I. Gearhart. Skalalatoot stories.
Rich. Why-so stories.
For other entries, see 2d edition.

How the turkey got his beard. II. Parker. Skunny Wundy and other Indian tales. (How moose and turkey scalped the giants.)

How the turtle got his shell. *See* Turtle's shell. I.

How the turtle saved his own life. Applegarth. Missionary stories for little folks. 1st series.
See also Why turtles stay near the water #.

How the turtle won the race. Morris. Stories from mythology: North American. (How turtle beat coyote in a race. *In* Ch. 9.)
For other entries, see 2d edition.

How the waggoner filled his sack, yet brought nothing home in it. Housman. What-o'clock tales.

How the water lily came. I. *See* 2d edition.

How the water lily came. II. Gearhart. Skalalatoot stories. (How water-lilies came.)
See also Star maiden. I ; Water lily. IV.

How the water spider brought the fire. *See* How fire was brought to the Indians. VI.

How the waterfall came. Phillips. Far peoples.

How the wildcat got its spots. Cooper. Argosy of fables.

How the wood duck got his red eyes and Sojy had his coat spoiled. Parker. Skunny Wundy and other Indian tales.
See also Iktomi and the ducks.

How the woodpecker got his red crest. *See* Why the woodpecker's head is red. II.

How the world was made. *See* Creation of the world (Norse).

How the wren became king. *See* King Wren.

How the wren brought fire to earth. *See* Wren who brought fire.

How the wren made a bid for the crown. *See* King Wren.

How the youth journeyed to the house of the Sun. Nusbaum. Seven cities of Cibola.
Nusbaum. Zuni Indian tales.

How there came to be a katydid. *See* Katydid.

How they bring back the village of cream puffs. Sandburg. Rootabaga country.
Sandburg. Rootabaga stories.

How they came to have kite day in China. Fun folk and fairy tales.
For other entries, see 2d edition.

How they go . . . to the Rootabaga country. Sandburg. Rootabaga country.
Sandburg. Rootabaga stories.

Hubert the shepherd. Baldwin. Pedlar's pack.

Huckabuck family. Sandburg. Rootabaga country.
Sandburg. Rootabaga pigeons.

Hudden and Dudden and Donald O'Neary. Lee. Folk tales
of all nations. (Donald and his neighbors.)
For other entries, see 2d edition.

Hugh John and the Scots Greys. Coe. Third book of
stories.

Hugh Midity tells a story. Shannon. Eyes for the dark.

Hugh of Lincoln and Jocelin of Wells. Butterfield. Young
people's story of architecture. (*In* Ch. 38.)
See also Why Rheims church was built.

Hugo of Egisheim. Henderson. Wonder tales of Alsace-
Lorraine.

Hugolina, Count of Pisa. Farjeon. Tales from Chaucer.
(*In* Monk's tale.)

Huia. *See* How Kahukura learned to make nets.

Humble vulture. Purnell. Merry frogs.

Humbo and Mumbo. Silvester and Peter. Happy hour
stories.
See also Munacher and Manacher.

Humbug. Cozad. Story talks.

Humming bird and heron. James. Happy animals of Atagahi. (*In* Rabbit is banished to the island.)

Humming bird and the crane. Cooper. Argosy of fables.

Humming bird and the flower. Harper and Hamilton.
Winding roads.
For other entries, see 2d edition.

Humming bird and the traveller. Cooper. Argosy of fables.
Johnson and Scott. Anthology of children's literature.

Humpty, dumpty, dickery Dan. *See* Gingerbread man. II.

Humpy. *See* Little humpbacked horse.

Hunchback and the elves. Masson. Folk tales of Brittany.
See also Knockgrafton, Legend of; You must not work on
Sunday.

Hundred crowns for a song. *See* Cobbler's song.

Hundred-wit, Thousand-wit, and Single-wit. Cooper. Ar-
gosy of fables. (Two fishes and the frog.)
Lee. Folk tales of all nations.
Power. Bag o' tales.
See also Fox and cat. I; Three fish. I.

Hundreds and thousands. Fyleman. Forty good-morning
tales.

Hungry chicks (poem). Shimer. Fairyland.

Hungry=boy. *See* How the bread came to the children.

Hungry fox and his breakfast. Dorey. Three and the
moon. (How on one day of great hunger Master Renard
tricked three fishermen.)
For other entries, see 2d edition.

Hungry Hans. Davis. Baker's dozen.
Keller. Fat of the cat.

Hungry old witch. Davis. Baker's dozen.
Harper. Ghosts and goblins.
For other entries, see 2d edition.
Hungry wolf. I. Carrick. More Russian picture tales.
Hutchinson.' Fireside stories.
Quinn. Stories for the six-year-old.
Hungry wolf. II. Martinez Del Rio. Sun, the moon and a
rabbit.
Hunted hare. Rhys. English fairy book. (Black rider.)
Williams-Ellis. Fairies and enchanters. (Old woman who
went to market at midnight.)
For other entries, see 2d edition.
Hunter and his wife. *See* Language of beasts.
Hunter and the fisherman. Cooper. Argosy of fables.
Hunter and the horseman. Æsop. Fables (Jones).
Hunter and the serpent. *See* Man and the snake. II.
Hunter and the woodman. Æsop. Fables (Jones).
Cooper. Argosy of fables.
Hunter, the fox and the leopard. Æsop. Fables (Whit-
man ed. Hunter, the fox and the tiger.)
For other entries, see 2d edition.
Hunter, the fox, and the tiger. *See* Hunter, the fox, and
the leopard.
Hunter who became a partridge. *See* Magic wigwam.
Hunters and their fairy brides. Pogány. Hungarian fairy
book.
Hunting nest of old Echtebé. Carpenter. Tales of a Basque
grandmother.
Huon of Bordeaux. Cross. Music stories. (Oberon.)
Echols. Knights of Charlemagne. (Decline of the court of
Charlemagne.)
See also Cold iron.
For other entries, see 2d edition.
Hurroo, Coupal Bawn! *See* O'Donoghue, The. II.
Husband shut out. Darton. Wonder book of old romance.
Husband who was left to mind the house. *See* Man who
was going to mind the house.
Husband who was to mind the house. *See* Man who was
going to mind the house.
Husbandman and the sea. *See* Shipwrecked man and the
sea.
Husbandman and the stork. *See* Farmer and the stork.
Hush=a=bye, baby. Hall. Godmother's stories.
See also Four clever brothers.
Hut in the forest. *See* House in the wood.
In 2d edition there are entries under each title.
Hyacinthus. Bulfinch. Golden age. (Apollo and Hyacin-
thus. *In* Ch. 8.)
Carey. Flower legends. (Wild hyacinth; or bluebell.)
Forbush. Myths and legends of Greece and Rome. (Apollo
and Hyacinthus.)
Lang. Book of myths.

Hyacinthus—*continued.*
Power. How it happened. (How the hyacinth was made.)
Pyle. Tales from Greek mythology. (Phœbus and Hya-
cinthus.)
For other entries, see 2d edition.

I

"I am Clockface." Cozad. Story talks.
I don't care. Harriman. Stories for little children.
For other entries, see 2d edition.
I don't want to (play). Elson and Runkel. Child-library
readers. Book 2.
I once knew a cat. Fyleman. Forty good-morning tales.
"I ride to=day, Geddes." *See* Parrot and the hawk.
I wish it would rain. Chrisman. Shen of the sea.
I won't. Coussens. Diamond story book.
For other entries, see 2d edition.
Ibycus. *See* Cranes of Ibycus.
Icarus. *See* Dædalus and Icarus.
Ice king. Skinner. Child's book of country stories.
For other entries, see 2d edition.
Ictinike. *See* Iktomi.
Idalwin's long sleep. Browne. Indian nights.
See also Rip Van Winkle.
Idas and Marpessa. Forbush. Myths and legends of Greece
and Rome. (Apollo, Idas and Marpessa.)
Lang. Book of myths.
For other entries, see 2d edition.
Idiotic trade. Cendrars. Little black stories.
Idle=paws and I-did-it. Potter. Captain Sandman.
Idol and the whale. Henderson and Calvert. Wonder tales
of old Japan. (Buddha and Kujira.)
Price. Legends of the seven seas. (Bronze Buddha and
the whale. Adapted.)
Whitehorn. Wonder tales of old Japan.
For other entries, see 2d edition.
Iduna's apples. Curtis. Stories in trees. (Yggdrasil, the
ash.)
Johnson and Scott. Anthology of children's literature.
(Magic apples.)
Miller. My book of history. v. 3. (*In* Norse tales of crea-
tion and the gods. Ch. 7.)
Power. Bag o' tales. (Apples of youth.)
Pyle. Tales from Norse mythology. (Idun's magic apples.)
Skinner. Child's book of country stories. (Spring maiden
and the frost giants.)
For other entries, see 2d edition.
Idun's magic apples. *See* Iduna's apples.
Idwal of Nant Clwyd. Henderson and Jones. Wonder tales
of ancient Wales.
See also Rip Van Winkle.

If heaven will it. I. *See* 2d edition.
If heaven will it. II. Sawyer. Picture tales from Spain. (Frog.)
Iktomi, Adventures of. *See* Shooting of the red eagle; Tree bound.
Iktomi and the buzzard. *See* Why the turkey-buzzard is bald-headed.
Iktomi and the ducks (play). Lamkin and Jagendorf. Around America with the Indians. (Iktomi, the Dakota, and the ducks.)
   See also How the wood duck got his red eyes.
   For other entries, see 2d edition.
Iktomi goes visiting. Spence. Myths of the North American Indians. (Ictinike and the creators. *In* Ch. 5.)
   See also Blue Jay the imitator; Coyote and porcupine.
Iktomi's blanket. Egan. New found tales. (Mischief maker.)
   See also Old couple of the humble hut; So-bee-yit.
   For other entries, see 2d edition.
Ill=formed bride. *See* Sir Gawain's marriage. II.
Ill luck. *See* Stupid's cries.
Ill=tempered princess. Gunterman. Castles in Spain.
   See also Devil worsted #.
Ill wind. Broomell. Children's story caravan.
Illuminating fig. Egan. New found tales.
   See also Acorn and the pumpkin.
Ilmarinen the smith. I. Olcott. Wonder tales from Baltic wizards. (Forging of the magic Sampo.)
Ilmarinen the smith. II. Bowman and Bianco. Tales from a Finnish tupa. (Wooing of Seppo Ilmarinen.)
Ilse's crystal palace. *See* Princess Ilse.
Image seller. Æsop. Fables (Jones).
Imp and the crust. *See* How the little demon earned his stolen crust of bread.
Imp and the drum. Patten. Junior clasiscs. v. 9.
Impatient bird. Egan. New tales.
Impetussle. Shannon. Eyes for the dark.
Important gnat. Purnell and Weatherwax. Why the bee is busy.
   See also Goats in the turnip field; Little white rabbit. II.
Imposter. Æsop. Fables (Jones).
Impoverished man whom Elijah entrusted with wealth for a period of seven years. **Gaster. Ma'aseh book. v. 1.
Imprisoned by bears. James. Tewa firelight tales.
Imprisoned princess. Farjeon. Martin Pippin in the apple orchard.
Imps on the meadow of heaven. Baumbach. Tales from the Swiss alps.
   See also Star of Bethlehem.
"In a minute." White. School management, p. 248.
   See also Little In-a-minute #.
In a rose garden. Stewart. Tell me a story I never heard before.

In clean hay. Harper. Merry Christmas to you.
  Kelly. Christmas nightingale.
In Drumtown. Burnett. Children's book.
In moon land. *See* Children in the moon. III.
In the beginning. I. *See* Creation of the world (Polynesian).
In the beginning. II. Pyle. Tales from Norse mythology.
  See also Creation of the world (Norse).
In the days of the Amazons. Eells. Magic tooth.
In the Forest of Arden. Echols. Knights of Charlemagne.
In the great walled country. Perkins and Danielson. Second year Mayflower program book.
  Skinner. Christmas stories. (Great walled country.)
  Walters. Book of Christmas stories. (Great walled country.)
  For other entries, see 2d edition.
In the kitchen garden. Patten. Junior classics. v. 8. (Some voices from the kitchen garden.)
  For other entries, see 2d edition.
In the land of souls. Browne. Indian nights. (Flight of the stone canoe.)
  Spence. Myths of the North American Indians. (Spirit bride. *In* Ch. 3.)
  See also Ghost land. III; Sayadio in spirit-land; Shadow wife #.
  For other entries, see 2d edition.
In the magician's castle. Cook. Red and gold stories.
In the plate country. Aspinwall. Can you believe me stories.
  See also Willow ware, Story of.
Ina, the fairy voyager. *See* Hina's voyage.
Inch=worm and the mountain. *See* Rock of the measuring worm.
Inchcape rock (poem). Johnson and Scott. Anthology of children's literature.
  (poem). Southey. Poems.
  For other entries, see 2d edition.
Incident of the French camp (poem). Browning. Poems.
  (poem). Johnson and Scott. Anthology of children's literature.
  (poem). Patten. Junior classics. v. 10.
Incomparable archer. Aspinwall. Jataka tales.
Inconstant prince. *See* Rosanie.
Independence Day. *See* Fourth of July.
Indian Bluebeard. De Huff. Taytay's memories.
  See also Bluebeard; Pueblo Bluebeard #.
Indian boy and his flute. Kinscella. Music appreciation readers. Book 3.
Indian Cinderella. *See* Little Scar Face.
Indian corn, Origin of. *See* First corn. VI, XI.
Indian hunter and the seven dancers of the sky. *See* Pleiades. VI.

Indian pipe. *See* How the Indian pipe came.

Indian summer. Wells. How the present came from the past. Book 1, pt. 2. (Haze of Indian summer.)
For other entries, see 2d edition.

Indians and the Quaker family. Hodgkins. Atlantic treasury of childhood stories.

Indians and the ravens. *See* Napi and the famine.

Indian's blanket. Eckford. Wonder windows. (Spider man.)

Indians' flood. *See* Flood (Indian).

Ingiald. Niemeyer. Stories for the history hour.

Ingrate. *See* Grateful animals and ungrateful man.

Ingvald, the wolf king. Dunlap. Stories of the Vikings. (Wolf's heart.)

Inisfail. Young. Celtic wonder tales.

Inn that missed its chance. *See* Innkeeper's story. II.

Innkeeper's story. I. Campbell. Story of Christmas, p. 30. (Wonder of Christmas night.)

Innkeeper's story. II (poem). Campbell. Story of Christmas, p. 28. (Inn that missed its chance.)

Inquisitive man. Cooper. Argosy of fables.
For other entries, see 2d edition.

Inquisitive monkey. *See* Carpenter and the ape.

Inquisitive little girl. Fyleman. Forty good-morning tales.

Inquisitive woman. Brown. Curious book of birds.
Carey. Stories of the birds. (Woodpecker and her sack.)
Lee. Folk tales of all nations. (Why the woodpecker has a long beak.)
Purnell and Weatherwax. Why the bee is busy. (Why the woodpecker has a long nose.)
Rich. Why-so stories. (Why the woodpecker has a long beak.)
See also Pandora ; Why the pelican has a pouch.

Insect-man and the fox. De Huff. Taytay's memories.

Inseparables. Metzger. Tales told in Hawaii.
See also Scorpion and his family.

Inspired maid of France. *See* Joan of Arc.

Intelligence and luck. *See* Luck and intelligence.

Intelligent weaver. *See* Wise weaver.

Inventive father. Canfield. Made-to-order stories.

Invisible prince. I. *See* 2d edition.

Invisible prince. II. Aulnoy. Fairy tales (Planché. Prince Sprite.)
Aulnoy. White cat. (Prince Sprite.)
For other entries, see 2d edition.

Io. Bulfinch. Golden age. (*In* Ch. 4.)
Carey. Stories of the birds. (Tail of the peacock.)
Pyle. Tales from Greek mythology.
Rich. Why-so stories. (How the peacock got its beautiful tail.)
For other entries, see 2d edition.

Iolanthe. *See* Fairy bridegroom.

Ionians build to Diana. Butterfield. Young people's story of architecture. (Columns with a maiden's beauty. Ch. 9.)

Ipswich alarm. Buckingham. Elephant's friend.

Irashima Taro. *See* Uraschimataro and the turtle.

Ireland, Origin of. *See* Creation of Ireland.

Iris. I–II. *See* 2d edition.

Iris. III. Carey. Flower legends.
For other entries, see 2d edition.

Iris IV. Newman. Fairy flowers. (Flower-towers.)

Irish stew. Baker. Tell them again tales.

Irishman and the donkey. Lee. Folk tales of all nations.

Iron hand. Wolff. Pale mountains.

Iron Hans. Grimm. Fairy tales (Olcott. Iron John.)
For other entries, see 2d edition.

Iron=headed man. Pogány. Magyar fairy tales.

Iron Henry. *See* Frog prince.

Iron John. *See* Iron Hans.

Iron stove. Grimm. Fairy tales (Olcott).
Johnson and Scott. Anthology of children's literature.
For other entries, see 2d edition.

Iron wolf. Lee. Folk tales of all nations.
For other entries, see 2d edition.

Irrepressible pie. Aspinwall. Can you believe me stories.
See also Gingerbread boy. I.

Is it true? *See* Three sieves.

Isaac's loaves. Cross. Stories to tell.
For other entries, see 2d edition.

Isabella. *See* Pot of basil.

Ishtar and Tammuz, Story of. Miller. My book of history. v. 1. (*In* Ch. 11.)
See also Orpheus, and Eurydice; Proserpina.

Isis. I. *See* Isis and Osiris, Story of.

Isis. II. *See* Ra and Isis, Story of.

Isis and Osiris, Story of. Baikie. Wonder tales of the ancient world. (Osiris and his wicked brother; Wanderings of Isis.)
Bulfinch. Golden age. (Osiris and Isis. *In* Ch. 34.)
Miller. My book of history. v. 1. (Osiris and Isis, Story of. *In* Ch. 6.)
Wells. How the present came from the past. Book 2, pt. 2. (*In* Chief gods of Egyptian mythology.)
For other entries, see 2d edition.
In 2d edition this story is also indexed under the title "Quest of Isis."

Island of cheese. Raspé. Children's Munchausen (Martin. *In* Ch. 9.)

Island of herons. Martinez Del Rio. Sun, the moon and a rabbit.

Island of skeletons. Spence. Myths of the North American Indians. (Friendly skeleton. *In* Ch. 4.)
For other entries, see 2d edition.

Islands of flowers. Eells. Islands of magic.
Islands, Origin of. Brown. Curious book of birds. (How the bluebird crossed.)
Isle of flower's. Metzger. Tales told in Hawaii.
Isle of plenty. Farjeon. Old sailor's yarn ·box.
Israel and the enemy. *See* Werewolf. VII.
Issunboshi. *See* One inch fellow.
Issy=Ben=Aran. Gunterman. Castles in Spain.
Istar, the moon princess. Johnson. Sky movies. (Why the Princess Istar loses and gains her jewelled robes. *In* Ch. 3.)
It is quite true. Manner. Silver treasury. (It's quite true.) For other entries, see 2d edition.
It snows and it blows. Burnett. Children's book.
It was lucky Noah invited the elephants. Krohn and Johnson. Scales of the silver fish.
Italy, Origin of. Fyleman. Forty good-morning tales. (Wind's tale of the giant's boot.)
Ito and his friends #.
   See also Crab and the monkey. I. Man of the woods and the giant; Verlioka.
Its mission. Eggleston. Stories for special days in the church school.
   See also Handful of clay.
It's my own invention. *See* Alice and the white knight.
Iva and the King of the Trolls. Falkberget. Broomstick and Snowflake.
Ivan and the chestnut horse. *See* Princess to be kissed at a charge.
Ivan and the gray wolf. I. Zeitlin. Skazki. (Ivan Tsarevitch and the gray wolf.)
   For other entries, see 2d edition.
Ivan and the gray wolf. II. Byrde. Polish fairy book. (About Jan the Prince, Princess Wonderface, and the Flamebird.)
   See also Golden bird. II.
Ivan Buikovich. Carpenter. Tales of a Russian grandmother. (Chudo Yudo with twelve heads.)
   Ralston. Russian fairy tales. (*In* Ivan Popyalof.)
Ivan Popyalof. Ralston. Russian fairy tales.
Ivan the fool. Tolstoy. Ivan the fool and other tales.
   For other entries, see 2d edition.
Ivan the peasant's son #.
   See also Schmat-Razum #.
Ivan Tsarevitch and Bailoi Polyanyin. Curtin. Fairy tales of Eastern Europe.
Ivan Tsarevich and the gray wolf. *See* Ivan and the gray wolf. I.
Ivanhoe. Patten. Junior classics. v. 5. (Abridged.)
I've come for Poly. *See* Fairy bakeshop.
Ivon Torţik, Story of. Dorey. Three and the moon.

Ivon the twisted. Dorey. Three and the moon. (Ivon the twisted and the daughter of the Pleumeur miller.)
Ivy and the thyme (poem). Cooper. Argosy of fables.
Izdubar. *See* Gilgamesh.

J

Jack. Baker. Tell them again tales.
Jack and his fiddle. Hall. Godmother's stories.
Jack and his golden box. *See* Jack and his golden snuff-box.
Jack and his golden snuff=box. Freeman. Child-story readers. 3d reader. (Jack and his golden box.)
    Morris. Gypsy story teller.
    Steel. English fairy tales. (Golden snuff-box.)
    For other entries, see 2d edition.
Jack and his master. Lee. Folk tales of all nations.
    See also Bodach and the boy; Errua, the madman; Son of strength.
    For other entries, see 2d edition.
Jack and his mother. Lee. Folk tales of all nations.
    See also Foolish Fred; Lazy Jack; Prudent Hans.
Jack and his wonderful hen. Macmillan. Canadian wonder tales.
Jack and the bean=stalk. Adams and Atchinson. Book of giant stories.
    Arthur Rackham fairy book.
    Brock. Book of fairy tales.
    Bruce. Treasury of tales for little folk.
    Curry and Clippinger. Children's literature.
    De La Mare. Told again.
    Evans. Worth while stories.
    Johnson and Scott. Anthology of children's literature.
    Lang. Old friends among the fairies.
    Mackenzie. Book of nursery tales.
    Quinn. Stokes' wonder book of fairy tales.
    Quinn. Stories for the six-year-old. (Abridged.)
    Rich. Read-aloud book.
    Rhys. English fairy book.
    Steel. English fairy tales.
    See also Magic tree; Sun a prisoner. VI; Turkey bean and the moon.
    For other entries, see 2d edition.
Jack and the bean stalk (Indian). *See* Sun a prisoner. VI.
Jack and the giant. I. *See* Jack the giant killer.
Jack and the giant. II. Evans. Worth while stories.
Jack and the king who was a gentleman #.
    See also Bet; Lying for a wager.
Jack and the Lord High Mayor. MacManus. Lo, and behold ye!
    See also Little Claus and Big Claus; Little farmer #.

Jack Beanstalk and the pea princess. Morley. I know a secret.
See also Princess on the pea.

Jack Hannaford. Lee. Folk tales of all nations.
See also All women are alike; Visitor from hell.
For other entries, see 2d edition.

Jack Hornby. Williams-Ellis. Fairies and enchanters.

Jack Mulligan's fairies. Kinscella. Music appreciation readers. Book 6.

Jack=o'=lantern. I. *See* 2d edition.

Jack=o'=lantern. II. Olcott. Wonder tales from fairy isles.

Jack=o'=lantern. III. Told under the blue umbrella.

Jack Popcorn. Pogány. Hungarian fairy book.

Jack the cunning thief. Colum. King of Ireland's son. (*In* Gilly of the goat skin.)
Lee. Folk tales of all nations.
See also Three thieves.
For other entries, see 2d edition.

Jack the giant=killer. Arthur Rackham fairy book.
Brock. Valentine and Orson.
Johnson and Scott. Anthology of children's literature.
Lang. Old friends among the fairies.
Mackenzie. Book of nursery tales.
Power. Stories to shorten the road.
Quinn. Stokes' wonder book of fairy tales.
Rhys. English fairy book.
Steel. English fairy tales.
For other entries, see 2d edition.

Jack the hedgehog. *See* Hans my hedgehog.

Jackal and the alligator. I. *See* Jackal and the crocodile.

Jackal and the alligator. II. *See* Little jackal and the alligator.

Jackal and the cat. **Arnold. Book of good counsels. (Vulture, the cat and the birds.)
Cooper. Argosy of fables. (Vulture, the cat and the birds.)
See also Eagle, the cat, and the sow.
For other entries, see 2d edition.

Jackal and the crocodile. Hutchinson. Fireside stories. (Jackal and the alligator.)
See also Guinea-hen and the crocodile; Mouse-deer, the crocodile and the tiger.
For other entries, see 2d edition.

Jackal and the drought. Lee. Folk tales of all nations.
See also Tar-baby. III #.

Jackal and the drum. Lee. Folk tales of all nations.
See also Fox and the drum.

Jackal and the heron. Lee. Folk tales of all nations. (Dove and the heron.)
Rich. Why-so stories. (Why the heron's neck is bent.)
See also Fox and the crow. II.
For other entries, see 2d edition.

Jackal and the partridge #.
See also Blackbird and the fox ; Clever woodpecker.
Jackal, deer and crow. *See* Stag, the crow and the jackal.
In 2d edition there are entries under each title.
Jackal or tiger #.
See also Lioness, the whelps and the little jackal.
Jackal, the barber, and the Brahmin. Pyle. Fairy tales
from India. (Jackal, the barber, and the Brahmin who
had seven daughters.)
See also Two melons ; Two neighbors.
For other entries, see 2d edition.
**Jackal, the barber, and the Brahmin who had seven daugh=
ters.** *See* Jackal the barber and the Brahmin.
Jackal the deer and the crow. *See* Stag, the crow and the
jackal.
Jackal's bride. Lee. Folk tales of all nations.
Jackal's spell. Aspinwall. Jataka tales.
Jackanapes. Curry and Clippinger. Children's literature.
Power. Children's treasure chest.
Jackass in office. *See* Ass carrying an idol.
Jackbean, Story of. *See* Pea blossom.
Jackdaw and the borrowed plumes. *See* Vain jackdaw. I.
Jackdaw and the doves. *See* Jackdaw and the pigeons.
Jackdaw and the pigeons. Æsop. Fables (Jones).
Cooper. Argosy of fables. (Jackdaw and the doves.)
See also Vain jackdaw. I.
For other entries, see 2d edition.
Jackie, a little wild rabbit. Freeman. Child-story readers.
3d reader.
Jack's windowbox. Evans. Worth while stories. (How
Jack came to have a window box.)
Jacky=my=Lantern. Field. American folk and fairy tales.
For other entries, see 2d edition.
Jacob the factor. Schwarz. Jewish caravan. (*In* Clever
judge.)
Jacquard and his loom. Chambers' miscellany. v. 18.
(Story of Jacquard.)
Jacqueline of Holland. Miller. My travelship: Holland.
(Story of Lady Jacqueline.)
Jade slipper. *See* Pigling and her proud sister.
Jan and Jaantje. Hart. Picture tales from Holland.
See also Cat and the mouse in partnership; Long time # ;
Winter.
Jan, Jan, the cobbler's boy. Olcott. Wonder tales from
windmill lands.
Jan the grumbler. Hart. Picture tales from Holland.
See also Man who was going to mind the house.
Jan the prince, Princess Wonderface, and the Flamebird.
See Ivan and the gray wolf. II.
Jane Addam's burglars. Broomell. Children's story cara-
van.

Jane, Jane, don't complain. Harper. Fillmore folk tales.
See also Son of Adam.
For other entries, see 2d edition.
Japanese Big Four. *See* Four friends. III.
Japanese Tom Thumb. *See* Momotaro. I.
Japanese twins and Bot' Chan. Harriman. Stories for little children.
Perkins. Japanese twins. Ch. 1.
Japonel. Housman. Moonshine and clover.
Jar of olives #.
See also Woman who hid her gold in a jar of honey.
Jar of rosemary. Harper. Merry Christmas to you.
Harper. Selfish giant.
Perkins and Danielson. Second year Mayflower program book.
For other entries, see 2d edition.
Jas the fiddler. Bernhard. Master wizard. (Adapted.)
Jasmine. Carey. Flower legends.
Jason Squiff and why he had a popcorn hat. Sandburg. Rootabaga country.
Sandburg. Rootabaga stories.
Javotte and the jolly goat boys. Cook. To-day's stories of yesterday.
Jealous wife. Metzger. Tales told in Hawaii.
Jealousy of the blind man. Woodson. African myths.
Jean Malin and the bull-man. Field. American folk and fairy tales. (Compair Tareau and Jean Malin.)
For other entries, see 2d edition.
Jean Paul and his little white mice. Harper and Hamilton. Winding roads.
Jean Valjean and the bishop (play). Knight. Dramatic reader.
Jelly=fish and the monkey. *See* Monkey and the jelly-fish.
Jellyfish that wouldn't. Skipper. Jungle meeting-pool. (*In* Fourth meeting.)
Jenny Pumpkin and the black witch. Deihl. Holiday-time stories.
Jerome. *See* St. Jerome.
Jerry. Brown. Under the rowan tree.
Jesper who herded the hares. Coe. Third book of stories for the story teller.
See also Ashiepattle and the king's hares; Bag of stories; Eighteen rabbits; Enchanted whistle #; One hundred hares; Sack of truth.
For other entries, see 2d edition.
Jest of Little John (poem). Bennett. Pigtail of Ah Lee Ben Loo.
Jester who fooled a king. Bernhard. Master wizard.
See also Abou Hassan; April Fools' Day, Origin of; Death of Abu Nowas and his wife.

Jew among the thorns. Kinscella. Music appreciation readers. Book 5. (Magic fiddle.)
See also Bewitched violin; Friar and the boy; Louis and the three wishes.
For other entries, see 2d edition.

Jewel spring. *See* Ambitious hunter and skilful fisher.

Jewel tears. Henderson and Calvert. Wonder tales of old Japan. (Samebito; or, The jewel tears.)
See also Lantern of the pearl.
For other entries, see 2d edition.

Jeweller and the lace-maker (poem). Cooper. Argosy of fables.

Jewels of the tides. *See* Tide jewels.

Jewish child who was stolen. *See* Pope's game of chess.

Jezinkas. *See* Grandfather's eyes.

Jimmy Scarecrow's Christmas. Walters. Book of Christmas stories.
For other entries, see 2d edition.

Jimmy's made to order story. Harper and Hamilton. Winding roads.

Jim's tale of the Manx cats. *See* Why Manx cats have no tails.

Jo-bate and the siren of Bonifaccio. Hill and Maxwell. Napoleon's story book.

Joan of Arc. Bailey. Stories children want. (Shepherdess whose dream came true.)
Chandler. Magic pictures. (Joan, Maid of Orleans.)
Clément. Flowers of chivalry. (Mysterious ride.)
Hodgkins. Atlantic treasury of childhood stories. (Inspired maid of France.)
Kinscella. Music appreciation readers. Book 6. (Heroine of France.)
Lang. Red true story book. (Life and death of Joan the maid.)
Miller. My book of history. v. 3. (*In* Ch. 14.)
Tappan. Old world hero stories.
See also Little Ki and the pot of rice; Moolang; Warrior maid. I.
For other entries, see 2d edition.

Joan of Arc's banner. Clément. Once in France. (Her friend and her flag.)

John-a-dreams. Burnett. Children's book.

John and the ghosts. *See* Youth who could not shiver and shake.

John Dietrich, Adventures of #.
See also Arndt's night underground.

John Gilpin (poem). Cowper. Poems.
(poem). Patten. Junior classics. v. 10.
For other entries, see 2d edition.

Johnny Appleseed. Bailey. Stories children want. (Appleseed John.)

Johnny Appleseed—*continued.*
Patten. Junior classics. v. 7. (Old Johnny Appleseed.)
Skinner. Child's book of country stories.
For other entries, see 2d edition.
Johnny=cake. I. Johnson and Scott. Anthology of children's literature.
Lee. Folk tales of all nations.
Williams-Ellis. Fairies and enchanters.
For other entries, see 2d edition.
Johnny Chuck finds the best thing in the world. Curry and Clippinger. Children's literature.
For other entries, see 2d edition.
Johnny Gloke. Coussens. Diamond story book.
See also Brave little tailor; Gipsy and the dragon. III.
Johnny Inkslinger. Rounds. Ol' Paul.
Johnny Pick=a-bean. Cook. To-day's stories of yesterday.
Johnny Reed's cat. De La Mare and Quayle. Readings. (Mally Dixon and Knurremurre.)
For other entries, see 2d edition.
Johnny's rabbit. Evans. Worth while stories.
See also Benjy in Beastland.
Johnny's shoe (poem). Richards. More five minute stories. (Lesson song.)
John's garden. Potter. Giant of Apple Pie Hill.
Johnson, Samuel. *See* Dr. Johnson and his father.
Jolly good boots. Delineator. Dec. 1929, p. 18.
Jolly old whistle. Williams. Jolly old whistle and other tales.
Jolly valentine. Bowman. Little brown bowl.
Jombatiste and the forty devils. Canfield. Made-to-order stories.
Jorinde and Joringel. Grimm. Fairy tales (Olcott. Jorinda and Joringel.)
Tappan. Prince from nowhere. (Sweetheart bewitched.)
For other entries, see 2d edition.
Joro and the elephant. Fyleman. Forty good-night tales.
Jose the beast slayer. Eells. Islands of magic.
Joseph and Damien (poem). Broomell. Children's story caravan.
Joseph, the Sabbath lover. **Gaster. Ma'aseh book. v. 1. (Observance of the Sabbath rewarded.)
See also Cross surety; Treasure of Hasan Taj.
For other entries, see 2d edition.
Josephine de Beauharnis. Clément. Once in France. (Little girl from the island.)
Journey. Mitchell. Here and now story book.
Journey of a drop of water. *See* Water drop. III.
Journey of Khensu to Bekhten. Baikie. Wonder tales of the ancient world. (Princess and the demon.)
Chandler. Magic pictures of the long ago. (Fair princess of Behkten; or, The Kindness of the Egyption Moon-god.)
Gibson. Golden bird. (Princess and the Moon god.)

Journey of Khensu to Bekhten—*continued.*
**Maspero. Popular stories of ancient Egypt. (Daughter of the Prince of Bakhtan and the possessing spirit.)
For other entries, see 2d edition.
Journey of Rheinfrid. Canton. Child's book of saints.
See also Monk and the bird's song.
Journey of the Breton fishermen. Chamoud. Picture tales from the French.
See also Frog travellers.
Journey to the house of the sun. Hogner. Navajo winter nights.
Journey to the stars. Harper. More story-hour favorites.
Juan Half=Bear. De Huff. Taytay's tales.
Juan Osito. Otero. Old Spain in our Southwest.
Juanillo. Gunterman. Castles in Spain.
Juanita, Marianita, the cat, and the bear. De Huff. Taytay's tales.
See also Little Red Riding Hood.
Judas Iscariot. Colum. Voyagers. (Soul that was permitted to revisit the earth.)
Judas tree. I. *See* Red-bud tree.
Judas tree. II. Metzger. Picture tales from the Chinese. (Three brothers.)
See also Bundle of sticks.
Judge and the king. Schwimmer. Tisza tales.
Judge=monkey. *See* Judgement of the monkey. II.
Judge who took all he paid for. Williams-Ellis. Fairies and enchanters.
Judgement of Cormac MacArt. *See* Cormac's judgement.
Judgement of Karakash. Egan. New found tales. (Lawyer of Samarcand: Judgement of Karakash.)
Judgement of Midas. *See* Midas. II.
Judgment of Solomon. I. *See* King Solomon's wisdom; Snake's thanks.
Judgement of Solomon. II. Manner. Silver treasury.
See also All Saints' Day. II.
Judgement of the monkey. I. Metzger. Tales told in Korea.
See also Matter of arbitration.
Judgement of the monkey. II. Skeat. Tiger's mistake. (Judge-monkey.)
Judgement seat of Vikramaditya. Through story-land with the children.
For other entries, see 2d edition.
Judy and the fairy. Fyleman. Forty good-morning tales.
Jugurtha. Cooke. Stories of Rome. (Marius and Jugurtha.)
Jujube. Fyleman. Forty good-night tales. (Bag of goodies, pt. 1.)
Julius Caesar crossing the Rubicon. *See* Caesar, Julius.
Jump, jump, jump the highest. *See* Abel Stok's difficult task.

Jump=over=the=wall bird. Purnell and Weatherwax. Talking bird.
Jumping fire. Olcott. Wonder tales from fairy isles.
Jumping Jack's journey. Blaisdell. Rhyme and story second reader.
Junco Bill. Brown. Under the rowan tree.
Jupiter and a bee. Æsop. Fables (Jones. Bee and Jupiter.)
    Cooper. Argosy of fables. (Jupiter and the bee.)
    For other entries, see 2d edition.
Jupiter and the ass. Æsop. Fables (Whitman ed.).
    See also Discontented ass. I.
    For other entries, see 2d edition.
Jupiter and the bee. *See* Jupiter and a bee.
Jupiter and the camel. Æsop. Fables (Artzybasheff).
    Cooper. Argosy of fables.
    For other entries, see 2d edition.
Jupiter and the horse. *See* First camel.
Jupiter and the monkey. Æsop. Fables (Artzybasheff).
    Æsop. Fables (Jones).
    Cooper. Argosy of fables.
    See also Crow's children.
Jupiter and the oak. Curtis. Stories in trees.
Jupiter and the thunderbolts. La Fontaine. Fables (Tilney).
Jupiter and the tortoise. Æsop. Fables (Jones).
Jupiter, Neptune, Minerva and Momus. Cooper. Argosy of fables.
    For other entries, see 2d edition.
Jupiter's two wallets. Æsop. Fables (Jones. Two bags.)
    Cooper. Argosy of fables. (Two wallets.)
    See also Two packs #.
    For other entries, see 2d edition.
Jurma and the sea god. *See* Three chests.
Just a dauber. *See* Tintoretto.
Just as well (play). Knight. Dramatic reader. (So-so.)
    For other entries, see 2d edition.
Just imagine it. Retner. That's that.
Just judge and his angel guard. Guerber. Legends of Switzerland. (*In* Tessin.)
Just king. Friedlander. Jewish fairy tales (Dutton).
Justice and the oyster. *See* Two travellers and the oyster.
Justice of Omar. Egan. New found tales.
Justinian and Theodora, the circus=girl empress. Miller, My book of history. v. 3. (*In* Ch. 3.)

K

Kabouter mannikins. Olcott. Wonder tales from windmill lands. (Ha! ha! the kabouter mannikins.)
Kachi=Kachi Yama. *See* Farmer and the badger.

Kagsagsuk. Morris. Stories from mythology: North American. Ch. 31.

Kai Kaus. *See* Foolish Shah.

Kai Khosroo, Story of. Coit. Ivory throne of Persia. (Kai Khosru.)

Coit. Kai Khosru and other plays for children.

(play). Coit. Kai Khosru and other plays for children.

For other entries, see 2d edition.

Kails. Henderson and Calvert. Wonder tales of old Tyrol.

Kalevide of Estland. Olcott. Wonder tales from Baltic wizards. (Singing sword.)

Kalle and the wood grouse. *See* Enchanted grouse.

Kamehameha, the Great. Colum. Bright islands.

Kana and the fairies. *See* Shadow gifts.

Kara and Guja. Lee. Folk tales of all nations.

Kari Woodencoat. *See* Kari Woodengown.

Kari Woodengown. Olcott. Wonder tales from Baltic wizards. (Kari Woodencoat.)

See also Sheepskin coat.

For other entries, see 2d edition.

Karl Katz. Olcott. Wonder tales from goblin hills. (Peter Klaus the goat-herd.)

Karu and Rairu. Eells. Magic tooth.

Kassian, St. *See* St. Kassian.

Katcha and the devil. Power. Stories to shorten the road.

For other entries, see 2d edition.

Kate Mary Ellen and the fairies. Colum. Fountain of youth.

For other entries, see 2d edition.

Katydid. Skinner. Child's book of country stories. (How there came to be a katydid.)

Katydid's party. Patten. Junior classics. v. 8.

Kaulu. Colum. Bright islands. (Kaulu, the world's strongest boy.)

Kava. Metzger. Tales told in Hawaii. (Origin of Kawa.)

Kawa the cunning. Metzger. Tales told in Hawaii.

Kawelo. Colum. Bright islands. (Ka-welo: the overthrower of the giant champion.)

Kazuma's revenge. Mitford. Tales of old Japan.

Keang=Njamo. Martens. Wonder tales from far away.

See also Discontented grass plant. II # ; Fisherman and his wife.

Keeltya and his rabblement. Young. Tangle-coated horse. (King's candlestick.)

Keep cool! #.

See also Churl of the Town of Mischance ; Devil's hide ; Eurrua, the madman ; Son of strength.

Keep troth. *See* Well and the weasel.

Keeper of the Pharos. *See* Alexandria.

Keeping of the bridge. *See* Horatius at the bridge.

Kelpies go to school. Blaisdell. Rhyme and story second reader.

Kenach, St. *See* St. Kenach.
Kenach's little woman. Canton. Child's book of saints.
Kenawai and the water buffalo. Skipper. Jungle meeting-
pool. (*In* Sixth meeting.)
See also Frog and the ox.
Kenewa, the bravest of the Penacooks. Browne. Indian
nights.
See also Brave three hundred.
Keresaspa. Wells. How the present came from the past.
Book 2, pt. 2. (Keresaspa, or Kershasp, Legend of.)
Kettle that would not walk. Hutchinson. Fireside stories.
Starbuck. Familiar haunts. (*In* Wise men of Gotham.)
For other entries, see 2d edition.
Key of the golden palace. Perkins and Danielson. Second
year Mayflower program book.
Kid and the tiger. Faulkner. White elephant.
See also Pour, Katrientje, pour.
For other entries, see 2d edition.
Kid and the wolf. I. Curry and Clippinger. Children's lit-
erature.
For other entries, see 2d edition.
Kid and the wolf. II. Æsop. Fables (Jones. Kid on the
housetop.)
Æsop. Fables (Whitman ed. Wolf and the kid.)
Cooper. Argosy of fables.
See also Wolf and the kid. I.
For other entries, see 2d edition.
Kid and the wolf. III. *See* Wolf and the kid. II.
Kid on the housetop. *See* Kid and the wolf. II.
Kidnapping Santa Claus. Skinner. Christmas stories.
Kids and the wolf. *See* Wolf, the she-goat and the kid.
Kija, the wise. Metzger. Tales told in Korea.
Killing of Cabrakan. Lee. Folk tales of all nations. (Dis-
comfiture of Cabrakan.)
For other entries, see 2d edition.
Killing the birds. Evans. Worth while stories.
Kind=hearted policeman. Evans. Worth while stories.
Kinder=fairy and the chalk. Cook. Red and gold stories.
Kindness misunderstood. Woodson. African myths.
Kindness of the crocodile. Housman. What-o'clock tales.
Kindness of the Egyptian Moon=good. *See* Journey of
Khensu to Behkten.
Kindness returned. White. School management, p. 254.
Kindness to a beggar. White. School management, p. 244.
King. Eells. Magic tooth.
King Alexander's adventures. *See* Alexander the Great.
II.
King Alfred. Cather. Pan and his pipes. (Harp King Al-
fred played.)
Coussens. Diamond story book. (Alfred the Great.)
Farjeon, Mighty men from Beowulf to William the Con-
queror. (How Alfred made the peace.)

King Alfred—*continued.*
Kinscella. Music appreciation readers. Book 2. (Harp that saved England.)
Tappan. Old world hero stories.
Terry. Tales from far and near. (King Alfred's dream.)
For other entries, see 2d edition.
King Alfred and the cakes. Evans. Worth while stories.
For other entries, see 2d edition.
King Alfred's dream. *See* King Alfred.
King and his hawk. I. *See* 2d edition.
King and his hawk. II. **Gaster. Ma'aseh book. v. 2. (King and the hawk.)
King and queen. Fyleman. Forty good-night tales.
King and the apple. Lee. Folk tales of all nations.
See also Silent princess #.
For other entries, see 2d edition.
King and the brazen horse. *See* Cambuscan bold, Story of.
King and the cobbler. *See* Cobbler and the king.
King and the hawk. *See* King and his hawk.
King and the horses that turned the mills. Cooper. Argosy of fables.
See also Soldier and his horse; War-horse and the miller.
King and the ju-ju tree. Lee. Folk tales of all nations.
King and the little bells. Kinscella. Music appreciation readers. Book 1.
King and the magic stick. Kinscella. Music appreciation readers. Book 5.
King and the miller of Mansfield. Coussens. Diamond story book. (King Henry and the miller.)
Power. Stories to shorten the road.
See also Better than that; Dish of lentils.
For other entries, see 2d edition.
King and the oak. Bulfinch. Golden age. (Erisichthon. *In* Ch. 22.)
Lee. Folk tales of all nations.
See also King who cut down the enchanted wood.
For other entries, see 2d edition.
King and the sage #.
See also Bag of stories.
King and the statue. Baldwin. Pedlar's pack.
King Arthur. Curry and Clippinger. Children's literature. (Adventures of Arthur.)
Elson and Keck. Junior high school literature. (Days of chivalry.)
Evans. Worth while stories.
Tappan. Old world hero stories. (Legend of King Arthur.)
Terry. Tales from far and near.
See also Dream of Rhonabwy; Giant of St. Michael's Mount; King Ryence's challenge.
For other entries, see 2d edition.
King Arthur and his swords. *See* King Arthur's coming.

King Arthur and King Cornwall. Williams-Ellis. Fairies and enchanters.

King Arthur and the magic sword. See King Arthur's coming.

King Arthur's coming. Allen. Tales from Tennyson. (Coming of Arthur.)
Bailey. Stories of great adventures. (Drawing of the sword.)
Curry and Clippinger. Children's literature. (How Arthur became king.)
Elson and Keck. Junior high school literature. (Coming of Arthur.)
Farjeon. Mighty men from Beowulf to William the Conqueror. (Sword in the stone.)
Johnson and Scott. Anthology of children's literature. (King Arthur and his swords.)
Kinscella. Music appreciation readers. Book 5. (King Arthur and the magic sword.)
Power. Bag o' tales. (How Arthur proved his kingship.)
For other entries, see 2d edition.

King Arthur's death. Allen. Tales from Tennyson. (End of the Round Table, and the passing of Arthur.)
Bailey. Stories of great adventures. (Passing of Arthur.)
Elson and Keck. Junior high school literature. (Passing of Arthur.)
For other entries, see 2d edition.

King Arthur's dream. Johnson and Scott. Anthology of children's literature. (Great bear.)
Williamson. Stars through magic casements. (Great bear.)

King Arthur's sword. Johnson and Scott. Anthology of children's literature. (King Arthur and his swords.)

King Believe and Peasant Truth. Botsford. Picture tales from the Italian.

King Bran of Britain. See Bran the blessed.

King Cophetua and the beggar maid. Evans. Worth while stories.
For other entries, see 2d edition.

King Cormac's cup. See How Cormac MacArt went to faery.

King Coustans, the emperor. See Constans the emperor.

King Diarmid an' Pol. Dunbar. Sons o' Cormac.

King Dorus builds a temple. Butterfield. Young people's story of architecture. (In Ch. 8.)

King Dragon. Dasent. East of the sun and west of the moon (Nielsen).
See also King Lindorm #.

King Eumenes starts a library. Lansing. Great moments in science. (From papyrus to paper.)

King Fergus and the water-horse. See King Iubdan and King Fergus.

King Fergus and the wee men. See King Iubdan and King Fergus.

King finds a beautiful hair. Shimer. Fairyland.
See also Bata the Egyptian boy.
King for three days. **Gaster. Ma'aseh book. v. 2.
(Rashi and the Duke of Lorraine.)
Schwarz. Jewish caravan. (Rashi and the Duke of Lorraine.)
See also Godfrey de Bouillon.
For other entries, see 2d edition.
King Frost. I. Carpenter. Tales of a Russian grandmother.
(Frost king's bride.)
Carrick. More Russian picture tales.
Ralston. Russian fairy tales. (Frost.)
Ransome. Old Peter's Russian tales. (Frost.)
For other entries, see 2d edition.
King Frost. II. Phillips. Far peoples. (Morozko.)
Shimer. Fairyland. (Gentle Olga and spiteful Vera.)
King Hakon. Lang. Red true story book. (Death of Hacon the good.)
King Harold of England. Farjeon. Mighty men from Beowulf to William the Conqueror. (Fall of the golden man.)
Kipling. Rewards and fairies. (Tree of justice.)
King Henry and the miller. *See* King and the miller of Mansfield.
King Henry of Navarre. Clément. Flowers of chivalry.
(Lucky seed.)
King Herla. Olcott. Wonder tales from fairy isles.
King Horn. Darton. Wonder book of old romance.
For other entries, see 2d edition.
King is asleep. Baker. Tell them again tales.
King Iubdan and King Fergus. Colum. Big tree of Bunlahy. (When the Luprachauns came to Ireland.)
Colum. Forge in the forest. (King Fergus and the waterhorse.)
Olcott. Wonder tales from fairy isles. (King Fergus and the wee men.)
For other entries, see 2d edition.
King John and the Abbot of Canterbury. Coussens. Diamond story book.
(poem). Johnson and Scott. Anthology of children's literature.
See also Clown of San Cristobal; Kunz and his shepherd; Pint bottle of Cinkota.
For other entries, see 2d edition.
King John and the Magna Charta. Lansing. Great moments in freedom. (*In* Signing of the Magna Carta.)
Miller. My book of history. v. 3. (*In* Ch. 13.)
For other entries, see 2d edition.
King Kojata. Byrde. Polish fairy book. (About Prince Surprise.)
Coussens. Diamond story book.
See also Water king's daughter.
For other entries, see 2d edition.

King Khufu and the magicians. Baikie. Wonder tales of the ancient world. (Tales of the old magicians.)
**Maspero. Popular stories of ancient Egypt.
For other entries, see 2d edition.
King Lareyn's garden. Guerber. Legends of the middle ages. (*In* Dietrich von Bern.)
Henderson and Calvert. Wonder tales of old Tyrol.
Wolff. Pale mountains. (King Laurin's rose garden.)
King Laurin's rose garden. *See* King Lareyn's garden.
King Lear. Chandler. Magic pictures. (King Lear and his daughters.)
Lamb. Tales from Shakespeare.
Richardson. Stories from old English poetry. (Story of King Lear and his three·daughters.)
See also Salt. I.
For other entries, see 2d edition.
King Leo and the two little jackals. *See* Little jackals and the lion.
King Louis XIV of France. Clément. Flowers of chivalry. (Let Jean Bart smoke.)
King Mathias' laziest men. Schwimmer. Tisza tales.
See also Prince Vivien and Princess Placida.
King Mathias' three riddles. Schwimmer. Tisza tales.
See also Potter. I #.
King Midas of the golden touch. *See* Midas. I–II.
King Monkey. Olcott. Wonder tales from pirate isles. (King Monkey; or, Why I have curly hair.)
King Nectanebo. **Maspero. Popular stories of ancient Egypt. (Adventure of the sculptor Petesis and King Nectonabo.)
King o' the cats. *See* King of the cats.
King o' the three winds. Dunbar. Sons o' Cormac.
See also Wind an' wave an' wandherin' flame.
King of England and his three sons. Coussens. Diamond story book.
For other entries, see 2d edition.
King of France's daughter. Power. Bag o' tales.
For other entries, see 2d edition.
King of horses. *See* Alexander the Great. I.
King of nature. Egan. New found tales.
King of the birds. I. *See* Setuli #.
King of the birds. II. *See* King Wren.
King of the birds. III. Fun folk, and fairy tales. (Sparrow and the eagle.)
King of the birds. I–III.
See also Why chickens live with man.
King of the buffaloes. Lee. Folk tales of all nations. (Aggo Dah Gauda; or, The man with his leg tied up.)
For other entries, see 2d edition.
King of the cats. I. Bailey. Story-telling hour.
Coussens. Diamond story book. (King o' the cats.)
Fun folk and fairy tales. (King o' the cats.)

King of the cats—*continued.*
Harper. Ghosts and goblins. (King o' the cats.)
See also Johnny Reed's cat.
For other entries, see 2d edition.
King of the cats. II. *See* King of the cats comes to Ireland.
King of the cats comes to Ireland. Colum. King of Ireland's son. (When the king of the cats came to King Connal's dominion.)
Colum. Fountain of youth. (King of the cats.)
King of the Golden River. Curry and Clippinger. Children's literature.
Johnson and Scott. Anthology of children's literature.
(play). Knight. Dramatic reader. (Destruction of Treasure Valley. Abridged.)
See also Sar, Nar and Jinook.
For other entries, see 2d edition.
King of the jackals. De La Mare and Quayle. Readings.
King of the Land of Mist. Colum. King of Ireland's son.
King of the mice. Faulkner. White elephant. (Kingdom of mouseland.)
For other entries, see 2d edition.
King of the robins. La Rue. Under the story tree.
See also Robin's Christmas song.
King of the tigers is sick. Skeat. Tiger's mistake.
King of the winds. Skipper. Jungle meeting-pool. (*In* First meeting.)
See also Wind and the sun.
King of Tripoli brings the pasta. Farjeon. Italian peep-show.
King Olaf. Dunlap. Stories of the Vikings. (Adventures of the boy Olaf.)
Farjeon. Mighty men from Beowulf to William the Conqueror. (Queen Sigrid's collar.)
Farjeon. Mighty men from Beowulf to William the Conqueror. (Treasure of the isle.)
Lang. Red true story book. (Fight at Svolder Island.)
For other entries, see 2d edition.
King O'Toole and his goose. Curry and Clippinger. Children's literature.
Johnson and Scott. Anthology of children's literature.
For other entries, see 2d edition.
King Orgulous. Canton. Child's book of saints.
See also King Robert of Sicily.
King Orpheo and the fairies. Barbour. English tales retold.
See also Orpheus and Eurydice.
King Picus. Colum. Children who followed the piper. (*In* Children and the gods of old time.)
For other entries, see 2d edition.
King Robert of Sicily. Coussens. Diamond story book.
Darton. Wonder book of old romance.
See also King Orgulous; Miser converted.

King Robert of Sicily—*continued.*
For other entries, see 2d edition.

King Robert the Bruce. *See* Bruce, Robert.

King Ryence's challenge. Lanier. Book of giants. (*In* Giant of St. Michael's Mount.)
See also Mantle of kings' beards #.
For other entries, see 2d edition.

King Schahriar and Scheherazade. Kinscella. Music appreciation readers. Book 6. (Queen of story-tellers.)
Lee. Folk tales of all nations. (Shariar and Sharazad.)
For other entries, see 2d edition.

King Setnan and the Assyrians #.
See also Sennacherib's defeat.

King Shudraka and Hero's family. *See* Faithful Rajpoot.

King Solomon and the ants. I. Cowles. Stories to tell.
See also Solomon's ghost.
For other entries, see 2d edition.

King Solomon and the ants. II. *See* King Solomon and the demon. II.

King Solomon and the bees. *See* King Solomon's answer.

King Solomon and the birds. I. Brown. Curious book of birds.

King Solomon and the birds. II. Berry. Black folk tales. (Story of Solomon and the birds.)

King Solomon and the birds. III. Skeat. Tiger's mistake. (King Solomon and the birds.)

King Solomon and the demon. I. Gaer. Burning bush. (*In* Search for the magic shomeer.)
Garnett. Ottoman wonder tales. (Ashmedai and King Solomon.)
**Gaster. Ma'aseh book. v. 1. (Solomon and Ashmedai.)
For other entries, see 2d edition.

King Solomon and the demon. II. Colum. Forge in the forest. (King Solomon and the servitor of the Lord of earth.)
See also Carob tree, Legend of.

King Solomon and the hoopoes. Brown. Curious book of birds. (*In* King Solomon and the birds.)
Carey. Stories of the birds.
See also Cynical hoopoe.

King Solomon and the servitor of the Lord of earth. *See* King Solomon and the demon. II.

King Solomon, the merchant, and the mouse-deer. De Leeuw. Java jungle tales.
See also This for that.

King Solomon's answer (poem). Johnson and Scott. Anthology of children's literature. (King Solomon and the bees.)
Kinscella. Music appreciation readers. Book 2. (Wise king and the bee.)
(poem). Saxe. Poems.
For other entries, see 2d edition.

King Solomon's power pump. Mackaye. Tall tales of the Kentucky mountains.

King Solomon's throne. Gaer. Burning bush. (*In* Golden throne of Solomon.)

King Solomon's wisdom. I. **Gaster. Ma'aseh book. v. 2. (Judgement of Solomon ; or, Two mothers.)

Evans. Worth while stories. (Wisdom of Solomon.)

King Solomon's wisdom. II. Gaer. Magic flight. (Wisdom of King Solomon.)

King Thrushbeard. Grimm. Fairy tales (Olcott).

See also Crumb in the beard ; How Blanca the haughty became gentle.

For other entries, see 2d edition.

King Thunder. Capuana. Golden-feather.

King Uggermugger; or, The Princess Silver=silk. Wilson. Red magic.

King Under Wave's daughter. Young. Tangle-coated horse.

King who cut down the enchanted wood. Lindsay. Choosing book.

See also King and the oak.

King who died for love of his general's wife. Ryder. Twenty-two goblins.

King who had no daughter. Chrisman. Wind that wouldn't blow.

King who kept his word. Martens. Wonder tales from far away.

King who won a fairy as his wife. Ryder. Twenty-two goblins.

King who would be stronger than fate #.

See also Maria-in-the-forest ; Prince and the foundling.

King=with=a=hole=in=his=pocket. Shannon. California fairy tales.

King with the face of an angel. *See* St. Louis.

King Wren. Bailey. Tell me another story. (How the wren became king.)

Brown. Curious book of birds. (King of the birds.)

Carey. Stories of the birds. (How the wren made a bid for the crown.)

Colum. Fountain of youth. (King of the birds.)

Grimm. Fairy tales (Olcott. Hedge-king.)

Harriman. Stories for little children.

Power. Stories to shorten the road. (King of the birds.)

Rich. Why-so stories. (Another story of why the eagle is king.)

Rich. Why-so stories. (Why the birds hate the owl.)

Spaulding and Bryce. Aldine readers. Book 2. rev. ed. (King of the birds.)

See also How the birds chose a king ; Linnet and the eagle ; Peacock and the magpie ; Why the owl is not king of the birds.

For other entries, see 2d edition.

King Wren—*continued.*
In 2d edition this story is also indexed under the title "Why the wren flies close to the earth."

King Xerxes goes to war. Farjeon. Mighty men from Achilles to Julius Caesar.

Kingdom of mouseland. *See* King of the mice.

Kingdom of the lion. Æsop. Fables (Jones). Cooper. Argosy of fables.

Kingfisher. I. *See* Forgetful kingfisher.

Kingfisher. II. *See* Halcyon birds.

Kingfisher and the sparrow. Cooper. Argosy of fables.

King's ankus #.
See also Robbers and the treasure.

King's barn. Farjeon. Martin Pippin in the apple orchard.

King's candlestick. Young. Tangle-coated horse.

King's castle in the Graytop Mountains. Falkberget. Broomstick and Snowflake.

King's choice. Dane. Once there was and was not.
See also Why the fish laughed.

King's curing. MacManus. Lo, and behold ye!
See also Queen's conquest.

King's daughter. Capuana. Italian fairy tales.

King's daughter and the apothecary. Fyleman. Forty good-morning tales.

King's daughter of France. Lee. Folk tales of all nations.

King's flea. I. White. Made in Russia. (*In* Ch. 3.)

King's flea. II. Sawyer. Picture tales from Spain. (Flea.)

King's holiday. Baldwin. Pedlar's pack.

King's hungry. Chrisman. Wind that wouldn't blow.

King's life saved by spells. Aspinwall. Jataka tales.
See also Seller of words.

Kings of Kent. Farjeon. Mighty men from Beowulf to William the Conqueror.

Kings, Origin of. *See* King.

King's page. Bailey. Stories children want.
For other entries, see 2d edition.

King's promise. Eells. Brazilian fairy book.
See also Queen's conquest.

King's rijstepap. Hart. Picture tales from Holland.

King's servants. Friedlander. Jewish fairy tales (Dutton).
See also Prince of Engalien.

King's son and the apple. *See* King and the apple.

King's son and the dervish's daughter. *See* Baldpate.

King's son and the hermit. *See* Golden apple with the silver seeds.

King's son and the painted lion. Æsop. Fables (Whitman ed.).
La Fontaine. Fables (Tilney. *In* Horoscope.)
For other entries, see 2d edition.

King's Thanksgiving. Bailey. Stories children want.
Bailey. Tell me another story.
Perkins and Danielson. Second year Mayflower program book.
King's white elephant. *See* Grateful elephant.
Kinkach Martinko. Cowles. Stories to tell.
For other entries, see 2d edition.
Kintaro, the golden boy. Whitehorn. Wonder tales of old Japan. (Story of Kintaro, strong boy.)
For other entries, see 2d edition.
Kippie=kappie. Olcott. Wonder tales from goblin hills.
See also Benead and the moor elves.
Kiss me. Sandburg. Rootabaga pigeons.
Kit and Kat. Harriman. Stories for little children.
Perkins. Dutch twins. Ch. 1–2.
Kitchen god. Metzger. Picture tales from the Chinese.
Kite and the butterfly. Johnson and Scott. Anthology of children's literature.
Cooper. Argosy of fables.
For other entries, see 2d edition.
Kite and the nightingale. *See* Hawk and the nightingale.
Kite and the pigeons. Æsop. Fables (Artzybasheff).
Cooper. Argosy of fables.
See also Hawk, the kite, and the pigeons.
For other entries, see 2d edition.
Kites and the swans. Cooper. Argosy of fables.
See also Crow and the partridge.
Kitpooseagunow the avenger #.
See also Badger and the bear.
Kitten that forgot how to mew. Skinner. Happy tales.
See also Canary-dog.
Kitten that wanted to be a Christmas present. Elson and Runkel. Child-library readers. Book 2.
Skinner. Happy tales. (Kitten's Christmas wish. Adapted.)
For other entries, see 2d edition.
Kitten's Christmas wish. *See* Kitten that wanted to be a Christmas present.
Klaubautermann. *See* Kobold and the pirate.
Kling, klang, poor Dokkum. Olcott. Wonder tales from windmill lands.
Klose=kom=bau, Story of. Browne. Indian nights.
See also Beaver's tail.
Knapsack #.
See also Soldier and the demons.
Knave of hearts. I. Blondell. Keepsakes. (True story of the Knave of hearts.)
Knave of hearts. II. Carroll. Alice's adventures in Wonderland. (Who stole the tarts; Alice's evidence. Ch. 11–12.)

Knavish little bird. Lee. Folk tales of all nations.
Sawyer. Picture tales from Spain. (Picaro bird.)
For other entries, see 2d edition.
    In 2d edition this story is also indexed under the title
"Put it on my bill."
Knife and the naked chalk. Kipling. Rewards and fairies.
Knight and his charger. *See* Soldier and his horse.
Knight and the dragon. Fuller. Book of dragons. (Ballad
of the knight and the dragon.)
Knight and the greyhound. Darton. Wonder book of old
romance.
    See also Beth Gellert.
Knight and the nightingale. Carey. Stories of the birds.
Knight and the yeoman (poem). Bennett. Pigtail of Ah
Lee Ben Loo. (Ye olde tyme tayle of ye knight ye yeo-
manne and ye faire damosel.)
Knight of La Sarraz and the toads. Guerber. Legends of
Switzerland. (*In* Legends of Vaud and Valais.)
Knight of the leopard. Power. Children's treasure chest.
Knight of the Madonna. McNeer and Lederer. Tales from
the crescent moon.
Knight with the lion. Barbour. English tales retold.
Knighting of Rodrigo. *See* Cid, The.
Knight's dilemma. *See* Sir Gawain's marriage. II.
Knights of the Round Table. *See* Round Table, Founding of.
Knights of the silver shield. Coe. Third book of stories.
Curry and Clippinger. Children's literature.
    See also At his post; Royal errand; Sachem of the white
plume.
For other entries, see 2d edition.
Knight's tale. *See* Palamon and Arcite.
Knockgrafton, Legend of. Lee. Folk tales of all nations.
(Lusmore at Knockgrafton.)
    See also Benead and the moor elves; How Ivan Tortik be-
came straighter than the poplars; Hunchback and the
elves; Kippie-kappie; Singing goblins.
For other entries, see 2d edition.
Knockmany, Legend of. Adams and Atchinson. Book of
giant stories. (Finn McCoul.)
For other entries, see 2d edition.
Knoonie in the sleeping palace. Housman. Doorway in
fairyland.
Starbuck. Far horizons.
    See also Sleeping beauty.
Knot-holes. St. Nicholas. Sept. 1888, p. 819.
Knut Spelevink. Topelius. Canute Whistlewinks and other
stories. (Canute Whistlewinks.)
For other entries, see 2d edition.
Kobold and the pirate. Price. Legends of the seven seas.
Kongi and Potgi. Phillips. Far peoples.
    See also Cinderella.
Korobona, the strong of heart. Partridge. Joyful Star.

Koschei without death. Carpenter. Tales of a Russian grandmother. (Kostchey the One-who-never-dies.) Ralston. Russian fairy tales. (Koschei the deathless.) Zeitlin. Skazki. (Kostchei the deathless.) *See also* Marya Morevna.
For other entries, see 2d edition.
Kostchei the deathless. *See* Koschei without death.
Kostchey the One=who=never=dies. *See* Koschei without death.
Krazy Kat. Cross. Music stories.
Krencipal and Krencipalka. Byrde. Polish fairy book.
See also Bremen town musicians ; Herr Korbes ; Vagabonds.
Kriemhild's ditch. Guerber. Legends of Switzerland. (*In* Legends of Zurich.)
Kris and the bear. Evans. Worth while stories.
K'tonton, a mouse and a bit of leaven. Weilerstein. Adventures of K'tonton.
K'tonton arrives. Weilerstein. Adventures of K'tonton.
See also Thumbling.
K'tonton plans a palace for the sabbath queen. Weilerstein. Adventures of K'tonton.
See also Magic palace.
K'tonton takes a ride on a runaway trendel. Weilerstein. Adventures of K'tonton.
Kunigunde's lover. Henderson and Calvert. Wonder tales of old Tyrol.
Kunz and his shepherd, Story of. **Gaster. Ma'aseh book. v. 2.
See also King John and the Abbott of Canterbury.
Kura the ogress. Metzger. Tales told in Hawaii.
Kurage. *See* Monkey and the jellyfish.
Kuratko the terrible. Davis. Baker's dozen.
For other entries, see 2d edition.
Kutoyis, the avenger. Spence. Myths of the North American Indians. (Kutoyis, Story of. *In* Ch. 3.)
For other entries, see 2d edition.
Kuz'ma Skorobogaty. Lee. Folk tales of all nations.
See also Puss in Boots.
For other entries, see 2d edition.
Kyang the fox, the wolf and the hare. Lee. Folk tales of all nations.
Kyrilo the tanner. Zeitlin. Skazki.

L

La Hormiguita and the mouse. *See* Perez the mouse. II.
Labor Day. *See* Boy who wanted to play always ; Bundle of sticks ; Cobblers of Bruges # ; Dinner horses ; Farmer tries to sleep ; Fairy who grew up ; First hat ; Gold ducat ; Holidays are busy days ; Hungry chicks ; Land where people never die ; Lazy chair bearers ; Lil' Hannibal ; Man who was going to mind the house ; Magician's apprentice ; Mill

Labor Day—*continued.*
and the water nymphs; Piggywee's little curly tail; Planting an orchard; Prince who wasn't hungry; Rhinoceros and the dromedary; Sad princess; Solomon's ghost; Sunshine fairy; Toy of the giant child; Tubal Cain; Wages of seven years; Waring's "white wings"; When everybody played; Week of Sundays; Wife of Auchtermuchty #; Wish ring #; Wrong thing.
For other entries, see 2d edition.
Laborer and his master. Eells. Island of magic.
See also Bruin and Reynard partners. I.
Labourer and the nightingale. *See* Nightingale and the pearl.
In 2d edition there are entries under each title.
Labourer and the snake. Æsop. Fables (Jones).
Cooper. Argosy of fables.
See also Wound and the scar.
Lad and the fox #.
See also Peasant and the hare.
Lad and the north wind. *See* Lad who went to the north wind.
Lad and the old lassie's song. Lee. Folk tales of all nations.
Lad who cleaned the garden path. Miller. My travelship: Japan.
Lad who fooled the troll and won the princess. *See* Boots and the troll.
Lad who went to Next Town. Lindsay. Choosing book.
Lad who went to the north wind. Arnold. Folk tales retold. (Hans and the north wind.)
Dasent. East of the sun and west of the moon (Nielsen).
Evans. Worth while stories. (Gifts of the north wind.)
Faulkner. Road to enchantment. (Lad and the north wind.)
Hutchinson. Chimney corner fairy tales.
Johnson and Scott. Anthology of children's literature.
Power. Blue caravan tales.
Rasmussen. East o' the sun and west o' the moon.
Told under the green umbrella.
See also Table, the ass and the stick.
For other entries, see 2d edition.
Ladders to heaven. Power. Bag o' tales.
Laden ass and a horse. *See* Horse and the loaded ass.
Lady and the morning=glory. Miller. My travelship: Japan.
Lady Featherflight. Adams and Atchinson. Book of giant stories.
For other entries, see 2d edition.
Lady Godiva's Day. *See* Godiva.
Lady in the sun. Williams. Jolly old whistle.
See also Daylight, Origin of. V #.

Lady Jacqueline. *See* Jacqueline of Holland.
Lady Jane. La Rue. Under the story tree.
Lady mole. Rhys. English fairy book.
See also Mole, Origin of.
For other entries, see 2d edition.
Lady of Greifenstein. Henderson. Wonder tales of Alsace-Lorraine.
Lady of Stavoren. *See* Sunken city.
Lady of the forest. Tappan. Prince from nowhere.
See also Wood maiden #.
Lady of the lakes. Martinez Del Rio. Sun, the moon and a rabbit.
Lady slippers. Newman. Fairy flowers. (Princess Pity Patter.)
Lady Toad in the moon. Olcott. Wonder tales from China seas.
Lady Yolanda's thimble. Masson. Folk tales of Brittany.
See also First thimble.
Lady's room. De La Mare and Quayle. Readings.
Farjeon. Italian peepshow.
Lafayette, Marquis de. Coe. Third book of stories. (Brotherhood of long ago.)
Clément. Flowers of chivalry. (Way he left.)
Laidley worm of Spindleston (poem). Rhys. English fairy book.
Steel. English fairy tales. (Laidly worm.)
For other entries, see 2d edition.
Laird of Co'. Olcott. Wonder tales from fairy isles. (Elfin cup.)
For other entries, see 2d edition.
Laka and the menehunes. Metzger. Tales told in Hawaii. (Menehune canoe.)
See also Clever little fisherman; Fairy nets; Little people of Ao-tea-roa; Rata, Legend of.
For other entries, see 2d edition.
Lake of St. Anna. Pogány. Hungarian fairy book.
Lake princess. Wilson. Green magic.
Lake Tanganyika, Origin of. Woodson. African myths.
Lamb and the fox. De Huff. Taytay's memories.
See also Wolf and the kid. II.
Lamb and the wolf. *See* Lamb chased by a wolf.
Lamb chased by a wolf. Æsop. Fables (Jones).
Cooper. Argosy of fables. (Lamb and the wolf.)
Lambikin. Curry and Clippinger. Children's literature.
Harriman. Stories for little children.
Hutchinson. Candlelight stories.
Kinscella. Music appreciation readers. Book I. (Drum that saved Lambkin.)
Power. Bag o' tales.
See also Lion-hearted kitten.
For other entries, see 2d edition.

Lambton worm. Rhys. English fairy book.
See also Vouivre.
For other entries, see 2d edition.
Lame duck. Hutchinson. Candlelight stories.
For other entries, see 2d edition.
Lame fox. *See* Laughing Eye and Weeping Eye.
Lame prince. *See* Little lame prince.
Lame squirrel's Thanksgiving. Bailey. Stories children want.
Sheriff. Stories old and new. (Lame squirrel's Thanksgiving dinner.)
For other entries, see 2d edition.
Lament of the leaf. Wheelock. Kindergarten children's hour. v. 2. (*In* Ch. 17.)
Lamentations of the fellah. *See* Peasant and the workman.
Lamp. *See* Lamp and the sun.
Lamp and the sun. Æsop. Fables (Jones. Lamp.)
Cooper. Argosy of fables. (Farthing rushlight.)
For other entries, see 2d edition.
Lampy's Fourth of July. Harper and Hamilton. Winding roads.
Lance of Kanana. *See* Message of the caliph.
Lancelot and Elaine. *See* Sir Lancelot and Elaine.
Land of the blue flower. Burnett. Land of the blue flower.
Ladies Home Journal. Dec. 1908, p. 7.
Land of the impossible. Bennett. Pigtail of Ah Lee Ben Loo.
Land of the sky-blue water. Kinscella. Music appreciation readers. Book 3. (Making of a song.)
Land turtle and the hippopotamus. *See* How the elephant and the whale were tricked. II.
Land where people never die. Seredy. Good master.
See also Blue bird. II.
Language of beasts. Borski and Miller. Gypsy and the bear. (How a sensible peasant cured his wife's curiosity.)
Lee. Folk tales of all nations. (Animals' language.)
Ransome. Old Peter's Russian tales. (Hunter and his wife.)
Tappan. Prince from nowhere. (Adventures of the shepherd.)
See also Ass, the ox, and the labourer; Ohia and his sorrows; Secret of the animals.
For other entries, see 2d edition.
Language of the birds. I #.
See also Councillor and the orphan; Ravens; Three languages.
Lantern and the fan. Johnson and Scott. Anthology of children's literature.
For other entries, see 2d edition.
Lantern fairies. Cook. Red and gold stories.
Lantern of the fisherman's little lad. Perkins and Danielson. Mayflower program book.

Lantern of the pearl. Egan. New found tales.
See also Jewel tears.
Laocoön. Bulfinch. Golden age. (*In* Ch. 28.)
Miller. My book of history. v. 2. (*In* Ch. 2.)
For other entries, see 2d edition.
Laodamia. *See* Protesilaus.
Lapwing and the owl. Bryce. Folk lore from foreign lands.
For other entries, see 2d edition.
Lapwing's search. *See* Why the peewee looks for brother.
Lark and her young ones. I. Æsop. Fables (Artzyba-
sheff).
Æsop. Fables (Jones. Lark and the farmer.)
Æsop. Fables (Whitman ed.).
Cooper. Argosy of fables.
Curry and Clippinger. Children's literature.
Johnson and Scott. Anthology of children's literature.
(Lark and its young.)
Williams. Tales from Ebony. (Larks.)
See also Mouse family talks of moving.
For other entries, see 2d edition.
Lark and its young. *See* Lark and her young ones.
Lark and the farmer. *See* Lark and her young ones.
Lark, the wolf, and the fox. Borski and Miller. Gypsy and
the bear.
Larks. *See* Lark and her young ones.
Lark's advice. Carey. Stories of the birds.
Lassie and her godmother. Dasent. East of the sun and
west of the moon (Nielsen).
See also Girl who did not do as she was told.
For other entries, see 2d edition.
Last adventure of Tchamsen. *See* Raven and the cask. II.
Last battle of the revolution. Freeman. Child-story read-
ers. 3d reader.
Last class. *See* Last lesson in French.
Last days of Zahhak. *See* Faridoun.
Last dream of the old oak. Andersen. Fairy tales (Stick-
ney). v. 2.
For other entries, see 2d edition.
Last fly, Story of. Mamin. Verotchka's tales.
Last lesson in French. Bailey. Tell me another story.
(Last class.)
For other entries, see 2d edition.
Last of the dragons. Fuller. Book of dragons.
For other entries, see 2d edition.
Last of the Feni. Colum. Big tree of Bunlahy. (Story of
Usheen.)
Johnson and Scott. Anthology of children's literature. (Oi-
sin in the land of youth.)
Lane. Tower legends. (Leprechaun of Ardmore Tower.)
Stephens. Irish fairy tales. (Oisin's mother.)
Young. Tangle-coated horse. (Saba ; Three hundred years
after.)

Last of the Feni—*continued.*
For other entries, see 2d edition.
Last of the frost giants. Topelius. Canute Whistlewinks.
Last of the Leprechauns. Shannon. California fairy tales.
Last of the thunderbirds. Snell. Told beneath the northern lights.
For other entries, see 2d edition.
Last straw. *See* Old Hump.
Last tragedy of the Toltecs. Martinez Del Rio. Sun, the moon and a rabbit.
Latchstring. Boeckel. Through the gateway.
See also Indians and the Quaker family.
Latona and the country people. *See* Latona and the frogs.
Latona and the frogs. Bulfinch. Golden age. (Latona and the rustics. *In* Ch. 4.)
Evans. Worth while stories. (Latona.)
Forbush. Myths and legends of Greece and Rome. (Latona and the country people.)
Lang. Book of myths. (Latona and the rustics.)
For other entries, see 2d edition.
Latona and the rustics. *See* Latona and the frogs.
Laugh of the swamp-rail. *See* How Ma-ui strove to win immortality for men.
Laugh with those who laugh. Williams. Jolly old whistle.
See also Faithful Svend.
Laughing apples and the weeping quinces. Curtin. Fairy tales of Eastern Europe.
Laughing dumpling #.
See also O Jizo Sama and the rice ball.
Laughing Eye and Weeping Eye. Harper. Fillmore folk tales. (Little lame fox.)
Lee. Folk tales of all nations. (Lame fox.)
See also Water of endless youth.
For other entries, see 2d edition.
Laughing horse. Aspinwall. Can you believe me.
Laughing Jack o' lantern. Elson and Runkel. Child-library readers. Book 2.
Laughless. Lebermann. New German fairy tales.
Launcelot of the lake. *See* Sir Lancelot.
Laurel, Story of. *See* Daphne.
Lavender. Carey. Flower legends.
Lawful heir. *See* Slave's fortune.
Lawkamercyme (poem). Steel. English fairy tales.
Lawyer of Samarcand. Egan. New found tales.
Lawyer's opinion. *See* To-day or to-morrow.
Lazy boy. Metzger. Tales told in Hawaii.
Lazy chair-bearers. Gordon and Stockard. Gordon readers. 2d reader.
Lazy fox. Mitchell. Gray moon tales. (Mammy and the lazy fox.)
Lazy frog. Berry. Black folk tales.
See also Monkeys' house.

Lazy girl. De Huff. Taytay's memories.
Lazy girl and the lake spirit. James. Tewa firelight tales.
Lazy Heinz. Grimm. Tales from Grimm (Wanda Gag).
See also Milkmaid and her pail of milk.
Lazy hornet. Purnell and Weatherwax. Why the bee is busy.
Lazy husbands. Meeker. Folk tales from the Far East.
Lazy Jack. Curry and Clippinger. Children's literature.
Hervey and Hix. Fanciful tales for children. (Lazy Sam.)
Lee. Folk tales of all nations.
Rhys. English fairy book.
Spaulding and Bryce. Aldine readers. Book 2. rev. ed.
Steel. English fairy tales.
See also Jock and his mother.
For other entries, see 2d edition.
Lazy judge. Cendrars. Little black stories.
Lazy Lena. Wahlenberg. Old Swedish fairy tales.
Lazy Maria. *See* Gold Maria and Pitch Maria.
Lazy men of Fimber village. Egan. New found tales.
Lazy queen. Pogány. Magyar fairy tales.
See also Spinning queen ; Rumplestiltskin.
Lazy Sam. *See* Lazy Jack.
Lazy Taro. Whitehorn. Wonder tales of old Japan. (Story of lazy Taro.)
For other entries, see 2d edition.
Lazy Tok.
See Bayong of the lazy woman.
League of rats. La Fontaine. Fables (Tilney).
Leak in the dyke (poem). Cabot. Course in citizenship.
Evans. Worth while stories.
White. School management, p. 257. (Faithful little Hollander.)
For other entries, see 2d edition.
Lean Liesl and Lanky Lenz. Grimm. Tales from Grimm (Wanda Gag).
See also Milkmaid and her pail of milk.
Leap, frog, leap. *See* Prince Green-eyes.
Leaping match. Andersen. Fairy tales (Stickney). v. 1.
For other entries, see 2d edition.
Leather. *See* Shoes.
Leaves and the roots. Cooper. Argosy of fables.
Leaves of the aspen tree. *See* Why the aspen leaves tremble. I.
Leaves that hung but never grew. Morris. Gypsy story teller.
Williams. Jolly old whistle. (Bertha and the black boar.)
See also Beauty and the beast.
Leek. Carey. Flower legends.
Leetie and the wood fairies. Meeker. Folk tales from the Far East.
See also Thumbelina.

Left-handed Humming Bird. Martinez Del Rio. Sun, the moon and a rabbit.
Legend of, etc. *See* the first important word of the title.
Leif Ericson. Blaisdell. Log cabin days. (Vikings.)
    Colum. Voyagers. (Children of Eric the Red; Leif the Lucky.)
    Kinscella. Music appreciation readers. Book 4. (Of Vikings bold.)
    Lang. True story book. (How Leif the Lucky found Vineland the Good.)
    Miller. My book of history. v. 4. (*In* Adventurous Northmen. Ch. 8.)
    Morris. Stories from mythology: North American. (Coming of the Norsemen.)
    Spence. Myths of the North American Indians. (Norsemen in America; Leif the lucky. *In* Ch. 1.)
    Tappan. Old world hero stories.
Leif the Lucky. *See* Leif Ericson.
Lelia and Lulia Lobster. Burnett. Children's book.
Lend a hand. White. School management, p. 276.
LeNotre, André. *See* Gardener to the king.
Leo, the faithful. Fun folk and fairy tales.
Leonard, St. *See* St. Leonard.
Leonardo da Vinci. Chambers' miscellany. v. 9. (*In* Anecdotes of the early painters.)
    Miller. My book of history. v. 3. (*In* Ch. 16.)
    Steedman. Knights of art.
Leonidas at Thermopylae. *See* Brave three hundred.
Leonor, Legend of. *See* St. Leonor.
Leopard and the deer. Bacon. Lion-hearted kitten.
Leopard and the fox. Æsop. Fables (Artzybasheff).
    Cooper. Argosy of fables.
Leopard and the hare. Woodson. African myths.
    See also Spider's visit.
Leopard, the tortoise, and the bush rat. Woodson. African myths.
Lepe, the bird-maiden. Colum. Bright islands.
Leppa Polkky and the blue cross. *See* Log.
Lepracaun. I (poem). Power. Bag o' tales.
    For other entries, see 2d edition.
Lepracaun. II–III. *See* 2d edition.
Lepracaun. IV. Baker. Pedlar's wares. (Leprechaun.)
Lepracaun. V (poem). Guiterman. Poems.
    (poem). Olcott. Wonder tales from fairy isles. (Leprechaun.)
Lepracaun. VI. Through story-land with the children. (Leprechaun.)
    See also Tease, tease, tease again.
Lepracaun stories. *See* Basket of eggs; Gold bell; Last of the Leprechauns; When the Luprachauns came to Ireland; Wily leprechaun.
Leprechaun. *See* Lepracaun.

Leprechaun of Ardmore Tower. Lane. Tower legends.
See also Last of the Feni.
Leprechaun's honey. Casserley. Michael of Ireland.
Leshy. Ralston. Russian fairy tales.
Lesson for kings. Broomell. Children's story caravan.
(Two kings.)
Lee. Folk tales of all nations.
For other entries, see 2d edition.
Lesson in courtesy. Chidley. Fifty-two story talks.
Lesson in justice. Curry and Clippinger. Children's literature. (Lord helpeth man and beast.)
Schwarz. Jewish caravan. (Lord helpeth man and beast.)
See also Alexander the Great. I.
For other entries, see 2d edition.
Lesson of faith. Hart. Picture tales from Holland. (Caterpillar and the lark.)
Johnson and Scott. Anthology of children's literature.
(What the caterpillar learned.)
Patten. Junior clasiscs. v. 8. (Butterfly's children.)
For other entries, see 2d edition.
Lesson song. *See* Johnny's shoe.
Let Jean Bart smoke. Clément. Flowers of chivalry.
Let, the first artist. Through story-land with the children.
Letter to Santa Claus. Bailey. Wonderful tree.
Bryce. Short stories for little folks.
Major. Merry Christmas stories.
Leviathan. *See* About Leviathan.
Lexy and the dogs on his street. Buckingham. Elephant's friend. (To keep store with Bimbo.)
See also Dicky the brave.
Lie. Schwarz. Jewish caravan.
Lie-a-stove. *See* By the pike's command.
Life and perambulations of a mouse. *See* Mouse, Adventures of.
Life for the Tsar. Kinscella. Music appreciation readers.
Book 6.
Light o' me eyes. Dunbar. Sons o' Cormac.
Light of the earth. Dane. Once there was and was not.
Light-of-the-evening and Rainbow. De Huff. Taytay's memories.
Lighthouse. I. Evans. Worth while stories. (Lighthouse keeper's grand-daughter.)
Lighthouse. II. Blondell. Keepsakes.
Lights on the Christmas tree. Barrows and Cavanah.
Favorite pages from Child Life.
Liisa and the prince. Bowman and Bianco. Tales from a Finnish tupa.
See also Cinderella.
Li'l Hannibal. *See* Little Hannibal.
Lilac, Legend of. Newman. Fairy flowers.
Lilies white #.
See also White Lily ; Arum lily.

Lily and the rose (poem). Cooper. Argosy of fables.

Lily=maid and the tailors (poem). Bennett. Pigtail of Ah Lee Ben Loo. (Ye very ancient ballad of ye lily-mayden and ye lyttel taylor-boye.)

Lily nymph. *See* Water-lily. V.

Lily of the valley. *See* Dragon Sin; Ladders to heaven.

Lily=pad post. Krohn and Johnson. Scales of the silver fish.

Lincoln, Abraham. Bailey. Tell me another story. (Log cabin boy.)

Cozad. Story talks. (Something to think about.)

McVenn. Good manners and right conduct. Book 2. (Lincoln's story of his first dollar.)

For other entries, see 2d edition.

Lincoln and the little birds. White. School management, p. 245. (Lincoln's kindness to birds.)

For other entries, see 2d edition.

Lincoln's birthday. *See* Birdhouse of Lincoln logs; Polly Prichard, patriot.

Linda Branca and her mask. Eells. Islands of magic. *See also* Many-furred creature; Rashin-Coatie.

Linnet and the eagle. Cooper. Argosy of fables. *See also* King Wren.

Lion and a mouse. *See* Lion and the mouse.

Lion and Aissa. Lang. Red book of animal stories. (*In* Adventure of Gerard, the lion hunter.)

Lion and hyena. *See* Lion and the hyena.

Lion and little jackal. Lee. Folk tales of all nations (Story of lion and little jackal.)

Lion and other beasts. *See* Lion's share. I.

Lion and squirrel. *See* Lion and the squirrel.

Lion and the ass hunting. Æsop. Fables (Artzybasheff). Æsop. Fables (Jones).

Æsop. Fables (Whitman ed. Ass and the lion hunting.)

Cooper. Argosy of fables.

For other entries, see 2d edition.

Lion and the bear. Æsop. Fables (Artzybasheff. Lion, the tiger and the fox.)

Æsop. Fables (Jones. Lion, the bear and the fox.)

Cooper. Argosy of fables.

For other entries, see 2d edition.

Lion and the blackbirds. De Huff. Taytay's memories. *See also* Red-winged blackbirds and coyote.

Lion and the boar. Æsop. Fables (Artzybasheff. Lion and the goat.)

Æsop. Fables (Jones).

Cooper. Argosy of fables. (Lion and the goat.)

Lion and the bull. I. Æsop. Fables (Jones).

Cooper. Argosy of fables.

Lion and the bull. II. **Arnold. Book of good counsels. (Lion, the jackals and the bull, Story of.)

Mackenzie. Jackal in Persia. (Bull Shan, the two jackals, Damnah and Lilah, and the lion.)

Lion and the bull. II—*continued.*
  Phillips. Far peoples.
  See also Elephant and the jackal.
Lion and the bulls. *See* Lion and the four bulls.
Lion and the crocodile. Raspé. Children's Munchausen
    (Martin. *In* Ch. 1.)
  Raspé. Tales from the travels of Baron Munchausen.
Lion and the dolphin. Cooper. Argosy of fables.
  Power. Children's treasure chest.
Lion and the eagle. Cooper. Argosy of fables.
Lion and the four bulls. Æsop. Fables (Artzybasheff. Ti-
    ger and the bulls.)
  Æsop. Fables (Jones. Lion and the three bulls.)
  Æsop. Fables (Whitman ed. Lion and the four oxen.)
  Cooper. Argosy of fables. (Lion and the bulls.)
  For other entries, see 2d edition.
Lion and the fox. I. *See* 2d edition.
Lion and the fox. II. *See* Fox who served a lion.
Lion and the gnat. I. Æsop. Fables (Jones. Gnat and
    the lion.)
  Æsop. Fables (Whitman ed. Gnat and the lion.)
  Cooper. Argosy of fables. (Gnat and the lion.)
  For other entries, see 2d edition.
Lion and the goat. I. Gordon and Stockard. Gordon read-
    ers. 2d reader.
  For other entries, see 2d edition.
Lion and the goat. II. *See* Lion and the boar.
Lion and the hare. I. **Arnold. Book of good counsels.
    (Lion and the old hare.)
  Carrick. Tales of wise and foolish animals. (Hare and
    the lion.)
  Cooper. Argosy of fables. (Lion and the old hare.)
  Curry and Clippinger. Children's literature. (Lion tricked
    by a rabbit.)
  See also Bunny Rabbit and the king of beasts; Bunny the
    brave; Hare at the water-hole; Lion and the squirrel;
    Tiger and the shadow.
  For other entries, see 2d edition.
Lion and the hare. II. Noel. Magic bird of Chomo-lung-
    ma.
Lion and the hare. III. Æsop. Fables (Jones).
  Cooper. Argosy of fables.
  See also Fox and the piece of meat.
Lion and the hare. IV. Cooper. Argosy of fables.
Lion and the hyena. Carrick. Tales of wise and foolish
    animals. (Lion and hyena.)
  See also Spider's visit.
Lion and the jackal. Cooper. Argosy of fables.
  See also "Heyo, house" #.
Lion and the little jackals. *See* Little jackals and the lion.

Lion and the mosquitoes. Johnson and Scott. Anthology of children's literature.
See also Tiger with burning eyes.
For other entries, see 2d edition.
Lion and the mouse. Æsop. Fables (Artzybasheff).
Æsop. Fables (Jones).
Æsop. Twenty-four fables (L'Estrange. Lion and a mouse.)
Æsop. Fables (Whitman ed.).
Cady and Dewey. Picture stories from the great artists.
Cooper. Argosy of fables.
Curry and Clippinger. Children's literature.
Johnson and Scott. Anthology of children's literature.
Power. Children's treasure chest.
See also Elephant and the rats.
For other entries, see 2d edition.
Lion and the neighborly hippopotamus. Lobagola. Folk tales of a savage.
Lion and the old hare. *See* Lion and the hare. I.
Lion and the saint. *See* St. Jerome and the lion.
Lion and the shepherd. *See* Androcles and the lion.
Lion and the squirrel. Berry. Black folk tales. (Lion and squirrel.)
See also Lion and the hare. I.
Lion and the three bulls. *See* Lion and the four bulls.
Lion and the wild ass. *See* Lion's share. I.
Lion, ass, and fox. *See* Lion's share. II.
Lion-hearted kitten. Bacon. Lion-hearted kitten and other stories.
See also Lambikin ; Little Black Sambo.
Lion, hyena, and hare. *See* Lion, the hyena, and the rabbit.
Lion in love. Æsop. Fables (Artzybasheff).
Æsop. Fables (Jones).
Æsop. Fables (Whitman ed.).
Cooper. Argosy of fables.
For other entries, see 2d edition.
Lion, Jupiter and the elephant. Æsop. Fables (Jones).
Cooper. Argosy of fables.
Lion makers. Broomell. Children's story caravan.
See also Four brothers who brought a dead lion to life.
Lion of Lucerne. Eggleston. Stories for special days in the church school. (True-hearted, whole-hearted.)
For other entries, see 2d edition.
Lion of the Pharaohs. *See* Sphinx (Egyptian). II.
Lion, the ass and the fox. *See* Lion's share. II.
Lion, the ass, and the fox hunting. *See* Lion's share. II.
Lion, the bear and the fox. *See* Lion and the bear.
Lion, the bear, the monkey and the fox #.
In 2d edition this story is also indexed under the title "Sick lion. II."
Lion, the fox and the ass. I. *See* 2d edition.

Lion, the fox and the ass. II. Æsop. Fables (Jones. Ass, the fox and the lion.)
Æsop. Fables (Whitman ed.).
Cooper. Argosy of fables. (Ass, the fox and the lion.)
Lion, the fox, and the ass. III. *See* Lion's share. II.
Lion, the fox and the beasts. Æsop. Fables (Artzybasheff. Sick lion.)
Æsop. Fables (Jones. Old lion.)
Æsop. Fables (Whitman ed. Fox and the sick lion.)
(poem). Cooper. Argosy of fables. (Sick lion and the fox.)
Cooper. Argosy of fables. (Sick lion.)
Harriman. Stories for little children. (Old lion.)
For other entries, see 2d edition.
Lion, the fox and the stag. Æsop. Fables (Jones).
See also Ass's brains.
Lion, the fox and the wolf. Æsop. Fables (Jones. Lion, the wolf and the fox.)
Æsop. Fables (Whitman ed.).
Cooper. Argosy of fables. (Lion, the wolf and the fox.)
For other entries, see 2d edition.
Lion, the hyena and the rabbit. Carrick. Tales of wise and foolish animals. (Lion, hyena, and hare.)
For other entries, see 2d edition.
Lion, the jackals, and the bull. *See* Lion and the bull. II.
Lion, the leopard, and the dog. Woodson. African myths.
Lion, the monkey, and the two asses. La Fontaine. Fables (Tilney).
Lion, the mouse, and the cat. **Arnold. Book of good counsels. (Cat who served the lion.)
Cooper. Argosy of fables. (Cat who served the lion.)
See also Washerman's jackass.
For other entries, see 2d edition.
Lion, the mouse and the fox. Æsop. Fables (Jones).
Cooper. Argosy of fables.
Lion, the tiger, and the eagle. Lee. Folk tales of all nations.
See also King Falcon, King Dolphin and King Stag #.
Lion, the tiger and the fox. *See* Lion and the bear.
Lion, the wolf, and the fox. *See* Lion, the fox, and the wolf.
Lion tricked by a rabbit. *See* Lion and the hare. I.
Lionbruno. Coussens. Diamond story book.
For other entries, see 2d edition.
Lioness. *See* Lioness and the fox.
Lioness and the bear. La Fontaine. Fables (Tilney. Lioness and the she-bear).
For other entries, see 2d edition.
Lioness and the cow. Woodson. African myths.
Lioness and the fox. Æsop. Fables (Jones. Lioness and the vixen.)

Lioness and the fox—*continued.*
Cooper. Argosy of fables. (Lioness.)
For other entries, see 2d edition.
Lioness and the she=bear. *See* Lioness and the bear.
Lioness, the whelps and the little jackal. Cooper. Argosy of fables.
See also Jackal or tiger.
Lion's share. I. Æsop. Fables (Artzybasheff. Lion and other beasts.)
Æsop. Fables (Jones. Lion and the wild ass.)
Cooper. Argosy of fables. (Wild ass and the lion.)
For other entries, see 2d edition.
Lion's share. II. Æsop. Fables (Artzybasheff. Lion, the ass and fox hunting.)
Æsop. Fables (Jones. Lion, the fox and the ass.)
Æsop. Twenty-four fables (L'Estrange. Lion, ass, and fox.)
Æsop. Fables (Whitman ed. Lion, the ass and the fox.)
Cooper. Argosy of fables. (Lion, the ass and fox hunting.)
Lion's share. III. Cooper. Argosy of fables. (Cow, the goat, the sheep and the lion.)
Lipp the Lapp. Farjeon. Old nurse's stocking basket.
Lippi, Fra Filippo. Steedman. Knights of art.
Lippo and Tapio. Bowman and Bianco. Tales from a Finnish tupa.
Lisa's lamb. Wheelock. Kindergarten children's hour. v. 4. Ch. 28.
Listening king. Eells. Islands of magic.
See also Three sisters. I.
Little acorn. Bailey. Tell me another story.
Bryce. Short stories for little folks.
Harriman. Stories for little children.
For other entries, see 2d edition.
Little=and=good. Housman. Turn again tales.
For other entries, see 2d edition.
Little animal who didn't go for his tail. Babbitt. Animals' own story book.
Little Anklebone. Williston. Hindu stories. (Little toe bone.)
For other entries, see 2d edition.
Little Athen's message. Cabot. Course in citizenship.
Little baby zebra. Bacon. Lion-hearted kitten.
Little bag. Carrick. Tales of wise and foolish animals.
Little Baxters go marketing. Patten. Junior classics. v. 9.
Little bear. Bailey. Stories children want.
For other entries, see 2d edition.
Little bear and the big bear. *See* Great bear and the little bear. II.
Little bedesman of Christ. *See* St. Francis of Assisi.
Little Betty Buttonhole. Potter. Giant of Apple Pie Hill.
Little Bigtown. Potter. Giant of Apple Pie Hill.

Little birchen twig. Tappan. Prince from nowhere.
Little bird. I. *See* Son of Adam.
Little bird. II. Chardon. Golden chick.
Little birds and red roses. Martinez Del Rio. Sun, the moon and a rabbit.
Little birds' Christmas feast. *See* Mercy, Legend of.
Little black coal. Harper and Hamilton. Winding roads.
Little black lamb. Casserly. Whins on Knockattan.
Little Black Quasha. Quinn. Stories for the six-year-old.
Little Black Sambo, Story of. Bannerman. Little Black Sambo.
  Harriman. Stories for little children.
  Hutchinson. Chimney corner stories.
  Johnson and Scott. Anthology of children's literature.
  Piper. Gateway to storyland.
  Power. Blue caravan tales.
  Quinn. Stokes' wonder book of fairy tales.
  Quinn. Stories for the six-year-old. (Abridged.)
  See also Lion-hearted kitten; Trudi in the forest.
  For other entries, see 2d edition.
Little blond shark. Colum. Bright islands. (When the little blond shark went visiting.)
  Price. Legends of the seven seas.
Little blue dishes. Arnold. Folk tales retold.
  Told under the blue umbrella.
Little blue ox. Wadsworth. Paul Bunyan.
Little Blue Peter. Potter. Captain Sandman.
Little boy pie. Farjeon. Old sailor's yarn box.
  See also Benjy in Beastland; Robin's eggs.
Little boy who said, "I don't want to eat it." Beard. Tucked-in tales.
Little boy who wanted a castle. Bailey. Stories children want.
  Bailey. Tell me another story.
Little boy who wouldn't get up. Fyleman. Forty good-morning tales.
Little brawl at Allen. Stephens. Irish fairy tales.
Little Briar=rose. *See* Sleeping beauty. I.
Little brother. Chrisman. Wind that wouldn't blow.
Little brother and little sister. *See* Brother and sister. I.
Little brother of long ago. Wiggin and Smith. Twilight stories.
Little brown bowl. Bowman. Little brown bowl and other stories.
Little bucket. Botsford. Picture tales from the Italian.
  See also Mother Holle.
Little Burnt=face. *See* Little Scar Face.
Little Buzz=man. *See* Sir Buzz.
Little Cacinella, Story of. Mamin. Verotchka's tales.
Little cat. Freeman. Child-story readers. 3d reader.
Little Chicken Cross=the=road. Potter. Giant of Apple Pie Hill.

Little Cinderella. De Huff. Taytay's tales.
See also Cinderella ; Turkey maiden.
Little Claus and Big Claus. Andersen. Fairy tales (Sie-
wers. Little Klaus and Big Klaus.)
Andersen. Fairy tales (Stickney. v. 2. Great Claus and
Little Claus.)
Andersen. Four tales.
De La Mare and Quayle. Readings. (Big Claus and Little
Claus.)
Quinn. Stokes' wonder book of fairy tales. (Big Claus and
Little Claus.)
See also Jack and the Lord High Mayor ; Stupid boy and the
wand.
For other entries, see 2d edition.
Little cock and little hen. Nemcova. Disobedient kids.
See also Cock and the hen. III.
Little cock who sang coplas. Sawyer. Picture tales from
Spain.
Little Cossette and Father Christmas (play). Knight.
Dramatic reader.
Little cream cheese. Botsford. Picture tales from the Ital-
ian.
See also Milkmaid and her pail of milk.
Little cricket. I. Capuana. Golden-feather.
Little cricket. II. Chamoud. Picture tales from the French.
Little crookedbill. Meeker. Folk tales from the Far East.
Little crown. De La Mare and Quayle. Readings.
Little cup of tears #.
See also Dream of the white lark ; Miller's daughter. I.
**Little Czar Novishny, the false sister and the faithful
beasts.** Morris. Gypsy story teller. (Twelfth dragon.)
For other entries, see 2d edition.
In 2d edition this story is also indexed under the title
"Witch princess."
Little dark=green man. Williams. Jolly old whistle.
Little daughter of the snow. *See* Snowflake. I.
Little dawn boy and the rainbow trail. Johnson and Scott.
Anthology of children's literature.
For other entries, see 2d edition.
Little Daylight. Adams and Atchinson. Book of princess
stories.
For other entries, see 2d edition.
Little duck. Skinner. Merry tales.
Little duckling tries his voice. Barrows and Cavanah. Fa-
vorite pages from Child Life.
For other entries, see 2d edition.
Little elephant who wanted to fly. Lobagola. Folk tales
of a savage.
Little elf's valentine. Potter. Captain Sandman.
Little engine that could #.
See also Horse that b'lieved he'd get there.

Little farmer #.
See also Jack and the Lord High Mayor; Little Claus and Big Claus; Rusty Jack.
Little feather of Fenist the bright falcon. *See* Bright-Hawk's feather.
Little feather of the splendid falcon. *See* Bright-Hawk's feather.
Little Federigo Gonzaga. Chandler. Magic pictures.
Little fir tree. *See* Fir tree.
Little fool Ivan #.
See also Princess to be kissed at a charge.
Little footsteps upon the water. Bailey. Stories children want.
For other entries, see 2d edition.
Little Fred and his fiddle #.
See also Fiddle bow of the nixie; Louis and the three wishes.
Little friend. Smith and Hazeltine. Christmas in legend and story.
See also Christ-child. III.
Little friend coyote #.
See also Medicine wolf.
Little frog that did not mind. Elson and Runkel. Child-library readers. Book 2.
Little giant. Kennedy. Red man's wonder book.
Little gildmaster. *See* Mouse merchant.
Little girl from the island. *See* Napoleon and Josephine.
Little girl lost in the woods. Potter. Giant of Apple Pie Hill.
Little girl who couldn't wait. Wiggin and Smith. Twilight stories.
Little girl who saved her parents. Fleming. Round the world in folk tales.
Little girl with the light. Perkins and Danielson. Mayflower program book.
Little girl's odd collection. Burnett. Children's book.
Little glass shoe. Olcott. Wonder tales from goblin hills.
For other entries, see 2d edition.
Little glass slipper. *See* Cinderella.
Little gold penny. Baker. Tell them again tales.
Little Goldenhood. Curry and Clippinger. Children's literature. (True history of little Golden-hood.)
Lang. Old friends among the fairies. (True story of little Golden-hood.)
For other entries, see 2d edition.
Little grain of wheat, Story of. Skinner. Child's book of country stories.
For other entries, see 2d edition.
Little gray elephant. Bacon. Lion-hearted kitten.
Little gray goat. Carrick. Still more Russian picture tales.
Little gray lamb. I. *See* 2d edition.

Little Ida's flowers—*continued.*
Johnson and Scott. Anthology of children's literature.
For other. entries, see 2d edition.
Little Indian boy who was changed into an owl. De Huff.
Taytay's tales.
Little island. Farjeon. Mighty men from Beowulf to William the Conqueror.
Little jackal and the alligator. Bryce. Folk lore from foreign lands. (Jackal and the alligator.)
Faulkner. White elephant. (Alligator and the jackal.)
For other entries, see 2d edition.
Little jackals and the lion. Bruce. Treasury of tales for little folk. (Lion and the little jackals.)
Faulkner. White elephant. (Singh Rajah and the cunning little jackals.)
Hervey and Hix. Fanciful tales for children. (King Leo and the two little jackals.)
For other entries, see 2d edition.
Little John's first adventure. *See* Robin Hood.
Little Joseph and the parade. *See* Haydn, Joseph.
Little June Rose. Potter. Captain Sandman.
Little Ki and the pot of rice. Olcott. Wonder tales from China seas.
Little Klaus and Big Klaus. *See* Little Claus and Big Claus.
Little lady in green. Tappan. Little lady in green and other tales.
See also Golden goose. I.
Little lady's roses. Farjeon. Italian peepshow.
Little lamb. Dane. Once there was and was not.
Little lame fox. *See* Laughing Eye and Weeping Eye.
Little lame prince. Evans. Worth while stories. (Lame prince. Abridged.)
Large. Famous children of storybook land. (Abridged.)
See also Prince's dream.
For other entries, see 2d edition.
Little light=spirit. Lebermann. New German fairy tales.
Little lights. Wheelock. Kindergarten children's hour. v. 4. (*In* Ch. 10.)
For other entries, see 2d edition.
Little lion with the big voice. Freeman. Child-story readers. 3d reader.
Little maid who was wise. Eells. Islands of magic.
Little man and the big problem. Metzger. Tales told in Korea.
Little man and the dog cart. Miller. My travelship: Holland.
Little Master Misery. *See* Gore-Gorinskoe.
Little match girl. Andersen. Fairy tales (Siewers tr.).
Andersen. Fairy tales (Stickney). v. 1.
See also Stranger child. I–III.
For other entries, see 2d edition.

Little men of the mountains. Buckingham. Elephant's friend.

Little mermaid. Andersen. Fairy tales (Siewers tr.). Andersen. Fairy tales (Stickney). v. 2.
For other entries, see 2d edition.

Little mermaid and the star. Burnett. Children's book.

Little Mer=miss Neptune. Krohn and Johnson. Scales of the silver fish.

Little Milk, Little Cereal, and grey kitten, Moorka. Mamin. Verotchka's tales.

Little Miss Goosey. Burnett. Children's book.

Little Monk of St. Gall. Miller. My book of history. v. 3. (*In* Ch. 6.)

Little Mook. Hauff. Arabian days' entertainment. (Little Muck.)
For other entries, see 2d edition.

Little mother and big child. Potter. Captain Sandman.

Little mouse. Potter. Fairy caravan. (*In* Ch. 6.)

Little Muck. *See* Little Mook.

Little mud sparrows. *See* Christ-child and the clay birds.

Little nation that wanted to hide. Perkins and Danielson Mayflower program book.

Little Nell. Kaphan. Tell us a Dickens story. (Angel from heaven. Adapted.)
Large. Famous children of storybook land.
For other entries, see 2d edition.

Little nymph who loved bright colors. Carey. Flower legends. (Tulip, pt. 2.)
For other entries, see 2d edition.

Little old man of the mountain. Tappan. Prince from no-where.

Little old woman. I. Capuana. Italian fairy tales.
For other entries, see 2d edition.

Little old woman. II. Fyleman. Forty good-morning tales.

Little One=eye, Two=eyes and Three=eyes. *See* One-eye, Two-eyes, Three-eyes.

Little pagan beggars. Shannon. California fairy tales.

Little pan. Capuana. Golden-feather.

Little path. Lindsay. Choosing book.

Little peach child. *See* Momotaro. I.

Little Peachling, Adventures of. *See* Momotaro. I.

Little people of Ao=tea=roa. Colum. Bright islands.
See also Fairy nets; Laka and the menehunes; Shadow gifts.

Little people of Tanagra. Chandler. Magic pictures.

Little Persian. White. School management, p. 256. (Truthful Persian.)
For other entries, see 2d edition.

Little Peter and the giant. Bennett. Pig tail of Ah Lee Ben Loo.

Little pig and the wolves. Pogány. Magyar fairy tales.
See also Three little pigs.

Little pig that grumbled. Skinner. Happy tales.
Little pine tree who wished for new leaves. Egan. New
found tales. (Discontented fir tree.)
Evans. Worth while stories.
Harriman. Stories for little children.
Piper. Folk tales children love. (Pine tree and its needles.)
Piper. Road in storyland. (Pine tree and its needles.)
For other entries, see 2d edition.
Little Pitch and Tchamsen. *See* Raven and Pitch.
Little pony. Lee. Folk tales of all nations.
Little post=boy. Hodgkins. Atlantic treasury of childhood
tales.
Little Princess Sunshine. Harriman. Stories for little
children.
See also Blacksmith's sons #.
Little Quaker boy. *See* West, Benjamin.
Little rabbit and the lynx, Story of. Phillips. Indian
tales for little folks.
Little rabbit who wanted red wings. Bailey. Stories chil-
dren want.
For other entries, see 2d edition.
Little Red=cap. *See* Little Red Riding Hood.
Little red flower. Phillips. Far peoples.
Little red hen. I. Evans. Worth while stories.
(poem.) Harriman. Stories for little children.
Hutchinson. Chimney corner stories. (Little red hen and
the grain of wheat.)
Piper. Gateway to storyland. (Little red hen and the
grain of wheat.)
For other entries, see 2d edition.
Little red hen. II. *See* 2d edition.
Little red hen. III (poem). Bailey. Story telling hour.
(Mouse, the frog and the little red hen.)
(poem). Blaisdell. Rhyme and story second reader.
(Mouse, the frog and the little red hen.)
Bruce. Treasury of tales for little folk.
For other entries, see 2d edition.
Little red princess. Bailey. Tell me another story.
Little Red Riding Hood. Arthur Rackham fairy book.
Bruce. Treasury of tales for little folk. (Red Riding
Hood.)
Curry and Clippinger. Children's literature.
De La Mare. Told again.
Evans. Worth while stories.
Grimm. Fairy tales (Olcott. Little Red-cap.)
Johnson and Scott. Anthology of children's literature.
Lang. Old friends among the fairies.
Lee. Folk tales of all nations.
Mackenzie. Book of nursery tales.
Quinn. Stokes' wonder book of fairy tales.
Rich. Read aloud book.
Rhys. English fairy book.

Little Red Riding Hood—*continued*.
Steel. English fairy tales.
See also Juanita, Marianita, the cat and the bear; Tiger aunt.
For other entries, see 2d edition.
Little red shoes. Bowman. Little brown bowl.
Little roadster. Buckingham. Elephant's friend.
Little Rock, Story of. Linderman. Kootenai why stories.
Little Roman shepherd. Skinner. Christmas stories.
See also Shepherd who turned back.
Little rooster #.
See also Farmer tries to sleep.
Little rooster and the Turkish sultan. Seredy. Good master. (*In* Ch. 9.)
See also Drakesbill and his friends.
Little Scar Face. Johnson and Scott. Anthology of children's literature. (Little Burnt-face.)
Macmillan. Canadian wonder tales. (Indian Cinderella.)
Partridge. Joyful Star. (Oochigeaskw the little scarred girl.)
Told under the green umbrella.
See also Cinderella.
For other entries, see 2d edition.
Little Scotch Granite. Cabot. Course in citizenship and patriotism.
White. School management, p. 262.
Little shepherd. Cabot. Course in citizenship. (Abridged.)
For other entries, see 2d edition.
Little shiner. Denton. Homespun stories.
Little shoe. Olcott. Wonder tales from fairy isles.
Little singing frog. Harper. Fillmore folk tales.
For other entries, see 2d edition.
Little sister. Bowman and Bianco. Tales from a Finnish tupa. (Girl who sought her nine brothers.)
For other entries, see 2d edition.
Little sister of the giants #.
See also Sleeping Tsarevna and the seven giants.
Little sister of the sun. *See* Witch and the sister of the sun.
Little Smart Aleck. Beard. Tucked-in tales.
Little snow girl. *See* Snow image.
Little Snow-White. *See* Snow-White and the seven dwarfs.
Little soldiers of the cross. *See* Children's crusade.
Little Squeaky Shoes and the dragon. Potter. Captain Sandman.
Little stars of gold. Nemcova. Disobedient kids.
See also Star dollars.
Little steam engine. Harriman. Stories for little children.
For other entries, see 2d edition.
Little Sunshine. I. *See* 2d edition.
Little Sunshine. II. Bailey. Stories children want.
For other entries, see 2d edition.

Little table set thyself, gold=ass, and cudgel out of the sack. *See* Table, the ass and the stick. I.
Little Thumb. I–IV. *See* 2d edition.
Little Thumb. V. *See* Palececk.
Little Thumb. VI. *See* Ditu Migniulu.
Little Thumbalina. *See* Thumbelina.
Little toe bone. *See* Little Anklebone.
Little Town of Upside Down. Beard. Tucked-in tales.
Little town pink and clean. Olcott. Wonder tales from windmill lands.
Little true American. Forbes. Good citizenship. (*In* Ch. 5.)
Little Tuk. Andersen. Fairy tales (Stickney). v. 1.
Johnson and Scott. Anthology of children's literature.
For other entries, see 2d edition.
Little turtle that could not stop talking. *See* Talkative tortoise.
Little Two Sticks. Buckingham. Elephant's friend.
Little Ugly Boy. *See* Ugly wild boy.
In the 2d edition there are entries under each title.
Little water=drop's journey. *See* Water-drop. III.
Little water fairy. *See* Tom, the water baby.
Little white bed that ran away. Beard. Tucked-in tales.
Little white daisy. Carey. Flower legends. (Daisy.)
For other entries, see 2d edition.
Little white dog. Olcott. Wonder tales from Baltic wizards.
See also Frog prince.
Little white duck. *See* White duck.
Little white flower. Bryce. Short stories for little folks.
Little white horse. Olcott. Wonder tales from Baltic wizards.
Little white rabbit. I. *See* 2d edition.
Little white rabbit. II. Lee. Folk tales of all nations. (White rabbit.)
See also Fox and the hare; Goats in the turnip field; Important gnat #.
For other entries, see 2d edition.
Little White=thorn and the talking bird. Masson. Folk tales of Brittany.
Little Wind's birthday. Potter. Captain Sandman.
Little Wolff's wooden shoes. *See* Sabot of little Wolff.
Little wooden doll. Bianco. Little wooden doll.
Johnson and Scott. Anthology of children's literature.
Little zinc house in the trees. Olcott. Wonder tales from pirate isles.
Lively day in lovely Sicily. Crew. Saturday's children.
Living Buddha. Metzger. Tales told in Korea.
Living kantele. Olcott. Wonder tales from Baltic wizards.
Livingstone, David. Broomell. Children's story caravan. (Word of a gentleman.)
Lizard, tiger and lame man. Lee. Folk tales of all nations.

Lizard's necklace. Hill and Maxwell. Napoleon's story book.
Lizzie Thumb. *See* Thumbelina.
Llew. Henderson and Jones. Wonder tales of ancient Wales.
See also Elves and the shoemaker.
Lludd and Llevelys, Story of. Fuller. Book of dragons.
For other entries, see 2d edition.
Llyn Tegid. *See* Bala lake.
Lo-Sun, the blind boy. Lee. Folk tales of all nations.
For other entries, see 2d edition.
Lob Lie-by-the-fire. Ewing. Lob Lie-by-the-fire and other stories.
Lobster trees. Raspé. Children's Munchausen (Martin. *In* Ch. 12.)
Raspé. Tales from the travels of Baron Munchausen.
Lock and the key. Cooper. Argosy of fables.
Locust and the coyote. Johnson and Scott. Anthology of children's literature.
Nusbaum. Zuni Indian tales.
Nusbaum. Seven cities of Cibola.
Locust, the beetle, the goldfinch and the hunter. Cooper. Argosy of fables.
Log. Bowman and Bianco. Tales from a Finnish tupa. (Leppa Polkky and the blue cross.)
For other entries, see 2d edition.
Log cabin boy. *See* Lincoln, Abraham.
Lohengrin. Cather. Pan and his pipes. (Holy Grail.)
Cross. Music stories.
For other entries, see 2d edition.
Loik Guern. Lee. Folk tales of all nations.
See also Orpheus and Eurydice.
Loki. Pyle. Tales from Norse mythology. (Punishment of Loki.)
For other entries, see 2d edition.
Lolomi and the giants. Williams. Jolly old whistle.
Long, Broad and Quick-eye. *See* Broad man, the tall man, and the man with eyes of flame.
Long, Broad and Sharpsight. *See* Broad man, the tall man, and the man with eyes of flame.
Long, Broad, and Swift Glance. *See* Broad man, the tall man, and the man with eyes of flame.
Long Cromachy of the crows. MacManus. Lo, and behold ye!
Long leather bag. *See* Old hag's long leather bag.
Long-legs, Big-mouth, Burning-eyes. Kovalsky and Putnam. Long-legs, Big-mouth, Burning-eyes.
See also How six men traveled through the wide world.
Long-life name. I. Sugimoto. Picture tales from the Japanese.
Long-life name. II. Through story-land with the children. (Tiki-Tiki-Tembo.)

Long-life name. I–II. *See also* Master of all masters.

Long porter's tale. Adams and Atchinson. Book of enchantment.

Long time #.
See also Winter.

Longnose the dwarf. Hauff. Arabian days' entertainment. (Nosey the dwarf.)
See also Proud cook of Manila.
For other entries, see 2d edition.

Longstaff, Pinepuller and Rockheaver. Eells. Islands of magic.
See also Four hunters; Giant twins; How six men traveled through the wide world.

Look three times. Eells. Brazilian fairy book.

Looking-glass witch. Evans. Worth while stories.

Lord Bag of Rice. Henderson and Calvert. Wonder tales of old Japan. (Lord Sack of Rice.)
Whitehorn. Wonder tales of old Japan. (Hidesato of the rice bale.)
For other entries, see 2d edition.

Lord helpeth man and beast. *See* Lesson in justice.

Lord Mayor's Day. Graham. Happy holidays.

Lord of Pengerswick. I. Williams-Ellis. Fairies and enchanters. (Pengersec and the witch of Fraddom.)
For other entries, see 2d edition.

Lord of Pengerswick. II. Rhys. English fairy book. (Pengerswick.)

Lord of the dark cloud. Martinez Del Rio. Sun, the moon and a rabbit.

Lord Peter. Lee. Folk tales of all nations.
For other entries, see 2d edition.

Lord Sack of Rice. *See* Lord Bag of Rice.

Lord Thorny's eldest son. MacManus. Lo, and behold ye!

Lordship of the Fianna. *See* Coming of Finn.

Lorelei. I. Cross. Music stories.
Lang. Book of myths.
Olcott. Wonder tales from goblin hills. (Rhine enchantment.)
For other entries, see 2d edition.

Loss of a great gambler. *See* Gambler's loss.

Lost bell. Choate and Curtis. Little people of the hills.
For other entries, see 2d edition.

Lost brother, Story of. Canton. Child's book of saints.

Lost button. Potter. Giant of Apple Pie Hill.

Lost camel. Cooper. Argosy of fables.
See also Abner the Jew who had seen nothing; Perplexity of Zadig; Wisdom of the men of Jerusalem.
For other entries, see 2d edition.

Lost charm. I. *See* 2d edition.

Lost charm. II. Aspinwall. Jataka tales.
Lost child. I. Bryce. Folk lore from foreign lands.
Cowles. Stories to tell. (Adapted.)
See also Sit Bdour.
For other entries, see 2d edition.
Lost child. II. *See* 2d edition.
Lost child. III. Egan. New found tales.
Rhys. English fairy book.
Lost city of Ys. *See* Ys, Story of.
Lost doll. Whiteman. Playmates in print.
Lost fisher. *See* Missing man found.
Lost Indian boy. Sheriff. Stories old and new.
Lost key. Hooker. Garden of the lost key.
Lost legs. Starbuck. Familiar haunts. (*In* Wise men of
Gotham.)
See also McAndrew family; Persian jest; Wise men of
Gotham.
For other entries, see 2d edition.
Lost purse. Bryce. Folk lore from foreign lands.
For other entries, see 2d edition.
Lost spear. Egan. New found tales. (Golden spear.)
For other entries, see 2d edition.
Lotus eaters. Bulfinch. Golden age. (*In* Ch. 29.)
For other entries, see 2d edition.
Louis and the three wishes. Evans. Worth while stories.
See also Jew among the thorns; Little Fred and his fiddle.
Louis of France. *See* St. Louis.
Louise's garden. Morley. I know a secret.
Louise's mischief=day. Aspinwall. Can you believe me
stories.
Love. White. School management, p. 255.
Love and Folly. La Fontaine. Fables (Tilney).
Love=bird. I. Farjeon. Italian peepshow. (Lovebirds.)
Love=bird. II. Chardon. Golden chick.
Love of Heipua. Metzger. Tales told in Hawaii.
See also Orpheus and Eurydice.
Love of Joyful Star. Partridge. Joyful Star. (Love of
Cusi Coyllur—Joyful Star.)
Lovebirds. *See* Love bird. I.
Lovely Ilonka. Lang. Old friends among the fairies.
For other entries, see 2d edition.
Lovely Myfanwy. De La Mare. Dutch cheese.
Lovely one out of the sky. Olcott. Wonder tales from
China seas.
Lovers of Kufstein. Henderson and Calvert. Wonder tales
of old Tyrol.
Loves of Gompachi and Komurasaki. Mitford. Tales of
old Japan.
Loving brother. Metzger. Picture tales from the Chinese.
Loving pair. *See* Top and ball.

Lucio and the flies. Chardon. Golden chick.

Luck and blessing. Schwimmer. Tisza tales.
See also Cogia Hassan Alhabbal.

Luck and intelligence. Lee. Folk tales of all nations.
(Intelligence and luck.)
For other entries, see 2d edition.

Luck and pluck, Story of. Elson and Runkel. Child-library readers. Book 2.

Luck and thrift. Broomell. Children's story caravan (What luck!)

Luck boat of Lake Geneva. Guerber. Legends of Switzerland. (*In* Legends of Geneva.)
For other entries, see 2d edition.

Luck=child. Young. Celtic wonder tales.

Luck egg. Olcott. Wonder tales from Baltic wizards.

Luck, luck in the red coat. Olcott. Wonder tales from Baltic wizards.
See also Gore Gorinskoe.

Luck of Nahum. Friedlander. Jewish fairy tales (Dutton).
**Gaster. Ma'aseh book. v. 1. (Nahum Ish Gamzo.)

Luck of the goldenrod. Tappan. Prince from nowhere.

Luck of the roses. Housman. Moonshine and clover.

Luckless pigwidgeon. Shannon. Eyes for the dark.

Lucknow pipers. *See* Campbells are coming.

Lucky beggar. Bernhard. Master wizard.

Lucky farmer. Hart. Picture tales from Holland.

Lucky frog. Williams. Jolly old whistle.

Lucky Lialil. Wahlenberg. Old Swedish fairy tales.

Lucky seed. Clément. Flowers of chivalry.

Lucy. No. 2 Joy Street.

Ludwig and Marleen. Wheelock. Kindergarten children's hour. v. 3. Ch. 48.
See also Fisherman and his wife.
For other entries, see 2d edition.

Lugh, the long handed. Young. Celtic wonder tales. (Coming of Lugh.)

Lugh's birth. Young. Celtic wonder tales. (*In* Cow of plenty.)

Lup, Story of. Through story-land with the children.

Lusmore at Knockgrafton. *See* Knockgrafton, Legend of.

Lutey and the mermaid. Williams-Ellis. Fairies and enchanters.

Lutzelburg Castle. Henderson. Wonder tales of Alsace-Lorraine.

Lydia Doane celebration. Burnett. Children's book.

Lying for a wager. Lee. Folk tales of all nations.
See also Goatherd who won a princess; Jack and the king who was a gentleman #.

Lynx and the hare. Cooper. Argosy of fables.

Lyre and the dolphin. *See* Arion and the dolphin.

M

Ma-ui. *See* Maui.

Maroof, Story of. Arabian nights. Adventures of Haroun Er Raschid (Olcott).

McAndrew family. Lee. Folk tales of all nations. (Story of the McAndrew family.)
See also Lost legs; Mare's nest.
For other entries, see 2d edition.

Macbeth. Lamb. Tales from Shakespeare.
Richardson. Stories from old English poetry. (Macbeth, king of Scotland.)
For other entries, see 2d edition.

MacDonald plaid. Crew. Saturday's children.

Machiavelli's Prince. Miller. My book of history. v. 3. (*In* Ch. 16.)

Mad cloak. Raspé. Children's Munchausen (Martin. *In* Ch. 19.)

Mad dogs. Martinez Del Rio. Sun, the moon and a rabbit.

Mad man, the dead man and the devil. MacManus. Lo, and behold ye!
See also Believing husbands; Silly men and cunning wives.

Mad tea party. Carroll. Alice's adventures in Wonderland. (Ch. 7.)
De La Mare and Quayle. Readings.
(play). Knight. Dramatic reader.
For other entries, see 2d edition.

Mad Wolf. Capuana. Italian fairy tales.

Madam Sage and Madam Tea. *See* Tea and the sage.

Madam Work-basket's "At Home." Wiggin and Smith. Twilight stories.

Madama Piccinina. *See* Madame Teeny Tiny.

Madame Teeny Tiny. Botsford. Picture tales from the Italian.
See also Wee, wee woman.

Madame Tulip and Princess Violet. Carey. Flower legends. (Tulip, pt. 3.)

Madej, the brigand. Bernhard. Master wizard.

Maelström, Origin of. Farjeon. Old nurse's stocking basket. (You can't darn that hole.)

Maganda and the banyan fairy. Meeker. Folk tales from the Far East.

Magic almonds. Lee. Folk tales of all nations.

Magic apples. I. *See* Iduna's apples.

Magic apples. II. *See* 2d edition.

Magic apples. III. **Gaster. Ma'aseh book. v. 2. (Story of two young men who wanted to marry the same girl.)
For other entries, see 2d edition.

Magic awl. James. Tewa firelight tales. (Copetuengh; or Magic awl.)

Magic bird of Chomo-lung-ma. Noel. Magic bird of Chomo-lung-ma.

Magic broom. Fyleman. Forty good-morning tales.
Magic caftan. McNeer and Lederer. Tales from the crescent moon.
Magic cap. Borski and Miller. Gypsy and the bear. (How a clever cottager outwitted seven thieves.)
Bowman and Bianco. Tales from a Finnish tupa. (Pekka and the rogues.)
Hart. Picture tales from Holland.
See also Brahman and the goat.
For other entries, see 2d edition.
Magic carpet. *See* Prince Ahmed and the fairy Perie Banou; Three gifts. V.
Magic casements. No. 2 Joy Street.
Magic cherry tree. Pogány. Hungarian fairy book.
Magic crocodile. Baikie. Wonder tales of the ancient world. (Waxen crocodile, Story of.)
**Maspero. Popular stories of ancient Egypt. (*In* King Khufui and the magicians.)
For other entries, see 2d edition.
Magic curtain. Arnold. Folk tales retold.
Magic dog #.
See also Three birds and a little black dog.
Magic dumplings. *See* Why the dog and cat are enemies. I.
Magic egg #.
See also Enchanted grouse.
Magic fiddle. I. *See* 2d edition.
Magic fiddle. II. Williston. Hindu stories.
See also Singing bone #.
Magic fiddle. III. *See* Jew among the thorns.
Magic fife. Byrde. Polish fairy book.
Magic fishbone. Coussens. Diamond story book.
Dickens. Magic fishbone.
Harper. Selfish giant.
Harper. More story-hour favorites.
Power. Children's treasure chest.
Magic flask. Tappan. Prince from nowhere.
Magic flower. Harriman. Stories for little children.
For other entries, see 2d edition.
Magic flute. I. Chambers' miscellany. v. 18.
Magic flute. II. Metzger. Tales told in Korea.
Magic hair pins #.
See also Snow-White and the seven dwarfs.
Magic harp of Dagda. *See* Dagda's harp.
Magic jar. Coussens. Diamond story book.
For other entries, see 2d edition.
Magic ladder. *See* House of beautiful days.
Magic lake. Kennedy. Red man's wonder book.
See also Ponce de Leon and the fountain of youth.
Magic lamp. I. **Gaster. Ma'aseh book. v. 2. (R. Jehiel of Paris and the king.)
For other entries, see 2d edition.

Magic lamp. II. Curtin. Fairy tales of Eastern Europe.
Lee. Folk tales of all nations.
See also Aladdin.
Magic leaf #.
See also Rash magician.
Magic mirrors. Cook. Red and gold stories.
Magic mountain. Cook. Red and gold stories.
Magic mouth. Egan. New found tales.
Magic mouthful. Eells. Islands of magic.
Magic music #.
See also Monk and the bird's song.
Magic necklace. Williams. Jolly old whistle.
Magic nut. Brown. Under the rowan tree.
Magic palace #.
See also K'tonton plans a palace for the sabbath queen.
Magic pears from nowhere. *See* Miserly farmer.
Magic pillow. *See* Pillow of content.
Magic playing mice. Rowe. Moon's birthday.
Magic portrait. Gunterman. Castles in Spain.
Magic pot. I. *See* 2d edition.
Magic pot. II. *See* Wonderful porridge pot.
Magic rice. Olcott. Wonder tales from pirate isles.
See also Why the rice stopped rolling.
Magic ring. I. Sheriff. Stories old and new.
See also Gigi and the magic ring.
For other entries, see 2d edition.
Magic ring. II–III. *See* 2d edition.
Magic ring. IV. Friedlander. Jewish fairy tales (Dutton).
**Gaster. Ma'aseh book. v. 2. (Rabbi whose wife turned
him into a werewolf.)
Schwarz. Jewish caravan. (Medieval Jezebel.)
Magic robe. Kovalsky and Putnam. Long-legs, Big-mouth,
Burning-eyes.
Magic rocks and the beggar. *See* Thirst of the standing
stones. I.
Magic sandals. Gate. Tales from the secret kingdom.
Magic saucepan. *See* Hillman and the housewife.
Magic scythe. Lee. Folk tales of all nations.
Magic singing. Fillmore. Wizard of the north. Ch. 4.
(Contest.)
Olcott. Wonder tales from Baltic wizards.
Magic skipping-rope. Fyleman. Forty good-night tales.
Magic snuff box. Carpenter. Tales of a Basque grand-
mother.
Magic stone. I. Pogány. Hungarian fairy book.
Magic stone. II. Martinez Del Rio. Sun, the moon and a
rabbit.
Magic thread. Howes. Long bright land.
Magic tooth. Eells. Magic tooth, and other tales from the
Amazon.
Magic top. Williston. Hindu stories.

Magic tree. Kovalsky and Putnam. Long-legs, Big-mouth, Burning-eyes.

Magic well. Adams and Atchinson. Book of princess stories. (Princess Fior Usga.)
For other entries, see 2d edition.

Magic wigwam. Leland. Algonquin legends. (Story of a partridge and his wonderful wigwam.)
For other entries, see 2d edition.
In the 2d edition this story is also indexed under the title "How the hunter became a partridge."

Magical dancing doll. Macmillan. Canadian wonder tales. (Boy and the dancing fairy.)
For other entries, see 2d edition.

Magical moon. *See* Mirror that made trouble.

Magical serpent. *See* Shawano who killed the Uktena. II.

Magician and the cat. Nemcova. Disobedient kids.

Magician of Samarkand. Katibah. Other Arabian nights. (Tale of Prince Salem and the magician of Samarkand.)

Magician's apprentice. Lebermann. New German fairy tales.

Magician's castle in the sea. Gunterman. Castles in Spain.

Magician's daughter and the high-born boy. Stockton. Reformed pirate.
For other entries, see 2d edition.

Magician's pupil. Bernhard. Master wizard. (Wizard's pupil.)
For other entries, see 2d edition.

Magna Charta. *See* King John and the Magna Charta.

Magpie. I. *See* Magpie's nest. I.

Magpie. II. Darton. Wonder book of old romance.

Magpie and the Wahroogah. Lee. Folk tales of all nations. (Gooloo the magpie, and the Wahroogah.)

Magpie bridge o'er the silver stream of heaven. *See* Sky bridge of birds.

Magpie maidens. Rich. Why-so stories. (Why the magpie chatters.)
For other entries, see 2d edition.

Magpies and the greedy spider. *See* Greedy spider and the magpies.

Magpies and the river of stars. *See* Sky bridge of birds.

Magpie's nest. I. Brown. Curious book of birds. (Mother Magpie's kindergarten. Adapted.)
Carey. Stories of the birds. (Magpie.)
For other entries, see 2d edition.

Magpie's nest. II. Harriman. Stories for little children. (Why the magpie's nest is not well built.)
Rich. Why-so stories. (Why the magpie builds a poor nest.)
Williams-Ellis. Fairies and enchanters. (Why the magpie makes a half-finished nest.)
For other entries, see 2d edition.

Magpie's tail. Carrick. Tales of wise and foolish animals.

Maid and the pail of milk. *See* Milkmaid and her pail of milk.

Maid in the house. Carpenter. Tales of a Basque grand-mother. (Maid in the house of the fairy Laminak.)

Maid Maleen. Grimm. Fairy tales (Olcott).

Maid of Holland. King. Golden cat head.

Maid of the mist. Howes. Long bright land.

Maid of Zaragoza. Eggleston. Stories for special days in the church school. (Her father's daughter.)

See also Molly Pitcher.

Maid who married the morning star. Morris. Stories from mythology: North American. (Poia the star boy. *In* Ch. 9.)

Macmillan. Canadian wonder tales. (Star-boy and the sun dance.)

Spence. Myths of the North American Indians. (Poia, Legend of. *In* Ch. 3.)

See also Scar Face. III–IV.

For other entries, see 2d edition.

Maid with her basket of eggs #.

See also Eggs and beans.

Maiden. La Fontaine. Fables (Tilney).

Maiden and Sarakin Pumpkin. Berry. Black folk tales.

Maiden and the grizzly bear. Partridge. Joyful Star.

Maiden huntress. Nusbaum. Seven cities of Cibola.

Nusbaum. Zuni Indian tales.

Maiden in green. Metzger. Picture tales from the Chinese.

Maiden of Matsaki. Partridge. Joyful Star.

Maiden of the milky way. Olcott. Wonder tales from Baltic wizards.

See also Sky bridge of birds.

Maiden of the mountain. Beston. Starlight wonder book.

Maiden of Yellow Rocks. *See* Witch maiden.

Maiden who was blessed by the buffalo. Partridge. Joyful Star. (Maiden who was blessed by the buffalo and the corn.)

Maiden who was wiser than an emperor. Gordon and Stockard. Gordon readers. 2d reader. (Clever daughter.)

Martens. Wonder tales from far away. (Girl who knew more than the emperor.)

See also Sage damsel.

For other entries, see 2d edition.

Maiden with the beautiful face and the evil heart. *See* Dance of death. II.

Maiden with the wooden helmet. Lee. Folk tales of all nations. (Maiden with the wooden bowl.)

For other entries, see 2d edition.

Maiden's curiosity. *See* Sayadio in spirit land.

Maiden's secret. Egan. New found tales.

Partridge. Joyful Star. (Secret of Dowanhotaninwin.)

Maize spirit. *See* First corn. III.
Major's birthday. Forbes. Good citizenship. (*In* Ch. 6.)
Makila, Tale of. Carpenter. Tales of a Basque grandmother.
Making of a song. *See* Land of the sky-blue water.
Making of the buffalo dance. James. Tewa firelight tales.
Making of the sun and moon. *See* Sun, moon and stars. VIII.
Making the stars. *See* Sun, moon and stars. VIII.
Malicious mother-in-law. *See* Snowbird and the water tiger.
Mally Dixon and Knurre=Murre. *See* Johnny Reed's cat.
Mammy and a modern problem. *See* Why children lose their teeth. II.
Mammy and Mr. Mean Fox. *See* Mr. Mean Fox.
Mammy and Mr. Tadpole. Harper. More story-hour favorites.
Mitchell. Gray moon tales.
Mammy and Mr. Wolf. *See* Mr. Wolf and the flint stones.
Mammy and the butterflies. *See* First butterflies. III.
Mammy and the fireflies. *See* Fireflies, Origin of. II.
Mammy and the lazy fox. *See* Lazy fox.
Mammy and the mocking bird. *See* Mocking bird. IV.
Mammy and the rabbit. *See* How rabbit lost his tail. IV.
Mammy and the rainbow elves. *See* Violet and the rainbow elves.
Mammy and the shadow blankets. *See* Shadow blankets.
Mammy and the twins. Mitchell. Gray moon tales.
Mammy and the wicked elves. *See* Giving game.
Man. Carrick. Tales of wise and foolish animals.
See also Smart young tiger; What is a man #; Wolf and the man #.
Man and a satyr. *See* Satyr and the traveller.
Man and his boots. Field. American folk and fairy tales.
For other entries, see 2d edition.
Man and his coat (poem). Cooper. Argosy of fables.
Man and his image. La Fontaine. Fables (Tilney).
Man and his piece of cloth. Broomell. Children's story caravan.
For other entries, see 2d edition.
Man and his two sweethearts. *See* Man and his two wives.
Man and his two wives. Æsop. Fables (Artzybasheff).
Æsop. Fables (Jones. Man and his two sweethearts.)
Cooper. Argosy of fables.
For other entries, see 2d edition.
Man and his wooden god. Æsop. Fables (Jones. Man and the image.)
For other entries, see 2d edition.
Man and the acorn. *See* Acorn and the pumpkin.
Man and the crocodile. *See* Foolish fish.
Man and the flea. *See* Flea and the man. II.
Man and the image. *See* Man and his wooden god.

Man and the lion. Æsop. Fables (Artzybasheff).
Æsop. Fables (Jones).
Æsop. Fables (Whitman ed.).
Cooper. Argosy of fables.
For other entries, see 2d edition.
Man and the satyr. *See* Satyr and the traveller.
Man and the snake. I. *See* 2d edition.
Man and the snake. II. Coussens. Diamond story book.
(Hunter and the serpent.)
Curtin. Fairy tales of Eastern Europe. (World's reward.)
Lee. Folk tales of all nations. (White man and the snake.)
See also Camel driver and the adder; Foolish fish; Reward
of kindness; Way of the world. I.
Man and turtle. Babbitt. Animals' own story book. (Tur-
tle's trick.)
For other entries, see 2d edition.
Man and woman. I. *See* Creation of man (Polynesian).
Man and woman. II. *See* Pet turkey whose feelings were
hurt; Turkey-given corn.
Man bitten by a dog. Cooper. Argosy of fables.
For other entries, see 2d edition.
Man=eater. De Huff. Taytay's tales.
Man from the North, the girl, and the turtle. De Huff.
Taytay's tales.
Man from the South. Metzger. Picture tales from the Chi-
nese.
Man, his wife, and her lover who all died for love. Ryder.
Twenty-two goblins.
Man in the boat. Otero. Old Spain in our Southwest. (*In*
Early schooling in New Mexico.)
Man in the Christmas moon. Potter. Captain Sandman.
See also Stranger child. I.
Man in the moon. I. *See* 2d edition.
Man in the moon. II. Chamoud. Picture tales from the
French.
Dane. Once there was and was not. (Old man in the
moon.)
Olcott. Wonder tales from windmill lands. (He who
picked up sticks.)
Man in the moon. III (poem). Potter. Giant of Apple Pie
Hill.
Man in the moon. IV. Marzials. Stories for the story hour.
Man in the moon and the orphan boy. Snell. Told be-
neath the northern lights. (Azazruk and the man-in-the-
moon.)
For other entries, see 2d edition.
Man in white. Lang. Red true story book.
Man of law's tale. *See* Faithful Constance.
Man of Nod. Potter. Giant of Apple Pie Hill.
Man of the family. Broomell. Children's story caravan.
Man of the North. Snell. Told beneath the northern lights.
Man of the wildwood. Beston. Starlight wonder book.

Man of the woods and the giant. Meeker. Folk tales from the Far East.
See also Ito and his friends; Vagabond.

Man, the boy and the donkey. Æsop. Fables (Artzybasheff. Miller, his son and their ass.)
Æsop. Fables (Jones. Miller, his son and their ass.)
Cooper. Argosy of fables. (Miller, his son and their ass.)
Curry and Clippinger. Children's literature. (Miller, his son and their ass.)
Johnson and Scott. Anthology of children's literature. (Miller, his son and the ass.)
For other entries, see 2d edition.

Man, the horse, the ox and the dog. Æsop. Fables (Jones).
Cooper. Argosy of fables.

Man who came back from Tlalocan. Martens. Wonder tales from far away.

Man who changed into a woman at will. Ryder. Twenty-two goblins.

Man who could not keep a secret. Bryce. Folk lore from foreign lands.

Man who did not believe in fairies. Guerber. Legends of Switzerland. (*In* Legends of Vaud and Valais.)
See also Unbelieving king.

Man who discovered the moon. Olcott. Wonder tales from pirate isles.

Man who found a lion in his cave. Fleming. Round the world in folk tales.

Man who found Bird Land. Snell. Told beneath the northern lights.

Man who killed the cuckoo. Housman. Moonshine and clover.

Man who lived with dragons. *See* Good natured dragons; Shepherd and the dragon.

Man who lived with thunder. Sexton. Gray wolf stories.

Man who lost himself. Whitman. Navaho tales.

Man who lost his legs. Lanier. Book of giants.
See also Ulysses and Polyphemus.

Man who lost his spade. Æsop. Fables (Jones).

Man who married a buffalo. Spence. Myths of the North American Indians. (Sacred bundle. *In* Ch. 6.)

Man who meant what he said. Tappan. Little lady in green.

Man who never laughed. Quiller-Couch. Twelve dancing princesses.

Man who never was a child. Potter. Giant of Apple Pie Hill.

Man who obeyed his father's last will. *See* About Leviathan, king of the fish.

Man who ran after Fortune, and the man who waited for her in his bed. La Fontaine. Fables (Tilney).

Man who rode a tiger. *See* Valiant chattee maker.

Man who stole all the animals. *See* Napi and the famine.

Man who tamed his wife. Darton. Wonder book of old romance.

Man who tamed the first caribou. Rasmussen. Eagle's gift.

Man who thought he was a god. *See* Paradise in the sea.

Man who thought that he was foolish. Lobagola. Folk tales of a savage.

Man who understood animals' conversation. *See* Ass, the ox, and the labourer.

Man who understood the speech of animals. *See* Ass, the ox, and the labourer.

Man who wanted to jump to the moon. Fyleman. Tea time tales.

Man who was always in a hurry. *See* First clock.

Man who was captured by ants. Sexton. Gray wolf stories.

Man who was going to mind the house. Coe. Third book of stories. (Husband who was to mind the house.)

Curry and Clippinger. Children's literature. (Husband who was to mind the house.)

(poem). Curry and Clippinger. Children's literature. (Change about.)

Dasent. East of the sun and west of the moon (Nielsen. Husband who was to mind the house).

Hutchinson. Candlelight stories. (Husband who was left to mind the house.)

Lee. Folk tales of all nations. (Husband who was to mind the house.)

Power. Stories to shorten the road.

Rasmussen. East o' the sun and west o' the moon. (Husband who was to mind the house.)

See also Jan the grumbler.

For other entries, see 2d edition.

Man who went home with a grizzly. Sexton. Gray wolf stories.

For other entries, see 2d edition.

Man who went to find his angel. Wheeler. Albanian wonder tales.

See also Fate. III ; What luck !

Man who would dream. MacManus. Lo, and behold ye !

Man whose library passed into strange hands. **Gaster. Ma'aseh book. v. 2.

Man with his leg tied up. *See* King of the buffaloes.

Man with the bag. Colum. Big tree of Bunlahy.

See also Apple dumpling # ; Travels of a fox.

Man with the name of a city. *See* Coriolanus.

Man with the wen. Lee. Folk tales of all nations. (How an old man lost his wen.)

Metzger. Tales told in Korea. (Old man with the wens.)

Mitford. Tales of old Japan. (Elves and the envious neighbour.)

Phillips. Far peoples. (Old man with a wen.)

Man with the wen—*continued.*
Sugimoto. Japanese holiday picture tales. (Apple-bump Ojii San.)
Whitehorn. Wonder tales of old Japan. (Old man with the wen.)
See also Discontented tailor; Victi and Antonio feast with the fairies.
For other entries, see 2d edition.
Man without a country. Power. Children's treasure chest.
Man without a shadow. Carpenter. Tales of a Basque grandmother.
See also Shadow. I.
Manabozho. Morris. Stories from mythology: North American. (Deeds of Nanaboojoo. Ch. 7.)
For other entries, see 2d edition.
Manabozho and his toe. Spaulding and Bryce. Aldine readers. Book 2, rev. ed. (Boaster and the baby.)
See also Why the baby says "goo."
For other entries, see 2d edition.
Manciple's tale. *See* Why the crow is black. I.
Mandioca. Eells. Magic tooth.
Manly apology. White. School management, p. 277.
Mannikin Long Beard. Olcott. Wonder tales from Baltic wizards.
See also Muzicheck-as-big-as-your-thumbs.
Manoel Littlebean. Eells. Islands of magic.
See also Thumbling. I.
Manslayer. Cooper. Argosy of fables.
Many enchantments. *See* Bradamante, Adventures of.
Many-furred creature. Williams. Tales from Ebony. (Gallimaufry.)
See also Linda Branca and her mask; Rashin-Coatie #.
For other entries, see 2d edition.
Many-horse stable. Mitchell. Here and now story book.
Many, many weddings in one corner house. Sandburg. Rootabaga pigeons.
Many wives. Chrisman. Shen of the sea.
Maple flute. Teall. Batter and spoon fairies. *In* Ch. 24.
See also Singing bone.
Marama and Ina. *See* Hina, the woman in the moon. II.
Marathon. *See* First Marathon race; Swiss Marathon.
Marble boy. Brown. Under the rowan tree.
Marble spout. Denton. Homespun stories.
March. Bryce. Folk lore from foreign lands. (March and the shepherd.)
March wind's picnic. Potter. Captain Sandman.
Marching music. *See* Campbells are coming.
Marco Polo. McDonald. Dick and the spice cupboard. (*In* Dick's eighth adventure.)
Miller. My book of history. v. 4. (Marco Polo explores the East. *In* Ch. 1.)

Marco Polo—*continued.*
Miller. My book of history. v. 4. (Marco Polo in the service of Kublai Khan. *In* Ch. 5.)
Olcott. Wonder tales from China seas. (Youth who gathered jewels.)
Tappan. Old world hero stories.
Marco the rich and Basil the luckless. *See* Three wonderful beggars.
Marda's masterpiece. Crew. Saturday's children.
Mare's nest. Guerber. Legends of Switzerland. (*In* Legends of Vaud and Valais.)
Harris. Uncle Remus, his songs and his sayings. (*In* Introduction.)
See also Donkey's eggs; McAndrew family; Simpleton. III; Watermelon.
Mares of Diomed. *See* Labors of Hercules.
Margaret of Fresingfield. Richardson. Stories from old English poetry. (Margaret, fair maid of Fresingfield.)
Margaret of New Orleans. McVenn. Good manners and right conduct. Book 2.
Margaret, St. *See* St. Margaret.
Margil vine. Otero. Old Spain in our Southwest.
Maria=of=the=forest. Eells. Islands of magic.
See also King who would be stronger than fate.
Marie Madeleine and her spinning. Guerber. Legends of Switzerland. (*In* Legends of Geneva.)
Marigold. Carey. Flower legends.
Mariposa. Shannon. California fairy tales.
Mariuccia and the magic ring. Hill and Maxwell. Napoleon's story book.
See also Nettle spinner.
Marius. *See* Jugurtha.
Mark, St. *See* St. Mark.
Marklake witches. Kipling. Rewards and fairies.
Marko of Servia. *See* Prince Marko.
Marko the rich, and Vasily the luckless. *See* Three wonderful beggars.
Marni gets dressed. Mitchell. Here and now story book.
Marni takes a ride. Mitchell. Here and now story book.
Marouf. *See* Maaroof.
Marpessa. *See* Idas and Marpessa.
Marriage of Geraint. *See* Sir Geraint.
Marriage of Ioi. *See* Blue Jay visits the ghosts.
Marriage of Sir Gawain. *See* Sir Gawain's marriage.
Marriage of the sun. Æsop. Fables (Artzybasheff).
Cooper. Argosy of fables.
Mars. Harshaw. Council of the gods. (Athene and Ares in conflict.)
For other entries, see 2d edition.
Marseillaise. Clément. Once in France. (Baleful cart.)
Marseilles, Founding of. Clément. Flowers of chivalry. (Nuptial cup.)

Marshall, John. Baldwin. Fifty famous people. (Why he carried the turkey.)
McVenn. Good manners and right conduct. Book 2. (Story of Chief Justice Marshall.)
Marsyas and Apollo. Bulfinch. Golden age. *In* Ch. 24.
For other entries, see 2d edition.
Martha (play). Kinscella. Music appreciation readers. Book 6.
For other entries, see 2d edition.
Martin, St. *See* St. Martin.
Martin of Valencia. Martinez Del Rio. Sun, the moon and a rabbit. (Little birds and red roses.)
Martinmas. *See* St. Martin.
Martyn's flying trip. Perkins and Danielson. Mayflower program book.
Mary Ann's party. Potter. Captain Sandman.
Mary, Mary, so contrary. Bowman and Bianco. Tales from a Finnish tupa. (Pig-headed wife.)
For other entries, see 2d edition.
Marya Morevna. Carpenter. Tales of a Russian grandmother.
Ralston. Russian fairy tales.
See also Koschei without death.
For other entries, see 2d edition.
Mary's baby brother. Shimer. Fairyland.
Masaccio, Tommaso. Steedman. Knights of art.
Masha and her friends. Kovalsky and Putnam. Long-legs, Big-mouth, Burning-eyes.
See also Dreadful boar.
Masquerading crow. Brown. Curious book of birds.
See also Vain jackdaw. II.
Master and his pupil. I #.
See also Mop servant # ; Sorcerer's apprentice.
Master and his pupil. II. Boggs and Davis. Three golden oranges. (Black magic.)
See also Master of magic.; Oh.
For other entries, see 2d edition.
Master-carpenter and southeast wind. Spence. Myths of the North American Indians. (*In* Ch. 7.)
Master Genever. Darton. Wonder book of old romance.
Master-maid #.
See also Fedelma, the enchanter's daughter ; Three feathers. II.
Master Mend-and-spoil. Capuana. Golden-feather.
Master Mustapha of the whiskers. Morris. Gypsy story teller.
See also Cottager and his cat # ; Fortune seekers. I.
Master of all masters. Hutchinson. Candlelight stories.
Johnson and Scott. Anthology of children's literature.
Steel. English fairy tales.
Through story-land with the children.
Williams. Tales from Ebony.

Master of all masters—*continued.*
See also Long-life name; Shepherd who laughed last.
For other entries, see 2d edition.
Master of magic. Eells. Islands of magic.
See also Master and his pupil. II.
Master of masters. *See* Three brothers. I.
Master of the boat. Harper and Hamilton. Winding roads.
Master of the gold. Egan. New found tales.
Master Rabbit. De Huff. Taytay's memories.
Evans. Worth while stories. (Rabbit tries to catch fish.)
Leland. Algonquin legends. (Amazing adventures of Master Rabbit.)
For other entries, see 2d edition.
Master Rabbit again encounters the pine-gum baby. De Huff. Taytay's memories.
See also Big long man's corn patch; Rescue of rabbit.
Master Rabbit has a ride. De Huff. Taytay's memories.
See also Brother Rabbit's riding horse; Wolf as bridegroom.
Master Rabbit has a toothache. De Huff. Taytay's memories.
Master Sparrow, Master Stickleback, and the jolly chimney-sweep, Yasha. Mamin. Verotchka's tales.
Master wizard, Pan Twardowski, and his spider. Bernhard. Master wizard and other Polish fairy tales.
Mastersingers of Nuremberg. Kinscella. Music appreciation readers. Book 4.
For other entries, see 2d edition.
Mastiff and the goose. Æsop. Fables (Whitman ed.).
For other entries, see 2d edition.
Matariki. Howes. Long bright land. (Matariki's star.)
For other entries, see 2d edition.
Matsuyama Kagami. *See* Mirror of Matsuyama.
Matsys, Quintin. Chambers' miscellany. v. 10. (Quintin Matsys, the blacksmith of Antwerp.)
Matter of arbitration. Cooper. Argosy of fables. (Quarrelsome cats.)
Lee. Folk tales of all nations. (Dividing the cheese.)
See also Cat, the rat, the cheese and the fox; Judgement of the monkey. I–II; Otters and the wolf; Quarrel in the pantry; Two travelers and the oyster.
For other entries, see 2d edition.
Matter of habit. Cozad. Story talks.
Matyi of the geese. Schwimmer. Tisza tales.
Maui and death. *See* How Maui strove to win immortality for men.
Maui and the birds. Metzger. Tales told in Hawaii.
Maui and the dragon. Howes. Long bright land.
See also How Maui overcame Kuna Loa the long eel.
Maui and the fish. *See* How Maui fished up the great island.
Maui and the goddess of fire. *See* Secret of fire. II.
Maui and the sun. *See* Sun a prisoner. V.

Maui the baby. *See* How Maui won a place for himself in the house.
Maui the mischievous. *See* Search that Maui's brother made for his sister Hina-of-the-sea.
Maui's boyhood. *See* How Maui won a place for himself in the house.
Maui's christening. *See* Christening of Maui.
Maui's kite=flying. Colum. At the gateways of the day. (How Maui lifted up the sky.)
May Day. Bailey. Wonderful tree. (Apple tree May basket.)
May eve. Casserly. Michael of Ireland.
May=pole fairy. Bailey. Wonderful tree.
Mayblossom. Fairy garland (Dulac).
See also Veil of Irazade.
Mazeppa. Colum. Forge in the forest. (Horse.) (poem). Byron. Poems. (Mazeppa's ride.)
For other entries, see 2d edition.
Me=ne=hu=ne. *See* Menehunes.
Meadow dandelion. *See* Prairie dandelion.
Meadow lark and the fox. De Huff. Taytay's tales.
Meadow larks. Cowles. Stories to tell.
Meamei. *See* Pleiades. VII.
Measure for measure. Lamb. Tales from Shakespeare.
Measure of rice. Broomell. Children's story caravan.
Measure=worm rock. *See* Rock of the measuring worm.
Meat of a snowball. Mackaye. Tall tales of the Kentucky mountains.
Meave. *See* Queen Maeve.
Meave demands the brown bull of Cooley. *See* Cattle raid of Cooley.
Meddlesome Matty. Beard. Tucked-in tales.
Meddlesome piggy. Meeker. Folk tales from the Far East.
Medea's cauldron. Bulfinch. Golden Age. (Medea and Æson. *In* Ch. 17.)
For other entries, see 2d edition.
Medicine legend. Spence. Myths of the North American Indians. (*In* Ch. 4.)
Medicine pipe. Field. American folk and fairy tales. (Origin of the medicine pipe.)
For other entries, see 2d edition.
Medicine wolf. Spence. Myths of the North American Indians. (*In* Ch. 3.)
See also Little friend coyote #.
Medicines, Origin of. Bailey. Stories from an Indian cave. (When the plants were kind.)
Spence. Myths of the North American Indians. (*In* Ch. 4.)
For other entries, see 2d edition.
Medieval Jezebel. *See* Magic ring. IV.
Medio Pollito #.
See also Little half-cock, Story of.

Medusa. *See* Perseus.

Meinrad's watchers. Guerber. Legends of Switzerland. (*In* Legends of Zug.)
See also Bright sun brings it to light; Cranes of Ibycus; Singing bone; Will on the wind.

Melampus. Bulfinch. Golden age. (*In* Ch. 24.)
For other entries, see 2d edition.

Meleager and Atalanta. *See* Calydonian hunt.

Melia and the seven goats. Hill and Maxwell. Napoleon's story book.

Melibeus, Tale of. Farjeon. Tales from Chaucer.

Memehunes. *See* Menehunes.

Memnon. Bulfinch. Golden age. (*In* Ch. 26.)

Memoirs. *See* the first important word of the title.

Men and the beasts. *See* How the animals lost their freedom. II.

Men-eating bird. Metzger. Tales told in Hawaii.

Men of the earth get into trouble. Snell. Told beneath the northern lights.

Men of the wallet. Bowman and Bianco. Tales from a Finnish tupa.
See also Table, the ass and the stick.

Men-serpents. Spence. Myths of the North American Indians.

Mencius. Metzger. Tales told in Korea. (Wise mother of China.)

Menehune canoe. *See* Laka and the menehunes.

Menehunes. Metzger. Tales told in Hawaii. (Memehunes.)

Menehune's canal. Colum. At the gateways of the day. (*In* Menehune.)
Metzger. Tales told in Hawaii. (Menehune watercourse.)

Mercenary camel. Bacon. Lion-hearted kitten.

Merchant and his friend. *See* Country where the mice eat iron.

Merchant and his iron. *See* Country where the mice eat iron.
In 2d edition there are entries under each title.

Merchant and his three sons. Mackenzie. Jackal in Persia.

Merchant of dreams. Stewart. Tell me a story I never heard before.

Merchant of Venice. Lamb. Tales from Shakespeare.
Patten. Junior classics. v. 5.
Richardson. Stories from old English poetry. (Witty Portia, or Three caskets.)
See also Slice of tongue.

Merchant who buried his money in a field and the advice of King Solomon by which he recovered it. **Gaster. Ma'aseh book. v. 2.

Merchants and the golden bowl. *See* Grandmother's golden dish.

Merchant's daughter. I. *See* 2d edition.

Merchant's daughter. II. Shannon. Eyes for the dark.
Merchant's son and the iron scale. *See* Country where the mice eat iron.
Merchant's tale. I. *See* 2d edition.
Merchant's tale. II. Farjeon. Tales from Chaucer.
Mercury and the man bitten by an ant. *See* Philosopher, the ants and Mercury.
Mercury and the sculptor. Æsop. Fables (Jones). Cooper. Argosy of fables.
Mercury and the tradesmen. Æsop. Fables (Jones).
Mercury and the woodman. *See* Honest woodman.
Mercury the mischievous. *See* Hermes and Apollo.
Mercy and Miranda. Bacon. Mercy and the mouse.
Mercy and the birds. Bacon. Mercy and the mouse.
Mercy and the cur. Bacon. Mercy and the mouse.
Mercy and the midget. Bacon. Mercy and the mouse.
Mercy and the minnows. Bacon. Mercy and the mouse.
Mercy and the monster. Bacon. Mercy and the mouse.
Mercy and the mouse. Bacon. Mercy and the mouse, and other stories.
Mercy, Legend of. Topelius. Canute Whistlewinks. (Little birds' Christmas feast.)
For other entries, see 2d edition.
Meredydd. Henderson and Jones. Wonder tales of ancient Wales.
Merlicoquet. Chamoud. Picture tales from the French.
See also All change # ; Travels of a fox.
Merlin and Vivien. *See* Merlin the enchanter.
Merlin the enchanter. Colum. Boy apprenticed to an enchanter. (Merlin and Vivien. *In* Two enchanters.)
Cross. Music stories. (Viviane.)
Olcott. Wonder tales from fairy isles. (Coming of Merlin.)
See also King Fortrager ; Why the red dragon is the emblem of Wales.
For other entries, see 2d edition.
Merlin's tomb. Echols. Knights of Charlemagne. (*In* Many enchantments.)
Mermaid of Edam. Miller. My travelship: Holland.
See also Escaped mermaid.
Mermaid of the Magdalenes. Macmillan. Canadian wonder tales.
Mermaid of the moving sands. Olcott. Wonder tales from windmill lands.
Mermaid's comb. Price. Legends of the seven seas.
Mermaid's revenge. Rhys. English fairy book.
Merman. Lee. Folk tales of all nations.
Merry bells of Wraye. Lindsay. Choosing book.
Merry Dun of Dover. Wilson. Green magic.
Merry frogs. Purnell. Merry frogs.
Merry=go=round and the Griggses. Emerson. Merry-go-round of modern tales.

Merry little breezes. Blaisdell. Rhyme and story second reader.
Merry little fox. Lee. Folk tales of all nations.
See also Fox and the crane; Fox in the well; Ups and downs #.
Merry March hare. Burnett. Children's book.
Merry pieman and the don's daughter. Bennett. Pigtail of Ah Lee Ben Loo.
Merry tale of the king and the cobbler. *See* Cobbler and the king.
Merrymind, Story of. Starbuck. Far horizons.
For other entries, see 2d edition.
Message of the Caliph. Kinscella. Music appreciation readers. Book 6.
Messenger of the moon. Skipper. Jungle meeting-pool. (*In* Sixth meeting.)
Messengers. Eells. Islands of magic.
Metal pig. *See* Bronze boar.
In 2d edition there are entries under each title.
Metamorphosis of the Dnieper, the Volga, and the Dvina. *See* Dnieper, the Volga, and the Dvina.
Mexican people, Origin of. Allen. Whispering wind. (Loss of a great gambler.)
Mexico city, Founding of. *See* Eagle and the snake.
M'hemd Lascheischi's flute. Martens. Wonder tales from far away.
Mice and the screech=owl. La Fontaine. Fables (Tilney).
Mice and the weasels. Æsop. Fables (Jones).
Cooper. Argosy of fables.
Mice in council. *See* Belling the cat.
Mice that ate an iron balance. *See* Country where the mice eat iron.
Michael. Fyleman. Forty good-night tales.
Michael Martin who became Sir Michael de Vaufort. Dorey. Three and the moon. (Story of a Norman peasant boy.)
Michael, St. *See* St. Michael.
Michaelangelo. Chambers' miscellany. v. 9. (Michael-Angelo Buonarotti. *In* Anecdotes of the early painters.)
Miller. My book of history. v. 3. (*In* Ch. 16.)
Steedman. Knights of art.
Michaelmas. *See* St. Michael.
Michael's painted ball. Casserly. Michael of Ireland.
Midas. I. Bulfinch. Golden age. (*In* Ch. 6.)
Curry and Clippinger. Children's literature.
Evans. Worth while stories. (Golden touch.)
Forbush. Myths and legends of Greece and Rome. (Midas of the golden touch.)
Lang. Book of myths. (King Midas of the golden touch.)
Piper. Road in storyland. (King Midas.)
Pyle. Tales from Greek mythology. (Midas and the golden touch.)

Midas—*continued.*
Starbuck. Familiar haunts. (Golden touch.)
See also Cruche, Legend of; Precious gem palace; Stone curse.
For other entries, see 2nd edition.

Midas. II. Bulfinch. Golden Age. (*In* Ch. 6.)
Johnson and Scott. Anthology of children's literature. (Judgment of Midas.)
Lang. Book of myths. (King Midas of the golden touch.)
Pyle. Tales from Greek mythology. (Choice of Midas.)
For other entries, see 2d edition.

Midridge, Myth of. Olcott. Wonder tales from fairy isles. (Sillie Willy.)
For other entries, see 2d edition.

Midsummer night's dream. Lamb. Tales from Shakespeare.
Patten. Junior classics. v. 5.
Rich. Read-aloud book.
See also Titania's sleep.
For other entries, see 2d edition.

Mielikki and her nine sons. Bowman and Bianco. Tales from a Finnish Tupa.
See also Three sisters. I.

Mighty men. *See* How six men traveled through the wide world.

Mighty Mikko. Davis. Baker's dozen.
Harper. Fillmore folk tales.
For other entries, see 2d edition.

Mignon. Cross. Music stories.
Menefee. Child stories.
For other entries, see 2d edition.

Mignonette. Carey. Flower legends.
For other entries, see 2d edition.

Mikado. Cross. Music stories.
Untermeyer. Last pirate. (Executioner of Titipu.)

Miklosh and the magic queen. Curtin. Fairy tales of Eastern Europe.

Mikulas, bearer of gifts. *See* St. Nicholas.

Miladi's ear=drops. Newman. Fairy flowers.

Milesians come to Ireland. Young. Celtic wonder tales. (Inisfail.)

Milk=woman and her pail. *See* Milkmaid and her pail of milk.

Milkmaid and her pail of milk. Æsop. Fables (Artzybasheff. Country maid and her milk can.)
Æsop. Fables (Jones. Milkmaid and her pail.)
Æsop. Fables (Whitman ed. Maid and the pail of milk.)
(poem). Cooper. Argosy of fables. (Milk woman and her pail.)
(poem). Curry and Clippinger. Children's literature. (Dairywoman and the pot of milk.)

Milkmaid and her pail of milk—*continued.*
Curry and Clippinger. Children's literature. (Milkmaid and her pail.)
Johnson and Scott. Anthology of children's literature. (Milkmaid and her pail.)
La Fontaine. Fables (Tilney. Dairywoman and the pail of Milk.)
(poem). Patten. Junior classics. v. 10. (Milkmaid.)
See also Broken pot # ; Barber's fifth brother ; Lazy Heinz ; Lean Liesl and Lanky Lenz ; Little cream cheese ; Peasant and the hare ; Poor man and the flask of oil.
For other entries, *see* 2d edition.
Milky way. I. *See* 2d edition.
Milky way. II. Olcott. Wonder tales from Baltic wizards. (Maiden of the milky way.)
See also Sky bridge of birds.
Milky way. III. Pogány. Hungarian fairy book.
See also Skyway of the warriors.
Mill and the water-nymphs. Wahlenberg. Old Swedish fairy tales.
Mill of dreams. Farjeon. Martin Pippin in the apple orchard.
Miller. Capuana. Golden-feather.
Miller and the king. *See* Bruce, Robert.
Miller at the professor's examination #.
See also Day of the scholars ; Wise weaver.
Miller, his son, and their ass. *See* Man, the boy, and the donkey.
Miller's boy and his cat. Grimm. Fairy tales (Olcott. Poor miller's boy and the cat.)
Lee. Folk tales of all nations. (Poor miller's boy and the cat.)
See also Dick Whittington and his cat.
For other entries, *see* 2d edition.
Miller's cloak. Eells. Islands of magic.
Miller's daughter. I. Shimer. Fairyland.
For other entries, *see* 2d edition.
Miller's man who became an ass. Henderson. Wonder tales of Alsace-Lorraine.
Miller's tale. Farjeon. Tales from Chaucer.
Millionaire and the angel. Manner. Silver treasury.
Outlook (N. Y.). Sept. 29, 1906. p. 277.
Millitinkle. Cooper. Tal. (*In* Ch. 7.)
Mince pie. Richards. More five minute stories.
Minerva. Bryant. Children's book of celebrated legends. (Birth of Athena.)
Minerva and Arachne. *See* Arachne.
Minerva's olive #.
See also Trees under the protection of the gods.
Ming the miser. Chrisman. Wind that wouldn't blow.
Miniature. McNeer and Lederer. Tales from the crescent moon.

Minister who lost his head from revealing a secret. Mackenzie. Jackal in Persia.
Mink and the eagle. Parker. Skunny Wundy and other Indian tales.
Mink goes to sun's house. Morris. Stories from mythology: North American. (Mink, the son of the sun. *In* Ch. 14.)
Mink, the pike and the pickerel. Cooper. Argosy of fables.
Mink, the son of the sun. *See* Mink goes to Sun's house.
Minon=Minette. Quiller-Couch. Twelve dancing princesses.
Minotaur and the labyrinth. *See* Theseus.
Minstrel and the cobbler. Gunterman. Castles in Spain. (Ballads and boots.)
Kinscella. Music appreciation readers. Book 5.
Minstrel's song. Kinscella. Music appreciation readers. Book 5.
For other entries, see 2d edition.
Minute guns of the gods. Metzger. Tales told in Hawaii.
Miracle. *See* Bacchus and the vine.
Miracle in the pitcher. Gaer. Burning bush.
Miracle that happened to a fish. Gaer. Burning bush.
Miraculous fish. Lee. Folk tales of all nations.
Miraculous fox. Morris. Gypsy story teller. (Fox.)
Pogány. Magyar fairy tales.
See also Golden bird. II; Ivan and the gray wolf.
Miraculous pitcher. *See* Baucis and Philemon.
Miraculous stag. Pogány. Hungarian fairy book.
See also Skyway of the warriors.
Miraculous tea-kettle.
See Accomplished and lucky tea kettle.
Mirage. Seredy. Good master. (*In* Ch. 6.)
Mirri the cat. Harper. Fillmore folk tales.
Harper and Hamilton. Winding roads.
For other entries, see 2d edition.
Mirror. I–II. *See* 2d edition.
Mirror. III. Andersen. Wonder stories. (*In* Snow Queen.)
Evans. Worth while stories.
Mirror of Matsuyama. Applegarth. Missionary stories for little folks. 1st series. (Fairy mirror.)
Curry and Clippinger. Children's literature.
Faulkner. Little Peachling. (Matsuyama Kagami.)
Lee. Folk tales of all nations.
Sugimoto. Picture tales from Japanese. (Clear round gift.)
Whitehorn. Wonder tales of old Japan.
For other entries, see 2d edition.
Mirror of Matsuyama.
In Ballard #, Ozaki #, and Sugimoto an extra incident of a jealous stepmother is added to the story.
Mirror of the sun goddess. Teall. Batter and spoon stories. (*In* Ch. 26.)
For other entries, see 2d edition.

Mirror that made trouble. Lee. Folk tales of all nations. Metzger. Tales told in Korea. (Magical moon.)
For other entries, see 2d edition.

Mirrors of fairyland. Bowman. Little brown bowl.

Misana, who was swept away to the land of beads. Rasmussen. Eagle's gift.

Mischief maker. *See* Iktomi's blanket.

Mischievous crow. Lee. Folk tales of all nations.

Mischievous dog. Æsop. Fables (Artzybasheff).
Æsop. Fables. (Jones).
Cooper. Argosy of fables.
For other entries, see 2d edition.

Mischievous knix #.
See also Child's wish.

Mischievous March wind. Bowman. Little brown bowl.
See also Wind's surprise.

Mischievous monkey. Bacon. Lion-hearted kitten.

Miser. I. Æsop. Fables (Jones).
Æsop. Fables (Whitman ed. Covetous man.)
Cooper. Argosy of fables.
See also Folly of avarice.
For other entries, see 2d edition.

Miser. II. Ralston. Russian fairy tales.

Miser and the banyan tree. Meeker. Folk tales from the Far East.
See also Rip Van Winkle.

Miser converted. Aspinwall. Jataka tales. (Converted miser.)
See also King Robert of Sicily.

Miserly farmer. Egan. New found tales. (Peaches of chance.)
Lee. Folk tales of all nations. (Wonderful pear-tree.)
Olcott. Wonder tales from China seas. (Magic pears from nowhere.)
See also Peach from the sky.
For other entries, see 2d edition.

Miser's daughter and the wicked steward. Guerber. Legends of Switzerland. (*In* Legends of Zurich.)

Misfortunes of Wenamon. Miller. My book of history. v. 1. (*In* Ch. 10.)
**Maspero. Popular stories of ancient Egypt. (Voyage of Unamunu to the coasts of Syria.)

Mishy the surf=baby. No. 2 Joy Street.

Miss Betty Buttercup. Potter. Giant of Apple Pie Hill.

Miss Cow falls a victim to Mr. Rabbit. Field. American folk and fairy tales.
For other entries, see 2d edition.

Miss Emery Threadneedle. Potter. Giant of Apple Pie Hill.

Miss Matilda's birthday. Potter. Captain Sandman.

Miss Merry Christmas. Harper. Merry Christmas to you.
Harper. Selfish giant.
Harper and Hamilton. Winding roads.
Miss Mouse's tail=ring. Potter. Giant of Apple Pie Hill.
Miss Peppermint Jones (poem). Potter. Giant of Apple
Pie Hill.
Miss Pound=the=stones. Partridge. Joyful Star.
Miss Sparrow's party. Potter. Giant of Apple Pie Hill.
Missing Fanchette. Cook. To-day's stories of yesterday.
Missing man found. Lee. Folk tales of all nations. (Lost
fisher.)
See also Wise men of Gotham.
For other entries, see 2d edition.
Mist. Patten. Junior classics. v. 8.
Mist caps. I. Olcott. Wonder tales from goblin hills.
Mist caps. II. Olcott. Wonder tales from goblin hills.
(Thousands of dwarfs.)
Mist Maid and Rain Boy. Metzger. Tales told in Hawaii.
Mister. *See also* Brother.
Owing to the inconsistent use of these terms, entries under
both heads should be consulted.
Mr. A. and Mr. P. Bianco. Street of little shops.
Mr. and Mrs. Vinegar. *See* Mr. Vinegar.
Mr. Badger. Grahame. Kenneth Grahame book.
Mr. Bear's party. Brown. Under the rowan tree.
Mr. Coyote and two pretty girls. De Huff. Taytay's tales.
Mr. Coyote's melon patch. De Huff. Taytay's memories.
See also Big long man's corn patch.
Mr. Cricket's airplane. Buckingham. Elephant's friend.
Mr. Dog and Mr. Bear. *See* Strange story of Mr. Dog and Mr.
Bear.
Mr. E. and the spelling man #.
See also Alphabet party.
Mr. Elephant and Mr. Frog. *See* Elephant and the frog.
Mr. Finney's turnip. Baldwin. Fifty famous people.
(Writing a composition.)
See also Turnip. II.
Mr. Fox. Rhys. English fairy book.
Steel. English fairy tales.
For other entries, see 2d edition.
Mr. Fox goes a=hunting but Mr. Rabbit bags the game.
Skinner. Happy tales. (Red Fox and Bunny Rabbit.
Adapted.)
For other entries, see 2d edition.
Mr. Fox's Christmas dinner. Walker. Sandman's Christ-
mas stories.
Mr. Frog has a party. Babbitt. Animals' own story book.
Mr. "Get=even" Coyote. De Huff. Taytay's tales.
Mr. Goat's Thanksgiving. Potter. Captain Sandman.
Mr. Gobbage and the brownie. Potter. Captain Sandman.
Mr. Horner of Grumble Corner (poem). Richards. More
five minute stories.

Mr. Turtle goes riding in the clouds. Babbitt. Animals' own story book.
Mr. Vinegar. Curry and Clippinger. Children's literature.
De La Mare and Quayle. Readings.
Hutchinson. Chimney corner stories. (Mr. and Mrs. Vinegar.)
Lee. Folk Tales of all nations.
Rhys. English fairy book.
Steel. English fairy tales. (Mr. and Mrs. Vinegar.)
For other entries, see 2d edition.
Mr. Whirlwind, shoemaker. Bernhard. Master wizard.
Mr. Wolf and the flint stones. Mitchell. Gray moon tales.
(Mammy and Mr. Wolf.)
Mistress and her servants. *See* Old woman and her maids.
Mrs. Bobby de Bunny. Potter. Giant of Apple Pie Hill.
Mrs. Bonny-Bunny and the orphan. Potter. Captain Sandman.
Mrs. Laura Lollipop. Potter. Giant of Apple Pie Hill.
Mrs. Moodle. Fyleman. Forty good-night tales.
Mrs. Moodle and the tea-tray. Fyleman. Forty good-morning tales. (Mrs. Moodle. I.)
Mrs. Mud-pie and the Hill-topper. Potter. Captain Sandman.
Mrs. Mudge and Mrs. Midge. Potter. Giant of Apple Pie Hill.
Mistress of magic. MacManus. Donegal wonder book.
See also Farmer Weatherbeard; Oh.
Mrs. Overboops and the magic broom. Potter. Giant of Apple Pie Hill.
Mrs. Partridge's babies. Brown. Curious book of birds.
Mrs. Sandman's pie. Potter. Captain Sandman.
Mistress Sweet P. the Quaker blossom. Newman. Fairy flowers.
Mrs. Tabitha Tortoiseshell (poem). Wilson. Red magic.
Mrs. Topknot's Easter surprise. Bailey. Wonderful tree.
Mrs. Turtle's nest. Buckingham. Great idea.
Misty-Moisty Mary. Shannon. California fairy tales.
Mizgir. Ralston. Russian fairy tales.
Moaning boots. Rounds. Ol' Paul.
Mock Turtle's story. *See* Alice and the Mock Turtle.
Mocking bird. I–II. *See* 2d edition.
Mocking bird. III. Lee. Folk tales of all nations. (Weedah the mocking bird.)
Mocking bird. IV. Mitchell. Gray moon tales. (Mammy and the mocking bird.)
Mocking bird. V. Æsop. Fables (Whitman ed.).
Modest sisters. Metzger. Picture tales from the Chinese.
Modest Syrithe. Adams. Swords of the Vikings.
Modest young herd. Williams. Jolly old whistle.
Modred, the Druid. Henderson and Jones. Wonder tales of ancient Wales.

Mohammed. Miller. My book of history. v. 3. (*In* Ch. 4.)
For other entries, see 2d edition.

Moi=keha, the voyager. Colum. Bright islands. (Moi-keha
the voyager and the sons of Moi-keha.)

Moko and the twelve little earth men. Meeker. Folk tales
from the Far East.
See also Old man who made withered trees to flower; Two
melons; Swallow king's reward.

Mole, Adventures of. Grahame. Kenneth Grahame book.
(River bank.)

Mole and her mother. Cooper. Argosy of fables.
For other entries, see 2d edition.

Mole, Origin of. Johnson and Scott. Anthology of children's
literature. (Story of the first moles.)
See also Lady mole.
For other entries, see 2d edition.

Molière at the barber's. Clément. Flowers of chivalry.

Molly Pitcher, Story of. Blaisdell. Log cabin days. (Her-
oine of Monmouth.)
Lang. Red true story book.
See also Maid of Zaragoza.

Molly Whuppie. Adams and Atchinson. Book of giant
stories.
De La Mare. Told again.
Lee. Folk tales of all nations.
Steel. English fairy tales. (Molly Whuppie and the double-
faced giant.)
For other entries, see 2d edition.

Molly's Easter hen. Bailey. Tell me another story.

Momotaro. I. Fleming. Round the world in folk tales.
(Japanese Tom Thumb.)
Faulkner. Little Peachling and other tales of old Japan.
(Little Peachling.)
Lanier. Book of giants. (Peach's son.)
Mitford. Tales of old Japan. (Adventures of Little Peach-
ling.)
Phillips. Far peoples. (Momo-Taro.)
Shimer. Fairyland. (Peach-prince and the demons.)
Sugimoto. Picture tales from the Japanese. (Peach boy.)
Whitehorn. Wonder tales of old Japan. (Momotaro, or
Little peach-child.)
Williams. Tales from Ebony. (Peachling.)
For other entries, see 2d edition.

Mona and the Morgans. Lee. Folk tales of all nations.

Mondawmin. *See* First corn.

Money box. *See* Money-pig.

Money chest. Lee. Folk tales of all nations.

Money makes the mare to go. Hall. Godmother's stories.

Money=pig. Andersen. Fairy tales (Stickney. v. 1. Money
box.)
Bailey. Tell me another story. (Adapted.)

Money-pig—*continued.*
Johnson and Scott. Anthology of children's literature. (Money box.)
For other entries, see 2d edition.
Mongan's frenzy. Stephens. Irish fairy tales.
Moni and his goats. Hodgkins. Atlantic treasury of childhood stories.
Monk and the bird's song. Coussens. Diamond story book. (Brother Bernard.)
Lane. Tower legends. (Raven of the Giralda.)
See also Dreamer-the-giant; Journey of Rheinfrid; Magic music #.
For other entries, see 2d edition.
Monkey and gun. Mukerji. Hindu fables.
Monkey and the camel. Æsop. Fables (Artzybasheff.)
Æsop. Fables (Jones).
Cooper. Argosy of fables.
For other entries, see 2d edition.
Monkey and the cat. *See* Cat, the monkey, and the chestnuts.
Monkey and the chipmunk, Adventure of. De Leeuw. Java jungle tales.
See also Mouse-deer, the crocodile and the tiger.
Monkey and the crab. I. *See* Crab and the monkey. I.
Monkey and the crocodile. Applegarth. Missionary stories for little folks. First series. (Crocodile tail and a monkey tail.)
Blaisdell. Rhyme and story second reader.
Cooper. Argosy of fables.
Fun folk and fairy tales.
Harriman. Stories for little children.
Mukerji. Hindu fables. (Monkey Vanaraj.)
See also Friendship of the squirrel and the creeping fish; Monkey and the jelly-fish.
For other entries, see 2d edition.
Monkey and the crows #. *See* Birds and the monkeys. I.
In 2d edition there are entries under each title.
Monkey and the dolphin. *See* Ape and the dolphin.
Monkey and the fishermen. Cooper. Argosy of fables.
Monkey and the heron. Noel. Magic bird of Chomo-lung-ma.
Monkey and the jelly-fish. Coe. Third book of stories. (How the jellyfish lost his bones.)
Henderson and Calvert. Wonder tales of old Japan. (Kurage.)
Lee. Folk tales of all nations. (Jelly-fish and the monkey.)
Power. How it happened. (Why the jellyfish is soft.)
Price. Legends of the seven seas. (How the jellyfish lost his bones.)
Sugimoto. Picture tales from the Japanese. (Why the jellyfish has no bones.)

Monkey and the jelly=fish—*continued.*
Whitehorn. Wonder tales of old Japan. (Why the jelly-fish has no shell.)
See also Monkey and the crocodile.
For other entries, see 2d edition.
Monkey and the peas. Skinner. Happy tales.
See also Boy and the filberts # ; Owl and the two rabbits.
Monkey and the spectacles. Cooper. Argosy of fables.
Monkey and the star fish. De Leeuw. Java jungle tales.
Monkey and the wedge. *See* Carpenter and the ape.
Monkey as king. *See* Fox, the monkey and the animals.
Monkey=gardeners. Aspinwall. Jataka tales. (Stupid monkeys.)
Cooper. Argosy of fables. (Stupid monkeys.)
Harper and Hamilton. Winding roads. (Stupid monkeys.)
For other entries, see 2d edition.
Monkey holding court. *See* Wolf, the fox, and the ape.
Monkey king. Metzger. Picture tales from the Chinese.
See also Ape, Sun Wu Kung #.
Monkey that kicked the trepang. De Leeuw. Java jungle tales. (Monkey who stepped on a sea star.)
Olcott. Wonder tales from pirate isles.
Monkey that set out to see the world. *See* Monkey who had seen the world.
Monkey, the tiger, the cat, and the goat. De Leeuw. Java jungle tales.
Monkey Vanaraj. *See* Monkey and the crocodile.
Monkey who had seen the world. Cozad. Story talks. (Monkey that set out to see the world.)
See also Ape.
For other entries, see 2d edition.
Monkey who stepped on a sea star. *See* Monkey that kicked the trepang.
Monkey who would be king. *See* Fox, the monkey and the animals.
Monkey whose tail was not caught. Lobagola. Folk tales of a savage.
Monkeys and the bears. Lee. Folk tales of all nations.
Monkeys and the hollow canes. Aspinwall. Jataka tales. (Monkeys and the ogre.)
Babbitt. Animals' own story book. (Monkeys drink through straws.)
For other entries, see 2d edition.
Monkeys and the moon. Cowles. Stories to tell.
Skinner. Happy tales.
For other entries, see 2d edition.
Monkeys and the ogre. *See* Monkeys and the hollow canes.
Monkey's bargains #.
See also Bird from the waterfall; Cat's tail; Hodgepodge hold fast; How rabbit lost his tail. I. Rat's wedding # ; Travels of a fox; Uhla-kan-yan-a.
For other entries, see 2d edition.

Monkeys drink through straws. *See* Monkeys and the hollow canes.

Monkey's face. Cooper. Argosy of fables.

Monkey's heroic self-sacrifice. *See* How the monkey saved his troop.

Monkeys' house. Carrick. Tales of wise and foolish animals. *See also* Birds and the monkeys; Lazy frog.

Monkey's revenge. Walters. Book of Christmas stories.

Monkeys, the firefly and the bird. Cooper. Argosy of fables.

See also Glowworm and the jackdaw #.

Monks and the wood nymph. Criss. Martine and Michel. (*In* Ch. 3.)

Monk's statue, Story of. Pogány. Hungarian fairy book.

Monk's tale. Farjeon. Tales from Chaucer. *See also* Crœsus's dream; Hugolina, Count of Pisa; Zenobia.

Monsieur de Bayard's duel. See Bayard. I.

Monsieur Rosette. Newman. Fairy flowers.

Monster of Baylock. Lee. Folk tales of all nations.

Monstrous fish. Raspé. Children's Munchausen (Martin. *In* Ch. 6.) Raspé. Tales from the travels of Baron Munchausen.

Month of March. Faulkner. Road to enchantment. *See also* Optimistic thrush. For other entries, see 2d edition.

Mooin, the bear's child #. *See also* Boy who lived with the grizzlies. II.

Moolang. Phillips. Far peoples. *See also* Joan of Arc.

Moon and her mother. Æsop. Fables (Artzybasheff). Æsop. Fables (Jones). Cooper. Argosy of fables. For other entries, see 2d edition.

Moon and his frog=wife. Macmillan. Canadian wonder tales.

Moon bird. Nakazawa. Weaver of the frost.

Moon=bowl. Young. Tangle-coated horse.

Moon cake. I. *See* 2d edition.

Moon cake. II. *See* Chinese Emperor's visit to the moon.

Moon daughter's magic. Olcott. Wonder tales from Baltic wizards.

Moon=flower. I. Housman. Doorway in fairyland.

Moon=flower. II. Newman. Fairy flowers. (Prince Green-eyes, or "Leap, frog, leap!")

Moon in the mill pond #. *See also* Edam cheese.

Moon=maiden. I–III. *See* 2d edition.

Moon maiden. IV. Chrisman. Shen of the sea.

Moon, Origin of. *See* Sun, moon and stars. VII.

Moon=Princess. I. Kovalsky and Putnam. Long-legs, Big-mouth, Burning-eyes.

Moon=Princess. II. Purnell and Weatherwax. Talking bird.

Blondell. Keepsakes.

Moon=stroke. Housman. Moonshine and clover.

Moon table. Burnett. Children's book.

Moon that shone on the Porcelain Pagoda. *See* Chinese emperor's visit to the moon.

Moonlight sonata, Story of. Manner. Silver treasury.

For other entries, see 2d edition.

Moon's birthday. Rowe. Moon's birthday and other stories.

Moon's messenger #.

In 2d edition this story is also indexed under the titles "Rabbit and the moon" and "Why the rabbit is timid."

Moon's tears. Burnett. Children's book.

Moor woman. Wahlenberg. Old Swedish fairy tales.

Moor's legacy, Legend of. Adams and Atchinson. Book of enchantment.

Irving. Tales from the Alhambra.

For other entries, see 2d edition.

Moosli the roast. Martin. Fatma was a goose.

Moozipoo. Housman. What-o'clock tales.

Mop servant #.

See also Master and his pupil. I; Sorcerer's apprentice.

Morag, Story of. Colum. King of Ireland's son.

More than a bullfighter. Shannon. Eyes for the dark.

More with mind than with force. Pogány. Magyar fairy tales.

See also Fox, the bear and the poor farmer.

Morgan le Fay. Bailey. Stories of great adventures. (Treachery of Morgan le Fay.)

For other entries, see 2d edition.

Morgana. I. Echols. Knights of Charlemagne. (*In* Gardens of Falerina; Return of Ogier the Dane.)

Morgana. II. *See* Princess Morgana.

Morning=glory. *See* Lady and the morning-glory; Why the morning-glories wear pretty dresses.

Morning star. I. Lee. Folk tales of all nations. (Puck Wudj Ininee; or, He of the little shell.)

Morris. Stories from mythology: North American. (He of the little shell. *In* Ch. 4.)

Power. Children's treasure chest. (Puck Wudj Ininee.)

For other entries, see 2d edition.

Morning star. II–III. *See* 2d edition.

Morning star. IV. Purnell. Merry frogs.

Morozko. *See* King Frost.

Morraha. MacManus. Donegal wonder book. (Sword of light.)

See also Fedelma the enchanter's daughter; Green man of No Man's Land.

For other entries, see 2d edition.

Moses. *See* Dream of a great prophet; Prince Zipporah never dreamt of; Star child. II; Water babe.

Mosquito Long-nose and fuzzy bear, Mishka Short-tail, Story of. Mamin. Verotchka's tales.
Mosquitoes come to Lapland. Olcott. Wonder tales from Baltic wizards. (Naughty, naughty spider.)
Moss rose, Legend of. I. Carey. Flower legends. (Moss rose.)
  Cook. Red and gold stories. (First moss rose.)
  For other entries, see 2d edition.
Moss rose, Legend of. II. Bryce. Short stories for little folks. (Moss rose.)
Moss wife. Buckingham. Elephant's friend. (*In* Butterfly boy.)
Moss wifie. *See* Golden strawberries.
Most beautiful bird and the loveliest woman. Rasmussen. Eagle's gift.
Most magnificent cook of all. Olcott. Wonder tales from windmill lands.
Most wonderful jade treasure. Olcott. Wonder tales from China seas.
Mother. Eells. Magic tooth.
Mother Christmas. No. 2 Joy Street.
Mother Earth's children. Evans. Worth while stories.
  See also Old Winter Man and the Spring; Spring routs Winter.
Mother Good-Luck. Kovalsky and Putnam. Long-legs, Big-Mouth, Burning-Eyes.
Mother Goose. Forbes. Good citizenship. (*In* Ch. 5.)
Mother Holle. Evans. Worth while stories. (Gold girl and the tar girl. Abridged.)
  Grimm. Fairy tales (Olcott).
  Hutchinson. Fireside stories. (Mother Hulda. Adapted.)
  Williams. Tales from Ebony. (Old Mother Frost.)
  See also Chests of dust; Gold Maria and Pitch Maria; Little bucket; Three sisters. V.
  For other entries, see 2d edition.
Mother Hubbard and her dog. *See* Old Mother Hubbard.
Mother Hulda. *See* Mother Holle.
Mother Magpie's kindergarten. *See* Magpie's nest. I.
Mother Murre. Coe. Third book of stories.
Mother Popple's Christmas pudding. *See* Christmas pudding. II.
Mother Spider. Skinner. Child's book of country stories.
  For other entries, see 2d edition.
Mother's blessing. Garnett. Ottoman wonder tales.
Mother's Day. *See* Enchanted forest; Fairy fancy; Flight of Tiri; How Ryochi found his mother; Jar of rosemary; Johnny Chuck finds the best thing; Little mother and big child; Mother Murre; North wind's baby; Star child. I: Taken for granted; Washington goes to sea; What the moon saw; 25th evening; Wise mother of China; Wise mother of Korea; Young Count's heart.
  For other entries, see 2d edition.

Mother's song. Wheelock. Kindergarten children's hour. v. 4. Ch. 18.

Moufflou. Curry and Clippinger. Children's literature. For other entries, see 2d edition.

Mt. Aetna's eruptions explained. Raspé. Children's Munchausen (Martin. *In* Ch. 8.)

Mount Pilatus. *See* Pontius Pilate.

Mount Popocatepetl. Purnell and Weatherwax. Talking bird. (Moon princess. II.)

Mountain and the squirrel (poem). Cooper. Argosy of fables.
(poem). Emerson, R. W. Poems.
(poem). Johnson and Scott. Anthology of children's literature.
For other entries, see 2d edition.

Mountain ash, Legend of. I. *See* 2d edition.

Mountain ash, Legend of. II. Evans. Worth while stories.

Mountain in labor. Cooper. Argosy of fables.
For other entries, see 2d edition.

Mountain lion, coyote and wild horses. Hogner. Navajo winter nights.

Mountain Munchausen. Mackaye. Tall tales of the Kentucky mountains.

Mountain of life. Martinez Del Rio. Sun, the moon and a rabbit.

Mountain with summer in its heart. *See* How the birds got their colors. II #.

Mountains of the moon. Housman. What-o'clock tales.

Mountebank and the countryman. *See* Actor and the pig.

Mouse, Adventures of. Wilson. Green magic. (Life and perambulations of a mouse.)

Mouse and the bull. Æsop. Fables (Jones).
Cooper. Argosy of fables.

Mouse and the butterfly. Lee. Folk tales of all nations.

Mouse and the cat (poem). Cooper. Argosy of fables.

Mouse and the frog. *See* Mouse, the frog and the hawk.
In 2d edition there are entries under each title.

Mouse and the mermaid. Fyleman. Forty good-morning tales.

Mouse and the moonbeam. Harper. Merry Christmas to you. (Abridged.)
Harper. More story-hour favorites. (Abridged.)
Walters. Book of Christmas stories. (Mouse that didn't believe in Santa Claus. Adapted.)
For other entries, see 2d edition.

Mouse and the sun. *See* Sun a prisoner. I.

Mouse bride. *See* Forest bride.

Mouse-deer and King Solomon. De Leeuw. Java jungle tales.
See also Country where the mice eat iron.

Mouse-deer shows his true self. De Leeuw. Java jungle tales.

Mouse=deer stories. *See* Friend Mouse-deer; Pa Badak's lawsuit; Tiger and the mouse-deer; Tiger learns a lesson.

Mouse=deer, the crocodile and the tiger. De Leeuw. Java jungle tales.
See also Eighty-one brothers; Jackal and the crocodile; Monkey and the chipmunk; Tiger learns a lesson.

Mouse=deer, the wild dog, and the tiger, Story of. De Leeuw. Java jungle tales.

Mouse=deer's shipwreck. Lee. Folk tales of all nations. Skeat. Tiger's mistake.
For other entries, see 2d edition.

Mouse family talks of moving. Blaisdell. Rhyme and story second reader.
See also Lark and her young ones.

Mouse=king's story. **Arnold. Book of good counsels. (*In* Winning of friends.)
Cooper. Argosy of fables. (Golden-skin, the mouse.)
See also Pigeon-king and Mouse-king.

Mouse merchant. Aspinwall. Jataka tales. (Little gild-master.)
Cooper. Argosy of fables. (Story of the mouse merchant.)
Egan. New found tales. (Golden mouse.)
See also One straw.

Mouse metamorphosed into a girl. *See* So born, so die.

Mouse that didn't believe in Santa Claus. *See* Mouse and the moonbeam.

Mouse that turned tailor. Bowman and Bianco. Tales from a Finnish tupa.

Mouse that wanted to get to London. Fyleman. Forty good-morning tales.

Mouse that was turned into a maiden. *See* So born, so die.

Mouse, the bird and the sausage. De La Mare and Quayle. Readings.
For other entries, see 2d edition.

Mouse, the cat and the cock (poem). Cooper. Argosy of fables. (Cock, the cat and the young mouse.)
(poem). Curry and Clippinger. Children's literature. (Cock, the cat and the young mouse.)
For other entries, see 2d edition.

Mouse, the cricket and the bumblebee (poem). Skinner. Happy tales.

Mouse, the frog and the hawk. Æsop. Fables (Jones).
Cooper. Argosy of fables. (Mouse and the frog.)
De Leeuw. Java jungle tales. (Adventures of the mouse and the frog.)
For other entries, see 2d edition.
    In 2d edition this story is also indexed under the title "Mouse and the frog."

Mouse, the frog and the little red hen. *See* Little red hen. III.

Mouse tower. Chambers' miscellany. v. 3. (*In* Walter Ruysdael.)
Coussens. Diamond story book.
(poem). Power. Children's treasure chest. (Bishop Hatto and the rats.)
For other entries, see 2d edition.
Mouse tower of Güttingen. Guerber. Legends of Switzerland. (*In* Thurgau.)
Mouse-trap. De La Mare and Quayle. Readings.
Mouse who became a tiger. **Arnold. Book of good counsels. (Recluse and the mouse.)
Cooper. Argosy of fables. (Hermit and the mouse.)
For other entries, see 2d edition.
Mouse who was afraid. Bryce. Short stories for little folks.
See also Mouse who became a tiger.
Mouse with the bobbed whiskers. Fyleman. Forty goodnight tales.
Mouse with the eager nose. Potter. Giant of Apple Pie Hill.
Mousekin. Capuana. Italian fairy tales.
For other entries, see 2d edition.
Mozart, Wolfgang. Kinscella. Music appreciation readers. Book 2. (Wolfgang and Nannerl.)
Much ado about nothing. I. Lamb. Tales from Shakespeare.
Much ado about nothing. II. Chamoud. Picture tales from the French.
Much and more. Perkins and Danielson. Mayflower program book.
See also Selfish prince.
For other entries, see 2d edition.
Much noise, no fairies. *See* Fairies' passage. III.
Mucius and Lars Porsena. Cooke. Stories of Rome. (*In* Heroes of early Rome.)
Muckle-mou'ed Meg. Power. Bag o' tales.
For other entries, see 2d edition.
Mud people. Lee. Folk tales of all nations.
See also Builder of ability and builder of haste #.
Muffin man. Gordon and Stockard. Gordon readers. 2d reader.
See also Barring of the door.
Mule. Æsop. Fables (Artzybasheff).
Æsop. Fables (Jones).
Æsop. Fables (Whitman ed.).
Cooper. Argosy of fables.
(poem). Cooper. Argosy of fables. (Mule who boasted of his family.)
For other entries, see 2d edition.
Mule-humans. Field. American folk and fairy tales.
Mackaye. Tall tales of the Kentucky mountains.

Mule laden with corn and the mule laden with gold.
See Mules and the robbers.
   In 2d edition there are entries under each title.
Mule who boasted of his family. *See* Mule.
Mules and the robbers. Æsop. Fables (Whitman ed.).
   (Mule laden with corn and the mule laden with gold.)
Cooper. Argosy of fables.
La Fontaine. Fables (Tilney. Two mules.)
For other entries, see 2d edition.
   In 2d edition this story is also indexed under the titles
"Mule laden with corn and the mule laden with wheat,"
and "Two mules."
Munachar and Manachar. Lee. Folk tales of all nations.
See also Humbo and Mumbo.
For other entries, see 2d edition.
Munchausen cuts the Suez canal. Raspé. Tales from the
travels of Baron Munchausen.
Munchausen in America. Raspé. Tales from the travels of
Baron Munchausen.
Munchhausen, Mountain. *See* Shell, Solomon.
Munchausen, Travels of Baron. *See* Travels of Baron Mun-
chausen.
Murdoch's rath. Power. Stories to shorten the road.
Starbuck. Enchanted paths.
Johnson and Scott. Anthology of children's literature.
For other entries, see 2d edition.
Murray river, Tale of. Farjeon. Martin Pippin in the ap-
ple orchard. (*In* Epilogue.)
Music box. Cooper. Tal. (*In* Ch. 8.)
Musical ass. Curry and Clippinger. Children's literature.
Musician of the wooden shoe. Kinscella. Music apprecia-
tion readers. Book 3.
Musicians. *See* Bremen town musicians.
Musicians of Bremen. *See* Bremen town musicians.
Mutual service of King Fierce=Lion and Prince Good.
Ryder. Twenty-two goblins.
Muzhichek=as=big=as=your=thumb #.
See also Mannikin Long Beard.
My lady wind. Marzials. Stories for the story hour.
My own self. Lee. Folk tales of all nations. (Ainsel.)
Williams-Ellis. Fairies and enchanters. (Ainsel.)
See also Crafty servant; Fairy and the spinning woman.
For other entries, see 2d edition.
My Shilo. *See* Fairy caught. II.
Myrmidons. Bulfinch. Golden age. (*In* Ch. 12.)
Mysteries of the Kyffhauser. Olcott. Wonder tales from
goblin hills.
Mysterious caves of the Jungies. Parker. Skunny Wundy
and other Indian tales.
Mysterious mirage. McNeer and Lederer. Tales from the
crescent moon.
Mysterious ride. *See* Joan of Arc.

Mysterious star. Martinez Del Rio. Sun, the moon and a rabbit.
Mystic thorn. *See* Thorn of Glastonbury.

N

Nahum Ish Gamzo. *See* Luck of Nahum.
Nahum Prince. Bailey. Stories children want.
For other entries, see 2d edition.
Nail. I. McVenn. Good manners and right conduct. Book 2.
For other entries, see 2d edition.
Nakhoda Ragam. Skeat. Tiger's mistake. (Nakhoda Ragam who was pricked to death by his wife's needle.)
Nala and Damayanti, Story of. Coit. Kai Khosru. (play). Coit. Kai Khosru.
Name of the City of Flowers. *See* Haarlem.
Name that grew. Hervey and Hix. Fanciful tales for children.
Nameless one with the misfortunes, Story of. Morris. Book of the three dragons.
Naming of the animals. Garett. Coyote stories. (Spirit Chief names the animals.)
Naming of the land. *See* Amerigo Vespucci; Columbus, Christopher.
Nanaboojoo. *See* Manabozho.
Nancy Jane O. Pyrnelle. Diddie, Dumps, and Tot. (*In* Ch. 9.)
Nanni, Story of. Davis. Truce of the wolf.
Nannie's shoes. Colum. (Big tree of Bunlahy.)
Nanny who wouldn't go home to supper. Hutchinson. Candlelight stories.
Power. Blue caravan tales.
Power. Bag o' tales. (Adapted.)
For other entries, see 2d edition.
Naosuke. Williams. Tales from Ebony.
Napi and the buffalo-stealer. *See* Napi and the famine.
Napi and the famine. De Huff. Taytay's memories. (Indians and the ravens.)
Sexton. Gray wolf stories. (Man who stole all the animals.)
Spence. Myths of the North American Indians. (Napi and the buffalo-stealer. *In* Ch. 3.)
For other entries, see 2d edition.
Napoleon and Josephine. Clément. Once in France. (Little girl from the island.)
Napoleon at Arcola. *See* Brave drummer boy of France.
Napoleon at Ratisbon. *See* Incident of the French camp.
Narabee. Kennedy. Red man's wonder book. (Adventures of Narabee; Rescue.)
Narcissus. I. *See* Echo and Narcissus.

Narcissus. II. Kinscella. Music appreciation readers. Book 5. (*In* Grecian music contest.)
For other entries, see 2d edition.
Narcissus. III. *See* Chinese boy's garden.
Narwhal, Origin of. Snell. Told beneath the northern lights. (Blind boy who killed a bear.)
For other entries, see 2d edition.
Nasr=Eddin. *See* King and the sage # ; Nazir Din.
Naughtiness of Number Nine. Aspinwall. Can you believe me stories.
Naughty boy. I. *See* 2d edition.
Naughty boy. II. Metzger. Picture tales from the Chinese.
Naughty goblin and the village school. Fyleman. Forty good-night tales. (Naughty goblin, pt. 1.)
Naughty goblin at the garden party. Fyleman. Forty good-night tales.
Naughty spider. Olcott. Wonder tales from Baltic wizards. (Naughty, naughty spider.)
Nausicaa. Forbush. Myths and legends of Greece and Rome. (How Ulysses met with Nausicaa. *In* Ulysses.)
Navaho and the wizard. Whitman. Navaho tales.
Navaho story of the swallow. *See* Creation of the world (Indian).
Navajo blanket. *See* Indian's blanket; Her blanket. II.
Navajo land. *See* Creation of the world (Indian) ; Five worlds.
Nazir Din, Some adventures of. White. Made in Russia. (*In* Ch. 6.)
Necklace of pearls. Eells. Islands of magic.
Needle. Capuana. Golden-feather.
Neighboring families. Andersen. Fairy tales (Stickney. v. 1. Roses and the sparrows.)
For other entries, see 2d edition.
Nella's dancing shoes. Farjeon. Italian peepshow.
Nelson, Horatio (poem). Johnson and Scott. Anthology of children's literature. (Admiral's ghost.)
Neptune's city. Price. Legends of the seven seas. (Atlantis the lost land.)
Nerrivik, the old woman of the sea. Morris. Stories from mythology : North American. (*In* Ch. 2.)
Ness king. Coussens. Diamond story book.
For other entries, see 2d edition.
Nessus. *See* Hercules and his labors.
Nest. *See* Ekorn the squirrel.
Nettle spinner. Coussens. Diamond story book.
See also Mariucca and the magic ring.
For other entries, see 2d edition.
Never kick a slipper at the moon. Sandburg. Rootabaga stories.
Sandburg. Rootabaga country.
Nevermind. Shannon. Eyes for the dark.

New automobile. Emerson. Merry-go-round of modern tales.
New dresses. Mitchell. Here and now story book. (Children's new dresses.)
New home. *See* Ram and the pig.
New leaf. Richards. More five minute stories.
New light in the sky. *See* Sun, moon and stars. VII.
New neighbors. Hooker. Garden of the lost key.
New shoes. Baker. Tell them again tales.
   See also Duty shoes.
New song of sixpence. Blaisdell. Rhyme and story second reader. (New song.)
New Thann, Legend of. Henderson. Wonder tales of Alsace-Lorraine.
New year. *See* Year, Story of the.
New Year olives. *See* Thriftless wife.
New Year's Day. *See* Animals' New Year's eve; How K'tonton drove Satan out of the shofar; I am Clockface; Lighthouse. II; New leaf; Resolutions; Yang Glow-of-Dawn. For other entries, see 2d edition.
New Year's party. Richards. More five minute stories.
Newton and the apple. Lansing. Great moments of freedom. (Young man's vision.)
Ngurangurane, Legend of. Woodson. African myths.
Niagara, Story of. Browne. Indian nights.
Nianya's little pigeons. Carpenter. Tales of a Russian grandmother.
Nibelungenlied. Tappan. Old world hero stories. (Story of the Nibelungs.) For other entries, see 2d edition.
Nice quiet morning. Buckingham. Great idea.
   See also Wolf and the seven little kids.
Nicholas, St. *See* St. Nicholas.
Nideck, Legend of. Henderson. Wonder tales of Alsace-Lorraine.
Niels and the giants. Freeman. Child-story readers. 3d reader.
Night before Christmas. Skinner. Christmas stories (play). Skinner. Christmas stories. For other entries, see 2d edition.
Night of colored lanterns. Olcott. Wonder tales from China seas.
Night of the big wind. Mason. Wee men of Ballywooden.
Night with Santa Claus. Bryce. Short stories for little folks.
Nightingale. I. Andersen. Fairy tales (Siewers tr.).
   Bailey. Story-telling hour.
   Bailey. Tell me another story. (Adapted.)
   Cowles. Stories to tell.
   Curry and Clippinger. Children's literature.
   Johnson and Scott. Anthology of children's literature.
   Kinscella. Music appreciation readers. Book 3. (Chinese nightingale. Abridged.)

Nightingale. I—*continued*.
Starbuck. Familiar haunts.
Wilson. Green magic.
For other entries, see 2d edition.
Nightingale. II–III. *See* 2d edition.
Nightingale. IV. Cather. Pan and his pipes. (Holy bird.)
Nightingale and the dove. *See* Why the nightingale sings
    better than the dove.
Nightingale and the glow-worm (poem). Cooper. Argosy
    of fables.
    (poem). Patten. Junior classics. v. 10.
    (poem). Cowper. Poems.
    See also Grasshopper and the dove.
    For other entries, see 2d edition.
Nightingale and the hawk. *See* Hawk and the nightingale.
Nightingale and the peacock. Cooper. Argosy of fables.
    For other entries, see 2d edition.
Nightingale and the pearl. Curry and Clippinger. Chil-
    dren's literature. (Eastern garden.)
    Kinscella. Music appreciation readers. Book 3. (Boy and
        nightingale.)
    See also Father "Lime-stick" and the flower-pecker; Part-
        ridge and the fowler.
    For other entries, see 2d edition.
        In 2d edition this story is also indexed under the title
    "Labourer and the nightingale."
Nightingale and the swallow. Æsop. Fables (Jones).
Nightingale and the worm. I. Carey. Stories of the birds.
Nightingale and the worm. II. Brown. Curious book of
    birds. (Why the nightingale wakes.)
Nightingale of Sass=leng. Wolff. Pale mountains.
Nightingale valley. Olcott. Wonder tales from goblin hills.
Niilo and the wizard. *See* Wizard and his pupil. II.
Nils, Adventures of. *See* Boy and the elf; Glimminge castle;
    Nils and the bear; Thumbietot blows a pipe; Wild goose
    chase.
Nils and the bear. Bailey. Tell me another story.
    Lagerlöf. Further adventures of Nils. (*In* Ch. 4.)
    For other entries, see 2d edition.
Nimrod, the mighty hunter. Gaer. Burning bush. (*In*
    Tower that wasn't completed; Because of a pot of lentils.)
Nine enchantments of Gwiawn Llygad Cath the sea=thief.
    Morris. Book of the three dragons.
Nine lives of Mr. Tommy Tippycat. Potter. Giant of Ap-
    ple Pie Hill.
Nine pea=hens and the golden apples. Fuller. Book of
    dragons. (Golden apple-tree and nine peahens.)
    Harper. Fillmore folk tales. (Enchanted peafowl.)
    Wilson. Green magic. (Golden apple-tree and nine pea-
        hens.)
    See also Prince Argyilus and the fairy Ilona.
    For other entries, see 2d edition.

Ninth wave. Farjeon. Old sailor's yarn box.
Niobe. Bulfinch. Golden age. (*In* Ch. 14.)
Lang. Book of myths.
Pyle. Tales from Greek mythology.
For other entries, see 2d edition.
Nipon the summer maiden. Partridge. Joyful Star.
Nish=Fang, Story of. Partridge. Joyful Star.
Nis at the grocer's. Andersen. Fairy tales. (Stickney.
v. 2. Goblin and the huckster.)
For other entries, see 2d edition.
Nisus and Euryalus. Bulfinch. Golden age. (*In* Ch. 33.)
For other entries, see 2d edition.
Nisus and Scylla. *See* Scylla, daughter of Nisus.
Nix in the pond. Grimm. Fairy tales (Olcott. Nix of the
mill-pond.)
For other entries, see 2d edition.
Nix Nought Nothing. Lee. Folk tales of all nations.
Steel. English fairy tales. (Nix, naught, nothing.)
Williams-Ellis. Fairies and enchanters.
For other entries, see 2d edition.
Nix of the mill=pond. *See* Nix in the pond.
No ears. Capuana. Italian fairy tales. (Princess Lackears.)
For other entries, see 2d edition.
No=so=what. *See* Go, I know not whither—fetch, I know not
what. II.
Noble Burghers of Calais. *See* Siege of Calais.
Noble physician. Schwarz. Jewish caravan.
Noble sailor boy. White. School management, p. 260.
Noble servant. White. School management, p. 249.
Nobleman of Hawaii. Williams. Jolly old whistle.
Noodle pagodas. Rowe. Moon's birthday.
Noonday party. Bowman. Little brown bowl.
Norka. Ralston. Russian fairy tales.
For other entries, see 2d edition.
Norman peasant boy, Story of. *See* Michael Martin who
became Sir Michael de Vaufort.
North Mountain Giant and the boy in the mine. Falk-
berget. Broomstick and Snowflake.
North star. I. *See* 2d edition.
North star. II. De Huff. Taytay's memories.
North star. III. *See* Sailor's star.
North wind. I. Fyleman. Tea time tales.
For other entries, see 2d edition.
North wind. II. La Rue. Under the story tree.
North wind and the duck. Cooper. Argosy of fables.
(Wind and the duck.)
For other entries, see 2d edition.
North wind and the sun. *See* Wind and the sun.
North wind's baby. Harper. More story-hour favorites.
Stewart. Tell me a story I never heard before.

Northern lights. I. Williamson. Stars through magic casements. (*In* Finn and the great bear.)
For other entries, see 2d edition.
Northern lights. II. Applegarth. Missionary stories for little folks. 1st series. (What happens to the Eskimo sun in winter.)
See also Three strong men.
Nose. I. *See* Nose-tree.
Nose. II. *See* Widow who would be comforted. II.
Nose=tree. Bruce. Treasury of tales for little folk. (Nose.)
Lee. Folk tales of all nations. (Red Jacket; or, The nose tree.)
Quinn. Stokes' wonder book of fairy tales. (Nose.)
Through story-land with the children. (Nose.)
For other entries, see 2d edition.
Nosey the dwarf. *See* Longnose the dwarf.
Not as one thinks. Olcott. Wonder tales from pirate isles. (*In* String of pearls.)
(poem). Cooper. Argosy of fables. (Old man and the three young men.)
Nothing at all. Williams-Ellis. Fairies and enchanters.
Nothing child #.
See also Bata the Egyptian boy.
Noureddin Ali and his son. Arabian nights. Adventures of Haroun Er Raschid (Olcott. Story of Noureddin Ali and Bedredden Hassan.)
Williams. Tales from Ebony. (Agib and the cheese cakes. Adapted.)
See also Camaralzaman and Badoura, Princess of China #.
For other entries, see 2d edition.
Noureddin and the beautiful Persian. Arabian nights. Adventures of Haroun Er Raschid (Olcott. Story of Noureddin and the fair Persian.)
For other entries, see 2d edition.
Noureddin and the fair Persian. *See* Noureddin and the beautiful Persian.
Now it is written. Chrisman. Wind that wouldn't blow.
Numskull of Cyprus. Lebermann. New German fairy tales.
Nun's priest's tale. *See* Cock and the fox. IV.
Nuptial cup. Clément. Flowers of chivalry.
Nuremberg stove. Evans. Worth while stories. (Adapted.)
For other entries, see 2d edition.
Nurse and the wolf. Æsop. Fables (Jones. Wolf, the mother and her child.)
Æsop. Fables (Whitman ed.).
Cooper. Argosy of fables.
For other entries, see 2d edition.
Nutcracker and Mouse=king. Cross. Music stories (Nutcracker suite).
Kinscella. Music appreciation readers. Book 3.
Skinner. Christmas stories.
Nutcracker suite. *See* Nutcracker and Mouse-king.

Nutcrackers of Nutcracker Lodge. Skinner. Child's book of country stories.
For other entries, see 2d edition.
Nuts of Jonisgyout. *See* How the flying squirrel got his wings.

O

O Jizo Sama and the rice ball. Sugimoto. Picture tales from the Japanese.
See also Laughing dumpling.
Oak and the dryad. Browne. Indian nights.
Oak and the pig. Cooper. Argosy of fables.
Oak and the reed. Æsop. Fables (Jones. Oak and the reeds).
Æsop. Fables (Artzybasheff).
Æsop. Fables (Whitman ed. Oak and the reeds.)
(poem). Cooper. Argosy of fables.
For other entries, see 2d edition.
Oak and the snail. Patten. Junior classics. v. 8.
Oak and the woodcutters. Cooper. Argosy of fables.
See also Eagle and the arrow.
Oak-apple Day. *See* Royal Oak Day.
Oak planting festival. Guerber. Legends of Switzerland. (*In* Aargau.)
Oaks and Jupiter. Cooper. Argosy of fables.
Oath. White. School management, p. 267.
Oberlin, John Frederic. Cozad. Story talks. (John Frederic Oberlin—a real champion.)
Oberon. *See* Huon of Bordeaux; Midsummer night's dream.
Obeying orders. White. School management, p. 258.
Observance of the Sabbath rewarded. *See* Joseph the Sabbath lover.
Ocean, Origin of. I. *See* 2d edition.
Ocean, Origin of. II. Metzger. Tales told in Hawaii.
Odile, St. *See* St. Odile.
Odin. I. *See* 2d edition.
Odin. II. Dunlap. Stories of the Vikings. (Wonder-prince from Aasgaard.)
Odin and the dwarfs. *See* Dwarfs and the fairies.
Odin and the mead. Pyle. Tales from Norse mythology. (How the magic mead was brought to Asgard.)
Odin's search for wisdom. Curry and Clippinger. Children's literature.
Johnson and Scott. Anthology of children's literature.
Pyle. Tales from Norse mythology. (How Odin became the wisest of the wise.)
O'Donoghue, The. I. *See* 2d edition.
O'Donoghue, The. II. Olcott. Wonder tales from fairy isles. (Hurroo, Coupal Bawn.)
Odysseus. *See* Ulysses.

Œdipus. Bulfinch. Golden age. (Sphinx. *In* Ch. 16.)
Miller. My book of history. v. 2. (Œdipus Tyrannus of
Sophocles. *In* Ch. 5.)
Pyle. Tales from Greek mythology. (Œdipus and the
sphinx.)
For other entries, see 2d edition.
Oeyvind and his goat. *See* Oeyvind and Marit.
Oeyvind and Marit. Whiteman. Playmates in print. (Oey-
vind and his goat.)
For other entries, see 2d edition.
Of a tailor and a bear. *See* Clever tailor. II.
Of buying of sheep. *See* Wise men of Gotham.
Of counting. *See* Missing man found; Wise men of Gotham.
Of drowning eels. *See* Salt fish and the eel; Wise men of
Gotham.
Of hedging a cuckoo. *See* Wise men of Gotham.
Of sending cheeses. *See* Cheeses that ran away; Wise men
of Gotham.
Of sending rent. *See* Hare that was sent to York; Wise
men of Gotham.
Officer of police. Mackenzie. Jackal in Persia (Story of
the officer of police).
Og, King of Bashan. Lanier. Book of giants.
See also Giant of the flood; Giant who rode on the ark.
For other entries, see 2d edition.
Ogier the Dane. Adams and Atchinson. Book of enchant-
ment. (Enchanted knight.)
Echols. Knights of Charlemagne.
Farjeon. Mighty men from Beowulf to William the Con-
queror.
Johnson and Scott. Anthology of children's literature.
For other entries, see 2d edition.
Ogre and his dragon. Stewart. Tell me a story I never
heard before.
Ogre that played jackstraws. Boeckel. Through the gate-
way.
Coe. Third book of stories.
Freeman. Child-story readers. 3d reader.
For other entries, see 2d edition.
Ogre's plaything. Metzger. Tales told in Hawaii.
Ogress and mother. *See* Chipmunk and Owl-woman.
Oh. Lee. Folk tales of all nations. (Oh, the tsar of the
forest.)
See also Farmer Weatherbeard; Mistress of magic.
For other entries, see 2d edition.
Ohia and his sorrows. Woodson. African myths.
See also Ass, the ox and the labourer; Language of beasts.
Ohia and the thieving deer. Lee. Folk tales of all na-
tions.
Oil merchant's donkey. Lee. Folk tales of all nations.
See also Was-a-boy.

Oil vendor and the blind man. Metzger. Tales told in Korea.
See also Turkish judge.
Oisin in the land of youth. *See* Last of the Feni.
Oisin's mother. *See* Last of the Feni.
Ol' Paul and his camp. *See* Bunyan, Paul.
Olaf and the three goats. *See* Goats in the turnip field.
Olaf returns to his own. *See* Death of Earl Haakon.
Olaf, the mermaid's son. Lee. Folk tales of all nations.
See also Young giant.
For other entries, see 2d edition.
Olaf Triggvison. *See* King Olaf.
Old acquaintance is soon forgot. Carrick. Still more Russian picture tales.
See also Way of the world. I.
Old Bluebeard. Williams-Ellis. Fairies and enchanters.
See also Three princesses of Connaught.
Old complaint. Cozad. Story talks.
Old cook book. Brown. Under the rowan tree.
Old couple of the humble hut. Sugimoto. Japanese holiday picture tales.
See also Iktomi's blanket.
Old couple's house. *See* Baucis and Philemon.
Old crab and a young one. *See* Crab and his mother.
Old curiosity shop. *See* Little Nell.
Old dame and her silver sixpence. *See* Old woman and her pig.
Old fable of the cock. *See* Cock and the fox. II.
Old Father Christmas. Ewing. Lob Lie-by-the-fire.
Old Fortune. *See* Fortunatus.
Old Gally Mander. Field. American folk and fairy tales.
See also Old hag's long leather bag.
Old hag of the forest. Harper. Ghosts and goblins.
See also Two brothers. III.
For other entries, see 2d edition.
Old hag's long leather bag. Faulkner. Road to enchantment. (Long leather bag.)
See also Old Gally Mander; Old witch. I.
For other entries, see 2d edition.
Old hare and the elephants. *See* Rabbit and the elephants.
Old hermit who exchanged his body for that of the dead boy. Ryder. Twenty-two goblins.
Old home camp. Field. American folk and fairy tales.
See also Bunyan, Paul.
Old horse Proudfoot. Potter. Giant of Apple Pie Hill.
Old hound. Æsop. Fables (Jones).
Cooper. Argosy of fables.
For other entries, see 2d edition.
Old house. Andersen. Fairy tales (Stickney). v. 1.
Bailey. Tell me another story. (Adapted.)
For other entries, see 2d edition.

Old Hump. Hervey and Hix. Fanciful tales for children.
See also How the camel got his hump.
Old iron pot. *See* Wonderful pot.
Old jackal and the elephant. *See* Elephant and the jackal.
Old Jan the cobbler. *See* Elves and the shoemaker.
Old Johnny Appleseed. *See* Johnny Appleseed.
Old King Fork=Beard and the scarf that he gave. Colum.
Forge in the forest.
Old lady fox and the old hen. De Huff. Taytay's tales.
Old lady of Purchase. Broomell. Children's story caravan.
Old lion. I. *See* Sick lion. I.
Old lion. II. *See* Lion, the fox, and the beasts.
Old man and death. *See* Death and the woodman.
Old man and his ass. Æsop. Fables (Jones. Ass and the
old peasant.)
Cooper. Argosy of fables. (Ass and the old shepherd.)
For other entries, see 2d edition.
Old man and his sons. *See* Bundle of sticks.
Old man and the grain of wheat. *See* Grain that was like
an egg.
Old man and the mermaid. Rhys. English fairy book.
Old man and the robbers. Eells. Brazilian fairy book.
Old man and the snake and the judgment of Solomon.
See Snake's thanks.
Old man and the three young men. *See* Not as one thinks.
Old=Man and the Thunder=birds. Field. American folk
and fairy tales.
Linderman. Kootenai why stories.
Old Man Chrysanthemum. Egan. New found tales.
Old Man Hug=me=tight's Christmas party. Major. Merry
Christmas stories.
Old man in the moon. *See* Man in the moon. II.
Old man of Teutli. Purnell. Merry frogs.
See also Hare in the moon. II.
Old man of the mountain. Browne. Indian nights. (*In*
Indian names and meanings.)
See also Great stone face ; Pipe of peace.
Old man of the volcano. Snell. Told beneath the northern
lights.
Old Man Rabbit's Thanksgiving dinner. Bailey. Stories
children want.
Elson and Runkel. Child-library readers. Book 2. (Uncle
Rabbit's Thanksgiving dinner. Adapted.)
For other entries, see 2d edition.
Old man who could not abstain from wine. **Gaster.
Ma'aseh book. v. 2.
Old man who made withered trees to flower. Bryce.
Folk lore from foreign lands.
Mitford. Tales of old Japan. (Story of the old man who
made withered trees to blossom.)
Sugimoto. Picture tales from the Japanese. (Flower
blooming old man.)

Old man who made withered trees to flower—*continued.*
Whitehorn. Wonder tales of old Japan. (Old man who made withered trees to blossom.)
See also Moko and the twelve little earth men.
For other entries, see 2d edition.

Old man with a wen. *See* Man with the wen.

Old man with the wens. *See* Man with the wen.

Old man's dreams. *See* Copernicus and his book.

Old=Man's eyes. Linderman. Kootenai why stories. (Coyote and Old-Man's eyes.)
See also Coyote's eyes; Wonderful bird; Why our sight fails in old age.

Old man's son. Byrde. Polish fairy book.
See also Bee, the mouse, the muskrat and the boy.

Old miser. Lee. Folk tales of all nations.

Old Mr. Toad and the little green frog. Buckingham. Great idea.

Old Mr. Toad shows his tongue. Burgess. Adventures of old Mr. Toad. Ch. 12.
Johnson and Scott. Anthology of children's literature.

Old Mr. Toad's babies. Burgess. Adventures of old Mr. Toad. Ch. 8.
Johnson and Scott. Anthology of children's literature.

Old Mr. Toad's music bag. Burgess. Adventures of old Mr. Toad. Ch. 5.
Johnson and Scott. Anthology of children's literature.

Old Mother Bear's Christmas stocking. Major. Merry Christmas stories.

Old Mother Frost. *See* Mother Holle.

Old Mother Hubbard. Curry and Clippinger. Children's literature. (Mother Hubbard and her dog.)
(poem). Johnson and Scott. Anthology of children's literature.
(poem). Patten. Junior classics. v. 10. (Old Mother Hubbard and her dog.)
Power. Bag o' tales. (Old Mother Hubbard and her wonderful dog.)
See also Dog's clock.
For other entries, see 2d edition.

Old Pipes and the dryad. Curry and Clippinger. Children's literature.
Kinscella. Music appreciation readers. Book 6.
Stockton. Reformed pirate.
For other entries, see 2d edition.

Old Put. *See* Putnam and the wolf.

Old soldier. Pogány. Magyar fairy tales.
See also Faithful John.

Old soldier and his sack. Carpenter. Tales of a Basque grandmother. (Old soldier and his magic sack.)

Old stag and the young stag. Cooper. Argosy of fables.

Old street lamp. Andersen. Fairy tales (Stickney). v. 2.
Bailey. Stories children want. (Adapted.)
For other entries, see 2d edition.
Old Sultan. King. Golden cat head. (Dog Sultan.)
McVenn. Good manners and right conduct. Book 2.
For other entries, see 2d edition.
Old trolley car. Emerson. Merry-go-round of modern tales.
Old Tubby Toad. Potter. Giant of Apple Pie Hill.
Old warrior Tameyoshi. Sugimoto. Japanese holiday picture tales.
Old Winter Man and the Spring. I. Stewart. Tell me a
story I never heard before. (Spirit of winter. Adapted.)
For other entries, see 2d edition.
Old Winter Man and the Spring. II. Lee. Folk tales of
all nations. (Winter spirit and his visitor.)
For other entries, see 2d edition.
Old Winter Man and the Spring. III. Sheriff. Stories
old and new. (Where they came from.)
Old witch. I. Steel. English fairy tales. (Two sisters.)
Harper. Ghosts and goblins.
See also Old hag's long leather bag.
For other entries, see 2d edition.
Old witch and the little bears. Hervey and Hix. Fanciful
tales for children.
Old woman and her maids. Æsop. Fables (Artzybasheff).
Æsop. Fables (Jones. Mistress and her servants).
Cooper. Argosy of fables.
For other entries, see 2d edition.
Old woman and her pig. I. Curry and Clippinger. Children's literature.
Harriman. Stories for little children.
Hutchinson. Chimney corner stories.
Johnson and Scott. Anthology of children's literature.
Patten. Junior classics. v. 10. (Old woman who bought
a little pig.)
Power. Bag o' tales. (Old dame and her silver sixpence.)
Steel. English fairy tales.
Told under the green umbrella.
Wilson. Green magic. (Tom, Dick, and Harry.)
For other entries, see 2d edition.
Old woman and her pig. II. Olcott. Wonder tales from
windmill lands. (There was an old wifey.)
Old woman and the doctor. Æsop. Fables (Jones).
Cooper. Argosy of fables. (Old woman and the physician.)
For other entries, see 2d edition.
Old woman and the pecans. Partridge. Joyful Star.
Old woman and the physician. *See* Old woman and the
doctor.
Old woman and the tides. Hillyer. Box of daylight.
(Tchamsen and the tides.)
See also Cause of tides.
For other entries, see 2d edition.

Old woman and the tramp. Fun folk and fairy tales.
Power. Bag o' tales.
Power. Stories to shorten the road.
See also Soldier's soup; Stone broth #.
For other entries, see 2d edition.
Old woman and the wine jar. Æsop. Fables (Jones).
Cooper. Argosy of fables.
For other entries, see 2d edition.
Old woman of the mountains. Perkins and Danielson.
Second year Mayflower program book.
Old woman, the rooster, and the chafing dish. Egan. New
found tales. (*In* Lawyer of Samarcand.)
Old woman who bought a little pig. *See* Old woman and
her pig.
Old woman who lived in a shoe. *See* Giant who married a
mortal princess.
Old woman who wanted all the cakes. *See* Why the wood-
pecker's head is red. I.
Old woman who went to market at midnight. *See* Hunted
hare.
Old woman's cat. Cooper. Argosy of fables. (Greedy cat.)
Mackenzie. Jackal in Persia. (Story of the old woman's
cat.)
For other entries, see 2d edition.
Old yew tree. Housman. What-o'clock tales.
Ole=Luk=Oie, the dream god. Andersen. Fairy   tales
(Stickney). v. 1.
Bailey. Tell me another story. (Adapted.)
Power. Bag o' tales. (Ole Shut-Eye. Abridged.)
Told under the green umbrella. (Olé Luköié, the dustman.)
For other entries, see 2d edition.
Ole Shut=eye. *See* Ole-Luk-Oie.
Olelbis. *See* Flood.
Olive tree. *See* Athens.
Olive tree and the fig tree. Æsop. Fables (Jones).
Cooper. Argosy of fables.
Olle's ski trip. Harper. Merry Christmas to you.
Omi Seijin—the farmer saint. Sugimoto. Picture tales
from the Japanese. (Farmer saint.)
On Christmas Day in the morning. Hall. Godmother's
stories.
On Christmas eve (play). Skinner. Christmas stories.
On the shores of longing. Canton. Child's book of saints.
On the wings of an arrow. *See* Death of King Haakon the
Good.
One calabash of water. Egan. New found tales.
One cannot help an unlucky man. Lee. Folk tales of all
nations.
See also Cogia Hassan Alhabbal.
One-eye, Two=eyes, Three=eyes. Evans. Worth while
stories.
Grimm. Fairy tales (Olcott).

One-eye, Two-eyes, Three-eyes—*continued.*
Hutchinson. Chimney corner fairy tales. (Little One-eye, Two-eyes, and Three-eyes.)
Johnson and Scott. Anthology of children's literature.
Power. Blue caravan tales. (Little One-eye, Two-eyes, and Three-eyes.)
For other entries, see 2d edition.
One-eyed doe. Æsop. Fables (Jones. Stag with one eye.)
Æsop. Fables (Whitman ed.).
Cooper. Argosy of fables.
For other entries, see 2d edition.
One-eyed Likho. Ralston. Russian fairy tales.
One good giant. *See* St. Christopher.
One hundred hares. Olcott. Wonder tales from Baltic wizards.
See also Enchanted whistle; Jesper who herded the hares.
One inch fellow. Henderson and Calvert. Wonder tales of old Japan. (Issunboshi.)
Sugimoto. Japanese holiday picture tales.
See also Tom Thumb. I.
One laugh too many. Nakazawa. Weaver of the frost.
One of the oldest stories in Japan. *See* Uraschimataro and the turtle.
One step at a time. *See* Hill.
One straw. Sugimoto. Japanese holiday picture tales.
See also Five pennies; Mouse merchant.
One swallow does not make a summer. *See* Spendthrift and the swallow.
One that is dead kills two, and two that are dead kill forty. *See* Riddle. I.
1, 2, 3, 4, 5, 6, 7— Hogner. Navajo winter nights.
One who would not weep for Balder. Pyle. Tales from Norse mythology.
See also Baldur and the mistletoe.
One's own children are always the prettiest. Dasent. East of the sun and west of the moon (Nielsen).
Rasmussen. East o' the sun and west o' the moon.
See also Crow's children; Eagle and the owl; Jupiter and the monkey.
For other entries, see 2d edition.
Onesimus. Niemeyer. Stories for the history hour.
Only a penny #.
See also Five pennies.
Only jealousy of Emer. *See* Fairy swan-maidens.
Only son of Aoiffe. *See* Death of Conla, son of Aiffe.
Only son rabbit. *See* Chekilli the Creek boy.
Oochigeaskw, the little scarred girl. *See* Little Scar Face.
Ootinna and the man of the North. Snell. Told beneath northern lights.
Open door. I. See 2d edition.
Open door. II. Housman. Turn again tales.
Open door. III. *See* Barring of the door. II.

Open road. Grahame. Kenneth Grahame book.
Open Winkins. Farjeon. Martin Pippin in the apple orchard.
Opium, Origin of. *See* Bad poppy seeds.
Opportunity. I. Black. Open door. (*In* Door of opportunity.)
  McVenn. Good manners and right conduct. Book 2. (Statue of Lysippus.)
  See also Morgana.
Opportunity. II. (poem). Patten. Junior classics. v. 10. (poem). Sill. Poems.
  See also Mouse merchant; One straw.
Optimistic thrush. Brown. Curious book of birds. (*In* Thrush and the cuckoo.)
  Carey. Stories of the birds.
  Rich. Why-so stories. (Why the thrush hides in a tree.)
  See also Month of March; Thrush and the cuckoo.
Oracle of Delphi. *See* Delphian oracle #.
Oracle of Trophonius. Bulfinch. Golden age. (*In* Ch. 34.)
  See also Treasure chamber of Rhampsinitus.
Orange=blossom, Legend of. Newman. Fairy flowers.
Oranges and lemons. Farjeon. Italian peepshow.
Orc. *See* Hippogriff.
Orchid. Newman. Fairy flowers. (Or-chis-a.)
Oriana. *See* Amadis of Gaul.
Origin of, etc. *See* the first important word of the title; also titles beginning with the word "First."
Orion. Bulfinch. Golden age. (*In* Ch. 26.)
  Forbush. Myths and legends of Greece and Rome. (Orion, unlucky hunter.)
  Johnson and Scott. Anthology of children's literature. (Artemis and Orion.)
  Kinney. Stars and their stories. (Great healing.)
  Lanier. Book of giants. (Giant who shines in the sky.)
  Williamson. Stars through magic casements. (Orion, the giant huntsman.)
  For other entries, see 2d edition.
Orpheus. I. *See* 2d edition.
Orpheus. II. Kinscella. Music appreciation readers. Book 5. (Grecian music contest.)
Orpheus. III. *See* Orpheus and Eurydice.
Orpheus and Eurydice. Bryant. Children's book of celebrated legends.
  Bulfinch. Golden age. (Orpheus and Eurydice. *In* Ch. 24.)
  Cross. Music stories.
  Forbush. Myths and legends of Greece and Rome.
  Johnson and Scott. Anthology of children's literature.
  Kinney. Stars and their stories. (Sad and lonely lover.)
  Lang. Book of myths. (Orpheus.)
  Pyle. Tales from Greek mythology.
  Williamson. Stars through magic casements. (Divine musician.)

Orpheus and Eurydice—*continued.*
See also Ishtar and Tammuz; King Orpheo and the fairies; Loik Guern; Love of Heipua.
For other entries, see 2d edition.
Orrelana, Story of. Browne. Indian nights.
See also Hero and Leander.
Orthon, Story of. Lang. Red true story book.
Osborn's pipe. *See* Ashiepattle and the king's hares.
Oseedah, the rabbit gambler. Parker. Skunny Wundy and other Indian tales.
Osiris and his wicked brother. *See* Isis and Osiris, Story of.
Osiris and Isis. *See* Isis and Osiris, Story of.
Ostrich. Cooper. Argosy of fables.
Ostrich chicks. Lee. Folk tales of all nations.
Othello. Lamb. Tales from Shakespeare.
Other side of the mountain. Casserley. Michael of Ireland.
Otokodate of Yedo, Story of. Mitford. Tales of old Japan.
Ottabec trapped with the Yellow=Feathers. Kennedy. Red man's wonder book.
Ottabec's adventure in the forest. Kennedy. Red man's wonder book.
Otter=heart. Spence. Myths of the North American Indians. (*In* Ch. 3.)
For other entries, see 2d edition.
Otters and the wolf. Cooper. Argosy of fables. (Otters and the jackal.)
See also Matter of arbitration.
For other entries, see 2d edition.
Ouphe of the woods #.
See also Pillow of content.
Our baby. Burnett. Children's book.
Our hen. Colum. Big tree of Bunlahy.
Our lady of Guadalupe, Legend of. Smith. Made in Mexico. (*In* Ch. 6.)
Out of the nest. Skinner. Child's book of country stories.
For other entries, see 2d edition.
Outlandish adventures of Bigger. Shannon. Eyes for the dark.
Outlaw king, Story of. *See* Bruce. Robert.
Outside the door like the mother of St. Peter. *See* Almost saved. II.
Outwitting of Polyphemus. *See* Ulysses and Polyphemus.
Outwitting of the Gedembai. Skeat. Tiger's mistake.
Outwitting the bogie. Williams-Ellis. Fairies and enchanters. (Hairy boggart.)
See also Bruin and Reynard partners. I.
Over the cat to the kitchen. Buckingham. Great idea. (Over the cat to the kitchen: Brownie turns cook.)
Over the moon. Blaisdell. Rhyme and story second reader.
Owain of Drws Coed. Henderson and Jones. Wonder tales of ancient Wales.
Owl. I. *See* 2d edition.

Owl. II (poem). Cooper. Argosy of fables.
Owl and the birds. Æsop. Fables (Jones).
Cooper. Argosy of fables.
See also Swallow and the other birds.
For other entries, see 2d edition.
Owl and the grasshopper. Æsop. Fables (Jones. Grasshopper and the owl.)
Æsop. Fables (Whitman ed.).
Cooper. Argosy of fables. (Grasshopper and the owl.)
For other entries, see 2d edition.
Owl and the lemming. Cooper. Argosy of fables.
See also Wolf and the kid. II.
Owl and the moon. Brown. Curious book of birds.
See also Giant Crump and Lady Moon.
Owl and the moon princess. Bryce. Folk lore from foreign lands.
Owl and the nightingale. Æsop. Fables (Whitman ed.).
For other entries, see 2d edition.
Owl and the peacock. Bailey. Story-telling hour.
Pyrnelle. Diddie, Dumps and Tot. (*In* Ch. 16.)
See also Why the peacock's tail is spotted.
For other entries, see 2d edition.
Owl and the two rabbits. Cooper. Argosy of fables.
See also Boy and the filberts # ; Fox and the piece of meat; Monkey and the peas #.
Owl as king. *See* Why the owl is not king of the birds.
Owl learns to see at night. *See* Why some animals see at night. I.
Owl man. Sexton. Gray wolf stories. (Owl man takes boy to mystery valley).
Owl, Tales of the. Rich. Why-so stories.
Owl, the fox and the crow. Carrick. Picture folk tales.
See also Fox and the crow. II.
Owls. *See* Boy who caught flies.
Owl's big eyes. Parker. Skunny Wundy and other Indian tales.
Owl's tufted cap. Brown. Curious book of birds. (Tufted cap.)
Carey. Stories of the birds. (How the long-eared owl came by his name.)
Ox and ass at the manger. Campbell. Story of Christmas. p. 50.
Ox and the calf. Cooper. Argosy of fables.
See also Bull and the calf.
Ox and the frog. *See* Frog and the ox.
Ox and the stag. Cooper. Argosy of fables.
Ox that helped. Lane. Tower legends.
Ox, the monkey, and the pig. Lebermann. New German fairy tales.
Ox who envied the pig. Cooper. Argosy of fables. (Discontented ox.)
See also Ass pretending that he was ill.

Ox who envied the pig—*continued.*
For other entries, see 2d edition.
Ox who won the forfeit. *See* Bull who demanded fair treatment.
Oxen and the axle=trees. Æsop. Fables (Jones).
Cooper. Argosy of fables. (Creaking wheels.)
For other entries, see 2d edition.
Oxen and the butchers. Æsop. Fables (Jones).
Cooper. Argosy of fables. (Beeves and the butchers.)
For other entries, see 2d edition.
Oyster and its claimants. *See* Two travelers and the oyster.
In 2d edition there are entries under each title.
Oyster and the heron. Cooper. Argosy of fables. (Bittern and the mussel).
Metzger. Picture tales from the Chinese.
Oyster and the pleaders. *See* Two travelers and the oyster.

P

Pa Badak's lawsuit. Skipper. Jungle meeting-pool. (*In* First meeting.)
See also Who killed the otter's babies.
Pack=ass and the wild ass. Æsop. Fables (Jones).
Pack=ass, the wild ass and the lion. Æsop. Fables (Jones).
Pack rat of Tuolumne. *See* Woodrat the trader.
Paddy's three pets. Told under the blue umbrella.
Padre and the negro. Lee. Folk tales of all nations.
Padre who never worried. Eells. Brazilian fairy book.
Pah=tay and the wind=witch. De Huff. Taytay's tales.
Pail of gold. Bryce. Short stories for little folks.
See also Fortune and the beggar # ; Stone lion. I.
Painted Death. Untermeyer. Donkey of God.
Painted spirits. Kennedy. Red man's wonder book.
Painter who forgot four colors. Perkins and Danielson. Mayflower program book.
Applegarth. Missionary stories for little folks. 1st series. (How the artist forgot four colors.)
Painting lady. Potter. Giant of Apple Pie Hill.
Pajaro. Shannon. California fairy tales.
Pak=su=ni and the chess=players. Metzger. Tales told in Korea.
See also Date-stone of forgetfulness ; Rip Van Winkle ; Vision of Tsunu.
Palace made by music. Kinscella. Music appreciation readers. Book 6.
Starbuck. Enchanted paths.
For other entries, see 2d edition.
Palace of Pharaoh's daughter. Vilnay. Legends of Palestine.
See also Acqueduct of Caesarea.
Palace of the night. Beston. Starlight wonder book.

Palamon and Arcite. Farjeon. Tales from Chaucer. (Knight's tale.)
Richardson. Stories from old English poetry. (Two noble kinsmen.)
For other entries, see 2d edition.
Pale mountains. Wolff. Pale mountains.
Palececk, "Little Thumb," Story of. Nemcova. Disobedient kids.
Palinurus. Bulfinch. Golden age. (*In* Ch. 31.)
Pali's luck. Pogány. Magyar fairy tales.
See also Go, I know not whither—fetch, I know not what.
Palissy, the potter. Clément. Flowers of chivalry. (Then he burnt the floor.)
Smith. Made in France. (*In* Ch. 1.)
See also Powdered wig.
Palm tree (poem). Curtis. Stories in trees. (Wonderful palm tree.)
See also Gifts the trees gave.
Pan. I. Cather. Pan and his pipes, and other stories. (Pan and his pipes.)
Forbush. Myths and legends of Greece and Rome. (Pan and his pipes.)
Johnson and Scott. Anthology of children's literature. (Syrinx and Pan.)
Kinscella. Music appreciation readers. Book 2. (Story of the flute.)
Lang. Book of myths. (Syrinx; Pan.)
Pyle. Tales from Greek mythology. (Story of Syrinx.)
Wheelock. Kindergarten children's hour. v. 3. (*In* Ch. 51.)
For other entries, see 2d edition.
Pan. II. Grahame. Kenneth Grahame book. (Piper at the gates of dawn.)
See also Ana Josepha.
Pan of peas (poem). Potter. Giant of Apple Pie Hill.
Pan Twardowski. *See* Master wizard, Pan Twardowski.
Pancake. Blaisdell. Rhyme and story second reader.
Hutchinson. Chimney corner stories.
Johnson and Scott. Anthology of children's literature.
Power. Bag o' tales.
Told under the green umbrella.
For other entries, see 2d edition.
Panch-Phul Ranee. Pyle. Fairy tales from India.
For other entries, see 2d edition.
Pandora. Bryant. Children's book of celebrated legends. (Hope.)
Bulfinch. Golden age. (*In* Ch. 2.)
Curry and Clippinger. Children's literature. (Paradise of children.)
Forbush. Myths and legends of Greece and Rome.
Johnson and Scott. Anthology of children's literature.

Pandora—*continued.*
(play).   Knight.   Dramatic   reader.   (Pandora's   box.
Adapted.)
Lang. Book of myths. (Prometheus and Pandora.)
Miller. My book of history. v. 2. (*In* Prometheus. Ch.
3.)
Pyle. Tales from Greek mythology.
See also Inquisitive woman.
For other entries, see 2d edition.
Pandora's box. *See* Pandora.
Pansies. I–II. *See* 2d edition.
Pansies. III. Carey. Flower legends. (Pansy.)
See also Heart's ease, Legend of # ; How pansies came col-
ored #.
For other entries, see 2d edition.
Pantagruel. Adams and Atchinson. There were giants.
For other entries, see 2d edition.
Panther and the shepherds. Cooper. Argosy of fables.
Papa Dragon's tale. St. Nicholas. April 1900, p. 816.
Paper daffodils. Morley. I know a secret.
Paphos, Story of. *See* Pygmalion and Galatea.
Papyrus to paper. *See* King Eumenes starts a library.
Parade in the City of Somewhere. Cook. To-day's stories
of yesterday.
Paradise in the sea. Gaer. Burning bush. (Man who
thought he was a god.)
See also Shah Jamshid.
For other entries, see 2d edition.
Paradise of children. *See* Pandora.
Paradise of the animals. Meeker. Folk tales from the Far
East.
Parasol of contentment. Martens. Wonder tales from far
away.
Pardoner's tale. *See* Three revellers and death.
Paris: Apple of discord. Bulfinch. Golden age. (*In* Ch.
27.)
Curry and Clippinger. Children's literature. (Apple of dis-
cord.)
Forbush. Myths and legends of Greece and Rome. (*In* Tro-
jan war: Decision of Paris.)
For other entries, see 2d edition.
Parrot #.
See also Confident parrot.
Parrot and the cat. Æsop. Fables (Jones).
Parrot and the hawk. Potter. Fairy caravan. (*In* Ch. 14.)
Parrot and the thrush. Ryder. Twenty-two goblins.
Parrot girl. James. Tewa firelight tales.
Parrot of Limo Verde. Eells. Brazilian fairy book.
See also East o' the sun and West o' the moon.
Parrot's story #.
See also Mr. Monk and the noisy gecko.

Parsee tale. Fyleman. Forty good-morning tales.
See also Wise priest.
Parsifal. *See* Sir Percival.
Parson and the deacon. *See* Priest and the clerk.
Parson's fiddle. Kinscella. Music appreciation readers. Book 6.
Parson's tale. Farjeon. Tales from Chaucer.
Partners. *See* Bruin and Reynard partners. II.
Partnership of the elephant and the rabbit. Woodson. African myths.
Partridge and his drum. *See* Pulowech and the sea maiden.
Partridge and his wonderful wigwam. *See* Magic wigwam.
Partridge and the cocks. Æsop. Fables (Artzybasheff).
Æsop. Twenty-four fables (L'Estrange. Cocks and a partridge.)
Cooper. Argosy of fables. (Game-cocks and the partridge.)
For other entries, see 2d edition.
Partridge and the crow. *See* Crow and the partridge.
In 2d edition there are entries under each title.
Partridge and the fowler. Æsop. Fables (Artzybasheff. Falconer and the partridge.)
Æsop. Fables (Jones).
Cooper. Argosy of fables. (Falconer and the partridge.)
For other entries, see 2d 'edition.
In 2d edition this story is also indexed under the title "Quail and the fowler."
Partridge and the fox. Cooper. Argosy of fables.
See also Cock and the fox. V.
Party. Fyleman. Forty good-night tales (Dolls' house, pt. 2.)
Parvarted bachelor. MacManus. Lo, and behold ye!
Pass of Thermopylae. *See* Brave three hundred.
Passable but unsafe. Emerson. Merry-go-round of modern tales.
Passing of Arthur. *See* King Arthur's death.
Passing of Glooskap. *See* Glooskap's departure.
Passing of the flowers. *See* Flowers, Legend of.
Passionate puppets. Housman. Doorway in fairyland.
Patch of snowdrops. Marzials. Stories for the story hour.
See also Snow man and the snowdrops.
Patched pot to the mended lid. Metzger. Tales told in Korea.
Path that never got anywhere. Fyleman. Tea time tales.
Patience. *See* Rival poets.
Patient Griselda. Bailey. Stories of great adventures.
Farjeon. Tales from Chaucer. (Clerk of Oxford's tale.)
Richardson. Stories from old English poetry. (*In* Three unknown poets.)
For other entries, see 2d edition.
Patrick, St. *See* St. Patrick.
Patriotic snowman. Bailey. Wonderful tree.

Patroclus. Bulfinch. Golden age. (*In* Ch. 27.)
  Farjeon. Mighty men from Achilles to Julius Caesar.
  (Friend. of Achilles.)
  For other entries, see 2d edition.
Paudeen and the merrow. Casserley. Whins on Knockat-
  tan.
Paul Bunyan. *See* Bunyan, Paul.
Paul goes hunting. Rounds. Ol' Paul.
Pea blossom. Andersen. Fairy tales (Stickney). v. 2.
  Elson and Runkel. Child-library reader: Book 2. (Five
    peas in a pod.)
  Evans. Worth while stories. (Story of the jackbean.
    Adapted.)
  Johnson and Scott. Anthology of children's literature. (Five
    peas in a pod.)
  See also Pea plant.
  For other entries, see 2d edition.
Pea plant. Baker. Tell them again tales.
  See also Pea blossom.
Peace-egg. Ewing. Lob Lie-by-the-fire.
Peace king. *See* First great adventure in thinking.
Peace queen. *See* How Genetaska deserted her trust.
Peaceful soldiers. Broomell. Children's story caravan.
Peacemaking duck. De Huff. Taytay's memories.
Peach boy. *See* Momotaro.
Peach from the sky. Olcott. Wonder tales from China seas.
  See also Miserly farmer.
Peach-prince and the demons. *See* Momotaro.
Peach-rocked deer. Mackaye. Tall tales of the Kentucky
  mountains.
  See also Stag and the cherry tree.
Peaches of chance. *See* Miserly farmer.
Peachling. *See* Momotaro.
Peach's son. *See* Momotaro.
Peacock and Juno. Æsop. Fables (Artzybasheff. Peacock's
  complaint.)
  Æsop. Fables (Jones).
  Æsop. Fables (Whitman ed.).
  Cooper. Argosy of fables.
  See also Peacock, the crow and the tortoise.
  For other entries, see 2d edition.
Peacock and the crane. Æsop. Fables (Artzybasheff).
  Æsop. Fables (Jones).
  Cooper. Argosy of fables.
  For other entries, see 2d edition.
Peacock and the magpie. Æsop. Fables (Artzybasheff).
  See also King Wren.
  For other entries, see 2d edition.
Peacock and the rooster. Johnson and Scott. Anthology of
  children's literature.
  Cooper. Argosy of fables.

Peacock=king. Carrick. Animal picture tales from Russia.
See also Princess Rosette.

Peacock, the crow and the tortoise. Cooper. Argosy of fables.
See also Peacock and Juno.

Peacock, the geese and the diver (poem). Cooper. Argosy of fables.

Peacock's complaint. *See* Peacock and Juno.

Peacock's cousin. Brown. Curious book of birds.
See also Why the crow is black. IV.

Peacocks of Baron's Hall. Colum. Big tree of Bunlahy.

Peacock's tail. *See* How the peacock was given colored feathers; Io; Owl and the peacock; Why the peacock's tail is spotted.

Peacock's wooing. Aspinwall. Jataka tales.

Peanut wagon. Morley. I know a secret.

Pear tree and the wise man. Independent (N. Y.). Aug. 29, 1895, p. 1179.

Peasant and the animals. Carrick. Animal picture tales from Russia.

Peasant and the apple tree. Æsop. Fables (Jones).
Cooper. Argosy of fables.
For other entries, see 2d edition.

Peasant and the bear. Carrick. More Russian picture tales.
Quinn. Stories for the six-year-old.
See also Bruin and Reynard partners. I; Outwitting the bogie.

Peasant and the hare. Carrick. Still more Russian picture tales.
See also Lad and the fox #; Milkmaid and her pail of milk.

Peasant and the workman. Lee. Folk tales of all nations.
**Maspero. Popular stories of ancient Egypt. (Lamentations of the fellah.)

Peasant, the saint and the prophet. *See* Elijah the prophet and St. Nicholas.

Peasant's clever daughter #.
See also Aunya's bargain; Basque maiden and the king; Clever daughter; Maiden who was wiser than an emperor; Sage damsel.

Peasant's journey. Guerber. Legends of Switzerland. (In Legends of Vaud and Valais.)
See also Frog travellers.

Peasie and Beansie. Johnson and Scott. Anthology of children's literature.
For other entries, see 2d edition.

Pebble and the diamond. Cooper. Argosy of fables.
For other entries, see 2d edition.

Pebbles. Richards. More five minute stories.

Peddler. King. Golden cat head.

Pedelestu and Mustaccio. Hill and Maxwell. Napoleon's story book.
See also Cock and the hen in the nut wood.

Pedlar of Swaffham. Hart. Picture tales from Holland. (Fortunate shoemaker.)
Lee. Folk tales of all nations. (Bridge of the kist.)
See also Fairy gold; Furze blossom gold; Treasure.
For other entries, see 2d edition.
Pedlar's pack. Shimer. Fairyland. (Scarlet blanket.)
For other entries, see 2d edition.
Pedro's feet. Mitchell. Here and now story book.
Peer Gynt. Cross. Music stories.
Kinscella. Music appreciation readers. Book 4.
See also Peter Gynt #.
Peerless knight Lancelot. *See* Sir Lancelot.
Pegasus. Barry and Hanna. Wonder flights of long ago. (Pegasus and Bellerophon.)
Bulfinch. Golden age. (Pegasus and the chimæra. *In* Ch. 16.)
Colum. Forge in the forest. (Bellerophon.)
Forbush. Myths and legends of Greece and Rome. (Bellerophon and Pegasus.)
Johnson and Scott. Anthology of children's literature (Chimæra.)
Pyle. Tales from Greek mythology. (Bellerophon and Pegasus.)
Williamson. Stars through magic casements. (Steed of the muses.)
Wilson. Red magic. (Chimæra).
For other entries, see 2d edition.
Pegasus in pound (poem). Williamson. Stars through magic casements.
Peggy feeds the minutemen. Buckingham. Elephant's friend.
Pekka. Topelius. Canute Whistlewinks. ("Aha!" said Pekka.)
Pekka and the rogues. *See* Magic cap.
Pele and the bad-tempered chief. Metzger. Tales told in Hawaii.
Pelican's punishment. Skeat. Tiger's mistake.
See also Crane and the crab; Undan the pelican.
Pelle's new suit. Told under the blue umbrella.
Pelops. Shimer. Fairyland. (Horses with wings.)
For other entries, see 2d edition.
Pemigewasset. *See* Old man of the mountain.
"Pen and ink" pagodas. Kinscella. Music appreciation readers. Book 6.
Pen and the ink stand. Andersen. Fairy tales (Stickney). v. 2.
For other entries, see 2d edition.
Penelope's web. Bulfinch. Golden age. (Penelope. *In* Ch. 23.)
See also Ulysses' return.
For other entries, see 2d edition.

Pengersec and the witch of Fraddom. *See* Lord of Pengerswick.

Pengerswick. *See* Lord of Pengerswick. II.

Penn, William. Boeckel. Through the gateway. (Why William Penn is famous.)

Pentheus. Bulfinch. Golden age. (*In* Bacchus. Ch. 21.)

People of the night. Egan. New found tales.

People's star. *See* Sailor's star.

Peppermint and pear=drops. Fyleman. Forty good night tales. (Bag of goodies, pt. 4.)

Perdita. Richardson. Stories from old English poetry. *See also* Winter's tale. I.

Perez the mouse. I. Coloma. Perez the mouse.
Harper. Merry Christmas to you.
Harper. Selfish giant.

Perez the mouse. II. Belpré. Perez and Martina.
Sawyer. Picture tales from Spain. (La Hormiguita and Perez the mouse.)
See also Little black ant # ; Spider and the flea.

Perfect gander. Shannon. Eyes for the dark.

Perfect ring (play). Boeckel. Through the gateway.

Pericles and Aspasia. Miller. My book of history. v. 2. (*In* Ch. 5.)

Pericles, Prince of Tyre. Lamb. Tales from Shakespeare.
Richardson. Stories from old English poetry. (Wonderful adventures of Pericles, Prince of Tyre.)

Perils of Sigrid. Adams. Swords of the Vikings.

Periplus . . . of Hanno. *See* Voyage of Hanno.

Peris' god=daughter. *See* Bath-boy's daughter.

Perjury punished. Guerber. Legends of Switzerland. (*In* Legends of Zug.)

Perlinette. Chardon. Golden chick.

Peronnik, Adventures of. Masson. Folk tales of Brittany. (Basin of gold and the diamond lance.)
Williams. Jolly old whistle. (Simple Peter.)
For other entries, see 2d edition.

Perpetua, St. *See* St. Perpetua.

Perplexity of Zadig. **Voltaire. Zadig. (Dog and the horse. Ch. 3.)
See also Abner the Jew ; Lost camel.

Perseus. Barry and Hanna. Wonder flights of long ago. (Perseus and the Gorgon's head.)
Bulfinch. Golden age. (*In* Ch. 15.)
De La Mare and Quayle. Readings. (How Perseus slew the Gorgon.)
Evans. Worth while stories. (Adventures of Perseus.)
Forbush. Myths and legends of Greece and Rome.
Johnson and Scott. Anthology of children's literature. (Gorgon's head.)
Lang. Book of myths.
Power. Bag o' tales. (How Perseus slew the Gorgon.)

Perseus—*continued.*
Pyle. Tales from Greek mythology.
Rich. Read-aloud book.
Williamson. Stars through magic casements. (Perseus and Andromeda.)
Wilson. Green magic.
For other entries, see 2d edition.
Perseverance wins. Cabot. Course in citizenship.
Coe. Third book of stories.
Persian cats, Origin of. Fyleman. Forty good-morning tales. (Persian tale.)
Persian Columbus. Bennett. Pigtail of Ah Lee Ben Loo.
Persian jest. Lee. Folk tales of all nations. (From a Persian jest book.)
See also Lost legs.
Persian tale. *See* Persian cats, Origin of.
Personal service. *See* Three questions. I.
Pert fire engine. Harper. More story-hour favorites.
For other entries, see 2d edition.
Perugino, Pietro. Steedman. Knights of art.
Pet raven. Olcott. Wonder tales from goblin hills. (Raven of Stolzeneck.)
For other entries, see 2d edition.
Pet turkey whose feelings were hurt. Allen. Whispering wind. (*In* Farm at the End-of-the-water.)
James. Tewa firelight tales. (Man and the woman.)
See also Turkey-given corn.
For other entries, see 2d edition.
Peter. Burnett. Children's book. (Story of Peter.)
Peter and the birch tree dryad. Curtis. Stories in trees. (*In* How trees grow.)
See also Blacksmith's sons.
Peter and the witch of the wood. Harper. Ghosts and goblins.
Starbuck. Far horizons.
Wahlenberg. Old Swedish fairy tales.
Peter Bloch, the treasure seeker. Olcott. Wonder tales from goblin hills.
Peter Cottontail. Burgess. Adventures of Old Mr. Toad. Ch. 4.
Johnson and Scott. Anthology of children's literature. (Peter Rabbit finds Old Mr. Toad.)
For other entries, see 2d edition.
Peter Klaus. *See* Karl Katz.
Peter Munk. *See* Stone-cold heart.
Peter of Lyons and the poor men. Miller. My book of history. v. 3. (Heretics. *In* Ch. 11.)
Peter=of=the=pigs. Eells. Islands of magic.
Peter, Paul, and Espen. *See* Boots and his brothers.
Peter Pot=luck. Potter. Giant of Apple Pie Hill.

Peter Pretty-Face. Morris. Gypsy story teller.
Peter Rabbit finds Old Mr. Toad. *See* Peter Cottontail.
Peter Rabbit, Tale of. Curry and Clippinger. Children's
literature.
Elson and Runkel. Child-library readers. Book 2.
Harriman. Stories for little children.
Hutchinson. Chimney corner stories.
Johnson and Scott. Anthology of children's literature.
Patten. Junior classics. v. 8.
Piper. Gateway to storyland.
Potter. Tale of Peter Rabbit.
Power. Blue caravan tales.
Quinn. Stokes' wonder book of fairy tales.
Quinn. Stories for the six-year-old.
For other entries, see 2d edition.
In 2d edition this story is indexed under the title "Peter
Rabbit, Story of."
Peter tries the world. Tappan. Prince from nowhere.
See also Queen bee.
Peter Tulip. Pogány. Magyar fairy tales.
See also Three sisters. I.
Peterchen. Olcott. Wonder tales from goblin hills.
Peterkins' Christmas tree. Johnson and Scott. Anthology
of children's literature.
Peter's ghost. Smith. Made in Sweden. (*In* Visby.)
Petronila of the coats. Shannon. Eyes for the dark.
Petru, Story of. Morris. Gypsy story teller.
See also Gold-spinners.
Pewter plate silver. Krohn and Johnson. Scales of the sil-
ver fish.
Phaeton. Barry and Hanna. Wonder flights of long ago.
Bryant. Children's book of celebrated legends. (Phaeton
and the chariot of the sun.)
Bulfinch. Golden age. (*In* Ch. 5.)
Colum. Forge in the forest. (Phaethon.)
Curtis. Stories in trees. (Poplar sisters.)
Curry and Clippinger. Children's literature. (Phaethon.)
Forbush. Myths and legends of Greece and Rome. (Phae-
thon.)
Johnson and Scott. Anthology of children's literature.
(Phaethon.)
Kinney. Stars and their stories. (Phaethon.)
Lang. Book of myths.
Pyle. Tales from Greek mythology. (Story of Phaethon.)
Rich. Read-aloud book.
Williamson. Stars through magic casements.
For other entries, see 2d edition.
Phantom banquet. McDonald. Dick and the spice cupboard
(*In* Dick's ninth adventure.)
See also Aicha's stratagem.
Phantom caravan. *See* Princess Morgana.
Phantom princess. Noel. Magic bird of Chomo-lung-ma.

Pharaoh and the little maid. Baikie. Wonder tales of the ancient world. (Zazamankh and the lost coronet.)
Miller. My book of history. v. 1. (Pharaoh Snefru and the maiden who lost her jewel. *In* Ch. 6.)
See also Lost talisman #.

Pharaoh Snefru and the maiden who lost her jewel. *See* Pharaoh and the little maid.

Pharos of Alexandria. *See* Alexandria, Founding of.

Pheidippides. *See* First Marathon race.

Phidias. Patten. Junior classics. v. 7. (How Phidias helped the image-maker.)

Philosopher, the ants, and Mercury. Æsop. Fables (Jones. Mercury and the man bitten by an ant.)
Cooper. Argosy of fables.
For other entries, see 2d edition.

Phips, Sir William. *See* Sunken treasure.

Phœbus and Boreas. *See* Wind and the sun.

Phœbus and Daphne. *See* Daphne.

Phœbus and Hyacinthus. *See* Hyacinthus.

Phœnix. Brown. Curious book of birds.
Bulfinch. Golden age. (*In* Ch. 36.)
Colum. Boy apprenticed to an enchanter. (*In* Story of Bird-of-gold.)
Lang. Red book of animal stories.
McDonald. Dick and the spice cupboard. (*In* Dick's fifth adventure.)
See also Vermilion bird, the dragon and the unicorn.
For other entries, see 2d edition.

Phyrrus. *See* Pyrrhus.

Physician and his cousin. Darton. Wonder book of old romance.

Picaro bird. *See* Knavish little bird.

Piccola (poem). Cabot. Course in citizenship.
Walters. Book of Christmas stories.
For other entries, see 2d edition.

Picnic basket, and the swan. Clark. Poppy seed cakes. (Picnic basket.)
Told under the blue umbrella. (Picnic basket.)

Picture princess. Chrisman. Wind that wouldn't blow.

Picus. *See* King Picus.

Pie that grew. Bailey. Wonderful tree.

Piece of gold. *See* Flanagan pig and his piece of gold.

Piece of liver. Wilson. Green magic. (Tom, Dick and Harry.)
For other entries, see 2d edition.

Pied piper of Hamelin. Bruce. Treasury of tales for little folk. (Pied piper.)
Colum. Children who followed the piper. (How the pied piper came.)
Coussens. Diamond story book. (Pied piper.)
Cowles. Stories to tell.
Evans. Worth while stories.

Pied piper of Hamelin—*continued.*
   (poem). Johnson and Scott. Anthology of children's literature.
Kinscella. Music appreciation readers. Book 3. (Pied piper of Hamelin and his flute.)
   (poem). Olcott. Wonder tales from goblin hills. (Rat-catcher of Hamelin.)
   (poem). Patten. Junior classics. v. 10.
See also Thumbietot blows a pipe.
For other entries, see 2d edition.
Pied piper (Indian). *See* Wonderful cave.
Pies of the princess. Chrisman. Shen of the sea.
   Power. Bag o' tales.
Pig and the captain. Canfield. Made-to-order stories. (Sally's story.)
Pig and the hen (poem). Boeckel. Through the gateway.
Pig and the sheep. I. *See* Ram and the pig.
Pig and the sheep. II. Æsop. Fables (Jones).
   Cooper. Argosy of fables. (Porker and the sheep.)
Pig brother. Perkins and Danielson. Mayflower program book.
For other entries, see 2d edition.
Pig-headed wife. *See* Mary, Mary, so contrary.
Pig let loose. Martin. Fatma was a goose.
Pig-pig and the three bears. La Rue. Under the story tree.
See also Three bears. I–II.
Pig Wisps. Sandburg. Rootabaga country.
   Sandburg. Rootabaga pigeons.
Pigeon and the dove. Aulnoy. Fairy tales (Planché).
For other entries, see 2d edition.
Pigeon-hawk and the tortoise. Cooper. Argosy of fables.
Pigeon-king and Mouse-king. **Arnold. Book of good counsels. (*In* Winning of friends.)
   Cooper. Argosy of fables. (Fowler and the pigeons.)
See also Mouse-king's story ; Quails.
For other entries, see 2d edition.
Pigeon's nest. Rich. Why-so stories. (*In* Why the magpie builds a poor nest.)
Pigeons of Paradise. Mukerji. Hindu fables.
Piggie Wiggie and his prize. Blaisdell. Rhyme and story second reader.
Piggywee's little curly tail. Harriman. Stories for little children.
Pigling and her proud sister. Lee. Folk tales of all nations.
   Metzger. Tales told in Korea. (Jade slipper.)
See also Cinderella.
For other entries, see 2d edition.
Pigmies. *See* Pygmies.
Pig's-head magician. Bernhard. Master wizard.
Pigtail of Ah Lee Ben Loo (poem). Bennett. Pigtail of Ah Lee Ben Loo.

Pike and other fish. Ransome. Old Peter's Russian tales. (*In* Chapter of fish.)

Pike and the cat. Cooper. Argosy of fables.
For other entries, see 2d edition.

Pike that pulled and pulled. Olcott. Wonder tales from windmill lands.

Pilgrim and the cloak. Guerber. Legends of Switzerland. (*In* Bern.)

Pilgrim of a night. Canton. Child's book of saints.
See also Two pilgrims.

Pilgrim's progress. *See* Christian and Hopeful in Doubting Castle; Great dream.

Pillar-box. Fyleman. Forty good-night tales.

Pillow of content. Lee. Folk tales of all nations. (Magic pillow.)
Olcott. Wonder tales from China seas.
See also Ouphe of the woods #.

Pilot light. Morley. I know a secret.

Pinafore. Untermeyer. Last pirate. (Uncommon common sailor.)

Pine cone, Story of. Warner. Carl Krinken.

Pine-gum baby. De Huff. Taytay's tales.
Lee. Folk tales of all nations.
See also Tar-baby stories.

Pine tree and its needles. *See* little pine tree who wished for new leaves.

Pine tree and the stars. *See* Pleiades. II.

Pine-tree shillings. Allen. Story-teller's house.
Blaisdell. Child life. 3d reader.
Hawthorne. Grandfather's chair. pt. 1, ch. 6.

Pine trees. Tuttle. Frightened tree. (Pious tree.)

Pink rabbit. Fyleman. Tea time tales.

Pinkel and the fur coat. *See* Golden lantern, the golden goat and the golden coat.

Pinkie, Winkie, and Peter. La Rue. Under the story tree.

Pinocchio. Johnson and Scott. Anthology of children's literature. (Pinocchio's first pranks.)
Kinscella. Music appreciation readers. Book 5. (Adventures of Pinocchio. Abridged.)
For other entries, see 2d edition.

Pint bottle of Cinkota. Schwimmer. Tisza tales.
See also King John and the Abbot of Canterbury.

Pious Constance. *See* Faithful Constance.

Pious man. I. **Gaster. Ma'aseh book. v. 1. (Pious man who was protected by a bear because he observed the Sabbath.)

Pious man. II. Vilnay. Legends of Palestine. (Pious men of Ascalon.)

Pious man and the two spirits. **Gaster. Ma'aseh book. v. 1.

Pious men of Ascalon. *See* Pious man. II.

Pious robin. I. Brown. Curious book of birds.
See also Why the robin has a red breast. V.
Pious robin. II. Carey. Stories of the birds. (Robin at the cross ; Straw in the Virgin's eye.)
Pious tree. Tuttle. Frightened tree and other stories.
Pipe of peace. I. Browne. Indian nights.
Pipe of peace. II. Spence. Myths of the North American Indians. (Sacred origin of smoking. *In* Ch. 27.)
Pipe of peace. I–II. *See also* Old man of the mountain.
Piper and the Puca. Lee. Folk tales of all nations.
For other entries, see 2d edition.
Piper at the gates of dawn. Grahame. Kenneth Grahame book.
Pippa passes. Bailey. Stories children want.
Evans. Worth while stories.
Kinscella. Music appreciation readers. Book 5. (Story of a joyful song.)
Menefee. Child stories. (Pippa.)
For other entries, see 2d edition.
Pirate and the pickled onions. Fyleman. Forty good-morning tales.
Pirate blue jay. Barrows and Cavanah. Favorite pages from Child Life.
Pirates. Marzials. Stories for the story hour.
Pirates of Penzance. Untermeyer. Last pirate. (Curious birthday.)
Piskey fine and piskey gay #.
See also Pixy thresher.
Piskie's cave. Olcott. Wonder tales from fairy isles.
Pitch doll. *See* Tar-baby. I.
Pitcher the witch and the black cats. Macmillan. Canadian wonder tales. (First mosquito.)
For other entries, see 2d edition.
Pit=mi=lussi marries the daughter of Thunder. Morris. Stories from mythology : North American. (*In* Ch. 14.)
Pixie cradles. *See* Tulip bed. I.
Pixies' vengeance. I. *See* 2d edition.
Pixies' vengeance. II. Olcott. Wonder tales from fairy isles. (Silver pennies.)
Williams-Ellis. Fairies and enchanters. (Water's locked.)
For other entries, see 2d edition.
Pixy fair. Olcott. Wonder tales from fairy isles.
See also Fairy fair #.
Pixy oven. Olcott. Wonder tales from fairy isles.
Pixy thresher. Rhys. English fairy book.
See also Piskey fine and piskey gay #.
Plain gold ring. Henderson and Calvert. Wonder tales of old Tyrol.
See also Frog prince # ; Prince Green-eyes.
Plaint of the camel. *See* Camel's complaint.
Plantaiη. Carey. Flower legends.
Planter and the pomegranate. Cooper. Argosy of fables.

Planting an orchard. Evans. Worth while stories.

Plaster cat. Capuana. Golden-feather.

Plasterer's ·ass. Capuana. Golden-feather.

Playful ass. Cooper. Argosy of fables.
For other entries, see 2d edition.

Playing the game. Through story-land with the children.

Playmates. Bailey. Tell me another story.

Please. I. Aspinwall. Can you believe me stories.

Please. II. White. School management, p. 242.

Pleiades. I. See 2d edition.

Pleiades. II. Bailey. Stories from an Indian cave. (Pine tree and the stars.)
Gearhart. Skalalatoot stories. (Seven bad boys become stars.)
Johnson and Scott. Anthology of children's literature. (Origin of the Pleiades.)
Williamson. Stars through magic casements. (Seven brothers of the star cluster.)
For other entries, see 2d edition.

Pleiades. III–V. See 2d edition.

Pleiades. VI. Williamson. Stars through magic casements. (Indian hunter and the seven dancers of the sky.)
See also Star wife.
For other entries, see 2d edition.

Pleiades. VII. Wells. How the present came from the past. Book 1, p. 120. (Meamei, the seven sisters.)

Pleiades. I–VII.
For other versions see Six boys go to the star country : Seven brothers.

Pliny. Niemeyer. Stories for the history hour.

Ploughman and his sons. See Gold in the orchard.

Ploughman and the wolf. Æsop. Fables (Jones).

Ploughman, the ass and the ox. Æsop. Fables (Jones).

Plowman. Williston. Hindu stories.

Plowman and his sons. See Gold in the orchard.

Plowman who found content. See Wishing ring.

Plum, the prune and the apricot. Cooper. Argosy of fables.

Plumed serpent. See Feathered snake. II.

Pluto. See Proserpina.

Pocahontas, Story of. Spence. Myths of the North American Indians.
For other entries, see 2d edition.

Pocahontas and John Rolfe. Colum. Voyagers. (In Virginia.)

Pocket-handkerchief park. Buckingham. Elephant's friend.
Field. Pocket-handkerchief park.

Poffertjes-pan. Hart. Picture tales from Holland.
See also Barring of the door.

Poh-ve and Pah-day. De Huff. Taytay's tales.

Poia. See Maid who married the morning star ; Scar Face. III.

Pointer Tray. Raspé. Children's Munchausen (Martin. *In* Ch. 17.)

Raspé. Tales from the travels of Baron Munchausen.

Poker Face the baboon, and Hot Dog the tiger. Sandburg. Rootabaga stories.

Polar bears. Raspé. Children's Munchausen. (Martin. *In* Ch. 15.)

Raspé. Tales from the travels of Baron Munchausen.

Polly Prichard, patriot. Barrows and Cavanah. Favorite pages from Child Life.

Pollywog princess. Potter. Giant of Apple Pie Hill.

Polyphemus and the Cyclops. *See* Ulysses and Polyphemus.

Pomegranate seeds. *See* Proserpina.

Pomegranate, the apple tree and the bramble. Æsop. Fables (Jones).

Cooper. Argosy of fables. (Pomegranate, the apple and the bramble.)

For other entries, see 2d edition.

Pomona. Bulfinch. Golden age. (Vertumnus and Pomona. *In* Ch. 10.)

For other entries, see 2d edition.

Ponaturi. *See* People of the night.

Ponce de Leon and the fountain of youth. Colum. Fountain of youth. (Fountain of youth.)

Colum. Voyagers. (Fountain of youth.)

Higginson. Tales of the enchanted islands of the Atlantic.

See also Magic lake.

For other entries, see 2d edition.

Pond lily, Legend of. *See* Star maiden. I.

Pontius Pilate. Guerber. Legends of Switzerland. (*In* Forest cantons.)

Fuller. Book of dragons. (*In* Dragons of Lucerne.)

For other entries, see 2d edition.

Pony-cart. Canfield. Made-to-order stories.

Pony engine. I. *See* 2d edition.

Pony engine. II. *See* Royal engine.

Pony with a past. Bacon. Mercy and the mouse.

Told under the blue umbrella.

Pooka. Colum. King of Ireland's son. (*In* Story of the fairy rowan tree.)

Pooka and King Bryan Boru. Olcott. Wonder tales from fairy isles.

Pooka stories. *See* Bogey beast; Huntsman's son #; Kildare pooka #; Piper and the Puca; Pwca of the Twryn #; Twelve silly sisters.

Poor Cecco. Harper and Hamilton. Winding roads.

Poor Count's Christmas. Harper. Merry Christmas to you.

Poor maid of Matsaki. *See* Turkey maiden.

Poor man and Never-enough. *See* Honest woodman.

Poor man and the flask of oil. Johnson and Scott. Anthology of children's literature.

Power. Stories to shorten the road.

Poor man and the flask of oil—*continued.*
See also Barber's fifth brother; Milkmaid and her pail of
milk.
For other entries, see 2d edition.
**Poor man, the snake, the cat, the dog, the mouse, and
the beaver, Story of.** De Leeuw. Java jungle tales.
See also Wonderful ring.
Poor Mary Jane. Elson and Runkel. Child-library reader.
Book 2.
Poor miller's boy and the cat. *See* Miller's boy and his cat.
Poor Mr. Fingle. Bianco. Street of little shops.
Poor turkey girl. *See* Turkey maiden.
Poor woman and the bell. **Arnold. Book of good coun-
sels. (Terrible bell.)
Cooper. Argosy of fables. (Terrible bell.)
For other entries, see 2d edition.
Poor woman's rooster. Pogány. Magyar fairy tales.
See also Drakesbill and his friends.
Pope's game of chess. **Gaster. Ma'aseh book. v. 2.
(Jewish child who was stolen by a servant and later be-
came Pope.)
For other entries, see 2d edition.
Poplar sisters. *See* Phaeton.
Poplar tree. Silvester and Peter. Happy hour stories.
For other entries, see 2d edition.
Poppet. Baker. Tell them again tales.
Poppy. *See* Bad poppy seeds.
Poppy seed cakes. Clark. Poppy seed cakes.
Told under the blue umbrella.
Porcelain Pagoda. Lane. Tower legends. (Moon that shone
on the Porcelain Pagoda.)
Porcupine and the snakes. Æsop. Fables (Artzybasheff).
(poem). Cooper. Argosy of fables. (Snake and the hedge-
hog.)
See also Arab and his camel; Puppies and their mother.
For other entries, see 2d edition.
In 2d edition this story is also indexed under the title
"Snake and the hedgehog."
Porcupine, elk and coyote. Hogner. Navajo winter nights.
Porcupine learns the sun dance. Garett. Coyote stories.
Porcupine's quills. Skunny Wundy and other Indian tales.
See also How the porcupine got its quills #.
Porgie's adventure. Fyleman. Forty good-night tales.
(Twinkles, pt. 3.)
Porker and the sheep. *See* Pig and the sheep. II.
Portugese duck. Andersen. Fairy tales (Stickney). v. 2.
For other entries, see 2d edition.
Portunes. Rhys. English fairy book. (Fairy farmers.)
Poseidon. *See* Neptune.
Possible—impossible. Cendrars. Little black stories.
See also Greedy cat. I.
Postman's valentine. Bailey. Wonderful tree.

Pot of basil. Bryant. Children's book of celebrated legends. (Isabella; or, The pot of basil.)
For other entries, see 2d edition.
Pot of butter. Carrick. Animal picture tales from Russia.
See also Stag at the lake.
Pot of carnations. *See* Fortunée.
Pot of fat. *See* Cat and the mouse in partnership.
Pot of gold. I–IV: *See* 2d edition.
Pot of gold. V. Gaer. Magic flight.
Pot of rosemary. *See* Jar of rosemary.
Pot of soup. *See* Wonderful porridge pot.
Potato Face Blind Man who lost the diamond rabbit. Sandburg. Rootabaga stories.
Potatoes come to France. Johnson and Scott. Anthology of children's literature. (History of the potato.)
Potter. I #.
See also King Matthias' three riddles.
Pottle o' brains. Coussens. Diamond story book.
For other entries, see 2d edition.
Poucinet. *See* Boots and his brothers.
Pound. Forbes. Good citizenship. (*In* Ch. 10.)
Pour, Katrientje, pour. Hart. Picture tales from Holland.
See also Kid and the tiger.
Powdered wig. Lansing. Great moments in science.
Smith. Made in Germany and Austria. (*In* Ch. 1.)
See also Palissy the potter.
Power of fables. Æsop. Fables (Jones. Demades and his fable.)
La Fontaine. Fables (Tilney. Power of fable.)
For other entries, see 2d edition.
Prairie dandelion. Buckingham. Elephant's friend. (Heads of gold. Adapted.)
Carey. Flower legends. (Dandelion.)
Sheriff. Stories old and new. (Meadow dandelion. Adapted.)
For other entries, see 2d edition.
Prairie dogs. I. Hogner. Navajo winter nights. (How little prairie dog was made.)
Prairie dogs. II. Hooker. Garden of the lost key.
Praying for rain. I. **Gaster. Ma'aseh book. v. 1. (Honi ha-Me'aggel and his prayer for rain.)
Vilnay. Legends of Palestine. (Honi the circle-maker.)
See also Wise priest.
Praying for rain. II. Weilerstein. Adventures of K'tonton. (How K'tonton prayed for rain.)
Praying for rain. III. Otero. Old Spain in our Southwest. (*In* Old Spanish hacienda.)
Precious gem palace. Olcott. Wonder tales from China seas.
See also Midas. I; Sovereign of the mineral kingdom.
Precious poison. Sugimoto. Japanese holiday picture tales.

Present. Fyleman. Forty good-night tales. (Dolls' house, pt. 3.)

Pretending woodchuck. Skinner. Child's book of country stories.

For other entries, see 2d edition.

Pretty Goldilocks. *See* Fair one with golden locks.

Price of curiosity. Fuller. Book of dragons.

Price of victory. Johnson and Scott. Anthology of children's literature.

Prickly bush. Bailey. Tell me another story.

Pride goeth before a fall. Curry and Clippinger. Children's literature.

For other entries, see 2d edition.

Pride of Peta Kway. Partridge. Joyful Star.

Priest and the clerk. Rasmussen. East o' the sun and west o' the moon. (Parson and the deacon.)

For other entries, see 2d edition.

Priest and the corpse. La Fontaine. Fables (Tilney).

Priest in his white woolen garment. Clément. Once in France.

Priest in spite of himself. Kipling. Rewards and fairies.

Priest with the envious eyes. I. Ralston. Russian fairy tales.

See also Smith and the devil.

For other entries, see 2d edition.

Priest with the envious eyes. II. Carpenter. Tales of a Russian grandmother. (Greedy priest.)

Priest's soul. Yeats. Irish fairy tales.

Primrose and elder. Olcott. Wonder tales from fairy isles.

Prince Ahmed al Kamel, Legend of. Irving. Tales from the Alhambra.

Prince Ahmed and the fairy Perie Banou, Story of. Arabian nights. (Eliot. Story of Prince Ahmed.)

See also Three gifts. V.

For other entries, see 2d edition.

Prince and his private raincloud. Shannon. California fairy tales.

Prince and the badger. Mitford. Tales of old Japan.

Prince and the dragon. Evans. Worth while stories.

Prince and the flea. *See* Flea and the man. I.

Prince and the foundling. Byrde. Polish fairy book.

See also Fate. II ; King who would be stronger than fate.

Prince and the piping boy. De La Mare and Quayle. Readings.

Prince and the procuress who suffered for their own faults, Story of. **Arnold. Book of good counsels.

Prince and the three dooms. *See* Prince and the three fates.

Prince and the three fates. Baikie. Wonder tales of the ancient world. (Doomed prince.)

Gibson. Golden bird. (Doomed prince.)

Lee. Folk tales of all nations. (Doomed prince.)

Prince and the three fates—*continued.*
**Maspero. Popular stories of ancient Egypt. (Doomed prince.)
Miller. My book of history. v. 1. (Prince and the three dooms. *In* Ch. 9.)
Wells. How the present came from the past. Book 2, pt. 2. (Doomed prince.)
For other entries, see 2d edition.
Prince and the wife of the merchant's son. **Arnold. Book of good counsels.
Prince Argyilus and the fairy Ilona. Pogány. Magyar fairy tales.
See also Nine pea-hens and the golden apples.
Prince Brave Heart. Purnell and Weatherwax. Talking bird.
Prince Bull. Coussens. Diamond story book.
Dickens. Works: Reprinted pieces.
Prince Bursten oudt Larrfen. Aspinwall. Can you believe me stories.
Prince Csihan. Lee. Folk tales of all nations.
See also Gazelle; Puss in boots.
Prince Darling. Lang. Old friends among the fairies.
For other entries, see 2d edition.
Prince Dawn and the magic flower. Forbes. Good citizenship. (*In* Ch. 10.)
Prince Desire and Princess Mignonetta (play). Going. Folklore and fairy tales. (Prince with the long nose.)
Harper. Magic fairy tales. (Prince Hyacinth and the dear little princess.)
For other entries, see 2d edition.
Prince from nowhere. Tappan. Prince from nowhere.
Prince Ganim. Katibah. Other Arabian nights. (Tale of Prince Ganim and his journey to the fountain of youth.)
See also Sham prince.
Prince Green-eyes. Newman. Fairy flowers. (Prince Green-eyes; or, Leap, frog, leap.)
See also Plain gold ring.
Prince had reason to cry. *See* Water-babe.
Prince Hedgehog. Byrde. Polish fairy book. (About the hedgehog who became a prince.)
For other entries, see 2d edition.
Prince Hyacinth and the dear little princess. *See* Prince Desire and Princess Mignonetta.
Prince in exile. Barbour. English tales retold.
Prince in the tower. Eells. Brazilian fairy book.
Prince Ivan, the witch baby, and the little sister of the sun. *See* Witch and the sister of the sun.
Prince Lindworm. *See* King Dragon.
Prince Manoel and the three princesses. Eells. Brazilian fairy book.
Prince Marko. Cruse. Young folk's book of epic heroes.
Prince number three. Williams. Jolly old whistle.

Prince of Engalien. Starbuck. Enchanted paths.
Wahlenberg. Old Swedish fairy tales.
See also King's servants.
Prince of the kingdom of Thankful. Deihl. Holiday-time stories.
Prince of the reed plains. *See* Eighty-one brothers.
Prince of travellers. *See* Marco Polo.
Prince plays tag. Quinn. Stories for the six-year-old.
Prince Rabbit. De La Mare and Quayle. Readings.
No. 2 Joy Street.
Prince Salem and the magician of Samarkand. *See* Magician of Samarkand.
Prince Sprite. *See* Invisible prince. II.
Prince Surprise. *See* King Kojata.
Prince, the faithful dog. *See* Hans and his dog.
Prince Underwave and the earth king's son. *See* Black horse.
Prince Vivien and the Princess Placida. Coussens. Diamond story book.
See also Dorji and Tipsi.
For other entries, see 2d edition.
Prince Weary's galoshes. Cook. To-day's stories of yesterday.
Prince who befriended the beasts. Lee. Folk tales of all nations.
For other entries, see 2d edition.
Prince who was not hungry. Bailey. Stories children want.
Bailey. Tell me another story. (Prince who wasn't hungry.)
See also Princess Aurora.
Prince whose father was blind. Eells. Brazilian fairy book.
See also Water of Kane.
Prince Wicked and the grateful animals. Aspinwall. Jataka tales. (Grateful animals.)
For other entries, see 2d edition.
Prince with the golden hand. Byrde. Polish fairy book. (Goldenhair and Goldenhand.)
Prince with the long nose. *See* Prince Desire and Princess Mignonetta.
Prince with the nine sorrows. Housman. Moonshine and clover.
Prince Zipporah never dreamt of. Gaer. Burning bush.
Prince's dream. Curry and Clippinger. Children's literature.
Stewart. Tell me a story I never heard before.
See also Little lame prince.
For other entries, see 2d edition.
Prince's elopement. Ryder. Twenty-two goblins.
Prince's parrot. Eells. Brazilian fairy book.
Prince's valentine. Bailey. Tell me another story.

Princess Ahez and the lost city. *See* Ys, Story of. II.
Princess Ahura, Story of. Baikie. Wonder tales of the ancient world. (*In* Setna and the magic roll.)
Princess and the beggar. I. *See* Princess of the tower.
In 2d edition there are entries under each title.
Princess and the beggar. II. Metzger. Tales told in Korea.
Princess and the beggar maid. Baker. Pedlar's wares.
Princess and the cucumbers. Marzials. Stories for the story hour.
Princess and the demon. *See* Journey of Khensu to Bekhten.
Princess and the greedy one. Chardon. Golden chick.
Princess and the moon god. *See* Journey of Khensu to Bekhten.
Princess and the pea. *See* Princess on the pea.
Princess and the rabbi. I. *See* 2d edition.
Princess and the rabbi. II. **Gaster. Ma'aseh book. v. 1. (R. Joshua b. Hananiah and the Emperor's daughter.)
Schwarz. Jewish caravan. (Rabbi Joshua and the princess.)
Princess and the shepherd. Partridge. Joyful Star.
Princess and the wizard. Hall. Godmother's stories.
Princess Aurora. Chardon. Golden chick.
See also Prince who was not hungry.
Princess Belle-Etoile and Prince Cheri. Aulnoy. Fairy tales (Planché).
For other entries, see 2d edition.
Princess Bluegreen of the seven cities. Eells. Islands of magic.
See also Atlantis.
Princess Carpillon. Adams and Atchinson. Book of princess stories.
Aulnoy. Fairy tales (Planché).
For other entries, see 2d edition.
Princess Dinar and the enchantress. Olcott. Wonder tales from pirate isles.
Princess Fairy-Story in masquerade. Hauff. Arabian days' entertainment. (*In-* Introduction.)
Princess Fior Usga. *See* Magic well.
Princess frog. *See* Frog queen.
Princess from the Troll Mountain. Falkberget. Broomstick and Snowflake.
Princess Helena the fair. *See* Princess to be kissed at a charge.
Princess Hotaru. Whitehorn. Wonder tales of old Japan.
See also Cinderella.
Princess Ilse. Olcott. Wonder tales from goblin hills. (Ilse's crystal palace.)
Princess in the chest. Martens. Wonder tales from far away. (Theophilus the Just.)
Ralston. Russian fairy tales. (Headless princess.)
See also Soldier's midnight watch.

Princess in the chest—*continued.*
For other entries, see 2d edition.
Princess Lackears. *See* No ears.
Princess Lemon-grass. *See* Fate of the silver prince.
Princess Lily. I. *See* 2d edition.
Princess Lily. II. Newman. Fairy flowers.
Princess Lily of the midnight palace. Olcott. Wonder tales from China seas.
Princes Lindagull. Topelius. Canute Whistlewinks. (Princess Lindengold.)
For other entries, see 2d edition.
Princess Lindengold. *See* Princess Lindagull.
Princess loses the foot race. *See* How the princess was beaten in a race.
Princess Melilot. Housman. Doorway in fairyland. (Bound princess, pt. 4.)
Princess Minon=Minette. Adams and Atchinson. Book of princess stories.
For other entries, see 2d edition.
Princess Morgana. Martens. Wonder tales from far away. (Phantom caravan; or, Tale of Saladin of Bagdad and the Princess Morgana.)
For other entries, see 2d edition.
Princess of Canterbury. Rhys. English fairy book.
For other entries, see 2d edition.
Princess of Cathay. Echols. Knights of Charlemagne.
Princess of China. Farjeon. Old nurse's stocking tales.
Princess of Colchester. *See* Three heads of the well.
In 2d edition, there are entries under each title.
Princess of Kensington. No. 2 Joy street.
Princess of Normandy. Darton. Seven champions of Christendom.
Princess of Pali=uli. Colum. Bright islands.
Princess of the genii's palace. Olcott. Wonder tales from China seas.
Princess of the lost island. Eells. Islands of magic.
Princess of the tower. Schwarz. Jewish caravan. (Legend of three and of four.)
For other entries, see 2d edition.
In 2d edition this story is also indexed under the title "Princess and the beggar."
Princess of Tiflis. Garnett. Ottoman wonder tales.
See also Donkey cabbage.
Princess on the glass hill. Dasent. East of the sun and West of the moon (Nielsen).
Faulkner. Road to enchantment.
Harper. Magic fairy tales.
Hutchinson. Chimney corner fairy tales.
Johnson and Scott. Anthology of children's literature.
Power. Blue caravan tales.
Rasmussen. East o' the sun and west o' the moon.
Told under the green umbrella.

Princess on the glass hill—*continued.*
See also Three horses.
For other entries, see 2d edition.
Princess on the glass mountain #.
See also Glass mountain.
In the 2d edition there are entries under each title.
Princess on the pea. Adams and Atchinson. Book of princess stories.
Andersen. Fairy tales (Stickney. v. 2. Real princess.)
Andersen. Four tales (Princess and the pea.)
Arthur Rackham fairy book. (Princess and the pea.)
Curry and Clippinger. Children's literature. (Real princess.)
Hutchinson. Candlelight stories. (Real princess.)
Johnson and Scott. Anthology of children's literature. (Real princess.)
Power. Bag o' tales.
Quinn. Stokes' wonder book of fairy tales.
Rich. Read-aloud book.
See also Jack Beanstalk and the pea princess; Specialist in food, specialist in women, and the specialist in cotton; Student who became king; Three delicate wives of King Virtue-banner.
For other entries, see 2d edition.
Princess Pan. Olcott. Wonder tales from pirate isles.
Princess Pat=a=cake. Potter. Giant of Apple Pie Hill.
Princess Petunia and the Fairy Grimbona. Baldwin. Pedlar's pack.
Princess Pity Patter. *See* Lady slippers.
Princess Printaniere. Aulnoy. Fairy tales (Planché).
For other entries, see 2d edition.
Princess Rosette. I. Adams and Atchinson. Book of princess stories.
Aulnoy. Fairy tales (Planché).
Fairy garland (Dulac).
See also Peacock-king; Queen who rose from the sea.
For other entries, see 2d edition.
Princess Sadong. Skeat. Tiger's mistake. (Princess Sadong of the caves, who refused her suitors.)
Princess Silver=silk. *See* King Uggermugger.
Princess Suil=dubh. MacManus. Donegal wonder book.
Princess to be kissed at a charge. Carpenter. Tales of a Russian grandmother. (Elena the fair.)
Dulac. Edmund Dulac's fairy book. (Ivan and the chestnut horse.)
Ralston. Russian fairy tales. (Princess Helena the fair.)
See also Little fool Ivan.
For other entries, see 2d edition.
Princess Ugly. Hervey and Hix. Fanciful tales for children.
Princess Unca. *See* Proud princess.
Princess who became a shepherdess. Clément. Once in France.

Princess who became a vestal virgin. *See* Vesta and the vestal virgins.

Princess who could not cry. Adams and Atchinson. Book of princess stories.

For other entries, see 2d edition.

Princess who couldn't sew. Fyleman. Forty good-morning tales.

Princess who had the silver tooth. Wheeler. Albanian wonder tales.

See also Warrior maids.

Princess who liked silken robes. Fleming. Round the world in folk tales.

Lansing. Great moments in science. (Secret kept for three thousand years.)

See also Silkworm. I.

Princess who lost her rings. Eells. Islands of magic.

See also Green bird. I; Sad princess, the green birds and the old granny of Capdepera.

Princess who vanished (poem). Adams and Atchinson. Book of princess stories.

Princess who would not smile #.

See also Bee, the harp, the mouse and the bum-clock.

Princess whom nobody could silence. Adams and Atchinson. Book of princess stories.

Hutchinson. Candlelight stories.

Power. Bag o' tales. (Adapted.)

Rasmussen. East o' the sun and west o' the moon. (Princess who would not be silenced.)

For other entries, see 2d edition.

Princess with the glass heart. St. Nicholas. April 1883, p. 427.

See also Three princesses with glass hearts.

Princess with the tired shadow. Cook. Red and gold stories.

See also Shadow. I #.

Princess with two lives. Martinez Del Rio. Sun, the moon and a rabbit.

Princesses who lived in a kailyard. Starbuck. Enchanted paths.

For other entries, see 2d edition.

Princess's handkerchiefs. Baker. Tell them again tales.

See also Green bird. I.

Prioress's tale. *See* Boy martyr.

Procne and Philomela. Rich. Why-so stories. (How the swallow came to be.)

See also Swallow and the crow.

For other entries, see 2d edition.

Prodigal son. Curry and Clippinger. Children's literature.

Profanity gently reproved. White. School management, p. 266.

Professional umpire and mascot keeper. Burnett. Children's book.

Professor and the custom officers. Guerber. Legends of
Switzerland. (*In* Legends of Neuchatel.)
Prometheus. Bulfinch. Golden age. (*In* Ch. 2.)
Forbush. Myths and legends of Greece and Rome.
Johnson and Scott. Anthology of children's literature.
Lang. Book of myths. (Prometheus and Pandora.)
Miller. My book of history. v. 2. (Prometheus and Epi-
metheus. *In* Ch. 3.)
Pyle. Tales from Greek mythology.
See also Pandora.
For other entries, see 2d edition.
Prometheus and the making of man. Æsop. Fables
(Jones).
Promise. I. *See* 2d edition.
Promise. II. Perkins and Danielson. Second year May-
flower program book.
Skinner. Christmas stories.
Walters. Book of Christmas stories.
For other entries, see 2d edition.
Promise of beauty. Housman. Turn again tales.
Promise of music. Rowe. Moon's birthday.
Prophecy of the djinn. McNeer and Lederer. Tales from
the crescent moon.
See also Bluebeard.
Prophecy of the silver florin. *See* Silver florin, Story of.
Prophet. I. *See* 2d edition.
Prophet. II. Æsop. Fables (Jones).
Cooper. Argosy of fables.
Prophet of the pines. Browne. Indian nights.
Proserpina. Bulfinch. Golden age. (Proserpine. *In* Ch. 7.)
Curry and Clippinger. Children's literature. (Story of the
springtime.)
Evans. Worth while stories. (Ceres and her daughter.)
Forbush. Myths and legends of Greece and Rome. (Pros-
erpine and Pluto.)
Harshaw. Council of the gods. (Demeter sits apart; De-
meter and Persephone.)
Johnson and Scott. Anthology of children's literature.
(Pomegranate seeds.)
(play). Knight. Dramatic reader. (Pomegranate seeds.
Adapted.)
Lang. Book of myths. (Proserpine.)
Lee. Folk tales of all nations. (Ceres and Proserpine; Re-
turn of Proserpine.)
Power. Bag o' tales. (Ceres and Proserpine.)
Pyle. Tales from Greek mythology. (Ceres and Per-
sephone.)
See also Ishtar and Tammuz; Sun of earth.
For other entries, see 2d edition.
Prospero and Miranda. Coit. Kai Khosru. (Story of the
Tempest.)
(play). Coit. Kai Khosru. (Tempest.)

Prospero and Miranda—*continued.*
Elson and Keck. Junior high school literature. (Tempest.)
Lamb. Tales from Shakespeare. (Tempest.)
Patten. Junior classics. v. 5. (Tempest.)
Rich. Read-aloud book. (Tempest.)
Richardson. Stories from old English poetry. (Tempest.)
See also Ariel; Francese's fairy letter.
For other entries, see 2d edition.
Protection of the devil. Eells. Brazilian. fairy book.
See also Smith and the devil.
Protesilaus. Bulfinch. Golden age. (Protesilaus and Laodamia. *In* Ch. 27.)
For other entries, see 2d edition.
Proteus. Forbush. Myths and legends of Greece and Rome. (Aristaeus and Proteus.)
For other entries, see 2d edition.
Proud biscuit. Fyleman. Tea time tales.
Proud cook of Manila. Meeker. Folk tales from the Far East.
See also Longnose the dwarf.
Proud foxglove. Fyleman. Forty good-night tales.
See also Buckwheat.
Proud Infanta. Farjeon. Old nurse's stocking basket.
Proud king. I. Curry and Clippinger. Children's literature. Starbuck. Familiar haunts.
For other entries, see 2d edition.
Proud king. II. *See* King Robert of Sicily.
Proud king. III. Evans. Worth while stories. (Proud king.)
Proud mouse. Lee. Folk tales of all nations.
For other entries, see 2d edition.
Proud peacock. Blaisdell. Rhyme and story second reader.
Proud prince who . . . gave his daughter . . . to a demon.
See Demon's marriage.
Proud princess. Olcott. Wonder tales from goblin hills. (Princess Unca.)
Williams. Jolly old whistle.
See also Sunken city.
Proud Rosalind and the hart-royal. Farjeon. Martin Pippin in the apple orchard.
Proud young scholar. Metzger. Tales told in Korea.
See also Why he carried the turkey #.
Proverb, Story of a. *See* Shoes.
Prudent Hans. Grimm. Fairy tales (Olcott. Clever Hans.)
See also As Hai Low kept house; Foolish Fred.
For other entries, see 2d edition.
Psyche. I. *See* 2d edition.
Psyche. II. *See* Cupid and Psyche.
Psychotherapist (play). Going. Folklore and fairy plays.
Puck Wudj Ininee. *See* Morning star. I.
Pueblo Bluebeard. I. *See* 2d edition.

Pueblo Bluebeard. II. De Huff. Taytay's memories. (Cliff-dweller and the corn maiden.)
See also Bluebeard.
Pulling red hairs. Olcott. Wonder tales from goblin hills.
Pulowech and the sea maiden. Leland. Algonquin legends. (Adventures of the great hero Pulowech, or the Partridge.)
Macmillan. Canadian wonder tales. (Partridge and his drum.)
See also How partridge built the birds' canoes.
For other entries, see 2d edition.
Pulque, Origin of. I. Martinez Del Rio. Sun, the moon and a rabbit. (Xochitl, the beautiful flower.)
Pulque, Origin of. II. Purnell and Weatherwax. Talking bird. (Green serpents.)
Pumpkin giant. Bailey. Story-telling hour.
Davis. Baker's dozen.
Skinner. Child's book of country stories.
For other entries, see 2d edition.
Pumpkin seed. Bowman. Little brown bowl. (Story about a pumpkin seed.)
Punch and Judy. Long. Folklore calendar. (*In* August.)
For other entries, see 2d edition.
Punishment of Loki. *See* Loki.
Punishment of the stingy. Spence. Myths of the North American Indians. (Myth of Stikua. *In* Ch. 7.)
See also How the selfish Goannas lost their wives.
For other entries, see 2d edition.
Punishment of Tisseyak. Partridge. Joyful Star.
Puppies and their mother. Cooper. Argosy of fables.
See also Arab and his camel; Porcupine and the snakes.
Puppy postman. Potter. Giant of Apple Pie Hill.
Purim, Feast of. Weilerstein. Adventures of K'tonton. (How K'tonton masqueraded on Purim.)
Purring when you're pleased. Hartshorne. Training in worship. (Purring when pleased.)
For other entries, see 2d edition.
Pushmi=pullyu. Johnson and Scott. Anthology of children's literature. (Rarest animal of all.)
Puss in boots. Arthur Rackham fairy book.
Brock. Book of fairy tales.
Bruce. Treasury of tales for little folk.
Curry and Clippinger. Children's literature.
De La Mare and Quayle. Readings.
Evans. Worth while stories.
Fairy garland (Dulac).
Lang. Old friends among the fairies.
Lee. Folk tales of all nations.
Mackenzie. Book of nursery tales.
Quinn. Stokes' wonder book of fairy tales.
Rich. Read-aloud book.
Wilson. Green magic.

Puss in boots—*continued.*
See also Fisherman and the monkey; Kuz'ma Skorobogaty; Prince Csihan.
For other entries, see 2d edition.
Pussy monks. Botsford. Picture tales from the Italian.
Pussy=willow kitten. Potter. Giant of Apple Pie Hill.
Pussy willows, Origin of. I–II. *See* 2d edition.
Pussy willows, Origin of. III. Rich. Why-so stories. (How rabbit lost his tail.)
For other entries, see 2d edition.
Pussy willows, Origin of. IV. Elson and Runkel. Child-library readers. Book 2. (Fairies' kittens. Abridged.)
Pussy willows, Origin of. V. Bowman. Little brown bowl. (How the pussies came on the willows.)
Put it on my bill. *See* Knavish little bird.
In 2d edition there are entries under each title.
Put your shoulder to the wheel. *See* Hercules and the wagoner.
Putnam and the wolf. Blaisdell. Log cabin days. (Old Put.)
Putri Balan, princess of the moon. *See* Owl and the moon.
Puzwuk, the orphan boy, and the starving time. Snell. Told beneath the northern lights.
Pwan=Ku. *See* Creation of the world (Chinese).
Pygmalion and Galatea. Bulfinch. Golden age. (Pygmalion. *In* Ch. 8.)
Gibson. Golden bird. (Story of Paphos.)
Lang. Book of myths. (Pygmalion.)
Pyle. Tales from Greek mythology.
For other entries, see 2d edition.
Pygmies. I. *See* Hercules and his labors.
Pygmies. II. Spence. Myths of the North American Indians. (Pigmies. *In* Ch. 4.)
See also Dwarf people #.
Pygmies and the cranes. Forbush. Myths and legends of Greece and Rome.
Pyramus and Thisbe. I. Bulfinch. Golden age. (*In* Ch. 3.)
Pyle. Tales from Greek mythology.
For other entries, see 2d edition.
Pyramus and Thisbe. II (poem). Manner. Silver treasury.
Saxe, J. G. Poetical works.
Pyrrhus. Cooke. Stories of Rome.
See also Phyrrhus #.
Pythias. *See* Damon and Pythias.

Q

Quack doctor. Æsop. Fables (Jones).
Quack frog. Æsop. Fables (Jones).
Cooper. Argosy of fables.

Queen Bertha and the spinners. Guerber. Legends of Switzerland. (*In* Legends of Vaud and Valais.)

Queen Elizabeth of England. Kipling. Rewards and fairies. (Gloriana.)

Marzials. Stories for the story hour. (Bright May morning.)

Queen Esther. Dane. Fate cries out. (Queens meet.)

Farjeon. Mighty men from Achilles to Julius Caesar.

Gaer. Magic flight. (How Esther became queen.)

Queen Lab and the magic cakes. Arabian nights. Adventures of Haroun Er Raschid (Olcott).

See also Gulnare of the sea.

Queen Maeve and Fedelm's foretelling. Hull. Cuchulain. (Queen Meave and the woman-seer.)

Gregory. Cuchulain of Muirthemne. (*In* War for the bull of Cuailgne.)

Queen Maeve of Connaght. Gregory. Cuchulain of Muirthemne. (Cruachan.)

Queen Marguerita. Stewart. Tell me a story I never heard before.

Queen of Armenia. Darton. Seven champions of Christendom.

Queen of elfland. *See* Thomas the rhymer.

Queen of hearts (play). Richards. More five minute stories.

Queen of night. Garnett. Ottoman wonder tales.

See also Snow-White and the seven dwarfs.

Queen of story=tellers. *See* King Schahriar and Scheherazade.

Queen of the Croderes. Wolff. Pale mountains.

Queen of the Lonely Isle. MacManus. Donegal wonder book.

Queen of the many=colored bedchambers. *See* Finn MacCool and the seven brothers.

Queen of the southern sea. Olcott. Wonder tales from pirate isles.

Queen Pumereta's magic ring. Dane. Once there was and was not.

Queen Ragnhild's dream tree. Dunlap. Stories of the Vikings.

Queen Sigrid's collar. Farjeon. Mighty men from Beowulf to William the Conqueror.

See also King Olaf.

Queen tree. Tuttle. Frightened tree and other stories.

Queen who rose from the sea. Eells. Brazilian fairy book.

See also Princess Rosette. I.

Queen's conquest. MacManus. Lo, and behold ye!

See also Aunya's bargain; King's curing; King's promise.

Queen's hat. Fyleman. Forty good-morning tales.

See also First hat.

Queens meet. *See* Queen Esther.

Queer chickens. Spaulding and Bryce. Aldine readers. Book 2. rev. ed.
  See also Hen that hatched ducks #.
Queer little baker man. Bowman. Little brown bowl. (Queer little baker.)
  See also Unselfish Frances.
  For other entries, see 2d edition.
Queer old man. Morris. Stories from mythology: North American. (*In* Ch. 3.)
Queer rag-bag. Cowles. Stories to tell.
Quentin and the clock. Gordon and Stockard. Gordon readers. 2d reader.
  See also Boy who wanted to play always.
Quern at the bottom of the sea. *See* Why the sea is salt. II.
Query Queer and the flowers. *See* How the flowers came.
  In 2d edition there are entries under each title.
Quest for truth. *See* Abelard and Heloise.
Quest of Isis. *See* Isis and Osiris, Story of.
  In 2d edition there are entries under each title.
Quest of the hammer. *See* Thor: Quest of the hammer.
Quest of the war gods. Whitman. Navaho tales.
Quest of World's Desire. Garnett. Ottoman wonder tales.
  See also Enchanted pomegranate branch and the beauty; Golden armlet; Princess of Tronkolaine.
Questin' o' Cleena. Dunbar. Sons o' Cormac.
Quinine, Discovery of. Curtis. Stories in trees. (*In* What trees give to us.)

R

R. D. P. Society. Wiggin and Smith. Twilight stories.
Ra and Isis, Story of. Baikie. Wonder tales of the ancient world. (How Isis stole the great name of Ra.)
  Lee. Folk tales of all nations.
  For other entries, see 2d edition.
Rabbi Akiba. **Gaster. Ma'aseh book. v. 1. (Romance of Rabbi Akiba the shepherd.)
Rabbi and the diadem. *See* Rabbi who found the diadem.
Rabbi Hanina and the frog. *See* Fairy frog.
Rabbi Jehiel of Paris and the king. *See* Magic lamp. I.
Rabbi Joshua and the princess. *See* Princess and the rabbi. II.
Rabbi who found the diadem. Curry and Clippinger. Children's literature. (Rabbi and the diadem.)
  Patten. Junior classics. v. 7.
Rabbi whose wife turned him into a werewolf. *See* Magic ring. IV.
Rabbit and hawk. James. Tewa firelight tales.
Rabbit and his ears. I–II. *See* 2d edition.
Rabbit and his ears. III. Potter. Giant of Apple Pie Hill.

Rabbit and his ears. IV. Carrick. Picture folk tales.
(Why hares have long ears.)
See also Rabbit and the animal wizard. II.
Rabbit and otter #.
See also How rabbit lost his tail. III.
Rabbit and Possum lose their tails. *See* How Mr. Rabbit
lost his fine bushy tail; Why the possum's tail is bare.
Rabbit and tar wolf. Bailey. Stories from an Indian cave.
(Rabbit and the pine-gum wolf.)
Morris. Stories from mythology: North American. (*In* Ch.
8.)
See also Big long man's corn patch; Tar-baby stories.
For other entries, see 2d edition.
Rabbit and the alligator. Lee. Folk tales of all nations.
(Rabbit and the crocodile.)
For other entries, see 2d edition.
Rabbit and the animal wizard. I. *See* 2d edition.
Rabbit and the animal wizard. II. Smith. Made in Mex-
ico. (Tehuantepec legend. *In* Ch. 8.)
See also Rabbit and his ears. IV.
Rabbit and the animal wizard. III.
Sale. Tree named John. (Why rabbit is pop-eyed. *In*
Spider-bitten.)
Rabbit and the antelope. Woodson. African myths.
Rabbit and the cocoanut. *See* Timid hare.
Rabbit and the crocodile. *See* Rabbit and the alligator.
Rabbit and the crow. De Huff. Taytay's tales.
Rabbit and the ducks. Bailey. Stories from an Indian cave.
(Why the rabbit winters in a hollow tree.)
Rich. Why-so stories. (Why the rabbit eats his fur when
he is starving.)
For other entries, see 2d edition.
Rabbit and the god of happiness. *See* Eighty-one brothers.
Rabbit and the monkey. Lee. Folk tales of all nations.
For other entries, see 2d edition.
Rabbit and the moon. *See* Moon's message.
In 2d edition there are entries under each title.
Rabbit and the other animals. Babbitt. Animals' own story
book. (Rabbit and all the other animals.)
See also Animals' winter quarters; Ram and the pig; Why
the tiger and the stag do not like each other #.
For other entries, see 2d edition.
Rabbit and the pine-gum wolf. *See* Rabbit and tar wolf.
Rabbit and the possum after a wife. Cooper. Argosy of
fables.
Rabbit and the rock soup. Babbitt. Animals' own story
book.
See also Stone broth #.
Rabbit and the turtle. *See* Rabbit's eyes.
Rabbit and the wild cat. I. Leland. Algonquin legends.
(Amazing adventures of Master Rabbit, pt. 4.)
For other entries, see 2d edition.

Rabbit and the wild cat. II. Rich. Why-so stories. (Why the wildcat has a wrinkled face.)

Rabbit and the woodpecker girls. Leland. Algonquin tales. (*In* Amazing adventures of Master Rabbit, pt. 2.)
For other entries, see 2d edition.

Rabbit in the corn=field. Babbitt. Animals' own story book.

Rabbit=person. *See* Rabbit who was afraid. II.

Rabbit scatters Flint to the winds. James. Happy animals of Atagahi.
See also Hare's lip. III; How arrow heads came.

Rabbit shows wildcat. James. Happy animals of Atagahi.

Rabbit tricks the tie snakes. James. Happy animals of Atagahi.

Rabbit tries to catch fish. *See* Master Rabbit.

Rabbit who was afraid. I. *See* Timid hare.

Rabbit who was afraid. II. Linderman. Kootenai why stories. (Rabbit-person.)

Rabbit who was grateful. Bailey. Tell me another story.

Rabbits. La Fontaine. Fables (Tilney).

Rabbits and the elephants. Allen. Story-teller's house. (How the rabbit fooled the elephant.)
**Arnold. Book of good counsels. (Old hare and the elephants.)
Mukerji. Hindu fables. (How a single bunny overcame a herd of elephants.)
For other entries, see 2d edition.

Rabbit's eyes. Metzger. Tales told in Korea. (Rabbit and the turtle.)
For other entries, see 2d edition.

Rabbit's self=respect. Bowman and Bianco. Tales from a Finnish tupa.
See also Hares and the frogs.

Rabbit's tail. I. Silvester and Peter. Happy hour stories.
See also Fox as herdsboy.

Rabbit's tail. II. Evans. Worth while stories. (How the rabbit got its cotton tail.)

Rabbit's tail. III. Bailey. Tell me another story. (Why Peter Rabbit wears a white patch.)

Rabbit's tail. I–III. *See also* How rabbit lost his tail.

Rabbits with wet eyes. Told under the blue umbrella. Morley. I know a secret.

Rabican the enchanted horse. Echols. Knights of Charlemagne. (*In* Gardens of Falerina.)

Raccoon and the three roasting geese. Parker. Skunny Wundy and other Indian tales.
See also Fox and the skunk.

Race between a reindeer and a tom=cod. Quinn. Stories for the six-year-old. (Reindeer and the tom-cod.)
See also Frog and the leopard #.
For other entries, see 2d edition.

Race between hare and hedgehog. *See* Hare and the hedgehog.

Race between the deer and the snail. *See* Deer and the snail.
Race for a wife. I. *See* 2d edition:
Race for a wife. II. Woodson. African myths.
Race for the boundary. Guerber. Legends of Switzerland. (*In* Forest cantons.)
For other entries, see 2d edition.
Radiant brow. *See* Taliesen.
Rag doll's Christmas. Bailey. Stories children want.
Skinner. Happy tales.
Walters. Book of Christmas stories.
For other entries, see 2d edition.
Raggy Ann. La Rue. Under the story tree.
Raghu, the son of a cook. Mukerji. Hindu fables.
Ragnar   Lodbrok. Fuller. Book   of   dragons. (Ragnar Shaggy-breeches.)
Lang. Red book of animal stories.
See also Aslaug and Ragnar.
For other entries, see 2d edition.
Ragnar Shaggy-breeches. *See* Ragnar Lodbrok.
Ragnarok. *See* Twilight of the gods. I.
Rags. I. *See* 2d edition.
Rags. II. Evans. Worth while stories.
Rags Habakuk, the two blue rats, and the circus man. Sandburg. Rootabaga country.
Sandburg. Rootabaga stories.
Rain child. Housman. What-o'clock tales.
Rain cloud. *See* Raincloud.
Rain drop. *See* Drop of rain.
Rain king's daughter. Chrisman. Shen of the sea.
Rain, rain, go away. Blaisdell. Rhyme and story second reader.
Rain tree. Tuttle. Frightened tree and other stories.
Rainbow lake. Wolff. Pale mountains.
Rainbow maiden. Olcott. Wonder tales from Baltic wizards. (Rainbow maiden.)
Rainbow, Origin of. Metzger. Tales told in Hawaii.
Raincloud. Cooper. Argosy of fables. (Rain cloud.)
For other entries, see 2d edition.
Raindrops' journey. Skinner. Happy tales.
Raining rock. Guerber. Legends of Switzerland. (*In* Legends of Vaud and Valais.)
Raising the stone. Perkins and Danielson. Mayflower program book.
Rakshas' palace. Pyle. Fairy tales from India.
For other entries, see 2d edition.
Ram. Aulnoy. Fairy tales (Planché).
Coussens. Diamond story book. (Wonderful sheep.)
For other entries, see 2d edition.
Ram and the leopard. Carrick. Picture folk tales.
No. 2 Joy Street.
See also Why the tiger and the stag do not like each other.

Ram and the pig. Bryce. Short stories for little folks. (New home.)
Evans. Worth while stories. (Pig and the sheep. Adapted.)
Johnson and Scott. Anthology of children's literature. (Ram and the pig who went into the woods to live by themselves.)
Perkins and Danielson. Second year Mayflower program book. (Sheep and the pig.)
Power. Bag o' tales. (Sheep and the pig who set up house.)
Told under the green umbrella. (Sheep and the pig that built the house.)
Whiteman. Playmates in print. (Sheep and pig who set up house.)
See also Animals' winter quarters; Rabbit and the other animals.
For other entries, see 2d edition.
Ram and the youngest son. Berry. Black folk tales.
Rama. Adams and Atchinson. There were giants. (Giant Pot-ear.)
Mukerji. Rama, hero of India.
Phillips. Far peoples. (Rama and Sita.)
For other entries, see 2d edition.
Ra=Mo and the Hindu. Leberman. New German fairy tales.
Rangi and Papatua. See Earth and the sky.
Ranunkulus. Baumbach. Tales from the Swiss alps.
Rape of the Sabines. See Sabine women and Roman wives.
Rapunzel. De La Mare. Told again.
Grimm. Fairy tales (Olcott).
Grimm. Tales from Grimm (Wanda Gag).
Quinn. Stokes' wonder book of fairy tales.
Williams. Tales from Ebony.
Wilson. Green magic.
For other entries, see 2d edition.
Rarest animal of all. See Pushmi-pullyu.
Rash magician. Aspinwall. Jataka tales.
See also Four brothers who brought a dead lion to life; Lion makers; Magic leaf.
Rashi and the Duke of Lorraine. See Godfrey de Bouillon; King for three days.
Rashin=Coatie #.
See also Linda Branca and her mask; Many-furred creature.
Raspberry worm. Topelius. Canute Whistlewinks.
For other entries, see 2d edition.
Rat and the elephant (poem). Cooper. Argosy of fables.
La Fontaine. Fables (Tilney).
For other entries, see 2d edition.
Rat and the toad. Cooper. Argosy of fables.
See also Wisdom of the rabbit.
For other entries, see 2d edition.
Rat=catcher of Hamelin. See Pied piper of Hamelin.

Rat=catcher's daughter. Davis. Baker's dozen.
Housman. Doorway in fairyland.
Rat retired from the world. La Fontaine. Fables (Tilney).
See also Rats and the cheese #.
Rata and the children of Puna. Colum. Bright islands.
(*In* Story of Rata.)
Price. Legends of the seven seas.
Rata, Legend of. Colum. Bright islands. (Story of Rata
the grandson of Ta-whaki.)
Howes. Long bright land. (Rata's search.)
Metzger. Tales told in Hawaii. (Rata's canoe.)
Price. Legends of the seven seas. (How Rata built his
canoe. Adapted.)
See also Laka and the menehunes.
For other entries, see 2d edition.
Rats and their son=in=law. Sugimoto. Picture tales from
the Japanese. (Bridegroom of O Chu San.)
See also Venus and the cat.
For other entries, see 2d edition.
Rats, the fox and the egg. La Fontaine. Fables (Tilney.
Two rats, the fox and the egg.)
For other entries, see 2d edition.
Rat's wedding #.
See also Fatty; Hodgepodge hold-fast; Monkey's bargains.
Ratteretalleratteratattertatatatterteta. *See* Giant king of
Limburg.
Rattlesnake and salmon. Garett. Coyote stories.
Raven and Pitch. Hillyer. Box of daylight. (Little Pitch ;
Little Pitch and Tchamsen.)
For other entries, see 2d edition.
Raven and the crab. I. *See* 2d edition.
Raven and the crab. II. Hillyer. Box of daylight. (Last
adventure of Tchamsen; Mouth at each end.)
Raven and the macaw. Nusbaum. Seven cities of Cibola.
Nusbaum. Zuni Indian tales.
Raven and the swan. *See* Why ravens croak.
Raven and the water chief. Hillyer. Box of daylight.
(Tchamsen and Axemag.)
Raven gets fire from Red Deer. Hillyer. Box of daylight.
(*In* Ch. 16.)
See also How fire was brought to the Indians. II.
Raven gets fish for his people. Hillyer. Box of daylight.
(Tchamsen gets the halibut; Gambles for the salmon;
Bright-cloud woman.)
Raven of Stolzeneck. *See* Pet raven.
Raven of the Giralda. Lane. Tower legends.
Raven who tried to walk like the dove. *See* Crow and the
partridge.
Ravens. Darton. Wonder book of old romance.
See also Language of the birds.
For other entries, see 2d edition.

Raven's adventures. Hillyer. Box of daylight.
For other entries, see 2d edition.
Raven's dancing blanket. Hillyer. Box of daylight. (Dancing blanket.)
For other entries, see 2d edition.
Raven's marriage. I. *See* 2d edition.
Raven's marriage. II. Hillyer. Box of daylight. (Tchamsen and Evening Sky; Tchamsen returns to the Town of the air.)
Raymond of Arles and Jeanne of Orange. Clément. Once in France. (Princess who became a shepherdess.)
Real champion. *See* Oberlin, John Frederic.
Real prince. Burnett. Children's book.
Real princess. I. *See* Princess on the pea.
Real princess. II. Howes. Long bright land.
Rebecca the drummer. *See* Army of two.
Recluse and the mouse. *See* Mouse who became a tiger.
Red apples in the snow. *See* Twelve months.
Red-bud tree. Cooper. Argosy of fables. (Judas tree.)
See also Blind men and the elephant; Chameleon.
For other entries, see 2d edition.
Red bull of Norroway. Lee. Folk tales of all nations.
Red cap. *See* Voyage of the red cap.
Red cent. Warner. Carl Krinken.
Red cherry and a little white mouse. Rowe. Moon's birthday.
Red Cross Knight's last battle. Bailey. Stories of great adventures.
See also Una and the Red Cross Knight.
Red dolly. Wiggin and Smith. Twilight stories.
Red-Ettin. Coe. Third book of stories.
Power. Stories to shorten the road.
Steel. English fairy tales.
For other entries, see 2d edition.
Red Fox and Bunny Rabbit. *See* Mr. Fox goes a-hunting but Mr. Rabbit bags the game.
Red geranium. Carey. Flower legends. (Geranium.)
For other entries, see 2d edition.
Red-haired girl's house. Casserley. Michael of Ireland.
Red heron. Martens. Wonder tales from far away.
See also Golden bird. II.
Red Jacket. *See* Nose tree.
Red king and the witch. Lee. Folk tales of all nations.
See also Witch and the sister of the sun.
Red leaf's Thanksgiving. Bailey. Wonderful tree.
Red lily. Carey. Flower legends.
Red leaves of autumn. *See* Why the autumn leaves are red. II.
Red palace. *See* Alhambra legend.
Red pepper. No. 2 Joy Street.
Red Riding Hood. *See* Little Red Riding Hood.

Red robe of heaven. Metzger. Tales told in Hawaii.
See also Earth and the sky.

Red roses of nectar. Carey. Flower legends. (Red roses.)
Olcott. Wonder garden. (*In* Adventures of Cupid among
the roses.)
For other entries, see 2d edition.

Red shoes. I. Andersen. Fairy tales (Stickney). v. 2.
Power. Children's treasure chest.
For other entries, see 2d edition.

Red snow. Guerber. Legends of Switzerland. (*In* Legends
of Vaud and Valais.)

Red thread of courage (poem). Johnson and Scott. Anthology of children's literature. (Red thread of honor.)
For other entries, see 2d edition.

Red thread of honor. *See* Red thread of courage.

Red wasp and the honey bee. Cooper. Argosy of fables.

Red Wing, Story of. Browne. Indian nights.

Red-winged blackbirds and coyote. James. Tewa firelight
tales.
See also Lion and the blackbirds.

Reed flute. Kovalsky and Putnam. Long-legs, Big-mouth,
Burning-eyes.

Reeve's tale. Farjeon. Tales from Chaucer.

Reformed pirate. I. Stockton. Reformed pirate.
For other entries, see 2d edition.

Reformed pirate. II. Olcott. Wonder tales from pirate
isles.

Regulus. Patten. Junior classics. v. 7. (Bravery of Regulus.)
For other entries, see 2d edition.

Reindeer and the tom-cod. *See* Race between a reindeer and
a tom-cod.

Reinicke's revenge on Isegrim #.
See also Reynard the fox.

Reinold. *See* Sons of Aymon.

Reluctant dragon. Grahame. Dream days.
Grahame. Kenneth Grahame book.
See also Dragon ; Last of the dragons.

Rembrandt. Chambers' miscellany. v. 8. (Sister of Rembrandt.)
Chandler. Magic pictures. (Feast of St. Nicholas.)
Miller. My travelship: Holland. (King of shadows, Rembrandt.)

Renard, the true Norman. *See* Reynard the fox.

Réné: Shepherd of Naussane. Crownfield. Feast of Noel.

Renowned history of little Goody Two-shoes. *See* Goody
Two-Shoes.

Repentance of Samuel Johnson. *See* Dr. Johnson and his
father.

Rescue of Arselik. Partridge. Joyful Star.

Rescue of Old Glory. Bailey. Tell me another story.

Rescue of rabbit. James. Happy animals of Atagahi.
See also Master Rabbit again encounters the pine-gum baby.
Rescue of Zita. *See* Alhambra legend.
Resolutions. I. Richards. More five minute stories.
Resolutions. II. Broomell. Children's story caravan.
Resonant cave. Schwimmer. Tisza tales.
Restless cuckoos. Carey. Stories of the birds.
See also Fisherman and his wife.
Resurrection of Dinny Muldoon. MacManus. Lo, and behold ye.
Return of Prosperine. *See* Proserpina.
Return of Ulysses. I. *See* Ulysses' return.
Return of Ulysses. II. Grahame. Kenneth Grahame book.
Revere, Paul #.
See also Peggy feeds the minutemen.
Reward for honesty. Woodson. African myths.
Reward of kindness. Bowman and Bianco. Tales from a Finnish tupa. (Fox as a judge.)
See also Man and the snake. II.
For other entries, see 2d edition.
Reward of virtue. Wilson. Red magic.
See also True and Untrue.
Reward of wisdom. **Gaster. Ma'aseh book. v. 2. **(Rich merchant of Jerusalem who died in a strange land . . .** and his wise son.)
Schwarz. Jewish caravan.
Reynard and Bruin. *See* How Bruin tried to bring Reynard to court.
Reynard the fox. Curry and Clippinger. Children's literature. (Battle between the fox and the wolf.)
Dorey. Three and the moon. (Adventures of Renard, the true Norman.)
See also Damnah the jackal ; How Bruin tried to bring Reynard to court ; Reinicke's revenge on Isegrim.
For other entries, see 2d edition.
Rhampsinitus, Story of. *See* Treasure chamber of Rhampsinitus.
Rheims cathedral. *See* Why Rheims church was built.
Rhine enchantment. *See* Lorelei.
Rhinoceros and the dromedary. Cooper. Argosy of fables.
Rhœcus. Bulfinch. Golden age. (*In* Ch. 22.)
Forbush. Myths and legends of Greece and Rome. (Rhœcus, the boy who forgot.)
For other entries, see 2d edition.
Rhyming prince. Fyleman. Forty good-night tales.
Harper and Hamilton. Winding roads.
Rhys and Llywelin. Choate and Curtis. Little people of the hills. (Dance of the Tylwythe Teg.)
See also Fiddler in the fairy ring.
For other entries, see 2d edition.
Rice and the sugar=cane. Lee. Folk tales of all nations.
Rice maiden. Olcott. Wonder tales from pirate isles.

Rich boy who chose to become poor. *See* St. Francis of Assisi.

Rich brother and poor brother. I #.
See also Beggar's gold; Shemyák the judge #.

Rich brother and poor brother. II. *See* Gore-Gorinskoe.

Rich goose. Bailey. Stories children want.
For other entries, see 2d edition.

Rich man and the tanner. Æsop. Fables (Jones).
Cooper. Argosy of fables.

Rich merchant of Jerusalem and his wise son. *See* Reward of wisdom.

Rich Peter the pedlar. Wilson. Red magic.
For other entries, see 2d edition.

Richard Coeur de Leon. Cather. Pan and his pipes. (When knighthood was in flower.)
Kinscella. Music appreciation readers. Book 3. (Faithful minstrel.)
Tappan. Old world hero stories.
For other entries, see 2d edition.

Richard, Duke of Normandy. Kinscella. Music appreciation readers. Book 6. (Bundle of straw.)

Riddle. I. Martens. Wonder tales from far away. (One that is dead kills two, and two that are dead kill forty.)
For other entries, see 2d edition.

Riddle of the Sphinx. I. *See* Œdipus.

Riddle of the Sphinx. II. Colum. Boy apprenticed to an enchanter. (*In* Story of Bird-of-gold.)

Ride on the gravestone. Ralston. Russian fairy tales.

Right=about=face. Housman. Turn again tales.

Right time to laugh. Carey. Stories of the birds. (Why the woodpecker laughs at frogs.)
Farmer. Nature myths. (Woodpecker's joke.)
For other entries, see 2d edition.

Righteous penny. *See* Honest penny.

Ring of Hallwyl. Guerber. Legends of Switzerland. (*In* Aargau.)

Ring: Siegfried. Evans. Worth while stories. (Abridged.)
Fuller. Book of dragons. (Story of Siegfried.)
Menefee. Child stories. (Siegfried.)
For other entries, see 2d edition.

Ring in the temple door. Dunlap. Stories of the Vikings.
See also King Olaf.

Rip Van Winkle. I. Arthur Rackham fairy book.
Field. American folk and fairy tales.
Rich. Read-aloud book.
See also Date-stone of forgetfulness; Dreamer-the-giant; Fairy huntsman; Four comrades who wanted to travel around the world; Idalwin's long sleep; Idwal of Nant Clwyd; Miser and the banyan tree; Pak-su-ni and the chess players; Visu, Story of #.
For other entries, see 2d edition.

Riquet with the tuft. Bruce. Treasury of tales for little folk.
Fairy garland (Dulac).
Power. Children's treasure chest.
For other entries, see 2d edition.
Rival poets. Untermeyer. Last pirate.
Rival roosters. Babbitt. Animals' own story book. (Black rooster and the red rooster.)
See also Bird with two beaks; Fox and the foolish blue jay.
For other entries, see 2d edition.
River bank. *See* Mole, Adventures of.
River magic. Howes. Long bright land.
River man. James. Tewa firelight tales.
River shark who would be king of the ocean. Cooper. Argosy of fables.
River Tisza, Origin of. Schwimmer. Tisza tales.
Rivers and the sea. Æsop. Fables (Jones).
Cooper. Argosy of fables.
Rivers that talked. *See* Brook Chorny; Dneiper and Sozh; Dneiper, the Volga, and the Dvina; Sadko; Vazuza and Volga.
Road of the loving heart. Forbes. Good citizenship. (*In* Ch. 2.)
See also Her roadway.
Road that went out West. Bailey. Stories children want.
Road to Canada. Broomell. Children's story caravan.
Road to the castle. Bailey. Stories children want.
For other entries, see 2d edition.
Roads of Rome. *See* Caesar, Julius.
Roast beef tree. Raspé. Children's Munchausen (Martin. *In* Ch. 21.)
Roast pig, Origin of. De La Mare and Quayle. Readings. (Roast pork.)
For other entries, see 2d edition.
Robber Caliph, Story of. Arabian nights. Adventures of Haroun Er Raschid. (Olcott. Story of the robber Caliph; or, The adventure of Haroun Er Raschid with the beautiful Zutulbe.)
Robber chief and the treacle pudding. Fyleman. Forty good-night tales.
Robber who became a poet. Mukerji. Rama. (Prelude: The singer of the epic.)
See also Caedmon.
Robbers. La Rue. Under the story tree.
Robbers and the treasure. Aspinwall. Jataka tales.
See also King's ankus.
Robe of feathers. Phillips. Far peoples. (Hagoromo.)
Lee. Folk tales of all nations.
Miller. My travelship: Japan.
See also Shadow crest.
For other entries, see 2d edition.

Robert, Duke of Normandy. *See* Arlette, the tanner's daughter; William the Conqueror.
Robin and the bear. I. De Huff. Taytay's tales.
See also Why the robin has a red breast. I.
Robin and the bear. II. *See* Why the robin has a red breast. I.
Robin and the rose. Bowman. Little brown bowl.
Robin at the cross. *See* Pious robin. II; Why the robin has a red breast. V.
Robin Goodfellow. Lee. Folk tales of all nations.
Rhys. English fairy book.
For other entries, see 2d edition.
Robin Hood. Bailey. Stories of great adventures. (How Robin Hood won the golden arrow; Robin Hood and Maid Marian.)
Coussens. Diamond story book. (Another recruit—Will Scarlet.)
Coussens. Diamond story book. (Robin Hood and the sheriff's prize.)
Coussens. Diamond story book. (Robin Hood meets Little John.)
Cruse. Young folk's book of epic heroes.
(poem). Curry and Clippinger. Children's literature. (Allen-a-Dale.)
Curry and Clippinger. Children's literature. (Robin and the merry little old woman.)
Evans. Worth while stories.
(poem). Johnson and Scott. Anthology of children's literature. (Robin Hood and Little John; Song of Sherwood.)
Johnson and Scott. Anthology of children's literature. (Little John's first adventure.)
(poem). Kinscella. Music appreciation readers. Book 5. (Robin Hood and the widow's three sons.)
(play). Kinscella. Music appreciation readers. Book 5. (Sheriff of Nottingham.)
Power. Bag o' tales. (Silver arrow.)
For other entries, see 2d edition.
Robin of the violin. Olcott. Wonder tales from fairy isles.
Robin, Origin of. *See* How the robin came.
Robin who was an Indian. *See* How the robin came.
Robin's Christmas song. Kinscella. Music appreciation readers. Book 1. (Wee Robin's Christmas song.)
Power. Bag o' tales. (Wee Robin's Yule song.)
Silvester and Peter. Happy hour tales.
Told under the green umbrella. (Wee Robin's Christmas Day.)
See also King of the robins.
For other entries, see 2d edition.
Robin's eggs. Evans. Worth while stories.
See also Benjy in Beastland; Little boy pie.
Robin's nest. Bryce. Short stories for little folks.

Robinson Crusoe. Johnson and Scott. Anthology of children's literature.
Patten. Junior classics. v. 5. (Abridged.)
Rich. Read-aloud book. (Robinson Crusoe meets Friday.)
For other entries, see 2d edition.
Rock of the measuring worm. Chidley. Fifty-two story talks. (Inchworm and the mountain.)
Cooper. Argosy of fables. (Measure-worm rock.)
Morris. Stories from mythology: North American. (*In* Ch. 14.)
For other entries, see 2d edition.
Rock that melted. *See* Tubal Cain. II.
Rockabye chair. Potter. Giant of Apple Pie Hill.
Rocking=horse land. Housman. Moonshine and clover.
Rocks removed. Bailey. Stories of great adventures. (Adapted.)
Farjeon. Tales from Chaucer. (Franklin's tale.)
For other entries, see 2d edition.
Roderick, the last of the Visigoths. Miller. My book of history. v. 3. (*In* Ch. 4.)
Rodney, Caesar. *See* Caesar Rodney's ride.
Roger and Bradamante. *See* Bradamante, Adventures of.
Rogue and the oracle. Æsop. Fables (Jones).
Rogue and the simpleton. Mackenzie. Jackal in Persia. (Cunning partner.)
Phillips. Far peoples. (Honesty and dishonesty.)
For other entries, see 2d edition.
Roland. I. *See* 2d edition.
Roland. II. Bailey. Stories of great adventure. (Story of Roland.)
Clément. Flowers of chivalry. (Death of Roland.)
Cruse. Young folk's book of epic heroes.
Echols. Knights of Charlemagne.
Johnson and Scott. Anthology of children's literature. (Roland and his horn.)
Kinscella. Music appreciation readers. Book 6. (Roland and his horn.)
Lang. Book of myths. (Roland the Paladin.)
Miller. My book of history. v. 3. (Minstrels' song of Roland. *In* Ch. 5.)
Power. Bag o' tales. (Roland's youth; Roland for an Oliver; Death of Roland.)
See also Ferragus who owned the brazen head; Sachem of the white plume.
For other entries, see 2d edition.
Roland and his horn. *See* Roland. II.
Rolf Stake. Lang. Red true story book.
Rolf the ganger. *See* Rollo.
Rolling stone. Carrick. Tales of wise and foolish animals.
See also Coyote steals a blanket #; So-bee-yit.

Rollo. Guerber. Myths of the Middle Ages. (Rolf the ganger. *In* Ragnar Lodbrok.)
Niemeyer. Stories for the history hour. (Rolf.)
Tappan. Old world hero stories. (Rollo the viking.)
For other entries, see 2d edition.

Romance of Alexander. *See* Alexander the Great. III.

Romeo and Juliet. Lamb. Tales from Shakespeare.
Rich. Read-aloud book.
For other entries, see 2d edition.

Romulus and Remus. Botsford. Picture tales from the Italian.
Cooke. Stories of Rome. (Founding of Rome.)
Farjeon. Mighty men from Achilles to Julius Caesar. (Children of the wolf.)
Miller. My book of history. v. 2. (Legend of the founding of Rome. *In* Ch. 8.)
Orvieto. Birth of Rome. (Two newborn babes; Twelve vultures and a square city.)
Terry. Tales from far and near.
Untermeyer. Donkey of God. (*In* Rome.)
For other entries, see 2d edition.

Ronan, St. *See* St. Ronan.

Rongo and the lizard-god. Lee. Folk tales of all nations.

Roof-tree. Farjeon. Old nurse's stocking basket.

Room with the window looking out on the garden. Mitchell. Here and now story book.

Rooster and the fox. *See* Cock and the fox. II and V.

Rooster and the hen. Bowman and Bianco. Tales from a Finnish tupa.
See also Cock and the hen in the nut wood.

Rooster and the hens. Mitchell. Here and now story book.

Rooted lover. Housman. Doorway in fairyland.

Rosalind and the turkeys. Burnett. Children's book.

Rosalind, Story of. *See* As you like it.

Rosanie. Quiller-Couch. Twelve dancing princesses. (Rosanie; or, Inconstant prince.)

Rosaura's birthday. Farjeon. Italian peepshow.

Rose and the amaranth. Æsop. Fables (Jones).

Rose-bud. *See* Sleeping beauty.

Rose-colored spectacles. Shannon. California fairy tales.

Rose, Legends of. Carey. Flower legends. (Rose, Dog rose, Red rose, Rose thorns.)

Rose of the Alhambra, Legend of. Irving. Tales from the Alhambra.

Rose queen. Tappan. Little lady in green.
See also Diamonds and toads.

Rose-Red and Rose-White. *See* Snow-White and Rose-Red.

Rose thorns. *See* Why roses have thorns. IV.

Rose tree. Steel. English fairy tales.
For other entries, see 2d edition.

Roses and the sparrows. *See* Neighboring families.

Rosetta Stone's secret. Lansing. Great moments in science. (*In* More stories of time and space.)

Round castle of the Red Sea. Wilson. Green magic.

Round Table, Founding of. I. Bailey. Stories of great adventures. (How the Round Table came.)⸴

Evans. Worth while stories. (Knights of the Round Table.)

For other entries, see 2d edition.

Round Table, Founding of. II. Johnson and Scott. Anthology of children's literature. (Great bear.)

Williamson. Stars through magic casements. (Great bear.)

See also King Arthur.

Rowan tree. *See* Fairy tree of Dooros.

Rowena. *See* Hengist and Horsa.

Royal eagle. Martinez Del Rio. Sun, the moon, and a rabbit.

Royal engine. Skinner. Merry tales. (Pony engine. Adapted.)

For other entries, see 2d edition.

Royal errand. Eggleston. Stories for special days in the church school.

See also Knights of the silver shield.

Royal Oak Day. Graham. Happy holidays. (Oak-apple Day.)

For other entries, see 2d edition.

Royal prince. Eells. Magic tooth.

Rubbydubble. Potter. Giant of Apple Pie Hill.

Rubezahl. Olcott. Wonder tales from goblin hills. (Rubezahl! Turnip counter!)

For other entries, see 2d edition.

Ruddigore. *See* Witch's curse. I.

Rugmakers. Blondell. Keepsakes.

See also Her blanket.

Rumble=stumble. *See* Rumpelstiltskin.

Rumpelstiltskin. Curry and Clippinger. Children's literature.

De La Mare. Told again.

Grimm. Fairy tales (Olcott).

Hervey and Hix. Fanciful tales for children. (Rumble-stumble.)

Johnson and Scott. Anthology of children's literature. (Rumpel-Stilts-Ken.)

Lang. Old friends among the fairies. (Rumpelstiltzkin.)

Quinn. Stokes' wonder book of fairy tales.

Williams. Tales from Ebony.

See also Age of the sorceror; Doubleturk; Girl who could spin gold from clay and long straw; Lazy queen; Sili go Dwt # ; Three guesses; Tom Tit Tot.

For other entries, see 2d edition.

Runaway dog and gadabout hen. Cook. Red and gold stories.

Runaway rabbit. Potter. Giant of Apple Pie Hill.

Runaway slave. Æsop. Fables (Jones).

Runaway sled. La Rue. Under the story tree.
Runaway train. I. Emerson. Merry-go-round of modern tales.
Runaway train. II. Barrows and Cavanah. Favorite pages from Child Life. (Adventures of Tilly.)
Running stick. Lee. Folk tales of all nations.
For other entries, see 2d edition.
Ruslán and Lyudmila. Zeitlin. Skazki.
Rustam. Coit. Ivory throne of Persia.
Rustam and the Div Akwan. Coit. Ivory throne of Persia.
Rustem. *See* Sohrab and Rustem.
Rustic and the nightingale. Mackenzie. Jackal in Persia. (Gardener and the nightingale.)
For other entries, see 2d edition.
Rusty Jack. Williams-Ellis. Fairies and enchanters.
See also Little farmer.
Ryantown Regulators. Burnett. Children's book.
Ryence. *See* King Ryence's challenge.

S

Saba. Young. Tangle-coated horse.
See also Last of the Feni.
Sabine women and Roman wives. Cooke. Stories of Rome. (*In* Women of Rome.)
Orvieto. Birth of Rome. (Roman women; Stolen maidens.)
Sabot of little Wolff. Kinscella. Music appreciation readers. Book 3. (Wolff and his wooden shoe.)
Harper. Merry Christmas to you.
Smith and Hazeltine. Christmas in legend and story.
Walters. Book of Christmas stories.
Wiggin and Smith. Twilight stories. (Little Wolff's wooden shoes.)
For other entries, see 2d edition.
Sacajawea, the bird woman. Partridge. Joyful Star.
Sachem of the white plume. Browne. Indian nights.
See also Knights of the silver shield.
Sack of barley and the pig. Broomell. Children's story caravan.
Sack of truth. Sawyer. Picture tales from Spain.
See also Bag of stories; Jesper who herded the hares.
Sacred bear spear. *See* Boy who lived with grizzlies.
Sacred bundle. *See* Man who married a buffalo.
Sacred fowls. Metzger. Tales told in Hawaii.
Sacred origin of smoking. *See* Pipe of peace. II.
Sacrifice. Cross. Music stories.
Sad and lonely lover. *See* Orpheus and Eurydice.
Sad ending of a picnic. James. Tewa firelight tales.
Sad princess. Baker. Pedlar's wares.
Sad princess, the green birds, and the old granny of Capdepera. Dane. Once there was and was not.
See also Princess who lost her rings.

Sad story of Halfcock. *See* Half-chick.

Sad story of Mr. Porium's family. Bianco. Street of little shops.

Sad tale of woodpecker and bluejay. *See* Woodpecker and bluejay.

Saddle to rags. Power. Bag o' tales.
For other entries, see 2d edition.

Saddler's horse. Bianco. Street of little shops.

Sadko. I. Ransome. Old Peter's Russian tales.
Kinscella. Music appreciation readers. Book 6.
Zeitlin. Skazki. (Sadko, the merchant.)

Sadko. II. Carpenter, Tales of a Russian grandmother. (Sadko the rich merchant.)

Sagacious lumbardar. Lee. Folk tales of all nations.

Sagacious monkey and the boar. Whitehorn. Wonder tales of old Japan. (Cunning monkey and the boar.)
See also Old dog; Old Sultan.
For other entries, see 2d edition.

Sagacious snake. **Arnold. Book of good counsels. (Frogs and the old serpent.)
Cooper. Argosy of fables. (Frogs and the old serpent.)
See also Frog and the serpent.
For other entries, see 2d edition.

Sage damsel. Tappan. Prince from nowhere. (Wise peasant girl. Adapted.)
See also Clever girl and the king; How the son of the Gobhaun Saor sold the sheepskin; Peasant's clever daughter.
For other entries, see 2d edition.

Sahan, the orphan. Partridge. Joyful Star.

Said, Adventures of. Hauff. Arabian days' entertainment. (Fortunes of Said.)
For other entries, see 2d edition.

Sailor's star. Cozad. Story talks. (People's star. Abridged.)
Fun folk and fairy tales. (North star. Adapted.)
Wheelock. Kindergarten children's hour. v. 3. (*In* Ch. 49.)
For other entries, see 2d edition.

St. Andrew of Scotland. Darton. Seven champions of Christendom.

St. Anthony is dead. *See* Farmer's ass.

St. Anthony of Italy. Darton. Seven champions of Christendom. (Castle of Blanderon.)
See also St. Andrew of Scotland; Why the owl flies by night. IV.
For other entries, see 2d edition.

St. Anthony's godchild. Eells. Islands of magic.

St. Basil. Canton. Child's book of saints. (Hermit of the pillar.)

St. Beatus. Guerber. Legends of Switzerland. (*In* Bern.)

St. Beuno and the curlew. Carey. Stories of the birds. (Curlew and the saint.)
For other entries, see 2d edition.

St. Boniface. Skinner. Christmas stories. (Legend of St. Boniface.)

St. Brandan. Colum. Voyagers. (Voyages of Saint Brendan.)

Eells. Islands of magic. (St. Brendan's island.)
See also Bran the blessed.
For other entries, see 2d edition.

St. Bride of the isles. *See* St. Bridget.

St. Bridget. Barclay. Saints by firelight. (St. Brigid of Kildare.)

Campbell. Story of Christmas, p. 41. (Bride and her Christmas dream.)

Campbell. Story of Christmas, p. 44. (St. Bride of the Isles.)

Farjeon. Ten saints.

Graham. Happy holidays. (St. Bridget's Day.)

Macleod, Fiona. Washers of the shroud. (St. Bride of the Isles.)

Stewart. Tell me a story I never heard before. (Candlemas eve.)
For other entries, see 2d edition.

St. Brigid of Kildare. *See* St. Bridget.

St. Cecilie. Farjeon. Tales from Chaucer. (Second nun's tale.)
For other entries, see 2d edition.

St. Christopher, Legend of. Broomell. Children's story caravan.

Coussens. Diamond story book.

Farjeon. Ten saints.

Lanier. Book of giants. (One good giant: St. Christopher.)

(poem). Macleod, Fiona. Poems. (St. Christopher of the Gael.)

Perkins and Danielson. Second year Mayflower program book.)

Smith and Hazeltine. Christmas in legend and story.

(poem). Smith and Hazeltine. Christmas in legend and story. (St. Christopher of the Gael.)

Starbuck. Familiar haunts.

Walters. Book of Christmas stories.
For other entries, see 2d edition.

St. Clare. Barclay. Saints by firelight.

St. Columba. Niemeyer. Stories for the history hour. (Columba.)

Stewart. Tell me a story I never heard before. (Cry of the eagle.)

St. Corentin. Lee. Folk tales of all nations. (Miraculous fish.)

St. Crispin. Graham. Happy holidays. (St. Crispin's story.)

St. Cuthbert. Niemeyer. Stories for the history hour. (Cuthbert.)
For other entries, see 2d edition.

St. Cuthbert and the eagle. Miller. My book of history. v.
3. (*In* Ch. 6.)
For other entries, see 2d edition.
St. David of Wales. Carey. Flower legends. (Leek.)
Darton. Seven champions of Christendom. (Enchanted
garden.)
St. Denis. Adams and Atchinson. Book of enchantment.
(Enchanted stag.)
Darton. Seven champions of Christendom. (Enchanted
stag.)
For other entries, see 2d edition.
St. Dorothea. Farjeon. Ten saints.
Canton. Child's book of saints. (Golden roses and apples
red.)
St. Eligius, or Eloi. Broomell. Children's story caravan.
St. Elizabeth and the roses. Carey. Flower legends.
Schwimmer. Tisza tales. (Legend of St. Elizabeth.)
For other entries, see 2d edition.
St. Elizabeth of Hungary. Barclay. Saints by firelight.
St. Francis of Assisi. Bailey. Story-telling hour. (Boy of
Italy who could tame all animals.)
Broomell. Children's story caravan.
This includes: St. Francis preaching to the birds; St.
Francis and the wolf of Agobio ; Brother Juniper.
Cabot. Course in citizenship. (Wolf of Gubbio.)
Canton. Child's book of saints. (Little bedesman of
Christ.)
Davis. Truce of the wolf and other stories. (Truce of the
wolf.)
Farjeon. Ten saints.
Lansing. Great moments in freedom. (Rich boy who chose
to become poor.)
Miller. My book of history. v. 3. (*In* Ch. 11.)
Untermeyer. Donkey of God. (Donkey of God.)
Untermeyer. Donkey of God. (*In* Gubbio-San Gimignano-
Siena.)
For other entries, see 2d edition.
St. Gall and the bear. Guerber. Legends of Switzerland.
(*In* St. Gall and Appenzell.)
Miller. My book of history. v. 3. (*In* Ch. 6.)
St. Genevieve, Legend of. Barclay. Saints by firelight.
Bryant. Children's book of celebrated legends. (St. Gene-
vieve watching over Paris.)
Clément. Once in France. (Genevieve! the Huns are com-
ing.)
Niemeyer. Stories for the history hour. (Genevieve.)
Patten. Junior classics. v. 7. (Fearless Saint Genevieve,
patron saint of Paris.)
For other entries, see 2d edition.
St. George and the dragon. I. Darton. Seven champions
of Christendom. (St. George of England.)
Evans. Worth while stories.

St. George and the dragon. I—*continued.*
Graham. Happy holidays. (St. George's Day.)
Johnson and Scott. Anthology of children's literature.
(How St. George fought the dragon.)
Power. Children's treasure chest.
Rhys. English fairy book.
Steel. English fairy tales. (St. George of Merrie England.)
Wilson. Red magic.
See also Egori the brave and the gipsy # ; Reluctant dragon.
For other entries, see 2d edition.
St. George and the dragon. II. *See* Una and the Red Cross
Knight.
St. Giles. Farjeon. Ten saints.
St. Helena and the cross. Bryant. Children's book of cele-
brated legends.
St. Hilary. Canton. Child's book of saints. (Ancient gods
pursuing.)
St. Hubert. Farjeon. Ten saints.
Saint Hubert's miracle. Baumbach. Tales from the Swiss
alps.
St. Jacob's roses. Guerber. Legends of Switzerland. (*In*
Basel.)
St. James of Spain. Darton. Seven champions of Christen-
dom. (Slaying of the boar.)
St. Jerome and the lion. Coe. Third book of stories.
Lang. Red book of animal stories. (Lion and the saint.)
For other entries, see 2d edition.
St. Kassian. Carpenter. Tales of a Russian grandmother.
(Kassian and Nicholas.)
Ralston. Russian fairy tales. (*In* Legends about saints.)
St. Kenach. Canton. Child's book of saints. (Kenach's lit-
tle woman.)
St. Leonard. Stewart. Tell me a story I never heard be-
fore. (Enchanted garden.)
For other entries, see 2d edition.
St. Leonor. Burt. Lanier book. (Legend of St. Leonor.)
See also Ear of wheat.
St. Louis. Clément. Flowers of chivalry. (King with the
face of an angel.)
For other entries, see 2d edition.
St. Margaret of Scotland. Barclay. Saints by firelight.
St. Mark of Venice. Untermeyer. Donkey of God. (*In*
Venice.)
St. Martin. Broomell. Children's story caravan. (St. Mar-
tin of Tours.)
Farjeon. Ten saints.
Graham. Happy holidays. (Martinmas.)
For other entries, see 2d edition.
Saint Martin and the honest man. Colum. Forge in the
forest.
St. Martin's summer. Marzials. Stories for the story hour.
St. Michael. Graham. Happy holidays. (Michaelmas.)

St. Michael and the conger eel. Price. Legends of the seven seas.

St. Michael and the dragon. Bryant. Children's book of celebrated legends.

St. Nicholas. Bryant. Children's book of celebrated legends. (Feast of St. Nicholas.)

Carpenter. Tales of a Russian grandmother. (Kassian and Nicholas.)

Farjeon. Ten saints.

Faulkner. Story lady's Christmas stories. (Legend of St. Nicholas.)

Graham. Welcome Christmas. (Story of Santa Claus.)

Miller. My travelship: Holland. (St. Nicholas legend.)

Olcott. Wonder tales from windmill lands. (Sinterklaas and Pieterbaas.)

Ralston. Russian fairy tales. (St. Nicholas and Kassian. *In* Legends about saints. Ch. 6.)

Seredy. Good master. (Mikulas, bearer of gifts. *In* Ch. 12.)

See also Beggar's gold; Priest with the envious eyes. II; Scarlet feather.

For other entries, see 2d edition.

St. Nicholas and black Pete. Hart. Picture tales from Holland.

Olcott. Wonder tales from windmill lands. (Sinterklaas and Pieterbaas.)

St. Nicholas and the children. Graham. Welcome Christmas. (*In* Story of Santa Claus.)

For other entries, see 2d edition.

St. Nicholas and the nobleman's son. Graham. Welcome Christmas. (Legend of St. Nicholas.)

For other entries, see 2d edition.

St. Nicholas in trouble. Harper. Merry Christmas to you.

St. Odile. Henderson. Wonder tales of Alsace-Lorraine.

St. Pagnoocious. *See* Judgement of Solomon.

St. Patrick. Darton. Seven champions of Christendom. (Six princesses of Thrace.)

Farjeon. Ten saints.

Graham. Happy holidays. (St. Patrick's Day.)

(poem). Potter. Giant of Apple Pie Hill. (St. Patrick's Day.)

For other entries, see 2d edition.

St. Patrick and the shamrock. Carey. Flower legends. (Shamrock.)

St. Patrick's thorn. Carey. Flower legends. (Blackthorn.)

St. Perpetua. Barclay. Saints by firelight.

St. Pirminius. Guerber. Legends of Switzerland. (*In* St. Gall and Appenzell.)

St. Ronan. Fleming. Round the world in folk tales.

Masson. Folk tales of Brittany. (Little White-thorn and the talking bird.)

St. Simeon Stylites. Farjeon. Ten saints.
For other entries, see 2d edition.
St. Swithin. Graham. Happy holidays. (St. Swithun's Day.)
Saint that was shot out of his own cannon. Skeat. Tiger's mistake.
St. Teresa. Barclay. Saints by firelight.
St. Tryphine. Dorey. Three and the moon. (Wonderful legend of St. Triphine.)
See also Bluebeard.
St. Ursula and the eleven thousand virgins. Bryant. Children's book of celebrated legends. (St. Ursula's dream.)
For other entries, see 2d edition.
St. Valentine. Sheriff. Stories old and new.
For other entries, see 2d edition.
St. Valentine's Day. *See* David's valentines; Fairy queen and the carrier doves; Jolly valentine; Postman's valentine; Prince's valentine; also titles beginning Valentine.
For other entries, see 2d edition.
St. Verena. Guerber. Legends of Switzerland. (*In* Legends of Soleure.)
St. Vincent de Paul. Broomell. Children's story caravan.
St. Winifred's well. Long. Folklore calendar. (*In* May: Wells.)
St. Yves. Lee. Folk tales of all nations. (St. Yves, the truth-giver.)
St. Zita. Barclay. Saints by firelight.
Brown. Under the rowan tree.
Sakata Kintoki, History of. Mitford. Tales of old Japan.
Sakka's presents. Lee. Folk tales of all nations.
Saladin of Bagdad and the Princess Morgana. *See* Princess Morgana.
Sally Gabble's cake. Potter. Giant of Apple Pie Hill.
Sally's story. *See* Pig and the captain.
Salmon of knowledge. Young. Tangle-coated horse. (Night of nights; Silver pool; Nuts of knowledge.)
Salmon of wisdom. Rolleston. High deeds of Finn. (*In* Boyhood of Finn MacCumhail.)
Salmon, Story of. Spence. Myths of the North American Indians. (*In* Ch. 5.)
Salt. I. Fleming. Round the world in folk tales.
See also King Lear.
Salt. II. Ransome. Old Peter's Russian tales.
See also Two bad bargains.
Salt fish and the eel. Lee. Folk tales of all nations. (Of drowning eels. *In* Wise men of Gotham.)
See also Wise men of Gotham.
For other entries, see 2d edition.
Salt smuggler. Fleming. Round the world in folk tales.
Saltness of the sea. *See* Why the sea is salt. I.
Salvator Rosa. Chambers' miscellany. v. 9. (*In* Anecdotes of early painters.)

Sambatyon river. *See* Alexander the Great and the river Sambatyon.

Samebito. *See* Jewel tears.

Sammy Squires and the pig family. Potter. Captain Sandman.

Samoa, Name of. Metzger. Tales told in Hawaii. (Sacred fowls.)

Sampler. Fyleman. Forty good-morning tales.

Sampo. Fillmore. Wizard of the North. (Forging of the Sampo. *In* Ch. 16.)
Olcott. Wonder tales from Baltic wizards. (Forging of the magic sampo.)

Sampo Lappelil. Topelius. Canute Whistlewinks.
For other entries, see 2d edition.

Sand flat shadows. Sandburg. Rootabaga stories.

Sandfly and the mosquito. Metzger. Tales told in Hawaii.

Sandman. I. *See* Ole-Luk-Oie.

Sandman. II. Bryce. Short stories for little folks.

Sands of Stavoren. *See* Sunken city.

Saneha, Story of. *See* Sinuhe, Adventures of.

Santa Claus, Story of. *See* St. Nicholas.

Santa Claus's helpers. Bryce. Short stories for little folks.
Walker. Sandman's Christmas stories.
For other entries, see 2d edition.

Santa Claus's home. Bryce. Short stories for little folks.

Santa Claus's present. Bryce. Short stories for little folks.

Santa Claus's sleepy story. Bailey. Stories children want.

Santa Claus's sleigh. Bryce. Short stories for little folks.

Sar, Nar, and Jinook. Cooper. Tal. (*In* Ch. 10 and 11.)
See also King of the golden river.

Sarto, Andrea del. Steedman. Knights of art.

Satni and the Magic Book of Thoth. Baikie. Wonder tales of the ancient world. (Setna and the magic roll.)
**Maspero. Popular stories of ancient Egypt. (Adventure of Satni-Khamois with the mummies.)
For other entries, see 2d edition.

Satni-Khamois and his son Senosiris. Baikie. Wonder tales of the ancient world. (Setna Khaemuas and his son Senosiris.)
**Maspero. Popular stories of ancient Egypt.
See also Senosoris, the wonder child #.

Saturday half-holiday. Baker. Tell them again tales.

Saturday mountain. Byrde. Polish fairy book.

Satyr and the traveller. Æsop. Fables (Artzybasheff. Man and the satyr.)
Æsop. Fables (Jones. Man and the satyr.)
Æsop. Twenty-four fables (L'Estrange. Man and a satyr.)
Æsop. Fables (Whitman ed.).
Cooper. Argosy of fables. (Man and the satyr.)
Curry and Clippinger. Children's literature. (Man and the satyr.)
Power. Children's treasure chest. (Man and the satyr.)

Satyr and the traveller—*continued.*
For other entries, see 2d edition.
Saucy fairy. Metzger. Tales told in Hawaii.
Saucy snow sprites. Cook. Red and gold stories.
Saul and David. Menefee. Child stories.
Sausage adventure. Fyleman. Forty good-night tales. (Twinkles, pt. 2.)
Saved by kindness. White. School management, p. 274.
Sayadio in spirit land. Partridge. Joyful Star. (Maiden's curiosity.)
Spence. Myths of the North American Indians. (*In* Ch. 4.)
See also Ghost land ; In the land of souls.
Saying of Socrates. *See* Socrates and his house.
Scales. Fyleman. Forty good-morning tales.
Scar Face. I–II. *See* 2d edition.
Scar Face. III. Spence. Myths of the North American Indians. (*In* Ch. 3.)
Morris. Stories from mythology: North American. *In* Ch. 9.)
See also Maid who married the morning star ; Star boy # ; Scar Face. IV.
For other entries, see 2d edition.
Scar Face. IV. Davis. Baker's dozen. (Legend of Scarface.)
Sexton. Gray wolf stories. (Scarface goes to the sun and meets morning star.)
For other entries, see 2d edition.
Scarecrow and the snow man. Bowman. Little brown bowl.
See also Snow man and the snowdrops.
Scarlet blanket. *See* Pedlar's pack.
Scarlet feather. Atkins. Pot of gold.
Scarlet Feather's Thanksgiving. Bailey. Wonderful tree.
Scarlet maple. Curtis. Stories in trees.
Scathach, woman warrior. Hull. Cuchulain. (Cuchulain's adventures in Shadow-land.)
Gregory. Cuchulain of Muirthemne. (*In* Courtship of Emer.)
Scheme of skunk and coyote. Hogner. Navajo winter nights.
See also Fox and the prairie dogs.
Scheming kitten. Morley. I know a secret.
Schildburgers. Lee. Folk tales of all nations.
See also Wise men of Gotham.
Schippeitaro. Faulkner. Little Peachling.
For other entries, see 2d edition.
Schmat=Razum #.
See also Go, I know not whither — fetch, I know not what. I–II ; Ivan the peasant's son #.
Schneider, Euloge. Clément. Once in France. (Baleful cart.)

Schoolboy, the pedant, and the owner of a garden. La Fontaine. Fables (Tilney).

Schwanau's ghost. Guerber. Legends of Switzerland. (*In* Forest cantons.)

Scorpion and his family. Martinez Del Rio. Sun, the moon and a rabbit.

See also Inseparables.

Scorpion and the tortoise. Mackenzie. Jackal in Persia. (Story of the tortoise and the scorpion.)

Scrapefoot. Power. Bag o' tales.

Power. Blue caravan tales.

Told under the green umbrella.

Whiteman. Playmates in print.

For other entries, see 2d edition.

Scrawny old man and woman. Lee. Folk tales of all nations.

Scrooge's Christmas. *See* Ebenezer Scrooge's Christmas.

Scrupulous cats (poem). Cooper. Argosy of fables.

Scullion Jack (poem). Bennett. Pigtail of Ah Lee Ben Loo. (Ye ballad of scullion Jack.)

Sculptor and the statue of Jupiter. La Fontaine. Fables (Tilney).

Sculptor Petesis and King Nectonabo. *See* King Nectanebo.

Scylla and Charybdis. Bulfinch. Golden age. (Glaucus and Scylla. *In* Ch. 7.)

Bulfinch. Golden age. (*In* Ch. 29.)

For other entries, see 2d edition.

Scylla, daughter of Nisus. Bulfinch. Golden age. (Nisus and Scylla. *In* Ch. 13.)

For other entries, see 2d edition.

Scythian philosopher. La Fontaine. Fables (Tilney).

Sea=baby. Farjeon. Old nurse's stocking tales.

Sea captain and the serpent. Carpenter. Tales of a Basque grandmother.

Sea horse. Raspé. Children's Munchausen (Martin. *In* Ch. 12).

Raspé. Tales from the travels of Baron Munchausen.

Sea king's gift. Topelius. Canute Whistlewinks. (Gift of the sea king.)

For other entries, see 2d edition.

Sea maiden. I. *See* 2d edition.

Sea maiden. II. Henderson and Jones. Wonder tales of ancient Wales.

Sea=side travelers. *See* What was it?

Sea Tsar and Vasilissa the wise #. *See* Vassilissa the cunning and the tsar of the sea.

In 2d edition there are entries under each title.

Seal maiden. I. Lee. Folk tales of all nations.

Seal maiden. II. Price. Legends of the seven seas.

Search for a charm. Cook. Red and gold stories.

Search for a good child. Wheelock. Kindergarten children's hour. v. 4. (*In* Ch. 29.)
For other entries, see 2d edition.
Search of the three princes. Cowles. Stories to tell.
Lee. Folk tales of all nations. (Seer.)
Morris. Gypsy story teller. (Seer.)
Search that Maui's brother made for his sister, Hina=of=the=sea.
Metzger. Tales told in Hawaii. (Maui the mischievous.)
For other entries, see 2d edition.
Seasons. Johnson and Scott. Anthology of children's literature. (Determination of the seasons.)
See also How summer came to the earth; How the seasons came to be; Little ice man #; Old Winter Man and the Spring; Proserpina; Why they have summer on St. Lawrence Island.
Second nun's tale. *See* St. Cecilie.
Secret kept for three thousand years. *See* Princess who liked silken robes.
Secret. I. Wheelock. Kindergarten children's hour. v. 4. (*In* Ch. 20.)
Secret. II. La Rue. Under the story tree.
Secret kingdom. Gate. Tales from the secret kingdom.
Secret of Dowanhotaninwin. *See* Maiden's secret.
Secret of fire. I. Metzger. Tales told in Hawaii. (Stingy mudhens.)
Howes. Long bright land. (Maui and the goddess of fire.)
For other entries, see 2d edition.
Secret of fire. II. Lansing. Great moments in science. (*In* Age of fire.)
Secret of fire. III. Lee. Folk tales of all nations. (Fire-makers.)
Secret of fire. I–III.
For other versions *see* Fire, Origin of; Wonderful lizard.
Secret of happiness. Cozad. Story talks.
Secret of success. Cozad. Story talks. (Buttons and rings and various things.)
Secret of the animals. Lebermann. New German fairy tales.
See also Language of beasts.
Secret of the fern jewel. Olcott. Wonder tales from goblin hills.
Secret path. *See* Brave three hundred.
Secret room. *See* Black bull of the Castle of Blood.
See no evil! hear no evil! speak no evil! Sugimoto. Picture tales from the Japanese. (Three wise little monkeys.)
See also Three apes.
Seed=babies' blanket. Harriman. Stories for little children.
Seeds and the wheat. Johnson and Scott. Anthology of children's literature.
Cooper. Argosy of fables.
Seeds of gold. Evans. Worth while stories.

Seeing's believing. Olcott. Wonder tales from fairy isles.
Seer. *See* Search of the three princes.
Self=made cat, Tale of a. Wiggin and Smith. Twilight stories.
Selfish ant. Botsford. Picture tales from the Italian.
Selfish giant. Adams and Atchinson. Book of giant stories. Harper. Selfish giant, and other stories. Werner's recitations. No. 51.
For other entries, see 2d edition.
Selfish little tree. Kinscella. Music appreciation readers. Book 3.
See also Spirit that lived in a tree.
Selfish prince. Cook. To-day's stories of yesterday.
See also Much and More.
Selfish princess. Metzger. Tale: told in Korea.
See also Tarpeia.
Seller of dreams. Harper and Hamilton. Winding roads.
For other entries, see 2d edition.
Seller of words. Katibah. Other Arabian nights.
See also King's life saved by spells.
Sending of the crystal egg. *See* Crystal egg.
Seneca's revenge. Spence. Myths of the North American Indians. (*In* Ch. 4.)
Senhor Black Art. Eells. Brazilian fairy book.
Senhor Black Art and the princess. Eells. Brazilian fairy book.
Sennacherib's defeat. Gaer. Burning bush. (*In* Battle that wasn't fought.)
**Maspero. Popular stories of ancient Egypt. (How Satni-Khamois triumphed over the Assyrians.)
See also King Setnan and the Assyrians #.
Senosoris, the wonder=child #.
See also Satni-Khamois and his son Senosiris.
Serafino and the four winds. Botsford. Picture tales from the Italian.
Seraphion. *See* Seven years of seeking.
Serpent and the eagle. I. Æsop. Fables (Jones).
Serpent and the eagle. II. *See* Eagle and the worm.
Serpent and the file. Æsop. Fables (Jones. Viper and the file.)
Æsop. Fables (Whitman ed. Viper and the file.)
Cooper. Argosy of fables. (Viper and the file.)
See also Fox and the bramble.
For other entries, see 2d edition.
Serpent and the peasant. Lee. Folk tales of all nations.
For other entries, see 2d edition.
Serpent of the sea. Nusbaum. Seven cities of Cibola. Nusbaum. Zuni Indian tales.
Serpent=peri and the magic mirror. Lee. Folk tales of all nations.
For other entries, see 2d edition.

Serpent prince. Dulac. Edmund Dulac's fairy book.
Serpent woman. I. *See* 2d edition.
Serpent woman. II. Lee. Folk tales of all nations.
Serpentina. Capuana. Italian fairy tales.
Servant of all. Cabot. Course in citizenship.
Perkins and Danielson. Second year Mayflower program book.
Servant who looked after a door. Cooper. Argosy of fables.
Servants who kept the rain off the trunks. Cooper. Argosy of fables.
Service of Alawn Alawon. Morris. Book of the three dragons.
Servin' o' Culain. Dunbar. Sons o' Cormac.
Sesostris. **Maspero. Popular stories of ancient Egypt. (Exploits of Sesostris.)
Sesshiu, painter of Japan. Gibson. Golden bird. (Sesshiu and the mouse.)
See also Painter of cats #.
For other entries, see 2d edition.
Set, Lord of evil. *See* Isis and Osiris.
Setna and the magic roll. *See* Satni and the Magic Book of Thoth.
Setna=Khaemuas and his son Senosiris. *See* Satni-Khamois and his son Senosiris.
Seven bad boys become stars. *See* Pleiades. II.
Seven brothers. Spence. Myths of the North American Indians. (*In* Ch. 3.)
See also Coyote and the bear maiden.
Seven brothers of the star cluster. *See* Pleiades. II.
Seven champions. I. Darton. Seven champions of Christendom. (Brotherhood of the seven champions; End of the brotherhood.)
Seven champions. II. Garnett. Ottoman wonder tales.
Seven cities of Cibola. Nusbaum. Seven cities of Cibola.
Nusbaum. Zuni Indian tales. (Seven cities.)
Seven colts. *See* Seven foals.
Seven conquerors of the queen of the Mississippi. Dulac. Edmund Dulac's fairy book.
Seven deadly sins. *See* Parson's tale; Why the peacock's tail is spotted.
Seven enchanted princes. Eells. Islands of magic.
See also Seven ravens.
Seven foals. Rasmussen. East o' the sun and west o' the moon. (Seven colts.)
For other entries, see 2d edition.
Seven giants. Martinez Del Rio. Sun, the moon and a rabbit.
Seven gifted brothers. Macdonnell. Italian fairy book. (*In* Wizard of Roccanero.)
Seven iron slippers. Lee. Folk tales of all nations.

Seven kingdoms and the hidden spring. Broomell. Children's story caravan.
For other entries, see 2d edition.
Seven pleas. Sugimoto. Picture tales from the Japanese.
Seven ravens. Grimm. Fairy tales (Olcott).
See also Little sister; Seven doves; Seven enchanted princes.
For other entries, see 2d edition.
Seven Rhine sisters. Olcott. Wonder tales from goblin hills.
Seven sheepfolds. Pogány. Hungarian fairy book.
Schwimmer. Tisza tales. (Legend of the Krasznahorka.)
For other entries, see 2d edition.
Seven sisters. I. *See* Pleiades. VII.
Seven sisters. II. Fyleman. Forty good-morning tales.
For other entries, see 2d edition.
Seven sleepers of Ephesus. Colum. Forge in the forest.
Williamson. Stars through magic casements.
For other entries, see 2d edition.
Seven sons. Friedlander. Jewish fairy tales (Dutton).
Seven sons of Sandy Saunderson. Lindsay. Choosing book.
See also Bundle of sticks.
Seven stages. *See* Brazen Hold.
Seven stars upon earth, Adventures of. Spurr. Dumas fairy tale book.
Seven Swabians. Evans. Worth while stories. (Six Swabians.)
See also Warlike seven. I–II.
For other entries, see 2d edition.
Seven white cats. Told under the blue umbrella.
Seven wise masters. Darton. Wonder book of old romance.
Seven years of seeking. Canton. Child's book of saints.
Seventeen camels. White. Made in Russia. (*In* Ch. 7.)
Seventh princess. Farjeon. Italian peepshow.
Severed hand. Hauff. Arabian days' entertainment.
Severi and Vappu. Bowman and Bianco. Tales from a Finnish tupa.
Seyf El Mulook. Arabian nights. Adventures of Haroun Er Raschid (Olcott. Story of Seyf El Mulook, sword of kings and the daughter of the genii.)
Shackles of frost. Egan. New found tales.
Shadow. I #.
See also Man without a shadow; Princess with the tired shadow.
Shadow blankets. Mitchell. Gray moon tales. (Mammy and the shadow blankets.)
Shadow crest. Sugimoto. Picture tales from the Japanese.
See also Robe of feathers.
Shadow gifts. Colum. Bright islands. (*In* Little people of Ao-tea-roa.)
Howes. Long bright land.
Metzger. Tales told in Hawaii. (Kana and the fairies.)
Shadow land. *See* Ghost wife. IV.

Shadow moose. Browne. Indian nights.
See also Sky elk #.
Shadow people (poem). Ledwidge, Francis. Complete poems.
(poem). Harper. Ghosts and goblins.
(poem). Olcott. Wonder tales from fairy isles.
Shaggy dog dance. *See* Dog dance. II.
Shah Jamshid. Coit. Ivory throne of Persia.
See also Paradise in the sea.
Shah Meram and Sultan Sade #.
See also Three brothers and three sisters.
Sham prince. Hauff. Arabian days' entertainment. (False prince.)
For other entries, see 2d edition.
Sham princes. *See* Boy who was fated to be king; Golden armlet; Golden lynx; Prince Ganim; Prince in exile; Princess of Tronkolaine.
Shamrock. *See* St. Patrick and the shamrock.
Shanavan Lee and Pangur Dhu. Casserley. Michael of Ireland.
Shariar and Sharazad. *See* King Schahriar and Scheherazade.
Shark and the menehunes. Colum. At the gateways of the day. (*In* Me-ne-hu-ne.)
Metzger. Tales told in Hawaii.
Shawano who killed the Uktena. I. Bailey. Stories from an Indian cave. (Winning of the crystal.)
See also Vouivre; Wyvern.
For other entries, see 2d edition.
Shawano who killed the Uktena. II. Spence. Myths of the North American Indians. (Magical serpent. *In* Ch. 4.)
She=goats and their beards. Æsop. Fables (Jones).
Cooper. Argosy of fables.
Sheep and a crow. *See* Crow and the sheep.
Sheep and pig who set up house. *See* Ram and the pig.
Sheep and the dog. Æsop. Fables (Jones).
Æsop. Fables (Whitman ed.).
For other entries, see 2d edition.
Sheep and the pig. *See* Ram and the pig.
Sheep and the pig that built the house. *See* Ram and the pig.
Sheep and the pig who set up house. *See* Ram and the pig.
Sheep and the shepherd's balur. Egan. New found tales.
Sheep and the swallow. Cooper. Argosy of fables.
Sheep, the wolf and the stag. Æsop. Fables (Jones).
Cooper. Argosy of fables. (Stag and the sheep.)
Sheep's petition (poem). Cooper. Argosy of fables.
Sheepskin coat. Byrde. Polish fairy book.
See also Cinderella; Kari Woodengown.
Sheik of Alexandria and his slaves. Hauff. Arabian days' entertainment.

Shell, Solomon. Mackaye. Tall tales of the Kentucky mountains. (Mountain Munchausen.)

Sheltering wings. Skinner. Child's book of country stories. For other entries, see 2d edition.

Shemyák the judge #.
See also Rich brother and poor brother. I.

Shen of colored cords. Chrisman. Wind that wouldn't blow.

Shen of the sea. Chrisman. Shen of the sea.

Shen who misunderstood. Chrisman. Wind that wouldn't blow.

Shepherd, Adventures of. *See* Language of beasts.

Shepherd and the dragon. Coussens. Diamond story book. Fuller. Book of dragons.
See also Good-natured dragons; Language of beasts.
For other entries, see 2d edition.

Shepherd and the sea. Cooper. Argosy of fables.
See also Shipwrecked man and the sea.

Shepherd and the sheep. Cooper. Argosy of fables.

Shepherd and the wolf. I. Æsop. Fables (Jones).

Shepherd and the wolf. II. Cooper. Argosy of fables.

Shepherd boy and the wolf. *See* Boy who cried "Wolf."

Shepherd boy who built a bridge. Kinscella. Music appreciation readers. Book 3.

Shepherd maiden's gift. *See* Christmas rose. II.
In 2d edition there are entries under each title.

Shepherd of Monte Cristallo. Wolff. Pale mountains.

Shepherd of Silfrunarstadir. Lee. Folk tales of all nations.

Shepherd pashaw. Starbuck. Far horizons. (Shepherd pacha.)
For other entries, see 2d edition.

Shepherd who laughed last. Boggs and Davis. Three golden oranges.
See also Master of all masters.

Shepherd who married a fairy. Hill and Maxwell. Napoleon's story book.

Shepherd who turned back #.
See also Little Roman shepherd.

Shepherd who won the king's daughter by a single word #.
See also Bet.

Shepherdess and the chimney sweep. Andersen. Fairy tales (Stickney). v. 2.
Power. Children's treasure chest.
For other entries, see 2d edition.

Shepherdess whose dream came true. *See* Joan of Arc.

Shepherd's boy. *See* Boy who cried "Wolf."

Shepherd's boy and the wolf. *See* Boy who cried "Wolf."

Shepherd's gift. Harper. Merry Christmas to you. (Holy night.)

Shepherd's gift—*continued.*
Van Buren and Bemis. Christmas in storyland. (Christmas night.)
Sheriff of Nottingham. *See* Robin Hood.
Shining beast. Young. Tangle-coated horse.
Ship Argo. *See* Argonauts.
Ship that sailed by land and sea. Bowman and Bianco. Tales from a Finnish tupa.
See also Ashiepattle and his goodly crew; Flying ship.
Shipman's tale. Farjeon. Tales from Chaucer.
Shipwrecked man and the sea. Æsop. Fables (Jones).
Cooper. Argosy of fables. (Husbandman and the sea.)
See also Shepherd and the sea.
For other entries, see 2d edition.
Shipwrecked sailor. Baikie. Wonder tales of the ancient world. (Shipwrecked sailor and the talking serpent.)
McDonald. Dick and the spice cupboard. (*In* Dick's first adventure.)
**Maspero. Popular stories of ancient Egypt.
Miller. My book of history. v. 1. (*In* Ch. 8.)
Wells. How the present came from the past. Book 2, pt. 2.
See also Sinbad the sailor.
Shirt=collar. Wilson. Green magic.
For other entries, see 2d edition.
Shirt of a happy man. *See* Happy man.
Shitakiri Suzume. *See* Tongue-cut sparrow.
Shoeing the wild mare. Hall. Godmother's stories.
Shoemaker and the elves. *See* Elves and the shoemaker.
Shoes. Burt. Lanier book. (Story of a proverb.)
Wheelock. Kindergarten children's hour. v. 3. (Leather. *In* Ch. 17.)
Wiltse. Kindergarten stories. (Leather.)
Shoes of Abu Kasim. *See* Slippers of misfortune.
Shoes of go=seek. Housman. What-o'clock tales.
Shoes of kindness. Freeman. Child-story readers. 3d reader.
Shoes that were danced to pieces. *See* Twelve dancing princesses.
Shooting of the red eagle. Adams and Atchinson. Book of enchantment.
Spence. Myths of the North American Indians. (Adventures of Ictinike. *In* Ch. 5.)
For other entries, see 2d edition.
Shooting round the corner. Guerber. Legends of Switzerland. (*In* Legends of Vaud and Valais.)
Shortening of the road. Power. Stories to shorten the road. (*In* Foreword.)
Young. Celtic wonder tales. (How the son of the Gobhaun Saor shortened the road.)
Young. Wonder smith and his son. (*In* How the son of the Gubbaun Saor talked with lords from a strange country.)

Shrove Tuesday visitor. Macmillan. Canadian wonder tales.

Shush, Shush, the big buff banty hen. Sandburg. Rootabaga country.

Sandburg. Rootabaga pigeons.

Shuttlecock. Fyleman. Forty good-night tales.

Si Crooker's fast fertilizer. Mackaye. Tall tales of the Kentucky mountains.

Siam=Siam. Phillips. Far peoples.

Siamese twins. Metzger. Tales told in Hawaii.

Sibyl. Bulfinch. Golden age. (*In* Ch. 32.)

For other entries, see 2d edition.

Sick fairy. Carpenter. Tales of a Basque grandmother.

See also Fairy nurse # ; Cherry of Zennor.

Sick kite. Cooper. Argosy of fables.

For other entries, see 2d edition.

Sick leopard and the friendly tree=cat. Lobagola. Folk tales of a savage.

Sick lion. I. Cooper. Argosy of fables. (Old lion.)

For other entries, see 2d edition.

Sick lion. II #.

See Lion, the bear, the monkey and the fox #.

In 2d edition there are entries under each title.

Sick lion. III. *See* Lion, the fox, and the beasts.

Sick man and the doctor. Æsop. Fables (Jones).

Sick stag. Æsop. Fables (Jones).

Æsop. Fables (Whitman ed.).

Cooper. Argosy of fables.

For other entries, see 2d edition.

Sidi Lion's shoemaker. Martin. Fatma was a goose.

See also Dog as cobbler.

Sidi=Nouman. Arabian nights. Adventures of Haroun Er Raschid (Olcott. Story told by Sidi Nonman.)

For other entries, see 2d edition.

Siege of Calais. Patten. Junior classics. v. 7. (Noble Burghers of Calais.)

Tappan. Old world hero stories. (*In* Edward, the Black Prince.)

For other entries, see 2d edition.

Siege of Gibraltar. Raspé. Children's Munchausen (Martin. *In* Ch. 11.)

Raspé. Tales from the travels of Baron Munchausen.

Siegfried. *See* Ring: Siegfried.

Siegfried and Handa. Graham. Welcome Christmas.

For other entries, see 2d edition.

Siegfried slays the dragon. *See* Ring: Siegfried.

Siegfried the dragon slayer. Olcott. Wonder tales from goblin hills.

Siegfried with the horny skin. Fuller. Book of dragons. (Legend of Drachenfels.)

For other entries, see 2d edition.

Sif's golden hair. *See* Dwarf's gifts.

Signora Lupa and the fig tree. Davis. Truce of the wolf.
See also Bear and the little old woman ; Bear's bad bargain.
Signs of baby. Coe. Third book of stories.
Sigrid the haughty. Dunlap. Stories of the Vikings. (*In*
Ring in the temple door.)
Sigrid's revenge. Dunlap. Stories of the Vikings.
Sigurd the Volsung. Bulfinch. Golden age. (Signy and
Sigmund. *In* Ch. 40.)
Colum. Fountain of youth. (Story of Sigurd.)
Coussens. Diamond story book. (Sigurd.)
Cruse. Young folk's book of epic heroes. (Sigurd.)
Johnson and Scott. Anthology of children's literature.
(Sigurd's youth.)
Power. Bag o' tales. (How Sigurd won the hand of Bryn-
hild.)
For other entries, see 2d edition.
Silencer. Denton. Homespun stories.
Silent cavalier. Eells. Islands of magic.
Silent drum. Cozad. Story talks.
Silent pool. Henderson. Wonder tales of Alsace-Lorraine.
Silent princess #.
See also Girl who transposed the heads of husband and
brother ; King and the apple ; Watchmaker.
Sili go dwt #.
See also Rumpelstiltskin.
Silken meadow. Williams. Jolly old whistle.
Silkworm. I. Lansing. Great moments in science. (Chi-
nese princess and her silk dress.)
See also Princess who liked silken robes.
For other entries, see 2d edition.
Silkworm. II (poem). Cooper. Argosy of fables.
Silkworm and the spider. I. Æsop. Fables (Whitman
ed.).
(poem). Argosy of fables.
For other entries, see 2d edition.
Silkworm and the spider. II. Cooper. Argosy of fables.
(Spider and the silk worm.)
For other entries, see 2d edition.
Silkworm and the spider. I–II. *See also* Spider's web.
Sillie Willy. *See* Midridge, Myth of.
Silly little woodpecker. Bacon. Lion-hearted kitten.
Silly Matt. Lee. Folk tales of all nations.
For other entries, see 2d edition.
Silly men and cunning wives. Lee. Folk tales of all na-
tions.
See also Believing husbands # ; Mad man, the dead man, and
the devil.
For other entries, see 2d edition.
Silly weaver girl. Lee. Folk tales of all nations.
See also Farmer's ass ; Three sillies.
Silly Will. I. Mitchell. Here and now story book.
Silly Will. II. *See* Midridge, Myth of.

Silver and gold. Gate. Tales from the secret kingdom.
Silver arrow. *See* Robin Hood.
Silver cones #.
See also Golden fir cones.
Silver florin, Story of. Hauff. Arabian days' entertainment. (Prophecy of the silver florin.)
For other entries, see 2d edition.
Silver flute. Boggs and Davis. Three golden oranges.
See also Friar and the boy.
Silver fox, Story of. Browne. Indian nights.
Silver magic. Gunterman. Castles in Spain.
Silver maple. Tuttle. Frightened tree. (Rain tree.)
Silver pennies. *See* Pixies' vengeance. II.
Silver peso. Broomell. Children's story caravan.
Silver pool. *See* How Finn obtained the tooth of knowledge.
Silver rose. I. Blaisdell. Rhyme and story second reader.
Silver rose. II. Henderson. Wonder tales of Alsace-Lorraine.
Silver saucer and the crystal apple. Ransome. Old Peter's Russian tales. (Tale of the silver saucer and the transparent apple.)
For other entries, see 2d edition.
Silver, silver. Potter. Captain Sandman.
Sim Chung, the filial daughter. *See* Dutiful daughter.
Simo the dolphin. Price. Legends of the seven seas.
See also Ape and the dolphin.
Simonides and Scopas. Bulfinch. Golden age. (Simonides. *In* Ch. 25.)
Simple Peter. *See* Peronnik, Adventures of.
Simple Simon. Kipling. Rewards and fairies.
Simpleton. I–II. *See* 2d edition.
Simpleton. III. Lee. Folk tales of all nations. (Story of a simpleton.)
See also Tiger and the frog.
Sin of the Prince Bishop. Canton. Child's book of saints. Smith and Hazeltine. Christmas in legend and story.
See also Ox that helped.
Sinbad the sailor, Story of. Arabian nights (Eliot). Arthur Rackham fairy book.
Barry and Hanna. Wonder flights of long ago. (Sinbad's second voyage.)
Kinscella. Music appreciation readers. Book 6. (Second voyage. Adapted.)
McDonald. Dick and the spice cupboard. (First to fourth voyages. Abridged. *In* Dick's fifth adventure.)
Miller. My book of history. v. 4. (Second voyage. Abridged. *In* Ch. 4.)
Patten. Junior classics. v. 5.
Price. Legends of the seven seas. (Fifth voyage. Adapted.)
Rich. Read-aloud book. (Voyages of Sinbad the sailor: First, second, and fifth voyages.)
See also Shipwrecked sailor.

Sinbad the sailor, Story of—*continued.*
For other entries, see 2d edition.
"Sing it." Hartshorne. Training for worship. (George and Willie.)
Singh Rajah and the cunning little jackals. *See* Little jackals and the lion.
Singing beggar. Egan. New found tales.
Singing bell. Starbuck. Far horizons.
Wahlenberg. Old Swedish fairy tales.
Singing bone #.
See also Bright sun brings it to light # ; Magic fiddle. II ; Maple flute ; Silver saucer and the crystal apple # ; Waving Locks ; Willow tree. II ; Will on the wind.
Singing competition. Fyleman. Forty good-night tales.
Singing fever. No. 2 Joy Street.
Singing goblins. Olcott. Wonder tales from goblin hills.
See also Knockgraften, Legend of.
Singing sack. Lee. Folk tales of all nations.
For other entries, see 2d edition.
Singing, soaring lark. *See* Soaring lark.
Singing spring. James. Tewa firelight tales.
Singing sword. *See* Kalevide of Estland.
Sinterklaas and Pieterbaas. *See* St. Nicholas.
Sintram's dragon. Guerber. Legends of Switzerland. (*In* Bern.)
Sinuhe, Adventures of. Baikie. Wonder tales of the ancient world.
**Frazer's magazine. 1865, p. 185. (Story of Saneha.)
**Maspero. Popular stories of ancient Egypt. (Memoirs of Sinuhit.)
Miller. My book of history. v. 1. (*In* Ch. 8.)
Sinuhit, Memoirs of. *See* Sinuhe, Adventures of.
Sir Accalon. Curry and Clippinger. Children's literature. (Arthur and Sir Accalon.)
For other entries, see 2d edition.
Sir Beaumains. *See* Sir Gareth.
Sir Bevis. Barbour. English tales retold. (Bevis of Hampton.)
For other entries, see 2d edition.
Sir Bobbie. Cabot. Course in citizenship.
Sir Buzz. Williston. Hindu stories. (Little buzz-man.)
For other entries, see 2d edition.
Sir Cleges, Tale of. Coussens. Diamond story book. (Sir Cleges and the cherries.)
Darton. Wonder book of old romance. (Sir Cleges and the cherries.)
Van Buren and Bemis. Christmas in storyland.
See also Dummling's request.
For other entries, see 2d edition.
Sir Degore and the broken sword. Darton. Wonder book of old romance.

Sir Ector. Burt. Lanier book. (King Arthur and his knights: Sir Ector and Sir Turquine.)

Sir Galahad. Evans. Worth while stories.

McVenn. Good manners and right conduct. Book 2.

For other entries, see 2d edition.

Sir Gamelyn. Farjeon. Tales from Chaucer. (Cook's tale of Gamelyn.)

For other entries, see 2d edition.

Sir Gammer Vans. Williams-Ellis. Fairies and enchanters.

For other entries, see 2d edition.

Sir Gareth. Allen. Tales from Tennyson. (Gareth and Lynette.)

Bailey. Stories of great adventures. (Beaumains, the knight of the kitchen.)

Burt. Lanier book. (King Arthur and his knights: Sir Beaumains and the black knight.)

Elson and Keck. Junior high school literature. (Story of Gareth.)

For other entries, see 2d edition.

Sir Gawain and the King of Man. Lanier. Book of giants. (Turke and Gawain.)

Sir Gawain's marriage. I (poem). Barbour. English tales retold. (Marriage of Sir Gawain.)

For other entries, see 2d edition.

Sir Gawain's marriage. II. Richardson. Stories from old English poetry. (Knight's dilemma.)

Farjeon. Tales from Chaucer. (Wife of Bath's tale.)

Williams-Ellis. Fairies and enchanters. (Ill-formed bride.)

For other entries, see 2d edition.

Sir Geoffrey. Dorey. Three and the moon. (Fabulous tale of Geoffrey, son of Dovon, knight of the Round Table.)

Sir Geraint. Allen. Tales from Tennyson. (Marriage of Geraint.)

Bailey. Stories of great adventures. (Geraint and Enid.)

For other entries, see 2d edition.

Sir Guyon's great adventure. Bailey. Stories of great adventures.

Sir Iwain. *See* Knight with the lion.

Sir Lancelot. Elson and Keck. Junior high school literature. (Peerless knight Lancelot.)

Rich. Read-aloud book. (Launcelot of the lake.)

For other entries, see 2d edition.

Sir Lancelot and Elaine. Allen. Tales from Tennyson.

For other entries, see 2d edition.

Sir Launcelot and Tarquin. Lanier. Book of giants.

Sir Launfal. Evans. Worth while stories. (Vision of Sir Launfal.)

Sir Launfal and the fairy princess. Barbour. English tales retold.

Sir Lazarus and the dragons. *See* Stan Bolovan.

Sir One Long Body and Madame Thousand Feet. Metzger. Tales told in Korea. (Broken engagement.)
For other entries, see 2d edition.
Sir Patrick Spens (poem). Johnson and Scott. Anthology of children's literature.
(poem). Power. Children's treasure chest.
For other entries, see 2d edition.
Sir Percival. Menefee. Child stories. (Parsifal.)
For other entries, see 2d edition.
Sir Topas, Tale of (poem). Farjeon. Tales from Chaucer.
Sir Turquine. Burt. Lanier book. (King Arthur and his knights: Sir Ector and Sir Turquine.)
For other entries, see 2d edition.
Sir Yvain. Lanier. Book of giants. (Adventures of Yvain.)
Sister Hen and the crocodile. Brown. Curious book of birds.
Sister without a name. *See* Hans the hunter.
Sisters. Richards. More five minute stories.
Sit Bdour and the Sultan Joseph. Katibah. Other Arabian nights. (Sit Bdour and the Sultan Joseph beyond the seven seas.)
See also Lost child. I.
Sita and Rama. *See* Rama.
Sita's birth, Story of. Mukerji. Rama.
Six and four are ten. Gordon and Stockard. Gordon readers. 2d reader.
For other entries, see 2d edition.
Six boys go to the star country. Sexton. Gray wolf stories.
Six men of Indostan. *See* Blind men and the elephant.
Six princesses of Thrace. *See* St. Patrick.
Six servants. *See* Five servants.
Six sirens. Browne. Indian nights.
Six Swabians. *See* Seven Swabians.
Six swans. Grimm. Fairy tales (Olcott).
Williams. Tales from Ebony.
Wilson. Red magic.
For other entries, see 2d edition.
Skadi. *See* How Skadi chose her husband.
Skald from Iceland. Dunlap. Stories of the Vikings.
Skillywidden. *See* Fairy caught.
In 2d edition there are entries under each title.
Skin and bones. Morris. Gypsy story teller.
Skippy is in the milk. La Rue. Under the story tree.
See also Spider and the flea.
Skitter cat. Harper and Hamilton. Winding roads.
Skrymsli. Pyle. Tales from Norse mythology. (How Loki saved a peasant's son.)
For other entries, see 2d edition.
Skull that saved the girl. Rasmussen. Eagle's gift.
Skunk. Linderman. Kootenai why stories. (Skunk-person.)

Skunny Wundy. Harper. More story-hour favorites.
Parker. Skunny Wundy and other Indian tales. (Skunny Wundy tricks Old Fox.)
Sky bridge of birds. Carey. Stories of the birds. (Magpies and the river of stars.)
Henderson and Calvert. Wonder tales of old Japan. (Tanabata-Matsuri.)
Kinney. Stars and their stories. (Weaving lady of the Milky Way.)
Miller. My travelship: Japan. (Herdboy and the weaver.)
Olcott. Wonder tales from China seas. (Magpie bridge o'er the silver stream of heaven.)
Phillips. Far peoples. (Tanabata.)
Williamson. Stars through magic casements. (Star lovers.)
See also Maiden of the milky way.
For other entries, see 2d edition.
Sky=goer and earth=goer. Egan. New found tales.
Sky High and Cloud Beard. Topelius. Canute Whistlewinks.
Sky spangles. Metzger. Tales told in Hawaii.
See also Earth and the sky.
Skyscraper to the moon and . . . the green rat. Sandburg. Rootabaga pigeons.
Skyway of the warriors. Seredy. Good master. (*In* Ch. 7.)
See also Milky way. III; Miraculous stag.
Slanderer. White. School management, p. 267.
Slapdash and Slambang. Potter. Captain Sandman.
See also Hinzelmann.
Slave and the lion. *See* Androcles and the lion.
Slave or son. Schwarz. Jewish caravan. (*In* Wise judge.)
Gaer. Burning bush. (*In* Boy judge.)
See also Haughty slave.
Slave's fortune. Schwarz. Jewish caravan. (*In* Reward of wisdom.)
Wells. How the present came from the past. Book 2, pt. 2. (Lawful heir.)
For other entries, see 2d edition.
Slayer of giants. Hogner. Navajo winter nights.
Slaying of the boar. *See* St. James of Spain.
Sleep of one hundred years. **Gaster. Ma'aseh book. v. 1. (Honi-ha-Me'aggel and his seventy-year-long sleep.)
For other entries, see 2d edition.
Sleeping beauty. I. Adams and Atchinson. Book of princess stories.
Arthur Rackham fairy book.
Bruce. Treasury of tales for little folk.
Cady and Dewey. Picture stories from the great artists.
Curry and Clippinger. Children's literature. (Rose-bud.)
De La Mare. Told again.
Evans. Worth while stories.
Faulkner. Road to enchantment.

Sleeping beauty. I—*continued.*
 Grimm. Fairy tales (Olcott. Little Briar-rose.)
 Harper. Magic fairy tales.
 Hutchinson. Chimney corner fairy tales. (Briar Rose.)
 Johnson and Scott. Anthology of children's literature.
  (Briar Rose.)
 Lang. Old friends among the fairies. (Sleeping Beauty in
  the wood.)
 Mackenzie. Book of nursery tales.
 Power. Bag o' tales.
 Power. Blue caravan tales.
 Quinn. Stokes' wonder book of fairy tales.
 Starbuck. Familiar haunts.
 Told under the green umbrella.
 Whiteman. Playmates in print.
 See also Knoonie in the sleeping palace.
 For other entries, see 2d edition.
Sleeping Tsarevna and the seven giants. Zeitlin. Skazki.
 See also Little sister of the giants # ; Snow-White and the
  seven dwarfs.
Sleepy Hollow, Legend of. Elson and Keck. Junior high
  school literature.
 For other entries, see 2d edition.
Sleepy story #.
 See also Go-to-sleep story ; Santa Claus' sleepy story.
Sleepytown palace. Potter. Giant of Apple Pie Hill.
Slice of tongue. Coussens. Diamond story book.
 See also Merchant of Venice.
 For other entries, see 2d edition.
Slipfoot. Sandburg. Rootabaga pigeons.
Slippers of Abdul of Kazan. White. Made in Russia. (*In*
  Ch. 5.)
Slippers of misfortune. Katibah. Other Arabian nights.
  (Shoes of Abu Kasim.)
 Williams. Tales from Ebony.
Slippers of the king. Mukerji. Rama. (Bharata's quest.)
 For other entries, see 2d edition.
Slow, the weaver. Broomell. Children's story caravan.
 Lee. Folk tales of all nations.
Slowboy and the blue goblins. Burnett. Children's book.
Small beginnings (poem). Patten. Junior classics. v. 10.
  (poem). Mackay. Poems.
Small story. Bailey. Story-telling hour.
Smart young tiger. Shimer. Fairyland.
 See also What is a man # ; Wolf and the blacksmith ; Wolf
  and the man #.
 For other entries, see 2d edition.
   In 2d edition this story is also indexed under the title
  "Tiger and the man."
Smiling Pool kindergarten. Burgess. Adventures of old
  Mr. Toad. Ch. 9.
 Johnson and Scott. Anthology of children's literature.

Smith and his dog. *See* Blacksmith and his dog.
Smith and the demon. *See* Smith and the devil. II.
Smith and the devil. I. *See* 2d edition.
Smith and the devil. II. Ralston. Russian fairy tales. (Smith and demon.)
> *See also* Priest with the envious eyes. I.
> For other entries, see 2d edition.
Smoke. Fyleman. Tea time tales.
> *See also* Smoker.
Smoke tree. Tuttle. Frightened tree. (Fire-ball dwarf tree.)
Smoker. Lebermann. New German fairy tales.
> *See also* Smoke.
Smoking. *See* Medicine pipe; Pipe of peace; Water pipe.
Smoking mirror. Martinez Del Rio. Sun, the moon and a rabbit.
Smolicheck. Nemcova. Disobedient kids. (About Smolinek.)
> For other entries, see 2d edition.
Snail and the monkey. Cooper. Argosy of fables.
Snail and the rose=tree. Harriman. Stories for little children. (Adapted.)
> For other entries, see 2d edition.
Snail, the red ant, and the shrimp. De Leeuw. Java jungle tales.
Snake #.
> *See also* Enchanted snake; Snake prince.
Snake and Jupiter. Æsop. Fables (Jones).
Snake and the crow. *See* Crow and the snake. II.
Snake and the hedgehog. *See* Porcupine and the snakes.
> In 2d edition there are entries under each title.
Snake and the lizard. Cooper. Argosy of fables.
Snake in the water. *See* Snake that the boy made.
Snake ogre. Lee. Folk tales of all nations.
> Spence. Myths of the North American Indians. (*In* Ch. 5.)
> For other entries, see 2d edition.
Snake prince #.
> *See also* Girl who took a snake for a husband; King Lindorm #; Snake #.
Snake princess. Zeitlin. Skazki. (Snake-Tsarevna.)
> For other entries, see 2d edition.
Snake that the boy made. Egan. New found tales.
> Purnell. Merry frogs. (Snake-in-the-water.)
Snake, the dog and the cat. Lee. Folk tales of all nations.
> *See also* Magic ring. I.
Snake=Tsarevna. *See* Snake princess.
Snake who became the king's son=in=law. *See* Enchanted snake.
Snake=wife. Spence. Myths of the North American Indians. (*In* Ch. 5.)
Snake with two heads. *See* Tail of the serpent. II.

Snake's thanks. **Gaster. Ma'aseh book. v. 1. (Old man and the snake and the judgment of Solomon.)
See also Camel driver and the adder.
For other entries, see 2d edition.
Snap=dragons. Fyleman. Forty good-night tales.
For other entries, see 2d edition.
Snapper brothers. Meeker. Folk tales from the Far East.
See also Chicken-Little.
Sneezer of Englebelmer. Chamoud. Picture tales from the French.
Snegorotchka. *See* Snowflake. I.
Snooks family and the candle. Williams. Tales from Ebony.
See also Twist-mouth family #.
Snorra Sturluson. Dunlap. Stories of the Vikings. (Skald from Iceland.)
Snow and the steeple. Raspé. Children's Munchausen (Martin. *In* Ch. 2.)
Raspé. Tales from the travels of Baron Munchausen.
Snow=drop. *See* Snow-White and the seven dwarfs.
Snow image. Arnold. Folk tales retold. (Little snow girl. Abridged.)
Bailey. Tell me another story. (Adapted.)
See also Snowflake. I.
For other entries, see 2d edition.
Snow lodge. Spence. Myths of the North American Indians. (*In* Ch. 3.)
Snow maiden. I. *See* Snowflake. I.
Snow maiden. II. Cross. Music stories.
See also Snowflake. I.
Snow man. I. Andersen. Fairy tales (Stickney). v. 2.
Shimer. Fairyland.
For other entries, see 2d edition.
Snow man. II. Harriman. Stories for little children. (Snowman.)
For other entries, see 2d edition.
Snow man and the snowdrops. Bowman. Little brown bowl.
See also Scarecrow and the snow man.
Snow=man husband. Spence. Myths of the North American Indians. (*In* Ch. 3.)
See also Girl who rejected her cousin #.
Snow queen. Andersen. Fairy tales (Siewers tr.).
Andersen. Fairy tales (Stickney). v. 1.
See also Three queens of winter.
For other entries see 2d edition.
Snow=White. I. *See* Snowflake. I.
Snow=White. II. *See* Snow-White and the seven dwarfs.
Snow=White and Rose=Red. Curry and Clippinger. Children's literature.
Faulkner. Road to enchantment.
Grimm. Fairy tales (Olcott).

Snow-White and Rose-Red—*continued.*
Grimm. Tales from Grimm (Wanda Gag).
Harper. Magic fairy tales.
Hutchinson. Chimney corner fairy tales.
Johnson and Scott. Anthology of children's literature.
Lang. Old friends among the fairies.
Quinn. Stokes' wonder book of fairy tales. (Rose-Red and Rose-White.)
Williams. Tales from Ebony.
For other entries, see 2d edition.
Snow-White and the seven dwarfs. De La Mare. Told again. (Snow-White.)
Faulkner. Road to enchantment. (Fair Snow-White.)
Grimm. Fairy tales (Olcott. Little Snow-White.)
Hutchinson. Chimney corner fairy tales. (Snowdrop and the seven little dwarfs.)
Johnson and Scott. Anthology of children's literature. (Snow-drop.)
Mackenzie. Book of nursery tales. (Snowdrop.)
Quinn. Stokes' wonder book of fairy tales. (Little Snow-White.)
Starbuck. Familiar haunts. (Little Snow-White.)
Shimer. Fairyland.
Williams. Tales from Ebony. (Snow-White.)
See also Magic hair pins # ; Queen of night; Sleeping Tsarevna and the seven giants.
For other entries, see 2d edition.
Snowball that didn't melt. Perkins and Danielson. Mayflower program book.
Skinner. Child's book of country stories.
For other entries, see 2d edition.
Snowbird and the water tiger. Spence. Myths of the North American Indians. (Malicious mother-in-law. *In* Ch. 3.)
Snowdrop. I. *See* 2d edition.
Snowdrop. II. See Snow-White and the seven dwarfs.
Snowdrop. III. *See* First snowdrops.
Snowdrop. IV. *See* Why the snow is white.
Snowdrops of Bride. *See* Coming of Angus and Bride.
Snowflake. I. Dulac. Edmund Dulac's fairy book. (Snegorotchka.)
Faulkner. Road to enchantment. (Snow maiden.)
Fleming. Round the world in folk tales. (Snow maiden.)
Ransome. Old Peter's Russian tales. (Little daughter of the snow.)
Tappan. Little lady in green. (Snowwhite.)
See also Snow image ; Snow maiden. II.
For other entries, see 2d edition.
Snowflake. II. *See* 2d edition.
Snowflake. III. Evans. Worth while stories.
See also Wolf and the seven little kids.
For other entries, see 2d edition.

Snowman. *See* Snow man.
Snowwhite. I. *See* Snow-White and the seven dwarfs.
Snowwhite. II. *See* Snowflake. I.
So=bee=yit. Harper. Ghosts and goblins.
  Harper. More story-hour favorites.
  See also Iktomi's blanket; Rolling stone.
So big and so little. Olcott. Wonder tales from windmill
  lands.
So born, so die. Cooper. Argosy of fables. (Mouse meta-
  morphosed into a girl.)
  Lee. Folk tales of all nations. (Mouse that was turned
  into a maiden.)
  See also Rats and their son-in-law.
  For other entries, see 2d edition.
So=so. *See* Just as well.
Soap bubble. Wahlenberg. Old Swedish fairy tales.
Soaring lark. Grimm. Fairy tales (Olcott. Singing, soar-
  ing lark.)
  For other entries, see 2d edition.
Socrates. Miller. My book of history. v. 2. (*In* Ch. 5.)
Socrates and his house (poem). Cooper. Argosy of fables.
  (Saying of Socrates.)
  For other entries, see 2d edition.
Sodewa Bai. Pyle. Fairy tales from India.
  For other entries, see 2d edition.
Sohrab and Rustem. Cruse. Young folk's book of epic
  heroes. (Rustem.)
  Lee. Folk tales of all nations. (Sohrab, child of many
  smiles; Death of Sohrab.)
  See also Zal and Rustem.
  For other entries, see 2d edition.
Soldier and his horse. Æsop. Fables (Jones).
  Æsop. Fables (Whitman ed. Knight and his charger.)
  Cooper. Argosy of fables. (Horse and his rider.)
  See also King and the horses that turned the mills.
Soldier and the demons. Zeitlin. Skazki.
  See also Knapsack #.
Soldier and the vampire. Ralston. Russian fairy tales.
Soldier who had served two years. Dane. Once there was
  and was not.
Soldier who lived in the drum. Kinscella. Music apprecia-
  tion readers. Book 2.
  For other entries, see 2d edition.
Soldier's midnight watch. Ralston. Russian fairy tales.
  See also Princess in the chest.
Soldier's soup. Kovalsky and Putnam. Long-legs, Big-
  mouth, Burning-eyes.
  See also Old woman and the tramp. Stone broth.
Solomon. *See* King Solomon.
Solomon and Ashmedai. *See* King Solomon and the demon.
Solomon and the birds. *See* King Solomon and the birds.
Solomon playing chess. **Gaster. Ma'aseh book. v. 2.

Solomon's ghost. Cooper. Argosy of fables.
Solon. Curry and Clippinger. Children's literature. (Croesus and Solon.)
Some voices from the kitchen garden. *See* In the kitchen garden.
Somebody's mother. White. School management, p. 251.
Something to think about. *See* Lincoln, Abraham.
Son of Adam. Coussens. Diamond story book.
　Faulkner. Road to enchantment. (Little bird.)
　See also Jane, Jane, don't complain.
　For other entries, see 2d edition.
Son of Anak. *See* Goliath.
Son of strength. MacManus. Lo, and behold ye!
　See also Jack and his master; Keep cool #.
Son of Ulé. Eells. Magic tooth.
Song of Roland. *See* Roland. II.
Song of the flute. Harriman. Stories for little children.
Song of the fox. *See* Fox sings. II.
Song of the mice. Cendrars. Little black stories.
Song of the minster. Canton. Child's book of saints.
Song of the pestle. Metzger. Tales told in Korea.
Song of the sirens. *See* Ulysses and the sirens.
Song of the spring. Bailey. Tell me another story.
　See also Flute music.
Song of the wolf. *See* Wolf sings.
Song that traveled. Perkins and Danielson. Second year Mayflower program book.
　For other entries, see 2d edition.
Song with riddles in it. Lindsay. Choosing book.
Sonless king. Chrisman. Wind that wouldn't blow.
Sons of Aymon. Echols. Knights of Charlemagne. (Passing of Roland and Reinold; Reinold and Bayard.)
　For other entries, see 2d edition.
Sons of Doel Dermait. Gregory. Cuchulain of Muirthemne.
　See also Destruction of Da Derga's hostel.
Sons of St. George. Darton. Seven champions of Christendom.
Soothsayer. I. *See* 2d edition.
Soothsayer. II. Garnett. Ottoman wonder tales.
Sorcerer and the apprentice. *See* Sorcerer's apprentice.
Sorcerer's apprentice. Cross. Music stories.
　Kinscella. Music appreciation readers. Book 4. (Sorcerer and the apprentice.)
　See also Master and his pupil. I.
Sorceress. Æsop. Fables (Whitman ed.).
　For other entries, see 2d edition.
Soreghina. Wolff. Pale mountains. (Children of the sun, pt. 2.)
Soria Moria Castle. Dasent. East of the sun and west of the moon (Nielsen).
　Rasmussen. East o' the sun and west o' the moon.
　For other entries, see 2d edition.

Sorrow #.
See also Gore Gorinskoe.
Sorrowful death of Usna's sons. *See* Deirdre.
Sorrowful tree. Tuttle. Frightened tree and other stories.
Soul of the great bell. *See* Great bell.
Soul that was permitted to revisit the earth. *See* Judas Iscariot.
Soup from a sausage skewer. Andersen. Fairy tales (Stickney). v. 2.
For other entries, see 2d edition.
Sour grapes. I. *See* Fox and the grapes.
Sour grapes. II. Olcott. Wonder tales from pirate isles. (*In* String of pearls.)
Soussanin, Ivan. Kinscella. Music appreciation readers. Book 6. (Life for the Tsar.)
South wind, Tale of. Carpenter. Tales of a Basque grandmother.
See also How summer came to the earth. III.
Sovereign of the mineral kingdom. Cowles. Stories to tell. (Bread of gold. Adapted.)
See also Midas. I; Precious gem palace; Stone curse. I.
For other entries, see 2d edition.
Sowittan, the grumbler. *See* Grumbler.
Sozh and Dnieper. *See* Dnieper and Sozh.
Spae woman. Colum. King of Ireland's son.
Spaeman, Story of. Colum. Big tree of Bunlahy. (Story of the Spaeman.)
Spaniel and the mastiff. Æsop. Fables (Whitman ed.).
Spanish savage. Martinez Del Rio. Sun, the moon and a rabbit.
Spare moments. White. School management, p. 275.
Spark neglected burns the house. Cabot. Course in citizenship.
Sparrow. *See* Tongue-cut sparrow.
Sparrow and the bush. I. *See* 2d edition.
Sparrow and the bush. II. Carrick. Still more Russian picture tales. (Sparrow and the blade of grass.)
Sparrow and the eagle. *See* King of the birds. III.
Sparrow and the washerwoman. *See* Tongue-cut sparrow.
Sparrow, the woodpecker, the fly, the frog and the elephant. Cooper. Argosy of fables.
See also Dog and the sparrow.
Sparrow whose tongue was clipped. *See* Tongue-cut sparrow.
Sparrows. Cooper. Argosy of fables.
Sparrows and the falcon. Mackenzie. Jackal in Persia. (Sparrows and the salamander.)
See also Crow and the snake. II; Sparrows and the snake #.
For other entries, see 2d edition.
Spartacus the slave. Cooke. Stories of Rome.

Spartan respect for the aged. White. School management, p. 260.
Speak gently. White. School management, p. 243.
Speaking bird. McNeer and Lederer. Tales from the crescent moon.
Speaking grapes, the smiling apple, and the tinkling apricot. Lee. Folk tales of all nations.
See also Beauty and the beast.
Spear of victory. Young. Celtic wonder tales.
Specialist in food, specialist in women, and the specialist in cotton. Ryder. Twenty-two goblins.
See also Princess on the pea.
Speckled axe. Cozad. Story talks. (*In* Benjamin Franklin.)
Spectacles. Cooper. Argosy of fables.
For other entries, see 2d edition.
Specter of Valorbes bridge. Guerber. Legends of Switzerland. (*In* Legends of Vaud and Valais.)
Spectral ship. Hauff. Arabian days' entertainment.
For other entries, see 2d edition.
Speed. Mitchell. Here and now story book.
Spell of the seven lanterns. Darton. Seven champions of Christendom.
Spendthrift and the swallow. Æsop. Fables (Artzybasheff. Young man and the swallow.)
Æsop. Fables (Jones).
Æsop. Fables (Whitman ed.).
Cooper. Argosy of fables.
For other entries, see 2d edition.
Sperrit of Akaluga Junior. Mackaye. Tall tales of the Kentucky mountains.
Sphinx. Fleming. Round the world in folk tales. (*In* Ch. 11.)
Sphinx (Egyptian). I. St. Nicholas. February 1900, p. 282. (Story of the Sphinx.)
Sphinx (Egyptian). II. Lamprey. Wonder tales of architecture. (Lion of the Pharaohs.)
Sphinx (Greek). *See* Œdipus; Riddle of the Sphinx.
Spider. Lee. Folk tales of all nations.
Spider and the crows #.
See also Greedy spider and the magpies.
Spider and the flea#.
See also All for the death of a flea; Ant and the rat called "Jemez"; Perez the mouse. II; Skippy is in the milk.
Spider and the silkworm. *See* Silkworm and the spider. II.
Spider and two chiefs. *See* Spider, the hippopotamus, and the elephant.
Spider man. I. *See* 2d edition.
Spider man. II. *See* Indian's blanket. I.
Spider passes on a debt. Lee. Folk tales of all nations.

Spider, the guinea=fowl, and the francolin. *See* Spider's visit.

Spider, the hippopotamus, and the elephant. Berry. Black folk tales. (Spider and two chiefs.)
See also How the elephant and the whale were tricked.
For other entries, see 2d edition.

Spider web, Legend of. *See* Arachne.

Spider webs. Fyleman. Forty good-morning tales.

Spider which bought a dog for a slave. Lee. Folk tales of all nations.

Spider who went round the world. Fyleman. Tea time tales.

Spider woman. *See* Bumble-bees, tumble-weeds, and eagles.

Spider's visit. Berry. Black folk tales. (Another story of the spider.)
Lee. Folk tales of all nations. (Spider, the guinea-fowl, and the francolin.)
See also Dog and the sparrow; How the monkey and the goat earned their reputations; Leopard and the hare; Lion and the hyena.

Spider's web (poem). Cooper. Argosy of fables.
See also Silkworm and the spider. I–II.

Spindle, shuttle and needle. Evans. Worth while stories.
Grimm. Fairy tales (Olcott).
Grimm. Tales from Grimm (Wanda Gag).
For other entries, see 2d edition.

Spindle=tree. Housman. What-o'clock tales.

Spinning queen #.
See also Lazy queen.

Spinning sisters. Schwimmer. Tisza tales.

Spinning=wheel of Omphale. Cross. Music stories.
See also Hercules and his labors.

Spirit bride. *See* In the land of souls.

Spirit Chief names the animal people. Garett. Coyote stories.

Spirit of Christmas. Van Buren and Bemis. Christmas in storyland.
See also Ebenezer Scrooge's Christmas.

Spirit of the air helps a poor boy. Rasmussen. Eagle's gift.

Spirit of winter. *See* Old Winter Man and the Spring. I.

Spirit that lived in a tree. Johnson and Scott. Anthology of children's literature.
See also Selfish little tree.
For other entries, see 2d edition.

Spoiled sugar. *See* Sugar moon.

Spriggan's child (poem). Rhys. English fairy book.

Spring fragrance. *See* Faithful dancing-girl wife. I.

Spring in the forest. Ransome. Old Peter's Russian tales.

Spring maiden and the frost giants. *See* Iduna's apples.

Spring of forgetting. Wolff. Pale mountains.

Spring, Story of the. *See* Year, Story of.

Springtime, Story of. *See* Proserpina.
Squeaky and the scare box. Faulkner. Story lady's Christmas stories.
Walters. Book of Christmas stories.
For other entries, see 2d edition.
Squire's bride. Power. Bag o' tales.
For other entries, see 2d edition.
Squire's half=crown. Broomell. Children's story caravan.
Squire's tale. *See* Cambuscan bold, Story of.
Squirrel and the fox. Morris. Gypsy story teller.
See also True and Untrue.
Squirrel and the spider. Woodson. African myths.
Squirrel and the thrush. Cooper. Argosy of fables.
Squirrel, the east wind and the west wind. De Leeuw. Java jungle tales.
Stag and the cherry tree. Raspé. Children's Munchausen (Martin. *In* Ch. 19.)
Raspé. Tales from the travels of Baron Munchausen.
See also Peach-rocked deer.
Stag and the lion. I. *See* 2d edition.
Stag and the lion. II. Æsop. Fables (Jones).
Stag and the sheep. *See* Sheep, the wolf, and the stag.
Stag and the vine. Æsop. Fables (Jones).
Cooper. Argosy of fables. (Hart and the vine.)
For other entries, see 2d edition.
Stag at the lake. Æsop. Fables (Artzybasheff. Stag looking into the water.)
Æsop. Fables (Jones. Stag at the pool.)
Æsop. Fables (Whitman ed. Stag at the pool.)
Æsop. Twenty-four fables. (L'Estrange. Stag drinking.)
Cooper. Argosy of fables. (Stag at the pool.)
See also Pot of butter.
For other entries, see 2d edition.
Stag at the pool. *See* Stag at the lake.
Stag drinking. *See* Stag at the lake.
Stag in the ox=stall. Æsop. Fables (Jones).
Æsop. Fables (Whitman ed.).
Cooper. Argosy of fables.
Power. Children's treasure chest.
For other entries, see 2d edition.
Stag looking into the water. *See* Stag at the lake.
Stag, the crow and the jackal. **Arnold. Book of good counsels. (Jackal, deer and crow.)
Cooper. Argosy of fables. (Jackal, the deer and the crow.)
See also True friendship.
For other entries, see 2d edition.
In 2d edition this story is also indexed under the title, "Jackal, deer and the crow."
Stag with one eye. *See* One-eyed doe.
Stan Bolovan. Lee. Folk tales of all nations. (Sir Lazarus and the dragons.)
Morris. Gypsy story teller. (Gypsy and the dragon.)

Stan Bolovan—*continued.*
Wilson. Green magic.
See also Brave little tailor; Gipsy and the dragon. II.
For other entries, see 2d edition.
Star. Marzials. Stories for the story hour.
Star and a song. Cather. Pan and his pipes.
Star angel. Major. Merry Christmas stories.
Star bearer (poem). Smith and Hazeltine. Christmas in legend and story.
Star boy. I. *See* 2d edition.
Star boy. II. Field. American folk and fairy tales. (Falling star.)
For other entries, see 2d edition.
Star-boy and the sun dance. *See* Maid who married the morning star.
Star child. I. Bailey. Tell me another story.
For other entries, see 2d edition.
Star child. II. Gaer. Burning bush. (*In* Abram discovers God.)
For other entries, see 2d edition.
Star dipper. *See* Dipper.
Star dollars. Grimm. Fairy tales (Olcott. Star-money.)
Hervey and Hix. Fanciful tales for children. (Star money.)
See also Little stars of gold.
For other entries, see 2d edition.
Star Eye. Topelius. Canute Whistlewinks.
Star flowers. *See* Field of angels; Imps on the meadows of heaven; Star of Bethlehem.
Star in the East (play). Skinner. Christmas stories.
Star lovers. *See* Sky bridge of birds.
Star maiden. I. Gordon and Stockard. Gordon readers. 2d reader. (Coming of the water-lily.)
Harriman. Stories for little children. (Legend of the pond lily.)
Kinscella. Music appreciation readers. Book 3. (First water lily. Adapted.)
See also How the water-lily came. II.
For other entries, see 2d edition.
Star maiden. II. *See* 2d edition.
Star maiden. III. *See* Star wife.
Star money. *See* Star dollars.
Star of Bethlehem. Skinner. Christmas stories.
Star that watches the moon. Farjeon. Old sailor's yarn box.
Star tree. I. *See* 2d edition.
Star tree. II. Tuttle. Frightened tree and other stories.
Star wife. Spence. Myths of the North American Indians. (Star maiden. *In* Ch. 3.)
For other entries, see 2d edition.
Star wives. Lee. Folk tales of all nations. (Fairy wives.)
Spence. Myths of the North American Indians. '(Fairy wives. *In* Ch. 3.)

Star wives—*continued.*
For other entries, see 2d edition.
Starkad's vow. Adams. Swords of the Vikings.
Stars and the child. Proudfoot. Child's Christ-tales.
Skinner. Christmas stories.
Stars and the sky-rocket. Cooper. Argosy of fables.
Stars in the sky. Cousseus. Diamond story book.
Elson and Runkel. Child-library readers. Book 2.
Hervey and Hix. Fanciful tales for children.
For other entries, see 2d edition.
Stars, Stories of. *See* Bar Beach; Capella; Cassiopeia;
Great bear; How we got our first daisies; How stars and
fireflies were made; Inseparables; Matarika's eyes; Scor-
pion and his family; Sky bridge of birds; Star that
watches the moon; Seven brothers; Temple boy; also titles
beginning with the word star.
Stars with wings. Harriman. Stories for little children.
For other entries, see 2d edition.
Statue and the nun. Keller. Fat of the cat.
Statue of Lysippus. *See* Opportunity.
Steadfast tin soldier. *See* Brave tin soldier.
Stealing the springtime. Field. American folk and fairy
tales.
Linderman. Kootenai why stories.
See also How summer came to the earth. III.
Steed o' bells. *See* Black Thief and Knight of the Glen.
Steed of the muses. *See* Pegasus.
Steel lock. Baumbach. Tales from the Swiss alps.
Steelpacha. Dulac. Edmund Dulac's fairy book. (Bashi-
chelik; or, True steel.)
Wilson. Red magic (Bash-Chalek; or True steel.)
For other entries, see 2d edition.
Stephen, boy crusader. *See* Children's crusade.
Stephen the child crusader. *See* Children's crusade.
Stephenson, George. White. School management, p. 277.
(Courage in danger.)
Stevenson, Robert Louis. Forbes. Good citizenship.
(Road of the loving heart. *In* Ch. 2.)
Stikua, Myth of. *See* Punishment of the stingy.
Stilts, Origin of. Metzger. Tales told in Hawaii.
Sting me! *See* Fleamie and the hornets.
Stingy mudhens. *See* Secret of fire. I.
Stocking's story. Graham. Welcome Christmas.
Warner. Carl Krinken.
Stolen by the fairies. Howes. Long bright land.
Stolen Fourth. Burnett. Children's book.
Stolen maidens. *See* Sabine women and Roman wives.
Stolen ploughshares. *See* Country where the mice eat iron.
Stolen plow #. *See* Country where the mice eat iron.
In 2d edition there are entries under each title.
Stolen prince. I. *See* Dulcetta.
Stolen prince. II. Untermeyer. Last pirate.

Stolen princess. Adams and Atchinson. Book of princess
stories.
For other entries, see 2d edition.
**Stolen turnips, the magic tablecloth, the sneezing goat,
and the wooden whistle.** Power. Bag o' tales.
Ransome. Old Peter's Russian tales.
See also Table, the ass and the stick.
Stolen wings. Williams. Jolly old whistle.
Stone. Fyleman. Forty good-morning tales.
Stone broth #.
For other versions, *see* Old woman and the tramp; Rab-
bit and the rock soup; Soldier's soup.
Stone=cold heart. Hauff. Arabian days' entertainment.
(Cold heart.)
For other entries, see 2d edition.
Stone curse. I. Olcott. Wonder tales from windmill lands.
See also Midas. I; Stones in the kettle; Sovereign of the
mineral kingdom.
Stone curse. II. Guerber. Legends of Switzerland. (In
Basel).
Stone cutter. Faulkner. Little Peachling.
Harriman. Stories for little children. (Hofus the stone-
cutter.)
Power. Stories to shorten the road. (Hafiz the stonecut-
ter.)
See also All too hard.
For other entries, see 2d edition.
Stone giantess. Lanier. Book of giants.
Spence. Myths of the North American Indians. (*In* Ch. 4.)
Stone in the cock's head. Tappan. Little lady in green.
(Wishing ring.)
For other entries, see 2d edition.
In 2d edition this story is also indexed under the title
"Cock's stone."
Stone in the road. I. Piper. Folk tales children love.
Piper. Road in storyland.
For other entries, see 2d edition.
Stone lion. I. Davis. Baker's dozen.
Lee. Folk tales of all nations.
For other entries, see 2d edition.
Stone lion. II. *See* Two travellers. II #.
Stone monkey. Lee. Folk tales of all nations.
See also Ape Sun Wu Kung #; Arrogant ape and the sea
dragon; Feast of magic peaches.
Stone of Haninah. Vilnay. Legends of Palestine.
Stone of refuge, Legend of. Schwimmer. Tisza tales.
Stone oxen. *See* Ox that helped; Sin of the Prince Bishop.
Stone princess. Pogány. Hungarian fairy book.
Stone=Shirt and the One=Two. Morris. Stories from my-
thology: North American. (*In* Ch. 11.)
For other entries, see 2d edition.
Stone twins. Eells. Brazilian fairy book.

Stones in the kettle. Tappan. Little lady in green.
See also Miraculous pitcher; Stone curse. II.
Stones of Plouvinec. *See* Thirst of the standing stones.
Stoop as you go through. White. School management, p. 275.
Store that gave things away. Emerson. Merry-go-round of modern tales.
Stork and the heron. Curtin. Fairy tales of Eastern Europe.
Stork kalif. *See* Caliph Stork.
Stork, the goose and the hawk. Cooper. Argosy of fables.
Storks. Andersen. Fairy tales (Siewers tr.).
Andersen. Fairy tales (Stickney). v. 2.
For other entries, see 2d edition.
Stork's mistake. Burnett. Children's book.
Stork's thanks. Olcott. Wonder tales from windmill lands.
Storm and the cucumber trees. Raspé. Children's Munchausen (Martin. *In* Ch. 1.)
Raspé. Tales from the travels of Baron Munchausen.
Storm coming. Lee. Folk tales of all nations.
Storm ship. Irving. Bold dragoon. (*In* Dolph Heyliger.)
Story of a joyful song. *See* Pippa passes.
Story of, etc. *See* The first important word of the title.
Story=teller. I. *See* 2d edition.
Story=teller. II. Capuana. Italian fairy tales.
See also Fairy story-shop #.
Story=telling time. Hauff. Arabian days' entertainment. (Princess Fairy-Story in masquerade.)
Story that is all lies. Katibah. Other Arabian nights.
See also Bag of stories.
Story that shattered King Cormac's cup. Colum. Big tree of Bunlahy.
See also Black Thief and Knight of the Glen.
Story told by the keeper of the Pharos. *See* Alexandria, Founding of.
Stove that would not stay in the kitchen. Emerson. Merry-go-round of modern tales.
Strand of the bitter cry. *See* Syfaddon lake.
Strange adventures of a wood sled. Skinner. Christmas stories.
Strange godfather. Dane. Fate cries out. (Godfather Death. Adapted.)
For other entries, see 2d edition.
Strange people of Nuglesock. Snell. Told beneath the northern lights.
Strange quest. *See* Fair unknown.
Strange September. Falkberget. Broomstick and Snowflake.
Strange story of Mr. Dog and Mr. Bear. Van Buren and Bemis. Christmas in storyland.
Strange wedding gift. Olcott. Wonder tales from goblin hills.

Stranger. I. *See* 2d edition.
Stranger. II. No. 2 Joy Street.
Stranger child. I. *See* Christmas tree. I.
Stranger child. II. Skinner. Christmas stories. (German legend.)
   See also Christ child. III; Little match girl; Man in the Christmas moon.
Stranger child. III (poem). Campbell. Story of Christmas, p. 151. (Stranger child's Holy Christ.)
Stranger pigeon. Martin. Fatma was a goose.
Straw in the Virgin's eye. Brown. Curious book of birds. (Pious robin.)
   Carey. Stories of the birds.
Straw ox. Arnold. Folk tales retold.
   Carrick. More Russian picture tales.
   Curry and Clippinger. Children's literature.
   Hutchinson. Fireside stories.
   Lee. Folk tales of all nations.
   Told under the green umbrella.
   For other entries, see 2d edition.
Straw that broke the camel's back. *See* Old Hump.
Straw, the coal and the bean. Evans. Worth while stories.
   Johnson and Scott. Anthology of children's literature.
   King. Golden cat head. (Straw, coal, and bean.)
   See also Bubble, the shoe and the straw.
   For other entries, see 2d edition.
Stray cow. Gordon and Stockard. Gordon readers. 2d reader. (Fairy cow.)
   For other entries, see 2d edition.
Stream and its source. Cooper. Argosy of fables.
Street musicians. *See* Bremen town musicians.
Street of the Good Children. Crew. Saturday's children.
String of pearls. I. *See* 2d edition.
String of pearls. II. Olcott. Wonder tales from pirate isles.
Strong brother. Snell. Told beneath the northern lights.
Strong man and the dwarf. Lee. Folk tales of all nations.
   For other entries, see 2d edition.
Strong man, Story of. *See* Gilgamesh.
Strongest boy. *See* Kaulu.
Strongest man in the world. *See* Hercules and his labors.
Struggles of a self-made man. Miller. My book of history. v. 2. (*In* Ch. 7.)
Student who became king. Pogány. Magyar fairy tales.
   See also Princess on the pea.
Stuffed horse. Martinez Del Rio. Sun, the moon and a rabbit.
Stupid bear. *See* Bear says, North.
Stupid boy and the wand. Macmillan. Canadian wonder tales.
   See also Little Claus and Big Claus.
Stupid monkeys. *See* Monkey gardeners.

Stupid Peikko. Bowman and Bianco. Tales from a Finnish tupa.

Stupid princess. Adams and Atchinson. Book of princess stories.

For other entries, see 2d edition.

Stupid Tartaro. Carpenter. Tales of a Basque grandmother.

See also Are you not satisfied; Fanch Scouranac.

Stupid wolf. Bowman and Bianco. Tales from a Finnish tupa.

See also Fox and the geese.

Stupid's cries. Borski and Miller. Gypsy and the bear. (Ill luck.)

For other entries, see 2d edition.

Sturmi. Niemeyer. Stories for the history hour.

Subterranean adventure. Spence. Myths of the North American Indians. (*In* Ch. 5.)

Subway car. Mitchell. Here and now story book.

Sugar and flour. Retner. That's that.

Sugar cakes for a kitchen god. Rowe. Moon's birthday.

Sugar cock. Fyleman. Forty good-night tales. (Bag of goodies, pt. 3.)

Sugar moon; or, The spoiled sugar. Cook. To-day's stories of yesterday.

See also How maple sugar came.

Sugar temple. Wahlenberg. Old Swedish fairy tales.

Sumé. Eells. Magic tooth.

Summer birds of K'yakime. Nusbaum. Seven cities of Cibola.

Nusbaum. Zuni Indian tales.

Summoner and the fiend. Farjeon. Tales from Chaucer. (Friar's tale.)

For other entries, see 2d edition.

Summoner's tale. Farjeon. Tales from Chaucer.

Sun a prisoner. I. Field. American folk and fairy tales. (Boy and his sister.)

Macmillan. Canadian wonder tales. (Mouse and the sun.)

Power. Children's treasure chest. (Boy who set a snare for the sun.)

Power. How it happened. (Why the mouse is small and grey.)

For other entries, see 2d edition.

Sun a prisoner. II. Piper. Folk tales children love. (How little bunny rabbit caught the sun.)

Piper. Road in storyland. (How little bunny rabbit caught the sun.)

Spence. Myths of the North American Indians. (How the rabbit caught the sun. *In* Ch. 5.)

Morris. Stories from mythology: North American. (*In* Ch. 11.)

For other entries, see 2d edition.

Sun a prisoner. III–IV. *See* 2d edition.

Sun a prisoner. V. Howes. Long bright land. (Maui and the sun.)
Metzger. Tales told in Hawaii. (How Maui snared the sun.)
For other entries, see 2d edition.
Sun a prisoner. VI. Kennedy. Red man's wonder book. (Sun-catchers.)
See also Jack and the bean stalk.
Sun and the moon. I. Morris. Stories from mythology: North American. (*In* Ch. 2.)
For other entries, see 2d edition.
Sun and the moon. II. *See* 2d edition.
Sun and the moon. III. Gearhart. Skalalatoot stories. (Story of the sun and the moon.)
See also Why the moon waxes and wanes. I.
Sun and the moon. IV. Phillips. Far peoples.
Sun and the wind. *See* Wind and the sun.
Sun and wind. *See* Wind and the sun.
Sun=catchers. *See* Sun a prisoner. VI.
Sun children kill the great monsters. Spence. Myths of the North American Indians. (Sun children. *In* Ch. 2.)
See also Boys who went to the sun.
For other entries, see 2d edition.
Sun conqueror, Sanpati. Mukerji. Rama. (*In* Monkeys' quest of Sita.)
See also Etana and his flight to heaven.
Sun, moon and stars. I–VI. *See* 2d edition.
Sun, moon and stars. VII. Howes. Long bright land. (New light in the sky.)
Metzger. Tales told in Hawaii. (Origin of the moon.)
Sun, moon and stars. VIII. Washburne. Indian legends. (*In* Flight from the fourth to the fifth world.)
Hogner. Navajo winter nights. (Making of the sun and moon; Making the stars.)
Sun, moon and stars. IX. Pyle. Tales from Norse mythology. (Sun, moon and stars and day and night.)
See also Creation of the world (Norse) #.
Sun of earth. Martinez Del Rio. Sun, the moon and a rabbit.
See also Proserpina.
Sun of fire. Martinez Del Rio. Sun, the moon and a rabbit.
Sun of water. Martinez Del Rio. Sun, the moon and a rabbit.
See also Earth and the sky.
Sun of wind. Martinez Del Rio. Sun, the moon and a rabbit.
See also When the sun fell from the sky.
Sun pays a call. Kovalsky and Putnam. Long-legs, Big-mouth, Burning-eyes.
Sun, Stories of. *See* Marriage of the sun; Modest sisters; Why the sun shines by day and the moon by night; When the sun fell from the sky.

Sun, the moon and a rabbit. Martinez Del Rio. Sun, the moon and a rabbit.

Sunball. Capuana. Italian fairy tales.

Sunbeam sprites. Gunterman. Castles in Spain.
See also Luck fairies # ; Three little crones each with something big.

Sunbeams. *See* Hickamore and Hackamore.

Sunflower. Burnett. Children's book.

Sunken city. Hart. Picture tales from Holland. (Wonder-wheat of Stavoren.)
King. Golden cat head. (Sands of Stavoren; or, Woman-sand.)
Miller. My travelship: Holland. (Lady of Stavoren.)
Olcott. Wonder tales from windmill lands. (Wonder-wheat of the Lady-sand.)
See also Lake of Issarles; Proud princess; Sea-baby; Two cities; Two gifts. II ; Ys, Story of.
For other entries, see 2d edition.

Sunken city in Zug lake. Guerber. Legends of Switzerland. (*In* Legends of Zurich.)
See also Biburg See.

Sunken treasure. Patten. Junior classics. v. 7.
Hawthorne. Grandfather's chair, pt. 1, ch. 10.

Sunken village. Howes. Long bright land.
See also Baucis and Philemon.

Sunny Boy. Harriman. Stories for little children.

Sun's waning glory. Cooper. Argosy of fables.

Sunshine fairy. Evans. Worth while stories.

Sunshine fairies #.
See also Dwarfs and the fairies #.

Sunshine stories. Andersen. Fairy tales (Stickney). v. 1.
For other entries, see 2d edition.

Sunshine tree. Wahlenberg. Old Swedish fairy tales.

Supervisor's mistake. Burnett. Children's book.

Surabo. Chevalier. Noah's children. (Legend of Surabo.)

Sura's seeds. Eells. Magic tooth.
See also Deucalion and Pyrrha.

Surprise Christmas tree. Bailey. Wonderful tree.
Major. Merry Christmas stories.

Surprised boy. Cowles. Stories to tell.

Susan Walker, what a talker. *See* How a fish swam in the air and a hare in the water.

Susan's manners. Burnett. Children's book.

Swallow. I. *See* 2d edition.

Swallow. II. Rich. Why-so stories. (Navaho story of the swallow.)

Swallow and crow. *See* Swallow and the raven.

Swallow and his forked tail. *See* Why the swallow's tail is forked. I.

Swallow and the crow. Æsop. Fables (Jones).
See also Procne and Philomela.

Swallow and the other birds. Æsop. Fables (Artzyba-sheff).
Æsop. Fables (Whitman ed. Swallow and other birds.)
Cooper. Argosy of fables. (Swallow and other birds.)
See also Owl and the birds.
For other entries, see 2d edition.
Swallow and the raven. Æsop. Fables (Whitman ed. Swallow and crow.)
Cooper. Argosy of fables.
Curry and Clippinger. Children's literature.
For other entries, see 2d edition.
Swallow in chancery. Cooper. Argosy of fables.
Swallow king's rewards. Carey. Story of the birds. (Grateful sparrow.)
Phillips. Far peoples. (Two brothers.)
See also Moko and the twelve little earth men; Two melons.
For other entries, see 2d edition.
Swallow who was once a wicked mother-in-law. *See* Why the swallow's tail is forked. IV.
Swallows, Origin of. I. Carey. Stories of the birds. (Children who were changed into swallows.)
Rich. Why-so stories. (How the swallow came to be.)
For other entries, see 2d edition.
Swallows, Origin of. II–III. *See* 2d edition.
Swallows, Origin of. IV. *See* Procne and Philomela.
Swallows war against the snakes. *See* Birds go to war. III.
Swamp robin. Rich. Why-so stories. (Why the swamp-robin foretells rain.)
Swan. Æsop. Fables (Jones).
Swan and the cook. Cooper. Argosy of fables. (Swan and the goose.)
For other entries, see 2d edition.
Swan and the goose. *See* Swan and the cook.
Swan and the linnet (poem). Cooper. Argosy of fables.
For other entries, see 2d edition.
Swan maidens. I #.
See also Lovely one out of the sky.
Swan maidens. II. *See* Fairy swan-maidens.
Swan Peter. Henderson. Wonder tales of Alsace-Lorraine.
Swan, the pike and the crab (poem). Curry and Clippinger. Children's literature.
Swanwhite and Ragner. Adams. Swords of the Vikings. (Warrior Princess.)
Swan's nest. I. *See* 2d edition.
Swan's nest. II (poem). Browning. Poems.
(poem). Patten. Junior classics. v. 10. (Romance of the swan's nest.)
Swastika egg devils. Noel. Magic bird of Chomo-lung-ma.
Sweet gum tree. Tuttle. Frightened tree. (Star tree.)
Sweet lavender. Marzials. Stories for the story hour.
Sweet porridge. *See* Wonderful porridge pot.

Sweet stringed dulcimer. *See* Tsarevich Ivan and the harp that harped without a harper.

Sweetheart bewitched. *See* Jorinde and Joringel.

Sweetheart of the flowers. Metzger. Tales told in Hawaii.

Swineherd. Andersen. Fairy tales (Stickney). v. 2.
Andersen. Fairy tales (Siewers tr.).
Johnson and Scott. Anthology of children's literature.
For other entries, see 2d edition.

Swiss Marathon. Guerber. Legends of Switzerland. (*In* Fribourg.)
See also First Marathon race.

Swiss wood carver. Evans. Worth while stories.

Switez lake. Cross. Music stories.

Swithin, St. *See* St. Swithin.

Swollen fox. Æsop. Fables (Jones).
Cooper. Argosy of fables.

Sword and the spit (poem). Cooper. Argosy of fables.
See also Sword blade #.

Sword in the stone. *See* King Arthur's coming.

Sword of light. I. *See* Morraha.

Sword of light. II. Colum. King of Ireland's son. (Sword of light and the unique tale.)

Syfaddon lake. Henderson and Jones. Wonder tales of ancient Wales. (Strand of the bitter cry.)
For other entries, see 2d edition.

Sylphs. Olcott. Wonder tales from goblin hills.

Symbol and the saint. Walters. Book of Christmas stories. (Adapted.)
For other entries, see 2d edition.

Sympathetic steam roller. Emerson. Merry-go-round of modern tales.

Syrinx and Pan. *See* Pan.

T

Table, the ass and the stick. I. Grimm. Fairy tales (Olcott. Little table set thyself, gold-ass, and cudgel out of the sack.)
Steel. English fairy tales. (Ass, the table and the stick.)
For other entries, see 2d edition.

Table, the ass and the stick. II. Coussens. Diamond story book. (Ass that lays money.)

Table, the ass, and the stick.
For other versions *see* Bastuncedo Dirigo; Donal O'Donnell's standing army; Gootom and the tree fairy; Lad who went to the north wind; Men of the wallet; Quarrelsome goat; Stolen turnips, magic tablecloth, sneezing goat, and the wooden whistle; Table, the sifter and the pinchers; Tailor and the hurricane; Two out of the knapsack; Wise simpleton; Wonderful horns.

Table, the sifter and the pinchers. Eells. Islands of magic.
See also Table, the ass and the stick.

Tail. Lee. Folk tales of all nations.

For other entries, see 2d edition.

Tail of Katoos. Martin. Fatma was a goose. (Tale of the tail of Katoos.)

See also Cat and the mouse. I.

Tail of Lemuel. Burnett. Children's book.

Tail of the peacock. *See* Io.

Tail of the serpent. I. Botsford. Picture tales from the Italian. (Head and tail of the snake.)

Friedlander. Jewish fairy tales (Dutton. Head or tail.)

Schwarz. Jewish caravan. (Anatomy of leadership.)

For other entries, see 2d edition.

Tail of the serpent. II. Cooper. Argosy of fables. (Snake with two heads.)

Tailor and a bear. *See* Clever tailor. II.

Tailor and the three beasts. De La Mare and Quayle. Readings.

For other entries, see 2d edition.

Tailor Havesoon and the Cobbler Neverdo. Lebermann. New German fairy tales.

Tailor of Gloucester. Potter. Tailor of Gloucester.

Starbuck. Enchanted paths.

Tailor of Limoise. Chamoud. Picture tales from the French.

Tailor of the dwarfs. *See* Dwarfs' tailor.

Tails of the storks. *See* Why the stork has no tail.

Tain bo Cuailgne. *See* Cattle raid of Cooley.

Taken for granted. Cozad. Story talks.

Taketori=Hime. *See* Bamboo cutter and the moon child.

Tale about words. *See* Diamonds and toads.

Tale of, etc. *See* the first important word of the title.

Tale from Timbuktu. Harper and Hamilton. Winding roads.

See also How the elephant and the whale were tricked. I.

Tale without end. *See* Endless tale. IV.

Tales of the old magicians. *See* King Khufu and the magicians.

Taliesen. Olcott. Wonder tales from fairy isles. (Radiant brow.)

For other entries, see 2d edition.

Talisman. I. *See* 2d edition.

Talisman. II. McNeer and Lederer. Tales from the crescent moon.

Talkative Christmas tree. Major. Merry Christmas stories.

Talkative sea gull. Broomell. Children's story caravan.

Talkative tortoise. **Arnold. Book of good counsels. (Tortoise and the geese.)

Curry and Clippinger. Children's literature.

Johnson and Scott. Anthology of children's literature. (Turtle who couldn't stop talking.)

Mackenzie. Jackal in Persia. (Story of the geese and the tortoise.)

Talkative tortoise—*continued.*
Piper. Folk tales children love. (Little turtle that could not stop talking.)
Piper. Road in storyland. (Little turtle that could not stop talking.)
Power. Bag o' tales.
Sheriff. Stories old and new. (Turtle who talked too much.)
For other entries, see 2d edition.
Talking bananas. Lee. Folk tales of all nations.
Talking bird. I. *See* Three sisters. I.
Talking bird. II. Lee. Folk tales of all nations.
Talking bird. III. Purnell and Weatherwax. Talking bird.
Talking birds. Egan. New found tales.
See also Ghost land.
Talking clock. Guerber. Legends of Switzerland. (*In* Legends of Neuchatel.)
Talking oak of Dodona. Curtis. Stories in trees. (Jupiter and the oak.)
Talking statues. Egan. New found tales.
Talking thrush. Gordon and Stockard. Gordon readers. 2d reader. (Thrush. Adapted.)
For other entries, see 2d edition.
Talking tree. Capuana. Italian fairy tales.
See also Wooden wife #.
Tall pine tree. *See* Flood (Indian).
Tally=High=Ho. Shannon. Eyes for the dark.
Tamanoi. *See* Ambitious hunter and skilful fisher.
Tamara lily. Newman. Fairy flowers.
Taming of Bucephalus. *See* Alexander the Great. I.
Taming of the shrew. Lamb. Tales from Shakespeare.
Taming of Tom. Hooker. Garden of the lost key.
Tamlane. Coussens. Diamond story book.
Harper. Ghosts and goblins.
Johnson and Scott. Anthology of children's literature.
Williams-Ellis. Fairies and enchanters.
For other entries, see 2d edition.
Tanabata. *See* Sky bridge of birds.
Tanabata=Matsuri. *See* Sky bridge of birds.
Tangle=coated horse. *See* Chase of the Gilla Dacar.
Tapa cloth, Origin of. Metzger. Tales told in Hawaii. (Origin of tapa.)
Tapestry prince. Starbuck. Enchanted paths.
See also Enchanted tapestry.
For other entries, see 2d edition.
Tar=baby. I. Carrick. Tales of wise and foolish animals. (Pitch doll.)
De Huff. Taytay's tales. (Pine-gum baby.)
See also Jackal and the drought.
For other entries, see 2d edition.
Tar=baby. II–III. *See* 2d edition.

Tar-baby. IV. Pyrnelle. Diddie, Dumps, and Tot. (*In* Ch. 5.)

Tar-baby stories.

For other versions see: Big long man's corn patch; Jackal and the drought; Master Rabbit again encounters the pine-gum baby; Mr. Monk and the noisy gecko; Monkey that kicked the trepang; Pine-gum baby; Rabbit and antelope; Rabbit and tar wolf.

Tar wolf. *See* Rabbit and tar wolf.

Tarantelle. Cross. Music stories.

Taro, Origin of. Egan. New found tales. (Despised maiden.)

Tarpeia. Cooke. Stories of Rome. (*In* Women of Rome.) Orvieto. Birth of Rome. (Girl who adored jewels.)

See also Selfish princess.

For other entries, see 2d edition.

Tarrandar's secret. Cooper. Tal. (*In* Ch. 16.)

Tartaro and Petit Perroquet. Lee. Folk tales of all nations.

See also Esben and the witch; Golden lantern, the golden goat and the golden cloak.

Tattercoats. Steel. English fairy tales.

For other entries, see 2d edition.

Tattoed one. Olcott. Wonder tales from pirate isles.

See also Why the crow is black. II.

Tavern in Spessart. Hauff. Arabian days' entertainment.

Ta=whaki, Story of. Colum. Bright islands.

See also Underworld.

Taxi that went mad. Buckingham. Elephant's friend.

Tchamsen. *See* entries under Raven.

Tchamsen and the tides. *See* Old woman and the tides.

Tchamsen gets the halibut. *See* Raven gets fish for his people.

Tchamsen regulates the seasons. *See* How the seasons came to be. IV.

Tea and the sage (poem). Cooper. Argosy of fables. (Madam Sage and Madam Tea.)

For other entries, see 2d edition.

Tea plant, Legend of. Olcott. Wonder tales from China seas.

Tea pot. Andersen. Fairy tales (Stickney). v. 2.

For other entries, see 2d edition.

Tease, tease, tease again. Olcott. Wonder tales from goblin hills.

See also Leprecaun. VI.

Teddy bears. I. *See* 2d edition.

Teddy bears. II. Hervey and Hix. Fanciful tales for children. (Old witch and the little bears.)

Teel=get, the monster. Hogner. Navajo winter nights.

See also Terrible giants.

Teeny-Tiny. I. Curry and Clippinger. Children's literature.

De La Mare and Quayle. Readings.

Harper. Ghosts and goblins.

Teeny-Tiny—*continued.*
Hutchinson. Fireside stories.
Johnson and Scott. Anthology of children's literature.
For other entries, see 2d edition.
Teeny-tiny story. Harriman. Stories for little children.
Teeth and no-teeth. Lee. Folk tales of all nations.
For other entries, see 2d edition.
Telegraph pots. Fyleman. Forty good-night tales.
Telemachus. *See* Ulysses' return.
Telephone's birthday party. Emerson. Merry-go-round of modern tales.
Tell, William. Coussens. Diamond story book. (William Tell and his great shot; William Tell's second shot.)
Cross. Music stories.
Cruse. Young folk's book of epic heroes.
Evans. Worth while stories.
Guerber. Legends of Switzerland. (*In* Forest cantons.)
(play). Knight. Dramatic reader. (Scenes from William Tell.)
Kinscella. Music appreciation readers. Book 5. (Brave mountaineer.)
Lansing. Great moments in freedom. (*In* Men of the forest cantons.)
Lee. Folk tales of all nations.
Tappan. Old world hero stories.
Terry. Tales from far and near.
See also Three Tells; Victory of Titanis.
For other entries, see 2d edition.
Telltale chalk. Chrisman. Wind that wouldn't blow.
Telltale grease. Lee. Folk tales of all nations.
See also Cat and the mouse in partnership; Fox as partner.
I #; Fox, the wolf and the cheese #; Two friends and the barrel of grease #; Wolf's butter #.
Temperamental typewriter. Emerson. Merry-go-round of modern tales.
Tempest. *See* Prospero and Miranda.
Temple boy. Untermeyer. Donkey of God.
Temple of the gods. Metzger. Tales told in Hawaii.
Ten at one stroke. *See* Valiant Vicky.
Ten hens go a-travelling. Potter. Giant of Apple Pie Hill.
Ten little prairie dogs. De Huff. Taytay's tales.
Ten years in the underwater country. *See* Underwater country.
Tender hearted monster. St. Nicholas. Jan. 1897, p. 236.
Tenene pove. James. Tewa firelight tales.
Teresa, St. *See* St. Teresa.
Terrapin's trick. James. Happy animals of Atagahi.
Terrible bell. *See* Poor woman and the bell.
Terrible Carlanco. *See* Carlanco.
Terrible giants, Story of. Hogner. Navajo winter nights.
See also Teel-get, the monster.

Terrible Olli. Lee. Folk tales of all nations.
For other entries, see 2d edition.
Tewa Cinderella. James. Tewa firelight tales.
See also Turkey maiden.
Thankful dead. Coussens. Diamond story book.
See also Traveling companion.
Thanksgiving at "Abner's Folly." Wiggin and Smith. Twilight stories.
Thanksgiving basket. Harriman. Stories for little children.
See also Lame squirrel's Thanksgiving.
Thanksgiving Day. *See* Apple that talked; Chip's Thanksgiving; First Thanksgiving; Gnomes who tried to stop Thanksgiving; Grateful Indian; King's Thanksgiving; Little Baxters go marketing; Mince pie; Mr. Goat's Thanksgiving; Mr. Horner of Grumble Corner; Pie that grew; Prince of the kingdom of Thankful; Pumpkin giant; Pumpkin seed; Red leaf's Thanksgiving; Scarlet Feather's Thanksgiving; Taken for granted; Their full Thanksgiving; Turkey and the ant; Turkey for the stuffing; When Jane changed her name.
For other entries, see 2d edition.
Thanksgiving turkey wishbone. Potter. Giant of Apple Pie Hill.
That beloved Duchess Anne. Clément. Once in France.
That boy! Crew. Saturday's children.
That lazy Ah Fun. Chrisman. Shen of the sea.
Thebes, Destruction of. Bulfinch. Golden age. (Antigone. *In* Ch. 23.)
For other entries, see 2d edition.
Theft of fire. *See* How fire was brought to the Indians. III.
Their flag. Bailey. Tell me another story.
Their full Thanksgiving. Bailey. Wonderful tree.
Then he burnt the floor. *See* Palissy, the potter.
Theodelind and the water sprite. Baumbach. Tales from the Swiss alps.
See also Zirbel.
Theodora. *See* Justinian.
Theophilus the Just. *See* Princess in the chest.
There are no dead. Skinner. Emerald story book.
There was an old wifey. *See* Old woman and her pig. II.
There was a war. Crew. Saturday's children.
Thermopylae. *See* Brave three hundred.
Theseus. Bulfinch. Golden age. (*In* Ch. 20.)
Coit. Kai Khosru.
(play). Coit. Kai Khosru.
Colum. Fountain of youth. (Theseus and the monster.)
Evans. Worth while stories. (Adventures of Theseus.)
Forbush. Myths and legends of Greece and Rome. (Theseus and Ariadne.)
Miller. My book of history. v. 2. (Tale of the Minotaur and the labyrinth. *In* Ch. 1.)

Theseus—*continued.*
Pyle. Tales from Greek mythology.
Rich. Read-aloud book.
Shimer. Fairyland. (How Ariadne helped Theseus.)
For other entries, see 2d edition.
They didn't think (poem). Cary. Poems.
Cooper. Argosy of fables.
Thiassa. *See* Iduna's apples.
Thidrandi and the goddesses. Fleming. Round the world
in folk tales.
Thief and his son. Darton. Wonder book of old romance.
See also Treasure chamber of Rhampsinitus.
Thief and the boy. Cooper. Argosy of fables. (Boy and
the thief.)
For other entries, see 2d edition.
Thief and the dog. Æsop. Fables (Whitman ed.).
Cooper. Argosy of fables. (Faithful dog.)
For other entries, see 2d edition.
Thief and the innkeeper. Æsop. Fables (Whitman ed.).
Æsop. Fables (Jones).
Cooper. Argosy of fables.
For other entries, see 2d edition.
Thieves and the cock. Æsop. Fables (Jones).
Cooper. Argosy of fables.
For other entries, see 2d edition.
Thieving foxes. De Huff. Taytay's tales.
Thin Helen. Fyleman. Forty good-morning tales.
Thing to be explained. Housman. Turn again tales.
No. 2 Joy Street.
Things of most worth. Perkins and Danielson. Second
year Mayflower program book.
For other entries, see 2d edition.
Things that loved the lake. Mitchell. Here and now story
book.
Third leg. I. Schwarz. Jewish caravan.
Third leg. II. *See* Dream of Paradise.
Thirst of the standing stones. I (play). Going. Folklore
and fairy plays. (Stones of Plouhinec.)
Dorey. Three and the moon. (How Ivon found more
golden pieces than all the golden apples on the apple tree
of Kerglas.)
Lee. Folk tales of all nations. (Stones of Plouvinec.)
Masson. Folk tales of Brittany. (Magic rocks and the beg-
gar.)
For other entries, see 2d edition.
Thirsty pigeon. Æsop. Fables (Whitman ed.).
Cooper. Argosy of fables.
For other entries, see 2d edition.
Thirsty well. Housman. Doorway in fairyland. (Bound
princess, pt. 3.)
Thirteen jeweled letters. Cabot. Course in citizenship.
For other entries, see 2d edition.

Thirteenth son. Lee. Folk tales of all nations. (Thirteenth.)
See also Esben and the witch.
Thirty=two teeth. Cooper. Argosy of fables.
This for that. Olcott. Wonder tales from pirate isles. (This for that, tit for tat.)
See also King Solomon, the merchant, and the mouse-deer.
This is the house that Jack built. *See* House that Jack built.
Thisbe. *See* Pyramus and Thisbe.
Thistle, Story of. I. Carey. Flower legends. (Thistle.)
Kinscella. Music appreciation readers. Book 5. (Land of the thistle.)
For other entries, see 2d edition.
Thistle, Story of. II. *See* 2d edition.
Thistle, Story of. III. Bowman. Little brown bowl. (Story of a thistle.)
Thistledown. Fyleman. Forty good-morning tales.
Thomas Berennikov #.
See also Brave little tailor.
Thomas the rhymer (poem). Adams and Atchinson. Book of enchantment. (Queen of elfland.)
Olcott. Wonder tales from fairy isles. (True Thomas.)
For other entries, see 2d edition.
Thor and Geirrod. *See* Geirrod and Thor.
Thor and his journey to Jötunheim. Adams and Atchinson. There were giants. (Thor's wonderful journey.)
Bulfinch. Golden age. (Thor's visit to Jötunheim. *In* Ch. 39.)
Curry and Clippinger. Children's literature. (Thor's visit to Jötunheim.)
Evans. Worth while stories. (Adventures of Thor; Thor contends with the giants.)
Johnson and Scott. Anthology of children's literature. (Thor's wonderful journey.)
Lanier. Book of giants. (When Thor went to Jötunheim.)
Miller. My book of history. v. 3. (*In* Ch. 7.)
Pyle. Tales from Norse mythology. (Thor visits Jötunheim.)
For other entries, see 2d edition.
Thor and Hrungnir. Pyle. Tales from Norse mythology. (Thor battles with Hrungnir.)
For other entries, see 2d edition.
Thor contends with the giants. *See* Thor and his journey to Jötunheim.
Thor: Quest of the hammer. Adams and Atchinson. Book of giant stories. (How Thor's hammer was lost and found.)
Bulfinch. Golden age. (Recovery of the hammer. *In* Ch. 38.)
Johnson and Scott. Anthology of children's literature. (Quest of the hammer.)

Thor: Quest of the hammer—*continued.*
Power. Bag o' tales. (How Thor's hammer was lost and found.)
Pyle. Tales from Norse mythology. (Thor brings a kettle from Jötunheim.)
For other entries, see 2d edition.
Thorkill. Adams. Swords of the Vikings. (Far journeys of Thorkill.)
See also Geirrod and Thor.
Thorn and the vine. Cooper. Argosy of fables.
Thorn of Glastonbury. Curtis. Stories in trees. (First Christmas tree.)
Long. Folklore calendar. (*In* May: Wells.)
Smith and Hazeltine. Christmas in legend and story. (Mystic thorn.)
(poem). Smith and Hazeltine. Christmas in legend and story. (Blooming of the white thorn.)
See also St. Patrick's thorn.
For other entries, see 2d edition.
Thor's visit to Jötunheim. *See* Thor and his journey to Jötunheim.
Thor's wonderful journey. *See* Thor and his journey to Jötunheim.
Thorstein. Colum. Voyagers. (Children of Eric the Red.)
For other entries, see 2d edition.
Thorwald. Colum. Voyagers. (Children of Eric the Red.)
Thousands of dwarfs. *See* Mist caps. II.
Three- and four, Legend of. *See* Princess of the tower.
Three apes. Egan. New found tales.
See also Three wise little monkeys.
Three apples. I. Arabian nights. Adventures of Haroun Er Raschid (Olcott. Story of the three apples.)
Three apples. II. Bailey. Tell me another story.
See also Two apples on a tree.
Three apples. III. Casserley. Michael of Ireland.
Three apples. IV. Warner. Carl Krinken.
Three aunts. *See* Three little crones each with something big.
Three bears. I. Hervey and Hix. Fanciful tales for children. (Golden Hair and the three bears.)
Hutchinson. Chimney corner stories.
Johnson and Scott. Anthology of children's literature.
Steel. English fairy tales.
See also Bears make a visit; Pig-pig and the three bears.
For other entries, see 2d edition.
Three bears. II. Arthur Rackham fairy book.
Curry and Clippinger. Children's literature.
Rich. Read-aloud book.
Quinn. Stokes' wonder book of fairy tales.
Rhys. English fairy book.
Wilson. Red magic.
See also Bears make a visit.

Three bears. II—*continued.*
For other entries, see 2d edition.
Three bears. III. Babbitt. Animals' own story book.
Three bears and the trolley car. Potter. Captain Sand-
man.
Three beautiful princesses, Legend of. Irving. Tales from
the Alhambra.
Three bells. Deihl. Holiday-time stories.
See also Bells of Christmas.
Three billy goats gruff. Bruce. Treasury of tales for little
folk. (Three goats named Gruff.)
Carrick. Picture folk tales. (Three Bruze goats.)
Curry and Clippinger. Children's literature.
Dasent. East of the sun and west of the moon (Nielsen).
Hutchinson. Chimney corner stories.
Johnson and Scott. Anthology of children's literature.
Power. Bag o' tales.
Power. Blue caravan tales.
Rasmussen. East o' the sun and west o' the moon.
Told under the green umbrella.
For other entries, see 2d edition.
Three birds and a little black dog. Purnell. Merry frogs.
See also Magic dog #.
Three birds go to the sun for tobacco. *See* Tobacco. III.
Three boys with jugs of molasses and secret ambitions.
Sandburg. Rootabaga stories.
Three brothers. I. Grimm. Fairy tales (Olcott).
Grimm. Tales from Grimm (Wanda Gag).
Hart. Picture tales from Holland. (Master of masters.)
King. Golden cat head.
See also Four clever brothers.
For other entries, see 2d edition.
Three brothers. II–V. *See* 2d edition.
Three brothers. VI. Bailey. Tell me another story.
Three brothers. VII. *See* Judas tree. II.
Three brothers. VIII. *See* Boots and his brothers.
Three brothers and their adventures with the queen.
Eells. Brazilian fairy book.
Three brothers and three sisters. Garnett. Ottoman won-
der tales. (Three brothers and their three sisters.)
See also Shah Meram and Sultan Sade.
For other entries, see 2d edition.
**Three brothers who went to King Solomon to learn wis-
dom.** *See* Three counsels of King Solomon.
Three Bruze goats. *See* Three billy goats gruff.
Three bugs (poem). Cooper. Argosy of fables.
For other entries, see 2d edition.
Three caskets. *See* Merchant of Venice.
Three chests. Bowman and Bianco. Tales from a Finnish
tupa. (Jurma and the sea god.)
See also Bluebeard; Forbidden room #.
For other entries, see 2d edition.

Three companions. I. Cooper. Argosy of fables.
Three companions. II. Colum. Big tree of Bunlahy.
See also Bremen town musicians.
Three copecks. Carpenter. Tales of a Russian grandmother
(Three kopecks and a cat.)
Ralston. Russian fairy tales.
See also Dick Whittington and his cat; Honest penny.
Three counsels of King Solomon. Dane. Once there was
and was not.
**Gaster. Ma'aseh book. v. 2. (Three brothers who went
to King Solomon to learn wisdom.)
Three cows. I–II. *See* 2d edition.
Three cows. III. Morris. Gypsy story teller. (A tale.)
See also Bee, the harp, the mouse and the bum-clock.
Three cows. IV. Macmillan. Canadian wonder tales. (Jack
and his magic aids.)
Three cranberries. Cooper. Argosy of fables.
Three delicate wives of King Virtue=banner. Ryder.
Twenty-two goblins.
See also Princess on the pea.
Three dwarfs. *See* Three little men in the wood.
Three feathers. I #.
See also Frog princess; Forest bride.
Three feathers. II. Steel. English fairy tales.
See also Fire bird; Goose girl; Master maid.
For other entries, see 2d edition.
Three fighting cocks. Martinez Del Rio. Sun, the moon
and a rabbit.
Three fish. I. **Arnold. Book of good counsels. (Fate
and the three fishes.)
Mackenzie. Jackal in Persia. (Story of the three fishes.)
Phillips. Far peoples.
See also Hundred-wit, Thousand-wit, and Single-wit.
For other entries, see 2d edition.
Three fish. II. *See* 2d edition.
Three fish. III. Evans. Worth while stories. (Three little
goldfish.)
Three fishes, Story of the. *See* Three fish. I.
Three freight trains. Bailey. Story-telling hour. (Three
freight trains take their loads to the city.)
Three gifts. I–II. *See* 2d edition.
Three gifts. III #.
See also Cogia Hassan Alhabbal.
Three gifts. IV. Masson. Folk tales of Brittany. (Wasp,
the winged needle and the spider.)
For other entries, see 2d edition.
Three gifts. V. Barry and Hanna. Wonder flights of long
ago. (Magic carpet.)
Tappan. Prince from nowhere.
Williams. Tales from Ebony. (Three magic gifts.)
Woodson. African myths. (Three rival brothers.)
See also Four clever brothers; Prince Ahmed and the fairy

Three gifts. V—*continued.*
Perie Banou ; Three lovers who brought the dead girl to life.
Three gifts. VI. Darton. Seven champions of Christendom.
Three goats. I. *See* Three billy goats gruff.
Three goats. II. *See* Goats in the turnip field.
Three goats named Gruff. *See* Three billy goats gruff.
Three golden apples. *See* Hercules and his labors.
Three golden hairs. I. *See* Giant with the golden hair. I.
Three golden hairs. II. Carpenter. Tales of a Russian grandmother. (Three golden hairs.)
See also Yvon and Finette.
Three golden hairs of Grandfather Know All. *See* Giant with the golden hair. II.
Three golden hairs of the old man Vsevede. *See* Giant with the golden hair. II.
Three golden hairs of the Sun=King. *See* Giant with the golden hair. II.
Three golden oranges. *See* Three oranges.
Three good giants #.
See also Wise inventor.
Three guesses. Tappan. Prince from nowhere.
See also Rumpelstiltskin ; Tom Tit Tot.
Three heads of the well. Lee. Folk tales of all nations. (Princess of Colchester.)
Rhys. English fairy book. (Princess of Colchester.)
Steel. English fairy tales.
For other entries, see 2d edition.
In 2d edition this story is also indexed under the title, "Princess of Colchester."
Three holy kings. *See* Three kings.
Three horses. Eells. Brazilian fairy book.
Harper. More story-hour favorites.
See also Princess on the glass hill.
Three hundred and sixty=five children. *See* Beggar's curse. I.
Three hundred wicked monkeys. Lobagola. Folk tales of a savage.
Three hundred years after. *See* Last of the Feni.
Three hundred zebras who spoke the truth. Lobagola. Folk tales of a savage.
Three hunters. Chamoud. Picture tales from the French.
Three images. Egan. New found tales.
Three kings (poem). Smith and Hazeltine. Christmas in legend and story.
Smith and Hazeltine. Christmas in legend and story. (Three holy kings.)
See also Christmas promise of the three kings ; Three kings of Cologne #.
Three kittens. Carrick. Animal picture tales from Russia.
See also Three little pigs. I.
Three kopecks and a cat. *See* Three copecks.

Three languages. Bruce. Treasury of tales for little folk. (Boy who learned the language of the beasts.)
Evans. Worth while stories. (What the stupid son learned. Adapted.)
See also Language of the birds.
For other entries, see 2d edition.
Three lazy brothers. Dane. Once there was and was not.
Three-legged stool. Harriman. Stories for little children.
Three lemons. I. *See* 2d edition.
Three lemons. II. Lee. Folk tales of all nations. (Three lemons.)
For other entries, see 2d edition.
Three lemons. I–II. *See also* How the pigeon became a tame bird; Three oranges.
Three little butterflies. Bailey. Tell me another story. (Three little butterfly brothers.)
For other entries, see 2d edition.
Three little crones each with something big. I. Lee. Folk tales of all nations. (Three aunts.)
See also Sunbeam sprites.
For other entries, see 2d edition.
Three little goldfish. *See* Three fish. III.
Three little kittens who lost their mittens (poem). Harriman. Stories for little children. (Three little kittens.)
(poem). Hutchinson. Candlelight stories. (Three little kittens.)
(poem). Johnson and Scott. Anthology of children's literature. (Three little kittens.)
(poem.) Patten. Junior classics. v. 10.
Piper. Gateway to storyland. (Three little kittens.)
(play). Wheelock. Kindergarten children's hour. v. 2. (*In* Ch. 14.)
For other entries, see 2d edition.
Three little men in the wood. Grimm. Fairy tales (Olcott).
Lang. Old friends among the fairies. (Three dwarfs.)
For other entries, see 2d edition.
Three little pigs. I. Curry and Clippinger. Children's literature.
Evans. Worth while stories. (Wise little pig. Abridged.)
Hutchinson. Chimney corner stories. (Three pigs.)
Johnson and Scott. Anthology of children's literature.
Power. Bag o' tales.
Piper. Gateway to storyland.
Steel. English fairy tales.
Told under the green umbrella.
Williams. Tales from Ebony.
See also Little pig and the wolves; Three kittens.
For other entries, see 2d edition.
Three little pigs and the ogre. Adams and Atchinson. There were giants.
For other entries, see 2d edition.

Three little wiggletails. Potter. Captain Sandman.
Three lovers who brought the dead girl to life. Ryder.
Twenty-two goblins.
See also Four clever brothers; Three gifts. V.
Three luck children. *See* Fortune seekers. I.
Three lucky sons. *See* Fortune seekers. I.
Three magic gifts. *See* Three gifts. V.
Three magicians. Meeker. Folk tales from the Far East.
Three Marys of the spring. Guerber. Legends of Switzerland. (*In* Aargau.)
Three meals shorten the day. *See* Hans Hannekemaier in Hindeloopen; Tailor of Limoise.
Three men of power. Ransome. Old Peter's Russian tales.
(Three men of power, Evening, Midnight, and Sunrise.)
See also Ivan the peasant's son #; Muzhicheck-as-big-as-your-thumbs-with-moustaches-seven-versts-long #.
Three mountain goats. Botsford. Picture tales from the Italian.
Three oranges. Boggs and Davis. Three golden oranges, and other tales. (Three golden oranges.)
See also Don Fernan and the orange princess; How the pigeon became a tame bird; Three lemons. I–II; Three orange peris.
Three orphan brothers. Phillips. Far peoples.
Three owls in a tree. Potter. Giant of Apple Pie Hill.
Three pigs. *See* Three little pigs.
Three platefuls and five squaws. Buckingham. Great idea.
Three powers. Starbuck. Far horizons.
For other entries, see 2d edition.
Three princesses. I. Fyleman. Forty good-morning tales.
Three princesses. II. Morris. Gypsy story teller.
Three princesses in the blue mountain. Dasent. East of the sun and west of the moon (Nielsen).
For other entries, see 2d edition.
Three princesses of Connaught. MacManus. Donegal wonder book.
Three princesses of Whiteland. Dasent. East of the sun and west of the moon (Nielsen).
For other entries, see 2d edition.
Three pumpkins. La Rue. Under the story tree.
Three queens of winter. Chardon. Golden chick.
See also Snow queen.
Three questions. I. Boeckel. Through the gateway.
Hartshorne. Training in worship. (*In* Personal service.)
For other entries, see 2d edition.
Three revellers and death. Farjeon. Tales from Chaucer.
(Pardoner's tale.)
For other entries, see 2d edition.
Three rings. Capuana. Italian fairy tales.
Three rival brothers. *See* Three gifts. V.
Three robes. Lang. Old friends among the fairies.
For other entries, see 2d edition.

Three roses. I. *See* 2d edition.
Three roses. II. Katibah. Other Arabian nights. (Tale of three roses.)
Three sieves. Cabot. Course in citizenship.
Three sillies. I. Curry and Clippinger. Children's literature.
De La Mare. Told again.
Steel. English fairy tales.
Williams. Tales from Ebony.
See also Farmer's ass; Silly weaver girl; Wife who bought herself a name.
For other entries, see 2d edition.
Three sillies. II. Lee. Folk tales of all nations. (Crazy priestess, and her crazy daughters.)
Three singers and the dragon=boat. Morris. Book of the three dragons.
Three sisters. I. Arabian nights (Eliot).
See also Golden fish, the wonder-working tree and the golden bird; Listening king; Mielikki and her nine sons; Peter Tulip; Tsar Saltan.
For other entries, see 2d edition.
Three sisters. II. *See* 2d edition.
Three sisters. III. Byrde. Polish fairy book.
See also Three sisters. I.
Three sisters. IV. Lee. Folk tales of all nations.
Three sisters. V. Morris. Gypsy story teller.
See also Mother Holle.
Three sisters. VI. *See* First corn. X; How corn and beans came to be. II.
Three sisters and Itrimobe. Lee. Folk tales of all nations.
Three sisters of Arth. Guerber. Legends of Switzerland. (*In* Forest cantons.)
Three sons and the chest bequeathed to them. **Gaster. Ma'aseh book. v. 2.
See also Cat and the mouse in partnership.
Three spinners. *See* Three spinning fairies.
Three spinning fairies. De La Mare and Quayle. Readings. (Three spinners.)
For other entries, see 2d edition.
Three strong men. Leland. Algonquin legends.
Macmillan. Canadian wonder tales. (Northern lights.)
See also Chib, Adventures of #; Three tests.
Three subtle crafts of Manawyddan. Morris. Book of the three dragons.
See also Escape of the mouse #.
Three Tells, Legend of. Guerber. Legends of Switzerland. (*In* Forest cantons.)
See also Tell, William.
Three tests. Spence. Myths of the North American Indians. (*In* Ch. 5.)
See also Coyote, the grey giant and the beautiful maiden; Three strong men.

Three thieves. Hart. Picture tales from Holland.
  See also Jack the cunning thief.
Three tradesmen. Æsop. Fables (Jones).
  For other entries, see 2d edition.
Three wise little monkeys. Sugimoto. Picture tales from
  the Japanese.
  See also Three apes.
Three wishes. I. *See* 2d edition.
Three wishes. II. Lee. Folk tales of all nations. (Wishes.)
  For other entries, see 2d edition.
Three wishes. III. Silvester and Peter. Happy hour
  stories.
  For other entries, see 2d edition.
Three wonderful beggars. Carpenter. Tales of a Russian
  grandmother. (Marco the rich, and Basil the luckless.)
  Lee. Folk tales of all nations. (Marko, the rich and Vasily
  the luckless.)
  For other entries, see 2d edition.
Three wonderful dresses. Garnett. Ottoman wonder tales.
  For other entries, see 2d edition.
Thriftless wife. Olcott. Wonder tales from China seas.
  (New Year olives.)
  For other entries, see 2d edition.
Thrifty squirrels. Evans. Worth while stories.
  See also Ant and the grasshopper.
Throne of Solomon. Vilnay. Legends of Palestine.
Thrush. *See* Talking thrush.
Thrush and the cuckoo. Brown. Curious book of birds.
  See also Optimistic thrush.
Thrush and the swallow. Æsop. Fables (Whitman ed.).
Thrush's nest, Story of. Morley. I know a secret.
Thumbelina. Andersen. Fairy tales (Siewers tr. Lizzie
  Thumb.)
  Andersen. Fairy tales (Stickney. v. 1. Little Thumbalina.)
  Johnson and Scott. Anthology of children's literature.
  (Thumbelisa.)
  See also Ditu Migniula ; Leetie and the wood fairies.
  For other entries, see 2d edition.
Thumbelisa. *See* Thumbelina.
Thumbietot blows a pipe. Freeman. Child-story readers.
  3d reader.
  Lagerlöf. Wonderful adventures of Nils. (*In* Ch. 4.)
  See also Pied piper of Hamelin.
Thumbling. I. Bruce. Treasury of tales for little folk.
  (Tom Thumb.)
  Evans. Worth while stories. (Tom Thumb.)
  Quinn. Stokes' wonder book of fairy tales. (Tom Thumb.)
  See also How K'tonton took a ride on a chopping knife ;
  K'tonton arrives ; Manoel Littlebean.
  For other entries, see 2d edition.
Thumbling the dwarf, and Thumbling the giant. *See*
  Young giant.

Thun-tsay and Cohn-Nah. De Huff. Taytay's tales.

Thunder bugs. Guerber. Legends of Switzerland. (*In* Basel.)

Thunder-child and the dragons. Kennedy. Red man's wonder book.

Thunder sends the great flood upon the earth. *See* Flood (Indian).

Thunderers. Spence. Myths of the North American Indians. (*In* Ch. 4.)

For other entries, see 2d edition.

Thunderer's son-in-law. Spence. Myths of the North American Indians. (*In* Ch. 7.)

Thunderstorm giant. Burnett. Children's book.

Thyrsis and Amaranth. La Fontaine. Fables (Tilney).

Ti tiriti ti. Capuana. Italian fairy tales.

For other entries, see 2d edition.

Tichborne dole. Long. Folklore calendar.

See also Countess Wilhelmine's long walk.

Tide jewels. I. Price. Legends of the seven seas. (Jewels of the tides.)

Whitehorn. Wonder tales of old Japan. (Great queen.)

For other entries, see 2d edition.

Tidy Tips. Shannon. California fairy tales.

Tiger and the antelope. De Leeuw. Java jungle tales.

Tiger and the bulls. *See* Lion and the four bulls.

Tiger and the frog. Noel. Magic bird of Chomo-lung-ma.

See also Simpleton. III.

Tiger and the grandmother. Metzger. Tales told in Korea.

See also Ito and his friends.

Tiger and the hare. *See* Bunny the brave.

Tiger and the man. *See* Smart young tiger.

In 2d edition there are entries under each title.

Tiger and the mousedeer. Skipper. Jungle meeting-pool. (*In* First meeting.)

Tiger and the shadow. De Leeuw. Java jungle tales. (Tiger and his image.)

Skeat. Tiger's mistake.

See also Bunny the brave; Hare at the water hole; Lion and the hare.

For other entries, see 2d edition.

Tiger and the traveler. *See* Traveler and the tiger.

Tiger aunt. Phillips. Far peoples.

See also Little Red Riding Hood.

Tiger gets his deserts. I. De Leeuw. Java jungle tales.

Skeat. Tiger's mistake.

See also Way of the world.

For other entries, see 2d edition.

Tiger gets his deserts. II. Mukerji. Hindu fables. (Bunny the brave saves Brahmin the priest.)

See also Brahman, the tiger and the jackal.

Tiger learns a lesson. De Leeuw. Java jungle tales. (Another mouse-deer adventure, and the tiger learns a lesson.)
See also Mouse-deer, the crocodile, and the tiger.

Tiger son. Metzger. Picture tales from the Chinese.
Olcott. Wonder tales from China seas. (Tiger sorrowful who had to work.)

Tiger sorrowful who had to work. *See* Tiger son.

Tiger, the Brahman, and the jackal. *See* Brahman, the tiger, and the jackal.

Tiger with burning eyes. Olcott. Wonder tales from pirate isles. (*In* String of pearls.)
See also Lion and the mosquitoes.

Tiger's fold. Skeat. Tiger's mistake.

Tiger's mistake. Skeat. Tiger's mistake.
See also Tune that makes the tiger drowsy.

Tiki-Tiki-Tembo. *See* Long-life name. II.

Tilly, Adventures of. *See* Runaway train. II.

Tilly Tattle and the Humpydoodle. Beard. Tucked-in tales.

Tilly's Christmas. Walters. Book of Christmas stories.
See also Little Gretchen and the wooden shoe.
For other entries, see 2d edition.

Tim Puss's Christmas. Walker. Sandman's Christmas stories.

Timid hare. Aspinwall. Jataka tales. (Flight of the beasts.)
Blaisdell. Rhyme and story second reader. (Hare and the elephant. Adapted.)
Bryce. Short stories for little folks. (What frightened the animal.)
Cowles. Stories to tell. (Flight of the beasts. Adapted.)
Davis. Baker's dozen.
Faulkner. White elephant. (Timid little rabbit.)
Hutchinson. Fireside stories. (Foolish timid rabbit.)
Johnson and Scott. Anthology of children's literature. (Hare that ran away.)
Whiteman. Playmates in print. (Rabbit and the cocoanut.)
See also Rabbit who was afraid; Chicken-Little.
For other entries, see 2d edition.

Timid little rabbit. *See* Timid hare.

Timid truck. Emerson. Merry-go-round of modern tales.

Timo and the Princess Vendla. Bowman and Bianco. Tales from a Finnish tupa.

Timon of Athens. Lamb. Tales from Shakespeare.

Timothy and Tabitha. Baker. Tell them again tales.

Timothy Brown. Skinner. Happy tales.

Timothy's shoes. Bailey. Tell me another story.
Coe. Third book of stories.
Ewing. Lob Lie-by-the-fire.
Silvester and Peter. Happy hour stories. (Bobby's fairy shoes. Adapted.)
See also Duty shoes.

Tims, (The). Farjeon. Italian peepshow.
Tinder=box. Adams and Atchinson. Book of enchantment.
Andersen. Fairy tales (Siewers tr.).
Andersen. Four tales.
Curry and Clippinger. Children's literature.
Johnson and Scott. Anthology of children's literature.
Quinn. Stokes' wonder book of fairy tales.
Shimer. Fairyland.
Skinner. Happy tales.
Williams. Tales from Ebony.
For other entries, see 2d edition.
Ting=a=ling. Stockton. Reformed pirate.
For other entries, see 2d edition.
Ting=a=ling and the five magicians. Stockton. Reformed
pirate.
For other entries, see 2d edition.
Ting=a=ling bome (poem). Carrick. Still more Russian pic-
ture tales.
Ting=a=ling's visit to Tur=i=lira. Davis. Baker's dozen.
Stockton. Reformed pirate.
For other entries, see 2d edition.
Tinker and the ghost. Boggs and Davis. Three golden or-
anges.
See also Youth who could not shiver and shake.
Tinker of Tamlacht. MacManus. Lo, and behold ye!
See also Smith and the devil #; Strange godfather #.
Tinker's cabbage=garden. Casserley. Whins on Knockattan.
Tinker's willow. Bailey. Tell me another story.
Tintil or Dicomill. Lindsay. Choosing book.
Tintoretto. Chambers' miscellany. v. 9.
Cozad. Story talks. (Giacomo Robusti—just a dauber.)
Tiny dog. *See* Little hunting dog.
Tiny little chicken who had not yet been born. *See* Why?
Why?
Tiny rain=drop. Kinscella. Music appreciation readers.
Book 1.
Tiny Tim. *See* Cratchit's Christmas dinner.
Tio Paco and his wonderful donkey. *See* Oil merchant's
donkey.
Tired trolley car. Starbuck. Enchanted paths.
'Tis faith which saves. Eells. Islands of magic.
Tit for tat. I. Curry and Clippinger. Children's literature.
Hutchinson. Candlelight stories.
Lee. Folk tales of all nations.
For other entries, see 2d edition.
Tit for tat. II. *See* This for that.
Titan of the north. Browne. Indian nights.
Titania's sleep. Cowles. Stories to tell.
Titans. Lanier. Book of giants. (How Zeus fought with
Titans and giants.)
Pyle. Tales from Greek mythology. (Battle between the
gods and Titans.)

Titans—*continued.*
For other entries, see 2d edition.
Titelli-Ture. *See* Girl who could spin gold from clay and long straw.
Titian. Chambers' miscellany. v. 9. (Titian Vecellio. *In* Anecdotes of the early painters.)
My Bookhouse. v. 4. (Boy of Cadore.)
Titty Mouse and Tatty Mouse. Curry and Clippinger. Children's literature.
Hutchinson. Fireside stories.
Lee. Folk tales of all nations.
Steel. English fairy tales.
For other entries, see 2d edition.
Titus, Emperor of Rome. Chandler. Magic pictures. (City of the seven hills.)
To-day or to-morrow? McVenn. Good manners and right conduct. Book 2. (Lawyer's opinion.)
For other entries, see 2d edition.
To keep store with Bimbo. *See* Lexy and the dogs on his street.
Toad and the frog. Cooper. Argosy of fables.
Toad and the kite. Woodson. African myths.
Toad brother's warts and the peeper's peep. Parker. Skunny Wundy and other Indian tales.
Toad's adventures. Grahame. Kenneth Grahame book.
Toads and diamonds. *See* Diamonds and toads.
Toadshead. Capuana. Italian fairy tales.
Toadstools, Origin of. I. *See* 2d edition.
Toadstools, Origin of. II. Shannon. California fairy tales. (Yellow elves.)
Tobacco. I. Spence. Myths of the North American Indians. (Sacred origin of smoking. *In* Ch. 2.)
Tobacco. II. *See* Water-pipe.
Tobacco. III. Sexton. Gray wolf stories. (Three birds go to the sun for tobacco.)
Tobacco. IV. Gila monster's tobacco ranch; or, How chipmunk got small feet.
Tobacco. I–IV. *See also* Fair earth; How the Indians got tobacco.
Tobias and the angel. Bryant. Children's book of celebrated legends.
Toboggan-to-the-moon dream. Sandburg. Rootabaga stories.
Tokutaro San. Henderson and Calvert. Wonder tales of old Japan.
Toller's neighbors. Choate and Curtis. Little people of the hills.
For other entries, see 2d edition.
Tom and the tinker. *See* Tom Hickathrift.
Tom, Dick and Harry. *See* Old woman and her pig; Piece of liver.
Tom goes down to the sea. *See* Tom, the water baby.

Tom Hickathrift. Coussens. Diamond story book.
Lee. Folk tales of all nations. (Tom Hickathrift the con-
queror.)
Rhys. English fairy book.
Williams. Jolly old whistle. (Tom and the, tinker.)
See also Giants of Towedneck.
For other entries, see 2d edition.
Tom,. the chimney sweep. *See* Tom, the water baby.
Tom, the water baby. Cabot. Course in citizenship. (Tom,
the chimney sweep.)
Freeman. Child story readers. 3d reader. (Little water
fairy; Tom goes down to the sea.)
For other entries, see 2d edition.
Tom Thumb. I. Curry and Clippinger. Children's litera-
ture.
Faulkner. Road to enchantment.
Johnson and Scott. Anthology of children's literature.
(History of Tom Thumb.)
Lee. Folk tales of all nations. (History of Tom Thumb.)
Mackenzie. Book of nursery tales.
Rhys. English fairy book.
Steel. English fairy tales. (True history of Sir Thomas
Thumb.)
For other entries, see 2d edition.
Tom Thumb. II. *See* Thumbling. I.
Tom Thumb. III. *See* Hop-o' my-thumb.
Tom Thumb. IV. My Bookhouse. v. 4. (Adventures of
General Tom Thumb.)
Tom Thumb, Japanese. *See* Monotaro. I; One inch fellow.
Tom Thumb, Jewish. *See* How K'tonton took a ride on a
chopping knife; K'tonton arrives.
Tom Tit Tot. Curry and Clippinger. Children's literature.
De La Mare and Quayle. Readings.
Faulkner. Road to enchantment.
Hutchinson. Chimney corner fairy tales.
Lee. Folk tales of all nations.
Rhys. English fairy book.
Steel. English fairy tales.
Williams-Ellis. Fairies and enchanters.
For other entries, see 2d edition.
See also Rumpelstiltskin; Three guesses.
Tomato peeler. Purnell. Merry frogs.
See also Cinderella.
Tomcat's meat dinner. Casserley. Whins on Knockattan.
Tommy Turtle. Beard. Tucked-in tales.
Tommy's Christmas stocking. Bowman. Little brown
bowl.
See also Boniface and Keep-it-all.
Tomorrow is Christmas. Potter. Captain Sandman.
Tomson's Hallowe'en. Baker. Tomson's Hallowe'en.
Harper. Ghosts and goblins.
See also Witch of Windy Hill.

Tongue-cut sparrow. Carey. Stories of the birds. (Sparrow and the washerwoman.)
Coussens. ' Diamond story book.
Curry and Clippinger. Children's literature.
Faulkner. Little Peachling. (Shitakiri Suzume.)
Henderson and Calvert. Wonder tales of old Japan. (Sparrow whose tongue was clipped.)
Mitford. Tales of old Japan.
Sugimoto. Japanese holiday picture tales. (Sparrow.)
Whitehorn. Wonder tales of old Japan.
For other entries, see 2d edition.
Tonia. Crew. Saturday's child.
Tonino and the fairies. Boggs and Davis. Three golden oranges.
See also Knockgrafton, Legend of.
Tontlawald, Tale of the. Olcott. Wonder tales from Baltic wizards. (Wood of Tontla.)
Tony Beaver. Field. American folk and fairy tales. (Big music.)
Too many daughters. Guerber. Legends of Switzerland. (*In* Legends of Vaud and Valais.)
Tooboo the short. Egan. New found tales.
See also Ghost land. III.
Tooty Tooty, the herb doctor. Retner. That's that.
Top and ball. Andersen. Fairy tales (Stickney. v. 1. Loving pair.)
See also Worsted dog.
For other entries, see 2d edition.
Top that could sing. Bailey. Stories children want.
Bailey. Tell me another story.
See also Why the top sings.
Topknot pigeons. Lee. Folk tales of all nations. (Goolah willeel, the topknot pigeons.)
Toplet. Capuana. Golden-feather.
Topmost apple. Potter. Giant of Apple Pie Hill.
Torch of courage. Bailey. Stories children want.
Harper. More story-hour favorites.
Toribio, the mountain boy. Phillips. Far peoples.
Torrone, Origin of. Untermeyer. Donkey of God. (*In* Prologue in Naples.)
Tortoise. *See* How a turtle fooled a little boy.
Tortoise and the eagle. *See* Foolish tortoise.
Tortoise and the elephant. I. See 2d edition.
Tortoise and the elephant. II. Carrick. Picture folk tales.
Tortoise and the geese. *See* Talkative tortoise.
Tortoise and the scorpion. *See* Scorpion and the tortoise.
Tortoise that gave the world music. *See* Hermes and Apollo.
Tournament. Cook. Red and gold stories.
Tournament day. *See* Birds' ball game.
Towel-land, Comb-land, and Brush-land. *See* Kari Woodengown.

Tower of Babel. Gaer. Burning bush. (Tower that wasn't completed.)

Tower of Babel (Aztec). *See* Giant pyramid builder.

Tower of Babel (Indian). *See* Seven giants.

Tower of Babylon. Colum. Boy apprenticed to an enchanter. (*In* Eean, the fisherman's son, pt. 3.)

Tower that sings. Lane. Tower legends.

Tower that wasn't completed. *See* Tower of Babel.

Town crier and the tailor. Buckingham. Elephant's friend.

Town mouse and the country mouse. I. *See* Country mouse and the town mouse. I.

Town mouse and the country mouse. II. Burnett. Children's book.

Town musicians. *See* Bremen town musicians.

Town of always play. Blaisdell. Rhyme and story second reader.

Town of Haveyourownway. Burnett. Children's book.

Town of nothing. Curtin. Fairy tales of Eastern Europe. *See also* Go I know not whither—fetch I know not what.

Town of the air. *See* Echo, chief of the Invisibles.

Town of the red castle. Colum. King of Ireland's son.

Town where no one slept. Berry. Black folk tales.

Toy of the giant child. Bailey. Tell me another story. (Giant's plaything.)
Guerber. Legends of Switzerland. (*In* Legends of Vaud and Valais.)
For other entries, see 2d edition.

Toy princess. Graham. Welcome Christmas.
Starbuck. Far horizons.
For other entries, see 2d edition.

Toymaker. I. Wiggin and Smith. Twilight stories. *See also* First doll.

Toymaker. II. Cooper. Tal. (*In* Ch. 17.)

Toys' departure. *See* Departure.

Trader meets a sokpar. Noel. Magic bird of Chomo-lung-ma.

Trail of two young warriors. Allen. Whispering wind.

Trailing arbutus, Legend of. Skinner. Child's book of country stories.

Train that would not stay on the track. Emerson. Merry-go-round of modern tales.

Training and restraint. *See* Wind and the flowers.

Trajan. Niemeyer. Stories for the history hour.

Tramp-cats. Richards. More five minute stories. (Tramps.)

Transformation donkey. Lee. Folk tales of all nations. *See also* Donkey cabbage.

Transformation of Cliff-dweller. De Huff. Taytay's memories.

Traveler and his dog. Æsop. Fables (Jones).
Æsop. Fables (Whitman ed.).
Cooper. Argosy of fables. (Dog and his master.)
For other entries, see 2d edition.

Traveler and fortune. Æsop. Fables (Jones).
Cooper. Argosy of fables.
See also Farmer and fortune.
Traveler and the tiger. **Arnold. Book of good counsels.
(Tiger and the traveller.)
Cooper. Argosy of fables. (Tiger and the traveler.)
For other entries, see 2d edition.
Travelers and the axe. Cooper. Argosy of fables. (Travelers and the hatchet.)
For other entries, see 2d edition.
Travelers and the bear. Æsop. Fables (Artzybasheff).
Æsop. Fables (Jones. Bear and the travelers.)
Æsop. Fables (Whitman ed.).
Cooper. Argosy of fables.
Curry and Clippinger. Children's literature.
Power. Children's treasure chest.
For other entries, see 2d edition.
Travelers and the hatchet. *See* Travelers and the axe.
Travelers and the plane=tree. Æsop. Fables (Jones).
Cooper. Argosy of fables.
Travelers by the seaside. *See* What was it?
In 2d edition there are entries under each title.
Traveler's money. Bryce. Folk lore from foreign lands.
Traveler's shoes. Housman. Doorway in fairyland.
See also Twelve dancing princesses.
Traveling cat. Chamoud. Picture tales from the French.
See also Bremen town musicians.
Traveling companion. Andersen. Fairy tales (Siewers tr.).
See also Thankful dead.
For other entries, see 2d edition.
Traveling musicians. *See* Bremen town musicians.
Travellers. *See* Travelers.
Travels of a fox. I. Elson and Runkel. Child-library readers: Book 2. (Fox that traveled. Abridged.)
Hutchinson. Chimney corner stories.
Told under the green umbrella.
Whiteman. Playmates in print. (Fox that traveled.)
For other entries, see 2d edition.
Travels of a fox. II. Carrick. Picture folk tales. (Fox who asked for a night's lodging.)
Travels of a fox. I–II.
For other versions *see* All change; Bird from the waterfall; Cat's tail; Giacco and his bean; Hodgepodge hold-fast; Little Miss Mouse and her friends; Man with the bag; Merlicoquet; Monkey's bargains.
Travels of Baron Munchausen. Patten. Junior classics. v. 5. (Startling adventures of Baron Munchausen.)
Raspé. Children's Munchausen (Martin).
Raspé. Tales from the travels of Baron Munchausen.
Rich. Read-aloud book.
See also Bunyan, Paul; Goatherd who won a princess; St Hubert's miracle; Shell, Solomon.

Travels of Baron Munchausen—*continued.*
For other entries, see 2d edition.
Treacherous conduct of the jackal Damnah. *See* Damnah the jackal.
Treacherous island. Wahlenberg. Old Swedish fairy tales.
Treacherous tree. Tuttle. Frightened tree and other stories.
Treachery of Morgan le Fay. *See* Morgan le Fay.
Treasure. I. *See* Endless tale. I.
Treasure. II. Ralston. Russian fairy tales.
Treasure beyond price. Egan. New found tales.
Treasure chamber of Rhampsinitus. Lee. Folk tales of all nations.
  **Maspero. Popular stories of ancient Egypt. (Story of Rhampsinitus.)
  See also Oracle of Trophonius; Thief and his son.
  For other entries, see 2d edition.
Treasure in the chest. Egan. New found tales.
  See also Duke William's treasure.
Treasure in the house. Bailey. Tell me another story.
Treasure of Cardona. Gunterman. Castles in Spain.
Treasure of Hasan Taj. Katibah. Other Arabian nights.
  See also Abraham the carpenter; Joseph, the Sabbath lover.
Treasure of the isle. Farjeon. Mighty men from Beowulf to William the Conqueror.
Treasure valley. Potter. Giant of Apple Pie Hill.
Treasure-wallet of Clan Bassna. Young. Tangle-coated horse. (Treasure wallet.)
Treasures. Egan. New found tales.
  See also Pedlar of Swaffham.
Treaty between the peacocks and the swans. **Arnold. Book of good counsels.
Tree bound. Spence. Myths of the North American Indians. (Adventures of Ictinike. *In* Ch. 5.)
  For other entries, see 2d edition.
Tree of justice. Kipling. Rewards and fairies.
Tree that trimmed itself. Bailey. Wonderful tree.
Major. Merry Christmas stories.
Tree who ran away from forest to plain. *See* Why! Why!
Tree with strange apples. *See* Hercules and his labors.
Tree with the softest heart. Skipper. Jungle meeting-pool (*In* Last meeting.)
Trees and the axe. *See* Woodman and the trees.
Trees choosing a king. Cooper. Argosy of fables.
  See also Bramble-bush king.
Trees, Origin of. Metzger. Tales told in Hawaii.
Trees under the protection of the gods. Cooper. Argosy of fables.
  See also Minerva's olive #.
Trembling tower. Meeker. Folk tales from the Far East.
  See also Queen bee. I.
Trip to the moon. I. Spurr. Dumas fairy tale book.
  See also Daniel O'Rourke.

Trip to the moon. II. Raspé. Children's Munchausen (Martin. *In* Ch. 18.)
Raspé. Tales from the travels of Baron Munchausen.
Trip to the moon. I–II.
For other versions *see* Chinese Emperor's visit to the moon; Chief in the moon; Goatherd who won a princess; Visit to the moon. II.
Trishka's caftan. Cooper. Argosy of fables.
For other entries, see 2d edition.
Triumph of Galatea. *See* Acis and Galatea.
Triumph of the East wind's daughter. *See* East wind and North wind.
Trojan war. Bulfinch. Golden age. (*In* Ch. 27.)
Forbush. Myths and legends of Greece and Rome.
Miller. My book of history. v. 2. (Greek minstrel's tale of the Trojan war. *In* Ch. 2.)
For other entries, see 2d edition.
Troll's Christmas. Topelius. Canute Whistlewinks.
See also Boniface and Keep-it-all.
Trolls in Hedale wood. Lee. Folk tales of all nations.
For other entries, see 2d edition.
Trophonius. Bulfinch. Golden age. (Oracle of Trophonius. *In* Ch. 34.)
Trott goes driving. Cabot. Course in citizenship.
Trott makes a visit. Cabot. Course in citizenship.
Trotty Veck's dinner. Cowles. Stories to tell.
Trouble, trouble, Mr. Alligator. Babbitt. Animals' own story book.
Trouble when one's young. Eells. Islands of magic.
See also Catherine and her destiny.
Truant vine. Bowman. Little brown bowl.
See also In the kitchen garden.
Truce of the wolf. *See* St. Francis of Assisi.
Trudi in the forest. Baumbach. Tales from the Swiss alps.
See also Little Black Sambo.
True and Untrue. Rasmussen. East o' the sun and west o' the moon. (Two brothers.)
See also Reward of virtue; Squirrel and the fox; Two brothers. VI; Two travellers. III; What witches tell.
For other entries, see 2d edition.
True charity. Curry and Clippinger. Children's literature.
True friendship. I. *See* 2d edition.
True friendship. II. Aspinwall. Jataka tales. (Woodpecker, tortoise and the antelope.)
Lee. Folk tales of all nations. (Four friends.)
See also Stag, the crow, and the jackal.
For other entries, see 2d edition.
In 2d edition this story is also indexed under the title "Zirac."
True-hearted, whole-hearted. *See* Lion of Lucerne.
True steel. *See* Steelpacha.
True Thomas. *See* Thomas the rhymer.

Trumbilloo the magician. Cooper. Tal. (*In* Ch. 9.)
Trumpeter taken prisoner. Æsop. Fables (Artzybasheff).
Æsop. Fables (Jones).
Cooper. Argosy of fables.
For other entries, see 2d edition.
Trusting lad. Chamoud. Picture tales from the French.
See also Hare that was sent to York.
Trustworthy one. Partridge. Joyful Star.
See also Sura and her seeds.
Trusty friend. *See* Country where the mice eat iron.
Truthful Jan. Choate and Curtis. Little people of the hills.
Truthful parrot. *See* Why the parrot repeats the words of men.
Truthful Persian. *See* Little Persian.
Truth's triumph. Pyle. Fairy tales from India.
For other entries, see 2d edition.
Tryphene, St. *See* St. Tryphine.
Tsarevich Ivan and the harp that harped without a harper. Carpenter. Tales of a Russian grandmother. (Sweet-stringed dulcimer.)
For other entries, see 2d edition.
Tsar Saltan. Zeitlin. Skazki.
See also Three sisters. I.
For other entries, see 2d edition.
Tschan-bolpin. Wolff. Pale mountains. (*In* Children of the sun, pt. 3.)
Tsenahale the Winged. *See* How the birds came. II.
Tuan MacCairill. Stephens. Irish fairy tales.
Tubal Cain. I. Evans. Worth while stories.
(poem). Kipling. Poems.
Tubal Cain. II. Lansing. Great moments in freedom. (*In* Fire stories: Rock that melted.)
Tubman, Harriet (poem). Broomell. Children's story caravan. (True ballad of glorious Harriet Tubman.)
Tufted cap. *See* Owl's tufted cap.
Tug of war. *See* How the elephant and the whale were tricked. I.
Tug of war between a whale and an elephant. *See* How the elephant and the whale were tricked. I.
Tuirean. *See* Birth of Bran; Finn MacCool.
Tulip. *See* Little nymph who loved bright colors; Madame Tulip and Princess Violet; Tulip bed. II.
Tulip bed. I. Carey. Flower legends (Tulip, pt. 1.)
Newman. Fairy flowers. (Pixie cradles. Adapted.)
Rhys. English fairy book.
Williams-Ellis. Fairies and enchanters. (*In* Water's locked.)
For other entries, see 2d edition.
Tulip bed. II. Cook. To-day's stories of yesterday. (How the tulips came to have bright colors. Adapted.)
For other entries, see 2d edition.

Tulip bed. III. Stewart. Tell me a story I never heard before. (Granny's garden.)

Tulisa. Martens. Wonder tales from far away.

Tumilkoontaoo. *See* Wuchowson the windblower.

Tune that makes the tiger drowsy. Skeat. Tiger's mistake.

See also Tiger's mistake.

For other entries, see 2d edition.

Tunny and the dolphin. Æsop. Fables (Jones. Tunny-fish and the dolphin.)

For other entries, see 2d edition.

Turke and Gawain. *See* Sir Gawain and the King of Man.

Turkey and the ant (poem). Cooper. Argosy of fables.

Turkey=bean and the moon. Raspé. Children's Munchausen (Martin. *In* Ch. 5.)

Raspé. Tales from the travels of Baron Munchausen.

See also Jack and the beanstalk.

Turkey for the stuffing. Skinner. Child's book of country stories.

Turkey girl. *See* Turkey maiden.

Turkey=given corn. Allen. Whispering wind. (Farm at the end-of-the-water.)

James. Tewa firelight tales. (Man and the woman.)

Sexton. Gray wolf stories. (Turkey helps his master find corn, cereals, and vegetables.)

See also Navaho and the wizard; Pet turkey whose feelings were hurt.

For other entries, see 2d edition.

Turkey helps his master find corn. *See* Turkey-given corn.

Turkey magic. *See* Turkey maiden.

Turkey maiden. Egan. New found tales. (Turkey magic.)

Johnson and Scott. Anthology of children's literature. (Poor turkey girl.)

Nusbaum. Seven cities of Cibola. (Poor maid of Matsaki.)

Nusbaum. Zuni Indian tales. (Poor maid of Matsaki.)

Partridge. Joyful Star. (Turkey girl.)

See also Little Cinderella; Tewa Cinderella.

For other entries, see 2d edition.

Turkey's nest. Elson and Runkel. Child-library readers. Book 2.

Turkey's singing lesson. James. Happy animals of Atagahi.

Turkish judge. Bryce. Folk lore from foreign lands.

See also Oil vendor and the blind man.

Turnip. I. De La Mare. Told again. (Adapted.)

For other entries, see 2d edition.

Turnip. II. Carrick. Animal picture tales from Russia.

Turnip. I–II. *See also* Mr. Finney's turnip.

Turnip counter. *See* Rubezahl.

Turnip-field godmother. Atkins. Pot of gold.

Turquoise princess. Noel. Magic bird of Chomo-lung-ma.

Turtle. Cooper. Tal. (*In* Ch. 4.)

Turtle and the deer run a race. Babbitt. Animals' own
story book.
Turtle and the fowl. Metzger. Tales told in Hawaii.
See also Hare and the tortoise.
Turtle and the joker. Kennedy. Red man's wonder book.
Turtle and Thunder-bird. Rich. Why-so stories. (How the
Thunder-bird scared the turtle.)
**Turtle gains a long neck and reveals that he is good for
soup.** Parker. Skunny Wundy and other Indian tales.
Turtle runs a race with bear. Parker. Skunny Wundy and
other Indian tales.
Turtle spots. Metzger. Tales told in Hawaii.
Turtle tales and chicken tails. *See* Hen and the Chinese
mountain turtle.
Turtle who couldn't stop talking. *See* Talkative tortoise.
Turtle who talked too much. *See* Talkative tortoise.
Turtle's shell. Lee. Folk tales of all nations. (How the
turtle got his shell.)
See also Was it the first turtle; Why the tortoise has a
round back.
For other entries, see 2d edition.
Turtle's trick. *See* Man and turtle.
Turtle's war party. *See* War party. III.
Tweedledum and Tweedledee. Carrol. Through the look-
ing glass. (*In* Ch. 4.)
Rich. Read-aloud book.
Twelfth dragon. *See* Little Czar Novishny, the false sister
and the faithful beasts.
Twelfth night; or, What you will. Lamb. Tales from
Shakespeare.
Twelve dancing princesses. I. De La Mare. Told again.
(Dancing princesses.)
Grimm. Fairy tales (Olcott. Shoes that were danced to
pieces.)
Kinscella. Music appreciation readers. Book 6. (Dancing
shoes.)
Quiller-Couch. Twelve dancing princesses.
Quinn. Stokes' wonder book of fairy tales.
Williams. Tales from Ebony.
For other entries, see 2d edition.
Twelve dancing princesses. II. Pogány. Hungarian fairy
book.
See also Traveler's shoes.
Twelve huntsmen #.
See also Curly-locks: White steed Bufanin.
Twelve labors of Hercules. *See* Hercules and his labors.
Twelve months. I. Bruce. Treasury of tales for little folk.
(Four seasons.)
Bryce. Folk lore from foreign lands.
Curtin. Fairy tales of Eastern Europe.
Faulkner. Road to enchantment.
Tappan. Prince from nowhere. (Red apples in the snow.)

Twelve months—*continued.*
Williams. Jolly old whistle. (Gentle sunshine.)
For other entries, see 2d edition.
Twelve silly sisters. *See* Twelve silly sisters that the Pooka
carried away.
Twelve silly sisters that the Pooka carried away. Colum.
Fountain of youth. (Twelve silly sisters.)
For other entries, see 2d edition.
Twelve vultures and a square city. *See* Romulus and Re-
mus.
Twelve wild ducks. Rasmussen. East o' the sun and west
o' the moon.
For other entries, see 2d edition.
Twelve wild geese. Colum. King of Ireland's son. (Unique
tale.)
For other entries, see 2d edition.
Twelve windows. De La Mare. Told again.
Tappan. Prince from nowhere. (Young man who used his
brains.)
See also Golden parrot.
In some editions not indexed here, this story has the title
"Sea-hare."
Twenty-one black and white chicks. Retner. That's that.
Twilight fairy. Marzials. Stories for the story hour.
Twilight of the gods. I. Bulfinch. Golden age. (Ragna-
rok. *In* Ch. 40.)
Miller. My book of history. v. 3. (*In* Ch. 7.)
Pyle. Tales from Norse mythology. (Ragnarok.)
For other entries, see 2d edition.
Twilight of the Indian gods. Leland. Algonquin legends.
(How Glooskap is making arrows for a great battle.)
Macmillan. Canadian wonder tales. (*In* Passing of Gloos-
kap.)
Twin brothers. I–III. *See* 2d edition.
Twin brothers. IV. *See* Castor and Pollux.
Twinkles. Fyleman. Forty good-night tales.
Twinkling Feet's Hallowe'en. Skinner. Topaz story book.
Twins with the dogs' eyes. Rasmussen. Eagle's gift.
Twist-mouth family #.
See also Snooks family and the candle.
Two apples on a tree. Potter. Captain Sandman.
See also Three apples. II.
Two bags. *See* Jupiter's two wallets.
Two bald men. Cooper. Argosy of fables.
Two billy goats, Fable of. Hogner. Navajo winter nights.
Two boys and a baby. Burnett. Children's book.
Two brothers. I–II. *See* 2d edition.
Two brothers. III #.
See also Old hag of the forest.
Two brothers. IV #.
See also Boy who was brother to a Drague.
Two brothers. V. *See* 2d edition.

Two brothers. VI. Through story-land with the children.
For other entries, see 2d edition.
Two brothers. VII–XII. *See* 2d edition.
Two brothers. XIII. *See* Bata, the Egyptian boy.
Two brothers. XIV. Bailey. Story-telling hour.
See also Two brothers. III–IV.
Two brothers. XV. Farjeon. Old nurse's stocking basket.
Two brothers. XVI. *See* Swallow king's rewards.
Two brothers. XVII. Faulkner. Road to enchantment.
See also Queen bee.
Two brothers. XVIII. Egan. New found tales.
Two brothers. XIX. *See* True and Untrue.
Two brothers and the forty=nine dragons. *See* Forty-nine
dragons.
Two bulls. *See* Cattle raid of Cooley.
Two children and two shoes. Potter. Giant of Apple Pie
Hill.
Two Cinderella stories. *See* Bones of Djuling; Cenerentola.
Two cities. Lagerlöf. Wonderful adventures of Nils. (*In*
Ch. 14.)
Two corpses. Ralston. Russian fairy tales.
Two daughters. Sheriff. Stories old and new.
For other entries, see 2d edition.
Two discreet statues, Legend of. Irving. Tales from the
Alhambra.
For other entries, see 2d edition.
Two dogs. Cooper. Argosy of fables.
For other entries, see 2d edition.
Two dreams. Darton. Wonder book of old romance.
Two fishes and the frog. *See* Hundred-wit, Thousand-wit,
and Single-wit.
Two flies and the bee (poem). Cooper. Argosy of fables.
Two foolish birds. Sheriff. Stories old and new. (Two
foolish jackdaws.)
For other entries, see 2d edition.
Two friends. Ralston. Russian fairy tales.
For other entries, see 2d edition.
Two frogs. I. Æsop. Fables (Jones).
Cooper. Argosy of fables. (Wise and the foolish frogs.)
For other entries, see 2d edition.
Two frogs. II. See 2d edition.
Two frogs. III. *See* Frog travelers.
Two frogs and the well. Æsop. Fables (Jones. Frogs and
the well.)
Cooper. Argosy of fables. (Two frogs and the well.)
Two gentlemen from Verona. Lamb. Tales from Shake-
speare.
Two gifts. I. Coussens. Diamond story book.
For other entries, see 2d edition.
Two gifts. II. Lindsay. Choosing book.
See also Sunken city.

Two girls and a devil. Pogány. Magyar fairy tales.
See also House in the wood.
Two goats. I. Boeckel. Through the gateway.
For other entries, see 2d edition.
Two goats. II. Hogner. Navajo winter nights. (Fable of
two billy goats.)
Two good-natured dragons. *See* Good-natured dragons.
Two grenadiers. Cross. Music stories.
Two imposters. Pogány. Magyar fairy tales.
See also Brahmin and his wife # ; Percy the wizard # ; Wise
soothsayer.
Two jars of honey. *See* Woman who hid her gold in a jar
of honey.
Two kings. *See* Lesson for kings.
Two kings at war. Cooper. Argosy of fables.
Two little cooks. Richards. More five minute stories.
For other entries, see 2d edition.
Two little kittens. La Rue. Under the story tree.
See also Three little kittens.
Two little maple leaves. Harriman. Stories for little children.
Two little owls. Kinscella. Music appreciation readers.
Book 2.
Two little pairs of shoes. Burnett. Children's book.
Two little roosters. La Rue. Under the story tree.
Two little stockings (poem). McVenn. Good manners and
good conduct.
Two lizards. I. Cooper. Argosy of fables.
For other entries, see 2d edition.
Two lizards. II. Patten. Junior classics. v. 1.
For other entries, see 2d edition.
Two marbles. Blaisdell. Rhyme and story second reader.
Two matches. De La Mare and Quayle. Readings.
Two melons. I. Egan. New found tales. (Golden melon.)
See also Jackal the barber and the Brahmin; Moko and the
twelve little earth men; Swallow king's rewards.
For other entries, see 2d edition.
Two melons. II. Olcott. Wonder tales from China seas.
(Two treasure-melons.)
Two merry princes. Gate. Tales from the secret kingdom.
Two millers. Beston. Starlight wonder book.
See also Wind against water.
For other entries, see 2d edition.
Two monks who tried to quarrel. Hartshorne. Training
in worship. (Two monks.)
Two mothers. *See* King Solomon's wisdom. I.
Two mule drivers. Carpenter. Tales of a Basque grandmother.
Two mules. *See* Mules and the robbers.
In 2d edition there are entries under each title.

Two neighbors. Lee. Folk tales of all nations. (Story of the two neighbours.)
See also Jackal, the barber and the Brahmin; Swallow king's rewards; Two melons.
Two noble kinsmen. *See* Palamon and Arcita.
Two old men. I. *See* Two pilgrims.
Two old men. II. Metzger. Tales told in Korea.
Two old people. Capuana. Golden-feather.
Two orphans. Wiggin and Smith. Twilight stories.
Two out of the knapsack. Lee. Folk tales of all nations.
For other entries, see 2d edition.
Two packs #.
See also Jupiter's two wallets.
Two pigeons, Story of. Mackenzie. Jackal in Persia.
Two pilgrims. Tolstoy. Ivan the fool. (Two old men.)
See also Pilgrim of a night.
For other entries, see 2d edition.
Two pine cones. Bowman and Bianco. Tales from a Finnish tupa.
See also Two wishes that came true.
Two pots. *See* Earthen pot and the pot of brass.
Two princesses. Marzials. Stories for the story hour.
Two rabbits (poem). Cooper. Argosy of fables.
For other entries, see 2d edition.
Two rats. I. Æsop. Fables (Whitman ed.).
For other entries, see 2d edition.
Two rats, the fox, and the egg. *See* Rats, the fox and the egg.
Two rocks. Partridge. Joyful Star. (Two rocks in Passamaquoddy Bay.)
Two sillies. Olcott. Wonder tales from pirate isles.
Two silver heads. Guerber. Legends of Switzerland. (*In* Legends of Neuchatel.)
Two sisters. I–IV. See 2d edition.
Two sisters. V. Wahlenberg. Old Swedish fairy tales.
Two sisters. VI. *See* Old witch. I.
Two skyscrapers who decided to have a child. Sandburg. Rootabaga stories.
Two soldiers and the robber. Æsop. Fables (Jones). Cooper. Argosy of fables.
For other entries, see 2d edition.
Two soldiers went a-fishing. Kovalsky and Putnam. Longlegs, Big-mouth, Burning-eyes.
Two tails. Skinner. Child's book of country stories. (Tale of two tails.)
For other entries, see 2d edition.
Two thrushes (poem). Cooper. Argosy of fables.
Two travelers. I. See 2d edition.
Two travelers. II. Harper. More story-hour favorites.
For other entries, see 2d edition.
Two travelers. III. Grimm. Fairy tales (Olcott).
See also True and untrue.

Two travelers and the oyster (poem).   Cooper.   Argosy of fables.   (Justice and the oyster . . .)
LaFontaine.   Fables (Tilney.   Oyster and the pleaders.)
See also Judgement of the monkey.   II ; Matter of arbitration.
For other entries, see 2d edition.
In 2d edition this story is also indexed under the title "Oyster and its claimants.
Two treasure-melons.   *See* Two melons.
Two trout in a pool.   Potter.   Giant of Apple Pie Hill.
Two wallets.   *See* Jupiter's two wallets.
Two ways.   Cowles.   Stories to tell.
For other entries, see 2d edition.
Two wee thumb-oxen.   Pogány.   Magyar fairy tales.
Two wine merchants lose their heads.   Broomell.   Children's story caravan.
Two wishes that came true.   Gaer.   Burning bush.
See also Cloth of endless length ; How the good gifts were used by two ; Two pine cones.
Two worlds.   *See* Dragon fly.
Two young men who wanted to marry the same girl.
See Magic apples.   III.
Two youths whose father was under the sea.   Colum.   Big tree of Bunlahy.
Twopence halfpenny.   Morris.   Gypsy story teller.
Twopenny town.   Starbuck.   Enchanted paths.
For other entries, see 2d edition.
Tyl Ulenspiegel.   Hart.   Picture tales from Holland.   (Tyl Uilenspiegel.)
Miller.   My travelship: Holland.   (Glorious, joyous and heroic adventures of Tyl Ulenspiegel.)
Tylwith Teg.   *See* Forbidden fountain.

U

Uffe the silent.   Adams.   Swords of the Vikings.
Ugly boy and the bear.   *See* Ugly wild boy.
Ugly duckling.   Andersen.   Fairy tales (Siewers tr.).
Andersen.   Fairy tales (Stickney).   v. 1.
Arthur Rackham fairy book.
Bruce.   Treasury of tales for little folk.
Curry and Clippinger.   Children's literature.
Evans.   Worth while stories.   (Adapted.)
Johnson and Scott.   Anthology of children's literature.
Kinscella.   Music appreciation readers.   Book 2.
Quinn.   Stokes' wonder book of fairy tales.
Rich.   Read-aloud book.
Starbuck.   Familiar haunts.
Williams.   Tales from Ebony.
For other entries, see 2d edition.
Ugly little crows.   *See* Crow's children.
Ugly Tom.   Steedman.   Knights of art.   (Masaccio.)

Ugly wild boy (play). Lamkin and Jagendorf. Around
America with the Indians. (Ugly wild Zuni boy.)
Nusbaum. Seven cities of Cibola. (Ugly boy and the bear.)
Nusbaum. Zuni Indian tales. (Ugly boy and the bear.)
For other entries, see 2d edition.
In 2d edition this story is also indexed under the title,
"Little ugly boy."

Ugly wild Zuni boy. *See* Ugly wild boy.

Uhla=kan=yan=a. Fleming. Round the world in folk tales.
See also Monkey's bargains.

Ulda's old mother. Olcott. Wonder tales from Baltic wizards. (What happened to some Lapp children.)
See also Changeling.

Ulster, awake! *See* Awakening of Ulster.

Ulysses. Adams and Atchinson. Book of enchantment.
(Circe's palace.)
Colum. Fountain of youth. (Story of Odysseus.)
Cruse. Young folk's book of epic heroes.
Forbush. Myths and legends of Greece and Rome.
Miller. My book of history. v. 2. (Wanderings of Odys-
seus. In Ch. 2.)
Power. Bag o' tales. (Stories from the Odyssey.)
Rich. Read-aloud book. (Adventures of Ulysses.)
For other entries, see 2d edition.

Ulysses and Polyphemus. Bulfinch. Golden age. (*In* Ch.
29.)
Forbush. Myths and legends of Greece and Rome. (*In*
Ulysses: Adventures with the Cyclops.)
Johnson and Scott. Anthology of children's literature.
(Polyphemus and the Cyclops.)
Lanier. Book of giants. (Outwitting of Polyphemus.)
Power. Bag o' tales. (Cyclops.)
See also Man who lost his legs.
For other entries, see 2d edition.

Ulysses and the bag of winds. Bulfinch. Golden age. (*In*
Ch. 29.)
Lane. Tower legends. (Æolus and the tower of the
winds.)
See also Calabash of winds.
For other entries, see 2d edition.

Ulysses and the sirens. Chidley. Fifty-two story talks.
Forbush. Myths and legends of Greece and Rome. (*In*
Ulysses: Sirens.)
Power. Bag o' tales. (Song of the sirens.)
For other entries, see 2d edition.

Ulysses at Circe's palace. Bulfinch. Golden age. (*In* Ch.
29.)
Forbush. Myths and legends of Greece and Rome. (*In*
Ulysses: Circe.)
See also Companions of Ulysses.
For other entries, see 2d edition.

Ulysses' return. Bulfinch. Golden age. (*In* Ch. 30.)
Colum. Fountain of youth. (How Odysseus returned to his own land.)
Farjeon. Mighty men from Achilles to Julius Caesar. (Bow of Ulysses.)
Forbush. Myths and legends of Greece and Rome. (*In* Ulysses.)
Power. Bag o' tales. (How the swineherd welcomed Odysseus.)
See also Penelope's web.
For other entries, see 2d edition.
Umakichi. Sugimoto. Japanese holiday picture tales.
Umbrella-maker's Kozo. Sugimoto. Japanese holiday picture tales.
Umi the conqueror. Colum. Bright islands.
Una and the Red Cross Knight. Bailey. Stories of great adventures.
Fuller. Book of dragons. (St. George and the dragon.)
See also Red Cross Knight's last battle.
For other entries, see 2d edition.
Unabashed wife, Story of. **Arnold. Book of good counsels.
Unamiable child. Morley. I know a secret.
Unbelieving king. Shannon. California fairy tales.
See also Man who did not believe in fairies.
Unbidden guest. Bancroft. Goblins of Haubeck.
Uncle Rabbit's Thanksgiving dinner. *See* Old Man Rabbit's Thanksgiving dinner.
Uncommon common sailor. *See* Pinafore.
Unda Marina's footprints. Topelius. Canute Whistlewinks.
Unda Marina's silver cup. Topelius. Canute Whistlewinks.
Undan the pelican. Carey. Stories of the birds.
See also Crane and the crab.
Under the lemon tree. Wiggin and Smith. Twilight stories.
Under the lid. Egan. New found tales.
Under the rowan tree. Brown. Under the rowan tree.
Underworld. Howes. Long bright land.
See also Ta-whaki.
Underwater country. Sexton. Gray wolf stories. (Ten years in the underwater country.)
Undine. I. Guerber. Legends of the Rhine. (*In* Zündorf.)
For other entries, see 2d edition.
Undoing of Zipacna. *See* Zipacna.
Unforgiving monkey. Lee. Folk tales of all nations.
Ungrateful guest. Hartshorne. Training in worship. (*In* Ungrateful self.)
For other entries, see 2d edition.
Ungrateful rat. Metzger. Tales told in Hawaii.
Ungrateful self. *See* Ungrateful guest.
Ungrateful sons. Egan. New found tales.
Ungrateful tom-tit. Carey. Stories of the birds.
Unhappily married man. La Fontaine. Fables (Tilney).

Unhappy echo. Bailey. Story-telling hour.
See also Echo. I.
Unhappy king. Martinez Del Rio. Sun, the moon and a rabbit.
Unicorn. I. *See* 2d edition.
Unicorn. II. Bulfinch. Golden age. (*In* Ch. 36.)
Uninvited guest. Egan. New found tales.
Uninvited guests. Choate and Curtis. Little people of the hills.
Unique tale. Colum. King of Ireland's son. (*In* Sword of light; Town of the red castle.)
See also Sword of light. II ; Twelve wild geese.
Unkind beauty. Metzger. Tales told in Hawaii.
Unknown travelers. Tappan. Prince from nowhere.
Unktomee and his bundle of songs. Phillips. Indian tales for little folks. (Why the wood duck has red eyes.)
See also Iktomi and the ducks.
For other entries, see 2d edition.
Unseen friends. Bailey. Stories from an Indian cave.
See also Beloved warrior.
Unselfish Frances. White. School management, p. 271.
See also Queer little baker man.
Unwelcome gift. Van Buren and Bemis. Christmas in storyland.
Up to the moon. *See* Daniel O'Rourke.
Up to the sky and back. *See* Water-drop. II.
Uphill brook. Potter. Giant of Apple Pie Hill.
Upi, Story of. Fleming. Round the world in folk tales.
Up-side-down world. *See* Dionysius and Jupiter's cloak.
Upside-down moral. Canfield. Made to order stories.
Uraschimataro and the turtle. Bruce. Treasury of tales for little folk. (Urashima Taro.)
Coussens. Diamond story book. (Urashima, the fisher boy.)
Dulac. Edmund Dulac's fairy book. (Urashima Taro.)
Henderson and Calvert. Wonder tales of old Japan. (One of the oldest stories in Japan.)
Johnson and Scott. Anthology of children's literature. (Fisher-boy Urashima.)
Lee. Folk tales of all nations. (Irashima Taro.)
Martens. Wonder tales from far away. (Urashimataro.)
Phillips. Far peoples. (Urashima.)
Price. Legends of the seven seas. (Urashima Taro and the sea princess.)
Sugimoto. Picture tales from the Japanese. (Urashima.)
Whitehorn. Wonder tales of old Japan. (Story of Urashima the fisher-boy.)
For other entries, see 2d edition.
Urashima. *See* Uraschimataro and the turtle.
Urashima Taro and the sea princess. *See* Uraschimataro and the turtle.
Urashima, the fisher boy. *See* Uraschimataro and the turtle.

Urashimataro. *See* Uraschimataro and the turtle.
Urho and Marja. Bowman and Bianco. Tales from a Finnish tupa.
Ursula, St. *See* St. Ursula.
Usheen, Story of. *See* Last of the Feni.
Ut=Rost cormorants. *See* Cormorants of Udröst.

V

Vagabonds #.
See also Krencipal and Krencipalka ; Man of the woods and the giant.
Vain bear. Bowman and Bianco. Tales from a Finnish tupa.
Vain cereals. Cooper. Argosy of fables.
See also When the jungle plants quarrelled.
Vain jackdaw. I. Æsop. Fables (Whitman ed.).
Cooper. Argosy of fables. (Vain jackdaw.)
Johnson and Scott. Anthology of children's literature. (Jackdaw and the borrowed plumes.)
See also Jackdaw and the pigeons.
For other entries, see 2d edition.
Vain jackdaw. II. Æsop. Fables (Jones).
See also Masquerading crow.
Vain queen, Tale of. *See* Cassiopeia.
Vain Teddy=bear. Fyleman. Forty good-night tales. (Vain teddy.)
Vainamoinen. *See* Vanemuine.
Vaino and the swan princess. Bowman and Bianco. Tales from a Finnish tupa.
Valentine. *See* St. Valentine.
Valentine and Orson. Brock. Valentine and Orson.
Mackenzie. Book of nursery tales.
For other entries, see 2d edition.
Valentine box. Bailey. Tell me another story.
Valentine that flew away. Bailey. Wonderful tree.
Valentine that posted itself. Bailey. Wonderful tree.
Valentine's day. *See* St. Valentine's Day.
Valiant blackbird. Faulkner. White elephant. (Bold blackbird.)
Lee. Folk tales of all nations.
See also Drakesbill and his friends.
For other entries, see 2d edition.
Valiant chattee=maker. Faulkner. White elephant. (Man who rode a tiger.)
Gordon and Stockard. Gordon readers. 2d reader. (Dripping.)
Lee. Folk tales of all nations.
Pyle. Fairy tales from India.
See also Bear and the leak.
For other entries, see 2d edition.
Valiant dwarf. *See* Brave little bowman.
Valiant little tailor. *See* Brave little tailor.

Valiant tin soldier. *See* Brave tin soldier.
Valiant Vicky. Shimer. Fairyland. (Ten at one stroke.)
For other entries, see 2d edition.
Valmiki. *See* Robber who became a poet.
Value of a good name. White. School management, p. 265.
Vampire cat of Nabeshima. Mitford. Tales of old Japan.
Van Dyck, Antonio. Barrows and Cavanah. Favorite pages
from Child Life. (Antonio Van Dyck and his master Ru-
bens.)
Van Ness family. Burnett. Children's book.
Vanemuine, god of song. Baldwin. Sampo.
Fillmore. Wizard of the North.
Olcott. Wonder tales from Baltic wizards. (Magic sing-
ing.)
See also Voices of nature #.
Vanished island. Harper. More story-hour favorites.
For other entries, see 2d edition.
Vanka's birthday. Mamin. Verotchka's tales.
Vasilisa the beauty. Carpenter. Tales of a Russian grand-
mother. (Wonderful doll of Vasilissa the beautiful.)
Ralston. Russian fairy tales. (Vasilissa the fair.)
See also Baba Yaga.
For other entries, see 2d edition.
Vasilissa the fair. *See* Vasilisa the beauty.
Vasilissa the wise. *See* Vassilissa the cunning and the tsar
of the sea.
Vassilissa the cunning and the tsar of the sea. Fun folk
and fairy tales. (Vasilissa the wise.)
Ralston. Russian fairy tales. (Water king and Vasilissa
the wise.)
Wilson. Green magic. (Water king and Vasilissa the
wise.)
For other entries, see 2d edition.
In 2d edition this story is also indexed under the title "Sea
Tsar and Vasilissa the wise."
Vazuza and Volga. Carpenter. Tales of a Russian grand-
mother. (Rivers that talked.)
Ralston. Russian fairy tales. (Vazuza and Volga.)
Ransome. Old Peter's Russian tales. (*In* Christening in
the village.)
For other entries, see 2d edition.
Vega and Altair, the star lovers. *See* Sky bridge of birds.
Veil of Irazade. Farjeon. Old nurse's stocking basket.
See also Mayblossom.
Venediger Manndl. Henderson and Calvert. Wonder tales
of old Tyrol.
Vengeance of a god. Martinez Del Rio. Sun, the moon and
a rabbit.
Venice legend. Steedman. Knights of art. (*In* Giorgione.)
Venus. Harshaw. Council of the gods. (Aphrodite on her
sacred island.)
Venus and Adonis. *See* Adonis.

Venus and the cat. Æsop. Fables (Jones).
Cooper. Argosy of fables.
See also Dancing monkeys; Rats and their son-in-law.
For other entries, see 2d edition.
Venus's looking glass. Carey. Flower legends. (Campanula or Canterbury bell.)
For other entries, see 2d edition.
Verbatim from Boileau. *See* Two travellers and the oyster.
Vercingetorex. Clément. Flowers of chivalry. (Gloria victis.)
Verlioka. Lee. Folk tales of all nations.
See also Ito and his friends.
For other entries, see 2d edition.
Vermilion bird, the dragon and the unicorn. Olcott. Wonder tales from China seas.
See also Phœnix.
Verotchka and the flowers. Mamin. Verotchka's tales. (Bed time.)
Vertumnus. *See* Pomona.
Very crafty minnow. Bacon. Lion-hearted kitten.
Very first. Blondell. Keepsakes.
Very last story of all. *See* Chinese student who got in the cellar.
Very rich aunt. Blaisdell. Rhyme and story second reader.
Very strange friend. Retner. That's that.
Very untidy country. Baker. Tell them again tales.
Vesta and the vestal virgins. Forbush. Myths and legends of Greece and Rome.
Orvieto. Birth of Rome. (Princess who became a vestal virgin.)
Vicram's choice. Egan. New found tales. (Talking statues, pt. 2.)
Victi and Antonio feast with the elves. Hill and Maxwell. Napoleon's story book.
See also Man with the wen.
Victor's dragoon trousers. Burnett. Children's book.
Victory for English. Forbes. Good citizenship. (*In* Ch. 4.)
Victory of Titanis. Browne. Indian nights.
See also Tell, William.
Vikings. Blaisdell. Log cabin days.
Viking's cave. Fuller. Book of dragons. (Legend of the viking's cave.)
Viking's death. Adams. Swords of the Vikings.
Vincent de Paul. *See* St. Vincent de Paul.
Vine and the goat. *See* Goat and the vine.
Vine tree. Darton. Wonder book of old romance.
Vintem. Phillips. Far peoples. (Story of the vintem.)
Violet. Carey. Flower legends.
See also Wood violet that was a maiden #.
For other entries, see 2d edition.
Violet and the rainbow elves. Mitchell. Gray moon tales. (Mammy and the rainbow elves.)

Vows of the Jom Vikings. Dunlap. Stories of the Vikings.
Voyage of Columbus. *See* Columbus, Christopher.
Voyage of Hanno of Carthage. Miller. My book of history.
v. 2. (Periplus or circumnavigation of Hanno. *In* Ch. 9.)
Voyage of Maelduin. Colum. Voyagers.
For other entries, see 2d edition.
Voyage of the red cap. Bryce. Folk lore from foreign
lands. (Red cap.)
Olcott. Wonder tales from fairy isles. (By yarrow and
rue.)
Yeats. Irish fairy and folk tales. (Witches' excursion.)
See also Piskies in the cellar # ; Voyage of the wee red cap.
Voyage of the wee red cap. Starbuck. Enchanted paths.
Walters. Book of Christmas stories. (Abridged.)
For other entries, see 2d edition.
Voyage of Unumunu to the coasts of Syria. *See* Misfortunes of Wenamon.
Voyages of St. Brendan. *See* St. Brandan.
Vukub=Cakix. *See* Hero twins. I.
Vulcan. Bryant. Children's book of celebrated legends.
(Forge of Vulcan.)
Forbush. Myths and legends of Greece and Rome. (Blacksmith of the gods.)
Harshaw. Council of the gods. (Hermes visits Hephaestus.)
For other entries, see 2d edition.
Vulture and the kite. Cooper. Argosy of fables.
Vulture, the cat and the birds. *See* Jackal and the cat.

W

Wabaskaha, Story of. Spence. Myths of the North American Indians. (*In* Ch. 5.)
Wager. Eells. Brazilian fairy book.
Wager to keep awake. De Leeuw. Java jungle tales.
Wages of seven years. Egan. New found tales.
Waggoner and the butterfly (poem). Cooper. Argosy of
fables.
See also Flea and the camel; Gnat and the bull.
Wagon-pole cross. Otero. Old Spain in our Southwest.
Wagtail and the sea, Story of. **Arnold. Book of good
counsels.
Wainamoinen. *See* Vanemuine.
Wait-and-see pudding. Potter. Giant of Apple-pie-Hill.
Wait till Martin comes. Harper. Ghosts and goblins.
For other entries, see 2d edition.
"Wake up" story. Harriman. Stories for little children.
For other entries, see 2d edition.
Wakontas and the two maidens. Egan. New found tales.
(Gentle maiden.)
Partridge. Joyful Star. (How Wakontas tested the maidens.)

Wakontas and the two maidens—*continued.*
For other entries, see 2d edition.
Walking boy. Aspinwall. Can you believe me stories.
Walking doll. Brown. Wonderful tree.
Wallflowers. I. Carey. Flower legends. (Wallflower.)
Wallflowers. II. Fyleman. Forty good-morning tales.
Wall=paperville. Richards. More five minute stories.
Walnut tree. Æsop. Fables (Jones).
Cooper. Argosy of fables.
Walpurgis witch=night. Olcott. Wonder tales from goblin hills.
Walter von der Vogelweide. Kinscella. Music appreciation readers. Book 4. (Boy who sang with birds.)
(poem). Olcott. Wonder tales from goblin hills.
Wander=Hawk who went out into the world. Rasmussen. Eagle's gift. (Wander-Hawk who went out into the world to uproot the wickedness of life and the treachery of man.)
Wanderer who had forgotten who he was. Byrde. Polish fairy book.
See also Giant with the golden hair.
Wandering dryad. Denton. Homespun stories.
Wandering huntsman and his music. Guerber. Legends of Switzerland. (*In* Bern.)
Wandering Jew #.
See also Tinker of Tamlacht.
Wandering Jew in Switzerland. Guerber. Legends of Switzerland. (*In* Bern.)
Wandering monkey. Lobagola. Folk tales of a savage.
Wandering nymph. Eells. Brazilian fairy book.
Wanderings of Isis. *See* Isis and Osiris.
Wanderings of Odysseus. *See* Ulysses.
Wanderings of Vicram Maharajah. Pyle. Fairy tales from India.
For other entries, see 2d edition.
Wang and his star. Shimer. Fairyland.
Wang Spring=Flowers and the golden oranges. Olcott. Wonder tales from China seas.
Want of fidelity. White. School management, p. 278.
War between animals and sky people. I. *See* 2d edition.
War between animals and sky people. II. Linderman. Kootenai why stories. (War with Up-there-persons.)
See also Animals in the sky # ; Arrow trail.
War between the birds and the animals. De Huff. Tay-tay's tales.
See also Birds' ball game.
War for the bull of Cuailgne. *See* Cattle raid of Cooley.
War=horse and the miller. Æsop. Fables (Jones. Charger and the miller.)
Cooper. Argosy of fables.
See also King and the horses that turned the mills.

War in Asgard. *See* How the gods made war and peace with one another.

War of the winds. Hillyer. Box of daylight. (Four chiefs of the four winds.)

War of the wolf and the fox #.
See also Man who meant what he said.

War of words of the women of Ulster. *See* Bricriu's feast.

War party. I #. *See* Warlike seven.
In 2d edition there are entries under each title.

War party. II. Rich. Why-so stories. (Why the mosquito lives in swampy places.)
See also Seven Swabians; Warlike seven.

War party. III. Parker. Skunny Wundy and other Indian tales. (Turtle's war party.)

War with Up=there=persons. *See* War between animals and sky people. II.

Waring's "white wings." Forbes. Good citizenship. (*In* Ch. 10.)

Warlike seven. I. *See* 2d edition.
In 2d edition this story is also indexed under the title "War party."

Warlike seven. II. Sheriff. Stories old and new. (Warriors.)

Warlock. Ralston. Russian fairy tales.

Warrior maid. I. Phillips. Far peoples.
See also Joan of Arc; Vasilisa Popovna #.

Warrior maid. II. Metzger. Tales told in Korea.

Warrior maids. *See* Dance of the fairies #; Joan of Arc; Maid of Holland; Moolang; Princess who had the silver tooth; Rain king's daughter.

Warrior Princess. *See* Swanwhite and Ragner.

Warriors. *See* Warlike seven. II.

Warriors and the monkeys. Lee. Folk tales of all nations.

Wars of Manawyddan against Tathal Twyll Goleu. Morris. Book of the three dragons.

Warty frog lantern. Rowe. Moon's birthday.

Was=a=boy. Chrisman. Wind that wouldn't blow.
See also Oil merchant's donkey.

Was it the first turtle? I. *See* 2d edition.

Was it the first turtle? II. Lee. Folk tales of all nations. (Wayambeh the turtle.)

Washerman's jackass, Story of. **Arnold. Book of good counsels.
Cooper. Argosy of fables.
See also Cat who served the lion.

Washing machine. Emerson. Merry-go-round of modern tales.

Washington, George. Buckingham. Elephant's friend. (Wishing tree.)
Buckingham. Great idea. (When Washington came to town.)

Washington, George—*continued.*
    Freeman. Child-story readers. 3d reader. (George Washington's boyhood.)
    Hervey and Hix. Fanciful tales for children. (Name that grew.)
Washington and the cherry tree. Evans. Worth while stories. (George Washington.)
    For other entries, see 2d edition.
Washington and the colt. Curry and Clippinger. Children's literature. (Boyhood of Washington.)
    For other entries, see 2d edition.
Washington does not go to sea. Cabot. Course in citizenship. (Childhood of George Washington.)
    Cozad. Story talks. (Dearest wish of your heart.)
    For other entries, see 2d edition.
Washington goes to sea. Evans. Worth while stories. (George Washington.)
Washington lends a hand. White. School management, p. 276. (Lend a hand.)
Washington pie. Bailey. Wonderful tree.
Washington's Birthday. *See* Cherry tree adventure; Lie; Patriotic snowman; Their flag.
Wasp and the snake. Æsop. Fables (Jones).
Wasp, the winged needle, and the spider. *See* Three gifts. IV.
Wasps, the partridges and the farmer. Cooper. Argosy of fables.
Waste not, want not. Curry and Clippinger. Children's literature.
    See also Wise Pélé and his foolish friend.
    For other entries, see 2d edition.
Watchmaker. Morris. Gypsy story teller.
    See also Silent princess #.
Water-babe. Gaer. Burning bush. (Prince had reason to cry.)
    For other entries, see 2d edition.
Water babies. *See* Tom the water baby.
Water buffalo and the cow. De Leeuw. Java jungle tales. (Buffalo and the cow.)
    Power. How it happened. (Why the cow's skin is loose round the neck.)
Water-drop. I. *See* 2d edition.
Water-drop. II. Elson and Runkel. Child-library readers. Book 2. (Up to the sky and back.)
    For other entries, see 2d edition.
Water-drop. III. Evans. Worth while stories. (Journey of a drop of water.)
    Wheelock. Kindergarten children's hour. v. 3. Ch. 23. (Little water-drop's journey.)
Water king and Vasilissa the wise. *See* Vassilissa, the cunning, and the tsar of the sea.

Water king's daughter. Carpenter. Tales of a Russian grandmother.
  See also King Kojata.
Water-lily. I–III. *See* 2d edition.
Water-lily. IV. Carey. Flower legends.
  See also How the water lily came. II.
Water-lily. V. Newman. Fairy flowers. (Lily nymph.)
Water lily maidens. Olcott. Wonder tales from goblin hills.
Water music. *See* Handel, George Frederick.
Water nixie. I #.
  See also Flight.
Water nixie. II. Fun folk and fairy tales.
Water of Kane. Martens. Wonder tales from far away.
  Egan. New found tales. (Waters of life.)
Water of Ladi. Berry. Black folk tales.
  See also Wolf and the seven little kids.
Water of life. I–II. *See* 2d edition.
Water of life. III. Coe. Third book of stories.
  For other entries, see 2d edition.
Water-pipe. McNeer and Lederer. Tales from the crescent moon.
Water snake. Ralston. Russian fairy tales.
  For other entries, see 2d edition.
Water sprite (poem). Olcott. Wonder tales from goblin hills.
  For other entries, see 2d edition.
Water thief. *See* First clock.
Water wizard. Kennedy. Red man's wonder book.
Waterfall which flowed saké. Faulkner. Little Peachling. (Wonderful waterfall.)
  For other entries, see 2d edition.
Watermelon. Cooper. Argosy of fables.
  See also Mare's nest.
Water's locked. *See* Pixies' vengeance. II.
Waters of endless youth. Curtin. Fairy tales of Eastern Europe.
Waters of life. *See* Water of Kane.
Waters of life and death. Curtin. Fairy tales of Eastern Europe.
Waving Locks. Eells. Brazilian fairy book.
  See also Singing bone.
Wax wings. *See* Dædalus and Icarus.
Waxen crocodile. *See* Magic crocodile.
Way he left. Clément. Flowers of chivalry.
Way of the wind. Housman. Doorway in fairyland.
Way of the world. I. Lee. Folk tales of all nations. (Virtue is its own reward.)
  See also Camel driver and the snake; Foolish fish; Friend Mouse-deer; Mr. Monk and the tiger; Man and the snake; Old acquaintance is soon forgot; Tiger gets his deserts. I–II; Well done, ill paid.
  For other entries, see 2d edition.

Wayambeh the turtle. *See* Was it the first turtle? II.

Wayfarers all. Grahame. Kenneth Grahame l ook.

Wayland, the smith. Williams-Ellis. Fairies and enchanters. (Wayla'nd Smith.)
For other entries, see 2d edition.

"We always succeed in the end." Snell. Told beneath the northern lights.

We cannot escape our fate. **Gaster. Ma'aseh book. v. 1.
See also Ca-mee-no-wa-sit # ; Fate. III.

Weasel and Old Snowy Owl. Parker. Skunny Wundy and other Indian tales.

Weasel and the man. Æsop. Fables (Jones).

Weathercock. Fyleman. Forty good-morning tales.

Weaver birds and the monkeys. *See* Birds and the monkeys.

Weaver of the frost. Nakazawa. Weaver of the frost.

Weaving lady of the milky way. *See* Sky bridge of birds.

Weaving princess. *See* Sky bridge of birds.

Webster, Daniel. Cozad. Story talks. (Old complaint.)

Wedding of Maine Morgor. Gregory. Cuchulain of Muirthemne.

Wedding procession of the rag doll and the broom han=
, **dle . . .** Sandburg. Rootabaga country.
'Sandburg. Rootabaga stories.

Wednesday. Ralston. Russian fairy tales.

Wee bannock. Johnson and Scott. Anthology of children's literature.
Olcott. Wonder tales from fairy isles.
Steel. English fairy tales.
For other entries, see 2d edition.

Wee Miss Violet. Newman. Fairy flowers.

Wee red man. MacManus. Donegal wonder book.
See also Smith and the devil.

Wee Robin's Christmas Day. *See* Robin's Christmas song.

Wee Robin's Christmas song. *See* Robin's Christmas song.

Wee robin's Yule song. *See* Robin's Christmas song.

Wee, wee woman #.
See also Madame Teeny Tiny.

Weedah the mocking bird. *See* Mocking bird. III.

Weeds. Patten, Junior classics. v. 8.

Week of Sundays. Baker. Tell them again tales.

Weert, Weert the ray=fish stickers. Olcott. Wonder tales from windmill lands.

Weewillmekq. *See* Dance of death. II.

Well and the weasel. **Gaster. Ma'aseh book. v. 1.
(Keep troth ; Story of the well and the weasel.)

Well done, ill paid. I. *See* 2d edition.

"Well done; ill paid." II. Chamoud. Picture tales from the French.
See also Way of the world. I.

Well of St. Keyne. Long. Folklore calendar. (*In* May: Wells.)

Well of the moon. Dane. Once there was and was not.
Well of the world's end. Steel. English fairy tales.
See also Frog prince.
For other entries, see 2d edition.
Well of wisdom. I (poem). Olcott. Wonder tales from goblin hills.
Well of wisdom. II. Young. Tangle-coated horse. (Nuts of knowledge.)
Well of wisdom and the salmon of knowledge. Young. Tangle-coated horse. (*In* Night of the nights; Nuts of knowledge.)
Wellington and the plowboy. Cabot. Course in citizenship.
White. School management, p. 258. (Obeying orders.)
Wells Cathedral. *See* Hugh of Lincoln, and Jocelin of Wells.
Werewolf. I. Coussens. Diamond story book. (Werwolf.)
For other entries, see 2d edition.
Werewolf. II. *See* Mad Wolf.
Werewolf. III. *See* William of Palermo and the werwolf.
Werewolf. IV. *See* 2d edition.
Werewolf. V. *See* Magic ring. IV.
Werewolf. VI. Browne. Indian nights. (Were wolf, Story of.)
Werewolf. VII. Schwarz. Jewish caravan. (Israel and the enemy.)
Wesley, John. White. School management. (Profanity gently reproved.)
West, Benjamin. Chandler. Magic pictures. (Story of a little Quaker boy.)
For other entries, see 2d edition.
Whale and the man of war. Raspé. Children's Munchausen (Martin. *In* Ch. 13.)
Raspé. Tales from the travels of Baron Munchausen.
Whale and the ship. Raspé. Children's Munchausen (Martin. *In* Ch. 10.)
Whale's soul and its burning heart. Rasmussen. Eagle's gift.
Whales, turtles and mermaids. Martinez Del Rio. Sun, the moon and a rabbit.
What ailed the king. Starbuck. Enchanted paths.
For other entries, see 2d edition.
What are you going to do about it. Retner. That's that.
What became of the cry-baby. De Huff. Taytay's memories.
What became of the sugar. *See* Bees and the sugar. II.
What befell Sidi Abbess. Martin. Fatma was a goose.
What father does is always right. *See* What the goodman does is sure to be right.
What frightened the animal. *See* Timid hare.
What happened to Eliza. Field. Eliza and the elves.
What happened to Jeremy Jones. Fyleman. Tea time tales.

What happened to K'tonton on his Lag B'Omer picnic. Weilerstein. Adventures of K'tonton.

What happened to some Lapp children. Olcott. Wonder tales from Baltic wizards. (Boys who did not get a magic cow; Ulda's old mother.)

What happened to the lazy stickleback. Lebermann. New German fairy tales.

What happened to the thistle. Andersen. Fairy tales. (Stickney). v. 2.

For other entries, see 2d edition.

What happens to the Eskimo sun in winter. Applegarth. Missionary stories for little folks. 1st series.

What Hautchen did. Bancroft. Goblins of Haubeck.

What is a man? #

See also Man; Smart young tiger.

What luck! Broomell. Children's story caravan.

See also Man who went to find his angel.

What made the raven black. See Why the raven's feathers are black.

What men live by. Tolstoy. Ivan the fool.

For other entries, see 2d edition.

What Santa Claus told the toys. Walker. Sandman's Christmas stories.

What six girls with balloons told. Sandburg. Rootabaga country.

Sandburg. Rootabaga stories.

Through story-land with the children.

What the blind princess did. Perkins and Danielson. Mayflower program book.

What the caterpillar learned. See Lesson of faith.

What the flag said. Bailey. Wonderful tree.

What the four were for. Retner. That's that.

See also Clever peasant.

What the fox did to the wolf. Noel. Magic bird of Chomolung-ma.

See also Dog and the sparrow; Spider passes on a debt.

"What the goodman does is sure to be right!" Andersen. Fairy tales (Stickney. v. 2. What the goodman does is always right.)

Arthur Rackham fairy book. (What the old man does is always right.)

Bailey. Tell me another story. (What Father does is always right. Adapted.)

Bruce. Treasury of tales for little folk. (What the old man does is always right.)

Power. Bag o' tales. (What the good man does is always right.)

Quinn. Stokes' wonder book of fairy tales.

Quinn. Stories for the six-year-old. (Goodman is always right.)

For other entries, see 2d edition.

What the learned cat remembers. Shannon. California fairy tales.

See also Father and his daughters; Wise priest.

What the lily needed. Bailey. Stories children want.

For other entries, see 2d edition.

What the moon saw. Freeman. Child-story readers. 3d reader. (2d evening. Adapted.)

For other entries, see 2d edition.

What the old man does is always right. *See* "What the goodman does is sure to be right."

What the stupid son learned. *See* Three languages.

What the teacher said to Trove. Forbes. Good citizenship. (*In* Ch. 8.)

What the wind said. Bryce. Short stories for little folks.

What the woodcarver did. Bancroft. Goblins of Haubeck.

What was in the box. *See* Box with something pretty in it.

What was it? Cooper. Argosy of fables. (Seaside travelers.)

(poem). Johnson and Scott. Anthology of children's literature. (Camel, and the floating sticks.)

In 2d edition this story is also indexed under the title "Travelers by the seaside."

What witches tell. Olcott. Wonder tales from Baltic wizards.

See also True and Untrue; Two brothers. VI; Two soldiers; Vilas' spring.

Wheat-field. Blondell. Keepsakes.

Perkins and Danielson. Mayflower program book.

For other entries, see 2d edition.

When Brer Crickit en Brer Flea fell out. Sale. Tree named John.

When Brer Rabbit thundered. *See* How rabbit lost his tail. V.

When Cavillaca ran away. Eells. Magic tooth.

See also Daphne.

When Ernest was a soldier. Bowman. Little brown bowl.

When everybody played. Cook. To-day's stories of yesterday.

When grandmother was stolen by the Modocs. Buckingham. Elephant's friend.

See also Mother's song.

When I was a squantum wagon. Burnett. Children's book.

When I was an ark. Burnett. Children's book.

When Jane changed her name. Bailey. Wonderful tree.

When knighthood was in flower. Cather. Pan and his pipes.

When Mother Squirrel went to town. Potter. Giant of Apple Pie Hill.

When Navajos stole Tewa boys. James. Tewa firelight tales.

When Norma Catherine ran away. Bowman. Little brown bowl.

When one's luck turns. *See* Abu Taloot.

When Pierrot was young. Spurr. Dumas fairy tale book.

When the blackbird was white. Brown. Curious book of birds. (How the blackbird spoiled his coat.)
Carey. Stories of the birds.
Olcott. Wonder garden. (Greedy blackbird.)
Rich. Why-so stories. (Why the blackbird is black.)

When the bright sun rises. Topelius. Canute Whistlewinks.

When the cricket was a barber. *See* Why the possum's tail is bare. I.

When the fox was teacher. Eells. Brazilian fairy book.

When the garden played tag. Potter. Giant of Apple Pie Hill.

When the jungle plants quarrelled. Skeat. Tiger's mistake.
See also Vain cereals.

When the king of the cats came to King Connal's dominion. *See* King of the cats comes to Ireland.

When the little blond shark went visiting. *See* Little blond shark.

When the little boy ran away (poem). Spaulding and Bryce. Aldine readers. Book 2. rev. ed.

When the Luprachauns came to Ireland. *See* King Iubdan and King Fergus.

When the North Mountain giant raged. Falkberget. Broomstick and Snowflake.

When the plants were kind. *See* Disease, Origin of; Medicines, Origin of.

When the sun fell from the sky. Eells. Magic tooth.
See also Sun of wind.

When Thor went to Jötunheim. *See* Thor and his journey to Jötunheim.

When Toinette sang. Crownfield. Feast of Noel.

When Washington came to town. *See* Washington, George.

Where love is, God is. *See* Where love is, there God is also.

Where love is, there God is also. Broomell. Children's story caravan.
Power. Children's treasure chest. (Where there is love, there is God also.)
Smith and Hazeltine. Christmas in legend and story.
Starbuck. Enchanted paths. (Adyevich.)
Tolstoy. Ivan the fool. (Where love is, God is.)
See also What men live by.
For other entries, see 2d edition.

Where the coconut came from. *See* Coconut tree. II.

Where the frost comes from. Wells. How the present came from the past. Book 1, pt. 2.

Where the strawberries came from. *See* First strawberries.

Where the white man came from. *See* How the races obtained their colors (African).

Where the yellow jackets came from. Phillips. Indian tales for little folks.
Where there is love, there is God also. *See* Where love is, there God is also.
Where they came from. *See* Old Winter Man and the Spring. III.
Where Tom found his manners. White. School management, p. 272.
Where's Polly? Potter. Captain Sandman.
Whiffy-wiff (poem). Potter. Captain Sandman.
Whins on Knockattan. Casserley. Whins on Knockattan.
Whippity-Stourie. Lee. Folk tales of all nations.
For other entries, see 2d edition.
Whirling Whimpus. Rounds. Ol' Paul.
Whirlwind. Fyleman. Forty good-night tales. (Mrs. Moodle. pt. 1.)
For other entries, see 2d edition.
Whispering game. Buckingham. Great idea.
Whispering trees. Gate. Tales from the secret kingdom.
Whistle. I. Curry and Clippinger. Children's literature.
For other entries, see 2d edition.
Whistle. II. *See* Tinker's willow.
Whistling Colin. Lindsay. Choosing book.
Whistling River. Rounds. Ol' Paul.
Whistling uphill. Cozad. Story talks.
White ash tree. Tuttle. Frightened tree. (Treacherous tree.)
White birch. I. Housman. Moonshine and clover.
White birch. II. Tuttle. Frightened tree. (Ghost tree.)
White bird's wife. Harper. More story-hour favorites.
For other entries, see 2d edition.
White bull of Uri and, the demon ram. Guerber. Legends of Switzerland. (*In* Forest cantons.)
White butterfly boy and rain boy. Hogner. Navajo winter nights.
White Caroline and Black Caroline. Dulac. Edmund Dulac's fairy book.
White cat. I. Aulnoy. Fairy tales (Planché).
Aulnoy. White cat and other old French fairy tales.
Evans. Worth while stories.
Freeman. Child-story readers. 3d reader.
Lee. Folk tales of all nations.
Quinn. Stokes' wonder book of fairy tales.
For other entries, see 2d edition.
White cat. II. *See* Enchanted cat.
White Corn and her sons. De Huff. Taytay's tales.
White Corn and the grasshoppers. De Huff. Taytay's tales.
White cotton rabbit. Potter. Giant of Apple Pie Hill.
White dancer. Olcott. Wonder tales from windmill lands.
White doe. I. *See* Hind in the forest.
White doe. II. Housman. Moonshine and clover.

White duck. Carpenter. Tales of a Russian grandmother. (Little white duck.)
For other entries, see 2d edition.
White elephant. I. *See* Elephant and the ungrateful forester.
White elephant. II. *See* 2d edition.
White elephant. III. *See* Grateful elephant.
White elephant. IV. My Bookhouse. v. 4. (Memoirs of a white elephant.)
White elephant. V. Fun folk and fairy tales.
Stewart. Tell me a story I never heard before.
See also Bronze boar; Chop Chin and the golden dragon # ; Gods know.
White elephant. VI. Aspinwall. Jataka tales. (White elephant with the six-colored tusks.)
White elephant with the six=colored tusks. *See* White elephant. VI.
White Feather and the six giants. Spence. Myths of the North American Indians. (White Feather, the giant-killer. *In* Ch. 5.)
For other entries, see 2d edition.
White flower of happiness. *See* Blue flower; Flower of content; Wonderful flower.
White goddess, Story of. Browne. Indian nights.
See also How Genetaska deserted her trust.
White=headed Zal. Coit. Ivory throne of Persia.
Gibson. Golden bird and other stories. (Golden bird.)
Johnson and Scott. Anthology of children's literature. (Zal.)
Lee. Folk tales of all nations.
Power. Bag o' tales. (Zal, the white-haired.)
See also Zal and Rustem.
For other entries, see 2d edition.
White=horned bull. Casserley. Michael of Ireland.
White=horse=cut=in=two. Criss. Martine and Michel. (*In* Ch. 8.)
See also Baron's steed.
White horse girl and the blue wind boy. Blondell. Keepsakes.
Davis. Baker's dozen.
Sandburg. Rootabaga country.
Sandburg. Rootabaga stories.
White hound of Oluff. Adams. Swords of the Vikings.
White king. Housman. Doorway in fairyland.
White lady of Haldenstein. Guerber. Legends of Switzerland. (*In* Glarus and Grisons.)
White lily. I #.
See also Arum lily.
White lily. II. Carey. Flower legends.
White Lily, the captive. Blaisdell. Log cabin days.
White man and the snake. *See* Man and the snake. II.
White mate, Story of. Housman. What-o'clock stales.

White mare's son. Pogány. Magyar fairy tales.
See also Dwarf with the long beard #.
White palfrey. Williams. Jolly old whistle.
White pet. Lee. Folk tales of all nations.
For other entries, see 2d edition.
White rabbit. *See* Little white rabbit. II.
White rabbit and the crocodiles. *See* Eighty-one brothers.
White snake. Grimm. Fairy tales (Olcott).
For other entries, see 2d edition.
White spinner. Olcott. Wonder tales from windmill lands.
White steed, Bufanin. Eells. Brazilian fairy book.
See also Curly-locks; Twelve huntsmen.
White-thorn's story. Housman. What-o'clock tales.
Whither no one knows. *See* Go, I know not whither—fetch, I know not what.
Whittington and his cat. *See* Dick Whittington and his cat.
Whittington, History of. *See* Dick Whittington and his cat.
Who-all's black hat. Mackaye. Tall tales of the Kentucky mountains.
Who discovered America? Cozad. Story talks.
Who is guilty? De Leeuw. Java jungle tales. (How the cat and the mouse became enemies.)
Olcott. Wonder tales from pirate isles.
See also Who killed the otter's babies?
Who is my neighbor? Broomell. Children's story caravan.
Who killed Cock Robin? *See* Cock Robin.
Who killed the otter's babies? Skeat. Tiger's mistake.
See also Chain of anger; Pa Badak's lawsuit; Sparrow, the woodpecker, the fly, the frog and the elephant; Who is guilty; Why the bush fowl calls up the dawn.
For other entries, see 2d edition.
Who lived in the skull? Ransome. Old Peter's Russian tales.
See also Dance in a buffalo skull #.
Who shall be May Queen? Bowman. Little brown bowl.
Who stole the bird's nest? (poem). Patten. Junior classics. v. 10.
For other entries, see 2d edition.
Who was the mightier? #
See also Conceited ant; Goats in the turnip field; Rats and their son-in-law; Wind and the sun.
Why a swallow has a swallow tail. *See* Why the swallow's tail is forked. I.
Why all men love the moon. Bailey. Stories children want. (How the moon was kind to her mother. Adapted.)
Bailey. Tell me another story. (How the moon was kind to her mother.)
Lane. Tower legends. (Brahman's star.)
For other entries, see 2d edition.
Why ants carry bundles. Lee. Folk tales of all nations. (Why we see ants carrying bundles as big as themselves.)

Why ants have small waists. Metzger. Picture tales from the Chinese.

Why are cherries red? Gaer. Magic flight.

Why badger is so humble. Garett. Coyote stories.

Why bears sleep winters. *See* Why the bear sleeps all winter.

Why cats always wash after eating. Hart. Picture tales from Holland.

See also Cat and the sparrows. II; Fox and the geese; Frog and the crow; Why the cat washes after eating #.

For other entries, see 2d edition.

Why cats and dogs fight. *See* Why the dog and cat are enemies. III.

Why chickens live with man. Woodson. African myths.

Why children belong to the mother. Woodson. African myths.

Why children lose their teeth. I. *See* 2d edition.

Why children lose their teeth. II. Mitchell. Gray moon tales. (Mammy and a modern problem.)

Why coyote lives on the prairie. Rich. Why-so stories.

Why coyotes are hungry. *See* Coyote the hungry. II.

Why coyotes are numerous in Kaweah Canon. Shannon. Eyes for the dark.

Why crows are black. *See* Why the crow is black. IV.

Why dogs have long tongues. Rich. Why-so stories.

For other entries, see 2d edition.

Why dogs sniff. Eells. Islands of magic.

See also Why the dogs howl at night. I.

Why dogs wag their tails. Babbitt. Animals' own story book.

See also Why the dog and cat are enemies.

For other entries, see 2d edition.

Why Drayton was safe. Forbes. Good citizenship. (*In* Ch. 6.)

Why Elbruz peak is split. White. Made in Russia. (*In* Ch. 5.)

Why elefunts are skeered uv mices. *See* Why elephants are afraid of mice. II.

Why elephants are afraid of mice. I. Meeker. Folk tales from the Far East. (Mr. Monk and King Tumbo.)

Why elephants are afraid of mice. II. Sale. Tree named John. (Why elefunts is skeered uv mices.)

Why Europe loves the robin. *See* Ear of wheat.

Why every rose has a thorn. *See* Why roses have thorns. IV.

Why everyone loves the nightingale. *See* How the nightingale got his beautiful voice; Why the nightingale sings better than the dove.

Why Father Christmas got married. Good Housekeeping. Dec. 1929, p. 34.

Why ravens croak. Cooper. Argosy of fables. (Raven and the swan.)
See also Crow and the swan.
For other entries, see 2d edition.

Why Ra=wen=io made the sea clams. Parker. Skunny Wundy and other Indian tales.

Why Rheims church was built. Butterfield. Young people's story of architecture. (*In* Cathedrals that record history. Ch. 31.)
See also Hugh of Lincoln and Jocelin of Wells.

Why Robin Redbreast sings at Easter time. *See* Why the robin has a red breast. V.

Why roses a,re red. Buckingham. Elephant's friend. (*In* Butterfly boy.)

Why roses have thorns. I. See 2d edition.

Why roses have thorns. II. Partridge. Joyful Star. (How Lawiswis was rescued by the white roses.)
Johnson and Scott. Anthology of children's literature. (Why wild roses have thorns.)
For other entries, see 2d edition.

Why roses have thorns. III. *See* 2d edition.

Why roses have thorns. IV. Carey. Flower legends. (Rose thorns.)
Power. How it happened. (Why every rose has a thorn.)
For other entries, see 2d edition.

Why Skinkoots arms are thin. Linderman. Kootenai why stories.

Why skunk's tail is black and white. Garett. Coyote stories.

Why some animals and birds see at night. *See* Why some animals see at night.

Why some animals see at night. Bailey. Stories from an Indian cave. (How the evergreens came.)
Borland. Rocky Mountain tipi tales. (Owl learns to see at night.)
Gearhart. Skalalatoot stories. (Why some animals and birds see at night and why some trees wear their leaves all year.)

Why some folks is black en some is white. *See* Why the negro is black.

Why some trees are always green. *See* Why the evergreen trees keep their leaves in winter. I.

Why some trees wear their leaves all year. *See* Why the evergreen trees keep their leaves in winter. II.

Why some women never eat mutton. Woodson. African myths.

Why spider has such long legs. Garett. Coyote stories.

Why Ted=oh, the woodchuck, climbs a tree. Parker. Skunny Wundy and other Indian tales.

Why the almond tree blossomed. Curtis. Stories in trees.

Why the Alveloa bird received a blessing. Eells. Islands of magic.

See also Flight into Egypt.

Why the aspen leaves tremble. I. Curtis. Stories in trees. (Leaves of the aspen tree.)

For other entries, see 2d edition.

Why the aspen leaves tremble. II. *See* 2d edition.

Why the aspen leaves tremble. III. Stewart. Tell me a story I never heard before. (Chattering aspen.)

For other entries, see 2d edition.

Why the aspen leaves tremble. IV. *See* 2d edition.

Why the aspen leaves tremble. V. Tuttle. Frightened tree and other stories. (Frightened tree.)

Why the autumn leaves are red. I. Skinner. Child's book of country stories.

For other entries, see 2d edition.

Why the autumn leaves are red. II. Wells. How the present came from the past. Book 1. pt. 2. (Red leaves of autumn. Abridged.)

Williamson. Stars through magic casements. (Why the leaves turn yellow and red.)

For other entries, see 2d edition.

Why the autumn leaves are red. III. Curtis. Stories in trees. (Scarlet maple.)

Why the baby says "goo." Spence. Myths of the North American Indians. (Glooskap and the baby. *In* Ch. 3.)

For other entries, see 2d edition.

Why the banana belongs to the monkey. Eells. Fairy tales from Brazil.

For other entries, see 2d edition.

Why the bat flies at night. *See* Why Flitter the bat flies at night #; Why the sun shines by day and the moon by night.

Why the bean has a black stripe. Sheriff. Stories old and new.

See also Straw, the coal and the bean.

Why the bear has a stumpy tail. Arnold. Folk tales retold.

Bowman and Bianco. Tales from a Finnish tupa. (Bear goes fishing.)

Cooper. Argosy of fables. (Why the bears have short tails.)

Curry and Clippinger. Children's literature. (Why the bear is stumpy tailed.)

Harriman. Stories for little children. (Why the bear has a short tail.)

Hutchinson. Fireside stories. (Why the bear is stumpy-tailed. Adapted.)

James. Tewa firelight tales. (Bear's tail.)

Parker. Skunny Wundy and other Indian tales. (How Chief Bear lost his tail.)

Rasmussen. East o' the sun and west o' the moon. (Why the bear is stumpy-tailed.)

Why the bear has a stumpy tail—*continued.*
See also How Master Renard persuaded Master Ysegrim to enter Holy Orders; Wolf that went fishing.
For other entries, see 2d edition.

Why the bear is stumpy tailed. *See* Why the bear has a stumpy tail.

Why the bear sleeps all winter. Bailey. Stories children want.
Babbitt. Animals' own story book.
Silvester and Peter. Happy hour stories. (Why bears sleep winters.)
For other entries, see 2d edition.

Why the bears have short tails. *See* Why the bear has a stumpy tail.

Why the bee is busy and the spider sullen. Purnell and Weatherwax. Why the bee is busy.

Why the bees gather honey. Bailey. Tell me another story.

Why the big ball game . . . was a hot game. Sandburg. Rootabaga country.
Sandburg. Rootabaga pigeons.

Why the birds go south in winter. *See* How summer came to earth. III.

Why the birds hate the owl. *See* King Wren.

Why the birds sing different songs. Spaulding and Bryce. Aldine readers. Book 2. rev. ed.
See also Bird songs # ; How the Sarts tribe learned to sing; Why the nightingale sings better than the dove.

Why the blackbird is black. *See* When the blackbird was white.

Why the bluebird carries happiness. Evans. Worth while stories.

Why the bluebird is blue, and the coyote is grey. *See* Bluebird and coyote.

Why the buffalo works so hard. Olcott. Wonder tales from pirate isles.

Why the bush fowl calls up the dawn. Woodson. African myths.
See also How the sun was made; Who killed the otter's babies?

Why the cat catches rats. Woodson. African myths.

Why the cat dislikes wet feet. Bailey. Stories children want.
For other entries, see 2d edition.

Why the catfish has a flat head. *See* Catfish and the moose. II.

Why the chimes rang. Starbuck. Far horizons.
Walters. Book of Christmas stories. (Christmas bells. Adapted.)
See also Bells of Christmas.
For other entries, see 2d edition.

Why the chipmunk's back is striped. *See* Chipmunk's stripes. V.

Why the cock can fly no higher than the stable door. *See* Why the cock cannot fly.

Why the cock cannot fly. Carey. Stories of the birds. Power. How it happened. (Why the cock cannot fly high.) For other entries, see 2d edition.

Why the cock crows at dawn #. *See also* How the sun was made.

Why the Codorniz Bird received a curse. Eells. Islands of magic.

Why the cow's skin is loose round the neck *See* Water-buffalo and the cow.

Why the coyote lives on the prairie. *See* Why coyote lives on the prairies.

Why the crow hates the hawk. *See* Crow's children.

Why the crow is black. I. Farjeon. Tales from Chaucer. (Manciple's tale.) Rich. Why-so stories. For other entries, see 2d edition.

Why the crow is black. II #. *See also* Peacocks' cousin ; Tattooed one.

Why the crow is black. III. Bryce. Folk lore from foreign lands. (Crane and the crow.) Martens. Wonder tales from far away. (How the crow came to be black.) For other entries, see 2d edition.

Why the crow is black. IV. Quinn. Stories for the six-year-old. (Why crows are black.) Cooper. Argosy of fables. (Crow and the peacock.) *See also* Owl and the raven ; Peacock's cousin.

Why the crow is black. V. Carey. Stories of the birds. (*In* Raven who tried to walk like the dove.) Rich. Why-so stories. (*In* Tales of the crow.)

Why the crow is black. I–V. For other versions *see* Crane and the crow ; Owl and the raven.

Why the cuckoo has no nest. Hervey and Hix. Fanciful tales for children.

Why the cuckoo has no time to build her nest, and why she flies so heavily. Carey. Stories of the birds.

Why the cuckoo never sings in winter. Purnell and Weatherwax. Why the bee is busy.

Why the deer eats leaves. *See* Why the deer's teeth are blunt.

Why the deer's teeth are blunt. Bailey. Stories from an Indian cave. (Why the deer eats leaves.) Rich. Why-so stories. *See also* Deer's teeth. For other entries, see 2d edition.

Why the dog and cat are enemies. I. Olcott. Wonder tales from China seas. (Magic dumplings.) For other entries, see 2d edition.

Why the dog and cat are enemies. II. Cowles. Stories to tell. (Adapted.)
Metzger. Tales told in Korea. (Why the cat and dog are enemies.)
For other entries, see 2d edition.
Why the dog and cat are enemies. III. Kovalsky and Putnam. Long-legs, Big-mouth, Burning-eyes. (Dogs' diploma.)
La Fontaine. Fables. (Tilney. Quarrel between the dogs and the cats, and between the cats and the mice.)
Rich. Why-so stories. (Why cats and dogs fight.)
For other entries, see 2d edition.
Why the dog and cat are enemies. IV. Gaer. Burning bush. (Friends that quarreled.)
For other entries, see 2d edition.
Why the dog and cat are enemies. V. *See* 2d edition.
Why the dog and cat are enemies. VI. Gaer. Magic flight. (Cat and the dog.)
Why the dog and cat are enemies. I–VI.
For other versions *see* Donkeys! dogs! cats! rats!; Horned animals give a party; How the animals lost their freedom; Why cats hate rats; Why dogs wag their tails.
Why the dogs howl at night. I. *See* 2d edition.
Why the dogs howl at night. II. Sexton. Gray wolf stories. (Six boys go to the star country.)
Why the dogs howl at night. I–II. *See also* Why dogs sniff.
Why the dove is on our valentines. *See* Why the dove is timid.
Why the dove is timid. Bailey. Tell me another story. (Why the dove is on our valentines. Adapted.)
For other entries, see 2d edition.
Why the eagle is king of the birds. Rich. Why-so stories.
See also King Wren; Phœnix.
Why the evergreen trees keep their leaves in winter. I. Hervey and Hix. Fanciful tales for children. (Why some trees are always green.)
For other entries, see 2d edition.
Why the evergreen trees keep their leaves in winter. II. Bailey. Stories from an Indian cave. (How the evergreens came.)
Gearhart. Skalalatoot stories. (Why some animals and birds see at night and why some trees wear their leaves all year.)
For other entries, see 2d edition.
Why the evergreen trees keep their leaves in winter. III. Parker. Skunny Wundy and other Indian tales. (How the conifers flaunt the promise of spring.)
Why the fairies went to Corsica. Hill and Maxwell. Napoleon's story book.
Why the finch's feathers are ruffled. *See* How the finch got her colors.

Why the fish laughed #.
See also King's choice.
Why the flint rock cannot fight back. Garett. Coyote
stories.
See also How arrowheads came.
Why the flounder has a crooked mouth. Borski and Mil-
ler. Gypsy and the bear.
Why the fox has a dark tail. Eells. Magic tooth.
See also Fox as herdsboy.
Why the fox has a white tip to his tail. *See* Fox as herds-
boy.
Why the goat's knees are bare. Rich. Why-so stories.
Why the hare has a split lip. *See* Hare's lip. II.
Why the hartebeest weeps. Berry. Black folk tales.
(Why the hartebeest always has tears in his eyes.)
Why the Hawaiian islands are in a row. *See* How Maui
fished up the great island.
Why the hawk catches chickens. Woodson. African myths.
For other entries, see 2d edition.
Why the hawk's legs are thin. Rich. Why-so stories.
Why the heron's neck is bent. *See* Jackal and the heron.
Why the hippopotamus lives in the water. Woodson.
African myths.
Power. How it happened. (Why the hippopotamus took to
the water.)
For other entries, see 2d edition.
Why the jelly-fish has no bones. *See* Monkey and the jelly-
fish.
Why the jelly-fish has no shell. *See* Monkey and the jelly-
fish.
Why the jelly-fish is soft. *See* Monkey and the jelly-fish.
Why the lamb is meek. Eells. Fairy tales from Brazil.
Why the lark flies up at dawn. Purnell and Weatherwax.
Why the bee is busy.
Why the lark wears a crown. Purnell and Weatherwax.
Why the bee is busy.
Why the laurel makes wreaths. Bailey. Stories from an
Indian cave.
Why the leaves turn yellow and red. *See* Why the au-
tumn leaves are red. II.
Why the lizard moves his head. Lee. Folk-tales of all na-
tions. (Why the lizard continually moves his head up and
down.)
Why the magpie builds a poor nest. *See* Magpie's nest.
II.
Why the magpie chatters. *See* Magpie maidens.
Why the magpie makes a half-finished nest. *See* Magpie's
nest. II.
Why the magpie's nest is not well built. *See* Magpie's
nest. II.
Why the maiden lost her turquoises. Harper and Hamil-
ton. Winding roads.

Why the men of Gavi will not eat fish. Lee. Folk tales of all nations.
Why the mink, is black. Rich. Why-so stories.
Why the mole has pink hands. Power. How it happened.
Why the mole is blind. I. *See* 2d edition.
Why the mole is blind. II. Morris. Stories from mythology: North American. (*In* Ch. 12.)
Why the monkey still has a tail. Eells. Fairy tales from Brazil.
See also Cat and the mouse. I.
Why the moon waxes and wanes. I–IV. *See* 2d edition.
Why the moon waxes and wanes. V. Johnson. Sky movies. (Why the Princess Istar loses and gains her jewelled robes. *In* Ch. 3.)
See also Ishtar and Tammuz.
Why the morning=glories wear pretty dresses. Bowman. Little brown bowl.
Why the mosquito lives in swampy places. *See* War party. II.
Why the mosquito says Zum, Zzzz, Zzz. *See* Why the swallow's tail is forked. I.
Why the mouse is small and grey. *See* Sun a prisoner. I.
Why the negro is black. I. *See* 2d edition.
Why the negro is black. II. Sale. Tree named John. (Why some folks is black en some is white.)
Why the negro is black. III. Pyrnelle. Diddie, Dumps and Tot. (*In* Ch. 16.)
Why the negro is black. I–III. *See also* How the races obtained their colors.
Why the nightingale has many songs, but the dove only says, "Coo." *See* Why the nightingale sings better than the dove.
Why the nightingale sings better than the dove. Carey. Stories of the birds.
Blaisdell. Rhyme and story second reader. (Nightingale and the dove.)
Purnell and Weatherwax. Why the bee is busy. (Why everyone loves the nightingale.)
Rich. Why-so stories. (Why the nightingale has many songs, but the dove only says "Coo.")
See also How the nightingale got his beautiful voice; Why the birds sing different songs.
Why the nightingale wakes. *See* Nightingale and the worm.
Why the opossum's tail is bare. *See* Why the possum's tail is bare.
Why the owl cries hoot! hoot! Rich. Why-so stories. (*In* Tales of the owl.)
See also Wren who brought fire.
For other entries, see 2d edition.
Why the owl flies. by night. I–II. *See* 2d edition.
Why the·owl flies by night. III. Berry. Black folk tales (Why the owl flies only at night.)

Why the owl flies by night. IV. Eells. Islands of magic.
(Why the owl flies at night.)
See also St. Anthony of Italy.
Why the owl is not king of the birds. Aspinwall. Jataka
tales. (Owl as king.)
See also King Wren.
For other entries, see 2d edition.
Why the owl rules the night. Eells. Magic tooth.
See also How night came.
Why the owl says "who." Through story-land with the chil-
dren.
For other entries, see 2d edition.
Why the pansy has no scent. Power. How it happened.
Carey. Flower legends. (Pansy, pt. 4.)
Why the parrot repeats the words of men. Carey.
Stories of the birds. (Truthful parrot.)
For other entries, see 2d edition.
Why the peacock's tail is spotted. Rich. Why-so stories.
See also How the peacock was given colored feathers; Io;
Owl and the peacock.
Why the peetweet cries for rain. Ralston. Russian fairy
tales. (*In* Legends about saints. Ch. 6.)
Rich. Why-so stories. (Why the peewit cries "Peet, Peet.")
See also Thirsty heron.
For other entries, see 2d edition.
Why the peewee looks for brother. Carey. Stories of the
birds. (Lapwing's search.)
For other entries, see 2d edition.
Why the peewit cries "Peet, Peet!" *See* Why the peetweet
cries for rain.
Why the pelican has a pouch. Rich. Why-so stories.
See also Inquisitive woman.
Why the petrel lays its eggs on land. Rich. Why-so
stories.
See also Battle of the birds. II; Birds go to war. II.
Why the possum's tail is bare. I. Bailey. Stories from an
Indian cave. (When the cricket was a barber.)
Gearhart. Skalalatoot stories. (Why the opossum's tail is
bare.)
James. Happy animals of Atagahi. (Rabbit and possum
lose their tails.)
Morris. Stories from mythology: North American. (*In* Ch.
8.)
Rich. Why-so stories.
For other entries, see 2d edition.
Why the potato lives in the ground. Harper and Hamilton.
Winding roads.
Why the Princess Istar loses and gains her jewelled robes.
See Why the moon waxes and wanes. V.
Why the rabbit eats his fur when he is starving. *See*
Rabbit and the ducks.

Why the rabbit has a short tail. *See* How rabbit lost his tail. III.
Why the rabbit is timid. *See* Moon's message #.
  In 2d edition, there are entries under each title.
Why the rabbit winters in a hollow tree. *See* Rabbit and the ducks.
Why the raven is black. *See* Why the raven's feathers are black. III.
Why the raven's feathers are black. I. *See* 2d edition.
Why the raven's feathers are black. II. Snell. Told beneath the northern lights. (What made the raven black.)
  For other entries, see 2d edition.
Why the raven's feathers are black. III. Power. How it happened. (Why the raven is black.)
  For other entries, see 2d edition.
Why the red dragon is the emblem of Wales. Olcott. Wonder tales from fairy isles. (Coming of Merlin.)
  For other entries, see 2d edition.
Why the rice stopped rolling. Olcott. Wonder tales from China seas.
  See also Magic rice.
Why the robin brings the spring. *See* How the robin came.
Why the robin has a red breast. I. Carey. Stories of the birds. (Robin and the bear.)
  Kinscella. Music appreciation readers. Book 1. (How the robin got his red breast.)
  Power. How it happened.
  See also Robin and the bear. I.
  For other entries, see 2d edition.
Why the robin has a red breast. II–IV. *See* 2d edition.
Why the robin has a red breast. V. Carey. Stories of the birds. (Robin at the cross.)
  Deihl. Holiday-time stories. (Why Robin Redbreast sings at Easter time.)
  Werner's recitations. No. 51. (How robin's breast became red.)
  See also Pious robin.
  For other entries, see 2d edition.
Why the robin has a red breast. VI–VII. *See* 2d edition.
Why the robin has a red breast. VIII. Pyrnelle. Diddie, Dumps and Tot. (How the woodpecker's head and the robin's breast came to be red. *In* Ch. 12.)
Why the sea is salt. I. Power. How it happened.
  Wells. How the present came from the past. Book 1. pt. 2. (Saltness of the seas. Abridged.)
  For other entries, see 2d edition.
Why the sea is salt. II. Curry and Clippinger. Children's literature. (Quern at the bottom of the sea.)
  Harper. Magic fairy tales.
  Lang. Old friends among the fairies.
  Power. Stories to shorten the road.
  Rasmussen. East o' the sun and west o' the moon.

Why the tiger and the stag fear each other. Eells. Fairy
tales from Brazil.
See also Rabbit and the other animals; Ram and the leopard.
Why the top sings. Bailey. Wonderful tree.
Major. Merry Christmas stories.
See also Top that could sing.
Why the tortoise has a round back. Purnell and Weather-
wax. (Why the bee is busy.)
Gordon and Stockard. Gordon readers. 2d reader.
Lee. Folk tales of all nations.
Why the turkey buzzard is bald=headed. I–II. See 2d edi-
tion.
Why the turkey buzzard is bald=headed. III. Spence.
Myths of the North American Indians. (Ictinike and the
buzzard. In Ch. 5.)
Why the turkey buzzard is bald=headed. IV. Field.
American folk and fairy tales. (Compair Lapin and
Madam Carencro.)
Why the turkey buzzard is bald=headed. V. Phillips. In-
dian tales for little folks. (How the buzzard got his black
coat.)
Why the turkey gobbles. I. Bailey. Stories from an In-
dian cave.
Rich. Why-so stories.
Sheriff. Stories old and new.
For other entries, see 2d edition.
Why the turkey gobbles. II. Parker. Skunny Wundy and
other Indian tales. (How the gobbler got his warwhoop.)
Gearhart. Skalalatoot stories. (Why the turkey gobbles.)
Why the wagtail wags his tail. Carey. Stories of the
birds.
Power. How it happened.
Why the weasel is white. Field. American folk and fairy
tales.
For other entries, see 2d edition.
Why the wild cat has a wrinkled face. See Rabbit and the
wild cat. II.
Why the wombat lives in the ground. Rich. Why-so
stories.
Why the wood duck has red eyes. See Unktomee and his
bundle of songs.
Why the woodchuck's tail is short. Rich. Why-so stories.
Why the woodpecker has a long beak. See Inquisitive
woman.
Why the woodpecker has a long nose. See Inquisitive
woman.
Why the woodpecker laughs at frogs. See Right time to
laugh.
Why the woodpecker likes trees. See Woodpecker. II
Why the woodpecker's head is red. I. Carey. Stories of
the birds. (Gertrude and the cake.)
Evans. Worth while stories. (Legend of the woodpecker.)

Why the woodpecker's head is red. I—*continued.*
Kinscella. Music appreciation readers. Book 1. (Woodpecker.)
Piper. Folk tales children love. (Old woman who wanted all the cakes.)
Piper. Road in storyland. (Old woman who wanted all the cakes.)
Rich. Why-so stories. (*In* Tales of the woodpecker.)
For other entries, see 2d edition.
Why the woodpecker's head is red. II. Carey. Stories of the birds. (How the woodpecker got his red crest.)
Johnson and Scott. Anthology of children's literature. (Story of the first woodpecker.)
See also Ana Josepha.
For other entries, see 2d edition.
Why the wren flies close to the earth. *See* King Wren.
In 2d edition there are entries under each title.
Why the wren has no tail. *See* Why the wagtail wags his tail; Wren who brought fire.
Why the wren's feathers look scorched. *See* Wren who brought fire.
Why there are no tigers in Japan. Rich. Why-so stories.
Why there are no trees on the desert. Rounds. Ol' Paul.
Why there is a hare in the moon. *See* Hare in the moon. I.
Why they moved the old north pole. Krohn and Johnson. Scales of the silver fish.
Why tigers eat raw meat. Rich. Why-so stories.
Why turtles stay near the water. I #.
See also How the turtle saved his own life.
Why turtles stay near the water. II. Lee. Folk tales of all nations. (Jackal and the drought.)
Why we do not live forever on this earth. Hogner. Navajo winter nights.
See also How Maui strove to win immortality for men.
Why we have tides. *See* Cause of tides. III.
Why we see ants carrying bundles as big as themselves.
See Why ants carry bundles.
Why? Why? Cendrars. Little black stories. (Why? Why?; or, The adventures of a tiny little chicken who had not yet been born.)
See also Drakesbill and his friends.
Why wild roses have thorns. *See* Why roses have thorns. II.
Why Will=o'=the=wisp carries a light. *See* Will-o'-the-wisp. VI.
Why witches wear red flannel petticoats. Shannon. Eyes for the dark.
Wicked handmaiden. Metzger. Tales told in Hawaii.
Wicked herdsman. Guerber. Legends of Switzerland. (*In* Fribourg.)

Wicked hornet. Johnson and Scott. Anthology of children's literature.
For other entries, see 2d edition.
Wicked tree. ' Tuttle. Frightened tree.
Widow and her seven sons. Browne. Indian nights.
See also Great head. I.
Widow and the hen. *See* Woman and the fat hen.
Widow and the sheep. Cooper. Argosy of fables.
Widow who would be comforted. I. **Gaster. Ma'aseh book. v. 1. (*In* Women are fickle.)
Darton. Wonder book of romance.
See also Woman and the farmer.
Widow who would be comforted. II. **Voltaire. Zadig. (Nose. Ch. 3.)
Widow's son. I. Dasent. East of the sun and west of the moon (Nielson).
For other entries, see 2d edition.
Wife of Bath's tale. *See* Sir Gawain's marriage. II.
Wife of R. Hanina and the miracles that occurred to her.
See Dream of paradise.
Wife who ate no rice. Sugimoto. Picture tales from the Japanese.
See also Woman who could not eat.
Wife who bought herself a name. Katibah. Other Arabian nights.
See also Clever Alice ; Three sillies.
Wild and tame geese. Æsop. Fables (Whitman ed.).
For other entries, see 2d edition.
Wild apple tree. Cooper. Argosy of fables.
Wild apples an' golden grain. Dunbar. Sons o' Cormac.
Wild ass and the lion. *See* Lion's share. I.
Wild boar and the fox. Æsop. Fables (Jones).
Cooper. Argosy of fables.
For other entries, see 2d edition.
Wild cat and the rabbit. Cooper. Argosy of fables.
Wild ducks. Raspé. Children's Munchausen (Martin. *In* Ch. 3.)
Wild ducks and the black fox. Raspé. Tales from the travels of Baron Munchausen.
Wild Edric. Rhys. English fairy book. (Edric the Wild.)
For other entries, see 2d edition.
Wild=goose chase. Shannon. Eyes for the dark.
See also Two cities.
Wild hunt. Olcott. Wonder tales from goblin hills. (Wod ! Wod ! Wod !)
For other entries, see 2d edition.
Wild hunter. Choate and Curtis. Little people of the hills. (Wode the wild hunter.)
Wild huntsman. Cross. Music stories.
See also Dando and his dogs.
Wild huntsman of Grimmenstein. Guerber. Legends of Switzerland. (*In* Bern.)

Wild hyacinth. *See* Hyacinthus.
Wild pigs. Raspé. Children's Munchausen (Martin. *In* Ch. 3.)
Raspé. Tales from the travels of Baron Munchausen.
Wild pussy. Fyleman. Forty good-morning tales.
Wild swans. Andersen. Fairy tales (Siewers tr.).
Andersen. Fairy tales (Stickney). v. 2.
Johnson and Scott. Anthology of children's literature.
Quinn. Stokes' wonder book of fairy tales.
Starbuck. Familiar haunts.
See also Seven ravens; Six swans; Unique tale.
For other entries, see 2d edition.
Wilhelmina's wooden shoes. Cather. Educating by story-telling.
Will-o'-the-wisp. I–III. *See* 2d edition.
Will-o'-the-wisp. IV. *See* Bog of Ecsed.
Will-o'-the-wisp. V. Partridge. Joyful star.
See also Wandering star #.
Will-o'-the-wisp. VI. Bailey. Story-telling hour. (Why Will-o'-the-wisp carries a light.)
Will-o'-the-wisp. I–VI. *See also* Jack-o'-lantern; Robin Goodfellow.
Will on the wind. Noel. Magic bird of Chomo-lung-ma.
See also Singing bone.
William of Palermo and the werwolf. Darton. Wonder book of old romance. (William and the werewolf.)
For other entries, see 2d edition.
William Tell and his great shot. *See* Tell, William.
William the Conqueror. Clément. Flowers of chivalry. (Arlette, the tanner's daughter.)
Farjeon. Mighty men from Beowulf to William the Conqueror. (Church and the crown.)
Johnson and Scott. Anthology of children's literature. (Duke William's treasure.)
For other entries, see 2d edition.
Willow maiden. Stewart. Tell me a story I never heard before.
Willow tree. I. See 2d edition.
Willow tree. II. Pogány. Hungarian fairy book.
See also Singing bone; Silver saucer and the crystal apple.
Willow tree. III. Tuttle. Frightened tree. (Sorrowful tree.)
Willow tree ghosts. Curtis. Stories in trees.
Henderson and Calvert. Wonder tales of old Japan. (Yanagi.)
See also Green willow #.
Willow ware, Story of #.
See also In the plate country.
Willowman and Sunday's child. *See* Altchen and Berend-John.
Wily fox. *See* Fox and the crow. II.

Wily Leprechaun. Choate and Curtis. Little people of the hills.
See also Field of Boliauns.
Wily lion. Æsop. Fables (Jones).
Wily monkeys. Noel. Magic bird of Chomo-lung-ma.
Wind. Cendrars. Little black stories.
Wind against water. Lansing. Great moments in science. (*In* Romance of the wheel.)
See also Two millers.
Wind an' wave an' wandherin' flame. Dunbar. Sons o' Cormac.
See also King of the three winds.
For other entries, see 2d edition.
Wind and his wife (poem). Potter. Giant of Apple Pie Hill.
Wind and the duck. *See* North wind and the duck.
Wind and the flowers. Patten. Junior classics. v. 8.
Gatty. Parables from nature. (Training and restraint.)
Wind and the leaves. Skinner. Happy tales.
Wind and the sun. Æsop. Fables (Artzybasheff).
Æsop. Fables (Jones. North wind and the sun.)
Æsop. Twenty-four fables (L'Estrange. Sun and the wind.)
Æsop. Fables (Whitman ed.).
Boeckel. Through the gateway. (North wind and the sun.)
Chidley. Fifty-two story talks. (Sun and wind.)
Cooper. Argosy of fables.
Curry and Clippinger. Children's literature.
Evans. Worth while stories.
Johnson and Scott. Anthology of children's literature.
(poem). Power. Bag o' tales. (Phœbus and Boreas.)
See also King of the winds; Squirrel, the east wind and the west wind.
For other entries, see 2d edition.
Wind bells. Kinscella. Music appreciation readers. Book 3. (Bells in China.)
Wind that wouldn't blow. Chrisman. Wind that wouldn't blow.
Windmill girl and Master Wind. Olcott. Wonder tales from windmill lands.
Winds, Origin of. I–III. *See* 2d edition.
Winds, Origin of. IV. Snell. Told beneath the northern lights. (First doll.)
For other entries, see 2d edition.
Winds, Origin of. V. Eells. Magic tooth. (Children of the House of Dawn.)
Wind's surprise. Spaulding and Bryce. Aldine readers. Book 2, rev. ed.
See also Mischievous March wind.
Wind's tale of the giant's boot. Fyleman. Forty good-morning tales.
Windy story. Wiggin and Smith. Twilight stories.
Wine and water (poem). Cooper. Argosy of fables.

Wing Dow. Chrisman. Wind that wouldn't blow.
Winged burdens. *See* Wings. II.
Winged hero. Cowles. Stories to tell. (Adapted.)
Morris. Gypsy story teller.
See also Flying trunk; Dædalus and Icarus.
Winged horse. I. *See* Pegasus.
Winged horse. II. *See* Hippogriff.
Winged man. De Huff. Taytay's memories.
Wings. I. See 2d edition.
Wings. II. Eggleston. Stories for special days in the church
school. (Legend of wings.)
Carey. Stories of the birds. (Winged burdens.)
Wings. III. Gordon and Stockard. Gordon readers. 2d
reader.
Wink, the lazy bird and the red fox. Parker. Skunny
Wundy and other Indian tales.
See also Gold in the orchard.
Winkelried, Arnold. Guerber. Legends of Switzerlana.
(*In* Forest cantons.)
Tappan. Old world hero stories.
For other entries, see 2d edition.
Winning of the crystal. *See* Shawano who killed the Uk-
tena. I.
Winning of the pushmobile cup. Burnett. Children's book.
Winona. Partridge. Joyful Star. (Winona the Sioux
maiden.)
Winter. Bryce. Folk lore from foreign lands.
Morris. Gypsy story teller.
See also Jan and Jantje; Long time #.
Winter in town. Wiggin and Smith. Twilight stories.
Winter of the blue snow. Field. American folk and fairy
tales.
Wadsworth. Paul Bunyan.
Winter season. Phillips. Far peoples.
Winter spirit and his visitor. *See* Old Winter Man and the
Spring. II.
Winter's tale. I. Lamb. Tales from Shakespeare.
See also Perdita.
Winter's tale. II. *See* Animals' winter quarters.
Wisdom of Solomon. *See* King Solomon's wisdom.
Wisdom of the forest. Housman. What-o'clock tales.
Wisdom of the men of Jerusalem. **Gaster. Ma'aseh book.
v. 1.
Gaer. Burning bush. (*In* Slave and the rich man.)
Vilnay. Legends of Palestine. (Children of Mt. Carmel.)
See also Abner the Jew; Lost camel; Perplexity of Zadig.
Wisdom of the rabbit. Bowman and Bianco. Tales from a
Finnish tupa.
See also Rat and the toad.
Wisdom of Wah=co=nah. Browne. Indian nights.
Wise and the foolish brother. Noel. Magic bird of Chomo-
lung-ma.

Wise and the foolish frogs. *See* Two frogs.
Wise ant. Harriman. Stories for little children.
Wise elephant and the disagreeable leopard. Lobagola. Folk tales of a savage.
Wise father-in-law. Katibah. Other Arabian nights.
Wise inventor. Lebermann. New German fairy tales. *See also* Three good giants #.
Wise judge. I. Bryce. Folk lore from foreign lands. For other entries, see 2d edition.
Wise judge. II. Metzger. Tales told in Korea.
Wise king and the bee. *See* King Solomon's answer.
Wise little pig. *See* Three little pigs.
Wise man and the boy. Metzger. Picture tales from the Chinese.
Wise man of Gotham. *See* Cheeses that ran away.
Wise men of Gotham. Johnson and Scott. Anthology of children's literature.
Lee. Folk tales of all nations.
Starbuck. Familiar haunts.
Steel. English fairy tales.
See also Foolish fishermen ; Schildbergers ; Trusting lad ; Wise men of Helm ; Wise men of Holmola.
For other entries, see 2d edition.
Wise men of Helm. Schwarz. Jewish caravan.
Wise men of Holmola. Bowman and Bianco. Tales from a Finnish tupa.
Wise men of Kampen. Miller. My travelship: Holland.
See also Catch the canary if you can ; Green grass on the wall ; Most magnificent cook of all ; Sagacious lumbarder.
Wise men of Merlingen. Guerber. Legends of Switzerland. (*In* Bern.)
See also Bags of the sun.
Wise Moro and the Hindu riddle guesser. Meeker. Folk tales from the Far East.
Wise Mother Coon. Brown. Under the rowan tree.
Wise mother of China. Metzger. Tales told in Korea.
Wise mother of Korea. Metzger. Tales told in Korea.
Wise old frog. Buckingham. Great idea.
Wise old shepherd. Coussens. Diamond story book.
Lee. Folk tales of all nations.
For other entries, see 2d edition.
Wise peasant girl. *See* Sage damsel.
Wise Pélé. Carpenter. Tales of a Basque grandmother. (Wise Pélé and his foolish friend.)
See also Waste not, want not.
Wise Peter Foolish. Retner. That's that.
Wise priest. Chamoud. Picture tales from the French.
See also Father and his daughters ; Parsee tale ; Praying for rain ; What the learned cat remembers.
Wise simpleton. Byrde. Polish fairy book.
See also Table, the ass and the stick.
Wise soothsayer. Katibah. Other Arabian nights.

Wise Vizier. Katibah. Other Arabian nights.

Wise weaver. Martens. Wonder tales from far away. (Intelligent weaver.)

See also Day of the scholars; Miller at the professor's examination #.

Wise words of the Guru. *See* Five wise words of the Guru.

Wisest of all. Mamin. Verotchka's tales.

Wish to goodness. Housman. Turn again tales.

Wishes. I. *See* 2d edition.

Wishes. II. La Fontaine. Fables (Tilney).

Wishes. III. *See* Three wishes. II.

Wishing book. Harriman. Stories for little children.

Wishing pot. Housman. Doorway in fairyland.

Wishing ring. I. Bailey. Tell me another story. (Plowman who found content.)

For other entries, see 2d edition.

Wishing ring. II. *See* Stone in the cock's head.

Wishing ring. III. *Sec* Gigi and the magic ring.

Wishing stone. I. Egan. New found tales.

Wishing stone. II. Pyrnelle. Diddie, Dumps and Tot. (*In* Ch. 3.)

Wishing stone. III. Martens. Wonder tales from far away.

See also Aladdin.

Wishing tree. *See* Washington, George.

Wishing well. I. Harper. Ghosts and goblins.

For other entries, see 2d edition.

Wishing well. II. *See* Well of St. Keyne.

Wit wins the day. De Leeuw. Java jungle tales.

Skeat. Tiger's mistake.

Witch. I. *See* 2d edition.

Witch. II. *See* Baba Yaga.

In 2d edition there are entries under each title.

Witch. III. Æsop. Fables (Jones).

Witch. IV. Ralston. Russian fairy tales.

Witch and the sister of the sun. Carpenter. Tales of a Russian grandmother. (Little sister of the sun.)

Ralston. Russian fairy tales. (Witch and the sun's sister.)

Ransome. Old Peter's Russian tales. (Prince Ivan, the witch baby, and the little sister of the sun.)

See also Little Czar Novishny, the false sister and the faithful beasts; Red king and the witch.

For other entries, see 2d edition.

Witch and the sun's sister. *See* Witch and the sister of the sun.

Witch cloak. Bancroft. Goblins of Haubeck.

Witch girl. Ralston. Russian fairy tales.

Witch hare. Lee. Folk tales of all nations. (Enchanted hare.)

Rhys. English fairy book. (Witch that was a hare.)

For other entries, see 2d edition.

Witch=hazel tree. Tuttle. Frightened tree. (Fighting witch tree.)
Witch maiden. Nusbaum. Seven cities of Cibola. Nusbaum. Zuni Indian tales.
In some editions, not indexed here, this story has the title "Maiden of Yellow Rocks."
Witch of Lok Island. *See* Groac'h of the Isle of Loc.
Witch of Windy Hill. Potter. Captain Sandman.
See also Tomson's Hallowe'en.
Witch princess. *See* Little Czar Novishny, the false sister and the faithful beasts.
In 2d edition there are entries under each title.
Witch that was a hare. *See* Witch hare.
Witch wife. James. Tewa firelight tales.
See also Woman who could not eat.
Witches' eyes. Egan. New found tales. (Lawyer of Samarcand : Witches' eyes.)
Witches of Solstein. Henderson and Calvert. Wonder tales of old Tyrol.
Witch's curse. I. Untermeyer. Last pirate.
Witch's curse. II. Colum. Children who followed the piper.
See also Faithful John.
Witches' excursion. *See* Voyage of the red cap.
Witch's shoes. *See* Blacksmith's wife of Yarrowfoot.
Witty answer. Lee. Folk tales of all nations.
For other entries, see 2d edition.
Witty Portia. *See* Merchant of Venice.
Wives of Weinsberg (poem). Manner. Silver treasury. (Women of Weinsberg.)
See also Emma of Haarlem.
For other entries, see 2d edition.
Wixie and the wireless. Fyleman. Forty good-morning tales.
Wizard and his pupil. I. See 2d edition.
Wizard and his pupil. II. Bowman and Bianco. Tales from a Finnish tupa. (Niilo and the wizard.)
Wizard Didi. **Maspero. Stories of ancient Egypt. (*In* King Khufui and the magicians.)
Wizard Earl. *See* Earl Gerald.
Wizard of Creno, Story of. Hill and Maxwell. Napoleon story book. (*In* Why the fairies went to Corsica.)
Wizard's pupil. *See* Magician's pupil.
Wizards, Pretended. *See* Brahmin and his wife # ; Dr. Know-it-all ; First ants # ; Home bred boy # ; Old man and the robbers ; Percy the wizard # ; Spaeman ; Two imposters ; Wise soothsayer.
Wod! Wod! Wod! *See* Wild hunt.
Wode, the wild hunter. *See* Wild hunter.
Woe. *See* Gore-Gorinskoe.
Woeful tale of long tail rabbit and long tail lynx. Parker. Skunny Wundy and other Indian tales.

Wolf. I–II. *See* 2d edition.
Wolf. III. Rasmussen. Eagle's gift. (Story of wolf.)
Wolf. IV. *See* Boy who cried "Wolf."
Wolf. V. *See* Wolf and the blacksmith.
Wolf. VI. Cooper. Argosy of fables. (Wolf a hero.)
Wolf and his shadow. Æsop. Fables (Jones).
Cooper. Argosy of fables. (Wolf and the lion.)
Wolf and the ass. Æsop. Fables (Whitman ed.).
For other entries, see 2d edition.
Wolf and the blacksmith. I. Bernhard. Master wizard.
Wolf and the blacksmith. II. Borski and Miller. Gypsy
and the bear. (Adventures of a wolf.)
Wolf and the blacksmith. I–II. *See also* Smart young tiger ;
What is man? # ; Wolf and the man.
Wolf and the boy. Æsop. Fables (Jones).
Wolf and the crane. Æsop. Fables (Artzybasheff).
Æsop. Fables (Jones).
Æsop. Fables (Whitman ed.).
Cooper. Argosy of fables.
See also Wolf on his deathbed.
For other entries, see 2d edition.
Wolf and the fox. I. De La Mare. Told again.
For other entries, see 2d edition.
Wolf and the fox. II. La Fontaine. Fables (Tilney).
See also Dog and his shadow ; Fox and the piece of meat.
For other entries, see 2d edition.
Wolf and the fox. III. Bowman and Bianco. Tales from
a Finnish tupa.
Wolf and the fox in the well. La Fontaine. Fables (Til-
ney).
See also Fox, the wolf and the cheese # ; Ups and downs #.
Wolf and the goat. I. Æsop. Fables (Jones).
Æsop. Fables (Whitman ed. Goat and the lion.)
Cooper. Argosy of fables.
See also Wolf and the horse.
Wolf and the hare. Cooper. Argosy of fables.
See also Hare and the tortoise.
Wolf and the horse. Æsop. Fables (Jones).
Cooper. Argosy of fables.
See also Wolf and the goat.
Wolf and the kid. I. *See* Kid and the wolf. II.
Wolf and the kid. II. Æsop. Fables (Jones. Kid and the
wolf.)
Cooper. Argosy of fables. (Kid and the wolf.)
Kinscella. Music appreciation readers. Book 2. (How a
flute saved Wee Lamb.)
See also Lamb and the fox ; Owl and the lemming.
For other entries, see 2d edition.
Wolf and the lamb. I. Æsop. Fables (Artzybasheff).
Æsop. Fables (Jones).
Æsop. Fables (Whitman ed.).
Cooper. Argosy of fables.

Wolf and the lamb. I—*continued.*
Rich. Read aloud book.
See also Cat and the cock.
For other entries, see 2d edition.
Wolf and the lion. I. Æsop. Fables (Jones).
Cooper. Argosy of fables.
Wolf and the lion. II. *See* Wolf and his shadow.
Wolf and the man #.
See also Smart young tiger; Wolf and the blacksmith.
Wolf and the mastiff. *See* Dog and the wolf.
Wolf and the seven little kids. Grimm. Fairy tales (Ol-
cott).
Johnson and Scott. Anthology of children's literature.
Quinn. Stokes' wonder book of fairy tales. (Wolf and the
seven little goats.)
See also Budulinek; Disobedient kids; Nice quiet morning;
Snowflake. III; Water of Ladi; Wolf, the she-goat, and
the kids.
For other entries, see 2d edition.
Wolf and the sheep. I. Æsop. Fables (Jones).
Cooper. Argosy of fables.
For other entries, see 2d edition.
Wolf and the sheep. II. Dane. Once there was and was
not.
See also Fox, the wolf and the cheese #.
Wolf and the shepherd. I. Cooper. Argosy of fables.
For other entries, see 2d edition.
Wolf and the shepherd. II. Æsop. Fables (Jones).
Cooper. Argosy of fables.
Wolf and the shepherds. Cooper. Argosy of fables.
For other entries, see 2d edition.
Wolf as bridegroom. Carrick. Animal picture tales from
Russia.
See also Brother Rabbit's riding horse; Master Rabbit takes
a ride.
Wolf in a sheep's skin. *See* Wolf in sheep's clothing.
Wolf in disguise. Æsop. Fables (Whitman ed.).
For other entries, see 2d edition.
Wolf in harness. Raspé. Children's Munchausen (Martin.
In Ch. 2.)
Raspé. Tales from the travels of Baron Munchausen.
Wolf in sheep's clothing. I. Æsop. Fables (Artzybasheff).
Æsop. Fables (Jones).
Æsop. Twenty-four fables (L'Estrange. Wolf in a sheep's
skin.)
Cooper. Argosy of fables.
Curry and Clippinger. Children's literature.
Johnson and Scott. Anthology of children's literature.
For other entries, see 2d edition.
Wolf in sheep's clothing. II. Rich. Read-aloud book.

Wolf in sheep's clothing. III. Æsop. Fables (Whitman ed.).
See also Wolf in sheep's clothing. I.
Wolf of Gubbio. Bailey. Story-telling hour. (Boy of Italy who could tame all animals.)
See also St. Francis of Assisi.
Wolf on his death-bed. Cooper. Argosy of fables.
See also Wolf and the crane.
For other entries, see 2d edition.
Wolf sings. Bowman and Bianco. Tales from a Finnish tupa. (Song of the wolf.)
For other entries, see 2d edition.
Wolf that went fishing. Carrick. Still more Russian picture tales.
See also Why the bear has a stumpy tail.
Wolf, the fox and the ape. Æsop. Fables (Jones).
Æsop. Fables (Whitman ed.).
Cooper. Argosy of fables. (Monkey holding court.)
For other entries, see 2d edition.
Wolf, the hare and the fox. *See* Hare, the fox and the wolf.
Wolf, the mother and the child. *See* Nurse and the wolf.
Wolf, the she-goat and the kid. Carrick. Still more Russian picture tales. (Kids and the wolf.)
Cowles. Stories to tell. (Goat.)
See also Wolf and the seven little kids.
For other entries, see 2d edition.
Wolf upsets terrapin. James. Happy animals of Atagahi.
Wolfert Webber; or, Golden dreams. Irving. Bold dragoon.
Wolff and his wooden shoe. *See* Sabot of little Wolff.
Wolf's bride. Wilson. Green magic.
Wolf's dream. Carrick. Picture folk tales.
See also Possum eaten in a dream #.
Wolf's heart. *See* Ingvald the wolf king.
Wolves and the dogs. Æsop. Fables (Jones).
Cooper. Argosy of fables. (Wolves and the sheep-dogs.)
Wolves and the sheep. Cooper. Argosy of fables.
For other entries, see 2d edition.
Wolves and the sheep-dogs. *See* Wolves and the dogs.
Wolves, the sheep and the ram. Æsop. Fables (Jones).
Woman and the farmer. Æsop. Fables (Jones).
See also Widow who would be comforted.
Woman and the fat hen. Cooper. Argosy of fables. (Widow and the hen.)
Curry and Clippinger. Children's literature. (Widow and the hen.)
See also Goose that laid golden eggs.
For other entries, see 2d edition.
Woman in the canyon. Otero. Old Spain in our Southwest.
Woman in the moon. I–III. See 2d edition.
Woman in the moon. IV. *See* Hina, the woman in the moon.

Woman who could not eat. Eells. Brazilian fairy book.
See also Wife who ate no rice; Witch wife.

Woman who had no children. Botsford. Picture tales from the Italian.
See also Women and the children of the sycamore tree; Woman with three hundred and sixty-five children.

Woman who had what she wanted. Tappan. Little lady in green.
See also Fisherman and his wife.

Woman who hid her gold in a jar of honey. **Gaster. Ma'aseh book. v. 2.
Gaer. Burning bush. (*In* Two jars of honey.)
See also Ali Cogia.

Woman who killed the wind. Chamoud. Picture tales from the French.

Woman who made two lakes. Snell. Told beneath the northern lights.

Womansand. *See* Sunken city.

Women and the children of the sycamore tree. Lee. Folk tales of all nations.
See also Woman who had no children.

Women are fickle. *See* Widow who would be comforted.

Women of Weinsberg. *See* Wives of Weinsberg.

Wonder balls. I. Wiggin and Smith. Twilight stories.

Wonder balls. II. St. Nicholas. Oct. 1889, p. 922. (Dora Miller's wonder ball.)

Wonder of Christmas night. *See* Innkeeper's story. I.

Wonder prince from Aasgaard. *See* Odin. II.

Wonder shoes. Bailey. Tell me another story.

Wonder wheat of Stavoren. *See* Sunken city.

Wonder=wheat of the Lady=sand. *See* Sunken city.

Wonderful adventures of Funakoshi Jiuyémon. *See* Funakoshi Jiuyémon.

Wonderful adventures of Nils. *See* Nils, Adventures of.

Wonderful beer of poor Petrusha. *See* Beer and bread.

Wonderful bell. *See* Benkei and the bell.

Wonderful bird #.
See also Coyote's eyes; Old-Man's eyes.

Wonderful cave. Kennedy. Red man's wonder book.
See also Pied piper of Hamelin.

Wonderful cow #.
See also Cow of plenty.

Wonderful cow=that=never=was. Mitchell. Here and now story book.

Wonderful doll of Vasilissa the beautiful. *See* Vasilisa the beauty.

Wonderful flower. I. Olcott. Wonder tales from goblin hills. (Forget not the best.)
See also Forget-me-not. I.
For other entries, see 2d edition.

Wonderful flower. II. *See* Hans and the wonderful flower.

Wonderful flower. III. Burnett. Children's book.

Wonderful garden of dreams. Williston. Hindu stories.
Wonderful goat. *See* Capella.
Wonderful hair. Harper. Fillmore folk tales.
See also Wonderful ring.
For other entries, see 2d edition.
Wonderful head. Morris. Book of the three dragons.
Wonderful horns. Lee. Folk tales of all nations.
See also Billy Beg and the bull ; Table, the ass, and the stick.
Wonderful horse. Pogány. Hungarian fairy book.
Wonderful journey. Gate. Tales from the secret kingdom.
Wonderful kettle. *See* Chestnut kettle.
Wonderful lamb. Harper. Ghosts and goblins.
Pogány. Magyar fairy tales.
See also Golden goose.
Wonderful lamp. *See* Aladdin.
Wonderful lizard. Lee. Folk tales of all nations.
See also Fire-makers ; Secret of fire.
Wonderful palm tree. *See* Palm tree.
Wonderful pear tree. *See* Miserly farmer.
Wonderful plough. Choate and Curtis. Little people of the hills. (Wonderful plow.)
For other entries, see 2d edition.
Wonderful porridge pot. De La Mare and Quayle. Readings. (Sweet porridge.)
Evans. Worth while stories. (Magic pot. Adapted.)
Grimm. Fairy tales (Olcott ed. Sweet porridge.)
Williams. Tales from Ebony. (Pot of soup.)
For other entries, see 2d edition.
Wonderful pot. Hutchinson. Fireside stories.
Skinner. Happy tales. (Old iron pot.)
Told under the green umbrella.
See also Bayong of the lazy woman ; Clipped penny.
For other entries, see 2d edition.
Wonderful ring. Williston. Hindu stories. (Charmed ring.)
See also Poor man, the snake, the cat, the dog, the mouse, and the beaver ; Wonderful hair.
For other entries, see 2d edition.
Wonderful sheep. *See* Ram.
Wonderful tea=kettle. *See* Accomplished and lucky tea kettle.
Wonderful tree. Bailey. Wonderful tree. (Story for Arbor Day.)
Wonderful tune. Beston. Starlight wonder book.
Wonderful waterfall. *See* Waterfall which flowed saké
Wonders of the three Donals. MacManus. Donegal wonder book.
Wood and the clown. *See* Woodman and the trees.
Wood beyond the world. Beston. Starlight wonder book.
Wood carver of Rouen. Butterfield. Young people's story of architecture. (*In* Ch. 34–37.)
Wood=fairies. Housman. What-o'clock tales.

Wood-find. Housman. What-o'clock tales.
Wood friends. Bryce. Short stories for little folks.
Wood maiden #.
See also Lady of the forest.
Wood of Tontla. *See* Tontlawald. Tale of the.
Woodcutter's tales. Housman. What-o'clock tales.
Wooden horse. I. Bulfinch. 'Golden Age. (*In* Ch. 28.)
Forbush. Myths and legends of Greece and Rome. (*In* Trojan war.)
jan war.)
Rich. Read-aloud book. (Wooden horse of Troy.)
Terry. Tales from far and near. (Story of a wooden horse.)
See also Trojan war.
For other entries, see 2d edition.
Wooden horse. II. *See* Enchanted horse.
Wooden horse. III. Fyleman. Forty good-morning tales.
Wooden Indian and the shaghorn buffalo. Sandburg.
Rootabaga country.
Sandburg. Rootabaga stories.
Wooden Jack. Pogány. Magyar fairy tales.
Wooden shoe. I. *See* 2d edition.
Wooden shoe. II. Brown. Under the rowan tree. (Wooden shoes.)
en shoes.)
Wooden shoes and silver rings. Hill and Maxwell. Napoleon's story book.
leon's story book.
Wooden spoon who wanted to be silver. Chambers' miscellany. v. 9. (*In* Wooden spoon, pt. 1.)
lany. v. 9. (*In* Wooden spoon, pt. 1.)
Wooden wife #.
See also Talking tree.
Woodland fairy. Pogány. Magyar fairy tales.
Woodman and the goblins. Freeman. Child-story readers.
3d reader. (Woodman and the brownies.)
Harper. Ghosts and goblins.
For other entries, see 2d edition.
Woodman and the trees. Æsop. Fables (Jones. Trees and the axe.)
the axe.)
Æsop. Fables (Whitman ed. Wood and the clown.)
Cooper. Argosy of fables. (Trees and the axe.)
La Fontaine. Fables (Tilney). (Forest and the woodcutter.)
ter.)
For other entries, see 2d edition.
Woodman and the wishing stone. Bowman. Little brown bowl.
bowl.
Woodpecker. I. *See* Why the woodpecker's head is red.
Woodpecker. II. Rich. Why-so stories. (Why the woodpecker likes trees.)
pecker likes trees.)
Woodpecker and bluejay. Macmillan. Canadian wonder tales. (Sad tale of woodpecker and bluejay.)
tales. (Sad tale of woodpecker and bluejay.)
Woodpecker and her sack. *See* Inquisitive woman.
Woodpecker, Tales of the. Rich. Why-so stories.
Woodpecker, tortoise, and the antelope. *See* True friendship.
ship.

Woodpecker who was selfish. Bailey. Stories children want.
Evans. Worth while stories.
For other entries, see 2d edition.
Woodpecker's joke. *See* Right time to laugh.
Woodrat the trader. Barrows and Cavanah. Favorite pages from Child Life. (Pack rat of Tuolumne.)
Wooing of Becfola. Stephens. Irish fairy tales.
Wooing of Gerd. Curry and Clippinger. Children's literature. (Frey.)
Johnson and Scott. Anthology of children's literature.
Pyle. Tales from Norse mythology. (How Frey won a bride and lost a sword.)
For other entries, see 2d edition.
Wooing of Seppo Ilmarinen. *See* Ilmarinen, the smith. II.
Wooing of the maze. Housman. Doorway in fairyland.
Word of a gentleman. Broomell. Children's story caravan.
Words, Tale about. *See* Diamonds and toads.
Worker in sandal-wood. Starbuck. Far horizons.
Walters. Book of Christmas stories.
For other entries, see 2d edition.
World-beautiful Sharkan Roja. Curtin. Fairy tales of Eastern Europe.
World of chance. Katibah. Other Arabian nights.
World's reward. I. *See* Way of the world.
World's reward. II. *See* Man and the snake. II.
Worsted dog. Aspinwall. Can you believe me stories.
See also Top and ball.
Wound and the scar #.
See also Labourer and the snake.
Wounded seal. Faulkner. Road to enchantment.
Wreath of destiny. Egan. New found tales.
Wren. I. Cooper. Argosy of fables. (Wren and the camel.)
See also Frog and the ox.
For other entries, see 2d edition.
Wren and the camel. *See* Wren. I.
Wren, God's little hen. *See* Wren who brought fire.
Wren who brought fire. Babbitt. Animals' own story book. (Wren, God's little hen.)
Brown. Curious book of birds.
Carey. Stories of the birds. (How the wren brought fire to earth.)
Olcott. Wonder garden. (Why the owl cries hoot! hoot!)
Rich. Why-so stories. (Why the wren's feathers look scorched.)
Rich. Why-so stories. (*In* Tales of the owl.)
Wriggeldy school. Cook. Red and gold stories.
Writing a composition. *See* Mr. Finney's turnip.
Wrong thing. Kipling. Rewards and fairies.
Wry-mouth family. *See* Snooks family; Twist-mouth family.

Wuchowson the wind-blower. Leland. Algonquin legends.
(Tumilkoontaoo; or, Broken wing.)
Leland. Algonquin legends. (How Glooskap found Wuchowsem.)
See also Adapa and the south wind.
For other entries, see 2d edition.
Wuzzle. Denton. Homespun stories.
Wyvern. Henderson and Jones. Wonder tales of ancient Wales.
See also Vouivre.

X

Xelhua. *See* Giant pyramid builder.
Xerxes. Farjeon. Mighty men from Achilles to Julius Caesar. (Queen Esther; King Xerxes goes to war.)
For other entries, see 2d edition.
Xochitl, the beautiful flower. Martinez Del Rio. Sun, the moon and a rabbit.

Y

Yanagi. *See* Willow tree ghosts.
Yang Glow-of-Dawn. Olcott. Wonder tales from China seas.
Yang Yang and Hoo Hoo. Sandburg. Rootabaga country.
Sandburg. Rootabaga pigeons.
Yankee balloon. Brown. Under the rowan tree.
Yanni and the dragon. Fuller. Book of dragons.
Yannik, the fairy child. Masson. Folk tales of Brittany.
Yappy. Hooker. Garden of the lost key.
Yarg. Aspinwall. Can you believe me stories.
Ye olde tyme tayle of ye knight, ye yeomanne, and ye faire damosel.
See Knight and the yeoman.
Ye very ancient ballad of ye lily mayden and ye lyttel taylor-boye.
See Lily maid and the tailors.
Year, Story of. Cowles. Stories to tell. (Story of the spring. (Adapted.)
Wheelock. Kindergarten children's hour. v. 3. New Year. Adapted. *In* Ch. 52.
For other entries, see 2d edition.
Year's house. Marzials. Stories for the story hour.
Yellow calfskin mat in the house of the spinning-woman of Arfon. Morris. Book of the three dragons.
Yellow dwarf. Aulnoy. Fairy tales (Planché).
For other entries, see 2d edition.
Yellow elves. Shannon. California fairy tales.
Yellow flowers. Whiteman. Playmates in print.
Yellow primrose. Buckingham. Elephant's friend.
Yggdrasil, the ash. *See* Iduna's apples.

Youth who could not shiver and shake—*continued.*
Quiller-Couch. Twelve dancing princesses. (John and the ghosts.)
See also Tinker and the ghost.
For other entries, see 2d edition.
Youth who gathered jewels. *See* Marco˙Polo.
Youth who set out to learn what fear was. *See* Youth who could not shiver and shake.
Youth who went through the proper ceremonies. Ryder. Twenty-two goblins.
Youth without age and life without death. Lee. Folk tales of all nations.
For other entries, see 2d edition.
Yvain. *See* Sir Yvain.
Yvon and Finette. Adams and Atchinson. There were giants.
Lee. Folk tales of all nations.
See also Three golden hairs. II.
For other entries, see 2d edition.
Ys, Story of. I. Clément. Once in France. (Ys and her bells.)
Colum. Forge in the forest.
Colum. Fountain of youth. (Lost city of Ys.)
Ys, Story of. II. Masson. Folk tales of Brittany. (Princess Ahez and the lost city.)
See also Cathedral under the sea.
Yukpachen, Story of. Noel. Magic bird of Chomo-lung-ma.
Yves, St. *See* St. Yves.

Z

Zahhak, the snake-king. Coit. Ivory throne of Persia.
Zal and Rudaba. Coit. Ivory throne of Persia.
Zal and Rustem. Wells. How the present came from the past. Book 2,·pt. 2. (Some stories of Zal and the childhood of Rustem.)
Zal, the white-haired. *See* White-headed Zal.
Zane, Betty. Evans. Worth while stories. (How a girl saved a fort.)
Zauber See, Legend of the. Henderson. Wonder tales of Alsace-Lorraine.
Zazamankh and the lost coronet. *See* Pharaoh and the little maid.
Zenobia, queen of Palmyra. Farjeon. Tales from Chaucer. (*In* Monk's tale.)
Miller. My book of history. v. 3. (*In* Ch. 1.)
Zenon of Philadelphia. Miller. My book of history. v. 2. (Struggles of a self-made man. *In* Ch. 7.)
Zeus. *See* Jupiter; Titans.
Zipacna. Lee. Folk tales of all nations. (Earth giants.)
Lee. Folk tales of all nations. (Undoing of Zipacna.)
Miller. ˙ My book of history. v. 4. (*In* Story of creation. Ch. 10.)

LIST OF BOOKS ANALYZED IN THE INDEX

The titles of books, a part only of whose contents has been indexed in the foregoing list, have been indicated by the addition of a dagger (†). The double asterisk (**) is used to indicate source material needing abridging or adapting.

The prices given are usually those quoted at time of publication and are only for aid in estimating approximate cost.

Adams, Julia D.
Swords of the Vikings; stories from the works of Saxo Grammaticus. c1928. Dutton, $2.00; London. Dent, 7s. 6d.

Adams, Kathleen and Atchinson, Frances E., *comps.*
Book of enchantment. c1928. Dodd, $2.50.
Book of giant stories. c1926. Dodd, $2.00.
Book of princess stories. c1927. Dodd, $2.50.
There were giants. c1929. Dodd, $2.00.

Addison, Joseph.
Essays.

Æsop.
Fables; ed. and illus. by Boris Artzybasheff. 1933. Viking press, $2.00.
Fables; V. S. Vernon Jones, tr. 1933. c1912. London. Heinemann, 6s.
Fables; text based upon La Fontaine and Croxall. 1929. c1925. Whitman, A., $1.25. (World-wide Just-right book.)
Twenty-four fables of Æsop and other eminent mythologists as rendered into English by Sir Roger L'Estrange. 1929. Dutton, $3.00.

Alcover, A. M.
See Dane, G. E., and B. J., eds.

Aldine readers.
See Spaulding, F. E., and Bryce, C. T., eds.

Allen, George C.
Tales from Tennyson. 1900. Brentano's, $1.25.

Allen, Philippa.
†Story-teller's house. c1930. Rockwell, $1.25.
Whispering wind. c1930. Rockwell, $.50.

Andersen, Hans C.
Fairy tales; Carl Siewers, tr. 1927. c1919. Whitman, A., $1.25.
Fairy tales; J. H. Stickney, ed. 2 v. c1915. Ginn, v. 1, $.72; v. 2, $.76.
Four tales; R. P. Keigwin, tr. 1935. Cambridge Univ. Press, 3s. 6d; N. Y. Macm., $1.25.

Andress, J. M., and A. T.
†Journey to Health-land. c1924. Ginn, $.72.

Applegarth, Margaret T.
†Missionary stories for little folks. 1st series: primary. 1928. c1921. Doubleday, $1.75.

Arabian days' entertainment.
See Hauff, Wilhelm.

Arabian nights' entertainment.
Adventures of Haroun Er Raschid and other tales; F. J. Olcott,
ed. Illus. by Willy Pogány. c1923. Holt, $2.00.
Based on Lane's translation.
Selected stories from the Arabian nights; Samuel Eliot, ed. n.d.
new rev. ed. Houghton, $.92.
Arnold, Edwin, tr.
**Book of good counsels; from the Sanskrit of the "Hitopadesa."
1896. London. Allen, 7s. 6d. (Author's autograph ed.)
Arnold, Margaret G.
Folk tales retold. c1926. Bruce, $.96.
Arthur Rackham fairy book.
See Rackham, Arthur.
Artzybasheff, Boris, ed.
See Æsop.
Asbjornsen, Peter C.
See Dasent, George W.; Rasmussen, Inger M.
Ashton, Winifred.
See Dane, Clemence, pseud.
Aspinwall, Alicia.
Can you believe me stories. 1926. c1909. Dutton, $2.00.
Aspinwall, Marguerite.
Jataka tales out of old India, retold. 1927 ed. Putnam, $1.25.
Association for childhood education, Literature committee.
See Told under the blue umbrella.
Atchinson, Frances E., comp.
See Adams, Kathleen.
Atkins, Elizabeth Howard.
Pot of gold. c1930. Stokes, $2.00.
Aulnoy, M. C. J. deB., Comtesse de.
Fairy tales; tr. by J. R. Planché. 1923. McKay, $3.50.
Complete authoritative collection.
White cat and other old French fairy tales. Arranged and
abridged by Rachel Field. c1928. Macm., $3.50.
Babbitt, Ellen C.
Animals' own story book. 1930. Century, $1.50.
Bachmann, Frieda, tr.
See Lebermann, Norbert.
Bacon, Peggy.
Lion-hearted kitten and other stories. 1927. Macm., $2.00.
Mercy and the mouse, and other stories. 1928. Macm., $1.75.
Baikie, James.
Wonder tales of the ancient world. c1915. Macm., $2.00.
Bailey, Carolyn S.
Stories children want. c1931. Bradley, $1.75.
Stories from an Indian cave. c1924. Whitman, A., $1.25.
Stories of great adventures; adapted from the classics. c1919.
Bradley, $1.75.
†Story-telling hour. 1934. Dodd, $2.00.
Tell me another story. 1926. c1918. Bradley, $1.75.
Wonderful tree, and golden day stories. c1925. Whitman, A.,
$1.25.
Baker, Margaret.
Tell them again tales. 1934. Dodd, $1.75.
†Tomson's Hallowe'en. 1929. Duffield, $2.00; London. Black-
well, 2s. 6d.
Baker, Mary and Margaret.
Pedlar's wares. 1925. Duffield, $1.50.

Baldwin, Mrs. Alfred.
Pedlar's pack. [1925.] Stokes. $2.50; London. Chambers.
Bancroft, Alberta. (Mrs. A. B. Reid.)
Goblins of Haubeck. 1933. McBride, $1.75.
Bannerman, Helen.
Little Black Sambo. 1923. Stokes, $2.00.
Barber, Margaret F.
See Fairless, Michael, *pseud.*
Barbour, Harriot B.
Old English tales retold. 1924. Macm., $.96.
Barclay, Vera.
Saints by firelight. 1931. Macm., $1.50.
Barrows, Marjorie, and Cavanah, Frances, *comps.*
†Favorite pages from Child Life. c1931. Rand. (Tenth birth-
day anthology. 1921–1931.)
Barry, Mary E., and Hanna, Paul R.
Wonder flights of long ago. c1930. Appleton, $2.00.
Baumbach, Rudolf.
Tales from the Swiss alps; tr. from the German by H. W. Mitchell.
c1930. Rockwell, $2.00.
Beard, Patten.
Tucked-in tales. 1930. c1924. Rand, $1.00.
Belpré, Pura.
Perez and Martina. 1932. Warne, $1.75.
Bemis, Katherine I.
See Van Buren, Maud.
Bennett, John.
Pigtail of Ah Lee Ben Loo. 1928. Longmans, $2.50.
Bergstrom, Richard.
See Tappan. Eva M.
Bernhard, Josephine B.
Master wizard and other Polish fairy tales; revised and adapted
by E. F. LeValley. c1934. Knopf, $1.50; $2.25.
Berry, Erick, *pesud.* **(Mrs. A. C. Best.)**
Black folk tales. c1928. Harper, $2.00.
Best, Mrs. Allena C.
See Berry, Erick, *pseud.*
Beston, Henry B., *pseud.* **(H. B Sheahan.)**
Starlight wonder book. c1923. Atlantic, $2.50.
Bianco, Margery W.
Little wooden doll. c1925. Macm., $1.00. (Little library.)
Street of little shops. c1932. Doubleday, $1.50.
See also Bowman, James C.
Black, Hugh.
†Open door. 1915. Revell, $1.00.
Blaisdell, Albert F. and Ball, Francis K.
†Log cabin days. c1920. Little, $1.20.
Blaisdell, Etta A.
†Rhyme and story second reader. 1929. Little, $.70.
Contents are same as her "My garden of stories."
Blondell, Richard, *comp.*
Keepsakes. c1936. Nelson, $1.50.
Told for radio programs.
Boeckel, Florence B., *comp.*
†Through the gateway. c1925. Nat'l council for prevention of
war. $.50. (Books of goodwill. v. 1.)
Boggs, Ralph S., and Davis, Mary G.
Three golden oranges and other Spanish folk tales. c1936. Long-
mans, $2.00.

Book of nursery tales.
See Mackenzie, Compton.
Borski, Lucia M., and Miller, Kate B.
Gipsy and the bear. c1933. Longmans, $1.75.
Bosch y Roca, Pablo.
See Dane, G. E., and B. J., *eds.*
Botsford, Florence.
Picture tales from the Italian. c1929. Stokes, $1.25.
Bowman, James C., and Bianco, Margery.
Tales from a Finnish tupa; from the tr. by Ali Kolehmainen. c1936. Whitman, A., $2.50. (Junior Literary Guild book.)
Bowman, Phila B.
Little brown bowl, with other tales and verse. 1928. Nelson, $2.00.
Brock, H. M., *illus.*
Book of fairy tales. n.d., Warne, $3.00.
Also pub. as Old fairy tales, v. 1–2.
Valentine and Orson, and Jack the giant killer. n.d. Warne, $2.00. (Old fairy tales, v. 3.)
See also Mackenzie, Compton.
Broomell, Anna P., *ed.*
†Children's story caravan. c1935. Lippincott, $2.00.
Brower, Josephine.
See Irving, Washington.
Brown, Abbie F.
Curious book of birds. c1903. Houghton, $1.50.
Under the rowan tree. 1926. Houghton, $1.75.
Browne, G. Waldo.
Indian nights. c1927. Noble, $.85.
Bruce, Marjory, *comp.*
Treasury of tales for little folk. 1936. c1927. Grosset, $1.00.
Bryant, Lorinda M.
†Children's book of celebrated legends. c1929. Century, $2.50.
Bryce, Catherine T.
Folk lore from foreign lands. c1913, Newson, $.76. (Aldine supplementary readers.)
Short stories for little folks. c1910. Newson, $.76. (Aldine supplementary readers.)
See also Spaulding, F. E.
Buckingham, Burdette R., *comp. and ed.*
†Elephant's friend. c1934. Ginn, $.84. (Children's bookshelf.)
†Great idea and other stories. c1934. Ginn, $.80. (Children's bookshelf.)
Bulfinch, Thomas.
†Golden age of myth and legend; being a revised and enlarged edition of "The age of fable." n.d. Stokes, $4.00.
Burgess, Thornton W.
†Adventures of old Mr. Toad. c1916. Little, $.60.
Burnett, Frances H.
†Land of the blue flower. 1909. Moffat, $.75.
Burnett, Frances H.. and others.
†Children's book. c1907–1915. Cupples & Leon, $1.25.
Burt, Mary E., *ed.*
†Lanier book. 1914. c1904. Scribner, $.76.
Butterfield, Emily H.
†Young people's story of architecture. c1933. Dodd, $3.00.
Byrde, Elsie, *tr.*
Polish fairy book. c1927. Stokes, $2.50.

Cabot, Ella L., and others.
†Course in citizenship and patriotism. c1914–1918. Houghton, $1.90.
Calvert, Charles.
See Henderson, Bernard.
Campbell, R. J.
†Story of Christmas. c1934. Macm., $3.00.
Canfield, Dorothy. (Mrs. D. C. Fisher.)
Made-to-order stories. c1925. Harcourt, $2.50.
Canton, William. {
Child's book of saints. c1906–1924. London. Dent; N. Y. Dutton, $.80. (Everyman's library.)
Capuana, Luigi.
Golden-feather; tr. by Dorothy Emmrich. c1930. Dutton, $2.50.
Italian fairy tales; tr. by Dorothy Emmrich. 1929. Dutton, $2.50.
Carey, Mabel C.
†Flower legends. 1929. London. Pearson, 3s. 6d.
Stories of the birds from myth and fable. n.d. Houghton, $2.00; 2d ed. 1932. Harrap, 2s. 6d.
Carpenter, Frances.
Tales of a Basque grandmother. 1930. Doubleday, $3.50.
Tales of a Russian grandmother. 1933. Doubleday, $2.00.
Carrick, Valery.
Animal picture tales from Russia. 1930. Stokes, $1.50.
More Russian picture tales. 1920. c1914. Stokes, $1.25; also London. Blackwell, 2s. 6d.
Still more Russian picture tales; tr. by Neville Forbes. 1930. c1915-1922. Stokes, $1.25.
Tales of wise and foolish animals. 1928. Stokes, $1.50.
Valery Carrick's picture folk tales. c1926. Stokes, $1.50.
Carroll, Lewis, *pseud.* (Charles L. Dodgson.)
Alice's adventures in Wonderland; and Through the looking-glass. Illus. by John Tenniel. 2 v. in 1. 1931. Macm., $1.00. (Children's classics.)
Cary, Alice and Phoebe.
†Poetical works. Houghton, $2.25. (Household ed.)
Casserley, Anne.
†Michael of Ireland. n.d. Harper, $1.50.
†Whins on Knockattan. c1928. Harper, $1.50.
Cather, Katherine D.
Pan and his pipes, and other tales for children. 1916. Victor Talking Machine Co., $.35.
Cavanah, Frances.
See Barrows, Marjorie.
Cendrars, Blaise.
Little black stories for little white children; tr. from the French by Margery Bianco, illus. by Pierre Pinsard. c1929. Payson and Clarke, $2.00.
Chambers, William, *ed.*
†Chambers' miscellany of instructive and entertaining tracts. New and revised ed. n.d. London and Edinburgh. Chambers.
Chamoud, Simone.
Picture tales from the French. c1933. Stokes, $1.25.
Chandler, Anna C.
Magic pictures of the long ago. 1918. Holt, $1.30.

Chardon, Jeanne.
Golden chick and the magic frying pan; tr. by Ruth P. Tubby.
1935. Whitman, A., $1.50.
Chesterton, G. K.
See Number two Joy street.
Chevalier, Jules C.
†Noah's grandchildren. 1929. Doubleday, $2.00.
Chidley, Howard J.
†Fifty-two story talks to boys and girls. 1929. c1914. Double-
day, $1.25; also Harper.
Choate, Florence and Curtis, Elizabeth.
Little people of the hills. c1928. Harcourt, $2.50.
Chrisman, Arthur B.
Shen of the sea. c1925. Dutton, $2.00.
Wind that wouldn't blow. c1927. Dutton, $2.50.
Clark, Margery.
†Poppy seed cakes. 1935. c1924. Doubleday, $2.00.
Clément, Marguerite.
Flowers of chivlary; stories of heroes and heroines of old France.
1934. Doubleday, $2.50. (Junior books.)
Once in France. 1935. c1927. Doubleday, $2.00.
Clippinger, E. E.
See Curry, C. M.
Coe, Fanny E.
Third book of stories for the story teller. 1920. c1918. Hough-
ton, $2.00.
Coit, Dorothy.
Ivory throne of Persia. c1929. Stokes, $3.00.
Kai Khosru and other plays for children. c1934. Theatre Arts,
$1.50.
Coloma, Louis de.
Perez the mouse; adapted from the Spanish by Lady Moreton.
c1914. Dodd, $.85.
Colum, Padraic.
Big tree of Bunlahy. 1933. Macm., $2.25.
Boy apprenticed to an enchanter. 1928. c1920. Macm., $1.75.
Bright islands. 1925. Published for the Hawaiian legend and
folklore comm. by the Yale Univ. Press, $2.50.
(Tales and legends of Hawaii. v. 2.)
†Children who followed the piper. 1930. c1922. Macm., $1.75.
Forge in the forest. c1925. Macm., $2.25.
Fountain of youth. 1927. Macm., $2.00.
King of Ireland's son. 1929. c1916. Macm., $2.00.
Voyagers. c1925. Macm., $2.25.
Cook, Frances K., *ed.*
Red and gold stories. 1927. Whitman, A., $1.25. (Just right
books.)
To-day's stories of yesterday. c1925. Whitman, A., $.75.
(Junior press books.)
Cooke, Arthur O.
Stories of Rome in days of old. n.d. N. Y. Stokes; London.
Jack, 3s.
Coolidge, Susan.
†Verses. 1912. Lippincott, $1.00.
Cooper, Frederic T., *ed.*
Argosy of fables. c1921. Stokes, $5.00.
Cooper, Paul F.
Tal; his marvelous adventures with Noom-Zor-Noom. 1929.
Morrow, $2.50.

Couch, Arthur T. Quiller-
See Quiller-Couch, Arthur T.
Coussens, Penrhyn W., *ed.*
Diamond story book. 1921. c1914. Duffield, $2.00.
Cowles, Julia D., *comp.*
Stories to tell. 1923. c1906. Flanagan, $.64.
Cozad, Simeon E.
†Story talks for boys and girls. 1935. Round Table Press, $1.50.
Crew, Helen C.
†Saturday's children. 1927. Little, $2.00.
Criss, Mildred.
†Martine and Michel. 1931. Doubleday, $2.00. (Junior books.)
Cross, Donzella.
Music stories for boys and girls. c1926. Ginn, $.80.
Crownfield, Gertrude.
Feast of Noel. c1928. Dutton, $1.50.
Cruse, Amy.
Young folk's book of epic heroes. 1927. Little, $2.00; Harrap,
7s. 6d.
Curry, Charles M., and Clippinger, Erle E.
†Children's literature; a textbook of sources for teachers. 1926
ed. c1921. Rand, $3.50.
Curtin, Jeremiah.
Fairy tales of Eastern Europe. 1931. c1914. McBride, $2.00.
Curtis, Elizabeth.
See Choate, Florence.
Curtis, Herbert P., *tr.*
See Hauff, Wilhelm.
Curtis, Mary I.
Stories in trees. c1925. Lyons and Carnahan, $.88.
Dane, Clemence, *pseud.* **(Winifred Ashton.)**
†Fate cries out. 1935. Doubleday, $2.00.
Dane, George E., and Beatrice J., *eds.*
Once there was and was not; tales from Majorca adapted . . .
from A. M. Alcover and Don Pablo Bosch y Roca. 1931.
Doubleday, $2.00.
Danielson, Frances W.
See Perkins, Jeanette E.
Darton, Frederick J. H.
Seven champions of Christendom. n.d. N. Y., Stokes, $3.00;
London. Wells.
Retold from old chap books and Richard Johnson's text.
Wonder book of old romance. c1907–1925. Stokes, $2.50.
Prose versions of romances of Middle Ages.
Dasent, George W.
East of the sun and west of the moon; illus. by Kay Nielson.
n.d. Garden City Pub. Co., $1.00.
Davidson, Ray, *tr.*
See Mamin, D. N.
Davis, Mary G., *comp.*
Baker's dozen: thirteen stories to tell and to read aloud. c1930.
Harcourt, $2.00.
Truce of the wolf, and other tales of old Italy. 1931. Harcourt,
$2.00.
See also Boggs, Ralph S.
De Huff, Elizabeth W.
Taytay's memories. c1924. Harcourt, $2.25.
Taytay's tales. c1922. Harcourt, $2.25.

Deihl, Edna G.
†Holiday-time stories. c1930. Whitman, A., $1.00.
De La Mare, Walter J.
Dutch cheese. 1931. c1925. Knopf, $2.50.
Told again; old tales told again. 1927. Knopf, $3.50.
De La Mare, Walter J., and Quayle, Thomas, *comp.*
†Readings. 1927. Knopf, $5.00.
De Leeuw, Hendrik.
Java jungle tales. c1933. Doubleday, $2.00.
Del Rio, Amelia Martinez.
See Martinez Del Rio, Amelia.
Denton, Clara J.
Homespun stories. c1924. Whitman, A., $.60.
Dickens, Charles.
Works: Reprinted pieces.
Christmas carol. Illus. by F. D. Bedford. Macm., $1.00. (Children's classics.)
Magic fishbone. 1922. London. Warne, $1.50.
Dodgson, Charles L.
See Carroll, Lewis, *pseud.*
Dorey, Jacques.
Three and the moon. c1929. Knopf, $3.50. (Junior Literary Guild book.)
Dulac, Edmund, *illus.*
Edmund Dulac fairy book; fairy tales of the allied nations. [1916.] Doran, $3.75.
See also Fairy garland.
Dumas, Alexandre.
Dumas fairy tale book; ed. and tr. by H. A. Spurr.
See Spurr, Harry A.
Dunbar, Aldis.
Sons o' Cormac, an' tales of other men's sons. c1929. Dutton, $3.00.
Dunlap, Maurice.
Stories of the Vikings; retold from Snorra's Heimskringla. c1923. Bobbs-Merrill, $2.00.
Echols, Ula W.
Knights of Charlemagne. c1928. Longmans, $3.00.
Eckford, Eugenia. (Mrs. E. E. Rhodes.)
Wonder windows; stories and pictures of art in many lands. c1931. Dutton, $2.00.
Eells, Elsie S.
Brazilian fairy book. c1926. Stokes, $2.50.
Fairy tales from Brazil. c1917. Dodd, $2.00.
Islands of magic; legends, folk and fairy tales from the Azores. c1922. Harcourt, $1.75.
Magic tooth and other tales from the Amazon. 1927. Little, $2.00.
Egan, Joseph B.
New found tales from many lands. c1929–1930. N. Y. Children's book club; Phila. Winston, $2.00.
Eggleston, Margaret W.
†Stories for special days in the church school. c1922. Doran, $1.25.
Eliot, Samuel, *ed.*
See Arabian nights' entertainment.
Ellis, Amabel Williams-.
See Williams-Ellis, Amabel S.

Elson, William H., and Keck, C. M.
†Junior high school literature. Book 1. c1919. Scott, $1.40.
Elson, William H., and Runkel, Lura E.
†Child-library readers: Book 2. c1925. Scott, $.68.
Emerson, Caroline D.
Merry-go-round of modern tales. 1927. Dutton, $2.00.
Emmerich, Dorothea, *tr.*
See Capuana, Luigi.
Evans, Lawton B.
†Worth while stories for every day. 1930. c1917. Bradley, $1.75.
Ewing, Juliana H.
Lob Lie-by-the-fire and other stories. n.d. N. Y. Harcourt, $2.00; London. Bell. (Queen's treasures series.)
Fairy garland; being fairy tales from the old French, illus. by Edmund Dulac. 1928. London. Cassell; 1930. N. Y., Scribner, $2.00.
Falkberget, Johan.
Broomstick and Snowflake; tr. by Tekla Welhaven, ed. by H. S. Mazet. c1933. Macm., $1.75.
Norwegian title was "Magic mountains."
Farjeon, Eleanor.
†Italian peepshow and other tales. 1926. Stokes, $2.50.
Martin Pippin in the apple orchard. c1922. Stokes, $2.50.
Mighty men from Achilles to Julius Caesar. 1931. c1925. Appleton, $1.00.
Mighty men from Beowulf to William the Conquerer. 1929. c1925. Appleton, $1.00.
Old nurse's stocking-basket. c1931. Stokes, $1.75.
Old sailor's yarn box. c1934. Stokes, $1.75.
Tales from Chaucer; the Canterbury tales done into prose. 1930. Cape, $3.00.
Ten saints. 1936. Oxford Univ. Press, $2.50.
Faulkner, Georgene.
Little Peachling and other tales of old Japan. c1928. Volland, $1.25.
Road to enchantment. c1929. Sears, $2.50.
"Story lady's" Christmas stories. 1927. c1920. Sears, $1.25.
White elephant and other tales from old India. c1929. Volland, $1.25.
Told for radio programs.
Field, Rachel, *ed.* and *comp.*
American folk and fairy tales. 1929. Scribner, $2.50.
Eliza and the elves. 1926. Macm., $2.00.
Pocket-handkerchief park. 1929. Doubleday, $.75.
See also Aulnoy, M. C. J. deB.
Fisher, Dorothy (Canfield).
See Canfield, Dorothy.
Flack, Marjorie.
Angus and the ducks. 1930. Doubleday, $1.00.
Fleming, Rachel M.
Round the world in folk tales. c1925. Harcourt, $1.50.
Forbes, Mildred P.
†Good citizenship through story telling. c1923. Macm., $1.60.
Forbes, Neville, *tr.*
See Carrick, Valery.
Forbush, William B.
†Myths and legends of Greece and Rome. c1928. Winston, $1.10.

Foss, C. W., *tr.*
   See Topelius, Zacharias.
Freeman, Frank N., and others.
   †Child-story readers : 3d reader. 1934. c1927–1929. Lyons and
     Carnahan, $.88.
Frere, M. E. I.
   See Pyle, Katherine.
Friedlander, Gerald.
   Jewish fairy tales and stories. c1920. Dutton, $1.00.
Fuller, O. Muriel, *ed.*
   Book of dragons. c1931. McBride, $1.00.
Fun folk and fairy tales.
   See National Association of Junior Chautauqua Directors.
Fyleman, Rose.
   Forty good-morning tales. 1930. c1929. Doubleday, $1.00.
   Forty good-night tales. c1924. Doran, $2.00.
   Tea time tales. c1930. Doubleday, $2.00.
Gaer, Joseph.
   †Burning bush ; adapted folklore legends. c1929. Union of
     American Hebrew Congregations, $2.00.
   (Union story series, ed. by Emanuel Gamoran.)
   †Magic flight ; Jewish tales and legends. c1926. Frank-Maurice,
     $1.25.
Garett, Mrs. Fred. (Mourning Dove.)
   Coyote stories ; ed. and illus. by Hester D. Guie. c1933. Cax-
     ton Printers, $2.00.
Garnett, Lucy M., *tr.* and *ed.*
   Ottoman wonder tales. 1915. London. Black, 6s.
Gaster, Moses, *tr.*
   †**Ma'aseh book. 2 v. 1934. Jewish Publication Society of
     America, $4.00. (Schiff library of Jewish classics.)
Gate, Ethel M.
   Tales from the secret kingdom. 1919. Yale Univ. Press, $2.00.
Gatty, Mrs. Margaret S.
   †Parables from nature. 1912. Macm. Also in Everyman's
     library.
Gearhart, Ephraim M.
   Skalalatoot stories ; a book of real Indian bed time stories. c1922.
     Stratford, $1.25.
Gibson, Katharine.
   Golden bird and other stories. 1927. Macm., $2.50.
Going, Charles B.
   †Folklore and fairy plays. c1927. Baker, $1.50.
Gordon, Emma K., and Stockard, Marietta.
   †Gordon readers ; new series : 2d reader. c1918. Heath, $.68.
Graham, Eleanor.
   Happy holidays. c1933. Dutton, $2.00.
   †Welcome Christmas. c1932. Dutton, $2.00.
Grahame, Kenneth.
   †Kenneth Grahame book. 1932. London. Methuen, $2.50.
   This includes : Golden age ; Dream days ; Wind in the willows.
Gregory, Lady Augusta.
   Cuchulain of Muirthemne. 1919. c1902. London. Murray,
     6s.
Grimm, Jakob L. C., and Wilhelm C.
   Fairy tales ; ed. by F. J. Olcott. 1927. c1922. Penn, $2.50.
   Tales from Grimm ; freely translated and illustrated by Wanda
     Gag. c1936. Coward-McCann, $1.50.

Guerber, Helene A.
†Legends of Switzerland. c1899. Dodd, $1.50.
Guie, H. D., *illus.*
See Garett, Mrs. Fred.
Gunterman, Bertha L.
Castles in Spain, and other enchantments. 1928. Longmans, $2.00.
Hale, Edward E.
See Raspé, Rudolf E.
Hall, Alice. (Mrs. H. F. Hall.)
Godmother's stories; new legends to old rhymes. 1912. London. Nutt, 6s.
Hamilton, Aymer J.
See Harper, Wilhelmina.
Hanna, Paul R.
See Barry, Mary E.
Harper, Wilhelmina, *comp.*
Fillmore folk tales. 1922. Harcourt, $1.50.
Selections from Mighty Mikko and Laughing prince.
Magic fairy tales; selected from Andrew Lang's Blue fairy book. 1926. Library ed. Huntting, $1.35; Longman's, $1.50.
Merry Christmas to you. c1935. Dutton, $2.00.
More story-hour favorites. c1929. Century, $2.00.
Selfish giant, and other stories. c1935. McKay, $2.00.
Harper, Wilhelmina and Hamilton, Aymer J., *comp.*
Winding roads. c1928. Macm., $1.25. (Treasure trails for grade 4.)
Harriman, Susan S.
Stories for little children. c1920. Houghton. (v. 1 of Kindergarten children's hour, ed. by Lucy Wheelock.)
Harrison, Elizabeth.
†Christmastide. c1902, 1907. Chicago Kindergarten College.
Harshaw, Ruth.
Council of the gods. c1931. Rockwell, $2.00.
Hart, John.
Picture tales from Holland. c1935. Stokes, $1.25.
Hartshorne, Hugh.
†Manual for training in worship. 1926. c1915. Scribner, $1.50.
Hauff, Wilhelm.
Arabian days' entertainment; tr. from the German by Herbert Pelham Curtis. c1858. Phillips, Sampson; 1900. Houghton, $1.50.
Hawthorne, Nathaniel.
†Grandfather's chair; or, True stories from New England history. c1850–1896. Houghton, $.80. (Riverside literature series.)
Hazeltine, Alice I.
See Smith, Elva S.
Henderson, Bernard and Calvert, Charles.
Wonder tales of Alsace-Lorraine. 1925. Stokes, $2.50; London, P. Allan, 6s.
Wonder tales of old Japan. 1924. Stokes, $2.50; London. P. Allan, 6s.
Wonder tales of old Tyrol. n.d. Stokes, $2.50.
Henderson, Bernard, and Jones, Stephen.
Wonder tales of ancient Wales. 1924. Small, $3.00.
Henderson, William.
†Notes on folklore of the Northern counties of England and the Border. 1879. London. Satchell.

Hervey, Walter L., and Hix, Melvin.
Fanciful tales for children. 1927. c1924. Longmans, $1.00.
    Pub. in 1924 under the title "Horace Mann new second reader."
Hill, Helen and Maxwell, Violet.
Napoleon's story book. 1930. Macm., $2.00.
Hillyer, William H.
†Box of daylight. c1931. Knopf, $2.50.
Hix, Melvin.
See Hervey, W. L.
Hogner, Dorothy C.
Navajo winter nights. c1935. Nelson, $1.50.
Hooker, Forrestine C.
†Garden of the lost key. c1929. Doubleday, $2.00.
Housman, Laurence.
Doorway in fairyland. n.d. Harcourt; London. Cape, 5s.
    Selections from his Farm in fairyland; House of joy; Field of
    clover; Blue moon.
Moonshine and clover. n.d. Harcourt; London. Cape, 5s.
Turn again tales. 1930. London. Blackwell, 7s. 6d.
What-o'clock tales. n.d. Stokes; London. Blackwell, 6s.
Howes, Edith.
Long bright land. 1929. Little, $2.50.
Hull, Eleanor.
Cuchulain, the hound of Ulster. n.d. Crowell, $2.00.
Hutchinson, Isobel, *tr.*
See Rasmussen, Knud.
Hutchinson, Veronica, S., *ed.*
Candlelight stories. 1928. Minton, $2.50.
Chimney corner fairy tales. 1926. Minton, $2.50.
Chimney corner stories. 1925. Minton, $2.50.
Fireside stories. c1927. Minton, $2.50.
International Kindergarten Union, Literature committee.
See Told under the green umbrella.
Irving, Washington.
Bold dragoon and other ghostly tales; sel. and ed. by Anne C.
    Moore. c1930. Knopf, $2.50.
Tales from the Alhambra; adapted by Joesphine Brower. c1910.
    Houghton, $2.00.
Jagendorf, M.
See Lamkin, N. B.
James, Ahlee.
Tewa firelight tales. c1927. Longmans, $2.50.
James, Bessie R.
Happy animals of Atagahi. c1935. Bobbs, $2.00.
Johns, Mrs. C. H. W., *tr.*
See Maspero, Gaston.
Johnson, Edna and Scott, C. E., *comp.*
†Anthology of children's literature. 1935. Houghton, $3.50.
Johnson, Gaylord.
†Sky movies. 1923. Macm., $1.50.
Johnson, John N.
See Krohn, Gretchen.
Johnson, Richard.
See Darton, F. J. H.
Jones, Stephen.
See Henderson, Bernard.
Jones, V. S. Vernon.
See Æsop.

Kaphan, Mortimer.
†Tell us a Dickens story. c1930. Coward-McCann, $1.50.
Katibah, H. I.
Other Arabian nights. 1928. Scribner, $2.50.
Keck, C. M.
See Elson, William H.
Keigwin, R. P., *tr.*
See Andersen, Hans.
Keller, Gottfried.
Fat of the cat, and other stories, freely adapted by Louis Untermeyer. c1925. Harcourt, $3.00.
Kelly, Eric P.
Christmas nightingale. 1932. Macm., $1.00.
Kennedy, Howard A.
†Red man's wonder book. c1931. Dutton, $2.50.
Kindergarten children's hour.
See Wheelock, Lucy, ed.
King, Marian.
Golden cat head and other tales of Holland. c1933. Whitman, A., $1.50.
Kinney, Muriel.
†Stars and their stories. 1926. Appleton, $1.25; London. Blackwell, 2s. 6d.
Kinscella, Hazel G.
†Music appreciation readers. 6 v. 1927–1929. Univ. Pub. Co. Title of the 1930 ed. is Music readers.
Kipling, Rudyard.
†Rewards and fairies. c1910. Scribner; 1911, Doubleday, $1.90.
Knight, Marietta.
†Dramatic reader for grammar grades. c1910. Amer. Book, $.68.
Kolehmainen, Ali.
See Bowman, J. C.
Kovalsky, Olga and Putnam, Brenda.
Long-legs, Big-mouth, Burning-eyes. 1926. Bradley, $2.00.
Krohn, Gretchen and Johnson, John N.
Scales of the silver fish. c1928. Bobbs, $2.00.
La Fontaine, Jean de.
Fables; rendered into English prose by Frederick C. Tilney. n.d. London. Dent; N. Y. Dutton, $1.00. (Tales for children from many lands.)
LaMonte, Francesco, *tr.*
See Wolff, C. F.
La Rue, Mabel G.
Under the story tree; illus. by M. and M. Petersham. 1930. c1923. Macm., $.76.
Lagerlöf, Selma O. V.
†Further adventures of Nils; tr. from the Swedish by V. S. Howard. 1922. c1911. Doubleday, $2.50.
†Wonderful adventures of Nils; tr. from the Swedish by V. S. Howard. c1907. Doubleday, $2.50.
Lamb, Charles and Mary.
Tales from Shakespeare; illus. by M. and M. Petersham. c1923. Macm., $1.75. (Children's classics.)
Lamkin, Nina B., and Jagendorf, M.
†Around America with the Indians. 1935. c1933. French, $1.50.
Lamprey, Louise.
†Wonder tales of architecture. 1927. Stokes, $2.50.

Lane, Bertha P.
Tower legends. 1933. Beacon Press, $2.00.
Lang, Andrew.
Old friends among the fairies; chosen from the fairy books edited by Andrew Lang. 1928. Longmans, $1.50.
†Red book of animal stories. 1921. c1899. Longmans, $1.75.
†Red true story book. 1928. Longmans, $1.75.
See also Harper, Wilhelmina.
Lang, Jean. (Mrs. John Lang.)
Book of myths. n.d. Nelson, $1.50.
Lanier, Henry W.
†Book of giants. c1922. Dutton, $2.00. (Library of romance.)
Lansing, Marion F.
†Great moments in freedom. c1930. Doubleday, $2.50.
†Great moments in science. 1928. c1926. Doubleday, $2.50.
Large, Laura A.
†Famous children of storybook land. c1925. Wilde, $1.50.
Lawrence, R. M.
†Magic of the horseshoe. c1898. Houghton, $2.25.
Lebermann, Norbert.
New German fairy tales, tr. by Frieda Bachmann. c1930. Knopf, $2.00.
Originally pub. in Nuremberg as "Blaue Blumen."
Lederer, Charlotte.
See McNeer, May.
Ledwidge, Francis.
†Poems. 1919. Brentano's, $2.50.
Lee, Frank H., *ed.*
Folk tales of all nations. 1932. c1930. Coward-McCann, $3.00.
Lefèvre, Félicite.
Cock, the mouse and the little red hen. 1917. Macrae-Smith, $1.00; Platt, $.60.
L'Estrange, Roger, *tr.*
See Æsop.
LeValley, E. F., *ed.*
See Bernhard, J. B.
Linderman, Frank B.
Kootenai why stories. 1926. Scribner, $2.00.
Lindsay, Maud.
Choosing book. 1928. Lothrop, $1.50.
Literature Comm. of the International Kindergarten Union.
See Told under the green umbrella.
Lobagola.
Folk tales of a savage. 1930. Knopf, $2.00.
Logie, A. E.
See Macmillan, Cyrus, *pseud.*
Long, George.
†Folklore calendar. 1930. London. P. Allan, 12s. 6d.
Longfellow, Henry W.
†Poetical works. Houghton. (Household ed.)
Macdonald, George.
At the back of the north wind; illus. by Jesse Wilcox Smith. 1919. McKay, $2.50.
McDonald, Lucile S.
†Dick and the spice cupboard. c1936. Crowell, $1.75.
Mackay, Charles.
†Poems.
Mackaye, Percy.
Tall tales of the Kentucky mountains. c1926. Doran, $2.50.

Mackenzie, Colin F., *tr.*
Jackal in Persia. c1928. Doubleday, $2.00.
　Adapted and abridged from the Persian classic "Anwar-i-Suhaili."
Mackenzie, Compton.
Book of nursery tales; illus. by H. M. Brock, with introd. by Compton Mackenzie. 1934. Warne, $2.50.
Macleod, Fiona, *pseud.* **(William Sharp.)**
Poems and dramas. 1910. Duffield, $2.00.
MacManus, Seumas.
Donegal wonder book. c1926. Stokes, $2.00.
Lo, and behold ye! c1900–1919. Stokes, $2.00.
Macmillan, Cyrus, *pseud.* **(A. E. Logie.)**
Canadian wonder tales. 1918. London. Lane; N. Y., Dodd, $2.00 and $5.00.
McNeer, May and Lederer, Charlotte.
Tales from the crescent moon. c1930. Farrar, $2.50.
McVenn, Gertrude E.
†Good manners and right conduct. Book 2. c1918–1919. Heath. $.88.
Major, William M., *ed.*
Merry Christmas stories. 1929. c1926. Whitman, A., $.75.
Mamin, Dmitri Naskisovitch. (Mamin-Siberiak, *pseud.***)**
Verotchka's tales; tr. by Ray Davidson, illus. by Boris M. Artzybasheff. c1922. Dutton, $2.00.
Manner, Jane, *comp.*
†Silver treasury. 1935. French, $3.00.
Martens, Frederick H.
Wonder tales from far away. c1924. McBride, $2.50.
Martin, Dahris B.
Fatma was a goose; Tunis tales. 1929. Doubleday, $2.00.
Martin, John, *ed.*
See Raspé, R. E.
Martinez Del Rio, Amelia.
Sun, the moon and a rabbit. c1935. Sheed & Ward, $3.00.
Marzials, Ada M.
Stories for the story hour from January to December. 1916. Dodd, $1.25.
Mason, Arthur.
Wee men of Ballywooden. 1930. Doran, $2.50.
Maspero, Gaston.
**Popular stories of ancient Egypt; tr. from the 4th French ed. by Mrs. C. H. W. Johns. 1915. Putnam, $3.50.
Masson, Elsie.
Folk tales of Brittany; ed. by Amena Pendleton. c1929. Macrae-Smith, $3.00.
Matthews, Washington.
See Whitman, William.
Maud, Aylmer, *tr.*
See Tolstoy, Leo N.
Maxwell, Violet.
See Hill, Helen.
Mazet, H. S.
See Falkberget, Johan.
Meeker, Charles H.
Folk tales from the Far East. c1927. Winston, $1.10.
Menefee, Maud.
Child stories from the masters. c1899–1901. Rand, $.75.

Metzger, Berta.
Picture tales from the Chinese. c1934. Stokes, $1.25.
Tales told in Hawaii. c1929. Stokes. $1.25.
Tales told in Korea. 1932. Stokes, $1.75.
Miller, K. B.
See Borski, L. M.
Miller, Olive Beaupré, *ed.*
†My book of history. v. 1–4. c1929–1933. Bookhouse for children.
   Pub. as a subscription book. Special price to libraries for first 4 v., $23.60.
†My travelship. 3 v. c1926. Bookhouse for children, $17.25.
   v. 2. Little pictures of Japan; v. 3, Tales told in Holland.
Mitchell, Harley W., *tr.*
See Baumbach, Rudolf.
Mitchell, Lucy S.
†Here and now story book. c1921. Dutton, $2.00.
Mitchell, Minnie B.
Gray moon tales. c1926. Bobbs, $2.00.
Mitford, A. B.
Tales of old Japan. 1890. Macm., $1.25.
Moore, Anne C., *ed.*
See Irving, Washington.
Moreton, Lady, *tr.*
See Coloma, Louis de.
Morley, Christopher.
I know a secret. c1927. Doubleday, $2.00.
Morris, Cora.
Gypsy story teller. c1931. Macm., $2.00.
†Stories from mythology, North American. c1924. Marshall Jones, $2.00.
Morris, Kenneth.
Book of the three dragons. c1930. Longmans, $3.50.
Mourning Dove.
See Garett, Mrs. Fred.
Mukerji, Dhan Gopal.
Hindu fables for little children. 1929. Dutton, $1.75.
†Rama, the hero of India. c1930. Dutton, $2.00.
My book of history.
See Miller, O. B.
My travelship.
See Miller, O. B.
Nakazawa, Ken.
Weaver of the frost. 1927. Harper, $2.50.
Nash, M. C.
†Children's occupations. (v. 2 of Kindergarten children's hour. ed. by Lucy Wheelock.)
National Association of Junior Chautauqua Directors.
Fun folk and fairy tales; with introd. by Edmund Vance Cooke. c1923. Revell, $1.25. (Junior Chautauqua series.)
Through story-land with the children; with introd. by Georgene Faulkner. c1924. Revell, $1.25. (Junior Chautauqua series.)
Nemcova, Bozema.
Disobedient kids and other Czecho-Slovak fairy tales. Interpreted by W. H. Tolman and V. Smetanka, selected by V. Tille. illus. by A. Scheiner. 1921. Prague. B. Koci; Writer's Pub. Co., $1.25; London. P. Allan, 6s.

Newman, Isidora.
Fairy flowers; illus. by Willy Pogány. c1926. London. Oxford Univ. Press; N. Y., Holt, $5.00.

Niemeyer, Nannie.
Stories for the history hour, from Augustus to Rolf. 1917. Dodd, $1.25.

Noel, Sybille.
Magic bird of Chomo-lung-ma. c1931. Doubleday, $3.50. (Junior books.)

Noyes, Alfred.
†Poems. 1901. Macm.

Number two Joy street; a medley of prose and verse for boys and girls, by G. K. Chesterton and others. 1924. Appleton, $2.50; London. Blackwell, 6s.

Nusbaum, Aileen.
Seven cities of Cibola. Illus. by Margaret N. Finnan. 1926. Putnam, $2.00.
Zuni Indian tales. 1928. Putnam, $2.00.

Oberholtzer, B. C., tr.
See Orvieto, Laura.

O'Brien, Florence R. W. M.
See Wilson, Romer, pseud.

Olcott, Frances J.
Wonder tales from Baltic wizards. c1928. Longmans, $2.00.
Wonder tales from China seas. c1925. Longmans, $1.75.
Wonder tales from fairy isles. 1929. Longmans, $1.75.
Wonder tales from goblin hills. c1930. Longmans, $1.75.
Wonder tales from pirate isles. 1927. Longmans, $2.00.
Wonder tales from windmill lands. 1926. Longmans, $2.00.
See also Arabian nights' entertainment; Grimm, J. L. C.; Topelius, Zacharias.

Orvieto, Laura.
†Birth of Rome; tr. by B. C. Oberholtzer. 1935. Lippincott, $2.00. (Junior Literary Guild book.)

Otero, Nina.
†Old Spain in our Southwest. c1936. Harcourt, $2.00.

Packard, Alice.
†Talks to children. (v. 3 of Kindergarten children's hour, ed. by Lucy Wheelock.)

Parker, Arthur C.
Skunny Wundy and other Indian tales. c1926. Doran, $3.00.

Partridge, Emelyn N.
Joyful Star. 1915. Sturgis & Walton; N. Y., Macm., $1.25.

Patten, William, ed.
†Junior classics. 10 v. c1912. Collier.

Patterson, A. deC., tr.
See Wahlenberg, Anna.

Peck, Harry Thurston.
†Adventures of Mabel. 1916. Dodd, $1.50.

Pendleton, Amena, ed.
See Masson, Elsie.

Perkins, Jeanette E. and Danielson, F. W.
†Mayflower program book. c1920. Pilgrim Press, $2.00.
†Second year Mayflower program book. c1922. Pilgrim Press, $2.00.

Perkins, Lucy F.
†Dutch twins. 1911. Houghton, $1.75.
†Eskimo twins. 1914. Houghton, $1.75.
†Japanese twins. 1912. Houghton, $1.75.

Peter, E. M.
See Silvester, N. G.
Phillips, Grace D.
Far peoples. c1929. Univ. Chicago Press, $1.50.
Phillips, Walter S. (El Comancho.)
Indian tales for little folks. c1923. 1935. Platt & Munk, $1.00.
Piper, Watty, *ed.*
Folk tales children love. 1934. c1932. Platt & Munk, 1.25.
Gateway to storyland. 23d ed. c1925. Platt & Munk, $1.50.
Road in storyland. illus. by L. W. and H. C. Holling. c1932. Platt & Munk, $1.50.
Planché, J. R.
See Aulnoy, M. C. J. deB.
Pogány, Nandor.
Hungarian fairy book. illus. by Willy Pogány. n.d. Stokes, $2.50.
Magyar fairy tales from old Hungarian legends; illus. by Willy Pogány. 1930. Dutton, $2.00.
Potter, Beatrix.
Fairy caravan. c1929. McKay, $2.00.
Tailor of Gloucester. c1903. Warne, $.75.
Tale of Peter Rabbit. Warne, $.75.
Potter, Miriam C.
Captain Sandman; his book of tales and rhymes for children. c1926. Dutton, $2.00.
Giant of Apple Pie Hill, and other stories. c1923. Dutton, $2.00.
Power, Effie, *comp.*
Bag o' tales; a source book for story tellers. c1934. Dutton, $5.00.
Blue caravan tales. c1935. Dutton, $1.50.
Stories to shorten the road. c1936. Dutton, $1.50.
Power, Lenore St. John.
Children's treasure chest. c1926. Sears.
Power, Rhoda D.
How it happened; myths and folk tales retold. 1931. Houghton, $2.00.
Price, Margaret E.
Legends of the seven seas. c1929. Harper, $2.50.
Purnell, Idella.
Merry frogs. c1936. Sutton House, $1.50.
(Julia Ellsworth Ford foundation for children's literature.)
Purnell, Idella and Weatherwax, J. M.
Talking bird. 1930. Macm., $1.75.
Why the bee is busy, and other Rumanian fairy tales. 1930. Macm., $1.75.
Putnam, Brenda.
See Kovalsky, Olga.
Pyle, Katherine, *ed.* and *illus.*
Fairy tales from India; retold from "Old Deccan days." 1926. Lippincott, $3.50.
Tales from Greek mythology. 1928. Lippincott, $2.50.
Tales from Norse mythology. c1930. Lippincott, $2.50.
Pyrnelle, L. C.
†Diddie. Dumps and Tot. 1930. c1882, 1910. Harper, $2.50.
Quayle, Thomas.
See De La Mare, Walter.
Quiller-Couch, Arthur T.
Twelve dancing princesses and other fairy tales retold. 1930. Doubleday, $2.50.

Quiller-Couch, Arthur T.—*continued.*
Previously pub. as "In powder and crinoline."
Quinn, Elizabeth V., *ed.*
Stokes' wonder book of fairy tales. c1917. Stokes, $2.00.
Stories for the six-year-old. c1917, 1924. Stokes, $1.25.
Rackham, Arthur, *comp.* and *illus.*
Arthur Rackham fairy book. n.d. Lippincott, $2.50.
Ralston, W. R. S.
**Russian fairy tales. n.d. Hurst; c 1873. Smith & Elder.
Ransome, Arthur.
Old Peter's Russian tales. c1916. Nelson ; also Stokes, $1.25.
Rasmussen, Inger M.
East o' the sun and west o' the moon, with other Norwegian folk
tales. 1933. c1924. Whitman, A., $1.25.
Rasmussen, Knud.
†Eagle's gift ; Alaska Eskimo tales, tr. by Isobel Hutchinson, illus.
by Ernst Hansen. c1932. Doubleday, $2.50.
Raspé, Rudolf Erich.
Children's Munchausen, retold by John Martin. c1921. Hough-
ton, $2.25.
Tales from the travels of Baron Munchausen ; E. E. Hale, ed.
c1901. Heath, $.60. (Heath supplementary readers.)
Reid, Mrs. Alberta (Bancroft).
See Bancroft, Alberta.
Retner, Beth A.
That's that. 1925. Doubleday, $1.50.
Rhodes, Mrs. E. E.
See Eckford, Eugenia.
Rhys, Ernest.
English fairy book. [1912–1917] Stokes, $2.50.
Rich, Edwin G.
Why-so stories. 1928. c1918. Little, $1.75.
† Read-aloud book. c1934. Lippincott, $2.50.
Richards, Laura E.
†More five minute stories. 1920. c1903. Page, $1.75.
Richardson, Abby S.
Stories from old English poetry. 1899. c1871. Houghton,
$1.50.
Rounds, Glen.
Ol' Paul, the mighty logger ; being a true account . . . of the
great Paul Bunyan. 1936. Holiday House. Rudges, printer.
Rowe, Dorothy.
Moon's birthday. 1927. Macm., $2.00.
Runkel, L. E.
See Elson, W. H.
Ryder, Arthur W.
**Twenty-two goblins. Tr. from the Sanskrit. 1917. London.
Dent ; N. Y. Dutton, $3.00.
Saint Nicholas Magazine. N. Y. Century Co.
Sale, John B.
†**Tree named John. c1929. Univ. of North Carolina Press,
$2.00.
Sandburg, Carl.
Rootabaga country. c1922–1929. Harcourt, $2.50.
Rootabaga pigeons. c1923. Harcourt, $2.00.
Rootabaga stories. c1922. Harcourt, $2.00.
Sawyer, Ruth.
Picture tales from Spain. c1936. Stokes, $1.35.

Saxo Grammaticus.
See Adams, J. D.
Schwarz, Leo W., *ed.*
† **Jewish caravan; great stories of twenty-five centuries. 1935.
Farrar & Rinehart, $3.75.
Schwimmer, Rosika.
Tisza tales; illus. by Willy Pogány. c1928. Doubleday, $5.00.
Scott, C. E.
See Johnson, Edna.
Sechrist, Elizabeth H.
†Little book of Hallowe'en. c1934. Lippincott, $1.00.
Segur, Sophie, Comtesse de.
†Memoirs of a donkey.
There are various editions of this.
Seredy, Kate.
†Good master. c1935. Viking Press, $2.00. (Junior Literary
Guild book.)
Sexton, Bernard.
†Gray wolf stories: Indian mystery tales of coyote, animals and
men. 1923. c1921. Macm., $1.50.
Shannon, Monica.
California fairy tales. 1926. Doubleday, $2.50.
Eyes for the dark. 1928. Doubleday-Doran, $2.50.
Sharman, Lyon.
†Bamboo; tales of the Orient-born. c1914. Paul Elder, $1.00.
Sharp, William.
See Fiona Macleod, *pseud.*
Sheahan, Henry B.
See Beston, H. B., *pseud.*
Sheriff, Abigail O.
†Stories old and new. c1922. Ginn, $.60.
A primary supplementary reader.
Shimer, Edgar D.
Fairyland; new fairy stories of all nations for little girls and boys.
Illus. by Lucy Fitch Perkins. c1924. Noble, $.90.
Shuttleworth, F. K.
See Starbuck, E. D.
Siewers, Carl, *tr.*
See Andersen, Hans.
Silvester, M. G., and Peter, E. M.
†Happy hour stories. c1921. Amer. Book Co., $.60.
Skeat, Walter.
Tiger's mistake: tales of Malay magic, with introd. by Margery
Quigley. 1929. Macm., $1.00.
Skinner, Ada M., *ed.*
†Christmas stories and plays. c1915–1925. Rand, $1.00.
Skinner, Ada M. and Eleanor L., *ed.*
Child's book of country stories. 1935. Dial Press; 1925, Duf-
field, $2.50.
Happy tales for story time. c1918. Amer. Book Co., $.64.
Skipper, Mervyn.
Jungle meeting-pool. 1929. Stokes, $1.50.
Smetanka, V., *tr.*
See Nemcova, Bozema.
Smith, David E.
†Number stories of long ago. c1919. Ginn, $.60.
Smith, Elva S. and Hazeltine, Alice I., *comp.*
†Christmas in legend and story. c1915. Lothrop, $2.00.

Smith, Nora A.
See Wiggin, Kate D.
Smith, Susan.
†Made in France. c1931. Knopf, $2.00.
†Made in Germany and Austria. c1933. Minton, $1.50.
†Made in Mexico. c1930. Knopf, $2.00.
†Made in Sweden. c1934. Minton, $2.00.
Snell, Roy J.
Told beneath the northern lights. c1925. Little, $2.00.
Snorra, Sturluson.
See Dunlap, Maurice.
Spaulding, F. E. and Bryce, C. T.
†Aldine readers. rev. ed. Book 2. c1907, 1918. Newson, $.76.
Spence, Lewis.
† **Myths of the North American Indians. [1914–1922] London. Harrap. $5.00.
Spurr, Harry A., *tr.* and *ed.*
Dumas fairy tale book. 1924. London. Warne, $2.50.
Starbuck, Edwin D., and Shuttleworth, F. K., and others,
  ed.
Enchanted paths. 1930. Macm., $2.50. (Wonder road, v. 2.)
Familiar haunts. 1930. Macm., $2.50. (Wonder road, v. 1.)
Far horizons. 1930. Macm., $2.50. (Wonder road, v. 3.)
Steedman, Amy.
†Knights of art; stories of the Italian painters. n.d. London.
  Jack; 1907. Macrae-Smith, $2.50.
Steel, Flora A.
English fairy tales; illus. by A. Rackham. 1930. c1918. Macm.,
  $1.75 and $3.50.
Stephens, James.
Irish fairy tales. 1923. c1920. Macm., $2.50.
Stewart, Mary.
Tell me a story I never heard before. c1919. Revell, $1.75.
Stickney, J. H., *ed.*
See Andersen, H. C.
Stockard, Marietta.
See Gordon, E. K.
Stockton, Frank.
Reformed pirate; with foreword by M. G. Davis. 1936. Scrib-
  ner.
    Stories from Floating prince, Ting-a-ling tales, Queen's mu-
    seum.
Sugimoto, Chiyono.
Japanese holiday picture tales. c1933. Stokes, $1.50.
Picture tales from the Japanese. 1933. c1928. Stokes, $1.50.
Tappan, Eva M.
†Old world hero stories. c1909–1911. Houghton, $1.16.
Tappan, Eva M., *tr.*
Little lady in green, and other tales. 1925. Houghton, $1.75.
    From R. Bergstrom's "Ur Folksagens Rosengarden."
Prince from nowhere, and other tales. 1928. Houghton.
    From the Swedish of Richard Bergstrom.
Teall, Edna A.
†Batter and spoon fairies. 1929. Harper, $2.00.
Terry, A. G.
Tales from far and near. c1915. Row. (History stories of
  other lands. Book 1.)
Thomsen, Frede.
See Wahlenberg, Anna.

504 FAIRY TALES—SUPPLEMENT

Through story-land with the children.
See National Association of Junior Chautauqua Directors.
Tille, V., *ed.*
See Nemcova, Bozema.
Tilney, F. C., *tr.*
See La Fontaine, Jean de.
†**Told under the blue umbrella:** new stories for new children, selected by the Literature committee of the Association for childhood education. Illus. by Marguerite Davis. c1933. Macm., $2.00.
†**Told under the green umbrella:** old stories for new children, selected by the Literature committee of the International Kindergarten Union. Illus. by Grace Gilkison. 1934. c1930. Macm., $2.00.
Tolman, W. H., *tr.*
See Nemcova, Bozema.
Tolstoy, Leo N.
†Ivan the fool, and other tales; tr. by Mr. and Mrs. Aylmer Maude. 1932. Oxford University Press, $2.50.
Topelius, Zacharias.
Canute Whistlewinks and other stories; tr. from the Swedish by C. W. Foss; sel. and ed. by F. J. Olcott. 1927. Longmans, $2.50.
Treasure trails.
See Harper, W. and Hamilton, A. J.
Tubby, Ruth P., *tr.*
See Chardon, Jeanne.
Tuttle, Veryl B.
Frightened tree and other stories. c1925. Frank-Maurice, $2.50.
Untermeyer, Louis.
Donkey of God. c1932. Harcourt, $2.50.
Last pirate; tales from the Gilbert and Sullivan operas. c1934. Harcourt, $2.50.
See also Keller, Gottfried.
Van Buren, Maud and Bemis, Katherine I., *eds.*
†Christmas in storyland. c1927. Century, $2.00.
Van Dyke, Henry.
†Blue flower. 1902. Scribner, $2.00.
Vilnay, Zev.
† **Legends of Palestine. c1932. Jewish Publication Society of America, $2.50.
Voltaire, Francois
† **Zadig, or Destiny: an oriental history; tr. from the French, with introd. by A. B. Walkley. London. Chapman & Dodd. (Abbey classics.)
Wadsworth, Wallace.
†Paul Bunyan and his great blue ox. c1926. Doran, $2.00.
Wahlenberg, Anna.
Old Swedish fairy tales; tr. from the Danish of Frede Thomsen by A. DeC. Patterson. 1929. c1925. Penn, $3.00.
Walker, Abbie P.
†Sandman's Christmas stories. c1918. Harper, $.60.
Walters, M. O., *ed.*
Book of Christmas stories for children. 1930. Dodd, $2.50.
Warner, Susan and Anna B.
†Carl Krinken. c1853. Putnam. (Ellen Montgomery's book shelf.)
Weatherwax, J. M.
See Purnell, Idella.

Weilerstein, Sadie R.
Adventures of K'tonton, a little Jewish Tom Thumb.   c1935.
Woman's League Press, $1.65.
Welhaven, Tekla, *tr.*
See Falkberget, Johan.
Wells, Margaret E.
†How the present came from the past.   2 v.   1925.   c1917.
Macm., $.80 each.
Werner, Edgar S., *comp.*
†Werner's readings and recitations; ed. by Stanley Schell.   No.
51.   n.d.   E. S. Werner Co., Belmar, N. J., $.75.
Wheeler, Post.
Albanian wonder tales   c1936.   Doubleday, $2.00.   (Junior Lit-
erary Guild book.)
Wheelock, Lucy.
†Talks to mothers.   (v. 4 of Kindergarten children's hour, ed. by
Lucy Wheelock.)   1922.   Houghton, $2.00.
Wheelock, Lucy, *ed.*
†Kindergarten children's hour.   5 v.   c1920.   Houghton, $12.50.
v. 1.   Harriman, S. S.   Stories for little children.
v. 2.   Nash, M. C.   Children's occupations.
v. 3.   Packard, Alice.   Talks to children.
v. 4.   Wheelock, Lucy.   Talks to mothers.
White, Emerson E.
†School management.   1894.   Amer. Book Co., $1.25.
White, William C.
†Made in Russia.   c1932.   Knopf, $2.00.
See also Yershov, Peter.
Whitehorn, A. L.
Wonder tales of old Japan.   c1912.   Stokes; Jack, 3s. 6d.
Whiteman, Edna, *ed.*
Playmates in print.   1926.   Nelson, $2.00.
Whitman, William, 3rd.
Navaho tales.   1925.   Houghton, $1.75.
Retold from trans. of Dr. Washington Matthews.
Wiggin, Kate D. and Smith, Nora A.
Twilight stories.   c1925.   Houghton, $1.75.
Williams, Harcourt.
Tales from Ebony.   c1935.   Putnam, $2.50.
Williams, Herschel.
Jolly old whistle and other tales.   1927.   Nelson, $2.00.
Williams-Ellis, Amabel S.
†Fairies and enchanters.   c1934.   Nelson, $2.00.   (Junior Lit-
erary Guild book.)
Williamson, Julia.
†Stars through magic casements.   c1930.   Appleton, $1.00.
Williston, Teresa P.
Hindu stories.   1925.   c1916.   Rand, $.90.
Wilson, Romer, *ed.*
Green magic.   1928.   Harcourt, $2.50; London.   Cape, 7s. 6d.
Red magic.   c1931.   Harcourt, $2.50.
Wolff, Carl F.
Pale mountains; tr. by Francesca LaMonte.   c1927.   Minton,
$2.50.
Wonder road, 3 v.
See Starbuck and Shuttleworth.
Woodson, Carter G.
African myths.   c1928.   Associated publishers, $1.10.

Worthington, Frank.
Little wise one. 1932. Houghton, $1.50.
Yershov, Peter.
Humpy; tr. by William C. White. 1931. Harper, $2.50.
Young, Ella.
Celtic wonder tales. new ed. 1923. Dublin.   Talbot Press;
London.   Unwin, 3s. 6d; N. Y.   Dutton, $2.50.
Tangle-coated horse and other tales.   c1929.   Longmans, $2.50.
Wonder smith and his son; illus. by Boris Artzybasheff.   1927.
Longmans, $2.25.
Zeitlin, Ida.
Skazki; tales and legends of old Russia, illus. by. Theodore Na-
dejen.   c1926.   Doran, $5.00.

TITLES OF BOOKS ANALYZED

Adventures of Haroun Ed Raschid. Arabian nights (Olcott).
Adventures of K'tonton. Weilerstein.
Adventures of Mabel. Peck.
African myths. Woodson.
Albanian wonder tales. Wheeler.
Aldine readers. Rev. ed. Book 2. Spaulding.
Alice's adventures in Wonderland. Carroll.
American folk and fairy tales. Field.
Angus and the ducks. Flack.
Animal picture tales from Russia. Carrick.
Animals' own story book. Babbitt.
Anthology of children's literature. Johnson and Scott.
Arabian days' entertainment. Hauff.
Arabian nights' entertainment.
Argosy of fables. Cooper.
Around America with the Indians. Lamkin and Jagendorf.
Arthur Rackham fairy book. Rackham.
At the back of the north wind. Macdonald.
Bag o' tales. Power.
Baker's dozen. Davis.
Bamboo. Sharman.
Batter and spoon fairies. Teall.
Big tree of Bunlahy. Colum.
Birth of Rome. Orvieto.
Black folk tales. Berry.
Blue caravan tales. Power.
Blue flower. Van Dyke.
Bold dragoon and other ghostly tales. Irving.
Book of Christmas stories for children. Walters.
Book of dragons. Fuller.
Book of enchantment. Adams and Atchinson.
Book of fairy tales. Brock.
Book of giant stories. Adams and Atchinson.
Book of giants. Lanier.
Book of good counsels. Arnold.
Book of myths. Lang.
Book of nursery tales. Mackenzie.
Book of princess stories. Adams and Atchinson.
Book of the three dragons. Morris.
Box of daylight. Hillyer.
Boy apprenticed to an enchanter. Colum.
Brazilian fairy book. Eells.
Bright islands. Colum.
Broomstick and Snowflake. Falkberget.
Burning bush. Gaer.
California fairy tales. Shannon.
Can you believe me stories. Aspinwall.
Canadian wonder tales. Macmillan.
Candlelight stories. Hutchinson.

Fables. La Fontaine.
Fairies and enchanters. Williams-Ellis.
Fairy caravan. Potter.
Fairy flowers. Newman.
Fairy garland. (Dulac).
Fairy tales. Andersen.
Fairy tales. Aulnoy.
Fairy tales. Grimm.
Fairy tales from Brazil. Eells.
Fairy tales from India. Pyle.
Fairy tales of Eastern Europe. Curtin.
Fairyland. Shimer.
Familiar haunts. Starbuck.
Famous children of storybook land. Large.
Fanciful tales for children. Hervey and Hix.
Far horizons. Starbuck.
Far peoples. Phillips.
Fat of the cat. Keller.
Fate cries out. Dane.
Fatma was a goose. Martin.
Favorite pages from Child Life. Barrows and Cavanah.
Feast of Noel. Crownfield.
Fifty-two story talks. Chidley.
Fillmore folk tales. Harper.
Fireside stories. Hutchinson.
Flower legends. Carey.
Flowers of chivalry. Clément.
Folk lore from foreign lands. Bryce.
Folk tales children love. Piper.
Folk tales from the Far East. Meeker.
Folk tales of a savage. Lobagola.
Folk tales of all nations. Lee.
Folk tales of Brittany. Masson.
Folk tales retold. Arnold.
Folklore and fairy plays. Going.
Folklore calendar. Long.
Folklore of the Northern counties of England. Henderson.
Forge in the forest. Colum.
Forty good-morning tales. Fyleman.
Forty good-night tales. Fyleman.
Fountain of youth. Colum.
Four tales. Andersen (Keigwin).
Frightened tree. Tuttle.
Fun folk and fairy tales. National Assoc. of Jr. Chautauqua, Directors.
Further adventures of Nils. Lagerlöf.
Garden of the lost key. Hooker.
Gateway to storyland. Piper.
Giant of Apple Pie Hill. Potter.
Gipsy and the bear. Borski and Miller.
Goblins of Haubeck. Bancroft.
Godmother's stories. Hall.
Golden age of myth and legend. Bulfinch.
Golden bird. Gibson.
Golden cat head and other tales of Holland. King.
Golden chick and the magic frying pan. Chardon.
Golden-feather. Capuana.
Good citizenship. Forbes.
Good manners and right conduct. Book 2. McVenn.

Good master. Seredy.
Gordon readers, new series: 2d reader. Gordon and Stockard.
Grandfather's chair. Hawthorne.
Gray moon tales. Mitchell.
Gray wolf stories. Sexton.
Great idea. Buckingham.
Great moments in freedom. Lansing.
Great moments in science. Lansing.
Green magic. Wilson.
Gypsy story teller. Morris.
Happy animals of Atagahi. James.
Happy holidays. Graham.
Happy hour stories. Silvester and Peter.
Happy tales for story time. Skinner.
Here and now story book. Mitchell.
Hindu fables. Mukerji.
Hindu stories retold. Williston.
Holiday-time stories. Deihl.
Homespun stories. Denton.
How it happened. Power.
How the present came from the past. Wells.
Humpy. Yershov.
Hungarian fairy book. Pogány.
I know a secret. Morley.
Indian nights. Browne.
Indian tales for little folks. Phillips.
Irish fairy tales. Stephens.
Islands of magic. Eells.
Italian fairy tales. Capuana.
Italian peepshow. Farjeon.
Ivan the fool and other tales. Tolstoi.
Ivory throne of Persia. Coit.
Jackal in Persia. Mackenzie.
Japanese holiday picture tales. Sugimoto.
Japanese twins. Perkins.
Jataka tales. Aspinwall.
Java jungle tales. De Leeuw.
Jewish caravan. Schwarz.
Jewish fairy tales and stories. Friedlander.
Jolly old whistle. Williams.
Journey to Health-land. Andress.
Joyful Star. Partridge.
Jungle meeting pool. Skipper.
Junior classics. Patten.
Junior high school literature. Elson and Keck.
Kai Khosru and other plays for children. Coit.
Keepsakes. Blondell.
Kenneth Grahame book. Grahame.
Kindergarten children's hour. 5 v. Wheelock.
King of Ireland's son. Colum.
Knights of art. Steedman.
Knights of Charlemagne. Echols.
Kootenai why stories. Linderman.
Land of the blue flower. Burnett.
Lanier book. Burt.
Last pirate. Untermeyer.
Legends of Palestine. Vilnay.
Legends of Switzerland. Guerber.
Legends of the seven seas. Price.

GEOGRAPHICAL AND RACIAL LIST

‡ Indicates volume also contains stories from other nationalities.

Africa.
Berry, Erick. Black folk tales. 1928.
Cendrars, Blaise. Little black stories. 1929.
‡Cooper, F. T. Argosy of fables. 1921.
‡Lee, F. H. Folk tales of all nations. 1930.
Lobagola. Folk tales of a savage. 1930.
‡Phillips, G. D. Far peoples. 1929.
Woodson, C. G. African myths. 1928.
Worthington, Frank. Little wise one. 1932.

Alaska.
See Eskimo; Indians of North America.

Albania.
Wheeler, Post. Albanian wonder tales. 1936.

America.
See Canada; Eskimo; Indians of North America; Mexico; Negroes; South America; United States.

Arabia.
See Oriental.

Australia.
‡Cruse, Amy. Young folk's book of myths. 1925.
‡Lee, F. H. Folk tales of all nations. 1930.
‡Wells, M. E. How the present came from the past. 1917.

Austria.
‡Smith, Susan. Made in Germany and Austria. 1933.
See also Tyrol.

Aztec.
‡Purnell, I. and Weatherwax, J. M. Why the bee is busy. 1930.
‡My book of history. v. 4.
See also Mexico.

Basque.
Carpenter, Frances. Tales of a Basque grandmother. 1930.
‡Lee, F. H. Folk tales from all nations. 1930.
See also Spain.

Bohemia.
‡Curtin, Jeremiah. Fairy tales of Eastern Europe. 1931.
‡Lee, F. H. Folk tales of all nations. 1930.

Brittany.
Dorey, Jacques. Three and the moon. 1929.
‡Going, C. B. Folklore and fairy plays. 1927.
‡Lee, F. H. Folk tales of all nations. 1930.
Masson, Elsa. Folk tales of Brittany. 1929.
See also France.

Canada.
Macmillan, Cyrus. Canadian wonder tales. 1918.

China.
Chrisman, A. B. Shen of the sea. 1925.
—— Wind that wouldn't blow. 1927.
‡Cruse, Amy. Young folk's book of myths. 1925.

517

China—*continued.*
‡Cooper, F. T.   Argosy of fables.   1921.
‡Gibson, Katharine.   Golden bird.   1927.
‡ Lee, F. H.   Folk tales of all nations.   1930.
Metzger, Berta.   Picture tales from the Chinese.   1934.
Olcott, F. J.   Wonder tales from China seas.   1926.
‡Phillips, G. D.   Far peoples.   1929.
Rowe, Dorothy.   Moon's birthday.   1927.
Cornwall.
‡Olcott, F. J.   Book of elves and fairies.   1918.
——— Wonder tales from fairy isles.   1927.
Czechoslovakia.
Nemcova.   Disobedient kids.   1921.
See also Bohemia.
Denmark.
Adams, J. D.   Swords of the vikings.   1928.
Andersen, H. C.   Fairy tales.
‡Lee, F. H.   Folk tales of all nations.   1930.
Dutch.
See Holland.
East India.
**Arnold, Edwin.   Book of good counsels.   1896.
Aspinwall, Margaret.   Jataka tales.   1927.
‡Cooper, F. T.   Argosy of fables.   1921.
‡Cruse, Amy.   Young folk's book of myths.   1925.
Faulkner, Georgene.   White elephant.   1929.
‡Lee, F. H.   Folk tales of all nations.   1930.
Mukerji, D. G.   Hindu fables.   1929.
——— Rama.   1930.
‡Phillips, G. D.   Far peoples.   1929.
Pyle, Katharine.   Fairy tales from India.   1926.
**Ryder, A .W.   Twenty-two goblins.   1917.
Williston, T. P.   Hindu stories retold.   1925.
East Indies.
See Island stories.
Egypt.
Baikie, James.   Wonder tales of the ancient world.   1915.
‡Cruse, Amy.   Young folk's book of myths.   1925.
‡Gibson, Katharine.   Golden bird.   1927.
‡Lee, F. H.   Folk tales of all nations.   1930.
**Maspero, Gaston.   Popular stories of ancient Egypt.   1915.
‡My book of history.   v. 1.
England.
Allen, G. C.   Tales from Tennyson.   1900.
Barbour, H. B.   Old English tales retold.   1924.
Carroll, Lewis.   Alice's adventures in Wonderland.
‡Choate, F. and Curtis, E.   Little people of the hills.   1928.
‡Cooper, F. T.   Argosy of fables.   1921.
Dickens, Charles.   Magic fishbone.
Ewing, J. H.   Lob Lie-by-the-fire, and other stories.
Farjeon, Eleanor.   Martin Pippin in the apple orchard.   1922.
Grahame, Kenneth.   Kenneth Grahame book.   1932.
Hall, Alice.   Godmother's stories.   1912.
‡Johnson, E. and Scott, C. E.   Anthology of children's literature.
      1935.
Kipling, Rudyard.   Rewards and fairies.   1910.
‡Lee, F. H.   Folk tales of all nations.   1930.
Long, George.   Folklore calendar.   1930.
‡Olcott, F. J.   Wonder tales from fairy isles.   1929.

England—*continued.*
‡Power, Effie. Blue caravan tales. 1935.
—— Bag o' tales. 1934.
Rhys, Ernest. English fairy book.
Richardson, A. S. Stories from old English poetry. 1899.
Steel, F. A. English fairy tales retold. 1930.
Williams-Ellis, A. S. Fairies and enchanters. 1934.
Eskimo.
Hillyer, W. H. Box of daylight. 1931.
‡Lee, F. H. Folk tales of all nations. 1930.
Rasmussen, Knud. Eagle's gift. 1932.
Snell, R. J. Told beneath the northern lights. 1925.
Esthonia.
‡Olcott, F. J. Wonder tales of Baltic wizards. 1928.
Europe.
Bancroft, Alberta. Goblins of Haubeck. 1933.
Crew, H. C. Saturday's children. 1927.
Dulac, Edmund. Edmund Dulac's fairy book. 1916.
Keller, Gottfried. Fat of the cat, and other stories. 1925.
Tappan, E. M. Old world hero stories. 1909.
Finland.
Bowman, J. C. and Bianco, M. Tales from a Finnish tupa. 1936.
Harper, Wilhelmina. Fillmore folk tales. 1922.
‡Lee, F. H. Folk tales of all nations. 1930.
‡Olcott, F. J. Wonder tales from Baltic wizards. 1928.
Topelius, Zacharias. Canute Whistlewinks. 1927.
France.
Aulnoy, M. C. J. Fairy tales, tr. by Planché. 1923.
—— White cat and other tales, ed. by R. Field. 1928.
Chamoud, Simone. Picture tales from the French. 1932.
Chardon, Jeanne. Golden chick and the magic frying pan. 1935.
Clément, Marguerite. Flowers of chivalry. 1934.
—— Once in France. 1927.
‡Cooper, F. T. Argosy of fables. 1921.
Crownfield, Gertrude. Feast of Noel. 1928.
Dorey, Jacques. Three and the moon. 1929.
Echols, E. W. Knights of Charlemagne. 1928.
Fairy garland (Dulac). 1928.
‡Gibson, Katharine. Golden bird. 1927.
Henderson, B. and Calvert, C. Wonder tales of Alsace-Lorraine.
  1925.
‡Lee, F. H. Folk tales of all nations. 1930.
Smith, Susan. Made in France. 1931.
Spurr, H. A. Dumas fairy tale book. 1924.
See also Basque ; Brittany.
Georgia (Transcaucasia).
Chevalier, J. C. Noah's grandchildren. 1929.
‡Lee, F. H. Folk tales of all nations. 1930.
Germany.
‡Choate, F. and Curtis, E. Little people of the hills. 1928.
‡Cooper, F. T. Argosy of fables. 1921.
Grimm, J. L. C. and W. C. Fairy tales.
Leberman, Norbert. New German fairy tales. 1930.
‡Johnson, E. and Scott, C. E. Anthology of children's literature.
  1935.
‡Lee, F. H. Folk tales of all nations. 1930.
Olcott, F. J. Wonder tales from goblin hills. 1930.
‡Smith, Susan. Made in Germany and Austria. 1933.

Gipsy.
‡Lee, F. H. Folk tales of all nations. 1930.
Morris, Cora. Gypsy story teller. 1931.
Greece.
Æsop. Fables.
‡Bulfinch, Thomas. Golden age.
‡Cooper, F. T. Argosy of fables.
‡Cruse, Amy. Young folk's book of myths. 1925.
Forbush, W. B. Myths and legends of Greece and Rome. 1928.
‡Gibson, Katharine. Golden bird. 1927.
Harshaw, Ruth. Council of the gods. 1931.
‡Johnson, E. and Scott, C. E. Anthology of children's literature. 1935.
‡Power, Effie. Bag o' tales. 1934.
Pyle, Katharine. Tales from Greek mythology. 1928.
‡Tappan, E. M. Old world hero stories. 1911.
Hawaii.
Colum, Padraic. Bright islands. 1925.
‡Howes, Edith. Long, bright land. 1929.
‡Lee, F. H. Folk tales of all nations. 1930.
Metzger, Berta. Tales told in Hawaii. 1929.
Hebrews.
See Jewish.
Holland.
‡Atkins, E. H. Pot of gold. 1930.
De La Mare, W. J. Dutch cheese. 1925.
Hart, John. Picture tales from Holland. 1935.
King, Marian. Golden cat head. 1933.
Miller, O. B. My travelship : Tales told in Holland. 1926.
‡Olcott, F. J. Wonder tales from pirate isles. 1927.
——— Wonder tales from windmill lands. 1926.
Hungary.
‡Curtin, Jeremiah. Fairy tales of Eastern Europe. 1931.
McNeer, M. and Lederer, C. Tales from the crescent moon. 1930.
Pogány, Nandor. Hungarian fairy book. 1927.
——— Magyar fairy tales. 1930.
Schwimmer, Rosika. Tisza tales. 1928.
Seredy, Kate. Good master. 1935.
Iceland.
‡Lee, F. H. Folk tales of all nations. 1930.
India.
See East India.
Indians of North America.
Allen, Philippa. Whispering wind. 1930.
Bailey, C. S. Stories from an Indian cave. 1924.
Browne, G. W. Indian nights. 1927.
‡Cooper, F. T. Argosy of fables. 1921.
‡Cruse, Amy. Young folk's book of myths. 1925.
De Huff, E. W. Taytay's memories. 1924.
——— Taytay's tales. 1922.
‡Field, Rachel. American folk and fairy tales. 1922.
Garett, Mrs. Fred. Coyote stories. 1933.
Gearhart, E. M. Skalatoot stories. 1922.
Hillyer, W. H. Box of daylight. 1931.
Hogner, Dorothy. Navajo winter nights. 1935.
James, Ahlee. Tewa firelight tales. 1927.
James, B. R. Happy animals of Atagahi. 1935.

Indians of North America—*continued.*
‡Johnson, E. and Scott, C. E. Anthology of children's literature. 1935.
Kennedy, H. A. Red man's wonder book. 1931.
Lamkin, N. B. and Jagendorf, M. Around America with the Indians. 1933.
‡Lee, F. H. Folk tales of all nations. 1930.
Linderman, F. B. Kootenai why stories. 1926.
Macmillan, Cyrus. Canadian wonder tales. 1918.
Morris, Cora. Stories from mythology, North American. 1924.
Nusbaum, Aileen. Zuni Indian tales. 1928.
Parker, A. C. Skunny Wundy and other tales. 1926.
Partridge, E. N. Joyful Star. 1915.
Phillips, W. S. Indian tales for little folks. 1935.
**Spence, Lewis. Myths of the North American Indians. 1922.
Whitman, William. Navaho tales. 1925.

Ireland.
Casserley, Anne. Michael of Ireland.
—— Whins on Knockattan. 1928.
Colum, Padraic. Big tree of Bunlahy. 1933.
—— King of Ireland's son. 1929.
Dunbar, Aldis. Sons o' Cormac. 1929.
Gregory, Lady Augusta. Cuchulain of Muirthemne. 1919.
Hull, Eleanor. Cuchulain, the hound of Ulster.
‡Johnson, E. and Scott, C. E. Anthology of children's literature. 1935.
‡Lee, F. H. Folk tales of all nations. 1930.
MacManus, Seaumas. Donegal wonder book. 1926.
—— Lo, and behold ye! 1919.
Mason, Arthur. Wee men of Ballywooden. 1930.
‡Olcott, F. J. Wonder tales from fairy isles. 1929.
Stephens, James. Irish fairy tales. 1923.
Young, Ella. Celtic wonder tales. 1923.
—— Tangle-coated horse. 1929.
—— Wonder smith and his son. 1927.

Island stories.
Colum, Padraic. Bright islands. 1925. (Polynesia.)
Dane, G. E. and B. J. Once there was and was not. 1931. (Majorca.)
De Leeuw, Hendrik. Java jungle tales. 1933. (East Indies.)
Eells, E. S. Islands of magic. 1922. (Azores.)
Hill, H. and Maxwell, V. Napoleon's story book. 1930. (Corsica.)
Howes, Edith. Long, bright land. 1929. (Polynesia.)
‡Lee, F. H. Folk tales of all nations. 1930.
Meeker, C. H. Folk tales from the Far East. 1927. (East Indies.)
Olcott, F. J. Wonder tales from pirate isles. 1927. (East Indies.)
Skipper, Marvyn. Jungle meeting-pool. 1929. (East Indies.)

Italy.
Botsford, F. H. Picture tales from the Italian. 1929.
Capuana, Luigi. Golden-feather. 1930.
—— Italian fairy tales. 1929.
Davis, M. B. Truce of the wolf. 1931.
Farjeon, Eleanor. Italian peepshow. 1927.
‡Lee, F. H. Folk tales of all nations. 1930.
Untermeyer, Louis. Donkey of God. 1932.

Japan.
‡Cruse, Amy. Young folk's book of myths. 1925.
Faulkner, Georgene. Little Peachling. 1928.
Henderson, B. and Calvert, C. Wonder tales of old Japan. 1924.
‡Lee, F. H. Folk tales of all nations. 1930.
Miller, O. B. My travelship : Little pictures of Japan. 1926.
Mitford, A. B. Tales of old Japan. 1890.
Nakazawa, Ken. Weaver of the frost. 1927.
‡Phillips, G. D. Far peoples. 1929.
Sugimoto, Chiyono. Japanese holiday picture tales. 1933.
—— Picture tales from the Japanese. 1928.
Whitehorn, A. L. Wonder tales of old Japan. 1912.
Jewish.
Friedlander, Gerald. Jewish fairy tales (Dutton ed.). 1920.
Gaer, Joseph. Burning bush. 1929.
—— Magic flight. 1926.
**Gaster, Moses. Ma'aseh book. 1934.
Schwarz, L. W. Jewish caravan. 1935.
**Vilnay, Zev. Legends of Palestine. 1932.
Weilerstein, S. R. Adventures of K'tonton. 1935.
Jugoslavia.
Harper, Wilhelmina. Fillmore folk tales.
Korea.
‡Lee, F. H. Folk tales of all nations. 1930.
Metzger, Berta. Tales told in Korea. 1932.
‡Phillips, G. D. Far peoples. 1929.
Lapland.
‡Olcott, F. J. Wonder tales from Baltic wizards. 1928.
‡Topelius, Zacharias. Canute Whistlewinks. 1927.
Latvia.
‡Olcott, F. J. Wonder tales from Baltic wizards. 1928.
Lithuania.
‡Olcott, F. J. Wonder tales from Baltic wizards. 1928.
Malay.
‡ Lee, F. H. Folk tales of all nations. 1930.
Skeat, Walter. Tiger's mistake. 1929.
Mayan.
See Mexico.
Mexico.
‡Cruse, Amy. Young folk's book of myths. 1925.
‡Lee, F. H. Folk tales of all nations. 1930.
Martinez Del Rio. Sun, the moon and a rabbit. 1935.
Otero, Nina. Old Spain in our Southwest. 1936.
Purnell, Idella. Merry frogs. 1936.
Purnell, I. and Weatherwax, J. M. Talking bird. 1930.
Smith, Susan. Made in Mexico. 1930.
Negro.
‡Field, Rachel. American folk and fairy tales. 1929.
‡Lee, F. H. Folk tales of all nations. 1930.
Mitchell, M. B. Gray moon tales. 1926.
Pyrnelle, L. C. Diddie, Dumps and Tot. 1910.
**Sale, J. B. Tree named John. 1929.
See also Africa.
New Guinea.
‡Lee, F. H. Folk tales of all nations. 1930.
New Zealand.
Howes, Edith. Long, bright land. 1929.
Normandy, and Provence.
‡Dorey, Jacques. Three and the moon. 1929.

Norway.
‡Cruse, Amy. Young folk's book of myths. 1925.
Dasent, G. W. East of the sun and west of the moon.
Dunlap, Maurice. Stories of the vikings. 1923.
Falkberget, Johan. Broomstick and Snowflake. 1933.
‡Johnson, E. and Scott, C. E. Anthology of children's literature.
    1935.
‡Lee, F. H. Folk tales of all nations. 1930.
‡Power, Effie. Bag o' tales. 1934.
Pyle, Katherine. Tales from Norse mythology. 1930.
Rasmussen, I. M. East o' the sun and west o' the moon. 1933.
Oriental.
Arabian nights' entertainment: Adventures of Haroun Er Ras-
    chid. 1923.
‡Cooper, F. T. Argosy of fables. 1921.
Garnett, L. M. Ottoman wonder tales. 1915.
Hauff, Wilhelm. Arabian days' entertainment.
‡Johnson, E. and Scott, C. E. Anthology of children's literature.
    1935.
Katibah, H. I. Other Arabian nights. 1928.
‡Lee, F. H. Folk tales of all nations. 1930.
Martin, D. B. Fatma was a goose. 1929.
Meeker, C. H. Folk tales from the Far East. 1927.
Sharman, Lyon. Bamboo. 1914.
Voltaire, F. M. A. de. Zadig.
Papua.
See New Guinea.
Persia.
‡Gibson, Katharine. Golden bird. 1927.
Coit, Dorothy. Ivory throne of Persia. 1929.
‡Cooper, F. T. Argosy of fables. 1921.
‡Lee, F. H. Folk tales of all nations. 1930.
Mackenzie, C. F. Jackal in Persia. 1928.
Philippine islands.
‡Phillips, G. D. Far peoples. 1929.
‡Meeker, C. H. Folk tales from the Far East. 1927.
Poland.
Bernhard, J. B. Master wizard. 1934.
Borski, L. M. and Miller, K. B. Gipsy and the bear. 1933.
Byrde, Elsie. Polish fairy book. 1927.
‡Cooper, F. T. Argosy of fables. 1921.
Kelly, E. P. Christmas nightingale. 1932.
Portugal.
‡Lee, F. H. Folk tales of all nations. 1930.
Rome.
‡Bulfinch, Thomas. Golden age of myth and legend.
Cooke, A. O. Stories of Rome in days of old.
‡Cruse, Amy. Young folk's book of myths. 1925.
‡Curry, C. M. and Clippinger, E. E. Children's literature. 1926.
Farjeon, Eleanor. Mighty men from Achilles to Julius Caesar.
    1925.
‡Forbush, W. B. Myths and legends of Greece and Rome. 1928.
Orvieto, Laura. Birth of Rome. 1935.
‡Tappan, E. M. Old world hero stories. 1911.
Roumania.
Ispirescu. Petre. Foundling prince and other tales. 1917.
‡Lee, F. H. Folk tales of all nations. 1930.
Purnell, I. and Weatherwax, J. M. Why the bee is busy. 1930.

Russia.
Carpenter, Frances. Tales of a Russian Grandmother. 1933.
Carrick, Valery. Animal picture tales from Russia. 1930.
—— More Russian picture tales. 1920.
—— Still more Russian picture tales. 1922.
—— Tales of wise and foolish animals. 1928.
·—— Valery Carrick's picture folk tales. 1926.
‡Cooper, F. T. Argosy of fables. 1921.
‡Curtin, Jeremiah. Fairy tales of Eastern Europe. 1931.
Kovalsky, Olga and Putnam, Brenda. Long-legs, Big-mouth.
    Burning-eyes. 1926.
‡Lee, F. H. Folk tales of all nations. 1930.
Mamin, D. M. Verotchka's tales. 1922.
‡Phillips, G. D. Far peoples. 1929.
Ralston, W. R. S. Russian fairy tales.
Ransome, Arthur. Old Peter's Russian tales. 1916.
Tolstoy, L. N. Ivan the fool and other tales. 1932.
White, William. Made in Russia. 1932.
Yershov, Peter. Humpy. 1931.
Zeitlin, Ida. Skazki. 1926.
Scandinavia.
‡Cruse, Amy. Young folk's book of myths. 1925.
Choate, F. and Curtis, E. Little people of the hills. 1928.
‡Lee, F. H. Folk tales of all nations. 1930.
Olcott, F. J. Wonder tales from Baltic wizards. 1928.
‡Power, Effie. Bag o' tales. 1934.
See also Denmark, Norway, Sweden.
Scotland.
‡Lee, F. H. Folk tales of all nations. 1930.
‡Olcott, F. J. Wonder tales from fairy isles. 1929.
Servia.
‡Curtin, Jeremiah. Fairy tales of Eastern Europe. 1931.
‡Lee, F. H. Folk tales of all nations. 1930.
South America.
‡Cruse. Amy. Young folk's book of myths. 1925.
Eells, W. S. Brazilian fairy book. 1926.
—— Fairy tales from Brazil. 1917.
—— Magic tooth. 1927.
‡Finger. C. J. Tales worth telling. 1927.
‡Partridge. E. N. Joyful Star. 1915.
‡Phillips, G. D. Far peoples. 1929.
Spain.
Belpré, Pura. Perez and Martina. 1932.
Boggs, R. S. and Davis. M. G. Three golden oranges. 1936.
Carpenter. Frances. Tales of a Basque grandmother. 1930.
‡Cooper, F. T. Argosy of fables. 1921.
Dane, G. E. and B. J. Once there was and was not. 1931.
Coloma, Luis de. Perez the mouse. 1914.
Gunterman, B. L. Castles in Spain. 1928.
Irving. Washington. Tales from The Alhambra. 1910.
‡Lee, F. H. Folk tales of all nations. 1932.
Sawyer, Ruth. Picture tales from Spain. 1936.
Sweden.
Lagerlöf. S. O. V. Further adventures of Nils. 1911.
—— Wonderful adventures of Nils. 1907.
Smith, Susan. Made in Sweden. 1934.
Tappan. E. M. Little lady in green. 1925.
—— Prince from nowhere. 1928.
Wahlenberg, Anna. Old Swedish fairy tales. 1925.

Switzerland.
Baumbach, Rudolf. Tales from the Swiss Alps. 1930.
Criss, Mildred. Martine and Michel. 1931.
Guerber, H. A. Legends of Switzerland. 1899.
Keller, Gottfried. Fat of the cat. 1925.
‡Lee, F. H. Folk tales of all nations. 1932.
Thibet.
Noel, Sybille. Magic bird of Chomo-lung-ma. 1931.
‡Lee, F. H. Folk tales of all nations. 1930.
Turkey.
See Oriental.
Tyrol.
Henderson, B. and Calvert, C. Wonder tales of old Tyrol.
Wolff, C. F. Pale mountains. 1927.
United States.
Babbitt, E. C. Animals' own story book. 1930.
Bianco, M. W. Street of little shops. 1932.
Blaisdell, A. F. and Ball, F. K. Log cabin days. 1921.
Brown, A. F. Under the rowan tree. 1926.
Canfield, Dorothy. Made-to-order stories. 1925.
Emerson, C. D. Merry-go-round of modern tales. 1927.
Field, Rachel. American folk and fairy tales. 1929.
——— Pocket-handkerchief park. 1929.
Hawthorne, Nathaniel. Grandfather's chair.
Irving, Washington. Bold dragoon and other tales. 1930.
‡Lee, F. H. Folk tales of all nations. 1930.
Mackaye, Percy. Tall tales of the Kentucky mountains. 1926.
Otero, Nina. Old Spain in our Southwest. 1936.
Rounds, Glen. Ol' Paul, the mighty logger. 1936.
Shannon, Monica. California fairy tales. 1926.
——— Eyes for the dark. 1928.
Sandburg, Carl. Rootabaga country. 1929.
——— Rootabaga pigeons. 1923.
——— Rootabaga stories. 1922.
Wadsworth, Wallace. Paul Bunyan and his great blue ox.
1926.
See also Eskimo ; Indians of North America ; Negro.
Wales.
Henderson, B. and Jones, S. Wonder tales of ancient Wales.
1924.
‡Lee, F. H. Folk tales of all nations. 1930.
Morris, Kenneth. Book of the three dragons. 1930.
‡Olcott, F. J. Wonder tales from fairy isles. 1929.

SUBJECT LIST

This list was compiled to aid in identifying stories. It is given here with the thought that it might be of use to others; but, it is not to be considered as a complete subject list of the tales indexed.

Absentmindedness.
Barber's fifth brother; Blunder #; Day-dreaming; Milkmaid and her pail of milk; Poor Mr. Fingle.

Advice.
Cormac: Cormac's Brehon #; Five wise words of the Guru; Good advice #; Ivan #; King's life saved by spells; Lac of rupees for a piece of advice #; Look three times; Nightingale and the pearl; Partridge and the fowler; Seller of words; Three counsels of King Solomon; Three precepts #; Tims; To-day or to-morrow; Ways of giving advice #.
See also Words.

Agriculture.
Boy who became emperor; Bruin and Reynard partners; Corn for Italy; Farmer saint; Gold in the orchard; Good Little Corn and bad Big Corn; Honied clover; In the kitchen garden; Kings, Origin of; Little rooster #; Lucky seed; Magic rice; Outwitting the bogie; Potatoes come to France; Seeds and the wheat; Sperrit of Akaluga Junior; Stupid monkeys; Three-legged stool; Truant vine; Trustworthy one; Turnip-field godmother; Weeds; Why the rice stopped rolling.

Airplanes.
Last of the dragons; Mr. Cricket's airplane; Pajaro; Speed.

Alligators and crocodiles.
Aruman #; Foolish fish; Heyo, house #; Little jackal and the alligator; Magic crocodile; Why the crocodile has a wide mouth #.

Almond tree.
Flowering stick; Summer snow #; Why the almond tree blossomed.

Alphabet.
Alphabet party; Blue silver; How the alphabet was made #; Kiss me; Mr. E. and the spelling man #; Pig Wisps.
See also Writing.

Amateur art.
Theodelind and the water sprite; Zirbel.

Ambition.
Golden eggs and cock of gold #.
See also Overconfidence; Self conceit.

Americanization.
Christmas wreath; Lie; Little Athen's message; Little true American; Real Hallowe'en witch #; Rescue of Old Glory; Victory for English.

Ancestors, Pride in.
Bandi Angel; Foolish mother goat; Fox and the monkey; Geese whose ancestors saved Rome; Lydia Doane celebration; Mule.

Art.
Angelus; Apelles #; Beth Gellert; Boy and the moonlight; Boy of Cadore; Bronze boar; Campapse and the painter; Chinese fairy tale; Ghiberti's doors; Giotto's O; Goblin of Giotto's tower; Guido and his pupil; Her blanket; House that burned down; Neighboring families; Painter of cats #; Rose from Homer's grave #; Sesshiu, painter of Japan; Soap bubble; Thirsty pigeon; Tonia; Two great painters #; Water lily. III #; Wilhelmina's wooden shoes; Wood carver of Rouen. *See also* Names of painters in main index.

Asking too much.
Camel's neck #; Fairy borrowing #; Foolish weaver #.

Astronomy.
Animal in the moon; Milky way; Moon stories #; Naughty comet #; Stars, Stories of; Sky bridge of birds; Sun, Stories of. *See also* Eclipse; Northern lights.

Authors.
Theodelind and the water sprite.

Automobiles.
City garage; Dog that stole a ride; Foolish Mabel; Great gray touring car; Happy-go-lucky Henery; Little roadster; New automobile; Old horse Proudfoot; Speed; Taxi that went mad; Timid truck.

Autumn.
Gay little king; Happy forest; Haze of Indian summer; Scarlet maple; Two little maple leaves; Two ways; Why the autumn leaves are red.

Aviation.
Dædalus and Icarus; First aviator of the Pacific; Flying trunk; How the Baron rescued the prisoners; Ship that sailed by land and sea; Winged hero; Wings. *See also* Airplanes; Flying.

Babies.
Amir and the Afghan; Corner in babies; Finding of the treasure; How the baby named herself; Japanese twins and Bot Chan; Manabozho and his toe; Maribel and Mrs. Lark #; Our baby; Red dolly; Secret. I; Signs of baby; Trading babies #; Why the baby says "goo."

Baseball.
Professional umpire and mascot keeper; Why Drayton was safe; Why the big ball game was a hot game.

Bats.
Birds' ball game; Borrowed wings; Children with one eye #; Gipsy winds up in a belfry; How the bat saved the world; Ogre and his dragon; Plucked #; When old Mr. Bat got his wings #; Why Flitter the bat flies at night #; Why the swallows are not molested #; Why the bat is blind #; Why the sun shines by day and the moon by night.

Bears.
Old Man Hug-me-tight's Christmas party; Old Mother Bear's Christmas stocking; Lost prince of the poles #; Mooin the bear's child #; Teddy Bear and the mud-pie mask #; What the moon saw: 31st evening; Why grizzly bear goes on all fours #; Why the bear has a stumpy tail; Why the bear sleeps all winter.

Beauty, Real.
Angel and the gargoyle; Great stone face; Silver, silver.

Bed time.
Little chick that didn't like to go to bed # ; Sandman.   II ; Three owls in a tree ; Wakeful star baby, Story of #.

Bees.
Flowers, Legend of ; Hare, the buffalo, the lion and the bees ; King Solomon's answer ; Queen bee ; What happened in the bee's cannery # ; Why the bee buzzes # ; Why the bees gather honey.

Bells.
Benkei and the bell ; Flos mercatorum ; Great bell ; Inchcape rock ; Kling, klang, poor Dokum ; Lake of St. Anna ; Poor woman and the bell ; Three silver bells # ; Voice of the bell # ; Why the chimes rang.

Birch tree.
Peter and the birch tree dryad ; White birch.

Bird legends.
See in the following books :
Bailey.   For the children's hour ; Baldwin.   Fifty famous stories ; Brown.   Curious book of birds ; Carey.   Stories of the birds ; Cooke.   Nature myths ; Crommelin.   Famous legends ; Gask.   Legends of our little brothers ; Grinnell.   Birds in song and story ; Holbrook.   Book of nature myths ; Judd.   Classic myths ; Judd.   Wigwam stories ; Judson.   Old Crow stories ; Pitré.   Swallow book ; Young.   Plantation bird legends ; Zimmern.   Old tales from Rome.

Birds. Colors of.
Forgetful kingfisher ; Greedy raven ; How color came to the redbird ; How the birds and the flowers were given their colors ; How the birds came ; How the bluebird got its color ; How the finch got her colors ; How the nightingale got his beautiful voice ; How the peacock was given colored feathers ; How the redbird got his color ; Impatient bird ; Mountain with summer in its heart ; Owl and Raven # ; Peacock's cousin ; Why the crow is black ; When Mr. Bluebird won his beautiful coat #.

Birds. King of.
How the birds chose a king ; King Wren ; Peacock and the magpie ; Why chickens live with man ; Why the owl is not king of the birds.

Birds. Origin of.
Early girl ; How the birds came ; How the bluebird came ; Sun of fire.

Birds. Songs of.
Bird songs # ; When Cavillaca ran away ; Why the birds sing different songs ; Why the nightingale sings better than the dove.

Birthdays.
Carp rider ; Coming of the paper carp ; Hundreds and thousands ; Jar of rosemary ; Little Wind's birthday ; Major's birthday ; Mary Ann's party ; Miss Matilda's birthday ; Noodle pagodas ; Rosaura's birthday ; Warty frog lantern.

Blackbirds.
Kenach's little woman ; Valiant blackbird ; When the blackbird was white.

Blessing (Parents').
Mother's blessing ; Three brothers and their adventures with the queen ; Well of the moon.

Bluebird.
Bobby Bluebird's adventures # ; How the bluebird came # ; How the bluebird got its color ; How the bluebird was chosen herald ; When Mr. Bluebird won his beautiful coat # ; Why the bluebird carries happiness.

Blue jay.
Early girl; Po' jay # ; Woodpecker and bluejay.

Bluestockings.
Theodelind and the water sprite.

Boastfulness.
Arachne; Caterpillar and the wild animals; Four weavers; Hare
and the tortoise; Hary Janos; How brave Walter hunted
wolves # ; Shirt-collar.
See also Ancestors; Tall tales.

Book week.
Ah Mee's invention; Booker Washington's examination; Cow
that went to college; Gold tree; Joro and the elephant; King
Eumenes starts a library; Man whose library passed into
strange hands; New Year's party; Perseverance wins; "Read,
and you will know" # ; Spare moments.

Bored.
Adventurous cottontail and the princess; What ailed the king.
See also Laziness.

Borrowing.
Better of it; Fairy borrowing # ; How the terrapin lost his whis-
tle; How the turkey got his beard; Nightingale and the worm.
I.

Bows and arrows. *See* Archery.

Boy's day in Japan.
Carp rider; Coming of the paper carp.

Bramble.
Bat and his partners # ; Fox and the bramble.

Bravery.
Little Persian; Pierre and the pewter cup # ; Red thread of
courage; Sachem of the white plume; Two companions # ; Two
kings at war.
See also Fear overcome.

Bridge building.
Devil's bridge; Fairy bridge of Licq; Fairy in the oak; Shepherd
boy who built a bridge; Why goats have short tails.

Brownies.
Brown's little brownie; Caraway brodchen; Country bumpkin
and the hobgoblin; Crazy Jim and the pixies; Lob Lie-by-the
fire; On Christmas Day in the morning; Owl's answer to
Tommy # ; Tease, tease, tease again.

Budgeting.
Clever peasant; What the four were for; Wise girl #.

Buffalo.
How the buffalo and the grizzly bear went to war; King of the
buffaloes # ; Napi and the famine; Nothing child # ; Why the
buffalo works so hard; Woman who married a buffalo.

Building.
Builder of ability and the builder of haste # ; Carpenter builds
shelter for some animals # ; Forgetful carpenter; Hal o' the
draft; Hammer and plane and saw; How the home was built;
How the rooster built a house of his own # ; Hugh of Lincoln
and Jocelin of Wells; Men learn to make tipis # ; Mud people;
Ox that helped; Ram and the pig; Three little pigs; Why
Rheims church was built.

Burros.
Donkey of God; Outlandish adventures of Bigger.

Buttercups.
First buttercups; How buttercups came # ; How the butter-

Buttercups—*continued.*
cups grew yellow # ; Story that the buttercups told # ; Why the frogs call the buttercups #.
Butterflies.
Down in the meadow ; Easter story ; Fairy steeds # ; First butterflies ; How butterflies came # ; Lesson of faith ; Priest's soul ; Princess of China ; Noonday party ; Three little butterflies.
Buzzards.
Brother Buzzard's hat # ; Why the turkey-buzzard is bald-headed.
Cactus.
Absent-minded tailor ; Eagle and the snake ; Great-big-man.
Calla lily.
Golden goblets of gladness.
Camel.
Arab and his camel ; First camel ; How the camel got his hump ; How the camel unbent # ; Jupiter and the camel ; Old Humpy ; Tit for tat.
Canary.
Bird bride ; Borrowed plumage ; Flight of the golden bird ; Promise of music.
Candy.
Bag of goodies ; Caramel ; How maple sugar came ; Torrone.
Cane.
Fairy walking stick # ; Makila, Tale of ; Mr. Blake's walking-stick #.
Canterbury bells.
Little nymph who rang the bells # ; Venus's looking glass.
Cardinal flower.
Prince Scarlet #.
Carpenter. *See* Building.
Cats.
Belling the cat ; Belshazzar and the strange cat ; Black cat's journey # ; Cheshire cat ; Colony of cats # ; Cottager and his cat ; Country cat ; Dick Whittington and his cat ; Domingo's cat # ; Enchanted cat ; Faithful cat ; Fortune seekers. I # ; Gagliuso ; How cats came to purr ; How curiosity killed the cat ; How Spot found a home ; How the cat became head forester # ; How the cat got all the grain # ; How the cat kept Christmas # ; I once knew a cat ; Judy and the fairy cat # ; King of the cats ; King's cat # ; Kisa the cat # ; Kitten that forgot how to mew ; Kitten that wanted to be a Christmas present ; Lion and the cat ; Miller's boy and his cat ; Nine lives of Mr. Tommy Tippy cat ; Old Sultan ; Persian tale ; Puss in boots ; Pussy monks ; Pussy Tinker's Thanksgiving # ; Pussy willows, Origin of. II # ; Queer rag bag ; Rainbow cat # ; Scheming kitten ; Self-made cat ; Shanavan Lee and Pangar Dhu ; Tim Puss's Christmas ; Tom Connor's cat # ; Venus and the cat ; White cat ; Why cats always wash after eating ; Why cats hate rats # ; Why the cat always falls upon her feet # ; Why the cat came to man's house # ; Why the cat dislikes wet feet ; Why the cat scratches # ; Why the cat spits at the dog # ; Why the dog and cat are enemies ; Why there are tailless cats # ; Who is guilty ; Woman who forgot her cat #.
Centipedes.
Matter of habit ; Sir One Long Body and Madame Thousand Feet #.
Character testing.
Anselmo # ; Blue glove # ; Rondel # ; Testing of the two knights #.

Charity.
Avaricious woman; Miser, converted; Sir Launfal; St. Martin; True charity; Two gifts. I.

Charms.
Curmudgeon's skin #; Forget not the best; Primrose and elder.

Cheating punished.
Magic cap; Pied piper of Hamelin; Six and four are ten; Table, the ass and the stick.

Cheerfulness.
Cobbler's song; Peddler; Scarlet feather; Treasure in the house.

Chickens. *See* Hens and chickens.

Children ruling the house.
Uncle David's nonsensical story #; Uncle Jack's story #. *See also* Baby.

Children's kingdoms.
Caraiman #; Pandora; When everybody played.

China, Stories of.
Butterfly blossom; Crocodile pagoda; Flute player; Little duck; Pigtail of Ah Lee Ben Loo.

Chipmunks. *See* Squirrels.

Chivalry, Modern.
Dark day #; Sir Bobbie; Whisperers #.

Chocolate.
Dwarf and his confectionery #; Secret of the little dwarf #; Sura's seeds.

Christmas eve.
Babe in the manger #; Boy without a name; Holy night; Innkeeper's story; North wind. I; Pan and the Babe of Bethlehem #; Shepherd maiden's gift #; Shepherd's gift; Star and a song; Star angel; Star bearer; Stars and the child.

Christmas greens.
Holly; Margil vine; Mister Tall Pine's Christmas tree #; Talkative Christmas tree.

Churches and cathedrals.
Hugh of Lincoln and Jocelin of Wells; Ox that helped; Pious tree; Sin of the Prince Bishop; Song of the minster #; Sparrows; Why Rheims church was built.

Circus.
Merry-go-round and the Griggses; Pony with a past.

City life and country life.
Country mouse and the town mouse; Peronella #; When Mother Squirrel went to town.

Clams.
Why Rawenio made the sea clams.

Clean-up Week.
Coming of the king #; Land of the blue flower; Little cat; Magic flower; Prince Dawn and the magic flower; Tommy Turtle; Very untidy country; Waring's "white wings"; Yellow primrose.

Cleverness, Too much.
Jack the cunning thief; Jackal and the partridge #; Rabbit and the animal wizard.

Clocks.
Caliph's clock; Erratic clock; False-alarm clock; First clock; I am Clockface; Little rooster. I; Naughtiness of Number Nine; Quentin and the clock.

Clothes.
Emperor's new clothes; Flax; Gamelyn the dressmaker; How

Clothes—*continued.*
Polly saw the aprons grow # ; King's servants; Knavish little bird; New dresses; Parsee tale; Pelle's new suit; Prince of Enghalien; Silly Will.   I ; Spider webs; Talking thrush; Winter clothes #.
See also Sewing.

Clouds.
Cat's trousers; Raincloud; Shepherd of clouds # ; Thin Helen.
See also Weather.

Clover.
Filmy White; Four-leaved clover; Honied clover: How the red clover got the white marks on its leaves # ; Why some clover is red #.

Collecting and collectors.
Enchanted baby; Golden apple with the silver seeds; King Mathias' laziest men; Knot holes; Little girl's odd collection; Queen's museum #.

Comet.
Mysterious star.

Common sense.
Magic fishbone; Timms; Unbelieving king.

Community Christmas.
Fir tree.   IV.

Competition.
Beech and the oak; Selfish little tree; Two millers.

Complaining.   *See* Grumbling.

Conceit.
Eagle and the crow; Foolhardy wolf; Frog and the ox; Hans the shepherd boy.   II ; Three princesses.   I ; Wren.   I ; Young cuckoo.

Confidence.   *See* Self confidence.

Conscience, Guilty.
Bright sun brings it to light # ; Cranes of Ibycus; Meinrad's watchers.

Consequences.
Black doll; Chain of anger; Snake that the boy made; Three questions; Who killed the otter's babies?

Contentment.
Ducky Widdle-waddle and Fishy Flip-flop; Four gifts; Moon princess.   I ; Wishing ring.   I.
See also Discontent cured.

Cooks and cooking.
Agib and the cheesecakes; Better than that; Christmas cake; Christmas pudding; Dwarf's new cheese; Dwarf's secret # ; Enchanted doughnuts; Fairies of the kitchen # ; Fairy bakeshop; Family too large for the pie; Greatest egg-beater of them all; How the Christmas pudding came; Hundreds and thousands; Irish stew; King of Italy brings the pasta; King's rijstepap; Little pan; Longnose the dwarf; Mandioca; Most magnificent cook of all; Mr. Salt and Mrs. Pepper # ; Old cook book; Over the cat to the kitchen; Proud biscuit; Proud cook of Manila; Proud Infanta; Pumpkin giant; Red pepper; Roast pig, Origin of; Soup from a sausage skewer; Stone broth # ; Stove that would not stay in the kitchen; Thistledown; Three platefuls and five squaws; Three knocks on the door # ; Wait-and-see pudding; Washington pie.
See also Candy; Tea.

Cooperation.
Belly and the members; Blind man and the lame man # ; Bundle of sticks; Cattle of Mohos; First gang; Five pennies; How fire was brought to the Indians. I ; Javotte and the jolly goat boys; King Tongue # ; Palace made by music; Pebbles; Quails; Ram and the pig; Seven sons of Sandy Saunderson; Three-legged stool; What the learned cat remembers; Who discovered America.

Corn.
Corn chooses a mate # ; Don Calico Corn; First corn; How corn and beans came to be; Seven corn maidens # ; Spirit of the corn # ; Turkey-given corn.

Cotton.
Fairy spinner #.

Courage. See Bravery.

Courtesy. See Manners; Politeness.

Cows.
Cattle that came # ; Elf and the cow; Enchanted cow; Little boy and big cow # ; Mad cow # ; Water-buffalo and the cow; Wonderful cow # ; Wonderful cow that never was.

Cowslips.
Friendly cowslip bells #.

Coyote.
Bluebird and coyote; Why coyote lives on the prairies; Why Old Man Coyote has many voices # ; Why Skinhoots arms are thin; Why the coyote is so cunning #.

Crabs.
Crane and the crab; Fox and the crabs # ; How a crab learned the rights of others # ; How Joeagah, the raccoon, ate the crabs; Magic almonds.

Craftsmanship.
Four clever brothers; How the Gubbaun Saor got his trade and proved himself; Three subtle crafts of Manawyddan; Wrong thing.

Crickets.
Grillo the cricket # ; How Johnny Cricket saw Santa Claus # ; How the crickets brought good fortune # ; Singing insects; When Brer Cricket en Brer Flea fell out; When the cricket was a barber; Why little cricket sang # ; Why Mr. Cricket has elbows on his legs #.

Crocodiles. See Alligators and crocodiles.

Crocus.
Springtime. III # ; Why crocus holds up his golden cup #.

Crows.
Children of wind and the clan of peace; Eagle and the crow; Emu and the crows; Fox and the crow; Stag, the crow and the jackal; Why the crow has a hoarse voice # ; Why the crow is black.

Cuckoo.
Call of the cuckoo; Christmas cuckoo; How Nial won the beautiful princess # ; Thrush and the cuckoo; Why the cuckoo has no time to build her nest.

Curfew.
Husband shut out.

Curiosity.
Billy goat and the king # ; Boots and his brothers; Carpenter and the ape; Elephant's child; Hugh Midity tells a story; Inquisi-

Dolls.
Baby Gretel; Christmas joke; Coppelia; Doll who was sister to a princess; First doll; Funeral march of a marionette; Gretchen; Happiest doll; Lady Jane; Lost doll; Pillow dolly; Rag doll's Christmas; Rosaura's birthday; Tokutara San; Toymaker. I; Van Ness family; Walking doll.
See also Toys.

Donkey transformations.
How the ass became a man again #; Miller's man who became an ass; Oil merchant's donkey; Transformation donkey; Was-a-boy.

Doors.
Goblin who was turned into a door knocker.

Doughnuts.
Enchanted doughnuts.

Dove.
Children of wind and the clan of peace; Early girl; Why the dove is on our valentines.

Dragons.
Big worm; Bitter waters; Chop Chin and the golden dragon #; Dragon's story; Forty-nine dragons; Good-natured dragons; Green dragon; Last of the dragons; Papa Dragon's tale; St. George and the dragon; Shepherd and the dragon; Tender-hearted monster; Una and the Red Cross Knight; Wyvern; Young dragon.

Dreams.
Merchant of dreams.

Dreams, Marvellous.
Daniel O'Rourke; Far adventures of Billy Burns; Gold tree; Little Lasse #; Man who would dream.

Dreams, Warning.
Ouphe of the woods #; Pillow of content; Woman who had what she wanted.

Dress. *See* Clothes; Millinery; Sewing; Shoes.

Drums.
Army of two; Brave drummer boy of France; In Drumtown; Napoleon and the drummer-boy; Silent drum.

Ducks.
Hen that hatched ducks #; How the ducks got their fine feathers; Iktomee and the ducks; Little duck; North wind and the duck; Portugese duck.

Echo.
Fine, fine; Saucy fairy; Unhappy echo.

Eclipse.
Columbus and the eclipse #; Sun and the moon. III; Terrapin's trick.

Education.
Old woman and the crowbar.

Efficiency.
Prince and the baker's daughter #; Queen who wished the flowers away #.

Egypt, Stories of.
Ali Mahmoud; Little Sosana and her gold wrought shoe #.

Electricity.
Wise inventor; Wixie and the wireless.

Elephants.
Hasteen saves the jewels of the king #; Moti Guj #; White elephant.

Envy.
Black doll; Dill # ; Two travellers. III.
European war.
Baby Gretel; Ernest service.
Exaggerations.
Embellishment # ; Long bow story # ; Much ado about nothing;
Necklace of truth # ; Story that is all lies; Travels of Baron
Munchausen.
See also Tall tales.
Explorers.
Harkouf; Marco Polo; Sinbad the sailor.
Eyesight.
Coyote and Old-Man's eyes; Eyes for the dark; Why our sight
fails with age # ; Why some animals see at night; Wonderful
bird #.
Fair play.
Wager.
Fairies, Belief in.
Boy and the fairies; Man who did not believe in fairies; Thing to
be explained; Unbelieving king.
Fairies, Creation of.
Dwarfs and the fairies; Giants and fairies # ; How the fairies
came to be.
Fairies, Visit with.
Elfin grove # ; Elfin hill # ; Elidore # ; Tontlawald, Tale of.
Fairy gifts.
Elf gifts; Four gifts; Poppet.
Fan, Origin.
Lantern and the fan; Wind that would not blow.
Fashion.
Emperor's new clothes; Fairyfoot; Prince Weary's galoshes;
Swineherd; Young Englishman.
Faithfulness.
At his post; Damon and Pythias; Hans the shepherd boy. I # ;
Knights of the silver shield.
Falling stars.
Little lost stars #.
Farming.
See Agriculture; Irrigation.
Fate.
Animals' New Year's eve; Antti and the wizard's prophecy; Bird
of sorrow # ; Catherine and her destiny; Constans the emperor;
Destiny # ; Fish and the ring; Foreordained match # ; Giant
with the golden hair; Hermit; Horoscope; King who would be
stronger than fate # ; King's son and the painted lion; Lord of
death # ; Man who went to find his angel; Maria-of-the-forest;
Œdipus; Prince and the foundling; Prince and the three fates;
Prince with the nine sorrows; Rashi and the Duke of Lorraine;
Three rings; We cannot escape our fate; What the stars fore-
told #.
Fate overcome.
Fate. III ; Prince and the three fates.
Father's Day.
Æneas and Anchises (Burning of Troy) ; Buy a father; Dr. John-
son and his father; How the knight of the sun rescued his
father # ; Seven fathers in the house; Seven sons of Sandy
Saunderson.
Fear.
Folly of panic # ; Goat and the hyena; Goat and the ram; How

Fear—*continued.*
fear came # ; Rabbit and the other animals; Ram and the leopard; Why the tiger and the stag do not like each other; Youth who could not shiver and shake.

Fear overcome.
Boy who conquered himself; Dicky the brave; Lexy and the dogs on his street; Over the cat to the kitchen; So-bee-yit.

Ferns.
How we came to have ferns # ; Magic ferns # ; Secret of the fern jewel; Why the ferns stand guard #.

Fire.
Bird with breast of fire # ; Fox and the fireflies # ; How fire was brought to the Indians; Mis' Swallow # ; Prometheus # ; Secret of fire # ; Wonderful lizard; Wren who brought fire.

Fire prevention week.
Fire neglected burns the house; Pert fire engine; Ting-a-ling-bome.

Fire-wood.
Gifts the trees gave # ; Why the laurel makes wreaths.

Fireflies.
Battle of the firefly and the apes # ; Butterfirefly # ; Lampy's Fourth of July; How stars and fireflies were made; How the firefly got its light # ; Light of the fly # ; Monkeys, the firefly and the bird; Prince Golden-Firefly # ; Princess Moonbeam #.

Fish.
About Leviathan; Coat of arms of Putsk; Coming of the paper carp; Enchanted fish of Polaman; How the fishes got their color # ; How the Indians obtained salmon # ; Lobster trees; Miracle that happened to a fish; Miraculous fish; Monstrous fish; Persevering carp # ; Raven gets fish for his people; Sun of Water; Why the flounder has a crooked mouth; Why the men of Gavi will not eat fish.

Fishing.
Better of it; Clever little fisherman; Fairy nets; Foolish fishermen; Fox and the peasant; Harbour buoy's story; How Kakahura learned to make nets; How Master Rabbit went fishing; How Maui fished up the great island; Hungry fox and his breakfast; I know what I have learned # ; Salt fish and the eel; Thor's fishing; Why the bear has a stumpy tail.

Flag stories.
Flag that waved in the north; In the flag house # ; Iris. III; Last battle of the Revolution; Rescue of Old Glory; Their flag; What the flag said; Why the red dragon is the emblem of Wales.

Flattery.
Crimson slippers; Fox and the crow; Fox and the grasshopper; Wily lion.

Fleas.
Fifine and the white mare; Flea-huntin'dest night; King's flea; Leaping match; Miss Race Hoss an' de fleas # ; Sir Skip-and-a-jump # ; Spider and the flea # ; When Brer Cricket en Brer Flea fell out.

Fleur-de-lis.
Iris. III; Prince's dream.

Flies.
Bad Indian's ashes; Bee and a housefly; Lucio and the flies; Madame Teeny Tiny.

Flint rock.
Hare's lip; Rabbit scatters Flint; Raven gets fire from Red Deer.

Floods.
Afloat on a roof.
Flowers.
Big, white, woolly lamb; Carnation; Christmas rose; Elf and the cow; Enchanted garden; Field of angels; Forget-me-not; Goldenrod and aster #; Heliotrope; How, the flowers came; How buttercups came #; Land of the blue flower; Maiden White and Maiden Yellow #; On the shores of longing; Passing of the flowers; Prickly bush; Queen who wished the flowers away #; Snapdragons; Star of Bethlehem #; Stray cow #.
See also names of flowers.
Flute.
Assemoka the sweet singer; Bird Feng; Everything in its right place; Fox and his flute; Gift of the flutes; Guillaume's flute; Indian boy and his flute; King and the magic stick; Reed flute; Sacrifice; Song of the flute; Two lizards. II.
Flying.
Dædalus and Icarus; Etana and his flight to heaven; Phaeton; Sun conqueror—Sunpati; Why the cock cannot fly; Wings.
See also Airplanes; Aviation.
Food waste punished.
Cheese floor; Dragon fly of Zuni; Girl who trod on the loaf; Why the rice stopped rolling.
Foolish people.
Foolish Fred; Foolish John; Jack and his mother; Lazy Jack; Prudent Hans; Silly Matt; Stupid's cries; Wise men of Gotham.
Football.
We always succeed in the end.
Forget-me-nots.
Water of forgetfulness #.
Forgetfulness.
God with a bad memory; Poor Mr. Fingle.
Fortune tellers.
Horoscope; Prophet. II; Sorceress.
Fraud.
Borrowed plumage; Sham princes; Wizards, Pretended.
Friendship.
Four friends; Friendship of the squirrel and the creeping fish; Travelers and the axe; Travelers and the bear; True friendship.
Frogs, Origin.
Cain's ducklings; First frogs #; First tree frog #; Glooskap and the bullfrog; How the peepers came to be #; Latona and the frogs.
Frogs, Stories of.
Fleamie, the tree frog; Green page; Hares and the frogs; How Old Mr. Tree Toad found out how to climb #; Little tadpole #; Mammy and Mr. Tadpole; Melilot #; Miss Peggy and the frog #; More ways than one #; Prince Green-eyes; Stylish Misses Woge #; Right time to laugh #; Tale of two tails; Three little wiggletails; Thumbelina; Why Mr. Frog is still a bachelor; Why the frog has no tail #.
Fuchsia.
Miladi's ear drops.
Future, Fear of. *See* Worry.
Games.
Birds' ball game; Ogre that played jackstraws; Pak-su-ni and the chess players; Pope's game of chess; Professional umpire and mascot keeper; Raja Rasalu #; Two dicers #; When I was a

Games—*continued.*
squantum wagon; When I was an ark; When the garden played tag; Whispering game.
Gardens.
Billy's garden; Christmas'rose. I; Enchanted garden; Ladders to heaven; Name that grew; Stone; Tulip bed; Wind and the flowers.
Gargoyles.
Angel and the gargoyle; Crown of gold.
Geography.
Acqueduct of Caesarea; Building the Rockies; Children of Spinalunga; Ditch of Czorsz; Giant's stairs; How a town was named; Little Tuk; Name of the City of Flowers; Rivers that talked; Why there are no trees on the desert; Wind's tale of the giant's boot; Wrekin #.
Giants.
Bells that ring-a-ting-a-ling; Bold giant; Geirrod and Thor; Giant king of Limburg; Giant twins; Haarlem; Hero twins; Killing of Cabrakan; Long, Broad and Quickeye; Longstaff, Pinepuller and Rockheaver; Outlandish adventures of Bigger; Rainbow cat and the giantess #; So big and so little; St. Christopher; Toy of the giant child.
Gipsies.
Happy Boz'll.
Girls.
Army of two; Betty's ride; Brave little Glory; Dance of the fairies #; Her friend and her flag; Little Ki and the pot of rice; Maid of Zaragoza; Melilot #; Moolang; Warrior maids; White elephant. V; Young head of the family.
Girls disguised as men.
Fair Jehane; Faithful little squire; Moolang; Rain king's daughter; Twelve huntsmen #; Vasilisa Popovna; White steed Bufanin.
Goats.
Billy goat and the king #; Billygoat's barnyard; Kid and the tiger; Kid and the wolf; Kid who would not go #; Lion and the goat; Little white rabbit. II; Nanny who wouldn't go home to supper; Snowflake; Table, the ass and the stick; Three billy goats gruff; Why goats have short tails; Why goats live with man; Why the goat left the jungle #; Why the goat's knees are bare; Wolf and the seven little kids.
Goldfish.
Finny and Funny; Fisherman and the goldfish; Three fish. III.
Golf.
Playing the game.
Gossip.
Adder that did not hear #; Eavesdropper, the ugly dwarf #; Fairy who judged her neighbors #; Ginger and Sandy; It is quite true; See no evil; Slanderer; Small story; Three sieves; Whispering game; Why Ra-wen-io made the sea clams.
Grasshopper, Origin of.
Aurora and Tithonus; Lazy girl.
Gratitude.
Lion and the mouse; Naosuke; Rabbit who was grateful; Unseen friends; Wonderful flower.
Greediness.
Boy and the filberts; Boy who was easily pleased; Fox and his piece of meat; Lucky beggar; Owl and the two rabbits; Pail of

Greediness—*continued*.
gold; Selfish prince; Stone lion. I; Swollen fox; Tommy's Christmas stocking; Troll's Christmas.

Grumbling.
Cock, the mouse and the little red hen; Cross-patch; Steamboat and the locomotive #.

Gunpowder.
That lazy Ah Fun.

Hands.
Beautiful hand; Clean hands; Helping hands; Judy and the fairy.

Hanukah, Feast of.
K'tonton takes a ride on a runaway trendel.

Happiness.
Cobbler's song; Crœsus and Solon; Golden apple with the silver seeds; Pippa passes #; Scarlet feather; Top that could sing; Treasure in the house; Why the bluebird carries happiness.

Hats. *See* Millinery.

Hayfever.
Outlandish adventures of Bigger.

Headache cure.
Dog, the snake and the cure of headache.

Health.
Black-toothed prince; David and the good health elves; Disobedient Dicky bird; Judy and the fairy; Kingdom of the greedy #; Prince who was not hungry; Raising the stone; Secret. II; Thin Helen; When Norma Catherine ran away; Why children lose their teeth.

Heliotrope.
Enchanted garden.

Helpfulness. *See* Chivalry; Kindness.

Hens and chickens.
Capons fat and lean; Cat and the hen #; Christmas in the woods; Guinea-hen and the crocodile; Half-chick; Hen and the falcon; How the speckled hen got her speckles; It is quite true; Medio Pollito #; Our hen; Queer chickens; Sister Hen and the crocodile; Small story; Ten hens go a-travelling; What the moon saw: 2d evening; Why chickens live with man; Why hens scratch in the ground; Why the hawk catches chickens.

Heroes, National.
Babarossa; Bruce, Robert; Charlemagne; Cid; King Alfred; King Arthur; Milky way. III; Rama; Roland. II; St. Denis; St. George; Tell, William; Sohrab and Rustem; Sons of Aymon; Three Tells; Toribio.
See also Patriotism.

Hide and seek, Magic.
Broad man, the tall man and the man with eyes of flame; Youth who used his own brains.

Hobbies. *See* Collecting.

Holly.
Holly, Legend of #; Holly-tree elf; Sprig of holly #.

Home.
Dreams of gold; Golden windows #; Little boy who wanted a castle; Three mountain goats; Timothy and Tabitha.

Honesty.
Gold ducat; Haughty butter dealer; Wang Spring-Flowers; What the flag said.
See also Cheating punished.

Ingratitude of masters.
Lion, the mouse and the cat; Old Sultan; Washerman's jackass; Way of the world.
Injustice.
Lazy judge; Lesson in justice; Jew among the thorns; Shemyak the judge #.
See also Unjust judgements.
Inquisitiveness. *See* Curiosity; Meddlesomeness.
Insects.
Camphor princess; Down in the meadow: Ephemera; Hickory Horn Devil # ; Noonday party; Why God made everything.
Inventions and inventors.
Alice and the white knight; Dædalus and Icarus; David Cameron's fairy god mother; Lantern and the fan; Rose-colored spectacles; That lazy Ah Fun; Three good giants # ; Watt and the teakettle # ; Wise inventor.
Irrigation.
Good Little Corn and bad Big Corn; Kings, Origin of.
Jealousy.
Bird with two beaks; Fox and the foolish blue jay; Fox and the wolf. V; Jealousy of the blind man; Resonant cave; Rival roosters; Twin lambs #.
Journeys, Magic.
Bronze boar; Chop Chin and the golden dragon # ; Daniel O'Rourke; Little Tuk; Man who did not believe in fairies; Pooka and King Bryan Boru; Ride on the gravestone; White elephant. V.
Joy. *See* Laughter.
Juggling.
Miserly farmer; Peach from the sky.
Jumping to conclusions.
Animal in the moon; What was it?
Justice and judges.
Ali Cogia; Cadi and the roguish monk # ; Cadi's decisions # ; Country where the mice eat iron; Diamond cut diamond # ; Dumb witness # ; Hero's tasks; King Solomon's wisdom; Lazy judge; Lost purse; Oil vendor and the blind man; Self-convicted # ; Shemyak the judge # ; Stolen garlic # ; Turkish judge; Widow and the sagacious magistrate # ; Woman who hid her gold in a jar of honey; Wise judge.
See also Wise judgements.
Kindness, Power of.
Androcles and the lion; Fairy Old Boy and the tiger # ; Mink and the eagle.
Kindness to animals.
Anton's errand # ; At grandpa's farm; Benjy in Beastland; Bobby Bluebird's adventures # ; Brownie and the farmer; Christmas witch: Dutch Boor and his horse; Fairy lamps: Forest's foster daughter; Fritz-and-Franz; Gerald's dream: Golden eggs. II; Gun for sale; Legend of mercy; Lincoln and the little birds; Little boy pie: Lucio and the flies; Lucky Lialil: Men and the beasts; Robin's eggs; Saturday half-holiday; Unamiable child; What happened to K'tonton on his Lag B'Omer picnic.
Kindness rewarded.
Apples of youth. II; Big, white, woolly lamb; Five pennies: Fresh figs; Golden eggs. II: Naosuke; Salt. II; Servant of all; Shadow crest; Stone; Three-legged stool; Two bad bargains # ; Unknown travelers.

Kite flying.
High as Han Hsin; How Maui lifted up the sky #; How they
came to have kite day in China.
Knitting.
Theodelind and the water sprite; Wonder balls.
Lace.
Marda's masterpiece.
Lady-bug.
Fat gnome; Why the lady-bug is said to be beloved of God #.
Lamb.
Big, white, woolly lamb; Lamb that went to fairy land #; Lambi-
kin; Little gray lamb; Moosli the roast; Twin lambs #; When
lamb was a hero #; White pet; Why the lamb is meek.
Lark.
Fairy who judged her neighbors #; How the lark got the crescent
on its breast #; Why the lark flies up at dawn; Why the lark
wears a crown.
Laughter.
Flute that blew from fairyland; Gay godmother; Harvestin' o'
Dermod.
Laziness.
Boy who wanted to play always; Castle Fortune #; Idle-paws
and I-did-it; Johnny Pick-a-bean; King Mathias' laziest men;
Lazy frog; Lazy raccoon #; Little boy who wouldn't get up;
Magic broom; Simon and the black-gum tree #; Stone lion.
II; Three lazy brothers; Three sleepy young men #; Three
sluggards #; Timothy and Tabitha; Town of always play;
Was-a-boy; What ailed the king; What happened to the lazy
stickleback.
Leap year.
Rescue of Arselik.
Leather.
Boot is a league of nations; Old house; Shoes; Slippers of Abdul
of Kazan.
Leaves.
Anxious leaf; Elder brother #; How the oak leaves came to have
notches #; How the poplar leaves were made #; Little pine
tree who wished for new leaves; Why the aspen leaves tremble;
Why the evergreen trees keep their leaves in winter; Why the
leaves shake #.
Leaves, Color in.
Gay little king; Maple, Legend of #; Scarlet maple; Vine '
dryad #; Why the autumn leaves are red.
Leisure, Use of.
Solomon's ghost.
Lepracaun stories.
Basket of eggs; Last of the Leprechauns; Outlandish adventures
of Bigger; Seeing's believing.
Life. *See* Long life.
Light.
Candles; Electric light and the candle; Magic lamp. I; Pilot
light.
Lilies.
Arum lily; Chinese boy's garden; Dragon Sin; How the water
lily came; Ladders to heaven; Princess Lily; Red lily; Star
maiden. I.
Lizards.
Chameleon; Fox and the lizard; Lantern of the pearl; Mr. Monk
and the noisy gecko; Parrot's story #; Rongo and the lizard-

Memorial Day.
Little boy who wanted to be a soldier #.
Memory.
Lad who went to Next Town; Land where people never die; Pig Wisps.
Mermaids.
Lutey and the mermaid; Pergrin and the mermaiden #; Pulowech and the sea maiden.
Mice.
Buffalo and the field-mouse #; Cat and the mouse; Ferdinand and the taste for cheese; Luck-mouse #; Song of the mice; When Mr. Wood Mouse learned from the birds #; Who is guilty?
Milky way.
Ga-do-waas and his star-belt; Little star flower #; Sky bridge of birds; Skyway of the warriors; Sun of water; Who-all's black hat.
Millinery.
Cap that mother made; First hat; Flyaway hat #; Hats for horses; Queen's hat.
Mineral springs, Origin
How the skunk helped the coyote #.
Mirage.
Ditch of Csorsz; Mirage; Princess Morgana.
Mirrors.
Cat and the looking glass; Family portrait; Magic mirror; Snow-white and the seven dwarfs; Young lady and the looking glass.
Miserliness.
Avaricious woman; Bantagooma; Folly of avarice; Judge who took all he paid for; Most frugal of men #; This for that; Two frugal men #.
Missions.
Thidrandi and the goddesses; What the blind princess did.
Mocking birds.
How the fairies were changed into mocking birds #; Mis' Mocking-bird's chillen; Mr. Bluebird and Mr. Mocking-bird #.
Moles.
Children with one eye #; Lady mole; Why the mole has pink hands; Why the mole is blind.
Monkeys, Origin.
How the monkey was made; Scrawny old man and woman; Sun of wind; When the sun fell from the sky.
Moon stories.
All too hard; Animal in the moon; Bobby's mud-pie man; Boy and the moonlight; Buried moon; Child that cried for the moon; Chinese emperor's visit to the moon; Cruel step-mother #; Fool in the moon; Giant Crump and Lady Moon #; Gods of the sun and moon; How Kana brought back the sun, moon and stars; How the moon became beautiful #; Istar, the moon princess; Lady Toad in the moon; Magic tree; Man who discovered the moon; Master wizard, Pan Twardowski; Modest sisters; Monkeys and the moon; Owl and the moon; St. Noth-burga #; Son of Ulé; Tidy Tips; Trip to the moon; Why all men love the moon; Woman in the moon.
Mosquitoes.
Bad Indian's ashes; First mosquitoes #; How mosquitoes came; Moaning boots; Naughty spider; Pitcher the witch; War party. II; Why mosquitoes bite people; Why the mosquito hates smoke #; Why the swallow's tail is forked. II.

Motherly vanity.
Crow's children; Frog's beautiful son; Jupiter and the monkey; Mrs. Partridge's babies; One's own children are always the prettiest; Ugly little crows; White Caroline and Black Caroline.
Mountains.
Building the Rockies; Cleft mountain #; Crab that played with the sea #; Great stone face; How the Bass was held for King James; How the cliff was clad #; How the waterfall came to the thirsting mountain #; Old Man of the mountain; Pipe of peace; Rock of the measuring worm; Why Elbruz peak is split.
Mud pies.
Bobby's mud-pie man; Mrs. Mud-pie and the Hill-topper; Pies of the princess; Teddy Bear and the mud-pie mask #.
Mushrooms and toadstools.
Elf and the dormouse; Jack Mulligan's fairies; Yellow elves.
Music.
Arion and the dolphin; Barrel-organ; Boy who played the bousouka; Campbells are coming; Dagda's harp; Dance of the nymphs; Enchanted whistle #; Fiddlebow of the nixie; First harp; Flute contest of the musical foxes; Friar and the boy; Gift of the flutes; Goat and the horse; Hawt #; How a song changed the world #; How music won two wives; How the harp came to Finland; How the rabbit escaped from the wolves; How the Swiss came to use the Alpine horn; Indian boy and his flute; Iron hand; Jack and his fiddle; King Alfred; Knockmany, Legend of; Kris and the bear; Land of the sky-blue water; Magic fiddle; Magic flute; Magical music #; Minstrel and the cobbler; Minstrel's song #; Moonlight sonata; Mr. Maple and Mr. Pine #; Naughty goblin and the village school; Old Pipes and the dryad; Orpheus. II; Orpheus and Eurydice; Palace made by music; Pan; Pied piper of Hamelin; Piper and the Puca; Pippa passes; Plowman; Resonant cave; Scales; Silent drum; Singing beggar; Singing spring; Soldier who lived in the drum; Song of the flute; Song of the minster; Song of the pestle; Tsar Ivan and the harp that harped without a harper; Vanemuine, god of song; Violin that sang to a king #; Vox Angelica and Lieblich Gedacht #; Walter von der Vogelweide; Wandering huntsman and his music; When Toinette sang; Wind bells; Wonderful musician; Wonderful tune; Wolf and the kid. II.
See also names of instruments, and musicians; Song; Singing.
Music, Power of.
Boy who played the bousouka; Duty that was not paid; Happy little song; How music won two wives; How the rabbit escaped from the wolves; Kris and the bear; Silver flute; Song of the spring; Wanderings of Arasmon #; Wonderful musician.
Names.
Crafty servant; How the baby named herself; Long-life name; Master of all masters; My own self; Shepherd who laughed last; What shall baby's name be #?
Nasturtiums.
Golden boy; Why nasturtiums have lines #.
Neatness.
Boy who wouldn't wash his face; Coming of the king #; Little cat; Missing Fanchette; Pig brother; Pound; Sammy Squires and the pig family; Tommy Turtle; Very untidy country; Washing machine; When Norma Catherine ran away; Yellow primrose.

Nemesis.
Cranes of Ibycus; Curse of Pantannas; Maple flute; Meinrad's watchers; Pope's mule #; Singing bone #; Syfaddon lake; Will on the wind.

Night.
Day and night; Daylight, Origin of #; How night came; Rescue of rabbit.

Nightingale.
Gloomy hippopotamus.

Nixies, Stories of.
Fiddlebow of the nixie; Mischievous knix #; Nix in the pond; Steel lock; Water nix #.

Northern lights. (Aurora Borealis).
Aurora, the white arch and the great bear #; Echo god and the Northern Lights #; Lost prince of the poles #; Raven gets fire from Red Deer.

Obedience.
Bag of dust; How the robin came; Knights of the silver shield; Mrs. Gray's family #.

Obstinacy.
Barring of the door; Goody 'Gainst-the-Stream; I won't; Mis' Mocking bird's chillen #; Poffertjes pan.

Olives.
Ali Cogia; Athens #; Thriftless wife.

Opium.
Bad poppy seeds; Why poppies make you sleep #.

Oracle.
Delphian oracle #; Œdipus; Rogue and the oracle.

Orphans.
Mrs. Bonny-Bunny and the orphan.

Owls.
Caliph Stork; Conjure wives; False woman who became a night owl; How the littlest owl came #; In de' swamp #; Why the owl cries hoot! hoot!; Why the owl eats only small creatures #; Why the owl flies by night; Why the owl is not king of the birds.

Palm tree.
Coconut tree; Date palm #; Fir-tree and the palm; Flight into Egypt; Giraffe and the palms; Timid hare.

Pansy.
How pansies came colored; Why the pansy has no scent.

Paper.
Flax; King Eumenes starts a library; Lantern and the fan; Parsee tale.

Paradise.
Almost-saved; Brother of Christ #; Dream of a great prophet; Dream of paradise; Garden of paradise; Leek; Moment in heaven #; Third leg; Visitor from paradise #.

Paris, City of.
Eudes; Lucky seed; St. Genevieve; Street of the Good Children.

Parks.
Alphabet park; Pocket-handkerchief park; Under the rowan tree.

Partridge.
How the hunter became a partridge #; How the partridge got his whistle; Magic wigwam; Why the partridge stays near the ground #; Why the sparrow stutters.

Passover, Feast of.
K'tonton, a mouse, and a bit of leaven.

Patriotism.
Army of two; Caesar Rodney's ride; Joan of Arc; Regulus; Surabo; Tell, William; Their flag; Warrior maids; Winkelried, Arnold.
See also Heroes, National.

Patriot's Day.
Ipswich alarm; Peggy feeds the minutemen; Revere, Paul #.

Peace.
Bird of love; Bird of paradise. I #; Boot is a league of nations; Forgiving Indian; Happy forest; Harping of Alain Alawon; Hercules and Pallas; Highwayman and the priest; How Genetaska deserted her trust; How the treaty of peace was made; Indians and the Quaker family; Kingdom of the lion; Land where people never die; Last peacemaker queen #; Latch-string; Maiden's secret; Melibeus, Tale of; Ogre that played jackstraws; One calabash of water; Pipe of peace; Serpent and the peasant; Sumé; Tubal Cain. I; White goddess.

Peace-makers, Fate of.
Frogs and the fighting bulls; Magic mouthful; Talking bird. III; Three magicians; Top that could sing.

Peach trees.
Raindrop's journey; Silent cavalier.

Peacock.
How jedge Peacock sowed his wild oats #; How the peacock was given colored feathers; Io; Owl and the peacock; Why the peacock's tail is spotted.

Perseverance.
Ambitious carp #; Blue hill; Bruce and the spider; Hill; Old woman and crowbar #; Puzwuk, the orphan boy, and the starving time; Raising the stone; We always succeed in the end.

Pessimism.
Robin and the raven #; Windows.

Pets.
At Mulberry Farm; Lady Brown Owl #; First friend; Fish which wanted a bath #; Pet turkey whose feelings were hurt; Thanksgiving dinners #; Woman who forgot her cat #.

Pies, First.
King's pie #; Pumpkin giant; Three knocks on the door #.
See also Cooks and cooking.

Pigeons.
How the pigeon became a tame bird; Messenger bird #; Topknot pigeons.

Pigs.
Five little pigs #; How the pigs can see the wind #; Little pig that grumbled; Old woman and her pig; Tail of Lemuel; Three little pigs and the ogre; Three piggy-wigs #; Why pigs have curly tails #.

Playmates, Imaginary.
Carrie-Barry-Annie; Child of the mist #.

Plates and dishes.
In the plate country; Palissy the potter; Pies of the princess; Willow ware, Story of #.

Pleiades.
Flight of Tiri; Six boys go to the star country; Star bearer; Thrush and the cuckoo.

Plumbing.
How the singing water got to the tub; It was lucky Noah invited the elephants.

Pyramid of animals.
Kara and Guyja ; Kid and the tiger ; Pour, Katrientje, pour.
Quack doctors.
Cobbler turned doctor ; Old woman and the doctor ; Quack frog.
See also Wizards, Pretended.
Quarantine.
Ana Josepha.
Quarrelling.
Magic mouthful ; Quails ; Spark neglected burns the house ; Three bugs.
Rabbits.
Adventurous cottontail ; Brother Rabbit and his famous foot ; Bunny Rabbit's journey ; Easter rabbit # ; Gift of swiftness ; God with a bad memory ; How bunny was named ; Little rabbits ; Little white rabbit ; Mr. Rabbit and Mr. Bear # ; Timid hare ; Witch hare.
See also titles beginning Brother ; Hare ; Mr.
Rabbit's ears.
Hare afraid of his ears ; Rabbit and his ears ; Rabbit and the animal wizard.
Rabbit's tail.
How Mr. Rabbit lost his fine bushy tail # ; How Rabbit lost his tail ; How the rabbit got its cotton tail ; Why Peter Rabbit wears a white patch.
Races.
Ambitious rocking horse # ; Animal races ; Atalanta's race ; Boar and the chameleon ; Deer and the snail ; First Marathon race ; Frog and the leopard ; Greatest race that ever was ; How a turtle outwitted a wolf # ; How badger won a race ; How deer won his antlers ; How the fox and the crab ran a race ; How the gopher raced ; How turtle got his tail ; How turtle won the race with beaver ; Humming bird and crane ; Pigeon-hawk and the tortoise ; Swiss Marathon ; Terrapin's trick ; Turtle runs a race with bear.
Radishes.
In the kitchen garden ; Traveler, the cook, and the little old man #.
Railroads.
Engine that wouldn't stop ; Kettle and the engines ; Little engine that could # ; Pony engine # ; Royal engine ; Runaway train ; Steamboat and the locomotive # ; Three freight trains ; Train that would not stay on the track.
Rain.
Cloud # ; Drop of rain ; Drouth witches ; Farmer and his two daughters ; Little red shoes ; Mr. Rabbit as a rain-maker # ; Parsee tale ; Praying for rain ; Prince and his private rain cloud ; Raincloud ; Tiny rain-drop ; Uncle Rain and Brother Drouth # ; Wang and his star ; Water-drop ; What the wind said ; Wise priest ; Yellow elves.
See also Weather.
Rainbow.
How color came to the world # ; How "To Wut In" made the rainbow # ; Iris. I ; Land of the northern lights # ; Little dawn boy and the rainbow trail ; Lost prince of the poles # ; Pot of gold. I #.
Rats.
Camel and the rat ; Glimminge castle ; Mouse tower ; Mr. Rat and Mr. Ratte # ; Mrs. Blackrat's house party # ; Pied piper of

Rats—*continued.*
Hamelin; When Old Mr. Rat became an outcast # ; Woodrat
and rabbits #.
See also Mice.
Revenge. *See* Nemesis; Vengeance.
Riddles.
Brother Rabbit has fun at the ferry # ; Cadi's decisions # ; City
of wise men; Clever girl and the king; Clever peasant; Courting of Emer; Day of the scholars; King John and the Abbot of
Canterbury; King Matthias' three riddles; King Solomon's an-
swer; King that talked biggity # ; King's choice; King's life
saved by spells; Œdipus; Peasant's clever daughter # ; Percy
the wizard # ; Prince from nowhere; Raven # ; Sage damsel;
Song with riddles in it; Why the fish laughed # ; Widow and the
sagacious magistrate # ; Wise Moro and the Hindu riddle
guesser; Wise weaver; Witty answer.
See also Justice; Wizards, Pretended.
Rip Van Winkle, Jewish.
Sleep of one hundred years.
Rip Van Winkle, East Indian.
Miser and the banyan tree.
Roads.
Buddy and the buried bone # ; How the path grew; Passable but
unsafe; Path that never got anwhere; Road of the loving heart;
Sandy road # ; Stone in the road.
Rocks.
Coyote and rolling rock; How arrow heads came; Niobe; Why the
flint rock cannot fight back.
Rogues outwitted.
Magic cap; Shepherd who laughed last.
Rome, Stories of.
Coriolanus; Cornelia's jewels # ; Geese save Rome; Horatius at
the bridge; How Decius Mus saved Rome # ; Princess who be-
came a vestal virgin; Regulus; Romulus and Remus; Sabine
women and Roman wives; Sibyl; Tarpeia; Virginia.
Rosemary.
How the rosemary was given its sweet scent; Jar of rosemary.
Roses.
Adonis; Blush rose and the sun # ; Christmas rose; Fairy rose;
Fruit on the rose bush # ; How roses came # ; How the wild
roses got their thorns # ; How we came to have pink roses # ;
In a rose garden; Little pink rose # ; Loveliest rose in the
world # ; Moss rose, Legend of; Neighboring families; Night-
ingale and the rose # ; Prickly bush; Saved by a rose # ; St.
Elizabeth and the roses # ; Sultana of the flowers # ; Why roses
have thorns; Why roses are red.
Rudeness.
Diamonds and toads; Landlord's mistake # ; Latona and the
frogs; Professor and the custom officers; Surly guest.
Runaways.
Flight of the dolls # ; When Norma Catherine ran away; When
the little boy ran away; Wooden horse. III.
Sabbath breaking.
Giants of the clock; Man in the moon; Pike that pulled and pulled.
Safety.
Imp and the drum; Kindhearted policeman; Mr. Monk and Mrs.
Graycat; Nail. I; Wishing wishes #.
Santa Claus, Existence of.
Santa Claus's helpers; What Santa Claus told the toys.

Scarecrows.
Jimmy Scarecrow's Christmas; Scarecrow and the snowman; Walking boy.

School.
Imp and the drum; How the griffin taught school; Last lesson in French; Little green goblin.

Sea serpent.
Castle that came from an egg; Klose-kom-bau, Story of; Sea captain and the serpent; Why the sea moans.

Seals.
Conversion of St. Wilfred; Na-Ha the fighter #; North wind's baby; White seal #.

Seashore.
Cause of tides; Star jewels #; Tidy Tips; Why the surf is broken.

Seasons.
Animals in council; Crown; Four winds; How summer came to the earth; How the seasons came to be; How the winter came #; Little ice man #; Nipon and the king of the Northland #; North wind and Star boy #; Old woman who met the months #; Raven and the macaw; Rescue of rabbit.

Secrets.
I know a secret; Midas. II; Minister who lost his head from revealing a secret.

Selfishness.
Ant and the glowworm; Boniface and Keep-it-all; Closed hand; Fight with dragons; Golden apple with the silver seeds; Half-chick; Leek; Mr. Monk and the smart young tortoises; Pebbles; Punishment of the stingy; Queer little baker man; Scheming kitten; Snake that the boy made; Stone curse; Travelers and the axe; What the learned cat remembers; Why the maiden lost her turquoises.

Sense. *See* Common sense; Wisdom.

Sequel stories.
Bears make a visit; Cinderella's sisters; How Olaf brought the brownie back #; Knoonie in the sleeping palace; Queens meet; Thousand-and-second tale of Scheherazade #; Tree of justice.

Service.
Gift of the shining stranger; Golden goblets of gladness; Its mission; Piggywee's little curly tail; Why the bluebird carries happiness.

Sewing.
Absent-minded tailor; Dress of scraps #; Dwarfs' tailor; Little Betty Buttonhole; Little Sister Kindness and the loving stitches #; First thimble; Flax leavings #; Lady Yolanda's thimble; Miss Emery Threadneedle; Petronila of the coats; Princess who couldn't sew; Sampler; Sham prince.

Shadows.
Desolate things #; Ghost and the shadow; Princess with the tired shadow.

Shams.
Ass in the lion's skin; Jay and the peacock #; Sham prince.
See also Imitations.

Sheep.
Greedy shepherd; Little gray sheep; Unknown travelers; Wolves and the sheep.

Shoes.
Bobby's fairy shoes; Cobbler; Crimson slippers; Dance of the shoes; Dominick's magic shoes; Duty shoes; Fairy cobbler; Green shoes; How the shoes went to the picnic #; Johnny's

Spring—*continued.*
Stealing the springtime; Who shall be May queen; Why the robin says, "cheer up" #; Year, story of.
Squirrels.
Bobby Squirrel plays a joke; Bunnytail, Tale of #; Bushy's bravery #; Chip and Munkey; Chip's Thanksgiving; How the flying squirrel got his wings; How the red squirrel got white eyelids; Lame squirrel's Thanksgiving; Merchant of dreams; Mountain and the squirrel; Mr. Gray-squirrel talks #; Mrs. Gray's family #; When Mother Squirrel went to town; Why the squirrel barks #; Why the squirrel lives in trees; Winter in town.
See also Chipmunks.
Stained glass.
Its mission.
Stamps. *See* Letters; Postage stamps.
Stars.
Bar Beach; Capella; Cassiopeia; Great bear #; How stars and fireflies were made; How we got our first daisies; Inseparables; Matariki; Scorpion and his family; Seven brothers; Sky bridge of birds; Star that watches the moon; Temple boy; Where the frost comes from.
Steam.
Ice king and his wonderful grandchild #; Moth and rust #; Mother Hotty and the little Hotties #; Three good giants #.
Storekeeping.
Lexy and the dogs on his street; Mr. A and Mr. P; Mr. Liverwurst's picnic; Mr. Murdle's large heart; Sad story of Mr. Porium's family; Store that gave things away.
Storks.
Caliph Stork; Courtship of Mr. Stork and Miss Heron; Fox and the stork; Homes a-fire; How the storks came and went #; Man who did not wish to die. II #; Marsh king's daughter #; Why the stork has no tail; Why the stork loves Holland #.
Story-telling.
Endless tale; Fairy story-shop #; King Schahriar and Scheherazade; Making a fairy story; Power of fables; Princess Fairy-Story in masquerade; Story-teller.
Strawberries.
Elves. VI #; First strawberries; Golden strawberries; Little white blossom #; Magic strawberries #.
Strongest, Who is.
Archer and the trumpeter #; Chib, Adventures of #; Five servants; Four hunters; Giant twins; Goats in the turnip field; How six men traveled through the wide world; How the elephant and the whale were tricked; Little white rabbit. II; Longstaff, Pinepuller and Rockheaver; St. Christopher; Rats and their son-in-law; Who is strongest #; Why the baby says "goo"; Wind and the sun.
Sugar.
Bees and the sugar; How maple sugar came; Precious poison.
Sulking.
Crocodile pagoda.
Sun.
How sun and moon came; How sun became so bright #; How sun was made #.
Sunday.
Joseph the sabbath lover; Pike that pulled and pulled; Week of Sundays; You must not work on Sunday.

Sunflowers.
Bronze heart; Clytie; Why the sunflowers hang their heads #.
Sunken cities.
Drowning of the bottom hundred # ; Princess Unca ; Sea-baby ;
Two cities ; Ys, Story of.
Sunshine.
Bags of the sun; Baskets of sunshine; Dark place; Hickamore
and Hackamore; Little Sunshine; Story that the buttercups
told # ; Sunbeam and the captive # ; Water of light #.
"Swapping," Stories of.
Apple dumpling # ; Hans in luck; Man with the bag; Monkey's
bargains # ; Travels of a fox; What the goodman does is always
right.
Tact.
Language of birds. II # ; Right answer # ; Three sworn broth-
ers # ; Ways of giving advice #.
Tadpoles. *See* Pollywogs.
Tailors.
Brave little tailor; Clothes make the man; Dwarfs' tailor; Giant
and the tailor # ; Little tailor # ; Sham prince; Sonless king;
Two travelers; Town crier and the tailor.
Tails.
Brother Mole; Cat and the mouse; Fairy tail; Fox that lost his
tail; Fox's trick; Guinea pig's tail; How George the tadpole
lost his tail; Little animal who didn't go for his tail; Rabbit's
tail; Tale that cost a dollar # ; Two tails; Why goats have short
tails; Why Manx cats have no tails; Why the bear has a stumpy
tail; Why the possum's tail is bare; Why the stork has no
tail; Woeful tale of long tail rabbit and long tail lynx.
Talents.
Four clever brothers; Poppet.
Talking too much.
Dwarfs' tailor; Talkative tortoise.
"Tall" tales.
Ashiepattle who made the princess tell the truth at last # ; Bet;
Bunyan, Paul; Conal and Donal, and Taig # ; Country where
the mice eat iron; Daniel O'Rourke; Flail which came from
the clouds # ; Goatherd who won a princess; Jack and the king
who was a gentleman # ; King and the sage # ; Lying for a
wager; Much ado about nothing. II ; Peach-rocked deer; Shell,
Solomon; Shepherd who won the king's daughter by a single
word # ; Shooting round the corner; Stag and the cherry tree;
Trip to the moon; Turkey-bean and the moon.
Taxes.
Countess Wilhelmine's long walk; Dog market in Buda; Tichborne
dole; What the four were for.
Taxi.
Hoppaway; Taxi that went mad; Timid truck.
See also Automobiles.
Tea.
Ah Tcha the sleeper; Bitter waters.
Teddy bears.
Black tower # ; Vain Teddy-bear.
See also Toys.
Teeth.
Thirty-two teeth; Why children lose their teeth; Why the ani-
mals no longer fear the sheep # ; Why the deer's teeth are blunt.

Temperance.
Bacchus and the vine; Devoted daughter; First vineyard; Four qualities of drunkenness; Giant of the flood; Magic lamp. I; Mountain giants, pt. 2 #; Mystic garden #; Sack of barley and the pig; Saved by kindness; Sir Guyon's great adventure; Two wine merchants lose their heads; Why the sparrow stutters; Wine and water; Young cupbearer #.

Thieves, Clever.
Brahman and the goat; Gilly of the goatskin; Jack Hannaford; Jack the cunning thief; Magic cap; Three thieves; Treasure chamber of Rhampsinitus.

Thrift.
Five pennies; Mouse merchant; One straw; Only a penny #; Solomon's ghost; Wages of seven years; Waste not, want not; What luck; What the four were for; Wise Pélé.
See also Labor Day.

Thunder.
Boy and his wife; Minute guns of the gods; Old-Man and the Thunder-birds.

Tidiness.
See Clean-up week; Neatness.

Time.
Bag of minutes #; Caliph's clock; Chinny; Enchanted watch #; First clock; Lost half-hour #; Monk and the bird's song; Why the bush fowl calls up the dawn; Why the cock crows at dawn #.

Time, Value of.
Quentin and the clock; Spare moments; Three questions. I.
See also Procrastination.

Toads.
Child's wish; How old Mr. Toad learned to sing #; How the toad got his bruises; Old Tubby Toad.

Tolerance.
Adder that didn't hear #; Bee and the beetle #.

Toys.
Ambitious rocking-horse #; Brave tin soldier; Carp rider; Christmas in the playroom; Christmas joke; Departure; Dobbin, Story of; Doll's wish; Flight of the dolls #; Happiest doll; In Drumtown; Irish stew; Jumping Jack's journey; Pink rabbit; Poor Cecco; Poor Mary Jane; Rag doll's Christmas; Rocking-horse land; Runaway sled; Shuttlecock; Top that could sing; Vanka's birthday; What Santa Claus told the toys; White cotton rabbit; Why the top sings; Wooden horse. III.
See also names of toys.

Trading bargains. *See* "Swapping" stories.

Treasure, Hidden.
Castle-treasure; Cavern of Steenfoll; Fairy gold; Furze blossom gold; Good orphan Sunblossom; Hans the otherwise; Haughty slave; Hidden treasure; Lord helpeth man and beast; Money chest; Moor's legacy; Pedlar of Swaffham; Rogue and the simpleton; Treasure of Hasan Taj; Treasure seeker #; Treasures; Under the lid; Young man and the big beast with a man's head.

Trees.
Bramble-bush king; Diablo and the dogwood #; Flight into Egypt; Gifts the trees gave #; Golden Mead, Legend of; Jupiter and the oak; Luck of the golden rod; Mountain ash; Pyramus and Thisbe; Quaking aspen #; Rondel #; Sighing pine tree #; Sky High and Cloud Beard; Sunshine tree; Talking tree;

Trees—*continued.*
Travellers and the plane tree; Why the laurel makes wreaths; Why the persimmon tree has its fruit in three colors #.
Trees, Spirit of.
Dryad # ; Fairy in the oak; Old Pipes and the dryad; Peter and the birch tree dryad; Rhœcus.
Trolley cars.
Old trolley car; Speed; Subway car; Three bears and the trolley car; Tired trolley car.
Truthfulness.
Ashes of deceit # ; Cap; King Believe and Peasant Truth; Lie; Little Persian; Magic flute; Peasant Truth; Washington and the cherry tree; What the teacher said to Trove; When Jane changed her name.
Tulips.
Little nymph who loved bright colors #.
Turkeys.
How the turkey got his beard; Pet turkey whose feelings were hurt; Rosalind and the turkeys; Wisest of all; Why the turkey gobbles.
Turquoise.
Why the maiden lost her turquoises.
Turtles.
How a turtle fooled a little boy; How the turtle saved his own life; How the turtle won the race # ; Man and turtle; Talkative tortoise; Terrapin's trick; Why turtles stay near the water.
See also titles under Tortoise.
Twins.
Beggar's curse; Carl and Carlo; Giant twins; Golden twins; Hero twins; Stone twins; Supervisor's mistake.
Typewriter.
Temperamental typewriter.
Ugliness.
Green serpent; King Uggermugger; Princess Petunia and the fairy Grimbona; Princess Ugly; Proud princess and the ugly prince #.
Umbrellas.
Elf and the dormouse; How the umbrella ran away with Ellie.
Unjust judgements.
Fairy who judged her neighbors # ; Officer of police; Shemyák the judge # ; Swan and the crow #.
Unselfishness rewarded.
Christmas gift. II # ; Little men of the mountains; Tonia; Two little stockings.
Untrustworthy servants.
Cock and cats who bore his litter.
Vegetables.
In the kitchen garden; Lucky seed; Some voices from the kitchen garden; Truant vine; Vain cereals; When the jungle plants quarreled; Why the potato lives in the ground; Why the rice stopped rolling.
Vengeance.
Creigfryn's bargain; Crow and the snake; Dog and the sparrow; Eagle and the beetle; Farmer and the fox; Hare, the secretary bird, the owl, the hyena and the crocodile; Jealousy of the blind man; Pour, Katrintje, pour; Sparrow, the woodpecker, the fly, the frog and the elephant; Sparrow's revenge; Strand of the bitter cry; Who killed the otter's babies?

Violin.
Bewitched violin ; Goat and the horse ; Mr. Maple and Mr. Pine #.
Violets.
Birth of the violet # ; Magic perfume # ; Secret of the violet # ; Why violets have golden hearts #.
Volcanoes.
Fire and beauty ; First humming bird # ; Giant of flaming mountain # ; Girl who had to be carried ; Mount Ætna's eruptions explained ; Mountain with summer in its heart # ; Moon princess. II.
Walled-up.
Surabo.
War.
Empty drum ; Ernest service ; Family portrait ; Farmer and the fox ; Fox who was the cause of his own death ; How a plowman won a battle ; King and the horses who turned the mills ; St. Jacob's roses ; Three bugs ; Trumpeter taken prisoner ; Two kings at war ; Wound and the scar #.
Wasps.
Bees, the drones and the wasp ; Where the yellow jackets came from ; Why the Jack-Spaniard's waist is small # ; Wicked hornet.
Water lilies.
How the water lily came ; Lonesome lake, Legend of # ; Star maiden. I.
Water of life, and death.
Prince Ganim ; Water of Kane ; Water of youth, water of life, and water of death #.
Waves.
Ninth wave ; Why the surf is broken.
Wealth, Curse of.
Cobbler's song ; Contented poor man ; Magic flask ; Magic pillow ; Midas. I ; Ouphe of the woods # ; Peronella # ; Precious gem palace ; Sky-goer and Earth-goer ; Sovereign of the mineral kingdom.
Weather.
Cat's trousers, Child's wish ; Fairies' weather # ; Father and his daughters ; God with a bad memory ; Good and bad weather ; Green page ; How the rain comes # ; How Tommy raised the wind ; Indian summer ; Jolly Mr. Wind # ; Little red shoes ; Man and the rain # ; March and the shepherd # ; Month of March ; Old woman who met the months # ; Parsee tale ; Praying for rain ; Rain tree ; Shepherd of clouds # ; That horrid rain # ; Thrush and the cuckoo ; Umbrella-maker's Kozo ; Wang and his star ; What are you going to do about it ; What the learned cat remembers ; What the wind said ; Where the harrycane comes from # ; Wise priest.
Weather vanes.
Discontented rooster ; Foolish weather cock ; Golden cock ; Golden horse and his rider # ; Half-Chick ; Pleasing everybody # ; Proud cock # ; Weathercock.
Well meaning, ill doing.
Blunder # ; Epaminondas and his auntie ; Prudent Hans ; Stupid's cries ; Yukpachen, Story of.
Whales.
Glooskap and th whale # ; How the elephant and the whale were tricked ; How the whale got his throat # ; How the white whales happened # ; Idol and the whale ; Killer whale # ; Narwhal, Origin of ; Punishment of the stingy.

Wheat.
Ear of wheat: How grain came to the Indians; Seeds and the wheat; Sunken city; Two gifts. II; Vain cereals.

Whining.
Chimborazo # ; Little boy who said, "I don't want to eat it."

Willow tree.
Golden willow; Tinker's willow; Willow-tree ghosts;

Windows.
Bags of the sun; Forgetful carpenter; Golden windows # ; Its mission; Twelve windows; Wing Dow; Wise men of Helm; Wise men of Holmola.

Winds.
Children of the House of dawn; Four winds; Girl who had to be carried; How the four winds were named; North wind and the South wind # ; Prairie dandelion; Wuchowson the wind blower.

Wings.
Dædalus and Icarus; Winged burdens; Why the cock cannot fly.

Winter.
City of the winter sleep; How the winter came # ; King Winter's harvest # ; Mother Hotty and the little Hotties # ; Seed-babies' blanket.
See also Seasons.

Wisdom, Acquiring.
How sense was distributed; Rabbit and the animal wizard.

Wisdom of fools.
King John and the Abbot of Canterbury; Miller at the professor's examination; Pekka and the rogues; Wise weaver.

Wise judgements.
Cormac's judgement; Justice of Omar; King Solomon, the merchant and the mouse-deer; Merchant who buried his money; Telltale chalk; Turkish judge; Wise old shepherd # .

Wishes.
Four wishes # ; How the good gifts were used by two; Lazy raccoon # ; Luck of the goldenrod; Three wishes; Two wishes.

Wishing gate.
Blunder # ; Secret. I.

Wizards, Pretended.
Brahmin and his wife # ; Black Robin # ; Doctor and detective # ; Doctor Know-all; First ants # ; Home-bred boy; Little bird. I; Little cricket. II; Old man and the robbers; Percy the wizard # ; Pig's-head magician; Spaeman; Two impostors; Wise soothsayer.

Women.
First woman # ; How the man found his mate # ; How woman came to earth # ; Why there are old maids # .

Women's rights.
Beware of the chest.

Wooden people.
Pinocchio; Saddler's horse; Talking tree; Wooden wife # .

Words, Power of.
City of wise men; Five wise words of the guru; Just imagine it; King Tongue # ; King's life saved by spells; Seller of words; Slanderer; Three sieves.

Work.
Giant Energy and Fairy Skill ;# ∙ Holidays are busy days; Sunshine fairy.
See also Labor Day.

Work done for one.
Big nosed bogy; Brownie #; Flies of Mendiondo; Elves and the shoemaker; Sir Buz; Schmat-Razum.

Worry.
Clock in the kitchen; Crazy priestess; Lippo and Tapio; Matter of habit.

Writing, Invention of.
Alcuin; How the alphabet was made #; How the first letter was written #; Now it is written.

Youth renewed.
Medea's cauldron; Tarrandar's secret; Two old men. II.

Zoo.
Alphabet park; Escape of the penguins; Escape of the stag.

DIRECTORY OF PUBLISHERS

Allen. W. H. Allen & Co., Ltd. 100 Southwark St., Southwark, S. E. 1, England.
Allan, P. Philip Allan & Co., Ltd. Quality House, 69 Great Russell St., London, W. C. 1, England.
Amer. Book. American Book Co., 88 Lexington Ave., New York City.
Appleton. D. Appleton & Co., New York City.
  See Appleton-Century.
Appleton-Century. D. Appleton-Century Co., Inc. 35 W. 32d St., New York City.
Associated publishers, Inc. 1538 9th St., N. W., Washington, D. C.
Atlantic. Atlantic Monthly Press, Inc. Boston, Mass.
  Books distributed by Little, Brown & Co.
Baker. Walter H. Baker Co. 178 Tremont St., Boston, Mass.
Beacon Press, Inc. 25 Beacon St., Boston, Mass.
Bell. George Bell & Sons, Ltd. York House, 6 Portugal St., Lincoln's Inn Fields, London, W. C. 2, England.
Black. A. & C. Black, Ltd. 4–6 Soho Square, London, W. 1, England.
Blackwell. Basil H. Blackwell & Mott, Ltd. 49 Broad St., Oxford, England.
Bobbs-Merrill Co. 724 N. Meridian St., Indianapolis, Indiana.
Bookhouse for Children. 360 N. Michigan Boulevard, Chicago, Ill.
Bradley. Milton Bradley Co. 74 Park St., Springfield, Mass.
Brentano's. New York City.
  See Coward-McCann.
Bruce. Bruce Publishing Co. 524–544 N. Milwaukee St., Milwaukee, Wis.
Burt. A. L. Burt Co. See Grossett & Dunlap.
Cambridge University Press. St. Dunstan's House, 133–137 Fetter Lane, London, E. C. 4, England.
Cape. Jonathan Cape, Ltd. 30 Bedford Square, London, W. C. 1, England.
Cassell & Co., Ltd. La Belle Sauvage, Ludgate Hill, London, E. C. 4, England.
Caxton Printers, Ltd. Caldwell, Ohio.
  See Reilly & Lee.
Century. Century Co., New York City.
  See Appleton-Century.
Chambers. W. & R. Chambers. 11 Thistle St., Edinburgh, Scotland; 38 Soho Square, London, W. 1, England.
Collier. P. F. Collier & Co. 250 Park Ave., New York City.
Coward-McCann, Inc. 2 W. 45th St., New York City.
  Acquired publications of Brentano's, excepting all titles by B. G. Shaw.
Crowell. Thomas Y. Crowell Co. 393 4th Ave., New York City.
Cupples & Leon Co. 470 4th Ave., New York City.
Dent. J. M. Dent & Sons, Ltd. Aldine House, 10–13 Bedford St., Strand, London, W. C. 2, England.
  See also Dutton.
Dial Press, Inc. 152 W. 13th St., New York City.

Dodd.   Dodd, Mead & Co., Inc.   443–449 4th Ave., New York City.
  Acquired the publications of Duffield, and also of Sears.
Doran, George H.
  See Doubleday.
Doubleday.   Doubleday, Doran & Co., Inc.   75 Franklin Ave.,
  Garden City, Long Island, N. Y.   •
  Acquired the publications of George H. Doran Co.
Duffield.   Duffield & Green, Inc., New York City.
  See Dodd.
Dutton.   E. P. Dutton & Co., Inc.   286–302 4th Ave., New York
  City.
Elder.   Paul Elder & Co.   239 Post St., San Francisco, Cal.
Farrar & Rinehart, Inc.   232 Madison Ave., New York City.
Flanagan.   A. Flanagan Co.   920 N. Franklin St., Chicago, Ill.
Follett Publishing Co.   1255 S. Wabash Ave., Chicago, Ill.
  Acquired publications of T. S. Rockwell.
Frank-Maurice, Inc., New York City.
French.   Samuel French, Inc.   25 W. 45th St., New York City.
Garden City Publishing Co., Inc.   75 Franklin Ave., Garden City,
  N. Y.
Ginn.   Ginn & Co.   15 Ashburton Place, Boston, Mass.
Grosset & Dunlap.   1140 Broadway, New York City.
  Have acquired the publications of A. L. Burt Co.
Harcourt.   Harcourt Brace & Co., Inc.   383 Madison Ave., New
  York City.
Harper.   Harper & Brothers.   49 E. 33d St., New York City.
Harrap.   George G. Harrap & Co., Ltd.   182 High Holborn, Lon-
  don, W. C. 1, England.
Heath.   D. C. Heath & Co.   285 Columbus Ave., Boston, Mass.
Heinemann.   William Heinemann, Ltd.   99 Great Russell St., Lon-
  don, England.
Holiday House.   225 Varick St., New York City.
Holt.   Henry Holt & Co., Inc.   1 Park Ave., New York City.
Houghton.   Houghton, Mifflin Co.   2 Park St., Boston, Mass.
Huntting.   H. R. Huntting Co.   Myrick Building, Springfield, Mass.
Hurst & Co.   New York City.
  Publications acquired by Platt & Munk.
Jack, T. C. & E. C. Jack.
  See Nelson, T. & Son.
Jewish Publication Society of America.   Broad and Spring Garden
  Sts., Philadelphia, Pa.
Junior Literary Guild, New York City.
Knopf.   Alfred A. Knopf, Inc.   730 5th Ave., New York City.
League Press.   Woman's League of the United Synagogues of
  America.   New York City.
Lippincott.   J. B. Lippincott Co.   227–231 S. 6th St., Philadelphia,
  Pa.
Little.   Little, Brown & Co.   34 Beacon St., Boston, Mass.
Longmans.   Longmans, Green & Co.   114 5th Ave., New York City.
Lothrop.   Lothrop, Lee & Shepard Co.   126 Newbury St., Boston,
  Mass.
Lyons and Carnahan.   2500 Prairie Ave., Chicago, Ill.
McBride.   Robert M. McBride.   116 E. 16th St., New York City.
McKay.   David McKay.   604–608 S. Washington Square, Phila-
  delphia, Pa.
Macm.   The Macmillan Co.   60 5th Ave., New York City.
  Acquired business of Sturgis and Walton.
Macrae-Smith Co.   1712–1714 Ludlow St., Philadelphia, Pa.
Marshall Jones Co.   Boston.

Methuen & Co., Ltd. 36 Essex St., Strand, London, W. C. 2, England.

Minton, Balch & Co. 2-6 W. 45th St., New York City.

Moffatt. Moffatt, Yard & Co.
  See Dodd.

Morrow. William Morrow & Co., Inc. 386 4th Ave., New York City.

Murray. John Murray. 50-a Albemarle St., London, W. 1, England.

National Council for Prevention of War. Washington, D. C.

Nelson. Thomas Nelson & Sons. 381-385 4th Ave., New York City.

Newson. Newson & Co. 73 5th Ave., New York City.

Noble. Noble & Noble, Publishers, Inc. 100 5th Ave., New York City.

Nutt. David Nutt. 212 Shaftesbury Ave., London, W. C. 2, England.

Oxford University Press. 11 Warwick Square, London, E. C. 4, England; 114 5th Ave., New York City.

Page. L. C. Page & Co. 53 Beacon St., Boston, Mass.

Payson & Clark. New York City.

Pearson. C. Arthur Pearson, Ltd. 16-18 Henrietta St., Covent Gardens, London, W. C. 2, England.

Penn Publishing Co. 925 Filbert St., Philadelphia, Pa.

Phillips, Sampson & Co., Boston.
  See Houghton, Mifflin.

Pilgrim Press. 14 Beacon St., Boston.

Platt & Munk Co., Inc. 200 5th Ave., New York City.

Putnam. G. P. Putnam's Sons. Putnam Building, 2-6 W. 45th St., New York City.

Rand. Rand McNally Co. 536 S. Clark St., Chicago, Ill.

Revell. Fleming H. Revell Co. 158 5th Ave., New York City.

Rockwell. Thomas S. Rockwell, Chicago.
  See Follett Publishing Co.

Round Table Press, Inc. New York City.

Row, Petersen & Co. 1911 Ridge Ave., Evanston, Ill.

Scott, Foresman & Co. 623-633 S. Wabash Ave., Chicago, Ill.

Scribner. Charles Scribner's Sons. 597 5th Ave., New York City.

Sears. S. H. Sears & Co. New York City.
  See Dodd.

Sheed. Sheed & Ward, Inc. 63 5th Ave., New York City.

Small, Maynard & Co. Boston.
  See Dodd.

Smith. Harrison Smith. 173 49th St., New York City.

Stokes. Frederick A. Stokes Co. 443-449 4th Ave., New York City.

Stratford Co. 89 Congress St., Boston.

Sturgis & Walton.
  Publications acquired by Macmillan.

Suttonhouse, Ltd. 523 H. W. Hellman Building, Los Angeles, California.

Talbot Press, Ltd. 89 Talbot St., Dublin, Ireland.
  English and U. S. agent is Longmans, Green & Co.

Union of American Hebrew Congregations. 1 W. 42d St., New York City.

Univ. Pub. Co., Normal, Ill.
  See Newson.

University of Chicago Press. 5750 Ellis Ave., Hyde Park Station, Chicago, Ill.

University of North Carolina Press.   Chapel Hill, North Carolina.
Unwin.   T. Fisher Unwin.   Bouverie House, Fleet St., London,
     E. C. 4, England.
Victor Talking Machine Co.   R. C. A. Victor Co., Educational Dept.,
     Camden, New Jersey.
Viking Press, Inc.   18 E. 48th St., New York City.
Volland.   P. F. Volland Co.   Joliet, Ill.
Warne.   Frederick Warne & Co., London, England; 381 4th Ave.,
     New York City.
Wells.   Wells, Gardner, Darton, & Co., Ltd.   3 Paternoster Build-
     ing, London, E. C. 4, England.
Werner. E. S. Werner Co.   Belmar, New Jersey.
Whitman, A.   Albert Whitman & Co.   560 W. Lake St., Chicago,
     Ill.
Wilde.   W. A. Wilde Co.   131 Clarendon St., Boston, Mass.
Winston.   John C. Winston Co.   1006–1016 Arch St., Philadelphia,
     Pa.
Wise-Parslow Co.   386 4th Ave., New York City.
     See also Volland.
Writers' Publishing Co., New York City.   (1921.)